D1534977

Testing Adolescents

Contributors

W. B. Apple, M.A.

Timothy A. Cavell, M.S.

Joan P. Cesari, Ph.D.

Stewart W. Ehly, Ph.D.

Kathryn C. Gerken, Ph.D.

Frank M. Gresham, Ph.D.

John Guidubaldi, D.Ed.

Robert G. Harrington, Ph.D.

Thomas H. Hohenshil, Ph.D.

E. Peter Johnsen, Ed.D.

Judith Kaufman, Ph.D.

Howard M. Knoff, Ph.D.

Steven Landau, Ph.D.

Brian W. McNeill, Ph.D.

Danny Mitchelson, M.A., MS.Ed.

Thorana Nelson, M.A.

Joseph D. Perry, Ph.D.

Patricia A. Petretic-Jackson, Ph.D.

Randal P. Quevillon, Ph.D.

Helen Reiner, Ph.D.

David Rosenthal, Ph.D.

Anne B. Spragins, Ph.D.

Michael M. Warner, Ph.D.

Testing Adolescents

A REFERENCE GUIDE FOR COMPREHENSIVE
PSYCHOLOGICAL ASSESSMENTS

Robert G. Harrington, Ph.D.
General Editor

Foreword by Jerome M. Sattler, Ph.D.

TEST CORPORATION OF AMERICA
KANSAS CITY

LIBRARY OF CONGRESS CATALOGING IN PUBLICATION DATA

Testing adolescents.

    Includes bibliographies and indexes.
    1. Youth--Psychological testing. 2. Handicapped
youth--Psychological testing. I. Harrington, Robert G.
(Robert Gerard), 1948-   . [DNLM: 1. Adolescent
Psychology. 2. Psychological Tests--in adolescence.
WS 462 T344]
BF724.25.T47 1987   155.5'028'7   87-1938
ISBN 0-933701-01-2

Printed in the United States of America

Contents

Foreword

JEROME M. SATTLER, PH.D.

Adolescent assessment is an overlooked topic in the testing literature and *Testing Adolescents* fills the void. The collective expertise of the contributing authors addresses a variety of real-life issues faced by adolescents today, including adolescent sexuality and self-concept, family life, vocational choice, social skills development and personal values. Areas of adolescent conflict that may lead to adjustment problems or psychopathology also are addressed, in chapters dealing with secondary learning disabilities, parental divorce, suicidal ideations, eating disorders, conduct disorders, juvenile delinquency, substance abuse, and psychological adjustment to handicapping conditions. These are special assessment problems faced by professionals that are not answered by referring to the child or adult literature.

Testing Adolescents provides a practical, research-based resource on adolescent assessment. Although each chapter is written by a different author or group of authors, some unifying trends appear. The focus is on both informal and formal assessment techniques, stressing interviews, behavioral observation, self-reports, peer rating scales, parent rating scales, teacher rating scales, and social skills assessment, all of which represent the multifactored assessment approach so necessary in conceptualizing adolescent case referrals. The writers discuss objective and projective personality assessment techniques, such as the MMPI, Rorschach, and Thematic Apperception Test, and show how each of these approaches can be used productively.

Testing Adolescents contains many useful features that assist in the practical application of the research forming the foundation of each of the individual chapters. For example, case studies are provided in each chapter to show how the epidemiological and assessment information can be integrated to address specific adolescent problems. The extensive appendix at the back of the book is valuable in describing commercially available tests mentioned in individual chapters. The extensive reference lists found at the end of each chapter are helpful for those desiring further information.

Readers will gain a wealth of information on assessing adolescent development, a critical point that marks a transition between childhood and adulthood. *Testing Adolescents* deals with assessment topics that are often overlooked in standard psychoeducational and clinical assessment texts. It is a welcome and needed addition to the field of assessment.

San Diego State University
San Diego, California
December, 1986

Preface

"If youth is a defect,
it is one that we outgrow too soon." ROBERT LOWELL

Adolescents are not children, nor are they adults. Rapid changes in physiology, personality, and social relationships make this a time of "becoming." The popular as well as research literature often describe adolescence as a period of stress and turmoil in which personal adjustments are being made and relationships renegotiated. As teens represent the next generation and thus the future itself, historically they have been given a clearly defined position in the social structure and thus the necessary time to adapt to their changing bodies, minds, and emotions. In addition to according them the time to make the expected transitions to adulthood, older members of the society extended adolescents support and guidance in the endeavor.

Our competitive, rapidly changing society has dispelled much of this protective developmental environment and thrusts a new set of expectations on its teenage members. Today they are expected to face life head on, to grow up quickly, to become independent thinkers early, to manage their own lives to a large extent. The fact of the matter is that adolescents are not prepared to make adult decisions and solve adult problems. Elkind (1984) has called this phenomenon the "hurried child" syndrome; children are expected to act like miniature adults for the convenience of society. Adolescence has become displaced in the sense that there may be no niche for a young person who needs a measured and controlled introduction to adulthood. The impact of premature adulthood on today's teenagers has had two negative results. First, adolescents are not being given sufficient time to construct their self-identities. Second, as a consequence, they are both more vulnerable to the added demands and less able to cope. Evidence of this increased stress and lack of coping skills can be found in the incidence of drug use, early sexual activity, suicide rates, and crime statistics.

Those in the helping professions who work with adolescents have been faced with a lack of up-to-date professional resources to which they may refer. Psychological assessment has been particularly problematic in this regard. The clinician has had little recourse but to extrapolate from either the child or adult assessment literature and apply what is known about these developmental periods to adolescence, as if adolescents do not face unique challenges requiring specialized forms of psychological assessment. The purpose of *Testing Adolescents* is first and foremost to recognize that adolescence *is* a unique developmental phase, the pressures of which are becoming increasingly evident.

Testing Adolescents provides the professional with a guide for constructing assessments of the developmental, adjustment, and educational problems faced by adolescents today. The book is organized around five themes, beginning with the *context* of adolescent assessment. Current practices and future prospects are critiqued, and the text establishes that most adolescent assessment depends on a family-based perspective. Next, the reader is introduced to the *developmental framework* of adolescent assessment. Strategies for assessing adjustment to "normal" developmental tasks are discussed, including the assessment of adolescent self-identity, value systems, and social skills. Techniques appropriate for assessing specific adolescent *adjustment problems* comprise the next section, which includes adolescent sexuality, eating disorders, substance abuse, and divorce adjustment. The fourth section offers discussion of the major areas of *adolescent psychopathology,* such as anxiety, depression, schizophrenia, suicidal risk, conduct disorders, and juvenile delinquency. The final series of chapters clusters around *social/educational considerations* in adolescent assessment, including the psychological adjustment of handicapped teenagers, learning disabilities, and vocational and career choice. Within each of these five themes effort has been made to differentiate normal adolescent difficulties from adjustment problems due to stress and the most severe forms of psychopathology.

Testing Adolescents will be most useful to the professional who has some background in testing, measurement theory, and personality assessment; however, novices in the area of adolescent assessment will find the chapter content useful as an introduction to this topic. More seasoned clinicians may look to *Testing Adolescents* for the most recent or novel approaches to assessing a specific area of interest. While the book includes a helpful test appendix, which offers additional information on every published test mentioned in the text, this is not meant to imply that a strictly psychometric approach should be taken in the assessment of adolescents. On the contrary, a multidimensional, multisourced approach is advocated, in which the participating professional is well versed in the factors that may contribute to the problem under consideration. For this reason, each chapter begins with an overview of the assessment problem/issue, including information about epidemiology and etiology, followed by a broad look at both formal and informal assessment methods, and finishes with a case study designed to show how one integrates instruments and other techniques to bring understanding to the problem and to develop appropriate interventions.

The various ethical and legal dilemmas, such as reporting suicide risk, that may confront the professional during the course of a psychological assessment are also discussed in relevant chapters. The reader must be aware, of course, that these are to be regarded as *general* recommendations; law pertaining to appropriate practice may vary from state to state, and practicing professionals are responsible for staying abreast of the legal idiosyncracies within their own states.

In sum, *Testing Adolescents* was designed to complement *Testing Children* and *Testing Adults,* its companion volumes, reflecting a lifespan approach and a philosophy that says adolescents are unique and deserving of well-trained professionals to assess their psychological needs.

ACKNOWLEDGEMENTS

My first acknowledgement goes to my family and specifically to my wife, Beth, who supported me in the writing process and encouraged me throughout.

Richard Sweetland, one of the founders of Test Corporation of America, deserves strong recognition for conceptualizing a series of books devoted to the specific assessment needs of individuals at various points within the life cycle. Daniel Keyser also deserves recognition for his strong support of this innovative writing project. Clark Smith, as CEO, lent consistent encouragement and enthusiasm, which was greatly appreciated.

As managing editor, Jane Doyle Guthrie served many roles in this undertaking. Throughout it all, she has been extremely dedicated to the project, has worked very hard to see it to its completion, and in the process has shown that not only is she a managing editor of the first order but also a very caring professional, sensitive to the special concerns involved in writing a book on adolescent assessment. The efforts of each member of the TCA editorial staff is acknowledged with gratitude, for the great many tasks involved in building a book.

The chapter authors have worked very hard for many months through several revisions of their chapters to produce a book that is balanced in its presentation. The expertise that each one brings to the field of adolescent assessment has been reflected in their chapters. The fact that such an array of professional psychologists, representing many specialties, contributed to this book is sure to be one of its greatest strengths. For the time and effort involved in making that contribution, the contributing authors have my deepest admiration and appreciation.

Ronda Consolver deserves my special gratitude for her assistance in typing several of the manuscripts.

Finally, the adolescents with whom many of the contributors worked and on whom they based their case studies merit a note of thanks, for making this book come to life and for helping us to see that they truly are special and deserving of the highest standard of professional care.

R.G.H.

REFERENCES

Elkind, D. (1984). *All grown up & no place to go: Teenagers in crisis.* Reading, MA: Addison-Wesley.

1

Adolescent Assessment: Current Practices and Future Prospects

KATHRYN C. GERKEN, PH.D.

Santrock (1984) has stated that we are in the midst of an explosion of knowledge about adolescent development, yet professionals continue to debate whether adolescence is a cultural creation (Proefrock, 1983) or a separate stage of development, a period of "storm and stress" or a relatively peaceful developmental phase (Looney, 1985; Siddique & D'Arcy, 1984). Siegel (1982) believes there is ample evidence to indicate that adolescence is a separate stage of development and suggests that investigations focus on the combination of physiological-anatomical and social-psychological changes that occur during this period. In view of the statistics regarding adolescent problems such as suicide, substance abuse, and unplanned pregnancies (Green & Horton, 1982; Ross-Reynolds & Hardy, 1985; Svobodny, 1982), continued investigation of the biological, psychological, and cultural events that mark the transition from childhood to adulthood appears essential.

In spite of public and professional awareness of adolescent problems, Looney (1985) reports that adolescent development remains relatively unstudied from a database perspective. He discusses the discrepancy between the "clinical care" that adolescents receive and the research on which "clinical care" is based. Looney suggests that research is needed to define further both the adolescent developmental process and its components—physiology, cognition, morals, sexual behavior, socialization, self-concept, educational and vocational competency, ideals, value systems, and identity. Large-scale epidemiological surveys, refined etiological studies, and rigorous follow-up studies should result in improved assessment and treatment.

Members of the National Middle School Association were asked to indicate research priorities concerning adolescents (Clark, Babich, & Burpeau, 1981). The majority of the respondents were male administrators, and at least 90% of them identified 16 priority areas for research. The top ten combined rankings were motivation/ interest; self-concept; attitudes toward adults; influence of different types of family structure on school-related behavior; attitude toward authority; social factors influencing behavior; how children learn; involvement with alcohol, tobacco, and drugs; attitudes toward peers; and involvement with sexual behavior.

Professionals must determine how to conduct adolescent assessments that will lead to positive changes and whether there are assessment instruments and techniques that are technically adequate, comprehensive, precise, economical, useful, and appropriate for adolescents. This age group traditionally has been given little atten-

1

tion by school psychologists, developmental psychologists, psychiatrists, and health-care providers (Green & Horton, 1982; Hobbs & Robinson, 1982; Looney, 1985; Nagle & Medway, 1982). Kiestenbaum (1985) points out that serious mistakes in adolescent intervention have been made because of lack of information. Assessment and treatment, for example, has often focused on a single symptom.

Messick (1983) states that one of the major goals of assessment is to maximize the validity of test interpretation and to minimize construct-irrelevant task difficulty. He emphasizes the necessity for considering context when assessing a child and for appraising under realistic conditions of functioning. Messick defines context as those aspects of the environment that illuminate or add to the meaning of the focal variables and their functioning. He reports that the three broad areas of child assessment are 1) cognition, 2) personal and social functioning, and 3) health and physical status, and he discusses the numerous aspects of context that must be considered when assessing an individual. There is a need to note, for example, characteristics of the examiner or researcher and the measurement procedures as well as the social and educational experiences the child/adolescent brings to the setting. The interaction of these variables must also be considered. Messick's major point is that child assessment results should never be interpreted in isolation.

Kagan (1983) believes that developmental psychology is about to experience a renaissance as tired dogma is refuted, more sensitive measurement techniques are introduced into the laboratory, and data, rather than unsubstantiated assumptions, provide the ideas for investigation. He believes that there will be new methods of assessment, such as computer analyses of electrocortical recordings for thought, using memory to measure motivational and additudinal variables, using selective recall to evaluate the position of an attribute in a hierarchy of related beliefs, and employing multidimensional scaling to assess the categories children and adults use to structure experiences.

Will these new methods be applicable and available to the adolescent? Has the adolescent fared any better than the child or adult who is being assessed in the 1980s? Have we created innovative approaches to adolescent assessment that are based on developmental theory, or have we simply produced downward/upward extensions of existing techniques? The purpose of this chapter is to review adolescent assessment both in the 1980s and as projected for the future. Excellent resources are available that list, describe, and evaluate existing instruments. Only a few instruments are described in this chapter; those described in detail are not necessarily the best instruments, but were chosen because they represent either a certain type of instrument, a revision of a widely used instrument, or an innovation.

There are many resources available besides test manuals to help examiners determine whether an assessment technique, procedure, or instrument is appropriate. Salvia and Ysseldyke (1985) describe three references provided by the Buros Institute of Mental Measurements: *Tests in Print* (three editions), *The Mental Measurements Yearbooks* (nine editions) and a computerized data base. In addition, Test Corporation of America publishes a series of volumes entitled *Test Critiques* (Keyser & Sweetland, 1984-86). *A Consumer's Guide to Tests in Print* is described by Brown and Bryant (1984). The authors have identified objective principles regarding the norms, reliability, and validity of standardized tests. In compiling this guide, assessment experts were asked to review tests and complete a Reviewer Evaluation Form, indicating whether the measure was Unacceptable, Acceptable, or Good. Contrary to some of the earlier such guides that considered all variables equally, an Acceptable rating in this instance can be obtained only with a combination of Acceptable and Good ratings for the norms, reliability, and validity.

There are numerous textbooks, such as those by Salvia and Ysseldyke (1985) and Taylor (1984), that provide critical reviews of assessment instruments, and of course professional journals such as *Remedial and Special Education, School Psychology Review, Journal of School Psychology, Journal of Psychoeducational Assessment,* and *Journal of Educational Measurement* often review tests.

Concern regarding the quality of available assessment instruments is evident in these publications, but also in the 30-year history of the publication of professional standards for educational and psychological tests by the American Psychological Association. The latest revisions of the *Standards for Educational and Psychological Testing* (American Educational Research Association, American Psychological Association, & National Council on Measurement in Education, 1985) provide criteria for the evaluation of tests, testing practices, and the effects of test use. Specifically, standards are provided for test construction, use, particular applications, and administrative procedures, and are considered of either Primary or Secondary importance. *Conditional* is used to describe those standards that vary in importance with the use of the test. It is stated that, ideally, all relevant Primary standards should be met at the time of publication or first operational use of the test. The major change in the 1985 versus 1974 *Standards* is the emphasis on appropriate test use. These standards are to be applied to constructed performance tasks, questionnaires, and to a lesser extent structured behavior samples.

AREAS OF ASSESSMENT

Thorough assessment of an adolescent must include information about the environment, health and physical status, social and emotional functioning, cognitive and academic abilities, linguistic competence and performance, and vocational interests and skills. Assessment in these areas cannot be conducted in isolation, as a student may exhibit competence in a specific setting or in a single area, yet not be able to perform in another setting or when a combination of skills are required.

Health and Physical Status

There is no question that the person who provides services to adolescents in a variety of settings must gather medical/health information and refer students in need for a physical examination. Information from a thorough health inventory or questionnaire may be the first step toward an appropriate intervention. Johnson and Tanner (1983) designed such a questionnaire for physicians that could be adopted for use by other human service providers. Anastasi (1982) briefly reviews two health status measures developed in the 1980s—the Sickness Impact Profile and The Index of Well-Being. Both instruments have been subjected to extensive research and have proved useful in planning intervention. Swisher, Shute, and Bibeau (1984) report on the reliability and validity of a survey instrument that assesses drug and alcohol abuse. Although limited geographically (Pennsylvania), their sample is large (N = 40,000), and the administration and reporting of scores and gathering of reliability and validity data meet acceptable standards.

Coleman (1986) has developed a computer-based health risk assessment called "Feeling Great," which soon will be available commercially. It has several unique features and could be used with adolescents in various settings, providing a link between assessment and intervention. One of the major components of the instrument is the Health Monitor, which consists of 50 or more questions about health history, smoking, nutrition, weight, exercise, stress, drugs and alcohol, accident prevention, and personal habits. The computer presents a histogram that displays the student's relative performance in each of the eight categories. A student may then proceed to the Health Advisor to learn about behavior that can be changed to improve the overall Feeling Great Index. This written material is similar to that typically found in a beginning health course, thus not of great interest even though valuable. The student may then set and review Health Goals and see graphically what effect meeting these goals will have on the overall Index. The student also has access to hotline information about alcohol/drug centers, crisis lines, emergency lines, and general medical and poison control centers. The teacher side of the diskette allows a teacher to modify the questionnaire and the Hotline Information by adding or deleting items and allows the teacher to update the student disk. An instructional manual will be available for consumer use. Information regarding development and technical adequacy is not available, but an initial review of the instrument shows good content validity.

Environment

Although the 1980s have not yielded innovative techniques for assessing the environment, the decade has produced a recognition of the necessity for such an evaluation. Environmental assessment, done either formally or informally, is an integral part of an evaluation. The process can be very structured and conducted via direct observation, checklists, inventories, interviews, and so on. Such an assessment examines the physical and social/emotional aspects of the environment in order to identify those elements that may affect the student's progress.

Perry (1982) believes that the major health problems evidenced by adolescents (e.g., unplanned pregnancy, smoking, drug and alcohol abuse, etc.) are social rather than physical in nature. Asserting that the school environment is one of the most potent variables affecting the presence or absence of health problems, he reports a study comparing schools judged "healthy" versus those considered "unhealthy." "Unhealthy" schools were those with a high rate of student absenteeism, both excused and unexcused, and suspensions for disciplinary actions, while "healthy" ones seemed more personalized and responsive and had clear organizational guidelines.

Adaptive Behavior

The adaptive behavior measures that were available during the 1970s had serious limitations. Reschly (1985) and Salvia and Ysseldyke (1985) discuss those limitations along with suggestions for the best practices in assessment of adaptive behavior, noting that these procedures are not sufficiently well developed to allow decisions to be based on single instruments. The technical adequacy and comprehensiveness were major shortcomings in the 1970s, and during the 1980s new adaptive behavior instruments and revisions of old ones have been introduced. Do they have the same problems? Reviews of the AAMD Adaptive Behavior Scales, School Edition, and the Vineland Adaptive Behavior Scale, Classroom Edition, indicate that reliability is too low for placement and programming decisions (Salvia & Ysseldyke, 1985). Additional validity studies are needed for these measures as well as for the Comprehensive Test of Adaptive Behavior, the Normative Adaptive Behavior Checklist, and the Scales of Independent Behavior in order to determine their value in assessing adolescent adaptive behavior. All the measures published in the 1980s seem to be based on a developmental model of adaptive behavior, and technical adequacy has improved in the majority of cases.

SOCIAL SKILLS

Assessing social skills has been emphasized during the last decade because they are believed to be related to cognitive development, academic achievement, classroom behavior, and teacher and peer acceptance (Gresham, 1985). Recent reviews of the literature on peer relations (Hartup, 1983; Newman, 1982) indicate that peer experiences can play a major role in the socialization of the individual child. Their precise impact is unknown, but it appears that situational social skills are prerequisites for acceptance by others.

Gresham and Elliott (1984) evaluated six methods for assessing social skills and concluded that assessment in this area is not well advanced. They believe normative data are needed on large samples of socially skilled children at various ages, and that examiners require fundamental skills in both behavioral assessment and knowledge of social development in order to perform valid assessments. Techniques such as peer nominations or ratings, behavioral role plays, interviews, self-reports, and naturalistic observation do not meet "ideal" standards; current data support ratings by others and naturalistic observation as the most appropriate techniques for this kind of assessment (Brockman, 1985; Gresham & Elliott, 1984). The need for a multimethod approach is evident, whether one is assessing for identification or intervention.

A recent article regarding social skills assessment by De Apodaca, Watson, Mueller, and Isaacson-Kailes (1985) offers an example of inappropriate assessment. The authors reworded items on the Peer Rating Scale, which was developed for students up to age 12, and asked peers to rate 29 orthopedically impaired students and 120 regular students in Grades 9-12; their assumption that the underlying dimensions, factor structure, and scores were appropriate for adolescents lacked merit.

Adams, Schvaneveldt, Jenson, and Jones (1982) expressed concern about the use of sociometric techniques with adolescents and attempted to validate a self-report alternative with 115 adolescents. Self-perceived social impact and social preference were measured, and it was revealed that self-report and teacher nominations were unrelated assessments of social relations categories during adolescence, and neither was effective in identifying social relations categories that differentiate adolescents on empathy or social sensitivity. The authors concluded that adolescents may be unable to provide an objective self-assessment of their social impact and peer-determined preferences, and teachers may lack the necessary background information to make appropriate and valid classifications of adolescents.

Matson, Rotatori, and Helsel (1983) developed a scale (the Matson Evaluation of Social Skills in Youngsters) for assessing the social skills of children between 4 and 18 years of age. The self-report form was completed on 422 children and the teacher report on 322 children. The authors attempted to look at developmental differences and found age differences on both forms. Not enough information, however, is provided in this study about subject characteristics, reliability, and validity.

Waksman (1985) developed a 21-item scale for Grades K-12 entitled the Waksman Social Skills Rating Scale (WSSRS). The scale was standardized on 331 students; 63 were from Grades 9-12 and 155 were in Grades 6-12. The two-factor structure of the instrument was determined via factor analysis. The author provides much of the information suggested in the 1985 *Standards for Educational and Psychological Testing*. Evidence of reliability was provided via internal consistency, test-retest, and interrater data. Criterion-related validity is presented through a correlation with the Portland Problem Behavior Checklist-Revised. The WSSRS total score correlation for 304 subjects was .65. Construct validity was evidenced by a comparative study of the normative sample and two groups of children classified as emotionally disturbed. The restricted geographic region and small sample size for some of the studies limits the generalizability of the findings. This instrument appears to be one of the few developed in the 1980s that may be reliable, valid, and practical.

Self-Esteem

The preponderance of recent literature regarding adolescents focuses on self-esteem, and the self-esteem literature overwhelmingly supports the view of a multidimensional construct that must be viewed from a developmental perspective (Byrne, 1984; Damon & Hart, 1982; Griffin, Chassin, & Young, 1981; Harter, 1983; Marsh & O'Neill, 1984; Petersen, Schulenberg, Abramowitz, Offer, & Jarcho, 1984; Savin-Williams & Jaquish, 1981; Savin-Williams & Demo, 1983).

Savin-Williams and colleagues Jaquish (1981) and Demo (1983) concluded that longitudinal studies of adolescent self-esteem were needed in which a diversity of measures and methods would be used. The 1981 study found low correlations between behavioral ratings, peer-ratings, and self-report ratings of self-esteem, leading to a suggestion that direct observation was needed using unobtrusive, nonreactive measures. The paging/beeper system they used for self-reports was problematic but unique. In 1983, Savin-Williams and Jaquish found that the intercorrelations among the variety of self-esteem instruments they used ranged from 0-.81 and suggested that a major portion of the professional literature provides too narrow a view of self-esteem for those concerned with adolescent development.

Openshaw, Thomas, and Rollins (1981, 1983) described two views of self-esteem in children: 1) as a function of parents' reflected appraisal of a child's inherent worth (evidenced during parent-child interactions) and 2) as positively related to parents' self-esteem, indicated by self-reports. These authors posited that both views may be viable and may influence self-esteem at different times. In studying 184 families with

14- to 18-year-olds (N = 368), they found that self-esteem was more a function of social interaction, reflecting the approval of significant others rather than modeling parental self-esteem.

In Harter's (1983) review of self-esteem, she reports there is no current scale that has adopted a developmental framework to assess self-esteem. No one knows whether the factor structure of self-esteem tests change across different developmental levels or in different populations. She has listed hypothesized dimensions of developmental changes in self-esteem, but has no data to support or refute these dimensions. Harter discusses the psychometric considerations in such assessments and provides a brief review of four assessment instruments.

Affective Variables

Professional and popular literature make it clear that stress, depression, and anxiety do occur in adolescents and Robbins and Alessi (1985) report that suicide is the third leading cause of death in adolescents. Controversy continues over the value and adequacy of methods used to assess personality functioning (Goh & Fuller, 1983).

Siegel and Griffin (1983) attempted to quantify the behavioral cues adolescents used to identify their peers as depressed. Ninety-nine 12- to 18-year-olds completed the Concept of Depression Questionnaire, which was designed to elicit their opinions regarding the characteristics of a depressed adolescent. A common element cited frequently in this study was social isolation. The adolescents also felt that substance abuse and trouble with the law were associated with depression among their peers. Siegel and Griffin (1983) factor-analyzed responses to the open-ended questions "What do you think a depressed teenager is like?" and "What causes a teenager to feel depressed?" There were two factors with sufficient loading for interpretation of the first question. Factor one consists of four items (dejected mood, angry, rejected by others, and not pleasant to be with); factor two had high loadings on bored and lonely. Relative to the second question (regarding causes of depression), three factors emerged. The first appeared to be general, without a specific theme (illness, loss of relationship, trouble with law, boredom, drugs, lack of money), whereas the second had a high loading on problems at school and moderate loadings on problems with parents and peers. The third factor consisted of two items, loneliness and rejection. Siegel and Griffin (1983) point out that their findings are highly consistent with the symptoms listed in the *Diagnostic and Statistical Manual of Mental Disorders* (DSM-III; American Psychiatric Association, 1980), specifically the "age-specific associated features."

Newcomb, Huba, and Bentler (1981) report that even though adolescence is viewed as a period vulnerable to life changes and stress, there have been relatively few studies regarding adolescent stress. These authors report that, typically, research in this area adopts a measure used to assess adult stress. Chandler (1983) has created an instrument specifically to assess children's (Grades K-8) reactions to stress, while Forman, Edison, and Hagan (1983) and Newcomb et al. (1981) have developed instruments to measure stress in adolescents. Information regarding the Life Events Questionnaire (Newcomb et al., 1981) and a brief version of the Adolescent Life Change Event Scale (Forman et al., 1983) makes it clear that additional validation of stress measures is needed. It appears that specific *types* of stress need to be investigated, not overall stress, and that a multitrait-multimethod validation design would be preferred.

Most of the instruments developed to assess assertiveness have been designed for adult populations, yet lack of assertiveness has been identified as an area of concern for children. Lee, Halberg, Slemon, and Haase (1985) have developed a situation-specific instrument for students in Grades 6-12 called the Assertiveness Scale for Adolescents. The ASA was administered to 682 sixth-, eighth-, tenth-, and twelfth-graders in Ontario. Lee et al. (1985) describe the content validation and provide reliability, validity (criterion-related and construct), and normative data. The internal consistency and test-retest reliability coefficients are at .76, and the criterion-related validity coefficients range from .03 to .55, depending on the criterion. The instrument needs to be validated against behavioral criteria.

Academic Issues

Gresham (1983) summarizes the major problems with psychoeducational assessment as (a) obtaining insufficient assessment information, (b) using technically inadequate tests, and (c) using measures that yield inappropriate or educationally irrelevant information. He advocates assessing the same student trait with more than one method in order to obtain more valid and relevant information. What Gresham says has been asserted before in different ways, but professionals have failed nonetheless to apply this knowledge.

It is unlikely that there will be any decrease in academic referrals during the next decade. PL 94-142 brought with it an increase in psychoeducational assessments as school personnel and parents sought services for students previously considered ineligible. Declining scores on standardized tests, the "back to basics" movement, and minimum competency testing have resulted in increased psychoeducational studies to find out why many students appear unable to do satisfactory academic work.

Regardless of the student's age, it is the responsibility of the person conducting or directing academic evaluation to ensure a differentiated assessment based on (a) factors within the student, such as overall ability and motivation, (b) factors in the student's instructional environment, such as the curriculum and teaching methods and materials, (c) factors in the student's physical environment, and (d) factors in the student's interpersonal environment, such as teacher-student interactions.

Academic skills. The scarcity of technically adequate, useful academic assessment instruments necessitates the combination of formal and informal techniques both for testing and teaching. Rather than using inadequate individual tests, the professional will find it necessary to reconsider the use of group tests for screening. The instrument selection process goes beyond group versus individual, screening versus diagnostic, or norm-versus criterion-referenced. The quest is for instruments that are technically adequate, provide large enough samples of behavior, and are linked to the curriculum. A technically adequate test that results in scores but no other information is not useful for planning intervention. The achievement test with content that does not reflect the curriculum in the school or classroom also has limited value.

Although there are innumerable diagnostic tests to assess academic areas, few of them provide sufficient information about individual strengths and weaknesses. If a technically adequate survey test has already been used to identify broad areas of difficulty, there is no need to waste time administering an inadequate diagnostic test. Some of the standardized diagnostic tests could be used as informal tests to identify specific problem areas.

Numerous books and articles have been written about the development of teacher-made tests or informal inventories. Guidelines differ but also share commonalities that are beneficial in developing a test. Such measures can take the form of very thorough inventories or checklists for specific instructional techniques. An example of a thorough mathematics inventory, for instance, is the 1985 Sequential Assessment of Mathematics Inventory (SAMI) developed by Reisman and Hutchinson. Hambleton (1982) describes the steps for building a criterion-referenced test, and Gerken (1983) summarizes various guidelines for developing informal evaluations of mathematics, spelling, and writing. Suggestions for developing an informal reading inventory are available from several sources (Elliott & Piersel, 1982; Hammill & Bartel, 1982; Wallace & Larsen, 1978).

Bejar (1984) discusses two traditional approaches to academic evaluation—deficit assessment and error analysis. He believes that academic assessment would be most effective if it were based on methods from cognitive psychology and artificial intelligence. Bejar states that a cognitive approach would enable the attribution of errors to specific causes, and he then explains how computers could assist in the analysis.

Numerous instruments have been developed in the 1980s to assess academic skills, but many have the same problems as those instruments they were intended to replace. For example, the Diagnostic Spelling Potential Test (DSPT), which would be age-appropriate for adolescents, was reviewed by Reynolds in 1983, and his final statement was that the DSPT was not recommended for the assessment of handicapped or other children at this time (p. 482). Salvia and Ysseldyke's (1985) review of the third edition of the Durrell Analysis of Reading Difficulty (DARD) suggests that it be used only as an informal assessment tool, because norm-referenced use is hindered by inadequate standardization, absence of a description of the norm group, and limited data on reliability and validity. Bryant and Brown (1985) also reviewed the DARD and found it wanting in its standardization and normative scores. Lipa (1985) reviewed the 1981 revised edition of the Diagnostic Reading Scales (DRS) and reported little advantage in using the DRS in preference to other published informal reading inventories. Salvia and Ysseldyke (1985) reviewed the 1984 Test of Mathematical Abilities (TOMA). Their evaluative comments are generally negative as they express concern about its technical adequacy, including norms, test-retest reliability, and content, criterion-related, and construct validity.

Four instruments that appear to add a new dimension to the assessment of adolescents who are experiencing academic difficulties are the Basic Achievement Skills Individual Screener (BASIS), the Kaufman Test of Educational Achievement (KTEA), the Sequential Assessment of Mathematics Inventories (SAMI), and the Brigance Diagnostic Inventory of Essential Skills. The BASIS and KTEA have been well standardized and can serve as efficient screening tests. The KTEA also provides information on conducting error analysis. The SAMI was initially developed as an informal math inventory and may still be most useful as such because of over- and underrepresentation in the standardization population and some low reliability coefficients for subtests. The Brigance inventory is useful in planning and evaluating instruction for adolescents who are functioning below average, but it cannot be used to classify students. Evidence of interrater reliability or alternate form reliability is needed even for its continued use as a criterion-referenced instrument.

Study skills. Kuepper (1985) has reviewed the area of study skills and offers suggestions for assessing and remediating study skill deficits in adolescents. Study skill deficits represent just one of the many variables that might account for lower-than-expected achievement. What is new in the 1980s is the recognition that such skills need to be assessed. For example, Deshler and his colleagues (Deshler, Schumaker, Lenz, & Ellis, 1984; Deshler & Schumaker, 1986) have developed a set of task-specific learning strategies for low-achieving adolescents. The first step in their learning strategy instructional process is to understand the types of curriculum demands that the student is failing to meet (such as listening and taking notes). The student is assessed to determine his or her current learning habits regarding a particular task and informed of strengths and weaknesses. The teaching methodology consists of a pretest, providing knowledge of the strategy, modeling the strategy, having the student use verbal rehearsal, practicing the strategy to a specified criterion in controlled materials, practicing the strategy to a mastery criterion in materials and situations that approximate classroom tasks, and taking a posttest. Reinforcement and corrective feedback are given after each practice attempt. The data that have been gathered regarding the effectiveness of the learning strategies indicate that significant student gains seem highly correlated with the level of staff training. The authors recognize that additional research is needed. It is important to determine what students benefit most/least from these interventions and to determine the long-term impact of these interventions on academic success and life adjustment.

Intelligence/Cognition

During the 1960s, the measurement of intelligence fell from a position of high respectability in psychology. Critics of intellectual assessment were concerned with the trivial content of tests and stated that such measures were scientifically unfounded and harmful. The value of intellectual assessment has been questioned in the 1970s and '80s because there appears to be no link between assessment of intelligence and intervention. Hobbs and Robinson (1982) express special concern about the limited research (both in quantity and quality) available on the cognitive functioning of adolescents. Investigations are needed that specifically explore cognitive development and modifiability in adolescents. Hobbs and Robinson suggest the following in order to enhance adolescent functioning: investigate the nature and use of intelligence under various circumstances, systematically assess cognitive skills, teach basic academic skills, and teach general cognitive competence.

The last 10 years have brought about a resurgence of efforts to translate laboratory findings into measures of human ability and to demonstrate the relationship between processes studied in controlled settings and processes involved in measures of individual differences in ability. There appear to be four major explicit conceptions of intelligence in the 1980s: learning/behaviorist perspective, psychometric perspective, Piagetian perspective, and information-processing perspective (Sternberg & Powell, 1983; Wagner & Sternberg, 1984). Clearly more of the professional literature and more research is devoted to the information-processing perspective. New and revised tests of intelligence and/or cognitive ability have appeared in the 1980s. Some have unique titles, formats, and proposed uses, while others have copied and closely resemble existing instruments.

The Test of Nonverbal Intelligence (TONI), published by PRO-ED in 1982, is a new performance measure that was developed for 5- to 85-year-olds. Adequate internal consistency and alternate form reliability coefficients have been obtained. However, limited validity data are reported, and the test assesses a single component of intelligence (problem solving). Cautious use of this test is recommended until additional data are provided about validity and stability across time.

The long-awaited revision of the Wechsler Adult Intelligence Scale appeared in 1981, showing few item changes. Kaufman (1985) expressed more concern about "non-changes" than changes; for example, there are still too few easy items for assessing low-functioning adults. Standardization of the WAIS-R and the evidence of its reliability are praised by Kaufman (1985) and Matarazzo (1985). However, concern regarding the lack of validity data was expressed as well as concern over the fact that 16- to 19-year-olds did not perform as well as 20- to 24-year-olds.

In 1986, the fourth edition of the Stanford-Binet Intelligence Scale was released as a major revision of Form L-M. The test authors present the instrument as a multistage adaptive test designed to measure the pattern and overall level of cognitive development from ages 2 to adult. To date there have been no critical reviews of the test or technical data provided other than that which is now available from the publisher. Reference is made in the *Guide for Administering and Scoring* manual to *The Expanded Guide for Interpreting Fourth Edition Results*. However, this guide is not currently available. Publication is expected in late 1986 or 1987.

Some of the apparent problems with the new Binet are discussed openly by the authors while others are not. The sample was overrepresented for the managerial/professional category of parental occupation and for the college graduate or beyond category of parental education. Weighting procedures were used in order to adjust for this discrepancy. A very positive aspect of the technical manual is that tables are provided that show the means and standard deviations obtained by persons representing numerous demographic breakdowns. Ages 18-23 are grouped together for each analysis. In view of the findings on the WAIS-R, it is reasonable to assume that some information of value to those who work with young adults may be missing. In every area except short-term memory, this age group obtained the lowest mean and largest standard deviation compared to other age groups. Test-retest reliability information is provided for only two samples (5- and 8-year-olds); thus, additional reliability data are needed, as well as validity studies that cover more diverse groups relative to age and other characteristics.

This brief overview of some of the measures of intellect or cognition developed in the 1980s underscores Hobbs and Robinson's concerns about the lack of information regarding adolescent cognitive skills. The developers of new instruments have not focused on the adolescent and in some instances have assumed that adolescents and young adults can be "lumped" together.

Language Skills

Language experts in the 1970s added a dimension to language assessment that must be appropriately assessed in children and adults (Gallagher, 1983; Prutting & Kirchner, 1983; Wiig & Semel, 1980): assessing the functional and social use of language, or *pragmatics,* has been deemed as important as assessing phonology, syntax, and semantics.

Very few recent articles or books are available about the assessment of adolescent language. O'Connor and Eldredge (1981), for example, present a very traditional approach to the assessment of adolescent language skills, emphasizing the need to compile a complete case study that includes language samples and traditional assessment instruments.

Wiig and Semel (1980) state that the assumption is proving erroneous that learning- and language-disabled students will outgrow their deficits as they reach adolescence and adulthood. Communication deficits may continue to exert a negative influence on the quality of interpersonal interactions. These authors also express concern about language deficits that begin early in life and go untreated; they may persist and emerge again and again as the individual ages. Circumstances such as a new job that places demands both on language processing skills and their use in speaking and writing may make these deficits reappear. Wiig and Semel (1980) believe that increased professional attention to developing functional and adequate communication skills, up to personal potential, should benefit both the individual and society. Are the language measures developed in the 1980s sufficiently comprehensive and appropriate for adolescents?

Reynolds (1983) briefly reviews the Language Inventory for Teachers, which was designed for children in preschool through junior high, and states that it should not be used for placement or programming until adequate validity data are obtained. Brown and Bryant's (1985) review of measures of spoken vocabulary rates the Peabody Picture Vocabulary Test-Revised (PPVT-R) and the Listening/Vocabulary subtest of the Test of Adolescent Language (TOAL) as unacceptable because of inadequate reliability and/or validity data. Salvia and Ysseldyke's (1985) review of the TOAL indicates that composite scores reliability is good and clear evidence for validity exists. They express concern, however, about insufficient data on the standardization sample.

Wiig developed the Let's Talk Inventory for Adolescents in order to provide a standardized method of eliciting and probing selected communication functions and speech acts, those that represent the ritualizing, informing, controlling, and feeling functions of verbal communication. The author indicates that the inventory provides diagnostic information relative to the need for pragmatic training and that it should not be used for an initial diagnosis of language disorders or to determine educational placement. Wiig (1982) reports that the analysis of strengths and weaknesses can be applied directly to intervention by using materials she developed entitled *Let's Talk: Developing Prosocial Communication Skills.*

The Let's Talk Inventory was standardized on a small sample of adolescents (N = 116), the majority of whom were Caucasian, lived in urban or suburban areas, and represented lower to upper-middle SES groups. Several geographic regions were represented, but some regions were clearly under- or overrepresented. Wiig cautions the user regarding the use of the test with groups different from the standardization group; it is intended to be of value only when evaluating adequacy in formulating Standard American English forms of speech acts and communication functions. Content validity is described in the manual, but the attempt to provide construct validity is limited to looking at the performance of already-diagnosed children as compared to that of "normals." Internal consistency reliability coefficients ranged from .56-.85, depending on the age of the subjects. Test-retest reliability (N = 52) for 1- to 2-week periods was .77 for Segment A of the test, .59 for Segment B, and .59 for the total test. Interexaminer reliability indicated that there was over 99% agreement by two examiners rating 56 students. There are problems with the Let's Talk Inventory relative to its technical adequacy, but it represents the initial attempt to measure the fourth dimension of adolescent language—pragmatics.

Vocational Issues

Hohenshil, Levinson, and Heer (1985) emphasize that although there are not any new techniques in vocational assessment, a new emphasis has emerged. Interestingly, just as human service providers have expanded their view of vocational assessment, some state and local governing agencies have decreased the financial support for vocational programs. The reform movement aimed at increasing academic standards in schools has in some instances resulted in a decrease in vocational programs. In spite of such decreases, however, the vocational needs of adolescents must be considered in the assessment process. Comprehensive evaluation of an adolescent demands that one consider the internal and external factors that will affect the student's vocational choices. Hohenshil, Levinson, and Heer (1985) suggest that the following areas be assessed: mental ability, achievement, small and large muscle coordination, personality, social maturity, vocational aptitude, vocational adaptive behavior, and career maturity.

Whether one agrees with these particular components, it is clear that using a paper-pencil vocational aptitude test alone may not be appropriate. Often the examiner does not know the reading level of such instruments or their technical adequacy, and such measures may provide limited information regarding vocational needs. Shepard and Levinson (1985) provide an overview of vocational assessment for adolescents, emphasizing that school psychologists can use traditionally elicited data to obtain vocationally relevant information. Assessment that includes actual or simulated work experience, performance tests, and direct behavioral observation will provide much more meaningful information than vocational aptitude scores alone.

Instruments that identify vocational interests are available for adolescents, but examiners must look at the content and vocabulary of these instruments as well as their technical adequacy to determine their usefulness. Anastasi (1982) and Aiken (1985) provide thorough reviews, for example, of the Kuder interest inventories and the Strong-Campbell Interest Inventory. Revisions of these inventories have included attempts to eliminate sex bias. The instruments appear to have sufficient stability to use as part of vocational planning, but validity varies depending on the type of validity assessed, which specific inventory is used, and with what group. The reviews on the Jackson Vocational Interest Survey (Aiken, 1985; Anastasi, 1982) indicate that it is based on an extensive research program, has high reliability coefficients, and shows evidence of adequate predictive validity. The Career Directions Inventory and the Career Assessment Inventory are noteworthy because they are somewhat easier in content and vocabulary and emphasize nonprofessional occupations. Additional technical data are needed for these instruments.

A subject's aptitude and/or knowledge level usually comprise part of a vocational battery, and new instruments have been developed to assess these areas. The Ball Aptitude Battery (1981) was developed to measure skill abilities of senior high school students and adults. The standardization group consisted of 1,600 individuals, male and female. Black, white, and Hispanic students were chosen so that all groups were similar in SES. A review by Layton (1985) indicates that reliabilities vary considerably across subtests and for males and females. Further investigation of reliability and validity is needed before using the instrument to make individual decisions.

Wiederholt and Larsen's Test of Practical Knowledge (TPK) was developed to assess the knowledge of everyday life situations of students in Grades 8-12. The standardization sample consisted of 1,398 white students from predominantly urban areas in 11 different states. Starkman (1985) reports that the internal consistency reliability coefficients are all within an acceptable range (.80 to .90) except for the Personal scale, which was .77. Test-retest stability coefficients ranged from .76 for the Occupational section to .89 for the Personal area, with a total TPK stability coefficient of .85. Relative to validity, Starkman expressed concern that the TPK may not focus solely on "practical" knowledge: its correlation with achievement batteries indicate it is to some extent a measure of academic achievement.

TECHNIQUES OF ASSESSMENT

Interviews

Edelbrock and Costello (1984) report that the interview, which has long been the cornerstone of child clinical assessment, has been refined only recently to the point of yielding valid and reliable data. Two important new trends are specialized interview materials (designed for different purposes, age ranges, and disorders) and recognizing the value of a child's report in the assessment and diagnosis of childhood disorders. Wiens and Matarazzo (1983) report a trend toward incorporating more adaptive, semistructured or structured interviews of demonstrable reliability alongside the classic interview skills of putting the client at ease, knowing how to elicit information, maintaining rapport and control, and bringing about closure. Kiestenbaum (1985) emphasizes the importance of taking an accurate developmental history and ensuring that multidimensional assessment has taken place. She believes that information regarding level of functioning, constitutional predisposition for problems, specific symptoms or behaviors, and environmental stresses must be derived from the interview process.

Paget (1984) has reviewed various interview techniques now available, only two of which are appropriate for adolescents. She proposes that one proceed with caution in using interviews because further research is needed to support their use. Baker (1983) reports that interviews are used widely with adolescents. She believes that interviews can yield valid information or biased information (which the interviewer should try to recognize and control) and can provide an encounter between an adult and adolescent that shares features of everyday life. Baker suggests that interviewers take another look at the interview as a social encounter in order to understand better the adolescent's responses.

Edelbrock and Costello's (1984) review of Kovacs' Interview Schedule for Children indicates that this measure has several unique features. Designed for 8- to 17-year-olds, it begins with a brief unstructured interview that focuses on the duration and chronicity of any recent problems. The more structured portion of the interview deals with specific symptoms or behaviors. The first few questions for each behavior directly concern the behavior itself; if these questions elicit negative replies, the interviewer may skip the remaining questions about that particular behavior. The order in which questions are asked may vary, there are follow-up questions to confirm a child's initial response, and standard inquiries are abbreviated on the form. The interviewer may also rate various characteristics of the child observed during the interview and record diagnostic impressions for Axis I and II of DSM-III. Data on validity were not available, but interrater reliability for 46 interviews was .86. One problem may be lack of access to the instrument, as the Kovacs (1982) reference cites an unpublished manuscript without an address.

Hodges, Kline, Stern, Cytryn, and McKnew's (1982) Child Assessment Schedule (CAS) was standardized on 32 outpatients, 18 inpatients, 37 normal controls, who ranged in age from 7-14. No additional demographic data are given, though more are needed (particularly before any generalizations can be made). The CAS measures 11 content areas and nine symptom complexes as well as total psychopathology. Reliability studies consist of two types of interrater agreement data. Independent ratings of 53 interviews resulted in a correlation coefficient of .90 for the total score. Reliability coefficients were lower for the specific areas and for individual items. Concurrent validity was measured by comparing the performance of contrast groups on the CAS with maternal reports and with child self-reports. Significant discriminations were found between the performances of the inpatient, outpatient, and normal control children. The correlations between the CAS and the Child Depression Inventory and State-Trait Anxiety Inventory for Children were .53 and .54, respectively. Hodges et al. (1982) recognize the need for further research regarding reliability and validity. Edelbrock and Costello (1984) suggest that the CAS be used in conjunction with a behavioral checklist.

Siegel, Matthews, and Leitch (1981) developed the Adolescent Structured Interview (ASI) in order to identify Type A behavior patterns in 13- to 18-year-olds. The interview consists of 22 content ratings and six behavior and speech ratings. Content and construct validation is described by the authors, and there is support for the ASI yielding three independent factors: interview behaviors, impatience, and hard-driving. These three factors in turn were found to relate to other measures of Type A behavior. Additional research is needed, including studies of reliability.

According to Edelbrock and Costello's review (1984), most of the structured interviews for children and adolescents yield global indices that are reliable enough to detect the presence or absence of a disorder, but few provide dependable information about specific behaviors. The validity of most of these interviews is weak, and more comprehensive studies are needed to determine their reliability. Edelbrock and Costello believe two trends will continue in interviewing: a synergistic combination of assessment methods and procedures, and the application of computers to the assessment and diagnosis of childhood disorders.

Standardized and Nonstandardized Testing

Hambleton (1982) states that the 10-year battle for supremacy in the testing world is nearly over and there is no winner. Both criterion- and norm-referenced tests play important roles in providing data for decision making. Standardized testing serves an important purpose when applied judiciously and in conjunction with other techniques. It is important that both quantitative and qualitative analyses of the results take place. For example, informal techniques such as error pattern analysis should be performed routinely in all types of assessment, yet the 1985 Kaufman Test of Educational Achievement is one of the few standardized tests to include such analysis.

Many criterion-referenced tests are available to the consumer and they range considerably in content, grade levels, and technical quality. Hambleton observes that there is substantial room for improvement in the preparation of commercially available criterion-referenced tests. There are usually no standardization data or information regarding the technical adequacy of these instruments. Content may be dated or too limited, the most critical component for scoring may be examiner expertise, and interpretation can be highly subjective. The most helpful academic assessment instruments are those developed from the student's own textbooks, but unless the examiner/ test developer has knowledge of both the specific academic area and test construction, these results must be interpreted cautiously as well.

Curriculum-based assessment (CBA) or curriculum-based measurement (CBM) have become the bywords in academic assessment. CBA is now recommended as the alternative to traditional psychometric testing. Recent issues of *Exceptional Children* (Tucker, 1985) and *School Psychology Review* (Fuchs & Fuchs, 1986) are devoted to this form of assessment; the articles describe a theoretical framework, applications in various settings, and a legal base of support for CBA. The term *direct assessment* has also been used by some authors to describe CBA. Gickling and Thompson (1985) identify curriculum-based assessment as "a methodology used to determine the instructional needs of students based upon their performances within existing course content" (p. 216). Deno (1985) states that CBM is an emerging alternative to commercial standardized tests and to informal observations because it combines the advantages of both. He goes on to point out certain limitations of CBM, but presents a case for its use at least as a supplement to current assessment practice. The success of CBM or CBA should be reflected in improved programs for students.

Computer-Assisted Assessment

Matarazzo (1983) expresses concern about administering and interpreting psychological tests via computer. A variety of human service providers and their staffs have access to low-cost microcomputers and software that can be used in various ways during the assessment process. Computers have been used to assist with test administration, scoring, and analysis, report writing, and data management (Brantley, 1984; Brown, 1984; McCullough, 1985; McCullough & Wenck, 1984). Presently there are few standardized tests that have been computerized for administration to school-aged youth, but many adult personality tests and interviews have been computerized and are often administered with the subject unattended and unsupervised. Without supervision, however, the examiner/interpreter cannot tell whether the subject needed assistance at any point in reading or responding to the questions asked. An intake interview with "If . . ., then" statements might look like a valuable time-saver for subject and examiner, but will prove so only if the subject is comfortable and competent while interacting with the computer. Normative data for many of these instruments are based on paper-pencil administrations (Brantley, 1984), and thus norms based on the computerized format are needed. Matarazzo (1983) points out that the predictive validity of such tests remains to be scientifically appraised.

The most controversial use of the computer is for test analysis or interpretation. One of the popular acronyms of the 1980s is CBTI—computer-based test interpretation (Kramer, 1985), based on automated clinical or actuarial predictions. Clinical predictions consist of a series of interpretive statements developed by an individual to fit a specific theoretical orientation. These statements are believed to have support in the research literature, and an attempt is made to determine the relationship between these statements and the input data. An actuarial system is based on statistical regularities that have been demonstrated between certain input and output data. McDermott and Watkins, for example, have developed a program called the McDermott Multidimensional Actuarial Classification (M-MAC), published by The Psychological Corporation in 1985. Although the initial software programs designed to interpret psychological tests were for adults, CBTI programs are now available for use with children and adolescents in a wide variety of assessment areas. Computer displays are in abundance at professional conventions, yet easy access to the software is a major concern. Kramer (1985) notes with concern that CBTI publishers seem to exhibit even more resistance to submitting their products for review than do the traditional test publishers.

Matarazzo (1983) states that "Psychological testing carried out by a console is no more synonymous with psychological assessment than is the printout from a laboratory computer synonymous with professional assessment in clinical medicine" (p. 323), and he points out that computerized interpretations in the hands of an untutored and unqualified user can be harmful. McCullough (1985) and McCullough and Wenck (1984) suggest that test analyses conducted via computer should be used only to generate hypotheses. They believe that an interpretation that focuses on scores alone without including environmental, behavioral, and personality variables could lead to misdiagnosis and inappropriate interventions.

Bejar (1984) and McArthur and Choppin (1984) are especially enthusiastic about computerized diagnostic assessment as they believe the computer will be able both to increase score precision and incorporate additional information such as response latency. They also believe that because diagnosis is an interactive process, the computer could best sort through all the possible causes for a student's problem. Kramer (1985), however, expresses concern because CBTI has no more treatment validity than the traditional interpretation. He believes that it is unlikely that there will be evidence to support such validity, when most of the popular CBTI programs are based on tests that themselves do not have treatment validity.

McArthur and Choppin (1984) cite the successful use of computers in medical diagnosis as reason enough to use this approach in education. Kramer (1985) and McArthur and Choppin agree that the development of expert systems (computer programs designed to match the ability of a human expert in a particular problem area) hold promise for understanding intellective functioning.

McCullough (1985) stresses the need to focus on using the computer only as a tool to assist in the assessment process, not as the process itself. Edelbrock and Costello (1984) advocate computer-assisted diagnosis rather than "computer diagnosis." Brantley (1984), Kramer (1985), McCullough (1985), and Thomas (1984) explicitly or implicitly stress the need to ensure that the ethical and professional standards that should be in effect for all assessments be in effect when using the computer as an assessment tool.

CONCLUSIONS

The most difficult task facing assessors can be the selection and interpretation of appropriate assessment procedures. Although, as a professional, this author would like to believe that assessors are aware of the importance and responsibility of this task, there is evidence (Ysseldyke & Mirkin, 1982) to indicate many are not. Anastasi's 1967 warnings to psychologists are still appropriate in 1986. Psychologists, educators, and others are still searching for the perfect test, and test developers are still trying to provide it. At workshops for consumers, presenters often spend more time criticizing a competitor's test than presenting data to support the use of their own instrument.

New approaches to assessment have appeared in the 1980s, and there are renewed efforts to provide data to support an assessment procedure. However, when reviewing assessment approaches intended specifically for the adolescent, one finds that few are multiple-component, data-based, developmental instruments that are also technically adequate. It is clear from the review of the literature on adolescent assessment that the traditional approaches have often lacked a bridge between diagnosis and intervention, and that what is desired in the 1980s is to provide the "missing link." An individual case study approach to assessment is still necessary—each adolescent is unique, and no one assessment system has been developed to meet all needs.

REFERENCES

Adams, G. R., Schvaneveldt, J. D., Jenson, G. O., & Jones, R. M. (1982). Sociometric research with adolescents: In search of a self-report alternative with evidence of psychometric validity. *Adolescence, 17*(68), 905-909.

Aiken, L. R. (1985). *Psychological testing and assessment* (5th ed.). Boston: Allyn & Bacon.

American Educational Research Association, American Psychological Association, & National Council on Measurement in Education. (1985). *Standards for educational and psychological testing.* Washington, DC: American Psychological Association.

American Psychiatric Association. (1980). *Diagnostic and statistical manual of mental disorders* (3rd ed.). Washington, DC: Author.

Anastasi, A. (1967). Psychology, psychologists, and psychological testing. *American Psychologist, 22,* 297-306.

Anastasi, A. (1982). *Psychological testing* (5th ed.). New York: Macmillan.

Baker, C. D. (1983). A "second look" at interviews with adolescents. *Journal of Youth and Adolescence, 12*(6), 501-519.

Bejar, I. J. (1984). Educational diagnostic assessment. *Journal of Educational Measurement, 21*(2), 175-189.

Brantley, J. C. (1984). Computers and school psychology training. *School Psychology Review, 13*(4), 449-454.

Brockman, M. P. (1985). Best practices in assessment of social skills and peer interaction. In A. Thomas & J. Grimes (Eds.), *Best practices in school psychology* (pp. 31-44). Kent, OH: National Association of School Psychologists.

Brown, D. T. (1984). Automated assessment in school and clinical psychology: Present status and future directions. *School Psychology Review, 13*(4), 455-460.

Brown, L., & Bryant, B. R. (1984). A consumer's guide to tests in print: The rating system. *Remedial and Special Education, 5*(1), 55-61.

Brown, L., & Bryant, B. R. (1985). The evaluation of selected measures of spoken vocabulary using the Consumer's Guide criteria. *Remedial and Special Education, 6*(1), 59-61.

Bryant, B. R., & Brown, L. (1985). A critical review of four measures of paragraph reading. *Remedial and Special Education, 6*(2), 52-55.

Byrne, B. M. (1984). The general/academic self-concept monological network: A review of construct validation research. *Review of Educational Research, 54*(3), 427-456.

Chandler, L. A. (1983). The Stress Response Scale: An instrument for use in assessing emotional adjustment reactions. *School Psychology Review, 12*(3), 260-265.

Clark, D. C., Babich, G., & Burpeau, M. Y. (1981). Priorities for research in early adolescent learner characteristics: A report of a national survey. *Journal of Early Adolescence, 1*(4), 385-390.

Coleman, K. A. (1986, March). *Development of a computer-based health risk assessment instrument.* Paper presented at the Eastern Educational Research Association, Miami Beach, FL.

Damon, W., & Hart, D. (1982). The development of self-understanding from infancy through adolescence. *Child Development, 53*, 841-864.

De Apodaca, R. F., Watson, J. D., Mueller, J., & Isaacson-Kailes, J. (1985). A sociometric comparison of mainstreamed, orthopedically handicapped high school students and non-handicapped classmates. *Psychology in the Schools, 22*, 95-101.

Deno, S. L. (1985). Curriculum-based assessment: The emerging alternative. *Exceptional Children, 52*(3), 219-222.

Deshler, D. D., & Schumaker, J. B. (1986). Learning strategies: An instructional alternative for low-achieving adolescents. *Exceptional Children, 52*(6), 583-590.

Deshler, D. D., Schumaker, J. B., Lenz, K., & Ellis, E. (1984). Academic and cognitive intervention for LD adolescents: Part II. *Journal of Learning Disabilities, 17*(3), 170-179.

Edelbrock, C., & Costello, A. J. (1984). Structured psychiatric interviews for children and adolescents. In G. Goldstein & M. Hersen (Eds.), *Handbook of psychological assessment* (pp. 276-290). New York: Pergamon.

Elliott, S. N., & Piersel, W. C. (1982). Direct assessment of reading skills: An approach which links assessment to intervention. *School Psychology Review, 11*(3), 267-280.

Forman, B. D., Edison, K., & Hagan, B. J. (1983). Measuring perceived stress in adolescents: A cross validation. *Adolescence, 18*(71), 573-576.

Fuchs, L. S., & Fuchs, D. (Eds.). (1986). Linking assessment to instructional intervention: An overview. *School Psychology Review, 15*(3), 318-323.

Gallagher, T. M. (1983). Pre-assessment: A procedure for accommodating language use variability. In T. M. Gallagher & C. A. Prutting (Eds.), *Pragmatic assessment and intervention issues in language* (pp. 1-28). San Diego: College-Hill.

Gerken, K. C. (1983). *Guidelines for the school psychologist: The diagnostic process in mathematics, spelling, and written expression.* Des Moines, IA: Iowa Department of Public Instruction.

Gickling, E. E., & Thompson, V. P. (1985). A personal view of curriculum-based assessment. *Exceptional Children, 52*(3), 205-218.

Goh, D. S., & Fuller, G. B. (1983). Current practices in the assessment of personality and behavior by school psychologists. *School Psychology Review, 12*(3), 240-243.

Green, L. W., & Horton, D. (1982). Adolescent health: Issues and challenges. In T. J. Coates, A. C. Petersen, & C. Perry (Eds.), *Promoting adolescent health* (pp. 23-43). New York: Academic Press.

Gresham, F. M. (1983). Multitrait-multimethod approach to multifactored assessment: Theoretical rationale and practical application. *School Psychology Review, 12*(1), 26-34.

Gresham, F. M. (1985). Best practices in social skills training. In A. Thomas & J. Grimes (Eds.), *Best practices in school psychology* (pp. 181-192). Kent, OH: National Association of School Psychologists.

Gresham, F. M., & Elliott, S. N. (1984). Assessment and classification of children's social skills: A review of methods and issues. *School Psychology Review, 13*(3), 292-301.

Griffin, N., Chassin, L., & Young, R. D. (1981). Measurement of global self-concept versus multiple-role, specific self-concepts in adolescents. *Adolescence, 6*(61), 49-56.

Hambleton, R. K. (1982). Advances in criterion-referenced testing technology. In C. R. Reynolds & T. B. Gutkin (Eds.), *Handbook of school psychology* (pp. 351-379). New York: John Wiley & Sons.

Hammill, D. D., & Bartel, N. R. (1982). *Teaching children with learning and behavior problems* (3rd ed.). Boston: Allyn & Bacon.

Harter, S. (1983). Developmental perspectives in self-esteem. In P. H. Mussen (Ed.), *Handbook of child psychology* (Vol. 4, pp. 275-386). New York: John Wiley & Sons.

Hartup, W. W. (1983). Peer relations. In P. H. Mussen (Ed.), *Handbook of child psychology* (Vol. 4, pp. 103-196). New York: John Wiley & Sons.

Hobbs, N., & Robinson, S. (1982). Adolescent development and public policy. *American Psychologist, 37*(2), 212-223.

Hodges, K., Kline, J., Stern, L., Cytryn, L., & McKnew, D. (1982). The development of a child's assessment interview for research and clinical use. *Journal of Abnormal Psychology, 10*(2), 173-189.

Hohenshil, T. H., Levinson, E. M., & Heer, K. B. (1985). Best practices in vocational assessment for handicapped students. In A. Thomas & J. Grimes (Eds.), *Best practices in school psychology* (pp. 215-228). Kent, OH: National Association of School Psychologists.

Johnson, R. L., & Tanner, N. M. (1983). Approaching the adolescent patient. In A. D. Hoffman (Ed.), *Adolescent medicine* (pp. 8-19). Menlo Park, CA: Addison-Wesley.

Kagan, J. (1983). Epilogue/Classifications of the child. In P. H. Mussen (Ed.), *Handbook of child psychology* (Vol. 1, pp. 527-560). New York: John Wiley & Sons.

Kaufman, A. S. (1985). Wechsler Adult Intelligence Scale-Revised. In J. V. Mitchell, Jr. (Ed.), *The ninth mental measurements yearbook* (pp. 1700-1703). Lincoln, NE: Buros Institute.

Keyser, D. J., & Sweetland, R. C. (Eds.). (1984-86). *Test critiques: Vols. I-IV.* Kansas City, MO: Test Corporation.

Kiestenbaum, C. J. (1985). Putting it all together: A multidimensional assessment of psychotic potential in adolescence. In S. C. Feinstein, M. Sugar, A. H. Esman, J. G. Looney, A. Z. Schwartzberg, & A. D. Sorosky (Eds.), *Adolescent psychiatry* (Vol. 12, pp. 5-16). Chicago: University of Chicago Press.

Kovacs, M. (1982). *The longitudinal study of child and adolescent psychopathology: The semi-structured psychiatric Interview Schedule for Children (ISC).* Unpublished manuscript.

Kramer, J. J. (1985, August). *Computer-based test interpretation in psychoeducational assessment.* Paper presented at the annual meeting of the American Psychological Association, Los Angeles.

Kuepper, J. E. (1985, April). *Assessment and remediation of study skill deficits in secondary students.* Paper presented at the annual meeting of the National Association of School Psychologists, Las Vegas.

Layton, W. L. (1985). Ball Aptitude Battery, In J. V. Mitchell, Jr. (Ed.), *The ninth mental measurements yearbook* (pp. 123-125). Lincoln, NE: Buros Institute.

Lee, D. L., Halberg, E. T., Slemon, A. G., & Haase, R. F. (1985). An assertiveness scale for adolescents. *Journal of Clinical Psychology, 41*(1), 51-57.

Lipa, S. (1985). Test review: Diagnostic Reading Scales. *Journal of Educational Measurement, 22*(2), 162-165.

Looney, J. G. (1985). Research priorities in adolescent psychiatry: Report of the Committee on Research of the American Society for Adolescent Psychiatry. In S. C. Feinstein, M. Sugar, A. H. Esman, J. G. Looney, A. Z. Schwartzberg, & A. D. Sorosky (Eds.), *Adolescent psychiatry* (Vol. 12, pp. 104-114). Chicago: University of Chicago Press.

Marsh, H. W., & O'Neill, R. (1984). Self-Description Questionnaire III: The construct validity of multidimensional self-concept ratings by late adolescents. *Journal of Educational Measurement, 21*(2), 153-174.

Matarazzo, J. D. (1983). Computerized psychological testing. *Science, 221*(4608), 323.

Matarazzo, J. D. (1985). Wechsler Adult Intelligence Scale-Revised. In J. V. Mitchell, Jr. (Ed.), *The ninth mental measurements yearbook* (pp. 1703-1705). Lincoln, NE: Buros Institute.

Matson, J. L., Rotatori, A. F., & Helsel, W. J. (1983). Development of a rating scale to measure social skills in children: The Matson Evaluation of Social Skills in Youngsters (MESSY). *Behavioral Research Therapy, 21*(4), 335-340.

McArthur, D. L., & Choppin, B. H. (1984). Computerized diagnostic testing. *Journal of Educational Measurement, 21*(4), 391-397.

McCullough, C. S. (1985). Best practices in computer applications. In A. Thomas & J. Grimes (Eds.), *Best practices in school psychology* (pp. 301-310). Kent, OH: National Association of School Psychologists.

McCullough, C. S., & Wenck, L. S. (1984). Current microcomputer applications in school psychology. *School Psychology Review, 13*(4), 429-439.

Messick, S. (1983). Assessment of children. In P. H. Mussen (Ed.), *Handbook of child psychology* (Vol. 1, pp. 477-526). New York: John Wiley & Sons.

Mitchell, J. V., Jr. (Ed.). *Tests in print III.* Lincoln, NE: Buros Institute.

Mitchell, J. V., Jr. (Ed.). *The ninth mental measurements yearbook.* Lincoln, NE: Buros Institute.

Nagle, R. J., & Medway, F. J. (1982). Issues in providing psychological services at the high school level. *School Psychology Review, 11*(4), 359-369.

Newcomb, M. D., Huba, G. J., & Bentler, P. M. (1981). A multidimensional assessment of stressful life events among adolescents: Derivation and correlates. *Journal of Health and Social Behavior, 22,* 400-415.

Newman, P. R. (1982). The peer group. In B. B. Wolman (Ed.), *Handbook of child psychology* (pp. 526-536). Englewood Cliffs, NJ: Prentice-Hall.

O'Connor, L. C., & Eldredge, P. D. (1981). *Communication disorders in adolescence.* Springfield, IL: Charles C. Thomas.

Openshaw, D. K., Thomas, D. L., & Rollins, B. C. (1981). Adolescent self-esteem: A multi-dimensional perspective. *Journal of Early Adolescence, 1*(3), 273-282.

Openshaw, D. K., Thomas, D. L., & Rollins, B. C. (1983). Socialization and adolescent self-esteem: Symbolic interaction and social learning applications. *Adolescence, 18*(70), 317-329.

Paget, K. D. (1984). The Structured Assessment Interview: A psychometric review. *Journal of School Psychology, 22*(4), 415-427.

Perry, C. (1982). Adolescent health: An educational-ecological perspective. In T. J. Coates & A. C. Petersen (Eds.), *Promoting adolescent health: A dialogue in research and practice* (pp. 73-86). New York: Academic press.

Petersen, A. C., Schulenberg, J. E., Abramowitz, R. H., Offer, D., & Jarcho, H. D. (1984). A Self-Image Questionnaire for Young Adolescents (SIQYA): Reliability and validity studies. *Journal of Youth and Adolescence, 13*(2), 93-111.

Proefrock, D. W. (1983). The uncertainty principle in adolescent research. *Adolescence, 18*(70), 339-343.

Prutting, C. A., & Kirchner, D. M. (1983). Applied pragmatics. In T. M. Gallagher & C. A. Prutting (Eds.), *Pragmatic assessment and intervention issues in language* (pp. 29-64). San Diego: College-Hill.

Reschly, D. J. (1985). Best practices: Adaptive behavior. In A. Thomas & J. Grimes (Eds.), *Best practices in school psychology* (pp. 353-368). Kent, OH: National Association of School Psychologists.

Reynolds, C. R. (1983). Some new and some unusual psychological and educational measures: Description and evaluation. *School Psychology Review, 12*(4), 481-488.

Robbins, D. R., & Alessi, N. E. (1985). Depressive symptoms and suicidal behavior in adolescents, *American Journal of Psychiatry, 142*(5), 588-592.

Ross-Reynolds, G., & Hardy, B. S. (1985). Crisis counseling for disparate adolescent sexual dilemmas: Pregnancy and homosexuality. *School Psychology Review, 14*(3), 300-312.

Salvia, J., & Ysseldyke, J. E. (1985). *Assessment in special and remedial education* (3rd ed.). Boston: Houghton Mifflin.

Santrock, J. W. (1984). *Adolescence* (2nd ed.). Dubuque, IA: William C. Brown.

Savin-Williams, R. C., & Demo, D. H. (1983). Conceiving or misconceiving the self: Issues in adolescent self-esteem. *Journal of Early Adolescence, 3*(1-2), 121-140.

Savin-Williams, R. C., & Jaquish, G. A. (1981). The assessment of adolescent self-esteem: A comparison of methods. *Journal of Personality, 49*(3), 324-335.

Shepard, J. W., & Levinson, E. (1985). Vocational assessment procedures for school psychologists at the secondary level. *Journal of Psychoeducational Assessment, 3*(3), 257-265.

Siddique, C. M., & D'Arcy, C. (1984). Adolescence, stress, and psychological well-being. *Journal of Youth and Adolescence, 13*(6), 459-473.

Siegel, J. M., Matthews, K. A., & Leitch, C. J. (1981). Validation of the Type A interview assessment of adolescents: A multidimensional approach. *Psychosomatic Medicine, 43*(4), 311-321.

Siegel, L. J., & Griffin, N. J. (1983). Adolescents' concepts of depression among their peers. *Adolescence, 18*(72), 965-973.

Siegel, O. (1982). Personality development in adolescence. In B. B. Wolman (Ed.), *Handbook of child psychology* (pp. 537-548). Englewood Cliffs, NJ: Prentice-Hall.

Starkman, S. (1985). Test of Practical Knowledge. In J. V. Mitchell, Jr. (Ed.), *The ninth mental measurements yearbook* (pp. 1585-1587). Lincoln, NE: Buros Institute.

Sternberg, R. J. (1981). Testing and cognitive psychology. *American Psychology, 36*(10), 1181-1189.

Sternberg, R. J., & Powell, J. D. (1983). The development of intelligence. In P. H. Mussen (Ed.), *Handbook of child psychology* (Vol. 3, pp. 341-419). New York: John Wiley & Sons.

Svobodny, L. A. (1982). Biographical self-concept and educational factors among chemically dependent adolescents. *Adolescence, 17*(68), 847-853.

Swisher, J. D., Shute, R. E., & Bibeau, D. (1984). Assessing drug and alcohol abuse: An instrument for planning and evaluation. *Measurement and Evaluation in Counseling and Development, 17*(2), 91-97.

Taylor, R. L. (1984). *Assessment of exceptional students.* Englewood Cliffs, NJ: Prentice-Hall.

Thomas, A. (1984). Issues and concerns for microcomputer uses in school psychology. *School Psychology Review, 13*(4), 469-472.

Tucker, J. A. (Ed.). Curriculum-based assessment [Special issue]. *Exceptional Children, 52*(3).

Wagner, R. K., & Sternberg, R. J. (1984). Alternative conceptions of intelligence and their implications for education. *Review of Educational Research, 54*(2), 179-223.

Waksman, S. A. (1985). The development and psychometric properties of a rating scale for children's social skills. *Journal of Psychoeducational Assessment, 3*(2), 111-121.

Wallace, G., & Larsen, S. C. (1978). *Educational assessment of learning problems: Testing for teaching.* Boston: Allyn & Bacon.

Wiens, A. N., & Matarazzo, J. D. (1983). Diagnostic interviewing. In M. Hersen, A. E. Kazdin, & A. S. Bellack (Eds.), *The clinical psychology handbook* (pp. 309-328). New York: Pergamon.

Wiig, E. H. (1982). *Let's Talk Inventory for Adolescents manual.* Columbus, OH: Charles E. Merrill.

Wiig, E. H., & Semel, E. M. (1980). *Language assessment and intervention for the learning disabled.* Columbus, OH: Charles E. Merrill.

Ysseldyke, J. E., & Mirkin, D. (1982). The use of assessment information to plan instructional interventions: A review of the research. In C. R. Reynolds & T. B. Gutkin (Eds.), *The handbook of school psychology* (pp. 395-409). New York: John Wiley & Sons.

2

The Family as a Context for Adolescent Assessment

ROBERT G. HARRINGTON, PH.D.

For many years psychopathology has been defined as a mental disorder residing within the individual. This perspective is reflected in the third edition of the *Diagnostic and Statistical Manual of Mental Disorders* (DSM-III; American Psychiatric Association, 1980) and in various forms of individual therapeutic intervention, such as psychoanalysis. Within the past two decades, however, the focus of diagnostic assessment and intervention has been shifting to include not only the individual, but also the larger interpersonal context of the family in which the person interacts.

The interpersonal relationship found in a nuclear family has been referred to as a *system,* reflecting the impact that each member in the family network can have on the psychological health and well-being of every other adult, adolescent, and child member in the system (Hess & Howard, 1981). Within the systems paradigm, interpersonal conflict as well as personal stress are viewed as symptomatic of a dysfunctional system, not necessarily requiring individual psychotherapy. Unique diagnostic assessment and therapeutic intervention techniques have been developed to match the philosophy of the systems approach. Methods of family assessment have been developed that can assist the psychologist in understanding the family system.

Adolescents are influenced by three major social contexts: the peer network, the school, and the family (Csikszentmihalyi & Larson, 1984). Contrary to popular opinion, the family is among the interpersonal contexts or systems with the most influence on adolescent values and psychological development. As adolescents grow older, the amount of time families have to influence their teenage members diminishes. In this regard, freshmen in high school spend about 25% of their waking hours with their families and seniors only about 15% (Csikszentmihalyi & Larson, 1984). This trend should not be surprising, because the major task of adolescence is to become gradually independent of parents, without undue stress to self or to other family members.

If one were to believe the popular literature it would appear that the successful resolution of adolescent crises is nearly impossible. Adolescent family relationships often are depicted as one turmoil after another (Douvan & Adelson, 1966; Offer, 1969). In fact, current research suggests that the amount of stress actually occurring between parents and teenagers probably has been overestimated. Nevertheless, certain characteristics of families in general and American families in particular make some family stress and conflict inevitable. Since Davis (1940) first identified the broad cultural trends that promote conflict in families, subsequent researchers up to the present have verified the validity of each of these sources of conflict. Because each of these factors sheds light on the epidemiology of family conflict, they will be reviewed before the specific precursors of dysfunctionality within individual families are described. With this understanding of the major factors that contribute to family stress, the reader will be prepared for a review of specific psychological instrumentation and techniques for assessing the family and home environments of adolescents.

SOCIAL TRENDS CONTRIBUTING TO FAMILY STRESS

Rapid Sociocultural Change

One of the social trends contributing to family stress and conflict is the rapid rate of sociocultural change the family institution has had to endure. These sociocultural changes have had profound effects on both the role of the American family in society and its impact on its adolescent members. First, families have been urbanized. About 75% of the U.S. population currently live in urban areas, on only about 1.5% of the available land (U.S. Department of Commerce, 1974, 1977, 1980). The effect of families abandoning small-town life for overcrowded urban centers is that the strong influence of traditional institutions, such as schools, churches, neighborhood organizations, law enforcement, and local government, has been diluted. The sense of community, of neighborhood, is missing (Conger, 1981).

A second factor contributing to the rapidity of social change is the increasing geographic mobility in the United States. It has been estimated that 50% of all American families move every 5 years, or, in other words, 13 or 14 times in the course of a lifetime (U.S. Department of Commerce, 1980). The net impact of urbanization and geographic mobility on the family unit has been that the stability and interdependence of neighborhood communities has been weakened, and the modern family has been left more isolated from personal, familial, and community support systems and thus more dependent on its own resources.

Without the benefits of nearby extended family members for encouragement and direction, parents in relatively isolated nuclear families have very few sources to turn to for help in learning and mastering new parenting skills when their own fail. Unlike parents living in traditional extended family systems, modern parents may seek advice from magazines, the popular psychology of radio call-in shows, or television. All of these alternatives may serve only to confuse because of their conflicting advice. Likewise, when adolescents are not raised in a close-knit, relatively homogeneous community, they also become victims of rapid sociological changes. For example, when adolescents are raised in families where parents are unable to communicate closely with other parents or where parents hold widely varying beliefs about parenting techniques, adolescents may become more skeptical about their own parents' values, beliefs, and parenting practices and may become more resistant to those parental expectations (Packard, 1974). Alternatively, adolescents living in a stable neighborhood community are more likely to accept parental rules, standards, and beliefs when they see that these rules are shared by their peer's parents (Conger & Petersen, 1984). The import of these two rapid social changes for family systems with adolescent members is that the more the intimate emotional relationships of both parents and adolescents are confined to the nuclear family, and the smaller this family unit is, the more intense family relationships are likely to be and the more difficult and stressful to modify. The adolescent developmental period is particularly prone to these stresses because of the necessary adjustments already inherent within it.

A third result of the increased rate of social change is that adolescents and their parents appear to have grown up in markedly different worlds. The developmental experiences that have shaped their personalities may have varied considerably (Conger, 1977). For example, parents who were adolescents in the turbulent 1960s grew up with the Vietnam War, the civil rights demonstrations, the Kennedy White House, and "American Graffiti," while the 1980's adolescent may experience a more conservative sociopolitical atmosphere. Consequently, when parents compare their adolescent's values, needs, and personal attitudes to their own adolescent experiences for guidance, they may be frustrated and bewildered by the vast differences.

A fourth societal change with impact on the family is related to role functions of family members. For example, the majority of married women now, including those with young children, work outside of the home. Whether this new role function is desirable is a source of debate. Meislin (1977) reports that when Americans were asked in a *New York Times*-CBS News poll "What kind of marriage do you think makes the more satisfying kind of life?", only 27% of the respondents in the 18- to 29-year-old age group preferred the traditional marriage. In contrast, of the respondents in the 30- to 44-year-old age group, which consisted of many parents of adolescents, 44% chose the traditional marriage while 56% chose the working wife arrangement. Clearly, there is a disparity between adolescents' and parents' views of the "traditional" versus the "modern" role of a mother and wife in marriage. Adolescents appear more likely to accept and encourage mothers working outside of the home, and parents in the 30- to 44-year-old range are more likely to be split almost evenly on the issue.

Whether the mother should work outside of the home is often a source of family conflict and stress, and the debate often centers on whether these working women make better or worse mothers. Opinions appear to be split on this issue also. Forty-three percent of working women believe that employed women make better mothers, only 24% believe that they make worse mothers, and the remaining 33% do not believe there is a difference. On the other hand, 45% of both men and nonworking women think employed women make worse mothers, and only 21% of men and 14% of nonworking women think they make better mothers. The trend is for younger age groups to be more likely than older age groups to believe that working women make better mothers. Interestingly, when high school seniors were polled in 1980 on the same question, only 13% of the boys and 4% of the girls considered the combination of a working husband and a nonworking wife desirable if no children are involved. Their opinions changed when preschool children became involved (Bachman, Johnston, & O'Malley, 1981): 44% of the boys and 39% of the girls considered the traditional arrangement desirable.

These results appear fairly clear-cut, but this working/nonworking mother dichotomy may oversimplify the situation. There are other factors, such as marital satisfaction, to consider. For example, marital satisfaction of both partners appears to be enhanced when the wife works by choice rather than necessity, has an interesting job, works part-time, or works when children are beyond the preschool age (Smith,

1979). Marital satisfaction tends to decline when these factors are not present and when the burden of home responsibilities is great and little relief or external help is available (Smith, 1979). For the most part, wives typically retain the major responsibility for household tasks whether they work outside the home or not. Consequently, whether wives and mothers work outside of the home or not, someone in the family system is likely to be dissatisfied with the situation.

Increased Divorce Rate

When the rapid changes in the functions of the family and its members are added to increased pressures of urban living and decreased support systems due to geographic mobility, it should be no surprise that the result has been more parental separations, desertions, and divorces. The increased divorce rate is the second major social trend contributing to family stress. A report by the U.S. Bureau of the Census (Calhoun, Grotberg, & Rackey, 1980; Carter & Glick, 1976; Glick & Norton, 1979; U.S. Department of Commerce, 1981) indicates that there is one divorce for every two new marriages. If current trends are predictive, 40-50% of new marriages will end in divorce by the early 1990s (Calhoun, Grotberg, & Rackey, 1980; Glick & Norton, 1979). For mothers born during the baby boom years of 1940 to 1949, the U.S. Bureau of the Census has projected that 34-38% will eventually obtain a divorce and 40-44% of those who remarry will be divorced again (Skolnick, 1978).

Predictably, the number of children of divorced families has risen steadily. Sixty percent of all divorces involve children or adolescents (U.S. Department of Commerce, 1980). More than one million children and adolescents under the age of 18, or 30% of all American youths, are not living with both of their natural parents (Glick & Norton, 1979). Predictions are that 40-50% of all children born during the 1980s eventually will live in a single-parent family due to divorce or death of a parent (Glick & Norton, 1979). Single parenthood is significantly more frequent among blacks only when studies do not control for residential setting and income (U.S. Department of Commerce, 1980). Finally, the percentages of births to unmarried women has quadrupled since 1950 and has doubled since 1965 (U.S. Department of Commerce, 1980). For all of these reasons, only 63% of all children under 18 in 1978 were living with both natural parents in their first marriage; nearly one in five was living in a single-parent family, almost doubling the rate reported 25 years previously (U.S. Department of the Census, 1980). Furthermore, the divorce rate is increasing. Only one in seven families today fits the stereotypic American pattern of working husband, homemaking wife, and two children (Toffler, 1981).

Beyond the adjustments required by divorce and separation there may be special psychological stresses for parents and children living in single-parent families. Most single-parent families are headed by divorced or separated women. The fact is that two-thirds of divorced mothers with school-age children and nearly 50% of those with children under 3 are not at home and are working (U.S. Department of Commerce, 1980). Furthermore, over 42% of families headed by women with children are currently living below the poverty level, compared to only 12% for all women with children (U.S. Department of Commerce, 1980). This group of single parents has been called the "fastest growing group in poverty" (U.S. Department of Commerce, 1980).

Among the specific family stressors associated with poor single-parent families are substandard housing, deteriorating neighborhoods, and lack of parental control due to the "latchkey child" phenomenon, in which children and adolescents find themselves unlocking the doors to their vacant and unsupervised homes. Likewise, single working parents may feel frustrated in assuming primary responsibility for parenting their adolescents. They may suffer guilt and feelings of inadequacy as they vascillate between wondering whether they are being good parents and wishing they never had children in the first place. Personal relationships with adolescent family members may also be in jeopardy. For example, male adolescents of divorced mothers who have been exceptionally affectionate and expressive seem to be under a great deal of stress as they work through the sexual conflicts involved in resolving the Oedipal complex. Likewise, it is very difficult for the mother to see an affectionate, comforting relationship with her son become tense just when they need each other most.

Blended Families

Despite high divorce rates, about 80% of all divorced people eventually remarry. Almost 25% of all American children are members of these "blended" families (Toffler, 1981; Walters & Stinnet, 1971). Consequently, these children have two or more sets of parents, natural siblings as well as step-brothers and step-sisters, and several sets of grandparents. In these circumstances, responsibilities for parenting and child support may be shared by several families (Toffler, 1981; Walters & Stinnet, 1971). The phenomenon of blended families represents the third major trend contributing to family stress.

Preliminary data suggest that there may be certain child-stepparent combinations that are less prone to problems than others. General findings (Stevens-Long & Cobb, 1983), for example, indicate that stepparents of the same sex as the child may encounter less resistance than those of the opposite sex. Stepparents of the opposite sex as the child are seen as "playing favorites" more often than biological parents. Stepmothers are more likely than stepfathers to be seen by children as playing favorites. When these instances of resistance are interpreted as rejection, the stepparent may be reluctant to assume any part of the parental role or even to disagree with a spouse over child-rearing practices. In addition, blended families often harbor unrealistic fantasies about an ideal family life and may become disappointed to realize that family cohesion requires time, effort, and hard work (Walters & Stinnet, 1971).

The "Generation Gap"

Considering the stress associated with rapid sociocultural change, the increased divorce rate, and the blended family phenomenon, it should not be surprising that many nuclear families are showing signs of strain. Some authors have proclaimed the American family "dead"; others have claimed that it is merely evolving. In either case, people will probably continue to live in some forms of small, intimate groups comprised of adults, adolescents, and children. The social trends that have been reviewed have clearly increased the difficulty of the adolescent period, both for parents and for young people. The situation thus would appear ripe for a "generation gap" between adolescents and their parents, such that contemporary adolescents may tend to forsake their parents' values and lean toward the values of the pervasive peer culture. The best answer to this statement is that there is a gap, but it is neither as wide nor as novel as popular stereotypes would suggest.

The term "generation gap" has been used in at least two different ways. When the term refers to generational conflict, it denotes the struggle for power that occurs between older and younger generations. The second phenomenon entails a difference in values and experiences between older and younger people. Such a difference can occur with or without conflict, but the shift is usually greatest and conflict is most likely in times of rapid social change (Skolnick, 1978).

From one generation to another, shifts in values may be inevitable. Where the pace of cultural change is swift, shifts may be very noticeable. On the other hand, research has revealed that there is also substantial generational continuity of values, even through three generations of the same family (Troll, 1971). For example, when a representative survey (Gallup, 1978) of American adolescents aged 13 to 18 were asked "How well do you get along with your parents?", 97% said that they got along very well or fairly well; only 3% said that they did not get along well at all. There were no sex differences. When these same adolescents were asked whether their parents' disciplinary actions were too strict, 54% said that their parents' discipline had been about right, 24% felt that their parents had been too strict, and 20% felt they had not been strict enough (Gallup, 1978). Of those adolescents who felt that their parents' discipline had been about right, 63% also reported that they got along very well with their parents. Only 49% of those who felt discipline had not been strict enough got along very well with their parents, and only 29% of those who felt their parents had been overly strict got along very well with them.

In another national survey (Sorensen, 1973), 88% of all adolescent respondents stated that they had a lot of respect for their parents as people, and 80% stated that they had a lot of respect for their parents' ideas and opinions. Only 21% stated that they did not feel any strong affection for their parents and only 6% reported that they felt that their parents really do not like them. When high school seniors were asked in a national survey (Bachman, Johnston, & O'Malley, 1981) how closely their ideas agreed with those of their parents on a wide range of topics, over 70% indicated that their ideas were very similar or mostly similar to those of their parents on what the young person should do with his or her life, what values in life are important, the value of education, issues of religion, and appropriate roles for men. Somewhat less, albeit substantial, agreement was found on issues of politics, race, conservation, pollution, and drug use other than marijuana. About as many adolescents agreed as disagreed regarding the use of leisure time, spending money, drinking and marijuana use, and dating behavior.

Several explanations may be offered for these discrepancies between the apparent facts reported in these national studies and popular stereotypes regarding the so-called "generation gap." First, there is a tendency on the part of the public at large to overgeneralize from the behavior of a relatively small number of young people to adolescents and youth in general. Second, these popular stereotypes often confuse comparisons between adults and adolescents *generally* with those between *individual* parents and *their* adolescent sons and daughters. For example, in one national study (Harris, 1971), two-thirds of adolescents aged 15 and older replied "yes" to the question "Do your parents approve of your values and ideals?" In contrast, a majority of these adolescents responded negatively to "Do they approve of the way your generation expresses their ideals?" Similarly, adolescents tend to be more critical of the older generation as a whole than of their own parents. In fact, adolescents occasionally may face conflicts with the values of some adult authority figures precisely because those values conflict with those the young person has acquired from and shares with his or her parents. A third reason for the differences between national reports and popular stereotypes is that parents and adolescents may differ in some of their values, but still remain capable of mutual respect. For example, in the previously cited national survey on adolescent sexuality in contemporary America (Sorensen, 1973), 80% of all adolescent respondents stated that they had a "lot of respect" for their parents' ideas and opinions, while disagreeing with them on specific issues. On the other hand, only 38% of this same sample agreed that "When it comes to sex, my attitudes and parents' attitudes are pretty much the same."

THE ROLE OF CONFLICT IN FAMILY SYSTEMS

An Alternative Perspective

Given the major social changes with which adolescents and their families have had to contend, one might assume that conflicted families produce maladapted adolescents. This position may not necessarily be true in all cases. Interestingly, recent literature has cast conflict between parent and adolescent in a slightly more positive role than might be expected. For example, a longitudinal study (Skolnick, 1978) found that stable, peaceful families are not necessarily prerequisite for optimal adolescent development. Instead, many of the most mature, integrated, and/or creative people in these studies had the most difficult childhoods and adolescent years.

In another classic study of child rearing, Baumrind (1975) discusses the relationship between conflict and identity. She contends that the parents of identity-achieved adolescents do not offer unconditional acceptance, but make clear demands for maturity, even appearing pushy and rejecting, while maintaining active communication with their children. Conflict may be especially important in understanding the development of identity achievement in females. Baumrind argues that conflict is necessary to stimulate the development of independence in girls. Girls may also require continuous positive reinforcement for independent behavior in the face of very strong cultural pressures toward submissiveness (Newman & Newman, 1978). Of course, independent thought and conduct cannot be reinforced if the opportunity to disagree or conflict is not present.

One author has described adolescents who are able to cope in homes characterized by intense conflict and even violence as "invulnerable" (Skolnick, 1978). Even in this very high-risk population, estimates are that 85-90% eventually will develop into reasonably well-adjusted adults (Garmezy, 1976). Other authors claim that modern life has certain beneficial effects on psychological development. Cottle (1975) believes that distance between generations encourages the questioning of authority and the development of a personal value system. In research supporting this hypothesis, Larson (1972) asked adolescent subjects whether the opinions of parents or friends would strongly influence their own decisions in a variety of hypothetical situations. Results showed that many adolescents make important decisions about issues such as career choice on their own, without resorting to peer or parental guidance pressure. Adolescents complied with parents or peers most often in instances when the decision involved a low priority issue such as whether to attend a party. Elder (1980) believes that there is insufficient empirical evidence to say that parent-youth conflicts produced by rapid social changes produce value differences. What does appear to be true is that young people are critical of the "older generation" in general, but these same adolescents are less likely to criticize their own parents.

Elkind (1979) argues that when conflict does arise between parent and child it may be due to renegotiations of basic parent-child arrangements. Children barter freedom for responsibility. Parents offer commitment in exchange for loyalty, and the young exchange achievement for support. There is a change in the expression of such family contracts as children move into adolescence, however. For example, in adolescence, parental support is still required, but public displays of affection and attention are not. Adolescents prefer more subtle displays of affection with their parents. Such changes imply increasing distance between parent and child and a shift toward less frequent, less intimate interactions. Parents still expect loyalty to family values and ideals, but they accept more abstract, less emotional parent-child involvement.

Elkind (1978) describes typical modern middle-class families as placing undue stress on adolescents for self-control, self-discipline, and independence, plus pressuring for school achievement, the development of poise, and athletic excellence. All of these pressures create self-consciousness in adolescents and may force a premature resolution of identity. They force adolescents to hurry and grow up and to act like "miniature adults."

Parents as well as professionals who work with adolescents sometimes expect the worst. Research has shown that parents expect adolescents as well as communication with them to be difficult. The widespread prevalence of this view is reflected in statistics indicating that 80% of high school teachers in one survey also believed that adolescence was a time of great emotional disturbance (Bakan, 1971).

Despite these misconceptions about the extent of adolescent turmoil, the fact is some ancient family tensions do heighten in adolescence. For example, many parents may feel uncomfortable with the increasing sexuality that accompanies puberty. Peskin (1972) reported a longitudinal study in which boys who had very affectionate, expressive mothers actually appeared to experience greater difficulty making the transition to puberty, and these families found it more problematic to assimilate and manage the sexualization of their relationships. Furthermore, psychoanalytic researchers appear to agree that regardless of social changes and raised expectations, families with adolescents seem to experience a "striking reappearance of the Oedipal drama" generation after generation.

A FAMILY SYSTEMS MODEL FOR ADOLESCENT ASSESSMENT

Having reviewed several major social trends and pervasive misconceptions regarding the role of conflict in modern family life, a model for assessing dysfunctional families is appropriate at this point. This model was adapted from two other assessment systems developed by Piercy, McKeon, and Laird (1983) and Hess and

Howard (1981), based on the kinds of information needed to understand a family from a systems framework and to intervene accordingly. The model consists of 12 components covering a wide range of assessment techniques. In the interests of time and cost efficiency, the examiner hoping to perform a family-based assessment of an adolescent should select from among the following areas of assessment based on the reason for referral and assessment collected as the assessment continues:

    I. Presenting problem(s)/change(s) desired
   II. Repetitive nonproductive behavioral sequences
  III. Family structure and function
     A. Family social climate
       1. Relationship dimensions (cohesion, expressiveness, conflict)
       2. Personal development dimensions (orientation toward independence, achievement, intellectual-cultural, recreational, and moral-religious emphases)
       3. System maintenance and system change (emphasis on neatness, structuring family activities, planning, punctuality, extent to which the family controls by relatively strict rules or procedures)
     B. Family roles
       1. Age appropriateness
       2. Role flexibility
       3. Cognitive awareness of role structure
       4. Personal growth allowed within role
       5. Successful filling of all necessary family roles
     C. Family patterns of behavior with relation to crisis and problem-solving
     D. Level of successful family task accomplishment
       1. Material provision
       2. Predictable need-meeting (mealtimes, children's bedtimes)
       3. Affective caretaking (support, expressing fondness and inclusion)
       4. Stimulation sufficient for personal growth (books, conversation)
       5. Organizational planning (coordination of schedules, allocation of financial resources, balancing individual family member's needs)
       6. Adolescent socialization and supervision
       7. Creation and maintenance of family support systems
     E. Boundaries—flexibility, permeability
       1. Willingness to incorporate newcomers
       2. Willingness to share information with other systems regarding family
       3. Methods of boundary protection
     F. Home environment
       1. Space adequate to accommodate the number of persons living within it
       2. Space adequate to allow for privacy of individual family members within individual territory, personal boundaries clearly defined
       3. Space adequate to allow for accomplishing family tasks (cooking, sleeping, recreation)
       4. Space allows for intergenerational boundaries (parent-adolescent)
       5. Space allows for common family-oriented areas

IV. Communication and interaction styles
   A. Nature (process), frequency, and topics forbidden and allowed
      1. Whole family
      2. Marital pair
      3. Subsystems
      4. Extended family
      5. Extrafamilial systems
   B. Problem and decision-making process
   C. Permitted affective expression and process
V. Hypotheses regarding symptom maintenance
VI. Family life stages/tasks
   A. Current developmental phase/tasks
   B. Current nature of developmental task mastery
   C. Family goals with relation to developmental tasks
VII. Pertinent family-of-origin information
VIII. External sources of stress and support
IX. Significant physical conditions/medication
X. Therapeutic goals
XI. Proposed therapeutic interventions
XII. Alternative assessment approaches

Each of the 12 components of the family systems assessment model described above will be reviewed, but only those sections directly related to selection and use of assessment instrumentation will be described in detail.

I. Presenting Problem(s)/Change(s) Desired

To begin the family assessment, a clear understanding of the problem is essential. When the psychological examiner asks each family member to describe the problem as he or she sees it, defining the problem for assessment is established as a family endeavor, and the importance of the parents' as well as the adolescent's subjective view is emphasized (Minuchin & Fishman, 1981). In defining the presenting problems of the family, it is often helpful to pose the question in terms of desired changes. Such reframing is more positive and brings into sharper focus the therapeutic goals family members would like to achieve.

At this initial stage of the assessment, the examiner should attempt to evaluate the complexity, urgency, and duration of the problem because chronic dysfunctional family patterns may be more difficult to modify than acute problems of recent origin (Dukette, Born, Gagel, & Henricks, 1978) and may require emergency attention. This feature of problem specification can be achieved by reviewing background information from past school, medical, social work, and psychological records and by consulting with professional sources who also may have dealt with the problem. The examiner may continue the problem-specification process by investigating to what extent the family members have tried to improve family functioning and which interventions have been most effective.

One of the most useful informal assessment techniques for gathering relevant information about the family's presenting problem is the family interview. This face-to-face meeting takes place between the psychologist and all the family members. Whenever possible, it is preferable to interview the entire family together to avoid distortions of information (Anderson & Schafer, 1979). Useful interview information can generally be elicited by asking both direct and indirect questions, encouraging comments, paraphrasing, reflecting feelings, and summarizing. Listening and reflecting are essential microcounseling skills and are implicit in every phase of interviewing (Schubert, 1971). Some family members may not have the insights or verbal expressive abilities necessary to describe the family's problems. Furthermore, because family members' personal descriptions of family functioning represent individual belief systems, they may have the effect of maintaining homeostasis in the family. Discrepancies between what is reported and what is observed may be quite large (Krill, 1968). Consequently, direct observation of family dynamics often may be required to clarify and validate family members' reports (Tomm & Leahey, 1980). Certain structured observation methods may be employed as well, to provide the examiner the opportunity to observe family interactions and to support the interview findings.

The Structured Family Interview (SFI; Watzlawick, 1966) was developed to facilitate this family interview and observation process. One of the most well-publicized informal clinical interview techniques to evaluate family conflicts, the SFI poses five consecutive tasks for family members to perform, which the examiner observes in the process. First, members of the family are asked individually what they feel are the main problems in their family. Second, the family is given the assignment to plan an activity or some other family event together. Third, without the adolescent siblings present, the parents are asked how the two of them met. Fourth, the parents are given a proverb and asked to discuss its meaning, then are told to teach it to their children. Fifth, each family member is asked to write down the main fault of the person sitting on his or her left. Then the interviewer reads aloud these faults and asks family members to designate the owner of each fault. The SFI has been employed to uncover patterns of scapegoating, overprotection, and defensiveness in the family, to observe how family boundaries operate, and to observe alliances, the closeness of family members, the kinds of parental support given to the adolescent family member(s), and the mood of the family.

In order to determine the urgency of a case and a family's ability to cope with immediate stressful events, the Family Functioning Index (FFI; Pless & Satterwhite, 1973) is an option. The FFI was constructed on the basis of 15 theoretically and empirically derived questions that the authors believe reflect the multidimensional nature of family functioning. Parallel forms of the FFI exist for parents solely; if these are used, methods other than the FFI would be necessary to assess the adolescent's perspective of the family situation.

II. Repetitive Nonproductive Behavioral Sequences

This component is included to alert the mental health counselor to perserving interactional patterns of behavior between family members that have not proven to be adaptive or productive in resolving their shared problem (Watzlawick, Weakland, & Fisch, 1974). An example might be the father who continues to engage in progressively stricter discipline with his adolescent son regardless of the outcome. In reaction to this misguided parenting, the adolescent male may become more and more rebellious in an unsuccessful attempt to gain autonomy. Reciprocally, the father may feel a need to counter his son's rebelliousness with even stricter discipline. The result is an escalating spiral of maladaptive interactions between the father and his son. When the family examiner identifies these kinds of repetitive patterns of maladaptive behavior, they should be considered as possible points of entry for interventions, once the remaining phases of the family assessment process have been considered.

III. Family Structure and Function

Family "structure and function" may be defined as either the repeated family interactions showing how, when, and with whom various family members relate (Minuchin, 1974) or the sum total of roles being played within a particular family (Duvall, 1977). The structural-functional approach to family assessment offers an excellent framework for examining the broad range of patterned sequences of family interaction (Terkelsen, 1980). Included among the areas for investigation in a structural-functional family assessment are overt and covert family rules, role tasks, boundaries, and family self-concept. Overt roles are socially expected behaviors prescribed for a person occupying a place in a particular social system (Biddle & Thomas, 1966). Covert roles are assigned informally to members so that the social and emotional needs of the family may be met. Some examples of informal role assignments are hero, victim, scapegoat, jokester, good daughter/son, black sheep, and rebel. Roles with negative connotations may be destructive to individual family members as well as to the entire family unit.

Dysfunctional families are more likely to have members occupying pejorative roles. For example, "scapegoat" is a role designed to shift responsibility from the stronger members of the family to the most vulnerable. When there is considerable anxiety between the marital pair, it is not uncommon for an adolescent to be drawn into the relationship as a buffer or distraction (Bowen, 1978). This family pattern of "triangulation" is common when the only shared parental interest is the problematic behavior of their teenager. Role behavior that conforms to the norms of a family elicits approval, while negative sanctions follow unapproved behavior. Role clustering occurs when a family member occupies a variety of roles simultaneously; when the demands of the roles conflict, the family balance is affected. In these situations, an assessment of the family's values system is required (Perlman, 1961). Flexibility and shifting of roles is an indicator of adaptive capabilities of the family.

Because the performance of roles is a significant indicator of how well a family may be expected to cope under stress, the examiner should assess why the family structure supports a negative role for one or more of its members. The clinical questions requiring answers are the following: Which family members occupy various roles? Is there complementarity between role performers? Do roles overlap? Are roles flexible, so that adaptation can be expected? Are roles congruent with societal expectations? Do certain roles label family members negatively? When working with ethnic, racial or cultural minorities knowledge of different values, customs and traditions is indispensable to the interpretation of the appropriateness of a role.

An area closely related to family roles is the relationship between functioning and the home environment (Hartman, 1979). Lennard and Lennard (1977) propose that physical home environments may be described as unsuitable when they do not complement the family's interaction patterns, role relationships, values, developmental stage, or structure. Among the concepts used in their analysis of physical home environments are territory (space identified as subject to the control of an individual or a family), boundary (that which defines territorial limits and separates territories), and orientation (the direction faced by the territory).

Approaches for assessing family functioning and the home environment include home visits, family interviews, ecomaps, family sculptures, formal measures (scales) of family environment, assignment of tasks to the family, and other assessment techniques developed by family therapists, such as family choreography. These assessment tools will be described in the context of structural and functional family assessment.

Certain system-focused assessment techniques have been developed as vehicles for enhancing the family interview. Two of the most widely used are the ecomap and the family sculpture (Hartman, 1978). These tools encourage active collaboration between typically unresponsive family members in operationalizing family structures and functioning. These methods have become recognized for their usefulness in family assessment because they permit the psychologist not only to gather factual information but also to observe personal reactions of family members and the meanings ascribed to family events and processes. These assessment tools may be used differentially, depending on the nature of the referral and the family's willingness to participate. As the examiner uses each of these techniques, the objective should be to learn something about the family's environment in terms of its relationship to the following systems: extended family, housing, health care, mental health, work, school, legal institutions, recreation, community, cultural or religious institutions, friends, and social services.

Ecomap. The ecomap (Hartman, 1979) was constructed as a dynamic way of diagramming the relationships within a family and the people and institutions tangential to it. As the ecomap develops, it provides the psychologist and the family with an understanding of stressors as well as available supports.

To construct an ecomap, family members are asked to label and connect a system of circles representing family members and related institutions. In the large circle at the center of the diagram, the family unit can be pictured by using symbols that represent members and their relationships. Squares depict male family members and small circles are used for females. These figures are joined to form a family tree that portrays relationships. Connections are drawn between circles on the map to show relationships between the family and significant institutions in its environment, such as the school, the church, or friends. The nature of these interconnections may be illustrated with a descriptive word, a drawing, or with different kinds of interconnecting lines (e.g., an unbroken line to depict a strong relationship, a broken line to show a tenuous relationship, or a line with slash marks to depict a stressful relationship). The ecomap may be useful in describing subsystem relationships, alliances, triangulations, blockages, or generational boundaries (Minuchin, 1974).

The process of ecomapping allows the psychologist to phrase initial questions in broad, general terms that may be less intrusive than a structured interview (e.g., "Please draw for me how your family members are related"; "What is your family's relationship with the schools?"). As information about family dynamics is gathered, more specific follow-up questions gradually can be posed: "Could you explain why you describe your relationship with your adolescent son as 'stressed'?"; "You show a close relationship with the church; what role has the church played in helping you with this problem?"; "What role have you played as mother in dealing with your adolescent son's sibling rivalry with his younger sister?"; and so on. Answers to these questions provide descriptions of family rules, roles played (e.g., good child, identified patient, spokesperson), uses of power (Haley, 1976), or leadership styles (Olson, Sprenkle, & Russell, 1979).

When family members actively participate in the process of ecomapping and in studying the finished diagram, discussions often follow about how family functioning might be improved. Furthermore, ecomapping often provides the psychological examiner entry into a closed family system, affording linkages to underused family coping resources. This process may also reveal a need for services that do not exist presently and that can become a focus for further planning. The examiner should be aware that adolescents asked to participate in constructing an ecomap may be fearful of negative consequences if they reveal forbidden stories about themselves or their parents. Consequently, the examiner should be personally accepting, avoid value judgments, and discuss the importance of honesty in the ecomapping process.

Family sculpture. Family interviewing and ecomapping can be further enriched through the use of family sculpture. This technique assesses family relationships and interactions, feelings, attitudes, moods, and activities by engaging the members in a dynamic process whereby they create a living family portrait. Like ecomapping, the family sculpture is a particularly effective technique with clients who are initially nonverbal. The examiner can introduce the technique to the family by telling each member in turn to imagine that they are stage directors and that they are to direct a typical scene that occurs in their household. By arranging the family "actors," they are to depict relationships, feelings, and actions (Papp, Silverstein, & Carter, 1973). The examiner can further explain that this is a useful way to find out what it is like to be in this family because sometimes it is easier to act out what happens in a family than it is to tell about it. Everyone in the family should get a turn to show his or her own version of what the family is like by constructing a family sculpture.

Each sculptor is encouraged to move the physical parts of each family member as if he or she were malleable and made of clay. The sculptor's task is to place each family character in a position that best characterizes that person's nonverbal behavior. As each person is added to the sculpture, the sculptor continues to shape and mold his creation until he or she is satisfied that the sculpture reflects his or her picture of the system of family relationships. It is important for family members to permit the sculptor to create the portrait according to his or her own interpretation, with the clear understanding that other members can sculpt their own interpretations when it is their turn.

Like pantomime, family sculpture is very expressive, although there is usually no movement involved. Papp (1976), however, expanded and refined the technique into an assessment tool that includes movement, which she called *family choreography.* In family choreography, participants are asked to make a slow motion picture of how the family lives together by directing and placing family members in representative positions or movements. The technique permits unspoken fears, hopes, and wishes to be played out in scenarios.

Another extension of the family sculpting technique involves the use of wooden dolls to assess psychological distance and interaction patterns within the family (Gerber & Kaswan, 1971). Using this procedure, individual family members are asked to relate a story revolving around each of the following themes: Loving Family, Happy Family, Worried Family, Sad Family, and Angry Family. Gerber and Kaswan claim that by using this technique it is possible to identify three general types of groupings of dolls: 1) a family unit, 2) two separate coalitions within the family unit, or 3) no subgroupings or diffuse relationships within the family unit.

Instrumentation. Probably the best known and most widely used formal measure of family structure and functioning is the 90-item, true/false Family Environment Scale (FES; Moos, 1974). The FES measures family interpersonal relationships, the directions of personal growth that the family emphasizes, and the basic structural organization of the family. Research on the FES has explored the difference between the perceived family environments of normal families and of those undergoing psychological distress. A tendency toward less cohesion and expressiveness, poorer organization, and the experience of greater conflict has been a consistent finding in families with one or more dysfunctional members (Scoresby & Christensen, 1976; White, 1978). In another study employing the FES, Steinbock (1978) compared the perceptions of adolescents who became runaways, adolescents who were in crisis but did not run away, and a control group of adolescents; each group also included parents. While the three groups of parents did not differ in perceptions of their families, the runaway adolescents perceived much less cohesion and independence but more conflict and control in their families than did either their parents or the control group.

A unique approach to the measurement of family structure and functioning is the Simulated Family Activity Measure (SIMFAM) (Straus & Tallman, 1971), which was designed to assess five aspects of family functioning: Power, Support, Communication, Problem-Solving Ability, and Creativity. This measure provides the psychological examiner the opportunity to observe and videotape family interactions in the simulated family activity of discovering the rules to shuffleboard. The family is to accomplish this by observing the patterns of red and green lights they receive as feedback to shape the various scoring strategies they employ. The game usually ends with the family in crisis, however. Russell (1980) altered the SIMFAM format to allow for a recovery period in which the family's ability to reorganize and adapt to new rules was assessed. Measurements are made by the examiner both during play and while reviewing a recording of the performance. Family cohesion is recorded by counting the number of times all members of the family are playing the game according to the rules in operation for that inning. Family adaptability is assessed during replays of the videotaped interactions by deriving a composite score, including a measure of cohesiveness (the number of times a person makes statements of direction intended to modify another's behavior) and control (the number of times a person's assertive statements actually modify the behavior of another person).

Like the SIMFAM, the Family Adaptability and Cohesion Evaluation Scales (FACES; Olson, Bell, & Portner, 1978) was designed to locate a family's style of functioning along the dimensions of family cohesion and family adaptability. FACES is a 111-item, self-report instrument comprised of 16 subscales, nine of which assess cohesion and seven of which measure adaptability. A family composite score can be obtained by summing the scores of individual family members; a discrepancy score is derived by comparing responses of different family members.

IV. Communication and Interaction Styles

Family members exchange interpersonal information through the process of verbal and nonverbal communication. Verbal communication is defined as not only spoken words but also laughter, moans, inflections, and tones of voice. Nonverbal communication is sent through body language and takes the form of changes in posture, position, facial expression, and gestures.

Certain dysfunctional communication patterns may occur in conflictual and symptomatic families (Johnson & Lobitz, 1974). A parent's conflicting messages can put an adolescent in a "double bind," with no way to gain parental approval. For example, the father who suggests that his teenage son get a job, but then criticizes him for not being around to go on family outings may be placing that adolescent in a no-win situation. Topics deemed appropriate for conversation may be influenced by sex-linked, stereotypical value systems—some fathers may prefer to discuss baseball with their sons, and daughters may talk about baby-sitting with their mothers.

Congruence of communications, conflict, role relations, and decision-making are interactive processes that, when observed, facilitate assessment of family functioning. Haley (1976) was one of the earliest researchers to discriminate between certain forms of normal and pathological communication in families. He found that very rigid, repetitive, and nonrandom patterns of interaction characterizes families with pathological communication patterns. For example, a mother and teenage son may have developed such a rigid pattern of interaction that each interaction between the father and son will be interrupted by a mother-son interchange.

In addressing this area of family assessment, the examiner should keep the following questions in mind: What are the topics of family discussion? Are certain topics forbidden? What is the atmosphere like surrounding family interactions: supportive, warm, happy, affiliative, mistrustful, fearful, defensive, cautious, formal, tense, hostile? Do family members seem to feel comfortable in expressing their needs and feelings, either directly or indirectly? Do certain family members provoke anxiety by their communications? Are messages clear, or do family members communicate "double" messages to each other? Are some family members excluded from discussion? Do some family members speak for other members? Is more communication time spent in attacking or defending others? Is there a pattern of scapegoating a particular family member? Are the patterns of communication influenced by sex-linked attitudes and values?

A number of formal and informal assessment techniques have been used successfully to disclose disturbed family communications and interaction patterns. Haley (1973) has suggested charting who communicates with whom, how often, for how long, under what circumstances, and discussing what topics. This informal technique may provide data on secret coalitions and alliances within the family. Charting may be done by one or more participants, observers within the family, and/or by the examiner in the course of the family interview.

Formal inventories have been developed as well to assess verbal communication behavior in families (Mishler & Waxler, 1968; Riskin, 1964; Riskin & Faunce, 1970; Thomas, 1974). One such measure is the Family Interaction Scales (FIS; Riskin, 1964), composed of six categories of family functioning: 1) Clarity, 2) Topic Continuity, 3) Commitment, 4) Agreement and Disagreement, 5) Affect Intensity, and 6) Relationship Quality. It should be noted that personality traits in early adolescents have been found to correlate with FIS scale scores (Riskin & Faunce, 1970). For example, children tend to become compulsive, intellectualized, and humorless when raised in families that demand extremely high levels of clarity in communication. When the family emphasizes moderate levels of clarity, the child's communication would be more likely to evidence good reality testing, a direct expression of wishes and feelings, a sense of identity, value rationality, and an ability to express humor. In families where there is a complete lack of clarity in communication, the children may learn to distrust their own perceptions and exhibit poor reality testing.

The Family Assessment Device (FAD; Epstein, Baldwin, & Bishop, 1981, 1983) is a 53-item self-report inventory that assesses family transactions and communications from a systems perspective. Responses are made in 4-point Likert format. The FAD has seven scales (Problem Solving, Communication, Roles, Affective Responsiveness, Affective Involvement, Behavior Control, and General Functioning), each of which contains between 5 and 12 items. Using this inventory, one can compare the perceptions of each family member over age 12 regarding the family's communication style and organization. The discriminant validity of FAD scores has been demonstrated with 218 nonclinical families and 98 clinical families (Epstein, Baldwin, & Bishop, 1983). True positive identifications were made in 64% of the clinical family members and in 67% of the nonclinical family members. The clinical mean scale scores were consistently higher (less healthy) than those of the nonclinical group.

A new scale to consider when assessing the characteristics of family communication is the Family Assessment Measure (FAM; Steinhauer, Santa-Barbara, & Skinner, 1985). The seven constructs assessed on the FAM are Task Accomplishment, Communication, Role Performance, Affective Expression, Affective Involvement, Control, and Values and Norms.

V. Hypotheses Regarding Symptom Maintenance

It may be that a long-standing family problem has continued because some or all family members benefit from it. In completing this item, the counselor must consider each family member, questioning "How might [the presenting problem] benefit him or her?" For example, certain family members may benefit from an adolescent's failing grades and drinking behavior because then the focus of family "scapegoating" is on him and not themselves.

VI. Family Life Stages/Tasks

All families pass through critical periods in which members must reorganize their views of themselves and their roles in the family. According to Rhodes (1977), the six stages of family life are the following: 1) intimacy versus idealization or disillusionment (newly married); 2) replenishment versus turning inward (parenting);

3) companionship versus isolation (family with adolescents); 4) regrouping versus binding or expulsion (family with children leaving home); 5) rediscovery versus despair (renegotiating a relationship divested of the parenting role); and 6) mutual aid versus usefulness (mutual, intergenerational assistance in old age). Likewise, marital pairs pass through a predictable sequence of stages. Developmental marital stages include courtship, early marriage, childbearing, child rearing, parenting teenagers, launching, middle years, and retirement (Piercy, McKeon, & Laird, 1983).

Each life stage has its own challenges, benefits, and problems. Behavior that was appropriate and effective at one stage (e.g., manner of exercising parental authority) may be ineffective at another. The life stages of families and marital pairs must complement the life stages of the developing adolescent. Erikson (1963) identified eight stages in the psychosocial development of the adolescent. The two pertinent stages here and the principal issues to be confronted within them are the adolescent stage, involving identity versus diffusion, and young adulthood, involving intimacy versus isolation.

An awareness of a particular family's life stage can sensitize the counselor to developmental tasks and problems associated with that particular stage (Carter & McGoldrick, 1980). Similarly, when the life stage of the marital pair is compared both to that of the family and that of the developing adolescent, it is important to look for discrepancies between the tasks involved in each to uncover sources of conflict. Problems are more likely to develop when the family or one of its adolescent members has experienced a change in life stage and/or when a major life event has taken place, such as an adolescent leaving for college (Hadley et al., 1974). When families have avoided resolutions of early tasks, chronic difficulties abound (Solomon, 1973). When the professional focuses on the predictable family life stages, attention is called to the individual or family not meeting the socially acceptable goals, thereby indicating potential for an impending or present problem. It is especially important to assess single-parent families with an understanding of how this phenomenon affects the roles and tasks of the various life stages.

VII. Pertinent Family-of-Origin Information

A consideration of the family tree and family history may be helpful in understanding the origins of present family issues and in planning effective interventions (Boszormenyi-Nagy & Spark, 1973; Bowen, 1978).

Genogram. The genogram (Holman, 1983) is a valuable assessment tool for learning about a family's history. Based on the concept of a family tree, it usually includes data depicting three or more generations, which provides the examiner a longitudinal perspective of the referred family. As a diagram of the family's relationship system, the genogram provides a graphic picture of genealogy, including significant life events (birth, marriage, separation, divorce, illness, death), identification (racial, social class, ethnic, religious), occupations, and places of residence. Family patterns emerge, providing vital information that frequently relates to behavior contributing to the family's problems. When developed in the course of an interview, the genogram offers a unique opportunity for family members and the professional examiner to visualize the gestalt of the family unit. This process offers a structured method for sharing information, yet at the same time it encourages the expression of feelings about the people and events being discussed.

Constructing a genogram may begin with the use of a photocopied genogram outline which shows the family that this is a usual procedure in this setting. Even reticent family members are generally willing to share abundant information and are often surprised to recognize that while they know much about some areas of family history, they know little about other areas. As information is discussed, it often becomes clear that spouses or children are unfamiliar with information that it was assumed they knew. Reluctance to share certain taboo information must be respected by the examiner, as it may be indicative of family history that is distressing or embarrassing. It is not unusual to find that previously withheld information is revealed at a later time, as trust in the psychologist develops.

Instrumentation. The Family Concept Assessment Method (FCAM; van der Veen, 1960, 1969) is a standardized assessment of each family member's perception of the cognitive, social, and emotional structures of his or her family. The FCAM can be used to characterize the real family concept as it presently exists, the ideal family concept as each family member would like it to be, and the concept of one's family of origin. The 80 items on the FCAM were constructed to apply to the entire family unit and not just to an individual family position or relationship. Direct comparisons between respondents are possible. The test comes in two principal versions, a Q-sort and multiple-choice format.

VIII. External Sources of Stress and Support

The family does not operate in a vacuum, but interacts either positively or negatively with many systems outside itself (Spiegel, 1971). The relationship of the family to its environment is a critical focus for assessment. External sources of stress and support could include relatives, work, friends, helping professionals, the referring person, and the local community. In any particular case, the psychologist might find him- or herself questioning how the family's income level affects life-style and self-esteem, whether the school is conducive to effective learning for the adolescent, whether appropriate health facilities are affordable for the family, whether services are available for a handicapped family member, and so on.

The social network of the family also should be assessed. This network includes the important people in the family's environment who provide the means for relatedness, identification, affirmation, socialization to belief systems, and cultural values. For example, neighbors and grandparents might function as mutual support systems. To determine whether a family system has adapted to its social environment, the examiner should look for either overdependence or alienation from extended family members, whether the family has a network of supportive friends, and whether the family conforms to neighborhood standards. It is sometimes helpful to know the strengths as well as the weaknesses of the family. By accentuating the positives, a family becomes more optimistic. In addition, a counselor can use these positive resources in planning therapeutic interventions.

IX. Significant Physical Conditions/Medication

Family members who have physical problems and/or who are taking medication should be noted, to determine the impact of the disability or the effects of the medication on the family constellation. Such information may lead the examiner to consult with a psychiatrist or family physician.

X. Therapeutic Goals

Therapeutic goals should be developed based on the assessment information gathered in the previous nine areas. These goals are usually described in terms of desired interactional changes within the family system.

XI. Proposed Therapeutic Interventions

The proposed therapeutic interventions reflect the family therapy techniques, such as "reframing" interpersonal communications (Haley, 1976) or behavioral contracting, which will be used to meet the therapeutic goals.

XII. Alternative Assessment Approaches

Besides the many assessment techniques already mentioned, there are several experimental or less frequently used approaches that should be mentioned. These techniques include videotaping, home visits, and projective assessments.

Family therapists increasingly are using videotaped sessions of family-based assessments. Once a family interaction is videotaped, it is played back to get members involved in assessing their own dysfunctions. These self-observations can be helpful in providing feedback about what family members actually said to each other, what kinds of facial expressions they displayed, gestures used, seating arrangements taken, and postures exhibited (Alger, 1976).

Home visits provide examiners the opportunity to observe the family on its own turf, noting the physical setting as well as in-home patterns of behavior. An informal checklist of environmental and family variables prepared by the examiner before visiting the home will guide and organize the observations.

The primary use of projective instrumentation in family-based assessments of adolescents has been to evaluate disturbed family interactional styles and communication patterns. Probably one of the most popular such instruments has been the Thematic Apperception Test (TAT). Kadushin, Cutler, Waxenberg, and Sager (1969) modified the TAT instructions so that a family story could be elicited from several stimulus cards that typically elicit interactional themes.

Other researchers have developed a Kinship Rating Scale and a Quality of Interpersonal Involvements Scale, two quantitative indices for measuring interpersonal themes on four TAT stimulus cards. The Kinship Rating Scale has a 5-point index of family relationships. The Quality of Interpersonal Involvements Scale analyzes those TAT responses characterized by positive or negative interpersonal involvements. Goldstein, Gould, Alkire, Rodnick, and Judd (1970) found that by using these rating scales it was possible to differentiate between four groups of adolescents and their parents: aggressive/antisocial, active family involvement, passive-negative, and withdrawn.

The Family Relations Indicator (FRI; Elbert, Rosman, Minuchin, & Guerney, 1964) and the Family Interaction Apperception Test (FIAT; Howells & Lickorish, 1969) represent two other TAT adaptations for use in family assessment. The FRI consists of 24 cards arranged in four series of six. This instrument may be useful in evaluating an individual's perception of the alliances, interpersonal relationships, and conflictual areas within the adolescent's family. The FIAT consists of 10 pictures, especially structured to explore the areas of nurturance, guidance, control, and aggression within a family.

In addition to the TAT, the Rorschach has been used also to evaluate family relationships. The Relation Rorschach (Loveland, 1967) asks the family to aim for interpretive agreement. It is intended to evaluate the quality of family communication content on the basis of exposition, grasp of meaning, and relationship. Behrens, Rosenthal, and Chodoff (1968) administered an adapted version of the Relation Rorschach to a group of families with a schizophrenic member and to a control group, reporting that families with a schizophrenic member demonstrated greater pathological communication than families without a schizophrenic member. Furthermore, Singer and Wynne (1975) have employed the Rorschach to evaluate three clusters of thinking-communication defects, including closure problems, disruptive behavior, and peculiar verbalizations.

In summary, videotaping and home visits promise to be objective assessment techniques for family assessment, but more research is needed to show how they can be used most effectively. On the other hand, the projective techniques described are subjective procedures that may be open to misinterpretation if not used judiciously. Examiners are cautioned especially about the limited reliability of diagnostic decisions when projective techniques alone are used to assess family functioning. Best practice would suggest that no family assessment technique should be used in isolation.

CASE STUDY

The Crawfords: A Family in Transition

The Crawford family was referred to the Adolescent Crisis Center because their 15-year-old son, Jim, was placed on probation and referred for counseling by the courts for his involvement in a stolen car incident. After the counselor interviewed Jim by himself it became fairly clear that this was not his problem alone, but represented a breakdown in the family system. The counselor requested that the entire family come to the next visit. After explaining his reasons for requesting their presence, the counselor proceeded to address various pertinent features of the family systems model of assessment and the family dynamics involved.

Presenting problem(s) and changes desired. In order to assess the presenting problem, the examiner interviewed the family members regarding their individual perceptions and then administered the Structured Family Interview to confirm the interview impressions. Jim's parents were agreed that Jim does not take discipline very well and that he is "irresponsible." They would like him to "straighten up and fly right." Jim claimed that neither of his parents cared about him, that they do not listen to him, and that he liked to "hang out" with his friends, who sometimes got into trouble with the law. In considering the family's interview comments, it seemed that one tentative goal both Jim and his parents might be willing to work toward was better family communication.

Repetitive nonproductive behavioral sequences. It appeared that both the parents and their adolescent son were engaged in a neurotic interchange of blaming. In fact, Jim seemed to be the scapegoat for some of his own parents' reported marital problems.

Family structure-functioning. The Crawford family was not a happy one. The boundaries erected between Jim and his parents seemed impermeable. Jim was isolated from them, and they spent much of their time discussing their own marital problems. Jim's father, who tried to dominate him, was an authoritarian figure within the family, but weak at work and in interpersonal relationships outside of their home. Jim's mother did not want to be passive, but feared what her husband's response might be if she were to stand up to him.

Ecomapping was helpful in discovering these family features. In addition, the counselor asked Jim to make a family sculpture of what it is like to be in his family. Jim staged his parents sitting on opposite sides of the room trying to talk to each other unsuccessfully and getting frustrated. At the end of the session, the counselor asked the family members to take the Family Environment Scale home with them and complete the surveys individually. The FES supported the counselor's impressions that the family had very few adaptive skills. The Crawfords really knew very little about how to change their dysfunctional communication patterns. In addition, they lacked cohesion as a family unit, which exacerbated their communication problems.

Communication and interaction style. The Family Assessment Device revealed rigid, almost ritualistic patterns of communication within the family. Affective expression was usually negative, and communications were not open, but controlled, mostly by Jim's father.

Hypotheses regarding symptom maintenance. The counselor hypothesized that the symptom of poor family communication may be maintained, in part, by Jim's father domineering and controlling family interactions, thus trying to compensate for his lack of assertiveness on the job and outside their home.

Family life stages. In formulating his hypotheses, the Crawfords examiner took into consideration the developmental stages of the family, the marital pair, and the adolescent. Obviously a certain amount of adolescent rebellion and movement toward independence was to be expected, but Jim's parents' marital discord seemed to exacerbate the problem. They seemed too involved with their own problems to communicate positively with him; instead, most communications were to discipline Jim for his "misbehaviors." The Crawfords seemed to be having great difficulty in making successful transitions within the marital and family stages.

Pertinent family-of-origin information and external sources of support. A genogram showed that Jim's father had not been very close to his own father. Neither parent had any extended family members living close by who could provide support and appropriate modeling on alternative methods for parenting their adolescent.

Therapeutic goals. Based on the family assessment, the counselor and the Crawfords agreed that they should begin family therapy to improve their interpersonal communication skills. Among the other issues they planned to address in the therapy was the family's scapegoating of Jim, his father's overcontrolling behavior, his mother's unmet need to assert herself, the parents' marital dissatisfaction as it related to improving communication within the family, and the family's transition and adjustment to their present life stage.

SUMMARY

There are both societal and intrafamilial reasons why families may become dysfunctional, and these reasons tend to change somewhat with each new generation. The benefit of implementing the Family Assessment Model is that it represents a concrete way to conceptualize the family evaluation process; only the portions of the model that relate to a particular case need to be applied.

Family assessment represents a unique perspective when dealing with adolescents' problems in the home. When the psychological examiner fully understands the factors that contribute to family conflict and knows how to frame the assessment of an adolescent problem from a family-based perspective, not only may the adolescent benefit but the entire family as well.

REFERENCES

Alger, I. (1976). Integrating immediate video playback. In P. J. Guerin (Ed.), *Family therapy: Theory and practice* (pp. 138-159). New York: Gardner Press.

American Psychiatric Association. (1980). *Diagnostic and statistical manual of mental disorders* (3rd ed.). Washington D.C.: Author.

Anderson, L. M., & Schafer, G. (1979). The character-disordered family: A community treatment model for family sexual abuse. *American Journal of Orthopsychiatry, 49,* 66-81.

Bachman, J. G., Johnston, L. D., & O'Malley, P. M. (1981). *Monitoring the future: Questionnaire responses from the nation's high school seniors 1980.* Ann Arbor, MI: University of Michigan, Institute of Social Research.

Bakan, D. (1971). Adolescence in America: From idea to social fact. *Daedalus, 100,* 979-995.

Baumrind, D. (1975). Early socialization and adolescent competence. In S. E. Dragastin & G. H. Elder, Jr. (Eds.), *Adolescence in the life cycle: Psychological change and social context* (pp. 117-143). New York: John Wiley.

Behrens, M. I., Rosenthal, A. J., & Chodoff, P. (1968). Communication in lower class families of schizophrenics. *Archives of General Psychiatry, 18,* 689-696.

Biddle, B. J., & Thomas, E. J. (1966). *Role theory: Concepts and research.* New York: John Wiley.

Boszormenyi-Nagy, I., & Spark, G. (1973). *Invisible loyalties.* Hagerstown, MD: Harper & Row.

Bowen, M. (1978). *Family therapy in clinical practice.* New York: Jason Aronson.

Calhoun, J. A., Grotberg, E. H., & Rackey, W. F. (1980). *The status of children, youth, and families 1979* (DHHS Publication No. OHDS 80-30274). Washington, DC: U.S. Government Printing Office.

Carter, E. A., & McGoldrick, M. (Eds.). (1980). *The family life cycle: A framework for family therapy.* New York: Gardner.

Carter, H., & Glick, P. C. (1976). *Marriage and divorce: A social and economic study* (rev. ed.). Cambridge, MA: Harvard University Press.

Conger, J. J. (1977). Parent-child relationships, social change, and adolescent vulnerability. *Journal of Pediatric Psychology, 2,* 93-97.

Conger, J. J. (1981). Freedom and commitment: Families, youth and social change. *American Psychologist, 36,* 1475-1484.

Conger, J. J., & Petersen, A. C. (1984). *Adolescence and youth* (3rd ed.). New York: Harper & Row.

Cottle, T. F. (1975). Of youth and the time of generations. In P. H. Mussen, J. J. Conger, &

J. Kagan (Eds.), *Contemporary issues in developmental psychology* (pp. 148-169). New York: Harper & Row.

Csikszentmihalyi, M., & Larson, R. (1984). *Being adolescent.* New York: Basic Books.

Davis, K. (1940). The sociology of parent-youth conflict. *American Sociological Review, 5,* 523-535.

Douvan, E., & Adelson, J. (1966). *The adolescent experience.* New York: John Wiley.

Dukette, R., Born, R., Gagel, B., & Henricks, M. (1978). *Structured assessment: A decision-making guide for child welfare.* Washington, DC: Department of Health, Education and Welfare.

Duvall, E. M. (1977). *Marriage and family development.* Philadelphia: Lippincott.

Elbert, S., Rosman, B., Minuchin, S., & Guerney, B. (1964). A method for the clinical study of family interaction. *American Journal of Orthopsychiatry, 34,* 885-894.

Elder, G. H. (1980). Adolescence in historical perspective. In J. Alderson (Ed.), *Handbook of adolescent psychology* (pp. 152-178). New York: John Wiley.

Elkind, D. (1978). Understanding the young adolescent. *Adolescence, 13,* 127-134.

Elkind, D. (1979, December). Growing up faster. *Psychology Today.* pp. 38-45.

Epstein, N. B., Baldwin, L. M., & Bishop, D. S. (1983). The McMaster Family Assessment Device. *Journal of Marital and Family Therapy, 9,* 171-180.

Erikson, E. (1963). *Childhood and society.* New York: Norton.

Gallup, G. (1978, January 22) Gallup poll. *Denver Post,* p. 16.

Garmezy, N. (1976). Vulnerable and invulnerable children: Theory, research and intervention. *JS: Catalog of Selected Documents in Psychology, 14,* 38-46.

Gerber, L. G., & Kaswan, J. (1971). Expressions of emotion through family grouping schemata, distance, and interpersonal focus. *Journal of Consulting and Clinical Psychology, 36,* 370-377.

Glick, P. C., & Norton, A. J. (1979). Marrying, divorcing and living together in the U.S. today. *Population Bulletin, 32,* 1-40.

Goldstein, J. M., Gould, E., Alkire, A., Rodnick, H. E., & Judd, L. L. (1970). Interpersonal themes in the Thematic Apperception Test stories of disturbed adolescents. *Journal of Nervous and Mental Disease, 150,* 351-365.

Hadley, T. R., Jacob, J., Milliones, J., Caplan, J., & Spitz, D. (1974). The relationship between family developmental crises and appearance of symptoms in family members. *Family Process, 13,* 72-85.

Haley, J. (1973). *Uncommon therapy: The psychiatric techniques of Milton H. Erikson, M.D.* New York: Norton.

Haley, J. (1976). *Problem solving therapy.* San Francisco: Jossey-Bass.

Harevan, T. K. (1978). Family time and historical time. In A. S. Ross, J. Kagan, & T. K. Harevan (Eds.), *The family* (pp. 109-133). New York: Norton.

Harris, L. (1971, January). Change, yes—upheaval, no. *Life,* pp. 22-27.

Hartman, A. (1978). A diagrammatic assessment of family relationships. *Social Casework, 59,* 465-476.

Hartman, A. (1979). *Finding families: An ecological approach to family assessment in adoption.* Beverly Hills, CA: Sage.

Hess, P., & Howard, T. (1981). An ecological model for assessing psychosocial difficulties in children. *Child Welfare, 15,* 499-518.

Holman, A. D. (1983). *Family assessment: Tools for understanding and intervention.* Beverly Hills, CA: Sage.

Howells, G. J., & Lickorish, R. J. (1969). A projective technique for assessing family relationships. *Journal of Clinical Psychology, 25,* 304-307.

Johnson, M. S., & Lobitz, G. K. (1974). Parental manipulation of child behavior in home observations. *Journal of Applied Behavior Analysis, 7,* 23-31.

Kadushin, P., Cutler, C., Waxenberg, E. S., & Sager, J. C. (1969). The Family Story Technique and intrafamily analysis. *Journal of Projective Techniques, 33*, 438-450.

Krill, D. F. (1968). Interviewing as an intake diagnostic method. *Social Work, 13*, 89-96.

Larson, L. E. (1972). The influence of parents and peers during adolescence: The situation hypothesis revisited. *Journal of Marriage and the Family, 34*, 64-74.

Lennard, S. C., & Lennard, H. (1977). Architecture effect of territory boundary and orientation on family functioning. *Family Process, 16*, 178-186.

Loveland, N. (1967). The Relation Rorschach: A technique for studying interaction. *Journal of Nervous and Mental Disease, 145*, 93-105.

Meislin, R. J. (1977, November 27). Poll finds more liberal beliefs on marriage and sex roles, especially among the young. *New York Times*, p. 75.

Minuchin, S., & Fishman, H. C. (1981). *Family therapy techniques.* Cambridge, MA: Harvard University Press.

Minuchin, S. (1974). *Families and family therapy.* Cambridge, MA: Harvard University Press.

Mishler, K. & Waxler, I. (1968). *Interaction in families.* New York: John Wiley.

Moos, R. H. (1974). *Family environment scale: Preliminary manual.* Stanford: Stanford University, California Social Ecology Laboratory.

Newman, B. M., & Newman P. R. (1978). The concept of identity: Research and theory. *Adolescence, 13*, 157-166.

Offer, D. (1969). *The psychological world of the teenager.* New York: Basic Books.

Olson, D. H., Bell, R., & Portner, J. (1978). *FACES: Family Adaptability and Cohesion Evaluation Scales (manual).* St. Paul, MN: University of Minnesota, Family Social Science.

Olson, D. H., Sprenkle, D. H., & Russell, C. S. (1979). Circumplex model of marital and family systems: I. Cohesion and adaptability dimensions, family types, and clinical applications. *Family Process, 18*, 30-28.

Packard, V. A. (1974). *A nation of strangers.* New York: Pocket Books.

Papp, P. (1976). Family choreography. In P. J. Guerin (Ed.), *Family therapy* (pp. 98-119). New York: Gardner.

Papp, P., Silverstein, O., & Carter, E. (1973). Family sculpting in preventive work with well families. *Family Process, 12*, 105-113.

Perlman, H. H. (1961). The role concept and social casework: Some explorations. *Social Science Review, 35*, 58-70.

Peskin, H. (1972). Multiple prediction of adult psychological health from preadolescent and adolescent behavior. *Journal of Consulting and Clinical Psychology, 38*, 155-160.

Piercy, F. P., McKeon, D., Laird, R. A. (1983). A family assessment process for community mental health clinics. *American Mental Health Counselors Association Journal, 5*, 94-104.

Pless, I. B., & Satterwhite, B. B. (1973). A measure of family functioning and its application. *Social Science and Medicine, 7*, 613-621.

Riskin, J. (1964). Family Interaction Scales. *Archives of General Psychiatry, 11*, 481-494.

Riskin, J., & Faunce, E. E. (1970). Family Interaction Scales. *Archives of General Psychiatry, 22*, 504-512.

Rhodes, S. (1977). A developmental approach to the life cycle of the family. *Social Casework, 58*, 158-172.

Russell, C. S. (1980). A methodological study of family cohesion and adaptability. *Journal of Marital and Family Therapy, 6*, 459-470.

Schubert, M. (1971). *Interviewing in social work practice.* New York: Council on Social Work Education.

Scoresby, A., & Christensen, B. (1976). Differences in interaction and environmental conditions of clinic and nonclinic families: Implications for counselors. *Journal of Marriage and Family Counseling, 2*, 63-71.

Singer, T. M., & Wynne, C. L. (1975). Principles for scoring communication defects and deviances in parents of schizophrenics: Rorschach and TAT scoring manuals. In P. Lerner (Ed.), *Handbook of Rorschach Scales*, (pp. 102-128). New York: International Universities Press.

Skolnick, A. (1978). *The intimate environment: Exploring marriage & family* (2nd ed.). Boston: Little, Brown.

Smith, R. E. (Ed.). (1979). *The subtle revolution: Women at work*. Washington, DC: Urban Institute.

Solomon, M. A. (1973). A development conceptual premise for family therapy. *Family Process, 12*, 73-89.

Sorensen, R. C. (1973). *Adolescent sexuality in contemporary America: Personal values and sexual behavior ages 13-19*. New York: Abrams.

Spiegel, J. (1971). *Transactions—the interplay between individual, family and society*. New York: Science House.

Steinhauer, P., Santa-Barbara, J., & Skinner, H. (1985). The process model of family functioning. *Canadian Journal of Psychiatry, 13*, 178-189.

Steinbock, L. (1978). Nest-leaving: Family systems of runaway adolescents (Doctoral dissertation, California School of Professional Psychology). *Dissertation Abstracts International, 38*, 4544A.

Stevens-Long, J., & Cobb, N. J. (1983). *Adolescence and early adulthood*. Palo Alto, CA: Mayfield.

Straus, M. A., & Tallman, I. (1971). SIMFAM: A technique for observational measurement and experimental studies of families. In J. Aldous (Ed.), *Family problem solving* (pp. 381-438). Hinesdale, IL: Dryden Press.

Terkelsen, K. G. (1980). Theory of the family life cycle. In E. A. Carter & M. McGoldrick (Eds.), *The family life cycle: A framework for family therapy* (pp. 58-84). New York: Gardner.

Thomas, L. E. (1974). Generational discontinuity in beliefs. An exploration of the generation gap. *Journal of Social Issues, 30*, 1-22.

Toffler, A. (1981). *The third wave*. New York: Bantam.

Tomm, K., & Leahey, M. (1980). Training in family assessment: A comparison of three teaching methods. *Journal of Marital and Family Therapy, 6*, 26-39.

Troll, L. E. (1971). The family in later life: A decade review. *Journal of Marriage and the Family, 33*, 263-290.

U.S. Department of Commerce. (1974). *Population of the United States, trends and prospects: 1950-1990* (Bureau of the Census, Current Population Reports, Series P-23, No. 49). Washington, DC: U.S. Government Printing Office.

U.S. Department of Commerce. (1977). *Projections of the populations of the United States: 1977 to 2050* (Bureau of the Census, Current Population Reports, Series P-25, No. 704). Washington, DC: U.S. Government Printing Office.

U.S. Department of Commerce. (1980). *Geographic mobility: March 1975 to March 1979* (Bureau of the Census, Population Reports, Series P-20, No. 353). Washington, DC: U.S. Government Printing Office.

U.S. Department of Commerce. (1981). *Population profile of the United States* (Bureau of the Census, Current Population Reports, Series P-20, No. 363). Washington, DC: U.S. Government Printing Office.

van der Veen, F. (1960). *Family Concept Q Sort*. Unpublished manuscript.

van der Veen, F. (1969). *Family Concept Inventory*. Unpublished manuscript.

Walters, J., & Stinnet, N. (1971). Parent-child relationships: A decade of research. *Journal of Marriage and the Family, 33,* 70-118.

Watzlawick, P. (1966). A structured family interview. *Family Process, 5,* 256-271.

Watzlawick, P., Weakland, J., & Fisch, R. (1974). *Change.* New York: Norton.

White, D. (1978). Schizophrenics' perceptions of family relationships (Doctoral dissertation, St. Louis University). *Dissertation Abstracts International, 39,* 1451A.

3

Assessing Adolescent Identity, Self-Concept, and Self-Esteem

HOWARD M. KNOFF, PH.D.

The collective assessment of identity, self-concept, and self-esteem may constitute the most fundamental and necessary step toward comprehensively understanding the adolescent's individual psychology and development. Such assessments also provide insight into adolescents' overall mental health, as well as their interpersonal and social competencies and their abilities to respond to the pressures of living and succeeding in today's pressure-filled world. As will be discussed, these three characteristics are related in important ways to adolescent and young adult mental health, interpersonal adjustment and competence, educational and vocational success, and ongoing personality and social development. There is, however, no real consensus—either theoretically or empirically—on how best to define and assess these areas. This chapter, nonetheless, will attempt to identify, as efficiently as possible, best practices in assessing adolescent identity, self-concept, and self-esteem, given the current status of the field.

DEFINITIONS

Despite the lack of agreement over definitions of adolescent identity, self-concept, and self-esteem, some appear more appropriate than others when used in the context of adolescent assessment.

An individual's *identity* does not develop and crystallize only during the period of adolescence. Indeed, identity development occurs across the lifespan, beginning with the young child's awareness of object permanence and initial sense of self (Wadsworth, 1984) and extending to the older adult's summation, integration, and evaluation of his or her life accomplishments (Erikson, 1963). Identity, therefore, is a broad term that describes the general components of an individual's total personality (Santrock, 1983)—that is, the establishment, assimilation, or interaction of, for example, societal norms, values, and standards; family, sibling, peer, and significant-other social interactions; sex-role and other (religious, vocational) identifications; and intrapersonal characteristics such as physiology, tolerance of stress, and locus of control. In a sense, then, identity is determined by the intrapersonal, interpersonal, and environmental characteristics, variables, and interactions of the significant components of an individual's unique ecology (Bronfenbrenner, 1979;

51

Knoff, 1983c). This ecology consists of both past and present events and interactions, although their differential influences vary for each adolescent.

Self-concept generally refers to how adolescents view and feel about themselves (Rice, 1984; Santrock, 1983). Initially requiring that adolescents recognize themselves as distinct and separate individuals, self-concept more specifically involves self-perceptions regarding, for example, physical and sexual, intellectual and vocational, social and emotional, and/or religious and moral selves. Contrasted with identity, self-concept is more discrete and easier to assess at specific points in time. Whereas identity is a more abstract, ongoing developmental process, self-concept assessment using one of the many self-concept scales can detect and analyze specific changes in specific areas (e.g., self-acceptance, self-security, social confidence, self-assertion) that occur over short periods of time.

Although self-concept involves self-appraisals, it also represents a conglomerate of six different selves: 1) the person you really are, 2) the person you think you are, 3) the person others think you are, 4) the person you think others think you are, 5) the person you really want to become, and 6) the person you think others want you to become (Rice, 1984). Thus, self-concept reflects a current perception of reality, an awareness of others' perceptions, a projection of future directions, and an overall cognitive process of self-evaluation. All of these selves are potentially important to the assessment and understanding of adolescents and their development, as will be discussed further.

Self-esteem involves the positive or negative evaluation that results when adolescents evaluate themselves; that is, once they have built concepts of themselves, to what degree can they accept and approve of themselves? Coopersmith (1967) noted that while self-concept refers more to adolescents' intellectual beliefs about themselves, self-esteem constitutes their feelings about themselves. As with the assessment of self-concept, specific scales measuring self-esteem are available. Carl Rogers (1961) has been most influential in this area, discussing how discrepancies between an individual's perceived sense of self and his or her desired or ideal sense of self can significantly affect self-esteem and its other behavioral correlates.

ADOLESCENT DEVELOPMENT AND THE SEARCH FOR IDENTITY

Identity, self-concept, and self-esteem are often discussed together in the theoretical and empirical literature. When considered separately, the theorists often address their notions of identity and identity development while the empiricists are operationalizing and correlating self-concept and self-esteem to other measurable variables. From among the large number available, three theorists have been chosen for discussion in this chapter: Erik Erikson, because his theory of identity development covers the entire lifespan; James Marcia, because his specific stages of adolescent identity formation also have some empirical support; and Albert Bandura, because his view of personality development will facilitate a later, pragmatic discussion of identity, self-concept, and self-esteem assessment.

Erik Erikson

The ego psychologist who modified Freud's theory of psychosexual development into a psychosocial perspective, Erikson believed that identity development was a dynamic, lifelong process in which previous developmental stages could influence successive or even later developmental stages. Separating identity development into eight stages from infancy to maturity, he felt that each stage contributed to an individual's integrated sense of identity through the resolution of its own developmental crisis. Each crisis (e.g., trust vs. mistrust during infancy, initiative vs. guilt during the preschool years, intimacy vs. isolation at young adulthood, integrity vs. despair at maturity) is considered normative and expected at its specific developmental level. Furthermore, resolution of each crisis—either positive or negative—is felt to contribute significantly to the current and ongoing personality and identity development of the individual (Erikson, 1959, 1963, 1968).

As a psychosocial theorist, Erikson emphasizes the impact of an individual's psychological and social-emotional status both on his or her social and environmental interactions and on identity formation; thus, he identifies a positively rewarding relationship with a parent, social interactions that nurture self-confidence and social skill-building, and the successful recognition and integration of societal mores and values as critical components of identity development and individual crisis resolution (Erikson, 1959). Clearly, although not specifically designated as such, Erikson's notions reflect a sensitivity to individuals' unique social and environmental ecologies or "ecosystems" and the impacts that various interactions have on one's individual psychology, identity, self-concept, and self-esteem.

Erikson emphasized that adolescence is a period when potential conflicts are expected as the individual struggles with the crisis of establishing a personal identity while avoiding the disruptions of role and identity diffusion. As he specifically cites the development of identity as *the* adolescent crisis, Erikson obviously views this developmental period as significant in crystallizing the overall identity formation of all individuals (Adams & Montemayor, 1983). Given this emphasis, Erikson further delineates the identity crisis into seven major parts or subcrises (Rice, 1984):

1. *Temporal perspective versus time confusion* represents the ability of the adolescent to understand the concept and implications of time, the fact that life is finite, and the importance of developing a sense of realistic lifetime goals.

2. *Self-certainty versus self-consciousness* entails the ability of adolescents to develop self-confidence and security in themselves, their abilities, their problem-solving and coping skills, and their personal judgments such that they can trust and feel comfortable with their life decisions and future goals.

3. *Role experimentation versus role fixation* draws on the adolescent's ability to assume different roles, perspectives, behaviors, and identities, both to experience the success that comes with taking such initiative and assertiveness and to operationally "find him- or herself" through active experimentation and experience.

4. *Apprenticeship versus work paralysis* is the ability of the adolescent to investigate and experiment with different occupations in the world of work in order to experience both tangible and emotional vocational success and to begin the process of vocational identity.

5. *Sexual polarization versus bisexual confusion* involves the adolescent's ability to develop a clear sexual identity, which can then form the foundation for heterosexual (Erikson believed that homosexuality was maladaptive) intimacy and the heterosexual roles and behaviors that culminate in adult relationships and marriage.

6. *Leadership and followship versus authority confusion* represents the adolescent's ability to discriminate (through social and interpersonal interaction) when to be a leader and when to be a follower, how to deal with authority and how to deal with power.

7. *Ideological commitment versus confusion of values* entails the adolescent's ability to develop and commit to a pattern of beliefs that guide behavior—personal, social, political, and moral.

Naturally, the seven subcrises do not exist concurrently and are not necessarily resolved at one specific time when the adolescent suddenly develops an "identity"; they are, like the entire process of identity development, ongoing, interactive, and interdependent. The subcrises do, however, according to Erikson, significantly determine the adolescent's success in resolving the identity versus identity-diffusion crisis. With respect to the assessment of identity in adolescents, these seven areas should be diagnostically considered, directly or indirectly, as part of the process. They may be especially involved in any case where an adolescent is referred due to interpersonal and/or intrapersonal problems or difficulties.

James Marcia

Marcia applied Erikson's concepts about the progressive and cumulative development of identity specifically to the period of adolescence by using two variables, *crisis* and *commitment,* to define four identity states. According to Marcia (1966), "crisis refers to the adolescent's period of engagement in choosing among meaningful alternatives; commitment refers to the degree of personal investment the individual exhibits" (p. 551). A "mature" identity results when the adolescent has experienced and resolved his or her identity crisis while also becoming committed to a religious, vocational, and ideological future (Rice, 1984). This occurs in the context of the four identity states: identity diffusion, foreclosure, moratorium, and identity achieved.

Marcia viewed the identity-diffused and identity-achieved states as polar opposites, comparable to those in Erikson's main adolescent crisis. The identity-diffused adolescent has not experienced a crisis and is not committed to any vocation or ideology. In essence, this adolescent has either withdrawn from any significant, developmental interactions (Bourne, 1978) or is sampling indiscriminantly whatever is available because "it is there." The identity-achieved adolescent, meanwhile, has experienced a religious, vocational, and ideological crisis, has resolved it by evaluating various alternatives and choices, and has become committed to a particular direction and belief system. This adolescent, according to Marcia (1967), has achieved a sense of stability and purpose and is less vulnerable to anxiety, yet can change these commitments—but only after a great deal of thought and introspection.

Maturationally between the identity-diffused and identity-achieved states are *foreclosure* and *moratorium.* Foreclosed adolescents identify commitments to specific vocations or ideologies, yet they have not experienced the crisis necessary for "true" commitment. These adolescents often assume or embrace the commitments of others—parents, significant role models, peers. Thus, they have not *achieved* their own identities; they have borrowed them. Moratorium adolescents significantly differ from the foreclosures: they seem always involved in their identity crises, yet they are unable to make the necessary decisions and commitments that resolve these crises. These adolescents are often unstable, bewildered, and rebellious, appearing to be on a continuous rollercoaster.

As noted, Marcia and others have operationalized these four identity states, developed assessment formats, and completed some significant empirical work. Most of these assessment formats have involved self-descriptive Q-sorts using adjectives or phrases, self-report questionnaires, or semistructured interviews (Bourne, 1978). Marcia (1966) developed his own interview technique to study identity formation, while Adams, Shea, and Fitch (1979) have recently published work with an objective measure of ego-identity status.

Some of the results of these studies indicate that identity-diffused adolescents conform in authority situations, but are more influenced by their peers than by these authority figures. These adolescents also have the lowest levels of intimacy with friends of all sexes. Foreclosed adolescents have low levels of anxiety, report themselves to be very close to their parents, and favor values like obedience and loyalty. Moratorium adolescents experience high levels of anxiety and conflict with authority figures and characterize their relationships with their parents as ambivalent. Finally, identity-achieved adolescents are very academically motivated, perform better than the other three states under stress, and have the highest levels of intimacy with friends of both sexes (Bourne, 1978; Rice, 1984). To summarize briefly, Marcia's theory offers both a specific view of adolescent identity development and a process of empirical assessment that can validate or invalidate the theory. It can be potentially useful to analyze adolescents at specific developmental points in time.

Albert Bandura

Bandura (1977, 1978) has provided one of the more comprehensive theoretical models, explaining behavior and personality development through his descriptions of social learning theory and reciprocal determinism. Social learning theory posits that there is a relationship between social and environmental factors and that individuals actively and vicariously learn both by observing others in their environments and by modeling or imitating their behavioral patterns. This modeling process requires that individuals can attend appropriately to their models, that they can remember what they have observed, that they are able motorically to reproduce the desired behaviors, and that they are motivated to do so. As with most behaviorists, Bandura relates motivation significantly to the concept of reinforcement. However, while Skinnerian psychology emphasizes reinforcement schedules that provide active, direct, and often tangible reinforcers, Bandura (1977) has extended this concept to include the effects of vicarious reinforcement and self-reinforcement on learning and behavior.

More important to the assessment of identity, self-concept, and self-esteem is Bandura's model of reciprocal determinism. Although earlier personality theorists felt that behavior was a function of the complex interactions between person and environmental variables or characteristics in an individual's life (Mischel, 1977), Bandura suggests that behavior, person, and environmental characteristics are actually *interactionally interdependent on one another.* Personality (or identity) development, thus, is a complex, continuous, reciprocal, and ecologically related process. In fact, given Bandura's definition of the person dimension as involving an individual's cognitions, beliefs, values, and perspectives, the reciprocal determinism model uses behavioral, ecological, *and* internal or cognitive developmental perspectives.

Related to adolescent identity development and assessment, the reciprocal determinism model suggests that a comprehensive understanding of the adolescent in this area requires an understanding of (a) his or her person-related characteristics and variables, (b) his or her behavior-related characteristics and variables, (c) his or her environment and, as noted previously, ecological characteristics and variables, and (d) the interdependent interactions among all of these as they influence identity development. This perspective is the conceptual foundation to the assessment process described later in this chapter. Before this discussion, however, some empirical results related to identity, self-concept, and self-esteem will be presented.

EMPIRICAL CONSIDERATIONS

Research in this area can be separated into (a) the social-emotional and behavioral correlates or implications of a positive or adequate self-concept and self-esteem, and (b) the variables, characteristics, and developmental influences that nurture a positive self-concept. In the former area, self-concept and self-esteem have been related to positive mental health, interpersonal competence and social adjustments, school achievement, vocational aspirations, and delinquency (Rice, 1984). Brief discussions of these correlates follow.

Social-Emotional and Behavioral Correlates

1) A significant relationship between mental health and identity achievement has been established clearly (Oshman & Manosevitz, 1974). Indeed, those with weak identities or low self-esteem have been found to manifest numerous symptoms of emotional illness, including anxiety, psychosomatic complaints, feelings of worthlessness, and instability. Those with high or adequate self-esteem appear less likely to exhibit or develop these difficulties and have less need for a facade, which often is used to avoid reality temporarily (Elliott, 1982).

2) While interpersonal competence and social adjustment often counterindicate mental health difficulties, positive social adjustment is also related to adequate or positive self-concept and self-esteem. Thus, those with these characteristics are often socially accepted by others (Gallatin, 1975). This complex interrelationship is a reminder that, when considering correlated variables, two characteristics may be related without one causing the other. Thus, though interpersonal competence and self-concept are related, this may be due to a third (or more) factor(s) (e.g., a positive home environment and family relationship while growing up). Some of these casual factors are discussed in the context of this section; however, further research is necessary to clarify these relationships.

3) School achievement and self-concept also have been positively correlated (e.g., Bell & Ward, 1980), with indications that this relationship develops quite early (Hansen & Maynard, 1973). Although possibly stronger for males than females, the relationship between academic achievement, school satisfaction, and self-esteem exists for all individuals across the elementary school through college levels (Strathe & Hash, 1979). Often these characteristics are mutually reinforcing: a positive self-

concept facilitates high achievement, which then (re)enhances the positive self-concept, and so on. However, Maruyama, Rubin, and Kingsbury (1981) suggest that educational achievement and self-esteem are not casually related, but related due to a third set of variables such as social class and academic ability. Purkey (1970) adds the emotional climate of the home and the personal success of one's parents as other variables that intervene in this school achievement and self-concept relationship.

4) Vocational aspirations as they relate to self-esteem have been investigated with career women versus homemakers; with boys aspiring to vocational levels that are higher versus lower than the vocational and socioeconomic status of their parents; and with low versus high self-esteem adolescents (Rice, 1984). Generally, it appears that women who have both a career and a marriage have high levels of self-esteem, that high self-esteem leads to aspirations of upward mobility, and that high self-esteem relates to patterns of accepting leadership and decision-making authority, respectively. The low self-esteem individual appears very similar to one with a dominating external locus of control: he or she anticipates failure without outside help, feels that any success is due to chance, and believes that "knowing the right people" is essential for vocational success.

5) Though delinquent youths show lower self-esteem than nondelinquent ones (Lund & Salary, 1980; Rathus & Siegel, 1973), a causal relationship is still being questioned (Bynner, O'Malley, & Bachman, 1981; Wells & Rankin, 1983). These studies suggest that self-esteem has little effect on subsequent delinquency and that delinquency does not have a subsequent effect on low self-esteem. Future research should examine the relationship between self-esteem and delinquency.

Variables, Characteristics, and Developmental Influences

Among the variables, characteristics, and influences that either nurture or interfere with positive self-concept are maternal and paternal relationship and identification; parental interest, concern, and discipline; intact versus broken family status; socioeconomic status and race; birth order; and physical and other handicaps (Rice, 1984). These are summarized briefly as follows:

1) Positive self-concept is related to warm, rewarding parental relationships, a low level of anxiety within the home environment, and a moderate degree of identification with both parents for both male and female adolescents (Kawash, 1982). When the adolescent closely identifies with parental models, he or she is able to develop a sense of stability and control while learning behaviors and roles that facilitate autonomy and self-reliance. Further, while same-sex relationships especially result in positive self-esteem and a stable self-image (e.g., Offer, Ostrov, & Howard, 1982), opposite-sex relationships result in the acceptance of one's sex roles and sexual self as well as in satisfactory heterosexual adjustment (Hamachek, 1976). However, extreme identification in either direction is potentially dangerous to the development of self-concept: too much identification can interfere with normal development and become pathological; too little can result in rebelliousness, poor self-control, and identity diffusion. Clearly, this variable, which involves both the adolescent's environmental influences and his or her interpersonal relationships, is important to the ongoing process of identity development.

2) Consistent with a warm, rewarding relationship is the parental interest, con-

cern, and disciplinary style shown the adolescent (Donovan, 1975). Parents of adolescents with high self-esteem exert more parental care and interest; are perceived as being more accepting, understanding, and friendly; are more supportive of the children's academic successes; and are democratic, yet less permissive disciplinarians (Hamachek, 1976). Thus, adolescents in these families understand parental expectations and rules of behavior, yet are able to experience and explore different roles and behaviors within these boundaries.

3) The effect of divorce on self-concept is dependent on a number of factors: how old the individual was at the time of the divorce, how long and how intense the pre-divorce tension was, the mother's age when the divorce occurred, the financial stability of the custodial parent, and the reactions of individual family members to the divorce (Hetherington, 1979; Kurdek, 1981). Research results, however, indicate that family conflict and divorce are related to lower self-concept scores (Raschke & Raschke, 1979; Rosenthal, Peng, & McMillan, 1980), and that remarriage can be a positive influence as long as the stepparent relationship is acceptable (Parish & Dostal, 1980). Adolescents who have lost a parent due to death seem to experience relatively fewer self-concept effects, while, clearly, intact families are most associated with positive self-concept (Parish & Taylor, 1979).

4) Adolescents from lower socioeconomic statuses (SESs) generally have lower self-esteems, but the variability here is dependent on parental self-esteem and what peer group is most highly represented in their schools. For example, if parental self-esteem is high, lower self-esteem due to the influence of lower SES can be overcome. Further, adolescents attending schools where they are similar to the dominant peer group, regardless of SES, will generally have higher self-esteems than those adolescents attending schools where they differ from the majority peer group (Rosenberg, 1975). This latter effect is also evident with blacks—that is, they tend to have higher self-esteems in segregated versus integrated schools, despite the other advantages of integration (Rosenberg & Simmons, 1972; Simmons, 1978). In general, however, blacks' self-esteems are as heterogeneous as those of whites, and they do not have a lower level of self-esteem as a group than whites (Hines & Berg-Cross, 1981; Paul & Fischer, 1980).

5) With respect to birth order, past research seemed to indicate little correlation between a child's place among his or her siblings and self-esteem, although only-children and firstborns who have no same-sexed siblings in the family seem to have some advantages. Recently, however, Kidwell (1982) has reported data indicating that middle-born children have lower self-esteems than first- or last-born children, and that their self-esteem is lower when adjacent siblings' ages are two years versus one year away. Clearly, additional research on this variable is necessary before definite conclusions can be drawn.

6) Adolescents with physical and other handicaps often have negative body- or self-images, and, thus, have greater difficulty attaining positive self-concepts and self-esteems. This is especially true when physical handicaps are evident, but it is also a potential problem with adolescents who are, for example, learning disabled (Bingham, 1980; Knoff, 1983b; Rosenberg & Gaier, 1977) or with adolescents who *perceive* their physical selves in significantly negative ways (e.g., Padin, Lerner, & Spiro, 1981; Pomerantz, 1979).

All of the preceding correlate with identity, self-concept, and self-esteem, whether they result *because* of these three factors or significantly *influence* their presence and development; thus, these correlates are important to the adolescent assessment process. Given an ecological perspective and adherence to the tenets of reciprocal determinism, these various correlates should be considered within the assessment process in order to have the most comprehensive understanding of the adolescent. This is not to say that these many correlates should necessarily be considered causal of either positive or negative self-concept; however, their presence may support other hypotheses or diagnostic conclusions. Thus, the empirical studies reviewed here do not contain isolated facts and results; instead, they contain potential hypotheses and conclusions that may guide an entire assessment, making its analyses and recommended directions more clear.

Stability and Prediction of Behavior

Before discussing a more pragmatic or applied approach toward assessing adolescent identity, self-concept, and self-esteem, it is important to note their developmental stability and their ability to predict behavior. Most of the research in stability has been with self-concept and its development. It appears that there is a high to moderate degree of stability in self-concept during adolescence (Blyth & Traeger, 1983). There is an apparent subtle reorganization of self-concept around ages 11 to 12, where Ellis and Davis (1982) identified eight dimensions of self-concept (self-acceptance, self-security, social confidence, school affiliation, teacher affiliation, peer affiliation, family affiliation, and self-assertion). This is followed by some consolidation until age 15, a reorganization in the self-acceptance dimension around age 16, and finally, a stabilizing crystallization around ages 17 to 18. Similarly, self-esteem appears to be stable during adolescence, with perhaps a slight increase from early to late adolescence (Blyth & Traeger, 1982).

Individuals, despite the group and longitudinal data, naturally have their own fluctuations in self-concept and self-esteem over the adolescent developmental period. Mental health practitioners should take care not to overgeneralize group data into expectations for individual adolescents. Further, practitioners must recognize that "being an adolescent" does not "cause" some of the emotional and behavioral reactions that we observe, perhaps in a biased way, during this developmental period. One still needs to understand the person, the behavior, and the environmental interactions that *are* causing, supporting, or maintaining that which we are observing or are concerned about.

As noted and as will become more evident, research has not yet arrived at the point where assessments of identity, self-concept, and self-esteem can be used to predict behavior. Actually, most assessments are directed to the correlated variables (e.g., school achievement) discussed previously, which, hopefully, are additionally related to actual observations of adolescent behavior.

CONCEPTUALIZING THE ASSESSMENT PROCESS

Assuming that the assessment goal with regard to identity, self-concept, and self-esteem is an in-depth understanding of the adolescent, it is evident that a multi-setting, multi-source, multi-instrument assessment process is necessary. Evaluations must include 1) the adolescent's perceptions of self, others, and environments; 2) *significant others'* perceptions of the adolescent; 3) the adolescent's actual behavior across numerous diverse environments; and 4) the environmental, situational, and ecological variables that have influenced or had impact on the adolescent. Conceptually, the reciprocal determinism model (Bandura, 1978), with its emphasis on person, behavior, and environmental variables and characteristics, appears best suited to guide this assessment process.

Person-Related Variables

As noted, Bandura (1978) defined the person dimension as including individuals' cognitions, beliefs, values, and perspectives. Given the breadth of their development, these psychological mechanisms are related to changes during adolescence in physiology; intellectual and cognitive growth and academic achievement; social skills, adaptive behavior, and emotional and self-concept areas; sexuality and sex roles; religious and moral development; and vocational experiences and aspirations. It is important to note here that adolescents' person characteristics necessarily involve their behaviors and environments, thus the clearly evident interdependent interactions in this assessment model.

Another, more operational way to assess the person dimension, as well as the other reciprocal determinism dimensions, is to use Arnold Lazarus' (1981) modality system, described as part of his multimodal therapy. Conceptualizing human functioning and development within seven modalities symbolized in the acronym BASIC ID (*B*ehavior, *A*ffective processes, *S*ensation, *I*magery, *C*ognition, *I*nterpersonal relationships, and *D*rugs/biological functioning), Lazarus assesses these modalities to understand individuals' social-emotional and psychological distresses. Four of the BASIC ID components are directly related to the person dimension of the reciprocal determinism model—*A*ffective processes (feelings), *S*ensation, *I*magery, and *D*rugs/biological functioning; two are directly related to the behavior dimension—the adolescent's *B*ehavior and *C*ognition; and the last, *I*nterpersonal relationships, is directly related to the environment dimension. This interaction between the reciprocal determinism dimensions and Lazarus' multimodal modalities is diagrammed in Table 1. Also included in this table are the differential placements of Rice's (1984) six adolescent "selves," the eight adolescent self-concept dimensions identified by Ellis and Davis (1982), and Bronfenbrenner's (1979) ecosystem components. All but the latter will be used now to discuss the Imagery modality (the most important in the person dimension, given our topic) in greater detail; the other person-related modalities will be discussed in later sections when specific assessment approaches are addressed.

Within the Imagery modality, self-concept involves (a) two of the six adolescent "selves" described previously (Rice, 1984)—adolescents as the people they really are and as the people they really want to become, and (b) three of the eight adolescent self-concept dimensions identified by Ellis and Davis (1982)—self-acceptance, self-security, and social confidence. Although assessing adolescents "as they really are" depends on the individual completing the assessment (who's to say what, in reality, an adolescent is—everyone has his or her own perspective of that individual), assessing

TABLE 1

INTEGRATING THE MODELS USED IN CONCEPTUALIZING THE ASSESSMENT OF
ADOLESCENT IDENTITY, SELF-CONCEPT, AND SELF-ESTEEM

	The Reciprocal Determinism Model (Bandura, 1978):		
	Person Dimension	*Behavior Dimension*	*Environment Dimension*
Lazarus (1981)	Affective processes Sensation Imagery Drugs/Biological functioning	Behavior Cognition	Interpersonal relationships
Rice (1984)	Adolescents as the people they really are Adolescents as the people they want to become	Adolescents as the people they think they are Adolescents as the people they think others think they are Adolescents as the people they think others want them to become	Adolescents as the people others think they are
Ellis & Davis (1982)	Self-acceptance Self-security Social confidence	Self-assertion	School affiliation Teacher affiliation Peer affiliation Family affiliation
Bronfenbrenner (1979)		Ecosystem	{ Microsystem Exosystem Macrosystem

what the adolescent "wants to become" can be accomplished easily through an interview, survey, or questionnaire format. Significantly, however, this assessment of the adolescent's "ideal self" must address a specific area (e.g., vocational, social, financial) and should be updated periodically to control for change over time. Diagnostically, discrepancies between the adolescent's current self (who "they really are") and ideal self (Rogers, 1961) may help to explain the presence of a poor self-concept. This analysis, however, must be integrated into the broader assessment process and tested as a "working hypothesis."

Assessments of adolescents' self-acceptance (their perceived competence, self-satisfaction, and happiness), self-security (their perceived emotional confidence or stability), and social confidence (their perceived ability to relate in social situations) emphasize the important connection between adolescent *perceptions* and reality.

While adolescents, their parents, and significant others sometimes agree on a specific assessment result (e.g., that the adolescent is able to get to school on time, is generally happy, is a good athlete, etc.), other perceptions and results are not shared. Regardless of how far from "reality" an adolescent's perceptions are, mental health practitioners must acknowledge these perceptions *as the adolescent's reality* in order to understand fully the individual and his or her self-concepts. From an intervention perspective, resolving discrepancies between an adolescent's perceptions and reality may become a psychotherapeutic goal. Alternatively, others (such as parents) may need help in understanding the adolescent's perceptions so *they* can adapt and change.

Behavior-Related Variables

From both Bandura's (1978) and Lazarus' (1981) perspectives, the assessment of behavior falls primarily into two areas: overt and cognitive behavior. Development and/or learning in both of these areas is best explained within four separate paradigms: classical conditioning, operant conditioning, social learning theory, and cognitive behavior. The development of overt behavior falls primarily into the first of these three paradigms; the development of cognitive behavior falls into the fourth.

Overt behavior generally is quite easy to assess. It is often discrete, observable, quantifiable, and can be operationally and reliably defined. Its assessment, however, varies with the type of behavior and the observation conditions and can involve evaluations of frequency, intensity, and duration as well as analyses of antecedent and consequent conditions. Although most behavioral assessments require that someone observe the adolescent, other approaches might involve self-assessments or the use of rating scales or behavioral interviews.

Cognitive behavioral assessment expands the notion of behavior to include thoughts, information processing, and the intrapersonal aspects of attention and problem-solving. Applying this assessment approach within the reciprocal determinism model, self-concept here involves (a) three more of the six adolescent "selves" (Rice, 1984)—adolescents as the people they think they are, as the people they think others think they are, and as the people they think others want them to become—and (b) the self-assertion dimension from Ellis and Davis' (1982) eight self-concept dimensions. *Now* included in the assessment of adolescent self-concept are adolescents' thoughts about how others think about them—a kind of metacognitive thinking. This is important in understanding adolescents when they are playing roles (e.g., macho man, dumb blonde) that they think others want them to play (note how metacognitive thinking can translate into actual behavior).

With respect to self-assertion, Ellis and Greiger (1977), in the context of rational emotive therapy, discuss specific rational and irrational beliefs, cognitions, or self-statements that influence adaptive or maladaptive emotions, feelings, and/or behaviors (note the relationship to both overt behavior and the person dimension). When these irrational beliefs (e.g., "I must be successful in everything I attempt") are identified and assessed, another facet of the adolescent's cognitive behavior and self-concept becomes apparent, leading to a greater overall understanding of the individual. Clearly, both overt and cognitive behavior comprise a significant component of the reciprocal determinism model and a necessary focus of assessment and analysis.

Environment-Related Variables

Environment-related variables involve an expansive number of settings, physical and psychological characteristics, and people and their interrelationships. From a personality or identity development perspective, Lazarus' (1981) interpersonal relationships modality is most related to this component of the reciprocal determinism model. This modality assesses the significant, nonsignificant, and/or potentially significant people in an adolescent's life. Stated another way, it assesses the positive, neutral, negative, or nonexistent (yet potentially significant) people who interact directly or indirectly with various aspects of adolescent's lives.

The ecological model (Bronfenbrenner, 1979; Knoff, 1983c) suggests other possible environmental variables or characteristics that contribute to every adolescent's unique ecosystem. These characteristics exist in the ecosystem's *microsystem* (a specifically defined system or environment; e.g., within a family system or a classroom environment), *exosystem* (systems or environments outside of the defined microsystem; e.g., within a legal or mental health system or a community environment), and *macrosystem* (societal systems or environments relevant to influential cultural attitudes and ideologies). Together, assessments of both interpersonal relationships and the characteristics within an adolescent's ecosystem should provide a thorough analysis of any significant environmental variables related to adolescent identity, self-concept, and self-esteem.

Within this dimension, self-concept involves (a) the last of the six adolescent "selves" (Rice, 1984)—adolescents as the people others think they are—and (b) the last of Ellis and Davis' (1982) eight self-concept dimensions—school affiliation, teacher affiliation, peer affiliation, and family affiliation. Just as adolescents have their own perceptions, which are based, simplistically here, on either reality or fantasy, others in the environment have their *own* accurate or inaccurate perceptions of the adolescent. Sometimes others' misperceptions about an adolescent's behavior or affect result in an inappropriate referral for identity or personality assessment. This referral and subsequent assessment may sensitize the adolescent regarding how "others think I am," which in turn may result in a change in self-concept (especially if the adolescent begins to believe that he or she is "disturbed" when, in fact, originally that was not so). Thus, as environmental variables can affect self-concept processes, they are a necessary part of a comprehensive assessment in this area.

As noted, affiliations with one's school, teachers, peers, and family are all aspects of one's ecosystem that may influence identity development, self-concept, and self-esteem. Again, assessing these areas may provide data critical to explaining specific adolescent behaviors, feelings, or difficulties.

PLANNING AND IMPLEMENTING THE ASSESSMENT PROCESS

Given the comprehensiveness necessary when evaluating adolescent identity, self-concept, and self-esteem, mental health practitioners must carefully select those who receive this type of assessment. Generally, adolescents having significant social-emotional problems or manifesting severe behavioral dysfunctions should be referred and assessed in this area. Often, evaluations of identity, self-concept, and self-esteem will be completed in the context of other, more specially defined problems, such as depression, conduct disorders, or juvenile delinquency. Often, identity, self-concept and self-esteem become related to or causative of these more specific problems.

Given the comprehensive perspective presented here, an abbreviated screening assessment process is not recommended and will not be discussed. Instead, as noted previously, a multi-setting, multi-source, multi-instrument process is recommended. Assuming the validity of the various tools and procedures, such a process will provide more reliable data and will be potentially less vulnerable to error. However, the extent of the assessment—that is, the number of settings, assessment sources, and instruments—remains an open question of both clinical and empirical importance. Although a full discussion of this area is beyond the scope of this chapter (see Cone, 1979; Gresham, 1983; Nay, 1979), mental health practitioners must consider these issues as they plan their assessments. Ideally, the practitioner is guided by a working and advocacy-oriented hypothesis that an adolescent's referred behavior and affect is typical of the developmental levels and environmental circumstances under which he or she currently functions.

There is no single "best assessment battery" for the assessment of adolescent identity, self-concept, and self-esteem. Instead, there are numerous ways to accomplish a multi-setting, multi-source, multi-instrument assessment that is organized to analyze (a) the person, behavior, and environment components of the reciprocal determinism model and (b) the various interactions within an adolescent's unique ecosystem. In Table 2, applicable procedures for assessing identity, self-concept, and self-esteem are organized both theoretically and by Lazarus' BASIC ID modalities. The theoretical organization is presented because there are many theoretical perspectives related to adolescent identity, self-concept, and self-esteem; no perspective has absolute empirical support and validation. As the behavioral and ecological theories have been discussed previously, the remaining five presented in Table 2 (neurobiological, psychoanalytic, humanistic, cognitive-developmental, and psychoeducational) will be briefly addressed here:

1. The neurobiological approach highlights the importance of genetic, chromosomal, biochemical, neurological, and physiological characteristics, variables, and predispositions and their effects on identity and personality development. While this approach primarily emphasizes the behavior and person components within the reciprocal determinism model, stress factors within the environment can also affect neurobiological reactions, which can have secondary affects on identity, self-concept, or self-esteem (Van Evra, 1983).

2. The psychoanalytic approach, in the Freudian tradition, evaluates identity and personality development within predetermined psychosexual stages and interrelationships between the id, ego, and superego. This approach is almost totally dependent on person variables and characteristics in its analysis and description of identity.

3. The humanistic approach significantly involves an adolescent's sense of reality, development of self-concept, and perceptions of desired or ideal relationships and life events. Depending primarily on person variables and self-comparisons with behavior and environmental variables, this approach particularly emphasizes consistencies between self and ideal-self perceptions for the development of a positive self-concept (Rogers, 1961).

4. The cognitive-developmental approach emphasizes the impact of cognitive

TABLE 2

IDENTITY ASSESSMENT APPROACHES ORGANIZED BY THE BASIC ID ACROSS SEVEN
THEORIES

Theory	BASIC ID Modality	Identity Assessment Approaches
Neurobiological	Behavior	Behavioral observations in the examining office and in specific other environmental settings; behavior rating scales and reports (including interviews and self-reports) of behavioral symptoms or incidents; behavioral changes and reactions to neurobiological (e.g., physical development and maturation) changes.
	Sensation	Self- or other report of physiological sensations such as aches, pains, dizziness, or tremors, along with when and where they occur and how they seem to go away
	Drugs/biological functioning	Comprehensive physiological assessments of growth, neurology, biochemical status, hormonal status, nutrition, hygiene, exercise, allergies, drug involvement; medical and developmental history-taking procedures; other specialized assessment and diagnostic procedures
Psychoanalytic	Behavior	Behavioral observations or self- and other reports of symptomatic behavior (e.g., obsessive or compulsive behaviors); interviewing
	Affective processes Imagery Cognition	Projective assessments; psychoanalysis; family history assessment; dream and wish analyses; assessment of psychosexual development and fixations
	Interpersonal relationships	Behavioral observations or self- and other reports; projective assessment; analyses of play and social development; assessment of transference processes in therapeutic environments
Humanistic	Behavior	Behavioral observations or self- and other reports of unacceptable intrapersonal and interpersonal behavior; interviewing
	Affective processes Imagery Cognition	Humanistic or supportive counseling/therapy; unconditional positive regard interactions; Q-sort assessment; analyses of wishes or future aspirations; self-concept assessments

(Continued)

TABLE 2 (CONT.)

Theory	BASIC ID Modality	Identity Assessment Approaches
	*I*nterpersonal relationships	Behavioral observations or self- and other reports; analyses of play and social interactions/development; assessment of therapy interactions
Cognitive-developmental	Behavior	Behavioral observations or self- and other reports; developmental scales (primarily norm- or criterion-referenced) assessing current status against developmental expectations; Piagetian behavioral tasks or assessment perspectives looking especially at cognitive development and its effects on other developmental processes; interviewing
	Cognition	Piagetian tasks that analyze the assimilation and accommodation processes of thinking and interpretation of one's world; assessment using, for example, Kohlberg's "moral dilemmas" to identify one's morals, values, and ethical standings
	*I*nterpersonal relationships	Behavioral observations or self- and other reports; analyses of play and social interactions/development with comparisons to normative development at a specific mental or chronological age; use of role-play situations to assess children's cognitive understanding of social situations and their resulting interpersonal behavior
	*A*ffective processes Sensation *I*magery Cognition *I*nterpersonal relationships	Any appropriate assessment strategy to develop a normative baseline or set of expectations such that assessed children may be compared to determine their conformity or discrepancy with these expectations; most assessment here is also based on children's norm- and criterion-referenced levels of intellectual and cognitive status
Behavioral	Behavior	Behavioral observation techniques; behavior rating scale approaches; analyses of children's behavior related to the operant, classical, social learning, and cognitive-behavioral paradigms; interviewing
	Cognition	Analyses of cognitive behavior, especially through the cognitive-behavioral and rational-emotive paradigms; assessment of cognitive self-statements, contingencies, reinforcements, and aversive conditions

(Continued)

TABLE 2 (CONT.)

Theory	BASIC ID Modality	Identity Assessment Approaches
	Interpersonal relationships	Similar to assessments of the cognition modality, with an emphasis on social learning paradigms and techniques; assessments could be in naturalistic, contrived, free-play, or variable-controlled conditions
	Affective processes Sensation Imagery Cognition Interpersonal relationships Drugs/biological functioning	May be behaviorally assessed to the extent that the target behaviors are defined and operationalized in ways that are discrete, reliably observable, and validly attributed to a specific modality characteristic
Psycho-educational	Behavior	Behavioral observations and behavior rating scale assessments, particularly of school and of academic behavior as it relates to acting-out and emotionally disturbed behavior; intellectual and psychoeducational assessment and criterion-referenced and task analyses tied to academic and curricular expectations; interviewing
	Imagery Cognitions	Assessments of self-concept primarily through self-concept scales and self-statements and behavioral manifestations; assessments of cognitive thoughts through *in vivo* statements and social interactions or milieu responses
	Interpersonal relationships	Assessments of social interactions in the environments where they occur; conscious comparisons/analyses of psychoeducational achievement, accomplishments, and desires and their relationships with peer, adult, and significant-other interactions
Ecological	Behavior	Analyzed using any appropriate assessment approach, but interpreted in a system's context of the microsystem, exosystem, and macrosystem; behavioral observation of positive, negative, neutral, and nonexistent behavioral interactions; interviewing
	Interpersonal relationships	Again, analyzed as systems interactions, which include all those relevant and influential to the referred child even if he or she is not a direct participant in the interaction; development of ecosystems analyses; use of surveys and observations

(Continued)

TABLE 2 (CONT.)

Theory	BASIC ID Modality	Identity Assessment Approaches
	Affective processes Sensation Imagery Cognition Drugs/biological functioning	Assessed only to the extent that the referred child interacts with a relevant subsystem individual (e.g., a psychologist or pediatrician) and that the results are applied to an ecosystem understanding and analysis

From H. M. Knoff (in press), *The Assessment of Child and Adolescent Personality.* Reprinted by permission of The Guilford Press.

processes on adolescents' perceptions and interpretations of self and environmental events and characteristics. In some ways a facet of the cognitive-behavioral component, this approach assumes that adolescents have the ability to *understand* the events around them and to draw appropriate conclusions about themselves and their environments. Piagetian theory is well represented within this approach.

5. The psychoeducational approach integrates a psychological and educational view that school success is important to adolescents' self-concept, social-emotional growth, and interpersonal change. Identity development in this case is dependent on the interaction of all three reciprocal determinism components, with an emphasis on the school environment as an important determinant of success and positive self-concepts.

Another way to organize potential assessment approaches is to use the reciprocal determinism components more directly. While these components are clearly interactive, making any organization somewhat artificial, this approach nonetheless can guide the comprehensive assessment process. A number of assessment techniques and approaches will be discussed briefly; a complete review of approaches is neither possible nor appropriate within this chapter. The most current resources in these areas are referenced, however. (The reader is also referred to the other chapters in this book in which assessment areas clearly overlap with those of identity, self-concept, and self-esteem.)

The Person Component

Within the person component of the reciprocal determinism model are four assessment areas: objective tests, projective techniques, special clinical scales, and self-concept scales. Because of their empirical base, objective tests are considered to have generally low susceptibility to errors due to assessment conditions or the process of test administration. Additionally, they often contain "lie scales," which identify implausible response patterns indicating that the respondent may be attempting to "look normal" or mask any significant diagnostic indicators. Interpretation of these tests, meanwhile, can be quite difficult as they often have numerous scales that require expertise in "profile analysis"—interpretation of diagnostic hypotheses that result from specific interscale patterns. Competent interpretation here often requires substantial experience with the test, a careful reading of the professional research, and an ability to integrate any results into the multimethod assessment process.

Among the most popular and useful objective tests in the area of identity, self-concept, and self-esteem assessment are the High School Personality Questionnaire (HSPQ) and the Minnesota Multiphasic Personality Inventory (MMPI). Like its adult version, the Sixteen Personality Factor Questionnaire, the HSPQ comprises 14 "source traits" (e.g., reserved, dominant, shy, tense, self-assured) that are considered factorially independent measures of personality. These factors and their profile analyses provide a current assessment of many facets of adolescent identity, especially as they occur from the adolescent's perception.

Although it does have adolescent norms, the MMPI has been primarily used with older adolescents and adults (both generally using the adult norms). Specific to identity, self-concept, and self-esteem, the Masculinity-Femininity and Social Introversion-Extroversion scales are most useful, as they evaluate identification with culturally acceptable gender interest patterns and social interaction patterns, respectively. Experientially, the MMPI is recommended only for juniors in high school or older as some of the test items deal with mature issues and topics. Additionally, because it is a long test to take, the individual's reading and motivation levels need to be adequate for useful results. With respect to other MMPI issues, the reader is referred to a recent article by Archer (1984), who discusses many critical administrative and interpretive cautions when using the inventory with adolescents. Most important is the decision regarding whether to use the adult or adolescent MMPI norms when diagnostically interpreting the test.

Projective techniques involve a wide variety of methods of presenting structured or unstructured ambiguous stimulus materials to the subject. Based on an individual's interpretations and responses to these materials, hypotheses about his or her identity, self-concept, and self-esteem may be identified. Although the utility and interpretation of projective tests has been much debated, (e.g., Batsche & Peterson, 1983; Knoff, 1983a), adolescents' responses may be interpreted to indicate their specific cognitive perceptions and self-statements that, as discussed earlier, can affect behavior, identity, self-concept, and self-esteem. Within the multimethod process, these techniques' hypotheses often require external validation or diagnostic consensus to be formally accepted. The most commonly used projectives (Prout, 1983) are the human figure drawings, the House-Tree-Person (H-T-P) Technique, the Kinetic Drawing System for Family and School, sentence completion techniques, thematic apperception tests, the Rorschach, and the Bender Visual Motor Gestalt Test (see Knoff, in press, and Koppitz, 1975 for reviews). Although each of these techniques varies in its response stimuli and the types of responses required, they all generate hypotheses relevant to the assessment of adolescent identity, self-concept, and self-esteem (Ogdon, 1982).

There are a number of scales available that specifically assess self-concept or self-esteem, including the Twenty Statements Test (see Noppe, 1983) and the Self-Observational Scales. The most cited, however, are the Coopersmith Self-Esteem Inventories (SEI), the Piers-Harris Children's Self-Concept Scale, and the Tennessee

Self Concept Scale (TSCS). These were most recently reviewed in an article by Gilberts (1983).

The SEI consists of 50 items concerned with children's and adolescents' perceptions in four areas (peers, parents, school, and self) and eight Lie Scale items. Adolescents check one column ("like me" or "unlike me") for each item, with the "like me" column indicating high self-esteem and "unlike me" indicating low self-esteem. The SEI appears to have adequate test-retest reliability in the few studies addressing this area, but its construct validity has been difficult to test due to the restricted sample used in its standardization. Currently, additional psychometric research is needed with the SEI before it can be used most validly in research and clinical assessment (Wylie, 1974).

Designed for children and adolescents in Grades 3 through 12, the Piers-Harris is one of the most accepted and psychometrically sound tools for the assessment of self-concept (Goodstein & Doller, 1978). Consisting of 80 first-person sentences answered "yes" or "no" by the adolescent, this tool can be administered individually or in groups and usually takes from 15 to 20 minutes to complete. Possessing adequate reliability, its factor structure nonetheless requires additional research. Various studies have supported a unidimensional factor structure (Bentler, 1972), a three-factor structure (physical appearance, socially unacceptable behavior, and academic confidence; Michael & Smith, 1975), and a six-factor structure (the three factors above plus anxiety, popularity, and happiness and satisfaction; Piers & Harris, 1964). Additionally, there is some construct validity support, but further research is necessary in the convergent and discriminant validity areas (Wylie, 1974). Overall, the Piers-Harris appears to be a sound test for the assessment of self-concept.

While one of the most used tools in research and assessment, the TSCS has extremely limited reliability data, conflicting factor analytic data, and minimal construct validity support. Consisting of 100 self-descriptive statements, 90 assessing self-concept and 10 from the MMPI Lie Scale assessing self-criticism, the TSCS is appropriate for individuals aged 12 or older. Each item is rated by the adolescent along a 5-point scale that ranged from "completely false of me" to "completely true of me." From there, the raw scores are interpreted within a two-dimensional classification scheme, one representing "the self" (the physical, moral-ethical, personal, family, and social selves) and the other representing self-concept (identity, self-satisfaction, and behavior). With criticisms ranging from its methodological limitations to its scoring awkwardness and questionable utility, the TSCS is not currently favored by those evaluating self-concept scales (Goodstein & Doller, 1978).

The Behavior Component

Specific to the overt behavior component of the reciprocal determinism model, there are two primary assessment areas: behavioral observation and behavior rating scales. Both of these areas are far too extensive to review here, although their theoretical components have been discussed previously. Whereas behavioral observation can be accomplished in multiple settings to assess an adolescent's differential behavior in different environments and under different constraints, behavior rating scales can assess perceptions of adolescent behavior from multiple sources. Both of these assessment areas are integrated easily into an ecological perspective (e.g., Wahler,

House, & Stambaugh, 1976), and they clearly facilitate the assessment of *what* adolescents do under quantifiable and generally replicable conditions.

The most important and most used observation approaches are interval recording, time sampling recording, event recording, and duration and latency recording. These often occur through naturalistic, analogue, or self-monitoring observation methods using observational equipment, selected protocol formats, and/or specific observation schedules. These areas are described and reviewed extensively by Keller (in press).

The most commonly used behavior rating scales are the Child Behavior Checklist and its forthcoming Teacher Version (Edelbrock & Achenbach, in press), the Conners parent and teacher rating scales (Conners, 1982), the Missouri Children's Behavior Checklist (Sines, Pauker, Sines, & Owen, 1969), and Quay and Peterson's (1983) Revised Behavior Problem Checklist. The Child Behavior Checklist, a well-standardized rating scale with both parent and teacher versions, can be used with adolescents through age 16. For the parent version, there are two broad-band factors (Internalizing and Externalizing Syndromes) and up to 13 narrow-band factors, depending on the adolescent's age and sex. The teacher version has the same two broad-band factors and eight narrow-band factors, including Social Withdrawal, Aggressive, and Inattentive. Both versions have sound psychometric properties.

Briefly analyzing the other behavior rating scales noted, the Conners parent and teacher rating scales are appropriate through age 17 for identifying multiple dimensions of psychopathology, particularly hyperkinetic behavior. Among the most useful self-concept-related scales are the Fearful-Anxious, Psychosomatic, Obsessional, Antisocial, and Immaturity scales. The Missouri Children's Behavior Checklist is completed by parents for subjects through age 16. With two broad-band factors that closely resemble the Child Behavior Checklist's Internalizing/Externalizing factors, the Missouri's Aggression, Inhibition, Activity Level, and Sociability scales are most related to adolescent identity, self-concept, and self-esteem. Finally, the Revised Problem Behavior Checklist, standardized through age 16, has four major (Conduct Disorder, Socialized Aggression, Attention Problems-Immaturity, Anxiety-Withdrawal) and two minor (Psychotic Behavior and Motor Excess) empirically derived factors. This scale can be completed by either parents or teachers. The Child Behavior Checklist and these other behavior rating scales contribute significantly toward identifying behavior patterns and issues that relate to adolescents' identities, self-concepts, and self-esteems.

For the cognitive behavior component of the reciprocal determinism model, many of the previously discussed person-oriented assessments may be used and integrated. Because these assessment tools and techniques are not equally direct in their abilities to identify adolescents' cognitive self-statements, follow-up interviews to clarify assessment responses or hypotheses are often necessary. For example, a sentence completion response of "I *hate myself*" should not be left to the examiner's interpretation. Through follow-up questioning, this "hatred" may be specified as a transient dislike of one's physical appearance rather than a deep-rooted obsession that suggests suicidal ideation. Clearly, interviews with a referred adolescent (and significant others) can identify how that individual feels and thinks about him- or herself and his or her world. Sometimes these beliefs or cognitions are directly related to the adolescent's behavior and immediately suggest ways to adapt or change that behavior. The clinical interview area has been much ignored in the research arena. Recent reviews (Gresham, 1984; Nuttall & Ivey, in press), however, do address conceptual, psychometric, and applied issues, practices, and critical needs. Although a common assessment approach (Prout, 1983), this area requires significant development and attention before its true contribution to the assessment process can be determined.

The Environmental Component

The environmental component of the reciprocal determinism model, in the spirit of its interactive nature, also depends heavily on many of the assessment approaches previously noted. Two assessment areas, however, can be added to the comprehensive assessment process here: family assessment approaches (discussed in detail in chapter 2 of this book) and ecological assessment approaches. Both of these assessment areas can identify people and interrelationships, issues and dynamics, and/or attitudes and circumstances that occur within the family or other significant environments that cause, support, or otherwise influence how the adolescent feels about him- or herself. Family assessments focus on such issues as parent and sibling interrelationships; the effects of divorce, parental strife, physical or emotional abuse; and/or the influences of financial strain, situational stresses, or health and other life crises. Ecological assessments involve evaluations of critical, specific areas of an adolescent's ecosystem (e.g., his or her neighborhood, school environment, or peer network). These assessments, usually entailing checklists, surveys, and/or interview formats, attempt to sample those environmental, interactive, and personal variables that significantly influence adolescent behavior and identity development in the chosen ecosystem area.

COMMUNICATING ASSESSMENT RESULTS

Once the assessment of identity, self-concept, and self-esteem is completed and analyzed, the results generally are summarized in an assessment report. Perhaps this report's primary goal is to communicate its information clearly and effectively to all relevant or concerned parties. This is best accomplished by discussing any specific concerns that led to the actual assessment, relating them to the assessment process, and then describing intervention directions *derived from the assessment results*. Knoff (in press) summarizes characteristics of such an appropriate report in the following manner:

1. The report clearly identifies the referral questions and concerns in the *Reason for Referral* section, discriminates those referral questions that emanated from different referring parties (if present), and responds directly to those concerns by the end of the report. All data and discussion are directly relevant to the referral concerns or additional practitioner concerns identified as a result of the assessment process.

2. The report discusses the most reliable behaviors and conclusions that have been sampled (or described) consistently across the case's interviews, conferences, and observations and across the individual assessments with the referred adolescent. As much as possible, this information should be described behaviorally, and all abstract constructs should be defined with behavioral or clarifying examples.

3. When used, raw data clarify or ensure the understanding of a specific point relative to the analysis or referral concerns. Raw data should not be presented indiscriminantly or out of context, nor left in the report for the reader's self-interpretation or conclusion.

4. The report describes the unique strengths and weaknesses of the referred adolescent and/or situation in such a way that his or her individuality and ecosystem are captured. As much as possible, the examinee should be viewed in a positive light and the report written with positive expectations for change.

5. The report does not omit essential information due to practitioner oversight or bias, nor does it include minor or irrelevant information or redundancy of information. That is, the presentation is straightforward and objective, and the report is concise.

6. Recommendations are explicit, specific, realistic, implementable, and oriented to curriculum (including social and behavioral) objectives that may be written into the student's individual educational and/or therapeutic plan. Recommendations should be described in such a way that they can be implemented (eventually) without the daily supervision of a mental health practitioner, and they must be realistic given the resources of the implementing parties.

A second, important aspect of writing the assessment report is the practitioner's ability to integrate all of the multi-setting, multi-source, multi-instrument data after their interpretation. Again, data interpretation in this area can be defined as involving the practitioner's choice of appropriate and technically sound assessment procedures and techniques (given the referral and assessment goals), his or her skill in utilizing the collected data effectively, and his or her ability to speculate when necessary beyond the data proper. Characteristics of a well-constructed integration (Knoff, in press-c) include the following:

1. Assessment procedures and techniques are presented with a brief description of their administration procedures and the skills, variables, or characteristics that they are purported to evaluate. Special limitations and conditions of the procedures and techniques are discussed if they directly relate to the referral concerns or assessment goals, and the rationales or procedures used to overcome these limitations are discussed.

2. The practitioner should responsibly interpret all assessment data, and the psychological report should reflect this through its stylistic and professional tone and format. Interpretations or conclusions are based on the assessment data and on a consistent pattern of behaviors and results taken from the various assessment procedures, which adequately sampled significant dimensions and characteristics of the referred child or situation. The practitioner does not overgeneralize from limited data, nor base his or her interpretations on personal ideas, bias, arbitrariness, or lack of objectivity.

3. Further, the practitioner does not assume a causal relationship between assessment data or results and diagnostic or interpretive characteristics unless there is clear support. Correlational effects do not necessarily indicate causal effects; the practitioner should distinguish these relationships when necessary in the psychological report.

4. When certain conclusions and predictions are necessary or important to the

referral and report and it is impossible or unrealistic to collect this information (e.g., can we expect this child to become openly violent again in this situation?), the practitioner should feel free to speculate in the report if he or she is comfortable with that speculation. However, this should occur only to answer specific referral questions or concerns and should be labeled in the report as speculative.

Finally, the organization of the assessment report is important to its ability to communicate assessment results effectively. While there are many formats toward this end, one possible approach is exemplified in the case study report that follows. This report has six distinct sections: a demographic data section; a delineation of the tests administered by the present examiner; referral, background, and assessment observations; cognitive and other psychoeducational assessment results; social-emotional assessment results and current status; and conclusions and recommendations. Among the assessment areas that might possibly relate to adolescent identity, self-concept, or self-esteem are cognitive functioning, academic achievement, vocational skills, adaptive and community-based behavior, individual talents and abilities, and social-emotional status. Analyses within any of these areas should report the adolescent's current status, his or her strengths and weaknesses, and how the particular area relates to the adolescent's current feelings or perceptions about him or herself.

An assessment report's description of an adolescent's current social-emotional status could be approached in two separate ways, (a) using an issues approach or (b) using a perceptions approach. In the former, the report writer identifies the issues pinpointed during the assessment process that are significantly affecting the adolescent and his or her identity, self-concept, or self-esteem. Examples of such issues would include antisocial tendencies, frustrations, interpersonal skills, sexual identity and desires, interrelationships with others (parents, siblings, peers, individuals of the opposite sex), or vocational skills or goals (see Tallent, 1976 for others). In the latter approach, the professional would identify the adolescent's perceptions of significant individuals or elements in his or her life, regardless of their accuracy or accordance with reality, and then analyze how these perceptions relate to a current identity, self-concept, or self-esteem status. It is important to note again that these two approaches are not mutually exclusive and often are used concurrently in very effective ways.

Case Study: Robert

Robert was a 13-year-old junior high-school student referred to his school psychologist after receiving social services for approximately one and one-half years. The social worker felt that she needed a "fresh" perspective of how Robert's various life crises were affecting him. Clearly to her, Robert's academic work had been floundering since he came to her attention; similarly, his emotional reactions and affect indicated a situational depression. The personality assessment completed involved multiple settings (i.e., in the classroom, at home through the social worker, in the testing setting, on the playground), multiple sources (i.e., the social worker, parent, classroom teachers, special education teachers, and Robert himself), and multiple instruments (i.e., behavioral observations, a behavior rating scale, cognitive assessments, projective assessments, and interviews). All of the assessment instruments and activities were geared toward identifying significant developmental levels and/or psychological issues in Robert's life; clearly, both elements directly related to Robert's self-concept and self-esteem in this particular case.

Some of the assessments, completed by or with adults who knew Robert, provided an external validity or "reality base" about him. For example, the home and classroom observations of Robert evaluated significant behaviors and affects that he exhibited both toward himself and toward others. The behavior rating scales assessed others' perceptions of his behavior both stylistically and interpersonally. The diagnostic interviews provided both background data and current evaluations of significant influential elements and dynamics in his life.

This information was compared and contrasted with results elicited directly from Robert, thus providing an opportunity to evaluate his accurate and inaccurate perceptions of his world and issues that might involve or be shared with others. Assessments administered to Robert, therefore, identified specific developmental levels and/or psychological issues as he *perceived* them at the time. For example, the intelligence test assessed Robert's current status in that developmental area and evaluated his learning and problem-solving style, yet it was sensitive to possible emotional influences that might interfere with his test performance. The projective tests identified Robert's perceptions of specific issues affecting his self-concept and self-esteem while also assessing his current psychological status and the extent of his personality development. Finally, all of these tests provided hypotheses to be further explored in a diagnostic interview, which more extensively evaluated Robert's perceptions of his world and his reactions to others' perceptions of him.

The assessment report reproduced in Figure 1 summarizes the referral and background information related to Robert's case, as well as the assessment results and their implications to his identity, self-concept, and self-esteem. Clearly, the extent of the testing indicates the comprehensiveness of the diagnostic process needed for this particular case. The assessment report reflects this comprehensive diagnostic process while attempting to integrate the "good report" characteristics described above. Importantly, the report can stand alone fairly well—it provides, in and of itself, a good presentation of Robert as a case study.

SUMMARY AND FUTURE DIRECTIONS

Although a great deal has been written about assessing identity, self-concept, and self-esteem, the assessment process and many of the tools and techniques need far more research and validation before their true differential contributions can be evaluated. Within the specific self-concept and self-esteem tests, reviews over the past three decades have noted the field's disarray and the lack of these tests' psychometric integrity and full clinical utility (Gilberts, 1983). Clearly, researchers need to address these specific self-concept and self-esteem assessment concerns with an eye toward a more defined integration within a comprehensive assessment process. Additional study should be directed toward (a) identifying and further validating the correlates and implications of positive and negative self-concept and self-esteem, (b) delineating more clearly patterns of identity development and how they are affected under various conditions, and (c) investigating how therapeutic and clinical interventions can influence self-concept and self-esteem.

FIGURE 1. SAMPLE PSYCHOLOGICAL REPORT

Psychological Report   CONFIDENTIAL

NAME: Robert   DATES OF TESTING: May 29
BIRTHDATE: 1/30   DATE OF REPORT: June 1
CHRONOLOGICAL AGE: 13-4   EXAMINER: Howard M. Knoff, Ph.D.
GRADE: 6, Central High School   Licensed Psychologist

Tests Administered

Classroom Observation   Incomplete Sentence Blanks
Devereux Behavior Rating Scale   House-Tree-Person Drawing
Wechsler Intelligence Scale for Children-Revised   Kinetic Family Drawing
The Hand Test   Parent and Child Interview

Referral, Background, and Assessment Observations

     Robert was referred for an intellectual assessment as part of his three-year
special education review. Social-emotional/personality assessment was requested
to clarify some of the significant issues currently in Robert's life/environment
in the resource room and counseling support with the school adjustment counselor
for the past number of years.
     Robert's home situation contains a number of significant stresses: Robert's
mother divorced his father when he was approximately two years old, remarried him
when Robert was about eight, and divorced him again two months later. Robert's
mother then married another gentleman, who Robert especially liked, who unfortunately died of an infection when Robert was 10. Robert now lives with his mother
and half-brother Aaron (aged 3) in a trailer park. Robert's mother worries about
his school grades--i.e., whether he'll be retained--but is generally supportive of
his counseling and resource room help.
     With me, Robert was somewhat tentative and interacted with little eye con-
tact. He was polite, answered my questions quite completely, but admitted he was
thinking about not coming for the evaluation. A reasonably good rapport was
developed, and Robert appeared to take the tests seriously with appropriate motivation and consideration. This evaluation, therefore, does appear valid and to
reflect Robert's current intellectual and social-emotional status.

Results

     On the Wechsler Intelligence Scale for Children-Revised (WISC-R), Robert with
a chronological age of 13-4 was assigned a Full Scale IQ of 79 ± 6 with a Verbal
Scale IQ of 79 and a Performance Scale IQ of 82. This places him in the Border-
line/Low Average classification of intelligence and at the 8th percentile rank of
those same-aged peers in the standardization sample.
     Robert's verbal subtests scored fairly consistently in the borderline intel-
lectual range (approximately four years below his chronological age). He demonstrated relative strengths in verbal concepts (Similarities) and expressive vocabulary, and relative weaknesses in general academic information and arithmetic.
Given the personality testing (below), I feel that Robert's intellectual potential
is somewhat higher than revealed here, and that it is depressed due to both
emotional reasons and a number of years of poor attention in school due to this
emotionality. This is evident in the higher conceptual skills (e.g., Similarities
subtest) yet the lower practical day-to-day academic skills.
     On the performance subtests, Robert scored fairly consistently in the low
average ability range. Robert was relatively strong in the Picture Arrangement
subtest (at an age-appropriate level), a test of sequencing picture stories into
logical orders. Here, Robert was able to analyze a number of stories and receive
bonus points for speed, but as the stories became harder he did not adapt his
speed, began to make errors, and did not review his work. This style was also

(Continued)

FIGURE 1 (CONT.)

evident in the Block Design subtest where Robert made two consecutive errors (the criterion to stop the test) due to poor analysis and review procedures. I continued the Block Design subtest to test the limits, and Robert correctly reproduced the next four designs (including all three 9-block designs)!! If I were allowed to use these results, Robert's Block Design performance would be age-appropriate, and his Full Scale IQ 87 + 6. Thus, Robert's learning/problem-solving seemed to interfere with his WISC-R performance, and may be affecting his academic progress.

Social-Emotional Status

Robert is reacting to and concerned with a number of social and emotional issues. These issues are significantly affecting his attitudes toward himself and his environment, and have created a very anxious, depressed child. Robert has a great need for both affection and security. His affective needs are almost infantile cravings for contact which may relate to significant frustrations during his early childhood. These affective needs are poorly integrated into and dominating his personality. Robert is still (emotionally) very much a child who is dependent on his mother's love and support. His security needs also relate to the family unit--Robert is afraid not only of losing his mother (she was recently hospitalized for emotional reasons), but even for the security of his home (one of his greatest worries is that a truck will run into his trailer home). Both these affective and security needs are out of Robert's control (he could not control his parents' divorces, his stepfather's death), thus he feels helpless in the face of these environment realities.

These realities have resulted in a number of other social-emotional reactions; Robert tends to withdraw from social interactions with both peers and adults, and tends to use fantasy to escape his pressures. Unfortunately, even his fantasy takes on a depressed tone; Robert's person drawing was an old, lonely man who lived in the alleys, was constantly drunk, and had walked the streets for 40 years. Interestingly, Robert enjoys science fiction books.

Robert's self-concept is very low indeed (he noted that sometimes he hates himself). Robert feels lonely, inferior, and socially rejected. He is very sensitive to being slightly overweight, and feels that his peers make fun of and abuse him physically. It was not surprising that school rarely came up during the personality assessment; Robert is dealing with so many other emotional issues that school is (has been) secondary to him. These issues were so strong that I feel they depressed his intellectual evaluation. Clearly, some of these issues need to be resolved before Robert can approach school and his coming adolescence in a free, unburdened way.

To summarize, Robert appears to be a depressed child who needs to work through some significant childhood issues. He is psychosexually immature, socially isolated, and has a very low self-concept.

Recommendations

Robert needs substantial emotional support. This requires counseling both in the school and through a community agency, and may include both individual and family involvement. Academically, Robert needs continued resource room support. It is not known to what extent Robert's emotionality is depressing his intellectual and academic progress--given counseling support, perhaps this can be addressed in the future. Nonetheless, Robert is missing academic work and exposure; a supportive learning environment is critical to maximize these losses.

Howard M. Knoff, Ph.D.

_____

From H. M. Knoff (in press), *The Assessment of Child and Adolescent Personality*. Reprinted by permission of The Guilford Press.

Projecting into the future, our improved technological and computer-based capabilities undoubtedly will assist significantly in meeting the research and clinical needs noted above. While automated, computer-assisted assessment is becoming a reality, the area of actuarial assessment (in which statistically derived pathways facilitate multiple data analyses and diagnoses) appears even more promising. Actuarial assessment has the potential to integrate the many variables and perspectives that have been identified as part of an ecological, multiple-setting, -source, and -instrument assessment process. Indeed, this assessment process will identify those variables that best predict certain outcomes.

This computer-assisted future is not too far away; however, it requires the careful conceptualization that guides and forms the entire assessment process. This chapter has addressed that process specific to adolescent identity, self-concept, and self-esteem, but it can be equally applied to any of the assessment areas included in this book.

REFERENCES

Adams, G. R., & Montemayor, R. (1983). Identity formation during early adolescence. *Journal of Early Adolescence, 3,* 193-202.
Adams, G. R., Shea, J. A., & Fitch, S. A. (1979). Toward the development of an objective assessment of ego-identity status. *Journal of Youth and Adolescence, 8,* 223-237.
Archer, R. P. (1984). Use of the MMPI with adolescents: A review of salient issues. *Clinical Psychology Review, 4,* 241-251.
Bandura, A. (1977). *Social learning theory.* Englewood Cliffs, NJ: Prentice-Hall.
Bandura, A. (1978). The self-system in reciprocal determinism. *American Psychologist, 33,* 344-358.
Batsche, G. M., & Peterson, D. W. (1983). School psychology and projective assessment: A growing incompatibility. *School Psychology Review, 12,* 440-445.
Bell, C., & Ward, G. R. (1980). An investigation of the relationship between Dimensions of Self Concept (DOSC) and achievement in mathematics. *Adolescence, 15,* 895-901.
Bentler, P. M. (1972). Review of Piers-Harris Children's Self-Concept Scale. In O. K. Buros (Ed.), *The seventh mental measurements yearbook.* Highland Park, NJ: Gryphon Press.
Bingham, G. (1980). Self-esteem among boys with and without specific learning disabilities. *Child Study Journal, 10,* 41-47.
Blyth, D. A., & Traeger, C. M. (1983). The self-concept and self-esteem of early adolescents. *Theory into Practice, 23,* 91-97.
Bourne, E. (1978). The state of research on ego identity: A review and appraisal: II. *Journal of Youth and Adolescence, 7,* 371-392.
Bronfenbrenner, U. (1979). *The ecology of human development.* Cambridge, MA: Harvard University Press.
Bynner, J. M., O'Malley, P. M., & Bachman, J. G. (1981). Self-esteem and delinquency revisited. *Journal of Youth and Adolescence, 10,* 407-441.
Cone, J. D. (1979). Confounded comparisons in triple response mode assessment research. *Behavioral Assessment, 1,* 85-95.
Conners, C. K. (1982). Parent and teacher rating forms for the assessment of hyperkinesis in children. In P. A. Keller & L. G. Ritt (Eds.), *Innovations in clinical practice: A source book* (Vol. 1). Sarasota, FL: Professional Research Exchange, Inc.
Coopersmith, S. (1967). *The antecedents of self-esteem.* San Francisco: W. H. Freeman.

Donovan, J. M. (1975). Identity status and interpretational style. *Journal of Youth and Adolescence, 4,* 37-55.

Edelbrock, C., & Achenbach, T. M. (in press). The Teacher Version of the Child Behavior Profile: I. Boys aged 6-11. *Journal of Consulting and Clinical Psychology.*

Elliott, G. C. (1982). Self-esteem and self-presentation among the young as a function of age and gender. *Youth and Adolescence, 11,* 135-153.

Ellis, A., & Greiger, R. (Eds.). (1977). *Handbook of rational-emotive therapy.* New York: Springer.

Ellis, D. W., & Davis, L. T. (1982). The development of self-concept boundaries across the adolescent years. *Adolescence, 17,* 695-710.

Erikson, E. H. (1959). *Identity and life styles: Selected papers* (Psychological Issues Monograph Series, Series I, No. 1). New York: International Universities Press.

Erikson, E. H. (1963). *Childhood and society* (2nd ed.). New York: Norton.

Erikson, E. H. (1968). *Identity: Youth and crisis.* New York: Norton.

Gallatin, J. F. (1975). *Adolescence and individuality.* New York: Harper & Row.

Gilberts, R. (1983). The evaluation of self-esteem. *Family and Community Health, 6,* 29-49.

Goodstein, L. D., & Doller, D. L. (1978). The measurement of the self-concept. In B. B. Wolman (Ed.), *Clinical diagnoses of mental disorders* (pp. 445-474). New York: Plenum.

Gresham, F. (1983). Multitrait-multimethod approach to multifactored assessment: Theoretical rationale and practical application. *School Psychology Review, 12,* 26-34.

Gresham, F. (1984). Behavioral interviews in school psychology: Issues in psychometric adequacy and research. *School Psychology Review, 13,* 17-25.

Hamachek, D. E. (1976). Development and dynamics of the self. In J. F. Adams (Ed.), *Understanding adolescence* (3rd ed.). Boston: Allyn & Bacon.

Hansen, J. G., & Maynard, P. E. (1973). *Youth: Self-concept and behavior.* Columbus, OH: Charles E. Merrill Publishing Co.

Hetherington, E. M. (1979). Divorce: A child's perspective. *American Psychologist, 34,* 851-858.

Hines, P., & Berg-Cross, L. (1981). Racial differences in global self-esteem. *Journal of Social Psychology, 113,* 271-281.

Kawash, G. F. (1982). A structural analysis of self-esteem from pre-adolescence through young adulthood: Anxiety and extraversion as agents in the development of self-esteem. *Journal of Clinical Psychology, 38,* 301-311.

Keller, H. R. (in press). Behavioral observation approaches to personality assessment. In H. M. Knoff (Ed.), *The assessment of child and adolescent personality.* New York: Guilford.

Kidwell, J. S. (1982). The neglected birth order: Middleborns. *Journal of Marriage and the Family, 44,* 225-235.

Knoff, H. M. (1983a). Justifying projective/personality assessment in school psychology: A response to Batsche and Peterson. *School Psychology Review, 12,* 446-451.

Knoff, H. M. (Ed.). (1983b). Learning disabilities in the junior high school: Creating the six-hour emotionally disturbed adolescent? *Adolescence, 18,* 541-550.

Knoff, H. M. (1983c). Personality assessment in the schools: Issues and procedures for school psychologists. *School Psychology Review, 12,* 391-398.

Knoff, H. M. (in press). *The assessment of child and adolescent personality.* New York: Guilford.

Koppitz, E. M. (1975). *The Bender Gestalt Test for Young Children, Volume II: Research and applications, 1963-1973.* New York: Grune & Stratton.

Kurdek, L. A. (1981). An integrative perspective on children's divorce adjustment. *American Psychologist, 36,* 856-866.

Lazarus, A. A. (1981). *The practice of multimodal therapy.* New York: McGraw-Hill.

Lund, N. L., & Salary, H. M. (1980). Measured self-concept in adjudicated juvenile offenders. *Adolescence, 15,* 65-74.

Marcia, J. (1966). Development and validation of ego-identity status. *Journal of Personality and Social Psychology, 3,* 551-558.

Marcia, J. E. (1967). Ego identity status: Relationship to change in self-esteem, general maladjustment, and authoritarianism. *Journal of Personality, 1,* 118-133.

Maruyama, G., Rubin, R. A., & Kingsbury, G. G. (1981). Self-esteem and educational achievement: Independent constructs with a common cause? *Journal of Personality and Social Psychology, 40,* 962-975.

Michael, W. G., & Smith, R. A. (1975). The factorial validity of the Piers-Harris Children's Self-Concept Scale for each of three samples of elementary, junior, and senior high school students in a large metropolitan school district. *Educational and Psychological Measurement, 35,* 405-414.

Mischel, W. (1977). On the future of personality assessment. *American Psychologist, 32,* 246-254.

Nay, W. R. (1979). *Multimethod clinical assessment.* New York: Gardner.

Noppe, I. C. (1983). A cognitive-developmental perspective on the adolescent self-concept. *Journal of Early Adolescence, 3,* 275-286.

Nuttall, E. V., & Ivey, A. E. (in press). The diagnostic interview process. In H. M. Knoff (Ed.), *The assessment of child and adolescent personality.* New York: Guilford.

Offer, D., Ostrov, E., & Howard, K. I. (1982). Family perceptions of adolescent self-image. *Journal of Youth and Adolescence, 11,* 281-291.

Ogdon, D. P. (1982). *Handbook of psychological signs, symptoms, and syndromes.* Los Angeles, CA: Western Psychological Services.

Oshman, H., & Manosevitz, M. (1974). The impact of the identity crisis on the adjustment of late adolescent males. *Journal of Youth and Adolescence, 3,* 207-216.

Padin, M. A., Lerner, R. M., & Spiro, A., III. (1981). Stability of body attitudes and self-esteem in late adolescents. *Adolescence, 16,* 371-384.

Parish, T. S., & Dostal, J. W. (1980). Evaluations of self and parent figures by children from intact, divorced, and reconstituted families. *Journal of Youth and Adolescence, 9,* 347-351.

Parish, T. S., & Taylor, J. C. (1979). The impact of divorce and subsequent father absence on children's and adolescents' self-concepts. *Journal of Youth and Adolescence, 8,* 427-432.

Paul, M. J., & Fischer, J. L. (1980). Correlates of self-concept among black early adolescents. *Journal of Youth and Adolescence, 9,* 163-173.

Piers, E. V., & Harris, D. B. (1964). Age and other correlates of self-concept in children. *Journal of Educational Psychology, 55,* 91-95.

Pomerantz, S. C. (1979). Sex differences in the relative importance of self-esteem, physical self-satisfaction, and identity in predicting adolescent satisfaction. *Journal of Youth and Adolescence, 8,* 51-61.

Prout, H. T. (1983). School psychologists and social-emotional assessment techniques: Patterns in training and use. *School Psychology Review, 12,* 377-383.

Purkey, W. W. (1970). *Self-concept and school achievement.* Englewood Cliffs, NJ: Prentice-Hall.

Quay, H. C., & Peterson, D. R. (1983). *Interim manual for the Revised Behavior Problem Checklist.* Coral Gables, FL: University of Miami, Department of Psychology.

Raschke, H. J., & Raschke, V. J. (1979). Family conflict and children's self-concepts: A comparison of intact and single-parent families. *Journal of Marriage and the Family, 41,* 367-374.

Rathus, S. A., & Siegel, L. J. (1973). Delinquent attitudes and self-esteem. *Adolescence, 8,* 265-276.

Rice, P. (1984). *The adolescent.* Boston: Allyn & Bacon.

Rogers, C. R. (1961). *On becoming a person: A therapist's view of psychotherapy.* Boston: Houghton Mifflin.

Rosenberg, B. S., & Gaier, E. L. (1977). The self-concept of the adolescent with learning disabilities. *Adolescence, 12,* 489-498.

Rosenberg, M. (1975). The dissonant context and the adolescent self-concept. In S. E. Dragastin & G. H. Edder, Jr. (Eds.), *Adolescence in the life cycle* (pp. 97-116). New York: John Wiley & Sons.

Rosenberg, M., & Simmons, R. G. (1972). *Black and white self-esteem: The urban school child* (Monograph series). Washington, DC: American Sociological Association.

Rosenthal, D. M., Peng, C. J., & McMillan, J. M. (1980). Relationship of adolescent self-concept to perceptions of parents in single and two-parent families. *International Journal of Behavioral Development, 3,* 441-453.

Santrock, J. W. (1983). *Adolescence: An Introduction.* Dubuque, IA: Brown.

Simmons, R. G. (1978). Self-esteem and achievement of black and white adolescents. *Social Problems, 26,* 89-96.

Sines, J. O., Pauker, J. D., Sines, L. K., & Owen, D. R. (1969). Identification of clinically relevant dimensions of children's behavior. *Journal of Consulting and Clinical Psychology, 33,* 728-734.

Strathe, M., & Hash, V. (1979). The effect of an alternative school in adolescent self-esteem. *Adolescence, 14,* 185-189.

Tallent, N. (1976). *Psychological report writing.* Englewood Cliffs, NJ: Prentice-Hall.

Van Evra, J. P. (1983). *Psychological disorders of children and adolescents.* Boston: Little, Brown & Co.

Wadsworth, B. J. (1984). *Piaget's theory of cognitive and affective development* (3rd ed.). New York: Longman.

Wahler, R. G., House, A. E., & Stambaugh, E. E. (1976). *Ecological assessment of child problem behavior.* New York: Pergamon.

Wells, L. E., & Rankin, J. H. (1983). Self-concept as a mediating factor in delinquency. *Social Psychology Quarterly, 40,* 11-22.

Wylie, R. C. (1974). *The self-concept.* Lincoln, NE: University of Nebraska Press.

4

Assessing Adolescent Value Systems

E. PETER JOHNSEN, ED.D.

Adolescence is a period of life that has beguiled and bewildered organized societies for many generations. Parents regard it with, perhaps, a mixture of awe over the youthful passion and energy that they have left behind and anxiety over losing control over the lives of their offspring, who gradually experiment with the roles open to them. The concern of the older generation and the "generation gap" are part of the transition of this period and seem to be based on the ambiguity adults experience regarding the outcomes of all their child-rearing efforts. Worries about the acceptance of responsibility, experimentation with sex and drugs, and the acceptance of adult prescriptions about religion, attitudes toward work and politics, and family relationships all reflect adult concerns about the young person's emerging value systems.

While our society sometimes confuses its own creations of cultural conventions, such as how we dress, social manners, and other indices of social acceptability, with the more central issues of honesty, hard work, compassion, and moral courage, it nevertheless seems clear that each generation looks to perpetuate itself through the inculcation of its values in youth who will soon become the leaders of the coming generation. Psychologists have addressed this issue in a variety of ways. Erik Erikson, the noted personality theorist who has written extensively on life-span development, suggests that adolescence is the time of life that requires a cystallization of identity. In resolving the many complex conflicts that young people face, Erikson suggests that each adolescent enhances his or her own individuality in some way. This process of seeking a genuine uniqueness is termed "the search for fidelity":

> The evidence in young lives of a search for something and somebody to be true to can be seen in a variety of pursuits more or less sanctioned by society. It is often hidden in a bewildering combination of shifting devotion and sudden perversity, sometimes more devotedly perverse, sometimes more perversely devoted. Yet in all youth's seeming shiftiness, a seeking after some durability in change can be detected . . . . (1968, p. 235)

Erikson continues by defining this search for fidelity as arising "only in the interplay of a life stage with the individuals and social forces of true community" (1968, p. 235). Such interactions then promote the commitment of young people to a personal ideology that is modified and adapted to their own view of their lives and the social order. And while such an opportunity for personalizing values and altering what the community has given them is necessary for the identity of the individual and the continued vitality of the society, each generation approaches these changes in values and beliefs with trepidation.

Our generation is no different. Each week we find various organizations decrying the vigor and care with which social agencies like families and schools do the job of passing on values. At the same time we find families and religious organizations complaining about the intrusion of educational and other social agencies into the values arena. Finally, we find families themselves in periods of more dramatic social change, quite confused about the kinds of values and expectations to suggest or impose on their own offspring. Thus, authors speak of children hurried into adolescence and adolescents rushed into adult roles when they still think more like children.

All of this foment suggests that we know exactly where our youth stand on a variety of value issues. Perhaps, even more significantly, it may imply that it is really a simple matter for any of us to determine what values any specific group of teenagers has developed for itself. The matter of defining what values are and which values are significant for consideration at this time of rapid change in adolescent development is a complex and controversial matter. The resolution from a scientific perspective of the value choices society has to make about values themselves and their inculcation awaits the resolution of the difficult questions regarding the determination of what values actually are and how best to assess them.

PROBLEMS IN DESCRIBING ADOLESCENT VALUES

Approaching the question of values and their assessment with a focus on adolescence is similar to attempting a very large jigsaw puzzle without knowing if all the pieces are in the box. Several problems present themselves to readers in this field: 1) How does one define values and differentiate them from attitudes, personality characteristics, interests, and moral processes? 2) How does one deal with the broad range of values, including aesthetic, political, and moral values? 3) Does scholarly interest in values and value systems exist for its own sake or for the predictable correlates of specific value patterns? 4) Must an interest in values during adolescence take account of the substantial changes that occur during this period of human development? If so, doesn't change itself add an ephemeral characteristic to the measurement process?

These questions outline what this chapter will address in describing the few psychometrically sound techniques that exist for measuring values during adolescence and in providing a backdrop of science's approach to values and to a lesser extent to adolescence itself. It is clear that the limited number of published assessment techniques does not diminish the importance of this topic for psychological examiners. In fact, many of the chapters in this book reflect the influence of value systems on adolescent development and decision-making. For example, under what circumstances may an adolescent adopt the value system of his parents regarding, for example, what should constitute appropriate dating behavior? What role do values play in vocational choice? Do delinquent adolescents share similar value systems, or is there a diversity of values within this group? What is the value system in an adolescent that precipitates self-destructive behaviors, such as substance abuse, eating disorders, or suicidal ideations? The writings of Norman Feather (1975, 1980) represent an excellent resource concerning the development of value systems in young people, and his ideas are featured prominently in this chapter.

Values have been the subject of examination since the time of the ancients. Current branches of social science, including sociology, anthropology, and psychology, have all dealt with the issue, each bringing its own peculiar assumptions to bear on defining the relevant questions and in describing the phenomena, their antecedents, and their consequences. This chapter will focus mainly on the psychological features of adolescent value systems. Arriving at a psychologically acceptable definition is no simple task. Two researchers, Feather (1975, 1980) and Rokeach (1973) stand out for their scholarly countributions to our understanding of adolescent values, with special concern for practical applied outcomes.

Rokeach has conceived of values as generalizable and enduring standards that people believe in and use as a basis for judging the appropriateness of actions and for guiding behavior. Values are not the same as needs, traits, interests, attitudes, or belief orientations toward specific objects or issues (e.g., attitudes toward organized religion). Values are more limited in number and occupy a "core" in the individual's cognitive-personality system, whether they refer to goals or to means (patterns of conduct to reach one's goals). Values serve at the pleasure of one's ego or to enhance one's sense of self.

Feather's conceptualizations of value are consistent with those of Rokeach, but go a bit further in helping one to understand the role of development in the study of values. Using a cognitive-structural model, Feather suggests that values belong to people, although they are influenced by interactions with value-laden objects and events in specific situations. Values represent a personally organized blueprint of prior experiences that helps to interpret the meaning of future experience in a normative, continuous way (what life experience ought to be like). Value structures can change of course, as new experiences that do not mesh into the existing system are encountered. Furthermore, values involve *means,* such as acting patriotically, and *ends,* such as equality and equity. Feather (1980) clearly states that individuals differ in many of the structural aspects of their value systems, including centrality, internal integration, and complexity or differentiation. Thus, mere names attached to values tell us little of the personal meaning of the value structure of a given person.

Values have behavioral implications not merely because they influence the processing of information, but because they also are linked to strong feelings of approach and avoidance. Thus, a value connected with standing up for one's own point of view may evoke the resentment of persons who are weak or silent in the face of opposition to their own moral or political perspectives; at the same time, it encourages one to be forthright and explicit in defense of one's own views.

THE STAGE OF ADOLESCENCE AND THE ROLE OF VALUES

Values according to Feather and Rokeach emerge over the life span as an interaction between an individual's existing belief or value structure and the policies and agencies of culture in a given society. These two authors have concentrated on highly generalizable and abstract ends and means states rather than on value-laden events or issues (e.g., abortion, *the* war, using drugs) that might be called the *contents* of values; as will be discussed later in this chapter, others use different definitions and catalogs of values.

How are such approaches as Rokeach's and Feather's germane to adolescence? Feather (1980) outlines some of the "themes" of current psychological writing about adolescent development that he considers relevant to values. Using Erikson's concepts of identity formation, one can suggest that many of the tasks and choices society requires of adolescents (preparing for occupations, developing an appropriate sex role, preparing for intimacy, reorienting toward the future, developing planning skills, identifying leadership skills, etc.) actually involve the acquisition of values. Erikson (1968) attaches to this period of development the notion of acquiring fidelity, a coherent, consistent and unique sense of "who I am and what I hold dear." If the process of identity formation is an accurate description of the development of self-knowledge, self-confidence, and a secure role in society, then many values should be actively taking shape at this time of life.

Structural concepts of intelligence like those of Piaget (Inhelder & Piaget, 1958) suggest that adolescence marks the beginning of a reorganized system of problem analysis and solution, characterized by greater abstraction, hypothetical reasoning, and the capacity for managing multiple aspects of complex problems simultaneously. Such sophistication eventually may allow teens to consider both complex value systems and the ramifications for choosing a priority of values within a given system.

The dynamic aspects of psychological change in no way simplify the assessment process. Rather, the emphemeral nature of adolescents' value systems may make reliable measurement that much more difficult. After offering a general description of values and some aspects of adolescence that bear on the role of values at this period of development, the remaining sections of this chapter will sketch some techniques for gathering evidence about human values. The chapter will conclude with a case study that demonstrates how values assessment might be conducted on a group level in an educational setting.

The process of values assessment is rife with problems. First, some techniques dismiss the issue of definition and avoid a clear conceptual or theoretical base for discussing what indeed is to be measured. Because of this, much of the research suffers from an incompatibility that makes comparisons of information gathered by different scales or techniques impossible. Conceptual fogginess also precludes careful validity studies of most of the instruments used, and thus reliability becomes the major focus of many studies. Many of the data-collection procedures use groups as the units of measurement; thus, the reliability of the findings when applied to single subjects is limited. These problems suggest that few well-established tests for measuring values are likely to be available, and of these most will be used mainly for research purposes with group data. Practitioners whose interest is clinical diagnosis or referral for adolescent problems involving values clarification may have to rely on more clinically oriented techniques.

APPROACHES FOR ASSESSING ADOLESCENT VALUE SYSTEMS

Feather (1980) lists several typical sources of data about personal values: 1) self-report information, 2) choices of objects or actions in the natural settings, 3) projective techniques, and 4) analysis of materials and documents. The discussion that follows here will focus on the first and, to some extent, the third source. The procedures for value assessment listed hereafter are ordered according to the breadth of value systems the techniques are intended to assess. Unlike other chapters in this book, very few endorsements of specific scales are made here and fewer are examined overall. The reasons, as noted previously, lie in the fact that the ambiguity of the concept (value) and the variety of operational definitions (when provided) have generated dozens of assessment procedures. Most of these procedures have proved to measure constructs highly related to other variables, such as attitudes, and to be less sophisticated than the work of Rokeach and Feather. The following sections will present some examples of the variety of available measures while at the same time emphasizing that many of these techniques are limited to research on groups.

Measures of Values as General Perspectives on Life

One of the earliest examples of these measures is found in Morris' (1956) work. The Paths of Life test presents 13 paragraphs representing philosophical attitudes towards life (e.g., an adolescent's attitude toward cultivating independence of persons and things). Subjects rate each set of statements on a Likert-type scale in order of acceptability, and they also rank order the paragraphs. Cross-cultural and national norms on college-age subjects are presented (including adolescents), but they are quite dated (Coffield & Buckalew, 1984), and little validity data seems available. A short form of the test has also been developed (Dempsey & Dukes, 1965).

The Paths of Life scale is applicable mainly to research on cross-generational and cross-cultural/ethnic groupings. Practitioners should not use such an instrument diagnostically due to its limited reliability and validity. In general, this scale represents the techniques used by those who approach values as broad-based views of life, having interest in group comparisons of late adolescents. For additional examples of this kind of instrument, see Kluckhohn and Strodtbeck (1961) and commentary by Triandis (1972, pp. 16-17). These scales may be described as principally measuring general belief systems rather than values (which connote desirability and preference).

Allport, Vernon, and Lindzey's Study of Values is a very well-known and examined assessment device that has been used in hundreds of published studies. Now in its third edition, the test measures value choices in six areas: theory, economics, aesthetics, social concerns, political issues, and religion. As an ipsative scale, the main interest lies in the peculiar patterns of preference shown by each subject. Norms are provided; that is, the performance of college and high school subjects who constituted the standardization on such preference pool patterns are described in the manual. Reliability is adequate, although many technical points could be debated, and more information in the manual would be useful. Validation studies are substantial in number, and the manual reports the performance of many individual difference groups on this scale, including culturally diverse samples, the gifted, and a variety of occupations, gender groups, religious denominations and students majoring in various college disciplines.

The Study of Values has been criticized for its fakeability. The format of many items makes it seem more a test of interest than of values, and the ipsative format creates negative responses from examinees as well as problems for statistical analyses. The test content appears to have a middle-class, college-oriented bias. Nevertheless, the Study of Values is one of the few tests used to look at longitudinal changes in value statements of college students. The number of values studied are constrained, the quality of the psychometric basis for the scale is limited, and many of the criticisms of the test have never been answered, but the scale is very popular. The manual's recommendations for applications to career selection and marriage counseling must be tempered by a realization that this is a 20-minute pencil-and-paper test measuring rather ambiguous constructs that reflect a confounding of interest and values. Although widely used, in applied situations the test can be described best as a starting point for interviews and counseling sessions.

Rokeach's Value Survey is perhaps the most interesting and thorough scale available for all post-childhood subjects. It looks at values broadly, but builds a careful research and theoretical base. Consistent with Rokeach's definition of value mentioned earlier, the scale distinguishes between *terminal values* (goals) and *instrumental values* (behavior modes). The survey presents 18 value statements on gummed labels in both the "terminal" and "instrumental" categories, which the subject then ranks from most to least important. Eighteen items are considered the maximum most subjects can comfortably rank. The result once again is ipsative, in that rankings reflect the relative importance to each examinee of one value compared to all the rest. The lists of instrumental and terminal values are equal in length, although one may argue, as Rokeach himself does, that there are no doubt many more instrumental values than terminal ones in any society. Some would suggest that the values themselves suffer from a middle-class basis.

The test-retest reliability of the Value Survey appears adequate, mostly in the .60-.79 range for a variety of age groups over a 2- to 50-week interval. Validity studies reported by Rokeach (1973) are substantial, including studies of religious affiliation, political activism, party affiliation, occupations and academic majors, and so on. Feather (1975) also reports correlations between the survey and delinquent and nondelinquent juveniles, and between age groups (adolescents and parents), income groups, and enculturated ethnic subcultural groups. The results indicate moderate support for the construct validity of the scale.

Rokeach suggests many practical implications for those using the Value Survey, including diagnosis in counseling, measuring the effects of psychotherapy, and locating the sources of conflicts between established social groups (e.g., black and white high school students). Practitioners may find the Value Survey thus a useful source of information. Obviously, human behavior results from more than the structure of *individual* human values, but this scale is perhaps one of the more useful and usable measures of values systems for adolescent or adult subjects.

Measures of Specific Values

Feather (1980) has outlined several other categories of scales whose purpose is to focus on special or limited categories of values. Most of these scales have proven their utility in research situations only. Yankelovich (1974) has achieved national visibility in his work on sexual attitudes ("moral norms"), values connected with the work place ("self-fulfillment"), and political values ("social values"). His focus has been on late adolescence, covering both college and noncollege youth. Yankelovich uses a lengthy interview, as do many other investigators who assess a similar range of values (Kenston, 1965). Scott's (1965) work on values in sororities and fraternities is a focused study of selected values (whether all would qualify as values—e.g., "physical development"—is debatable) relevant to such organizations. Scott used a questionnaire of moderate reliability with little validity data. Triandis (1972) reports a variety of other techniques used to study a restricted field of values defined in various ways, including observational techniques, projectives (including the TAT and drawings), semantic differential, sentence completion tests, content analysis of stories, and Q-sort methods. As noted by the author, many of the techniques present problems in coverage of values, difficulties in reliability and validity properties, and/or the failure of limited studies to relate their findings on selected values to any other psychological function. Some of these studies ignore age as a variable of interest. In general, the techniques yield a picture of values that is uncoordinated, unsystematic, and culture bound.

Morality: A Special Case of Selected Values

When approaching the question of changing moral values during adolescence, one is again struck with the ambiguity of social science findings and methods in the study of values. Rokeach (1973) has described moral values as a circumscribed set of instrumental values (not terminal or goal-state values) that focus on interpersonal relationships. Such values contrast with competence values that are concerned with personal rather than interpersonal concerns. Thus, the violation of instrumental competence values, such as behaving logically, may lead to a sense of shame over one's personal inadequacy; the violation of instrumental moral values, such as behaving honestly or with compassion, leads to guilt reactions based on judgments of wrongdoing.

While Rokeach organizes moral values quite elegantly in his paradigm of value types and related psychic constructs, his measurement scale, the Value Survey, measures moral values only incidentally as one of many sets of values. One must turn briefly to the developmental literature to note the work of Kohlberg and his colleagues on what is generally called *moral development*.

In considering values as events that are personally and/or socially preferred, one notes that Kohlberg's (1984) approach is more concerned with the rational basis for moral values. Rather than asking, for example, which values are more important, he asks "What is the conceptual basis for an individual's judgment about one course of action being more preferable than another?" Kohlberg has suggested that the answers to this question reveal a gradually emerging structure of ideas about social justice issues, which is reflective of developmental maturity in abstract problem-solving and growing social knowledge. These emerging networks of ideas can be described systematically as stages of moral development (see Hoffman [1980] for an alternative view).

To attempt to assess the structural constructs that he maintains best describe the changes in moral values so defined, Kohlberg began with a series of structured interviews centering on material that presents conflicts. Each interview includes at least three conflicts, such as between altruism and legal violations, between regard for one's personal conscience and meting out punishment, between maintaining a contract and upholding a broad legitimate social authority, and so on. The most well-known examples include questions about whether it is morally right for a doctor to give a terminal patient a lethal overdose of a drug when she requests it.

This approach to moral values attempts to ignore moral content and to evaluate the justification for the decision of each interviewee in terms of the form or structure of their rationale (Colby, Kohlberg, Gibbs, & Lieberman, 1983). The scoring system devised to accomplish this is quite complex, but results in very substantial reliability indices and stage-like outcomes that validate the theoretical formulation (see Kohlberg, 1984, and Rest, 1983, for more on validity). While the Moral Judgment Interview is a significant development in theorizing about moral values that begin to emerge in adolescence, it is a highly complex document intended for research outcomes that provides a limited view of moral concerns from a psychological perspective. Alternatively, it should be noted that Gibbs and Widaman (1982) have developed an abbreviated form of the Moral Judgment Interview that has impressive psychometric properties, including construct validity evidence. If this abbreviated version proves itself with longitudinal data, it may replace the full-length version for research purposes.

The only other instrument concerned with adolescent moral values from a cognitive-developmental perspective similar to the Moral Judgment Interview is the Defining Issues Test (Rest, 1979). This paper-and-pencil scale requires subjects to read six moral conflict stories and rate 12 rationale statements (e.g., upholding the laws of the community) on a 5-point scale. A variety of scores can be obtained from this procedure, and the resulting evidence seems to indicate good reliability and concurrent validity with the Moral Judgment Interview. However, these two tests are only mildly intercorrelated when social class and other variables are controlled (Froming & McClogon, 1979; Rest, 1979). Obviously, asking subjects to choose from prepared statements in order to justify moral choices reveals information quite different from procedures that require subjects to frame personal reasons in their own words. The Defining Issues Test, however, is easy to administer, has satisfactory reliability properties, and interesting correlational data supporting some aspects of construct validity. The longitudinal data are limited, and the test is perhaps questionably valid when used with the very young adolescent groups. The test is used most appropriately in research studying the values decisions of groups.

A CASE STUDY OF ADOLESCENT VALUES IN AN EDUCATIONAL SETTING

Given the "state of the art" in the individualized assessment of adolescent values systems the psychological specialist interested in assessing adolescent values might consider group assessment of values as a viable alternative. Such an approach might be considered to have three phases. First, the psychologist should define an area of generalized concern regarding the values of a group of adolescents. Second, a group measurement of adolescent values might be administered to the group, scored and interpreted in terms of group performance. Third, the psychologist should consider applying these group results in developing group, rather than individual, intervention stategies.

Feather's research (1975) in Australia on the relationship between student's reported values and those they attribute to their schools will be used as a case example of how group assessment of adolescent values might be applied to an educational setting. Before describing the study, it is important to understand how Feather defined values. Feather (1975) put it most clearly when he wrote:

> Thus, one can conceive a value as an abstract structure involving an associative network which may take different forms for different individuals. We would make the further assumption that this structure also involves feeling or affection—some of the associations involved are affective associations. (p. 16)

For this study, Feather sampled 19 secondary schools, both public and private, which included religiously affiliated schools and technical schools as well as the typical comprehensive high school. Students in the sample (N = 2,947) were in the last two years of secondary school and completed Rokeach's Value Survey with half of the sample ranking the terminal values only and the other half completing the instrumental values section. Each pupil performed the ranking twice, first ranking the values as reflecting their own priorities and then ranking them separately as reflecting the school's priorities. In addition, all subjects completed two indices of adjustment to school. One was a modified version of the Cornell Job Description Index (JDI), which results in a satisfaction score relevant to an educational environment. The other was a 9-point Likert-type scale asking students how much they enjoyed being in school. Each subject was given a score on a similarity index, which reflected the degree of their agreement between the repeated ratings given from the personal and the institutional perspectives respectively, on either the terminal or the instrumental values.

To examine whether there was a positive relationship between increasing adjustment at schools and congruence between personal and institutional values, Feather examined the correlations between similarity index scores and adjustment scores. The results indicated that there was a highly significant correlation between these values, but the correlations were very modest ($r = .23$ to $.28$). In separate analyses the subtest scores on the JDI (satisfaction with classwork, satisfaction with classmates, and satisfaction with teachers) were analyzed individually. In general, students exhibited stronger relationships between satisfaction with teachers and work and the similarity index than between peer satisfaction and value congruence. Some gender and age differences did occur among the JDI subtest scores.

Feather has interpreted the findings to indicate that only a small percent of the variability in school adjustment is related to the match between the perception of institutional values and one's own values. They suggest that several other factors need to be included in the study of adjustment and pupil/environmental factors, including (a) how mismatches in values between home or family and the adolescent might generalize to schools and other settings, and (b) how the misperceptions of generally unhappy or dissatisfied students may affect their judgments regarding the values structures of their schools.

While the results of this particular study may not have great application to our general understanding of adolescent values, it has demonstrated the complexity of the assessment process as well as having shown how schools can begin to collect data on group patterns of adolescent values development in a school system by conducting a series of group assessment studies. Furthermore, individual school systems could adapt this type of group assessment procedure for their own use by comparing Value

Survey results for several years with other measures of student characteristics. Then, the value similarity indices could be used to account for that portion of the student body unhappy with the school experience. It would be useful to identify these disenfranchised adolescents because the success of students, their compliance and contributions in the school setting, and even their perseverance in the educational enterprise may be related to this constellation of adolescent characteristics that includes values.

SUMMARY

From the treatment given to values during adolescence in many current textbooks one might conclude that the content of adolescent values, as well as the conflicts that this changing content evokes, is well established. The picture painted by this brief and selective review of the instrumentation used to collect evidence on adolescent values, however, suggests that the medium, not the message, requires considerably more scholarly attention before highly probable conclusions can be drawn.

One sees that, due to the ambiguities of definition, it has been problematic for researchers to determine how values differ from attitudes, interests, beliefs, and needs. Without such clarity of definition, techniques vary from highly global observational and analytic techniques to specific, forced-choice ratings. One also sees that the breadth of value types covered in such measurement procedures can include that which is personal, social, moral, sexual, aesthetic and philosophic.

While no single assessment procedure can resolve these scientific problems, this author feels Rokeach's Value Survey is the instrument of choice for group assessment of values because of 1) its psychometric properties, 2) the clear theoretical base for developing the constructs measured, 3) the varied validity studies indicating a picture of systematic correlations, and 4) the wide age ranges with which the scale can be used to examine developmental change.

The scale of course has its limits. Ipsative procedures restrict the coverage of values due to the rankings one must perform. With any specific and limited list of values, an ethnocentric bias is introduced that perhaps prevents the use of the scale in disparate cultures. Statistical analysis of data is constrained by the characteristics of nonindependent observations. However, given these limits, the Value Survey still qualifies as a fine research instrument. The limits of the instrument for diagnostic and clinical use are related to the lack of evidence in the literature on careful validity studies in clinical settings. Reliability, while respectable for groups, is limited in individual use. The need for longitudinal data to cast light on developmental change is strong. Multimethod-multitrait validation studies would enhance the uses of the Value Survey and strengthen its theoretical base.

No attempt has been made in the context of this chapter to cover the many published tests available for measuring specific sets of values, with the exception of tests for moral value changes during adolescence. Readers are encouraged to consult general sources like Laker, Miles, and Earle (1973) and Robinson and Shaver (1969) for the range of scales available, though most seem to suffer to a great extent from the limitations presented previously.

As Feather (1980) has noted, science is disposed quite correctly to discover the meaning and nature of human values, especially during those periods of life, such as adolescence, in which new values emerge and different values gain ascendancy. However, those who work "in the field" with adolescents must remind themselves that values are only one facet of human functioning, albeit an important one. Feather (1980) reminds us that

> inference from behavior must give due consideration to all of the variables involved in the dynamics of action, not just to those that define characteristics of an individual's dominant values. (p. 284)

The totality of psychic characteristics, the context of events, and the tapestry of culture, society, and history all interplay to produce human behavior. Values are but a part of that puzzle for whose pieces we continually search.

REFERENCES

Coffield, K., & Buckalew, L. (1984). The study of values: Toward revised norms and changing values. *Counseling and Values, 28,* 72-75.

Colby, A., Kohlberg, L., Gibbs, J., & Lieberman, M. (1983). A longitudinal study of moral judgment. *Monographs of the Society for Research in Child Development, 48*(4).

Dempsey, P., & Dukes, W. (1965). *An examination and revision of Morris's Paths of Life.* Unpublished manuscript, University of California, Institute of Behavior Assessment, Davis.

Erikson, E. (1968). *Identity: Youth and crisis.* New York: Norton.

Feather, N. T. (1975). *Values in education and society.* New York: Free Press.

Feather, N. T. (1980). Values in adolescence. In J. Adelson (Ed.), *Handbook of adolescent psychology* (pp. 247-294). New York: John Wiley.

Froming, W. J., & McClogon, E. B. (1979). Comparing the Defining Issues Test and the Moral Dilemma Interview. *Developmental Psychology, 15,* 658-659.

Gibbs, J. C., & Widaman, K. (1982). *Social intelligence: Measuring the development of sociomoral reflection.* Englewood Cliffs, NJ: Prentice-Hall.

Hoffman, M. (1980). Moral development in adolescence. In J. Adelson (Ed.), *Handbook of adolescent psychology* (pp. 295-343). New York: John Wiley.

Inhelder, B., & Piaget, J. (1958). *The growth of logical thinking from childhood to adolescence.* New York: Basic Books.

Kenston, K. (1965). *The uncommitted: Alienated youth in society.* New York: Harcourt, Brace, & World.

Kluckhohn, F., & Strodtbeck, F. (1961). *Variations in value orientations.* Evanston, IL: Row, Peterson.

Kohlberg, L. (1984). *The psychology of moral development.* San Francisco: Harper & Row.

Laker, D. G., Miles, M. B., & Earle, R. B., Jr. (1973). *Measuring human behavior.* New York: Teachers College Press.

Morris, C. (1956). *Varieties of human value.* Chicago: University of Chicago Press.

Rest, J. R. (1979). *Development in judging moral issues.* Minneapolis. University of Minnesota Press.

Rest, J. R. (1983). Morality. In P. Mussen (Ed.), *Handbook of child psychology: Vol. III. Cognitive development.* New York: John Wiley.

Rokeach, M. (1973). *The nature of human values.* New York: Free Press.

Robinson, J. P., & Shaver, P. R. (1969). *Measures of social psychological attitude.* Ann Arbor, MI: Institute for Social Research.

Scott, W. (1965). *Values and organizations.* Chicago: Rand McNally.

Triandis, A. (1972). *The analysis of subjective culture.* New York: John Wiley.

Yankelovich, D. (1974). *The new morality.* New York: McGraw-Hill.

5

Assessing Adolescent Social Skills

FRANK M. GRESHAM, PH.D., TIMOTHY A. CAVELL, M.S.

Most of the chapters in this volume address assessment procedures for specific types of behavior problems in the adolescent population—delinquency, substance abuse, suicide, and so on. Instead of viewing "psychopathology" in terms of excesses in maladaptive behavior patterns, one could interpret these same problems as deficiencies in adaptive behavior patterns or, more generally, *social competence* deficits.

Historically, a number of psychologists have been interested in the motivational underpinnings of competence. For example, the cognitive-developmental theory of Piaget (1952), the psychosocial theory of Erikson (1950), and the self-actualization theory of Maslow (1968) all recognize and emphasize the importance of competence or "sense of mastery" in explaining human behavior. White (1959) hypothesized that all individuals manifest an "urge toward competence," which he termed *effectance motivation*. Effectance motivation describes an individual's "need" to be successful or otherwise deal effectively with the environment.

More recently, Harter (1978) reconceptualized and expanded White's theory of effectance motivation such that this construct could be translated into researchable hypotheses. Based on factor analyses of her own measure (the Perceived Competence Scale for Children) across various age levels, Harter (1982) differentiated three dimensions of competence or effectance motivation: cognitive, physical, and social. It is important to isolate such effectance dimensions in order to assess the degree to which an individual invests energy in these different mastery domains.

Bandura (1977, 1982) has provided a more comprehensive theory of human motivation known as *self-efficacy*. The basic premise in self-efficacy, as in effectance motivation, centers on an individual's sense of personal power to produce and regulate effectively the events in his or her life. Perceived self-efficacy is concerned with judgments of how well one can execute behaviors required to deal with prospective situations. Bandura (1977, 1982) differentiates between *efficacy expectations* and *outcome expectations*. The former reflects an individual's belief that he or she can execute the behavior required to produce a given outcome; in contrast, the latter reflects the belief that a given behavioral performance will produce a given outcome. Efficacy and outcome expectations are differentiated because a person can believe that behaviors will produce certain outcomes (an outcome expectation), but may not believe that he or she can perform the requisite behaviors that will produce desired outcomes (an efficacy expectation).

What do the concepts of effectance motivation and self-efficacy have to do with the social competence deficiencies of adolescents? Many adolescents displaying

93

problem behavior patterns (e.g., conduct disorders, social withdrawal, depression, etc.) probably have low levels of self-efficacy (or effectance motivation). They have learned over a series of social interactions that their behavior is not effective in obtaining desired outcomes (reinforcers) in interpersonal relationships. In fact, their maladaptive social interaction patterns frequently result in punishment from significant others, such as peers, teachers, and parents. This history of negative experience in social relationships may result in low efficacy expectations concerning social interaction, in that the adolescent may perceive that he or she cannot perform those social behaviors that will lead to desired outcomes. Thus, while believing that certain positive social behaviors may result in beneficial outcomes, these adolescents may not believe that they can competently execute these behaviors in specific social situations.

The purpose of this chapter is to provide a description and evaluation of a number of social skills assessment procedures for adolescents. An overview of various theoretical conceptualizations of the social skills construct is presented, three definitions of social skills common to the literature are delineated, and a four-category conceptualization of social skill problems is offered. Methods of social skills assessment are divided into three broad categories based on the purposes of assessment: (a) Assessment for Classification, (b) Assessment for Treatment Planning, and (c) Assessment for Treatment Evaluation. Under each category appropriate assessment techniques are presented and critically evaluated. The social validation of social skill assessments is also discussed in relation to the social significance of given social behaviors and the social importance of the effects produced by social skill interventions.

Social Skill as a Behavioral Construct

In a seminal theoretical review of the concept of social skill, McFall (1982) identifies two general approaches that have been taken in conceptualizing social skill: 1) the *trait model,* which views social skills as an underlying, cross-situational response predisposition, and 2) a *molecular model,* which views social skills as discrete, situation-specific behaviors with no reference to an underlying personality characteristic or trait. McFall offers insightful criticisms of both.

The trait model is amorphous, highly abstract, and has little empirical data to support its adequacy as a "trait" (Bellack, 1979; Curran, 1977; Hersen & Bellack, 1977). Moreover, various measures of the trait of social skill typically have shown little or no empirical relationship to behavior in naturalistic or simulated situations (Bellack, Hersen, & Lamparski, 1979; Bellack, Hersen, & Turner, 1978; Chandler, 1973; Urbain & Kendall, 1980).

The molecular model, on the other hand, tries to correct the abstract, unobservable nature of the trait approach by providing operationally defined responses in specific situations. Although the behaviorist may perceive this as an improvement, it creates perhaps even more confusion and ambiguity than the trait model. McFall (1982) specifies several issues that the molecular model has not resolved, including (a) the selection of appropriate units of behavior (head nods, eye flinches, toe taps, etc.), (b) a classification of social situations (e.g., by physical characteristics of the situation or by the participants in the situation), and (c) a classification and evaluation of outcomes (e.g., short-term vs. long-term consequences, "success" vs. "failure," etc.). In evaluating the molecular model of social skill, McFall (1982) states

> the molecular model is of limited value to investigators who are interested in making behavioral predictions. The model states that the best predictor of a person's future behavior is that person's past behavior in the same situation. . . . to make such a prediction requires little or no special understanding either of human behavior generally, or of the individual subject. (p. 10)

There is obviously a need for a coalescence between the trait and molecular models of social skill. Perhaps a conceptualization that is intermediately placed on the trait-molecular continuum would be the most beneficial. Such a model, however, has not been developed, and social skill remains a construct in need of further conceptualization and theoretical refinement.

The following section provides a distinction between social competence and social skill from which a general conceptualization of social skill deficits will be derived.

Social Competence versus Social Skill

Social competence and social skill are not identical constructs. McFall (1982) clearly articulates key distinctions between the two concepts. *Social skills* are the specific behaviors that an individual exhibits to perform competently on a task. In contrast, *social competence* represents an evaluative term, based on judgments (given certain criteria) that a person has performed a task adequately. These "judgments" may be based on opinions of significant others (e.g., parents, teachers, etc.), comparisons to explicit criteria (e.g., number of social tasks correctly performed in relation to some criterion), or comparisons to some normative sample.

Competence does not imply exceptional performance; it only indicates that the performance was adequate (McFall, 1982). The issue of social competence can be recast in terms of *social validity:* the determination of the clinical, applied, and/or social importance of exhibiting certain social behavior in particular situations (Kazdin, 1977; Van Houten, 1979; Wolf, 1978). In other words, behavior can be considered socially competent if it predicts important social outcomes for individuals (Gresham, 1983b). The relationship between social competence and social validity is an important one and will be discussed in a subsequent section of this chapter.

Gresham (1985) has conceptualized social competence as comprised of two components: adaptive behavior and social skills. Adaptive behavior for adolescents would include independent functioning skills, physical development, language development, and academic competencies. Social skills on the other hand, would include (a) interpersonal behaviors (e.g., accepting authority, conversation skills, cooperative behaviors, assertion skills, etc.); (b) self-related behaviors (e.g., expressing feelings, ethical behavior, positive attitude toward self, etc.); and (c) task-related behaviors (e.g., attending behavior, completing tasks, following directions, independent work, etc.).

The notion of social competence is perhaps useful at a conceptual level, but requires much more empirical validation and clarification. Greenspan (1981) provides an interesting conceptualization of social competence based on three definitional approaches. This conceptualization differs from those described previously in that it focuses on the outcomes, contents, and processes of social competence rather than descriptive labels for socially competent behavior.

The first approach is termed the *outcome-oriented approach,* which focuses exclusively on the outcomes or results of exhibiting certain social behaviors in particular situations. Greenspan (1981) uses a golf analogy here, whereby competence as a golfer is defined by the end result of golfing behavior (i.e., the final score). This approach certainly allows one to define competence, but does not indicate what specific behaviors were emitted in what situations that resulted in competence.

The second approach can be termed the *content-oriented approach,* which focuses on the specific behaviors associated with successful outcomes. This conceptualization is similar to McFall's (1982) view of social competence/social skill, as well as Gresham's (1983b) social validity definition of social skills and Asher and Markell's (1978) competence correlates definition. Continuing with the golf analogy, an individual's swing, stance, grip, and coordination typically are associated with golfing competence (i.e., a low score). This approach has the distinct advantage of identifying specific behaviors that lead to golfing competence.

The final definitional approach to social competence is termed the *skill-oriented approach* and focuses on interpersonal processes (e.g., knowledge, attitudes, perceptions, etc.) that lead to socially competent outcomes. Using Greenspan's (1981) analogy, knowledge of golf rules, club selection, etiquette, controlling one's temper, judgment, and familiarity with the golf courses would be associated with golfing competence. Although this approach attempts to get at the "processes" underlying social competence, it tends to focus on somewhat intangible and nebulous aspects of social behavior.

These three approaches provide yet another view of social competence that may have some utility at both conceptual and practical levels. The bottom line in golf (and the only one that really counts) is the outcome (i.e., the score). Similarly, the bottom line in the social skills area is the outcome or result of social behavior. Unfortunately, we do not know what "score" to use because optimum outcomes have not been established. It would seem that a combination of the outcome- and content-oriented approaches would be the most useful way of conceptualizing social competence, because the focus would be on the selection of only those behaviors that predict important social outcomes. Given some general agreement about what these outcomes should be, this approach holds promise in defining social competence. Based on extensive research in the social skills area, the skill-oriented approach does not appear to be a fruitful perspective at this time because of its emphasis on private events and underlying psychological processes, which are difficult to measure reliably or accurately, rather than on observable behavior.

DEFINITIONS OF SOCIAL SKILL

As previously discussed, social skill may be viewed as part of a broader construct known as social competence (Gresham, 1981b; McFall, 1982; Kazdin, 1979).

Past conceptualizations of adolescents' behavior have highlighted deviant aspects of social behavior (Foster & Ritchey, 1979). Recent interest in social skills has focused primarily on building positive behaviors into the repertoire as well as eliminating negative behaviors (Asher & Hymel, 1981; Asher, Oden, & Gottman, 1977; Cartledge & Milburn, 1978, 1980; Greenwood, Walker, & Hops, 1977; Gresham, 1981a, 1981b, 1982a; Hops, 1983).

Several definitions of social skills have arisen during the past several years. Combs and Slaby (1977), for example, define social skills as "the ability to interact with others in a given social context in specific ways that are societally acceptable or valued and as they sometimes are personally beneficial, mutually beneficial or beneficial primarily to others" (p. 162). Libet and Lewinsohn's (1973) definition describes "the complex ability both to emit behaviors that are positively or negatively reinforced and not to emit behaviors that are punished or extinguished by others" (p. 304). Finally, Foster and Ritchey (1979) define social skills as "those responses which, within a given situation, prove effective, or in other words, maximize the probability of producing, maintaining, or enhancing positive effects for the interactor" (p. 626).

Each of these definitions provides a "ballpark" notion of what social skills are, but they remain somewhat vague and ambiguous. For example, it is unclear what terms such as "personally beneficial," "complex ability," "positive effect," and so forth mean in an operational sense. Clearly, the definition of social skill requires delineation, operationalization, and explanation in order to be conceptually and practically useful.

At least three general definitions can be gleaned from the expanding social skills literature. One of these can be termed the *peer-acceptance definition,* in that researchers primarily use indices of peer acceptance or popularity (e.g., peer sociometrics) to define social skill. Using a peer-acceptance definition, children and adolescents who are accepted by or popular with peers in school and/or community settings can be described as socially skilled. This definition has been implicit in the work of many prominent researchers in the area of social skills (Asher & Hymel, 1981; Asher et al., 1977; Asher, Singleton, Tinsley, & Hymel, 1979; Gottman, 1977; Gottman, Gonso, & Ramussen, 1975; Gottman, Gonso, & Schuler, 1976; Ladd, 1981; La Greca & Santogrossi, 1980; Oden & Asher, 1977).

In spite of its relative objectivity, the major drawback of a peer-acceptance definition is that it cannot identify what specific behaviors lead to peer acceptance or popularity. As such, one can identify a group of individuals who are poorly accepted or unpopular without any knowledge of what social behaviors (or absence thereof) lead to poor acceptance.

Some researchers, therefore, have opted for a *behavioral definition* of social skills. This approach essentially defines social skills as those situation-specific responses that maximize the probability of maintaining reinforcement and minimize the probability of punishment or extinction contingent on one's social behavior. Measures used to define social skills in this manner typically consist of observations of behavior in naturalistic or role-play situations and settings. Researchers adhering to a strict behavioral definition of social skills almost never utilize peer acceptance (via sociometric measures) as part of their criteria for defining social skills.

Many well-known investigators adopt primarily a behavioral definition of social skills (Bellack & Hersen, 1979; Bornstein, Bellack, & Hersen, 1977; Combs & Slaby, 1977; Foster & Ritchey, 1979; Greenwood, Todd, Hops, & Walker, 1982; Greenwood, Walker, Todd, & Hops, 1981; O'Connor, 1969, 1972; Rogers-Warren & Baer, 1976; Strain, 1977; Strain & Shores, 1977; Strain, Cooke, & Apolloni, 1976; Warren, Rogers-Warren, & Baer, 1976). This definition has the advantage over the peer-acceptance definition in that the antecedents and consequences of particular social behaviors can be identified, specified, and operationalized for assessment and remedial purposes. In spite of this, the behavioral definition does not ensure that these social behaviors are in fact *socially skilled, socially significant,* or *socially important;* that is, merely increasing the frequency of certain behaviors that researchers define a priori as "social skills" may have no impact on goals or outcomes valued by society at large.

A final and less-often discussed definition may be termed the *social validity definition,* according to which social skills are those behaviors that, within a given situation, predict important social outcomes for children. These so-called important social outcomes may be (a) peer acceptance or popularity; (b) significant others' judgments of social skill (e.g., parents, teachers, etc.); and/or (c) other social behaviors known to correlate consistently with peer acceptance/popularity and judgments of significant others.

This definition uses naturalistic observations of behavior, sociometric indices, and ratings by significant others to assess and define social skill. It has the advantage of not only specifying behaviors in which a child is deficient, but also defining these behaviors as socially skilled based on their relationships to socially important outcomes (e.g., peer acceptance, parental acceptance, teacher acceptance, etc.).

The social validity definition has received recent empirical support (Green, Forehand, Beck, & Vosk, 1980; Gresham, 1981c, 1982b, 1983a) as well as past indications of validity (Hartup, Glazer, & Charlesworth, 1967; Marshall & McCandless, 1957; McCandless & Marshall, 1957; McGuire, 1973; Moore & Updegraff, 1964; Singleton & Asher, 1977). Specific criteria for and discussion of social validity are presented in a subsequent portion of this chapter.

The aforementioned definitions of social skills emphasize social competence. The peer-acceptance definition equates peer acceptance or popularity with social skill; hence, an individual who is poorly accepted, socially rejected, or unpopular is, by definition, socially unskilled. The behavioral definition considers deficits or excesses in behaviors as indications of poor social skill; thus, persons exhibiting behaviors below or above certain levels specified a priori are considered socially unskilled. Finally, the social validity definition considers individuals socially unskilled if specific social behaviors predict standings on socially important outcomes. This definition is a hybrid of the peer-acceptance and behavioral definitions and is the most socially valid in the sense of predicting important social outcomes for children and adolescents. It seems reasonable to use a definition of social skill that is based on *criterion-related* or *social* validity. This definition should provide a basis for accumulating empirical evidence for the construct of social skills.

Classification of Social Skill Problems

Most classifications of social skill difficulty have been based on either the socio-metric or behavioral definitions. These definitions may be useful at a descriptive level, but they are less relevant in targeting specific types of social skill deficits. Gresham (1981a, 1981b, 1982c) has categorized social skill problems into four general areas that should be useful from assessment, diagnostic, and intervention stand-points: 1) skill deficits; 2) performance deficits; 3) self-control skill deficits; and 4) self-control performance deficits. The bases for these distinctions rest on whether the individual knows *how to perform the skill* in question and on the existence of *emotional arousal responses* (e.g., anger, impulsivity, etc.). This conceptualization represents a modification and extension of Bandura's (1977) distinction between acquisition versus performance of behavior, and although it is primarily speculative at this point, there is some empirical support for the majority of social skills problems described (Camp, Blom, Herbert, & van Doorninck, 1977; Gottman, 1977; Gresham, 1981a, 1981b; Meichenbaum, 1977; Van Hasselt, Hersen, Whitehill, & Bellack, 1979). The purpose of this conceptualization is to provide a heuristic framework for social skills problems that should be useful in the assessment, classification, and remediation of social skill difficulties.

Skill Deficits

Adolescents with social skills deficits do not have the necessary social skills to interact appropriately with peers or they do not know a critical step in the perform-ance of the skill. A social skill deficit is similar to what Bandura (1969, 1977b) refers to as an *acquisition deficit* or *learning deficit*.

Several examples can be cited to elucidate social skill deficits. For example, the adolescent may not know how to carry on a conversation with peers, ask appropri-ately to be recognized in class, or give a compliment. The barometer to use in deter-mining whether a skill deficit exists is based on *knowledge* or *past performance* of the skill; that is, if the adolescent does not know how to perform the skill or has never been observed to perform the skill, there is probably a skills deficit. An example of a skills deficit in which an individual leaves out a critical step in a chain of behaviors can be found in giving a compliment. The adolescent may be able to formulate a reason for giving a compliment, may know how to phrase a compliment, and may be able to discriminate the most appropriate time for giving a compliment, but may not know how to offer the compliment in a clear and sincere voice. Given this assessment, an intervention would focus on teaching the individul how to compliment clearly and sincerely. Most social skill deficits are remediated primarily through modeling, be-havioral rehearsal, and/or coaching (Gresham, 1981b; Gresham & Elliott, 1984; Ladd & Mize, 1983).

Performance Deficits

A *social performance deficit* describes individuals who have the necessary social skills in their repertoires, but do not perform them at acceptable levels. A perform-ance deficit can be thought of as a deficiency in the number of times a social behavior is emitted, perhaps related to a lack of motivation (i.e., reinforcement contingencies) or an absence of opportunity to perform the behavior (i.e., stimulus control problem). It is important to realize that fear, anxiety, or other emotional arousal responses do *not* enter into a social performance deficit.

The key in determining if a social skills problem is a performance deficit lies in whether the person can perform the behavior. Thus, if he or she does not perform a behavior in a classroom situation, but can perform the behavior in a behavioral role-play situation, one is confronting a social performance deficit. Also, if the individual has been observed to perform the behavior in the past, the problem is probably a performance rather than a skill deficit. Given that difficulties either in stimulus control or reinforcement contingencies are functionally related to social performance deficits, training strategies typically focus on antecedent and consequent control techniques. These strategies may include peer initiations (Strain, Shores, & Timm, 1977); sociodramatic activities (Strain, 1975); contingent social reinforcement (Allen, Hart, Buell, Harris, & Wolf, 1964); token reinforcement (Iwata & Bailey, 1974); and group contingencies (Gamble & Strain, 1979).

Self-Control Skill Deficits

This social skill problem describes an individual who has not learned a particular social skill because some kind of emotional arousal response has prevented the *acquisition* of the skill. Anxiety is an example of an emotional arousal response that interferes with learning and that prevents the acquisition of appropriate coping responses, particularly in cases of fears and phobias (see Bandura, 1969, 1977a, 1977b for comprehensive reviews). Hence, adolescents may not learn how to interact with peers because social anxiety or fear prevents social approach behavior. In turn, avoidance of or escape from social situations reduces anxiety, thereby negatively reinforcing social isolation behaviors.

Another emotional arousal response that may prevent the acquisition of social skills is impulsivity (i.e., the tendency toward short response latencies in social situations). Individuals who exhibit "impulsive" social behavior fail to learn appropriate social interaction strategies because their behavior often results in social rejection by peers. Thus, as peers avoid the impulsive person, he or she is not exposed to models of appropriate social behavior or is placed on an extinction schedule for his or her social responses.

This behavioral formulation suggests that the target person emits aversive social behaviors (i.e., as a result of a socially impulsive response style), which results in social rejection from peers, parents, teachers, and so forth. Other individuals in the environment are under aversive contingencies in that behaviors that lead to avoidance of or escape from the target person are negatively reinforced. In turn, this results in the target person's behavior either being punished (e.g., by verbal or physical reprimands, loss of reinforcement, etc.) or extinguished (e.g., by ignoring). The outcome of this sequence of events is that the target person does not learn the social skills for appropriate interaction (i.e., a skill deficit).

Several studies in the literature have described this type of individual (Bryan, 1978; Camp et al., 1977; Meichenbaum & Goodman, 1971; O'Leary & Dubey, 1979;

Zahavi & Asher, 1978). Determination of a self-control skill deficit rests on two criteria: 1) the presence of an emotional arousal response (e.g., anxiety, fear, impulsivity, anger, etc.), and 2) the person either not knowing or never having performed the skill in question. Training strategies typically take the form of anxiety-reducing techniques (e.g., desensitization, exposure, etc.) coupled with modeling/coaching and self-control strategies (e.g., self-talk, self-monitoring, self-reinforcement). (For reviews see Kendall & Braswell, 1982; Kendall & Wilcox, 1979; Meichenbaum, 1977; Urbain & Kendall, 1980).

Self-Control Performance Deficits

Adolescents with self-control performance deficits have the specific social skill in their repertoires, but do not perform it because of an emotional arousal response and problems in antecedent and/or consequent control. That is, the person knows how to perform the skill, but does so infrequently or inconsistently. The key difference between self-control skill deficits and self-control performance deficits is the presence of the social skill in the repertoire. In the former deficit, the skill has never been learned; in the latter, the skill has been learned, but is not exhibited consistently. Two criteria are used to determine a self-control performance deficit: the presence of an emotional arousal response (e.g., anger, fear, etc.) and the inconsistent performance of the skill in question.

Interventions with this type of problem typically focus on self-control strategies to teach the adolescent how to inhibit inappropriate behavior, on stimulus control training designed to teach discrimination of potentially conflictful situations, and/or on reinforcement contingencies for appropriate social behaviors (Blackwood, 1970; Bolstad & Johnson, 1972; Bornstein & Quevillon, 1976; Drabman, 1973).

PROCESS, TARGETS, AND METHODS OF SOCIAL SKILLS ASSESSMENT

Process

As with the psychological assessment of any disorder, the process of social skills assessment is characterized by a series of hypothesis-testing sequences. Hypotheses are generated in an attempt to answer questions related to the following stages of assessment: (a) identification/classification, (b) treatment planning, and (c) treatment evaluation. Hypotheses are generated based on whatever information is available at a given point in the assessment and then tested at subsequent points through the gathering of additional information. Comprehensive assessments allow one to draw conclusions regarding problem severity, role of contributory factors, treatment strategies needed, and extent of treatment success.

A standard procedure for assessing adolescent social skills does not exist; rather, hypotheses generated dictate the direction of the assessment, questions to be answered, and methods to be used. Assessment should proceed in such a manner that specific information needed for treatment planning is gathered eventually. Conversely, the assessment of treatment outcome typically proceeds in the opposite direction, moving from an examination of immediate and target-specific outcomes toward global analyses of the treatment's impact on important social outcomes (i.e., social validity).

Targets

Social skills assessment focuses on multiple targets. During the identification/ classification stage of assessment, adolescents in need of social skills intervention are the focus. Once such individuals have been identified, more specific foci evolve. Subsequent assessment targets primarily reflect one's conceptualization of human behavior, those factors capable of producing ineffective performance, and the type of intervention strategies adopted. The bias here is against personality structures and underlying intrapsychic conflict as useful assessment targets. Instead, observable behaviors occurring in specific situations and influenced by one's learning history and current environmental events are seen as more deserving of an assessor's attention.

The preference of these authors was reflected in the earlier discussion concerning conceptualizations of social skill problems. Comprehensive social skill assessments should include such targets as performance × situation interactions resulting in judgments of social incompetency plus any measurable factors contributing to poor performance. Specific skill deficits, inadequate reinforcement or opportunity for skilled performance, and interfering emotional arousal are all important considerations when conducting an assessment.

Methods

Methods for assessing adolescents' social functioning can vary along several dimensions. For example, methods can rely on different sources of information. Common sources include clients themselves, their peers, relevant adults, and trained observers. Information produced by assessment instruments can vary in specificity, ranging from indications of global traits to quantification of molecular behaviors. Methods of assessment can also differ with respect to the temporal proximity of performance and assessment. Thus, assessment information may stem from observations of ongoing behavior, ratings of recent behavior in certain situations, or recall of temporally distant social functioning.

These three factors—source, specificity, and temporal proximity of observation to performance—have an impact on three additional dimensions on which social skills assessment methods can be evaluated (Cone, 1977): reliability (consistency of measurement), validity (capability of answering a given assessment question), and practicality (costs of collecting information) (Anastasi, 1982; Cimenero, Calhoun, & Adams, 1977). Although a detailed discussion of these issues is beyond the scope of this chapter, one can see that information from sources familiar with an adolescent's behavior that is both specific in its focus and proximal to the occurrence of performance would result in greater reliability and validity, though it may be less practically obtained.

Ideally, practitioners should use assessment methods possessing all three of these attributes. Unfortunately, few social skill instruments meet all three criteria, except perhaps in the case of broadly stated questions such as whether a social skill problem actually exists. Easily administered instruments (e.g., self-report scales) useful for screening purposes, however, are of little help in designing an intervention. Also, other methods requiring considerably more effort from assessors and clients (e.g., naturalistic observations, self-monitoring) have equivocal or unknown psychometric properties (Dodge & Murphy, 1984; Gresham & Elliott, 1984; Hops & Greenwood, 1981). Further contributing to the difficulties involved in social skills assessment is a tendency for data from different methods or sources to correlate only moderately at times and often quite poorly (Gresham, Bruce, & Veitia, 1983; Matson, Esveldt-Dawson, & Kazdin, 1983). As a result, multiple sources of information are a must when assessing adolescent social skills.

The following discussion of social skills assessment methods is organized around the three stages of assessment (selection/classification, treatment planning, and treatment evaluation). Most of the techniques discussed were chosen primarily because they provide information on important targets of social skill interventions and do so in a manner that is fairly reliable, valid, and practical. A similar approach has been used by others (e.g., Gresham & Elliott, 1984; Hops & Greenwood, 1981) when discussing assessment of children's social skills. Developmental differences between children and adolescents are important to consider, however, when going from one population to the other. Limiting this discussion is the paucity of research in the area of adolescent social skills assessment, especially when compared to research focusing on adult and child populations (see Bellack, 1983; Hops & Greenwood, 1981). As a result, current recommendations regarding adolescent assessment are based, in part, on studies involving nonadolescent samples.

Identification/Classification

Given that adolescents engaged in social skills treatment programs generally are referred by parents, teachers, or other adults charged with their care, assessment at this stage typically involves confirmation of a reported or suspected social skills problem. (Although rarely done with adolescents, assessment at this stage also may include screening of large samples of adolescents in order to identify those at risk and in need of services.) An additional goal of this kind of assessment may be classification of social skill problems. Analysis here is still on a fairly global level and refers to placement of clients into such broad categories as *aggressive* or *withdrawn,* or along a continuum of social competency (e.g., very incompetent to very competent). Identification of the adolescent in need of social skill intervention is possible through a variety of assessment methods. A discussion of some of the more useful methods follows.

Sociometric techniques. These techniques were originally developed to study children's friendship patterns (Moreno, 1934), but have since been found to be quite predictive of later maladjustment (e.g., Roff, 1961; Ullman, 1957). Technically, *sociometrics* refers to procedures in which individuals, typically students within a class, are asked to *nominate* a small number of their peers fitting certain social roles (e.g., preferred work partner) or *rate* each class member on some nonspecific descriptor (e.g., likeability) (Asher & Hymel, 1981; Asher & Taylor, 1981). The term has been applied, however, to other variations, including ratings by peers on specific behavioral criteria. Depending on the type of information obtained via sociometrics, one can ascertain an adolescent's sociometric status (e.g., accepted vs. rejected), compute a rating score of perceived likeability, or identify specific behaviors that may be excessive or deficient in the eyes of peers.

Sociometric techniques have been used with both positively and negatively keyed criteria. For example, adolescents may be asked to nominate their three most-liked and three least-liked peers. An advantage to using both types of criteria is that they enable identification of three distinct social status groups: accepted, rejected, and neglected. Accepted students receive high likeability and low disliked scores, whereas rejected students receive low likeability and high disliked scores. Neglected children, on the other hand, receive low scores on both criteria, indicating neither acceptance nor rejection. Research efforts to distinguish between the two deviant statuses have found that neglected children tend to withdraw socially, whereas rejected children tend to engage in excessive, disruptive behaviors that peers quickly find intolerable (e.g., Dodge, 1983). Coie and Dodge (1983) have reported considerable stability in the sociometric status of younger adolescents over a five-year period, especially for rejected students.

Although the authors of this chapter are unaware of published data on adverse side effects resulting from the use of sociometrics with adolescent populations, school administrators and teachers may be reluctant to allow students to nominate or rate peers on negatively keyed criteria. A less intrusive approach to grouping students into neglected and rejected categories would be to combine positive nomination scores with scores from a likeability rating scale. Dodge and his colleagues (Dodge, McClaskey, & Feldman, 1985) were able to form separate rejected and neglected status groups using this approach.

A sociometric instrument developed specifically for adolescent populations is the Adjustment Scales for Sociometric Evaluation of Secondary School Students (ASSESS; Prinz, Swan, Liebert, Weintraub, & Neale, 1978). With this measure, students are asked to indicate which students exhibit any of 41 behaviors falling into five categories: Anxiety, Withdrawal, Aggression-Disruptiveness, Academic Difficulty, and Social Competence.

Sociometric techniques, even those utilizing specific behavioral criteria, are insufficient for planning social skills interventions. They provide little information about specific situations in which performance is inadequate or about factors maintaining poor performance. Their primary use is in screening, classifying, and predicting social incompetency (Dodge & Murphy, 1984; Gresham, 1984; La Greca, 1981). Other disadvantages relate to potential difficulty with administration. Problems may arise in gaining teachers' and students' cooperation, some procedures (e.g., peer ratings) require preparation of a different "test" for each class, and decisions need to be made about which of several classes to enter. Although Coie and Dodge (1983) obtained sociometric data from adolescents using grade-wise nominations, it is unlikely that practitioners would adopt such an approach for a single client. Unfortunately, little is known about the stability of an adolescent's sociometric status across classrooms.

Teacher- and parent-report instruments. An often-used social skill assessment method requires teachers to rate the extent to which students engage in various pro-social or socially dysfunctional behaviors. Information from teachers can be obtained easily and quickly relative to that derived from peer ratings. Like peer ratings, teacher ratings can confirm the existence of social skill problems, indicate the severity of the problem, and suggest more detailed investigations needed to plan an intervention. As in the case of peer ratings, empirical evidence supporting their use as predictors of later maladjustment has yet to be demonstrated for teacher ratings; therefore, information obtained from teacher ratings cannot be assumed to have social validity beyond the context of a particular classroom. Correlations between teacher and peer ratings, though often moderate in size (e.g., MacMillan, Morrison, & Silverstein, 1980), are not perfect. Information gained from teacher ratings should serve to complement, not replace, information from peer ratings.

The Social Behavior Assessment (SBA) scale is one of the most comprehensive rating scales whereby teachers can rate the degree to which students exhibit each of 136 social skills (i.e., acceptable level, less than acceptable level, or never). The 136 social skills are grouped into 30 subcategories, which in turn are grouped into four broad behavioral categories: environmental, interpersonal, self-related, and task-related. The SBA has good evidence for reliability (interrater, internal consistency, and stability) and validity (content, criterion-related, and construct). Stumme, Gresham, and Scott (1982) tested the SBA's discriminative efficiency and found the 30 subcategories correctly classified 83% of subjects into emotionally disturbed and nondisturbed categories. Thus, the evidence indicates the SBA has reasonable psychometric properties and is useful in selection and classification of children and younger adolescents with social skill difficulties. In a subsequent study, Stumme, Gresham, and Scott (1983) factor-analyzed the SBA and found that the factor structure was generally consistent with the four broad behavioral categories discussed by Stephens (1979) (i.e., environmental, task-related, self-related, and interpersonal).

Two teacher-report measures have been designed to interface with specific social skills training programs or curricula. Walker and his associates (Walker et al., 1983) developed a rating scale for use with *The Walker Social Skills Curriculum.* The Walker scale is a 28-item measure whereby teachers rate a target child on a 5-point Likert-type scale anchored by statements ranging from "not descriptive" to "very descriptive." Although this instrument has not received much research attention to date, it appears to be content valid. Similarly, Goldstein and his colleagues (Goldstein, Sprafkin, Gershaw, & Klein, 1980) have used a 50-item skills inventory completed by teachers (or parents) in order to identify unskilled adolescents and areas to be addressed via their Structured Learning Skills Training. This inventory also appears to be content valid, but further evaluation of its psychometric properties is required.

Gresham and Elliott (Clark, Gresham, & Elliott, 1985) recently developed the Teacher Rating of Social Skills (TROSS) scale. The TROSS was constructed by drawing items from empirically based studies of social skills training and from studies exploring correlates of positive peer status. An initial pool of 93 items was reduced to 50 via factor analysis. Four factors were retained and given the following labels: Academic Performance, Social Initiation, Cooperation, and Peer Reinforcement. Preliminary studies with the TROSS indicate a stable factor structure, adequate internal consistency of subscales, and efficiency in discriminating between handicapped and nonhandicapped students (Black, 1985; Clark et al., 1985). The TROSS was designed to provide information comparable to that offered by the SBA but requiring less time for teachers to complete.

Little attention has been given to parent-report measures of adolescent social skills. Parent-report measures typically used are designed to identify problems along much broader dimensions than social skills specifically. These measures include Achenbach and Edelbrock's Child Behavior Checklist (CBCL), Quay and Peterson's (1967) Behavior Problem Checklist, and the Walker Problem Behavior Identification Checklist. The CBCL does allow for normative comparisons on ratings considered indicative of social competency (e.g., number of friends, hobbies), but little is known of the actual relation between this information and adolescents' social functioning.

Self-report measures. Adolescent self-report measures have the potential to provide information unavailable from ratings by peers or adults. Self-descriptions of (a) behavior occurring in situations inaccessible to teachers and parents, (b) expected difficulty in handling problem situations, and (c) anxiety associated with particular external cues are potentially derivable from adolescent self-report instruments. However, few self-report measures have been developed with the explicit goal of assessing adolescent social competency, and most self-report instruments used with children have equivocal psychometric properties (Gresham, 1985; Gresham & Elliott, 1984).

A recently developed, 92-item self-report scale, the Matson Evaluation of Social Skills in Youngsters (MESSY; Matson et al., 1983) assesses a broad domain of social behavior (e.g., appropriate social interaction, negative interaction, expression of hostility, social isolation, and conversation skills). The MESSY requires children to rate each of the 92 items on a 1 to 5 Likert-type scale. Matson et al. (1983) found the MESSY was not correlated with performance on a behavioral role-play measure and demonstrated a low ($r = .27$) but significant correlation with a structured child interview. The MESSY did not relate to sociometric status, teacher estimates of child popularity, teacher ratings of social skills, or global ratings of social adjustment.

A somewhat different approach is taken by two measures of perceived social competency. Rather than have adolescents rate the extent to which they engage in specific behaviors, Wheeler and Ladd's (1982) Children's Self-Efficacy for Peer Interaction Scale and Harter's Perceived Competence Scale for Children ask respondents to judge the degree to which they see themselves as socially competent persons. Wheeler and Ladd's measure asks children to rate the difficulty of handling specific situations, whereas with Harter's scale, children rate the degree to which socially competent behaviors can be attributed to themselves.

Self-report measures have also been developed whereby an adolescent chooses his or her most likely response from a set of responses to hypothetical situations. These sets of responses had been rated previously by relevant judges (e.g., teachers, juvenile probation officers) as differentially effective solutions to problem situations. The Adolescent Problem Inventory (API; Freedman, Rosenthal, Donahoe, Schlundt, & McFall, 1978) and the multiple-choice version of the Problem Inventory for Adolescent Girls (MC-PIAG; Gaffney, 1984; Gaffney & McFall, 1981) have been developed for use with male and female delinquents, respectively. The self-report, multiple-choice formats of these two instruments were adopted from the open-ended, brief role-play format for which they were originally designed. Both measures have been shown to discriminate effectively between delinquent and nondelinquent adolescents. A notable characteristic of both the API and the PIAG is the manner in which test situations were generated. Using Goldfried and D'Zurilla's (1969) behavior-analytic model for assessing social competency, developers of these instruments relied on samples of delinquent adolescents to determine which situations were relevant and problematic (Freedman et al., 1978; Gaffney & McFall, 1981). A similar approach was used recently by Cavell and Kelley (Cavell, Kelley, & Buss, 1985) to construct an inventory of problem situations experienced by nondeviant samples of middle and high school students. Factor analysis, based on adolescents' ratings of the difficulty in dealing with each of 164 problem situations (generated by a previous sample of adolescents), yielded 13 principal components, reflecting such problem areas as making friends, keeping friends, and dealing with teachers, siblings, and parents.

Archival records. Occasionally, problems in social functioning are reflected in the records maintained by persons or agencies with whom the adolescent comes in contact. School administrators, juvenile authorities, and employers are examples of those who may routinely document incidents related to an adolescent's inadequate social skills. Recurring incidents of fighting with other students or cursing a teacher will be noted in the form of school suspensions or disciplinary referrals. Acts of vandalism or shoplifting, possibly resulting from ineffective handling of peer pressure or from deficits in the skills required to enter less deviant peer groups, may be noted in records of arrest and parole violations. Difficulty in interacting with fellow employees or employers could result in dismissal, demotion, pay cuts, or reduced work hours, all of which would be evident in work records (Schinke, 1981).

The value of archival information for assessing adolescent social competency should not be overlooked. Many of the behaviors documented by such records have considerable ramifications for adolescents, possibly biasing interactions with others in the future (e.g., criminal behavior) or interfering with achievement of important developmental outcomes (e.g., high school graduation). Archival information may also be useful in corroborating reports of the chronicity and severity of the social skills problem. Finally, once appropriate consent to examine records has been granted, obtaining archival information requires relatively minimal effort. For these reasons, archival records are often used to identify adolescents possibly at risk for social skills deficits (e.g., Dishion, Loeber, Stouthamer-Loeber, & Patterson, 1984).

TREATMENT PLANNING

In order to design a social skills intervention adequately, two basic types of information are needed. First, one must identify those situations in which poor performance is a recurrent problem (Dodge & Murphy, 1984; McFall, 1982; Goldfried & D'Zurilla, 1969). *Situational analyses* begin with an assessment of those situations frequently encountered by adolescents and with which judgments of social competency are often associated. Identification of relevant situations is then followed by a determination of which specific situations are too demanding or problematic for those adolescents receiving treatment.

Besides knowing which situations are relevant and problematic, successful treatment planning requires knowledge of factors contributing to poor performance (Dodge & Murphy, 1984; Gresham & Elliott, 1984). Conducting a thorough *functional analysis* involves delineation of specific behaviors and the variables having an impact on those behaviors that maintain poor performance. Earlier, a four-category system for conceptualizing social skill problems was presented. With this approach, factors potentially contributing to poor performance included specific skill deficits, inadequate reinforcement or opportunity for skilled performance, and interfering emotional arousal (Gresham & Elliott, 1984).

Dodge and McFall (Dodge & Murphy, 1984; McFall, 1982; McFall & Dodge, 1983), adopting more of a social-cognitive approach to social skills assessment, offer an alternative schema whereby sources of difficulty are linked to deficits in one of three skill areas: decoding skills, decision skills, and enactment skills. Currently, one cannot say which offers the more useful model for conceptualizing inadequate social performance. Suffice it to say that the respective models are, in effect, quite similar, and both emphasize the potential for varied and multiple sources of difficulty.

Planners of social skills interventions cannot assume uniformity among their clients when targeting variables for treatment. Unfortunately, such assumptions are often made by those social skill trainers who proceed with training before conducting adequate situational and functional analyses of social behavior (Dodge & Murphy, 1984; Gresham & Elliott, 1984). The following is a discussion of assessment methods useful in conducting situational and functional analyses of adolescent social skills. Emphasis is placed on methods that focus on those factors outlined by Gresham and Elliott (1984) as possible contributors to poor performance and as fruitful targets for treatment. Therefore, methods were chosen based on the extent to which they assisted in identifying problematic situations and assessed specific social skill deficits, the role of interfering emotional arousal, and reinforcement and opportunities for skilled social performance. Readers interested in assessing social-cognitive skill deficits are referred to Dodge and Murphy (1984).

Behavioral Interviews

Behavioral interviews can aid in identifying adolescents' relevant and problematic interpersonal situations (e.g., Sarason & Sarason, 1981). One useful interview tactic is to start with broad areas in an adolescent's life (e.g., school, home) that are the loci of reported problems. Specific interactants, events, and places are then surveyed and those circumstances that consistently occasion poor performance are noted. Interviews can be conducted with adolescent clients, their parents and teachers, and others with whom they are in frequent contact (Dodge & Murphy, 1984; Gresham & Elliott, 1984; Schinke, 1981).

Behavioral interviews also are very useful in conducting functional analyses of social behavior. Researchers have demonstrated that behavioral interviews are effective in (a) defining behaviors in observable terms, (b) identifying antecedent, sequential, and consequent conditions surrounding target behaviors, and (c) designing interventions (Haynes & Jensen, 1979; Witt & Elliott, 1985). Gresham (1983b) reviewed 21 studies investigating the psychometric characteristics of behavioral interviews and concluded there is some support for their reliability and validity. No systematic empirical investigation, however, has been conducted using a behavioral interview as a method to assess adolescents' social skills. Thus, this method of assessment deserves more attention because adolescents frequently are referred for social skills problems by sources (e.g., parents, teachers) who are interviewed before other assessment data are collected.

Self-Monitoring

Self-monitoring is an assessment procedure that requires an individual first to self-observe and then systematically to self-record occurrences of behavior. The use of this technique as a social skills assessment method deserves greater attention as one moves from child to adolescent populations. Nelson and Hayes (1979) offer valuable guidelines to users of this information-gathering approach. For example, the accuracy of self-monitoring data can suffer when instructions are too complex and recording is too time-consuming. Also, providing incentives for complete and accurate recording may be required in some cases. Often, a review of self-monitoring data during sessions serves as sufficient incentive, though this may not be the case with some adolescents (see Shapiro, 1984, for a comprehensive review).

Self-monitoring targets often change during the course of assessment and treatment depending on the type and specificity of information needed. Within the context of assessing social skill problems, adolescents may be asked to monitor problematic situations, frequency of aggressive or submissive behaviors, or antecedents and consequences of particular behaviors. Depending on the integrity with which adolescents monitor these variables, the assessment is greatly enhanced by information both unavailable otherwise and recorded soon after the behavior's occurrence. Usually, decisions regarding appropriate self-monitoring targets are made based on information gathered previously via other assessment methods (e.g., behavioral interviews, behavior checklists).

Behavioral Observations

Ideally, behavioral observations should take place in natural settings with minimal obtrusiveness. Rarely is the ideal possible when assessing adolescent social skills. Given that many forms of adolescent social incompetency involve low frequency behaviors (e.g., fighting), inaccessible situations (e.g., with peers), or both, it is not surprising to find that the most frequent use of "naturalistic" observation is in residential treatment centers (Schinke, 1981). It may be feasible, however, to observe some forms of adolescent social incompetency. For example, one could observe social withdrawal at school, especially at lunch time or during study halls.

Commonly used alternatives to in vivo observation are behavioral role play (BRP) tests. Researchers have used BRPs because they have several advantages over sociometrics, ratings by others, and naturalistic observation techniques; that is, (a) BRPs can assess important social skills that occur at low frequencies in the natural environment; (b) BRPs represent actual behavioral enactment of a skill rather than a rating or perception of that skill; (c) simulated settings can be controlled more tightly to assess an adolescent's response to selected social stimuli; and (d) BRPs are much less expensive than collecting data via naturalistic observation.

Numerous researchers have demonstrated that performance on BRPs shows little or no correspondence with the same behaviors in naturalistic settings and does not predict sociometric status (Bellack, Hersen, & Lamparski, 1979; La Greca & Santogrossi, 1980; Matson et al., 1983; Van Hasselt, Hersen, & Bellack, 1981). In one of the most comprehensive studies to date concerning the validity of BRPs for children, Van Hasselt et al. (1981) found low and nonsignificant relationships between role-play measures and both sociometric status (i.e., positive nominations, negative nominations, and peer ratings) and teacher ratings of social skills. Matson et al. (1983) found that role-play performance was not related consistently to sociometric status, self-report, or teacher ratings of social skills.

The previous studies call into question the validity of BRPs in predicting naturally occurring social behavior and sociometric status. Similar studies, however, have not been conducted with adolescent samples using measures developed especially for adolescents. The previously mentioned API (Freedman et al., 1978) and PIAG (Gaffney & McFall, 1981) are two brief role-play measures in which adolescents are asked to respond to empirically derived relevant and difficult problem situations. The API and PIAG have proven useful in evaluating the social competency of male and female delinquent adolescents, respectively. Additional work is needed, however, before these measures can be used to identify sources of social incompetency and thus aid in treatment design.

The lack of predictive validity associated with BRPs notwithstanding, other uses for observing role-played performance exist. For one, social skill interventions with adolescents often involve behavioral rehearsal and coaching (e.g., Goldstein et al., 1980), and thus may benefit from comparisons with pretreatment role-play performances. Secondly, BRPs can aid in distinguishing among social skill, self-control, and social performance deficits (Gresham & Elliott, 1984). Adolescents performing a given skill on a BRP test but not in other situations are likely experiencing self-control or social performance deficits. For example, McCullough, Huntsinger, and Nay (1977) successfully used role play techniques to identify antecedent emotional arousal in an adolescent experiencing problems with aggressive behavior. Dodge and Murphy (1984) have also noted the importance of modifying BRPs in order to assess specific sources of performance difficulty while controlling for the influence of nonrelevant factors. For example, one could not adequately assess skill deficits using a BRP if the adolescent were entirely unmotivated to participate. In this case, incentives to perform the skill as best one could may be needed to rule out this confounding variable.

Before concluding this discussion of assessment for the purpose of designing social skill interventions, it should be noted that analyses of relevant problem situations and factors contributing to poor performance are neither easy nor unimportant. No single assessment instrument or method can supply all the information one needs to design a social skills intervention successfully. The inexperienced practitioner, therefore, may be misled by various tests of social skills that appear to be more rigorous and informative than research evidence would suggest. Moreover, no single social skills training package exists that is powerful enough to produce significant and lasting changes, regardless of an individual's particular deficits. Practitioners interested in improving the probability of treatment success, therefore, are well advised to optimize the match between client deficits and treatment targets. This takes time, effort, and considerable "detective" work, though of course treatments not based on adequate assessment and thus doomed to fail can also require considerable time and effort.

Treatment Evaluation

Assessments to identify/classify social skill problems or design social skill interventions are successful to the extent that the therapist's behavior is guided effectively. Assessment information having no bearing on which adolescents receive treatment and what that treatment should be is of doubtful worth. Similarly, thorough evaluations of treatment effects are not simply academic exercises; it is information collected at this stage of assessment that should determine whether treatment is continued, modified, or terminated.

As mentioned previously, assessing treatment outcome can be viewed as a reversal of the global-to-specific process characterizing pretreatment data gathering (Dodge & Murphy, 1984). Ideally, instruments sensitive to small and immediate behavior changes are employed before evaluating the extent and significance of treatment's impact. The following discussion reflects this specific-to-global process of assessing treatment outcome and categorizes the information gathered into three related areas: (a) treatment process, (b) treatment generalization, and (c) social validity of treatment effects. The reader should keep in mind that few social skill assessment methods are reserved solely for evaluating treatment outcome. As Dodge and Murphy (1984) have noted, "Once the intervention has been completed, its effectiveness can be evaluated by conducting another assessment of social competence" (p. 84). Thus, repeating earlier assessment efforts using similar methods represents the most efficient manner of evaluating social skills interventions.

Treatment Process

An often overlooked aspect of assessment is the degree to which treatment has been implemented with integrity (Hops & Greenwood, 1981; Yeaton, Witt, & Sechrest, 1981). Occasionally, intervention strategies and techniques may be judged as inappropriate when in fact poor implementation comprises the real reason for treatment failure. Continuous self-monitoring of compliance to homework assignments (e.g., relaxation exercises) is a common example of assessing treatment integrity.

Treatment evaluation also requires one to look at immediate changes in specific treatment targets. Treatment targets will vary with each case, of course, depending on those variables judged to be maintaining socially inadequate performance. Hence, examining the immediate impact of treatment involves readministration of methods used initially to identify and quantify target behaviors. In addition, similar assessments throughout the course of treatment provide a feedback loop that can guide session-to-session use of certain strategies and techniques. Examples of this type of assessment include behavioral role-play tests (such as open-ended questions) and self-monitoring to evaluate specific target behaviors (such as level of subjective anxiety).

Treatment Generalization

Evaluation of treatment results should extend, of course, beyond assessments of role-play behaviors in analogue situations. Demonstrating significant treatment gains requires performance evaluations done over time, across situations, and with a variety of interactants.

Comparison of posttreatment and follow-up information is needed to draw any conclusions regarding maintenance of treatment effects over time (Hops & Greenwood, 1981). Follow-up assessments should be scheduled after treatment has faded and after treatment effects have had sufficient time to deteriorate, if such were to happen. Scheduling follow-up assessments also allows for treatment booster sessions and for an examination of treatment effects (e.g., enhanced sociometric status), which may lag behind more immediate indices of change (Asher & Hymel, 1981).

Evaluating treatment generalization also should include assessment of performance in situations other than those focused on during treatment. The extent to which treatment effects transfer to different situations involving different interactants is especially important when the performance level is a function of the presence of certain external cues. Situations targeted during treatment may have acquired nonthreatening cues (e.g., presence of the therapist or confederates) that are not present in other situations.

Social Validity

Social validity has become an important concept in the behavioral literature over the past several years (Kazdin, 1977; Van Houten, 1979; Wolf, 1978). Social validity refers to establishing the *social significance* of the goals for interventions, creating interventions that are *socially acceptable* to treatment consumers, and evaluating the *social importance* of the effects of interventions (Wolf, 1978). The issues of social significance and social importance are most relevant to the assessment of social skills and to the evaluation of outcomes produced by social skills training. The issue of social acceptability is most germane to the training of adolescent social skills. Because this chapter focuses on assessment considerations, the issue of social acceptability will not be discussed.

As stated, one aspect of social validity is the social significance of the goals specified for interventions; that is, are the goals for behavior change what society wants (Wolf, 1978)? For example, a practitioner may target increases in the number of "thank you" verbalizations emitted by an adolescent. Although this would appear to be an appropriate goal, significant others (e.g., teachers, parents, etc.) may *not* consider this a socially significant goal. A broader, albeit more socially valid goal may be increasing the frequency of all positive verbalizations toward others (including "thank you" responses).

It is important to recognize that the social significance of behavioral goals typically is based on subjective evaluation (Kazdin, 1977; Wolf, 1978; Van Houten, 1979). Subjective evaluations are judgments made by persons who interact with or who are in a special position to judge behavior (Kazdin, 1977). Parents, teachers, counselors, social workers, and other significant persons in an individual's environment are likely candidates for subjectively evaluating the goals of behavioral interventions.

Determining the social significance of the goals of a social skills training program is vital. Obviously, one would not want to teach social behaviors that are not considered valuable or important. The likely result of teaching socially insignificant behaviors is extinction (i.e., the behaviors simply do not get reinforced). Some years ago, Baer and Wolf (1970) stressed the importance of teaching only those behaviors that have a high probability of being "trapped" into natural communities of reinforcement.

Social significance has the most relevance for social skills assessment during the classification/diagnosis phase. The focus is to classify or diagnose the type of social skill problem and target the most important behaviors (i.e., the most socially significant) for remediation.

Evaluating the social importance of the effects produced by social skills training is crucial. The question here is "Does the quantity and quality of behavior change make a difference in terms of an individual's functioning in society?" In other words, do changes in targeted social behaviors predict an individual's standing on important social outcomes (Gresham, 1983a)?

It has been previously stated that social skills can be perhaps best defined in terms of their social validity. That is, to the extent that behaviors predict important social outcomes for individuals, they are (by definition) socially skilled behaviors. What are important social outcomes for adolescents? A vast literature in the area of social development would suggest that acceptance in the peer group, acceptance by significant adults (e.g., parents and teachers), school adjustment, mental health functioning, and lack of contact with the juvenile court system are socially important and valued outcomes for adolescents (see Asher et al., 1977; Cowen, Pederson, Babijian, Izzo, & Trost, 1973; Gilbert, 1957; Gresham, 1981a, 1981b; Hartup, 1970; Kohn & Clausen, 1955; Roff, 1970; Roff, Sells, & Golden, 1972; Strain, Cooke, & Apolloni, 1976, for reviews).

Sociometrics and teacher ratings have been the measures most frequently used to validate the outcomes of social skills training. Those measures reflect socially important outcomes for adolescents based on the literature in the area of adolescent social development. For example, sociometric status has been shown to predict juvenile delinquency (Roff et al., 1972); school maladjustment (Gronlund & Anderson, 1963); psychological functioning in adulthood (Cowen et al., 1973; Garmezy, 1974; Kohn, 1977); dropping out of school (Ullman, 1957); self-concept (Cowen et al., 1973); and vulnerability to psychopathology (Weintraub, Prinz, & Neale, 1978). Peer acceptance is also a highly valued and desirable outcome in our society (Asher et al., 1977; Hartup, 1970; Oden, 1980).

Teacher ratings or judgments of social behavior also reflect an important social outcome for children and youth. Teacher ratings correlate with sociometric status (Green, Forehand, Beck, & Vosk, 1980; Green, Vosk, Forehand, & Beck, 1981; La Greca, 1981; MacMillan & Morrison, 1980; Vosk, Forehand, Parker, & Rickard, 1982). Teachers also prefer to interact with popular children and dispense more attention and praise statements toward popular children than unpopular ones (Brophy, 1981).

In summary, it would seem that the most effective and socially valid way to evaluate the outcomes of social skills training would be to track behavior changes that best predict an individual's standing on socially important outcomes (e.g., sociometric status, teacher or parent ratings, etc.). This would ensure that changes are being effected in behavior that society considers important for adolescents.

Social validation of treatment outcomes can be assessed in at least two ways. First, social competency can be evaluated subjectively by significant others in the adolescent's environment (e.g., parents, peers, and teachers). Using methods described previously (e.g., rating, sociometrics, etc.), one can assess whether the adolescent has increased in socially competent behavior as judged by others. Also, behavior-analytic measures of social competency (Goldfried & D'Zurilla, 1969) such as the PIAG often have scoring systems based on ratings obtained from samples of relevant judges (e.g., teachers, probation officers, peers, parent, employers) and thus have built-in subjective judgments of social behavior.

A second manner in which the social validity of treatment effects can be evaluated is to compare an adolescent's posttreatment performance with the average performance exhibited by an appropriate norm group (Hops & Greenwood, 1981). An advantage of this approach over that of subjective judgments is that it allows for a more objective and detailed assessment. Disadvantages include the potential for making comparisons on behaviors that are unrelated to important social outcomes and the lack of readily available normative data on adolescent social behavior. Obtaining comparison data would require the social skills assessor to assess the social competency of a sample of unselected adolescents, matched for age, sex, race, and socioeconomic status with one's client. Practically speaking, of course, this option may not be available to many practitioners. Obtaining data on one or two adolescents who are available and have similar backgrounds may be possible, however, and still highly informative.

CASE STUDY

The following case study illustrates many of the issues and methods of assessing adolescent social skills. This particular case was seen as representative in that the methods chosen provide reliable and valid information within the constraints of practicality. Also, the evaluation process reflects an attempt to individualize assessment and link assessment findings with treatment targets. Finally, this case study demonstrates possible areas where newly developed instruments may be of some use.

Reason for Referral

Mike D. is a 14-year-old black male referred to our clinic because of a recent suicide attempt. He lives with his mother and a 9-year-old half-brother, Jake. Mike's natural father never lived with the family, whereas Jake's father left home approximately four years after Jake's birth. The boy's mother, Ms. D., reported that Jake's father often abused her and she often would call to Mike for help in such instances. It was during this period that Mike complained of frequent stomachaches.

Approximately one year ago, Ms. D. began seeing another man, Larry, who now visits three to four times per week. Because Ms. D. reported feeling guilty and anxious when disciplining her sons, she has allowed Larry to assume a prominent role as disciplinarian. His approach to handling conflicts with the boys tends to be fairly authoritative and characterized by loud demands and physical punishment.

Recently, Mike's behavior at school resulted in a temporary suspension. The school's guidance counselor (supported by documentation in Mike's school folder) reported that on separate occasions Mike had become quite upset with one of his teachers and with the school-bus driver. In both situations, he angrily cursed the adults when accused of "offenses" he had not committed. Immediately after the suspension ended, Mike was incorrectly prohibited by the driver from once again riding the school bus. Mike became upset and angrily cursed the bus driver. This behavior resulted in a second suspension, the news of which greatly upset his mother and his mother's boyfriend. As a result, Larry harshly disciplined Mike. Later that evening, Mike ingested 20 Tylenol capsules in an attempt to commit suicide.

Assessment Procedures

One part of the assessment and treatment focus in Mike's case was his interactions with school personnel. Behavioral interviews and school records had adequately identified several characteristics of the situations that resulted in Mike's angry outbursts. Based on interview data, the decision was made to have Mike initially self-monitor all interactions he had with the school-bus driver and his science teacher. An interaction was defined as any verbal response made by these two school personnel to him and vice versa. Specifically, Mike was asked to record a one- to two-sentence description of the event and to rate on a 9-point scale (where 1 = not at all and 9 = extremely) the degree of anger he experienced. A small spiralbound notepad was used as a record form, with Mike instructed to make his entries at the first convenient opportunity after the interaction.

Self-monitoring information suggested Mike was capable of engaging in positive exchanges with these adults except when the situations involved Mike's receiving negative feedback from them, especially in the presence of his peers. Two weeks of self-monitoring data indicated Mike had two negative (i.e., anger ratings of 5 or greater) interactions with the bus driver and one with his science teacher. Contrary to previous negative interactions, however, on these occasions Mike simply said nothing. The interaction with his science teacher was particularly noteworthy in that she had accused him of not studying for a test he had failed. For this interaction, Mike rated his anger as a "9" because he felt he had studied for the test and the teacher was simply picking on him.

When this particular scene was role-played with Mike given instructions to respond, not as he had, but as best he could, he was unable to generate appropriate alternative responses. When asked to relate what self-statements and emotional responses occurred when unjustifiably accused by the teacher, Mike pointed out that he could feel himself "heating up" but was trying not to curse at her. From the information collected, it appeared as though Mike's poor performance in these situations was a result of self-control skill deficits. In other words, he was unable to perform the skills required (i.e., appropriate assertive responses) *and* his anger and impulsivity were interfering with his ability to acquire these skills.

Though not particularly germane to changing his interactions with school personnel, Mike's tendency to respond with angry verbal outbursts may have been shaped through interactions with his mother. She had reported that she was ineffectual in disciplining Mike, especially when he would "blow up" at her; thus, Mike's angry outbursts had a history of negative reinforcement at home, which may have generalized to school situations.

The immediate impact of social skills training (consisting primarily of instructions, modeling, coaching, and feedback for assertive responses, coupled with techniques for reducing interfering emotional arousal) was evaluated through continued self-monitoring and behavior role-playing. Frequent phone contact also was made with the school's guidance counselor in order to corroborate Mike's self-monitoring data.

Assessment Results

The significance of changes associated with social skills training was evaluated in two ways. First, with Mike's consent, two different teachers were asked to participate in an assessment of the generalization of his newly acquired skills to novel situations. Without Mike knowing which teachers were contacted, two were asked to engage Mike in a potentially anger-provoking interaction (e.g., accusing him of making disruptive noises in class). Afterward, these teachers rated Mike's performance on certain aspects (e.g., appropriatenesss of verbal content) and reported these to us. The second method in which the significance of treatment's impact was assessed involved asking the bus driver and science teacher to report to the guidance counselor any incident in which Mike exhibited angry verbal outbursts. In this way, inquiries made to the counselor represented both a simple way to monitor Mike's performance over time and a return to very global, yet socially valid, information.

SUMMARY AND CONCLUSIONS

Based on the material reviewed in this chapter, these authors strongly believe that social skills are best defined as those behaviors that, within given situations, predict important social outcomes for adolescents. Important social outcomes for adolescents include peer acceptance, adult acceptance (teachers and parents), academic achievement, and adequate adjustment to school, home, and community settings. This view of social skills is based on criterion-related and social validity. That is, behaviors that predict an adolescent's standing on these outcomes are, by definition, socially skilled behaviors.

Several major themes can be extracted from the foregoing review of assessment strategies for adolescent social skills. First, the assessment of adolescent social skills should be multifactored, including a variety of assessment methods (e.g., ratings, behavioral role plays, direct observations, interviews, etc.), sources of information (e.g., teachers, parents, peers, the adolescent, etc.), and content foci (e.g., behaviors, situations, settings, etc). Second, the assessment of adolescent social skills can be conceptualized into three distinct stages: (a) assessment for classification, (b) assessment for treatment planning, and (c) assessment for treatment evaluation. These distinctions are important because differential assessment procedures are associated with each stage. Finally, it is critical to assess the social validity of social skills assessment and training with adolescents. This involves an assessment of the *social significance* of the behavioral goals of social skills interventions, an assessment of the *social acceptability* of social skills training procedures for the adolescent as well as significant others (e.g., teachers and parents), and an assessment of the *social importance* of the effects of social skills training. This social validation process ensures that practi-

SOCIAL SKILLS 117

tioners will be teaching socially significant behaviors using socially acceptable treatment procedures that produce socially important effects.

REFERENCES

Anastasi, A. (1982). *Psychological testing* (5th ed.). New York: Macmillan.
Allen, K. E., Hart, B. M., Buell, J. S., Harris, F. R., & Wolf, M. M. (1964). Effects of social reinforcement on isolate behavior of a nursery school child. *Child Development, 35,* 511-518.
Asher, S. R., & Hymel, S. (1981). Children's social competence in peer relations: Sociometric and behavioral assessment. In J. D. Wine & M. D. Smye (Eds.), *Social competence* (pp. 125-157). New York: Guilford Press.
Asher, S. R., & Markell, R. S. (1978). *Peer relations and social interaction: Assessment and intervention.* Unpublished manuscript.
Asher, S. R., Oden, S. L., & Gottman, J. M. (1977). Children's friendships in school settings. In L. G. Katz (Ed.), *Current topics in early childhood education* (Vol. 1). Norwood, NJ: Ablex.
Asher, S. R., Singleton, L., Tinsley, B. R., & Hymel, S. A. (1979). A reliable sociometric measure for preschool children. *Developmental Psychology, 15,* 443-444.
Asher, S. R., & Taylor, A. R. (1981). The social outcomes of mainstreaming: Sociometric assessment and beyond. *Exceptional Education Quarterly, 1,* 13-30.
Baer, D. M., & Wolf, M. M. (1970). The entry into natural communities of reinforcement. In R. Ulrich, T. Stachnik, & J. Mabry (Eds.), *Control of human behavior* (Vol. 2). Glenwood, IL: Scott Foresman.
Bandura, A. (1969). *Principles of behavior modification.* New York: Holt, Rinehart, & Winston.
Bandura, A. (1977a). Self-efficacy: Toward a unifying theory of behavior change. *Psychological Review, 84,* 191-215.
Bandura, A. (1977b). *Social learning theory.* Englewood Cliffs, NJ: Prentice-Hall.
Bandura, A. (1982). Self-efficacy mechanism in human agency. *American Psychologist, 37,* 122-147.
Bellack, A. S. (1979). A critical appraisal for strategies for assessing social skills. *Behavioral Assessment, 1,* 157-176.
Bellack, A. S., & Hersen, M. (Eds.). (1979). *Research and practice in social skills training.* New York: Plenum Press.
Bellack, A. S., Hersen, M., & Lamparski, D. (1979). Role-play tests for assessing social skills: Are they valid? Are they useful? *Journal of Consulting and Clinical Psychology, 47,* 335-342.
Bellack, A. S., Hersen, M., & Turner, S. M. (1978). Role-play tests for assessing social skills: Are they valid? *Behavior Therapy, 9,* 448-461.
Bellack, A. S. (1983). Recurrent problems in the behavioral assessment of social skill. *Behaviour Research and Therapy, 21,* 29-41.
Black, F. (1985). *Social skills assessment for mainstreamed handicapped students: The discriminative efficiency of the Teacher Ratings of Social Skills.* Unpublished doctoral dissertation, Louisiana State University.
Blackwood, R. O. (1970). The operant conditioning of verbal mediated self-control in the classroom. *Journal of School Psychology, 8,* 251-258.
Bolstad, O. D., & Johnson, S. M. (1972). Self-regulation in the modification of disruptive classroom behavior. *Journal of Applied Behavior Analysis, 5,* 443-454.

Bornstein, M. R., Bellack, A. S., & Hersen, M. (1977). Social skills training for unassertive children: A multiple baseline analysis. *Journal of Applied Behavior Analysis, 10,* 183-195.

Bornstein, P. H., & Quevillon, R. P. (1976). The effects of a self-instructional package on overactive preschool boys. *Journal of Applied Behavior Analysis, 9,* 179-188.

Brophy, J. (1981). Teacher praise: A functional analysis. *Review of Educational Research, 51,* 5-32.

Bryan, T. S. (1978). Social relationships and verbal interactions of learning disabled children. *Journal of Learning Disabilities, 11,* 107-115.

Camp, B. W., Blom, G. E., Herbert, F., & van Doorninck, W. J. (1977). "Think Aloud": A program for developing self-control in young aggressive boys. *Journal of Abnormal Child Psychology, 5,* 157-169.

Cartledge, G., & Milburn, J. (1978). The case for teaching social skills in the classroom: A review. *Review of Educational Research, 48,* 133-156.

Cartledge, G., & Milburn, J. (Eds.). (1980). *Teaching social skills to children: Innovative approaches.* New York: Pergamon.

Cavell, T. A., Kelley, M. L., & Buss, R. R. (1985, November). *Adolescents' perceptions of frequent and difficult interpersonal problem situations: Grade, sex, and race differences.* Presented at the 19th Annual Meeting of the Association for the Advancement of Behavior Therapy, Houston, TX.

Chandler, M. J. (1973). Egocentrism and antisocial behavior: The assessment and training of social perspective-taking skills. *Developmental Psychology, 9,* 326-332.

Ciminero, A. R., Calhoun, K. S., & Adams, H. E. (Eds.). (1977). *Handbook of behavioral assessment.* New York: Wiley.

Clark, L., Gresham, F. M., & Elliott, S. N. (1985). Development and validation of social skills assessment measure: The TROSS-C. *Journal of Psychoeducational Assessment, 4,* 347-356.

Coie, J. D., & Dodge, K. A. (1983). Continuity of children's social status: A five-year longitudinal study. *Merrill-Palmer Quarterly, 29,* 261-282.

Combs, M. L., & Slaby, D. A. (1977). Social skills training with children, In B. B. Lahey & A. E. Kazdin (Eds.), *Advances in child clinical psychology* (Vol. 1). New York: Plenum.

Cone, J. D. (1977). The relevance of reliability and validity for behavioral assessment. *Behavior Therapy, 8,* 411-426.

Cowen, E. L., Pederson, A., Babijian, H., Izzo, L. D., & Trost, M. A. (1973). Long-term follow-up of early detected vulnerable children. *Journal of Consulting and Clinical Psychology, 41,* 438-446.

Curran, J. P. (1977). Skills training as an approach to the treatment of heterosexual-social anxiety: A review. *Psychological Bulletin, 84,* 140-157.

Dishion, T. J., Loeber, R., Stouthamer-Loeber, M., & Patterson, G. R. (1984). Skill deficits and male adolescent delinquency. *Journal of Abnormal Child Psychology, 12,* 37-54.

Dodge, K. A. (1983). Behavioral antecedents of peer social status. *Child Development, 54,* 1386-1399.

Dodge, K. A., & Murphy, R. R. (1984). The assessment of social competence of adolescents. In P. Karoly & J. J. Steffen (Eds.), *Adolescent behavior disorders: Foundations and contemporary concerns.* Lexington, MA: Lexington Books.

Dodge, K. A., McClaskey, C. L., & Feldman, E. (1985). Situational approach to the assessment of social competence in children. *Journal of Consulting and Clinical Psychology, 53,* 344-353.

Drabman, R. S. (1973). Child-versus-teacher-administered programs in a psychiatric hospital school. *Journal of Abnormal Child Psychology, 1,* 68-87.

Erikson, E. (1950). *Childhood and society.* New York: Norton.

Foster, S. L., & Ritchey, W. L. (1979). Issues in the assessment of social competence in children. *Journal of Applied Behavior Analysis, 12,* 625-638.

Freedman, B. J., Rosenthal, L., Donahoe, C. P., Jr., Schlundt, D. G., & McFall, R. M. (1978). A social-behavioral analysis of skill deficits in delinquent and nondelinquent adolescent boys. *Journal of Consulting and Clinical Psychology, 46,* 1448-1462.

Gaffney, L. R. (1984). A multiple-choice test to measure social skills in delinquent and nondelinquent adolescent girls. *Journal of Consulting and Clinical Psychology, 52,* 911-912.

Gaffney, L. R., & McFall, R. M. (1981). A comparison of social skills in delinquent and nondelinquent adolescent girls using a behavioral role-playing inventory. *Journal of Consulting and Clinical Psychology, 49,* 959-967.

Gamble, R., & Strain, P. S. (1979). The effects of dependent and interdependent group contingencies on socially appropriate responses in classes for emotionally handicapped children. *Psychology in the Schools, 16,* 253-260.

Garmezy, N. (1974). Children at risk: The search for antecedents of schizophrenia—Part I: Conceptual models and research methods. *Schizophrenia Bulletin, 8,* 14-90.

Gilbert, G. M. (1957). A survey of "referral problems" in metropolitan child guidance centers. *Journal of Clinical Psychology, 13,* 37-42.

Goldfried, M. R., & Kent, R. N. (1972). Traditional versus behavioral personality assessment: A comparison of methodological and theoretical assumptions. *Psychological Bulletin, 77,* 409-420.

Goldfried, M. R., & D'Zurilla, T. J. (1969). A behavioral-analytic model for assessing competence. In C. D. Spielberger (Ed.), *Current topics in clinical and community psychology* (Vol. 1, pp. 151-196). New York: Academic Press.

Goldstein, A. P., Sprafkin, R. P., Gershaw, N. J., & Klein, P. (1980). *Skillstreaming the adolescent.* Urbana, IL: Research Press.

Gottman, J. M. (1977). The effects of a modeling film on social isolation in preschool children: A methodological investigation. *Journal of Abnormal Child Psychology, 5,* 69-78.

Gottman, J. M., Gonso, J., & Rasmussen, B. (1975). Social interaction, social competence, and friendship in children. *Child Development, 46,* 708-718.

Gottman, J. M., Gonso, J., & Schuler, P. (1976). Teaching social skills to isolated children. *Journal of Abnormal Child Psychology, 4,* 179-197.

Green, K. D., Forehand, R., Beck, S. J., & Vosk, B. (1980). An assessment of the relationship among measures of children's social competence and children's academic achievement. *Child Development, 51,* 1149-1156.

Green, K. D., Vosk, B., Forehand, R., & Beck, S. (1981). An examination of differences among sociometrically identified accepted, rejected, and neglected children. *Child Study Journal, 11,* 117-124.

Greenspan, S. (1981). Social competence and handicapped individuals: Practical implications and a proposed model. *Advances in Special Education, 3,* 41-82.

Greenwood, C., Todd, N., Hops, H., & Walker, H. (1982). Behavior change targets in the assessment and treatment of socially withdrawn preschool children. *Behavioral Assessment, 4,* 237-297.

Greenwood, C. R., Walker, H. M., & Hops, H. (1977). Issues in social interaction/withdrawal assessment. *Exceptional Children, 43,* 490-499.

Greenwood, C. R., Walker, H. M., Todd, N., & Hops, H. (1981). Normative and descriptive analysis of preschool free play social interaction rates. *Journal of Pediatric Psychology, 6,* 343-367.

Gresham, F. M. (1981a). Assessment of children's social skills. *Journal of School Psychology, 19,* 120-133.

Gresham, F. M. (1981b). Social skills training with handicapped children: A review. *Review of Educational Research, 51,* 139-176.

Gresham, F. M. (1981c). Validity of social skills measures for assessing the social competence in low-status children: A multivariate investigation. *Developmental Psychology, 17,* 390-398.

Gresham, F. M. (1982a). Misguided mainstreaming: The case for social skills training with handicapped children. *Exceptional Children, 48,* 422-433.

Gresham, F. M. (1982b). Social interactions as predictors of children's likeability and friendship patterns: A multiple regression analysis. *Journal of Behavioral Assessment, 4,* 39-54.

Gresham, F. M. (1982c). *Social skills: Principles, practices, and procedures.* Des Moines, IA: Iowa Department of Public Instruction.

Gresham, F. M. (1983a). Social skills assessment as a component of mainstreaming placement decisions. *Exceptional Children, 49,* 331-336.

Gresham, F. M. (1983b). Social validity in the assessment of children's social skills: Establishing standards for social competency. *Journal of Psychoeducational Assessment, 1,* 297-307.

Gresham, F. M. (1984). Behavioral interviews in school psychology: Issues in psychometric adequacy and training. *School Psychology Review, 12,* 17-25.

Gresham, F. M. (1985). Conceptual issues in the assessment of social competence in children. In P. Strain, M. Guralnick, & N. Walker (Eds.), *Children's social behavior: Development, assessment, and modification* (pp. 143-179). New York: Academic Press.

Gresham, F. M., & Elliott, S. N. (1984). Assessment and classification of children's social skills: A review of methods and issues. *School Psychology Review, 13,* 292-301.

Gresham, F. M., Bruce, B., & Veitia, M. (1983, December). *Convergent-discriminant validity in the assessment of adolescents' social skills.* Paper presented at the World Congress on Behavior Therapy, AABT 17th Annual Convention, Washington, DC.

Gronlund, H., & Anderson, L. (1963). Personality characteristics of socially accepted, socially neglected, and socially rejected junior high school pupils. In J. Sederman (Ed.), *Educating for mental health* (pp. 163-172). New York: Crowell.

Harter, S. (1978). Effectance motivation reconsidered: Toward a developmental model. *Human Development, 21,* 34-64.

Harter, S. (1982). The Perceived Competence Scale for Children. *Child Development, 53,* 87-97.

Hartup, W. W. (1970). Peer interaction in social organizations. In P. H. Mussen (Ed.), *Carmichael's manual of child psychology.* New York: Wiley.

Hartup, W. W., Glazer, J. A., & Charlesworth, R. (1967). Peer reinforcement and sociometric status. *Child Development, 38,* 1017-1024.

Haynes, S., & Jensen, B. (1979). The interview as a behavioral assessment instrument. *Behavioral Assessment, 1,* 97-106.

Hersen, M., & Bellack, A. S. (1977). Assessment of social skills. In A. R. Ciminero, K. S. Calhoun, & H. E. Adams (Eds.), *Handbook of behavioral assessment* (pp. 509-554). New York: Wiley.

Hops, H. (1983). Children's social competence and skill: Current research practices and future directions. *Behavior Therapy, 14,* 3-18.

Hops, H., & Greenwood, C. R. (1981). Social skills deficits. In E. J. Mash & L. G. Terdal (Eds.), *Behavioral assessment of childhood disorders.* New York: Guilford Press.

Iwata, B. A., & Bailey, J. S. (1974). Reward versus cost token systems: An analysis of the effects on students and teacher. *Journal of Applied Behavior Analysis, 7,* 567-576.

Kazdin, A. E. (1977). Assessing the clinical or applied importance of behavior change through social validation. *Behavior Modification, 1,* 427-451.

Kazdin, A. E. (1979). Situational specificity: The two-edged sword. *Behavioral Assessment, 1,* 57-75.

Kendall, P. C., & Braswell, L. (1982). Assessment for cognitive behavioral interventions in the schools. *School Psychology Review, 11*, 21-31.

Kendall, P. C., & Wilcox, L. E. (1979). Self-control in children: Development of a rating scale. *Journal of Consulting and Clinical Psychology, 47*, 1020-1029.

Kohn, M. (1977). The Kohn Social Competence Scale and Kohn Symptom Checklist for the preschool child: A follow-up report. *Journal of Abnormal Child Psychology, 5*, 249-262.

Kohn, M., & Clausen, J. A. (1955). Social isolation and schizophrenia. *American Sociological Review, 20*, 265-273.

Ladd, G. W. (1981). Effectiveness of a social learning method for enhancing children's social interaction and peer acceptance. *Child Development, 52*, 171-178.

Ladd, G., & Mize, J. (1983). A cognitive-social learning model of social skill training. *Psychological Review, 2*, 127-157.

La Greca, A. M. (1981). Peer acceptance: The correspondence between children's sociometric scores and teacher's ratings of peer interactions. *Journal of Abnormal Child Psychology, 9*, 167-178.

La Greca, A. M., & Santogrossi, D. A. (1980). Social skills training with elementary school students: A behavioral group approach. *Journal of Consulting and Clinical Psychology, 48*, 220-227.

Libet, J. M., & Lewinsohn, P. M. (1973). Concept of social skills with special reference to the behavior of depressed persons. *Journal of Consulting and Clinical Psychology, 40*, 304-312.

MacMillan, D. L., & Morrison, G. M. (1980). Correlates of social status among mildly handicapped learners in self-contained special classes. *Journal of Educational Psychology, 72*, 437-444.

MacMillan, D. L., Morrison, G. M., & Silverstein, A. B. (1980). Convergent and discriminant validity of Project PRIME's Guess Who? *American Journal of Mental Deficiency, 85*, 78-81.

Marshall, H. R., & McCandless, B. R. (1957). A study in the prediction of social behavior of preschool children. *Child Development, 28*, 149-159.

Maslow, A. H. (1968). *Toward a psychology of being.* New York: Van Nostrand Reinhold.

Matson, J., Esveldt-Dawson, K., & Kazdin, A. E. (1983). Validation of methods for assessing social skills in children. *Journal of Clinical Child Psychology, 12*, 174-180.

McCandless, B. R., & Marshall, H. R. (1957). Sex differences in social acceptance and participation of preschool children. *Child Development, 28*, 421-425.

McCullough, J. P., Huntsinger, G. M., & Nay, W. R. (1977). Case study: Self-control treatment of aggression in a 16-year-old male. *Journal of Consulting and Clinical Psychology, 45*, 322-331.

McFall, R. M. (1982). A review and reformulation of the concept of social skills. *Behavioral Assessment, 4*, 1-33.

McFall, R. M., & Dodge, K. A. (1983). Self-management and interpersonal skills learning. In P. Karoly & F. H. Kanfer (Eds.), *Self-management and behavior change: From theory to practice.* New York: Pergamon.

McGuire, J. M. (1973). Aggression and sociometric status with preschool children. *Sociometry, 36*, 542-549.

Meichenbaum, D. (1977). *Cognitive behavior modification.* New York: Plenum Press.

Meichenbaum, D., & Goodman, J. (1971). Training impulsive children to talk to themselves: A means of developing self-control. *Journal of Abnormal Psychology, 77*, 115-126.

Moore, S. G., & Updegraff, R. (1964). Sociometric status of preschool children related to age, sex, nurturance giving, and dependency. *Child Development, 35*, 519-524.

Moreno, J. L. (1934). *Who shall survive?* (Nervous and Mental Disease Monograph No. 58). Washington, DC: Nervous and Mental Disease Publishing Co.

Nelson, R., & Hayes, S. (1979). Some current dimensions of behavioral assessment. *Behavioral Assessment, 1*, 1-16.

O'Connor, R. D. (1969). Modification of social withdrawal through symbolic modeling. *Journal of Applied Behavior Analysis, 2*, 15-22.

O'Connor, R. D. (1972). Relative effects of modeling, shaping, and combined procedures for modification of social withdrawal. *Journal of Abnormal Psychology, 79*, 327-334.

Oden, S. (1980). A child's social isolation: Origins, prevention, intervention. In G. Cartledge & J. F. Milburn (Eds.), *Teaching social skills to children: Innovative approaches*. New York: Pergamon.

Oden, S. L., & Asher, S. R. (1977). Coaching children in social skills for friendship making. *Child Development, 48*, 496-506.

O'Leary, S. G., & Dubey, D. R. (1979). Applications of self-control procedures by children: A review. *Journal of Applied Behavior Analysis, 12*, 449-465.

Piaget, J. (1952). *The origins of intelligence in children*. New York: International Universities Press.

Prinz, R., Swan, G., Liebert, D., Weintraub, S., & Neale, J. (1978). ASSESS: Adjustment Scales for Sociometric Evaluation of Secondary School Students. *Journal of Abnormal Child Psychology, 6*, 493-501.

Quay, H., (1977). Measuring dimensions of deviant behavior: The Behavior Problem Checklist. *Journal of Abnormal Child Psychology, 5*, 277-287.

Roff, M. (1961). Childhood social interactions and young adulthood conduct. *Journal of Abnormal Psychology, 63*, 333-337.

Roff, M. (1970). Some life history factors in relation to various types of adult maladjustment. In M. Roff & D. Ricks (Eds.), *Life history research in psychopathology* (pp. 265-287). Minneapolis: University of Minnesota Press.

Roff, M., Sells, S. B., & Golden, M. M. (1972). *Social adjustment and personality development in children*. Minneapolis: University of Minnesota Press.

Rogers-Warren, A., & Baer, D. M. (1976). Correspondence between saying and doing: Teaching children to share and praise. *Journal of Applied Behavior Analysis, 9*, 334-354.

Sarason, I. G., & Sarason, B. R. (1981). Teaching cognitive and social skills to high school students. *Journal of Consulting and Clinical Psychology, 49*, 908-918.

Schinke, S. P. (1981). Interpersonal-skills training with adolescents. *Progress in Behavior Modification, 11*, 65-115.

Shapiro, E. S. (1984). Self-monitoring procedures. In T. H. Ollendick & M. Hersen (Eds.), *Child behavioral assessment: Principles and procedures* (pp. 148-165). New York: Pergamon.

Singleton, L. C., & Asher, S. R. (1977). Peer preferences and social interaction among third-grade children in an integrated school district. *Journal of Educational Psychology, 69*, 330-336.

Stephens, T. M. (1979). *Social behavior assessment*. Columbus, OH: Cedars Press.

Strain, P. S. (1975). Increasing social play of severely retarded preschoolers with sociodramatic activities. *Mental Retardation, 13*, 7-9.

Strain, P. S. (1977). An experimental analysis of peer social initiations on the behavior of withdrawn preschool children: Some training and generalization effects. *Journal of Abnormal Child Psychology, 5*, 445-455.

Strain, P. S., Cooke, R. P., & Apolloni, T. (1976). *Teaching exceptional children: Assessing and modifying social behavior*. New York: Academic Press.

Strain, P. S., Shores, R. E., & Timm, M. A. (1977). Effects of peer social initiations on the behavior of withdrawn preschool children. *Journal of Applied Behavior Analysis, 10*, 289-298.

Stumme, V. S., Gresham, F. M., & Scott, N. A. (1982). Validity of *Social Behavior Assessment* in discriminating emotionally disabled from nonhandicapped students. *Journal of Behavioral Assessment, 4,* 327-342.

Stumme, V. S., Gresham, F. M., & Scott, N. A. (1983). Dimensions of children's classroom social behavior. *Journal of Behavioral Assessment, 5*(3), 161-177.

Ullman, C. A. (1957). Teachers, peers, and tests as predictors of adjustment. *Journal of Educational Psychology, 48,* 257-267.

Urbain, E. S., & Kendall, P. C. (1980). Review of social-cognitive problem-solving interventions with children. *Psychological Bulletin, 88,* 109-143.

Van Hasselt, V. B., Hersen, M., & Bellack, A. S. (1981). The validity of role play tests for assessing social skills in children. *Behavior Therapy, 12,* 202-216.

Van Hasselt, V. B., Hersen, M., Whitehill, M. B., & Bellack, A. S. (1979). Social skill assessment and training for children: An evaluative review. *Behavior Research and Therapy, 17,* 413-437.

Van Houten, R. (1979). Social validation: The evolution of standards of competency for target behaviors. *Journal of Applied Behavior Analysis, 12,* 581-591.

Vosk, B., Forehand, R., Parker, J. B., & Rickard, K. (1982). A multimethod comparison of popular and unpopular children. *Developmental Psychology, 18*(4), 571-575.

Walker, H., McConnell, S., Holmes, D., Todis, B., Walker, J., & Golden, N. (1983). *The Walker Social Skills Curriculum.* Austin, Texas: Pro-Ed.

Warren, S., Rogers-Warren, A., & Baer, D. M. (1976). The role of offer rates in controlling sharing by young children. *Journal of Applied Behavior Analysis, 9,* 491-497.

Weintraub, S., Prinz, R. J., & Neale, J. M. (1978). Peer evaluations of the competence of children vulnerable to psychopathology. *Journal of Abnormal Child Psychology, 6,* 461-473.

Wheeler, V. A., & Ladd, G. W. (1982). Assessment of children's self-efficacy for social interactions with peers. *Developmental Psychology, 18,* 795-805.

White, R. W. (1959). Motivation reconsidered: The concept of competence. *Psychological Review, 66,* 287-333.

Witt, J. C., & Elliott, S. N. (1985). Acceptability of classroom intervention strategies. In T. R. Kratochwill (Ed.), *Advances in school psychology* (Vol. 4, pp. 251-288). Hillsdale, NJ: Lawrence Erlbaum.

Wolf, M. M. (1978). Social validity: The case for subjective measurement or how applied behavior analysis is finding its heart. *Journal of Applied Behavior Analysis, 11,* 203-214.

Yeaton, W. H., Witt, J. C., & Sechrest, L. (1981). Critical dimensions in the choice and maintenance of successful treatments: Strength, integrity, and effectiveness. *Journal of Consulting and Clinical Psychology, 49,* 156-167.

Zahavi, S. L., & Asher, S. R. (1978). The effect of verbal instruction on preschool children's aggressive behavior. *Journal of School Psychology, 16,* 146-153.

6

Normative and Non-Normative Issues in Assessing Adolescent Sexuality

JUDITH KAUFMAN, PH.D.

One of the essential characteristics of adolescent development is the integration of sexual drives into the psychosocial life of the teenager. The onset of puberty, the development of primary and secondary sexual characteristics, and the accomplishment of sexual and sex-role identity are hallmarks of this period, serving to distinguish adolescence from all other developmental periods. As is noted throughout this volume, at no other time in life do so many changes occur within such a short time span. The physical and sexual maturity that occurs in both sexes during adolescence can falsely imply concomitant psychological maturity and responsibility to cope with those changes. Parental and peer attitudes and expectations along with the teenager's self-perceptions combine to influence the adolescent's psychological response to sexual maturity. The social impact of significant others' responses to the developing adolescent's sexual identity may be greater than the biological changes themselves. Although the female's physical maturation is more overtly apparent and may draw more attention from male and female peers alike, the psychological impact of the onset of puberty is comparable for boys and girls.

In a survey of 541 adolescents, Sondheimer (1982) found that the most frequently asked personal questions and concerns regarding teenage sexuality concerned abnormality in sexual feelings, followed by emotional concerns (i.e., depression, suicidal ideation), and then moral, ethical, and social concerns. Responses to questionnaires like the Inventory of Attitudes Toward Sex (Eysenck, 1970) show marked shifts and changes in attitudes and actual sexual behavior among the adolescent population today. The average age of initial sexual intercourse, for example, has lowered for middle-class girls, and puberty also is occurring at a younger age (Kiestenbaum, 1979). Research data from several studies suggest that the more advanced kinds of sexual expression (petting and intercourse) are occurring at an earlier age (Miller & Simon, 1974; Zelnik & Kanter, 1977). Overall, more teenagers report more sexual activity (Hass, 1979). Adolescents assume adult-type roles while they may not attain their educational goals until their mid-to-late 20s.

Culture has a strong effect on adolescent development, as do class differences, and both play important roles in placing a "normative assessment" of adolescent sexuality in perspective. Masturbation, for example, is becoming a normal activity among middle-class adolescents, while among lower-class youth the act is stigmatized as shameful and sinful (Kiestenbaum, 1979). In contrast, lower-class males

124

are more ready to engage in sexual intercourse to prove manhood. Intercourse has become an acceptable alternative to masturbation as reflected in the early age and frequency of sexual activity in lower-class youngsters.

Ethnic differences, too, are reflected in figures for adolescent sexual activity. Black and Hispanic males (Finkel & Finkel, 1975) and black females (Kanter & Zelnik, 1972) adopt more sophisticated sexual behaviors earlier than their white counterparts; however, more recent research shows that the differences for females are beginning to disappear (Zelnik & Kanter, 1977). There was a 30% increase in premarital intercourse from 1971 to 1976 among unmarried females between 15 to 19 years of age; the increase was nearly twice as great for whites as blacks. The frequency of reported intercourse per individual adolescent seems to be about the same for both groups, although there are some differences in the number of partners. Both in 1971 and 1976 white females tended to have sex with more than one partner; most girls regardless of race were likely to have had 1 to 3 partners.

These data show a decline in adolescent male sexual behavior and an increase in adolescent female permissiveness when compared to the figures for 16- to 20-year-olds from the 1948 Kinsey, Pomeroy, and Martin study, in which a 70% activity rate for males and a 20% rate for females was reported. Apparently, the sexual revolution may be characterized by earlier ages of advanced sexual behavior and seemingly greater equality between the sexes.

PREASSESSMENT CONSIDERATIONS: UNDERSTANDING THE REFERRAL

Sexual issues are rarely the primary reason for referring an adolescent for psychological assessment, unless symptomatology is severe or apparent. Instead, the typical referral may describe general emotional concerns (i.e., depression, acting out, lack of motivation) or specific behavior patterns such as truancy, delinquency, or substance abuse. Sexual concerns might be mentioned as secondary issues, as when parents express anxiety over their daughter's preoccupation with sex, a teacher notes unusual or provocative behavior patterns, a physician reports an adolescent patient's sexual concerns subsequent to a physical examination, or a teenager frames a self-referral in terms of his or her concerns for a "friend's" sexuality.

Particularly with the younger adolescent, professionals must be sensitive to self-statements about physical development, wishes or fantasies about not growing up, fear of the opposite sex, and excuses designed to avoid gym classes or physical exercises. Sometimes an adolescent's physical and sexual concerns may be expressed through body language and posture. For example, a female may slouch in an attempt to hide her breast development, or a young man may strut in a "macho" swagger with his shirt sleeves rolled up, showing off his body hair.

Although professionals often mention the excitement and unique challenges of working with teenagers, few discuss the problems in dealing with the sexual issues they may present. When an adolescent's sexuality is blatant, some clinicians may feel uncomfortable. In other cases, watching an adolescent struggling with emerging sexuality may remind clinicians of similar issues they experienced as adolescents. Professionals may unwittingly choose to avoid certain topics and as a consequence never comprehend fully the difficulties the adolescent is facing (Gartner, 1985). Clinicians who experienced their own adolescence in an environment or time when it was not socially acceptable to discuss sex may tend to deny an adolescent's sexuality or over-interpret it due to vicarious identification. A professional may identify unconsciously with the adolescent and by doing so experience vicariously the same emotions over the problem that they themselves did as an adolescent (Anthony, 1969). Further, the adolescent may respond seductively to the clinician, expressing a need for affection or projection of forbidden affection for a parent onto the clinician, who may symbolize the fantasy parent. To deal with such cases and circumstances properly, the clinician must be aware of normative as well as non-normative adolescent sexual behavior. Furthermore, professionals must become aware of their own attitudes toward sex and sexuality and recognize those personal values and attitudes that might obstruct the objective assessment process. One useful technique for the clinician to self-evaluate his or her own attitudes would be to answer the questions on one of the adolescent sexual development questionnaires discussed in this chapter and compare their responses with the typical responses of teenagers of a particular age. Peer-group discussion as well as supervision can prove helpful as well.

The assessment of issues such as sex-role development is critical in understanding the adjustment as well as the symptomatology unique to the adolescent period. Success or failure in sexual adjustments during adolescence can have dramatic consequences for future relationships and provides the foundation for adult sexuality. Sometimes adolescents model adult forms of sexual behavior (often with marked distortion) as a vehicle for acting out and asserting their seeming maturity and independence. Multiple sex partners, provocative sexuality, and adolescent pregnancy might be seen as examples of such acting out. Often sexuality becomes the behavioral symptomatology indicative of more deeply rooted problems. Some adolescents, for example, may become sexually promiscuous in order to reinforce a poor self-image. Others may have questions and concerns about sexual issues that belie more obscure or generalized psychological problems, such as an adolescent concerned about frequent masturbation that in fact fits a more generalized problem of self-abusing behavior.

The rapid physical changes that occur in the course of "normal" adolescent development can cause confusion, questions, and temporary or transitory disruptions in development. The effects of additional elements of stress, such as early or late maturation or episodes of sexual abuse, may seriously impair body image, leave marked psychological scars, and create long-lasting negative attitudes about sexuality and self. Therefore, it is critical for the clinician to recognize the "normal" disruptions and concerns of adolescence and distinguish them from the signals and maladaptive features of non-normative or atypical adolescent sexual development. Through such knowledge, professionals are in a better position to develop programs and treatment interventions to meet adolescents' needs and address their confusion over sex and sexuality. What follows is a discussion of adolescent developmental issues as they impact normative and non-normative sexual development.

DEVELOPMENTAL ISSUES

In the past, adolescence has been characterized as a period of disruption and turmoil in which consistency was considered unusual (Blos, 1962). The more recent viewpoint (Offer, Ostrov, & Howard, 1981a) has suggested that it need not be a traumatic peiod; in fact, disruption may be the exception rather than the common experience. Coleman (1980) presents perhaps a more tenable position as compared to these two extremes. He describes the existence of certain standard adolescent stressors that are determined by the antecedent and current condition of an individual adolescent; for most adolescents the initial challenge is embodied in their physical development and changing bodies, which signal changing roles and increased expectations from their social environments. Therefore, the primary focal point for early adolescence is the integration of physical and sexual changes, which are considered primary stressors.

Normative versus Non-normative Sexual Development

Although puberty typically is considered to begin with the onset of menstruation in girls and the growth of pubic hair in boys, these observable changes represent only one aspect of the total complexity. Puberty affects not only the adolescent's reproductive system but also the functioning of the heart, the cardiovascular system, the lungs (affecting respirations), and the size and strength of many of the muscles. In addition, during puberty adolescents typically undergo a "growth spurt" in which they can be expected to increase dramatically in height and weight. There is considerable latitude among normal children in the age of onset and the duration of these physical changes accompanying puberty. The growth spurt and concomitant sexual maturation begin on the average almost two years earlier in females than in males. At age 6, there are no differences between the physical strength and stamina of boys and girls; as they reach adolescence, however, considerable differences emerge in motor development and physical strength. Boys, for example, double their strength between the ages of 11-14. Young adolescents tend to be awkward in their coordination and may appear quite clumsy, to the extent that self-image may be adversely affected. Typical of the asynchronization of growth during the early adolescent years, the hands, feet, and nose reach adult proportion first, while the rest of the body matures to adult size over the course of approximately two more years.

Although the fact that all adolescents exhibit comparable changes can serve as a valuable point of reference and reassurance for some adolescents, it can operate as an imaginary yardstick as well, against which an individual teenager may not "measure up" in his or her own estimation at any given time. More important than specific physical and sexual changes are the meaning and associations the adolescent attributes to these changes, the reactions of parents, siblings, and other significant individuals, and peer attitudes toward their own and their friends' changes. For example, if a late developer operates in a peer group with individuals who are sexually developed, he or she may begin to feel peculiar and different. These circumstances may have serious ramifications for healthy psychological growth. Furthermore, if an adolescent is not ready to accept his or her own physical maturation, atypical symptomatology may result at the expense of healthy development (e.g. anorexia nervosa, unhealthy sexual activity, early pregnancy, etc.).

The relative ease or difficulty with which a young person progresses through puberty and the adolescent developmental period in general is determined largely by past experiences, by the nature of unresolved conflicts, by existing coping abilities, and by familial and environmental support structures and systems. In order to make a successful transition to healthy adulthood, there are several psychological and psychosocial tasks the adolescent needs to master. These tasks begin with psychological and then later physical separation from parents, the formation of intimate attachments outside the family unit, the exploration and eventual consolidation of identity, the development of a sense of independence and competence, the generation of future plans and goals, the shift from concrete to hypothetical reasoning, and the development of empathic feelings.

Some individuals may reach adolescence without having fully developed the requisite psychological skills for progressing from childhood to adulthood. They have not or cannot complete the proscribed adolescent tasks because they do not have the necessary emotional resources. Failure to complete the tasks can lead to a prolonged adolescence, an incomplete adolescence, or to a superficial adolescent experience. Attributions regarding why adolescents have difficulties in completing and mastering developmental tasks have ranged from certain deficiencies in early parental care (e.g., mother-child interaction or environmental stability) to traumatic childhood events occurring through separation, illness, or loss and stressful environmental circumstances coinciding with the onset of adolescence. Such situations leave the young person particularly vulnerable to the stressors associated with growth and change.

Given the multitude of developmental concerns confronting the young adolescent, it is not surprising that certain problems may emerge that seem to be based in sexual adjustment problems. In the context of this chapter, the authors refer to nonnormative or "atypical" sexual development, not in the psychiatric sense (i.e., meaning psychopathological), but rather to indicate certain developmental circumstances that differ from the expected developmental norm. Any developmental change, even positive change, typically brings with it a degree of stress. As part of the developmental change process, adolescents will evaluate how "normal" they feel they are as well as how they feel others will react to the changes.

If developmental changes occur gradually and with the assistance of a good support system, accurate information, and adequate internal psychological resources, adolescents usually are able to examine, analyze, and integrate their experiences successfully and outgrow any perceived problems. However, a peer support network may exist only in that its members share common anxieties; information sources can be inaccurate or incomplete; and psychological defenses are often burdened by fears of disclosure, denial, and negation. Consequently, the adolescent may not see him- or herself as experiencing "typical stress" (Coleman, 1980). What begins as a normative developmental concern may become a major problem without the necessary environmental and psychological support.

Atypicality and non-normative sexual behavior are highly complex constructs and in general are not attributable to a single factor. The assessment of atypicality itself is a multidimensional process, requiring a range of instruments, appropriate training, good clinical skills, and knowledge of adolescent sexual development. For example, examiners should know that males tend to be more open, sexually provocative, and exhibitionistic during adolescence, while female sexual acting out tends to be more subtle, initially unrecognizable and very often with longer lasting consequences. As there is no male counterpart to menstruation, adjustment to the onset of puberty for male adolescents has not been as rich an area for assessment or research. However, it is important to note, for example, the growth of body hair and facial hair, although envied later in development, can be traumatic for the early developing male. Males have been known to be devastated by physical education classes and locker room experiences if they perceive themselves to be physically different from their peers. Male adolescents' reactions to changes in physical development may be observed in terms of the kinds of outward behavioral changes mentioned previously; however, these changes in behavior may not be as overtly dramatic as those of females.

SELECTION OF ASSESSMENT PROCEDURES

It is difficult to assess whether an adolescent is adjusting successfully to physical transformations and emerging sexuality. Few standardized tests have been developed to measure directly the factors affecting adolescent sexual development. Those that are available frequently are intended for research purposes only. Adolescent sexuality scales may be found embedded as subtests in more general instruments or one may have to infer attitudes about adolescent sexuality by interpreting self-concept and body image scales.

The assessment challenges faced by a psychological examiner reach far beyond discerning what is typical versus atypical adolescent behavior; the assessment must distinguish cause and effect, what is the symptom and what is the problem. Although the most common instruments employed have been self-report scales, their poor reliability is emphasized in the literature and responses to such questionnaires may be influenced by the situation, the examiner, and the psychological state of the individual at the time of testing. The inherent problems of such scales are exacerbated with an adolescent population because their self-evaluations are so contingent upon how they think they appear to others. The previously mentioned complications arising when psychological examiners have their own difficulties in acknowledging the sexuality of adolescents and engage in intellectual denial may account in part as well for the paucity of available assessment instruments for these purposes.

In the discussion that follows, direct and indirect assessment measures useful in general assessments of adolescent sexual development will be described first, followed by specialized instrumentation useful in assessing certain specific concerns in adolescent sexual development.

Direct and Indirect Assessment

Most direct measures of adolescent sexuality involve self-report techniques, utilizing either an interview or questionnaire format in which the examinee is asked to respond to a number of focused areas and concerns. Although self-report inventories have the problems noted previously, there may be no better way to get an answer to a question than by asking it. Clinicians, in contrast to psychometricians, often believe that an interview yields more reliable impressions than a questionnaire because the interviewer is present to determine (through clinical judgment) the candor of the interviewee. A questionnaire dealing with anxiety-provoking content may yield responses reflective of how the adolescent thinks others expect him or her to be rather than how he or she actually feels.

In his extensive examination of adolescent development, Coleman (1980) developed a series of interview questions that he used to evaluate teenagers' subjective responses to various domains of development. The physical/sexual domain, only one of the areas discussed in the interview, is assessed in the following ways:

> It's a well-known fact that teenagers are becoming physically mature at a younger age these days. Do you think this makes things more difficult for young people of today?

> In early adolescence, usually about age eleven or twelve, young people experience something called the growth spurt, when their bodies change and grow very quickly. Do you remember this? How did you feel at the time? (Coleman, 1980, p. 189)

According to Coleman's (1980) research using this interview technique, 150 randomly selected 15- to 17-year-olds attending schools throughout England presented themselves as open, honest, and thoughtful in response to all questions. Kaufman (1983, 1985) studied the interview transcripts of 500 American adolescents, spanning ethnic groups, socioeconomic status, and cognitive levels, and observed behavior comparable to that reported by Coleman. Kaufman expanded the questions on physical development to include concerns about sexual behavior, perceptions of sexual freedom and its impact on behavior, and attitudes and views about birth control and abortion.

Based on both the Coleman (1980) and Kaufman (1983, 1985) interview material, it may be hypothesized that the more troubled adolescents are about physical and sexual development, the less likely that they will be able to acknowledge the impact of the changes or admit that they have taken place. Denial, distortion, and reaction formation are the most prevalent defense patterns. Such avoidant behaviors are often reflected in the other domains of the adolescent's life and may indicate more deeply rooted problems. Similarly, blatant precocious sexuality may also be indicative of inappropriate or difficult sexual adjustment. Coleman (1980) found that questions about the adolescent growth spurt and the body itself were the most difficult for teenagers to answer, and inhibitions about their changing bodies were reflected in their answers.

As open and peer-oriented as adolescents may appear, Kaufman (1983) found that if they had a concern with their bodies, their development, or their sexuality, it was not shared with anyone, including parents and peers. When these kinds of preoccupations are concealed they may generate confusion, myths, and fears, which are difficult to remediate because they are not rationally based. It is important, therefore, to create opportunities for the adolescent client to discuss his or her physical and sexual development during the interview. Rates of change in physical characteristics and emotions do not necessarily correspond, and teenagers inevitably compare themselves to one another. Reassurances coupled with information about the ranges of normal development are of paramount importance. It is equally essential for the examiner to discuss the various kinds of relationships into which adolescents enter, some of which may include sexual thoughts and shared physical experiences. Of course, it is difficult to generalize about total personality development when only a few questions are abstracted from a much larger interview. The interpretations generated should be taken with caution and placed within a more comprehensive assessment context.

Although the interview technique is one of the most frequently used, it has not been subjected to rigorous tests of reliability and validity. The idiosyncratic nature of interviewers, of the questions generated in the interpersonal process, and of the research conducted has contributed to that lack. Certainly, there are methods for quantifying interview material and subjecting it to statistical analysis, if that were its intended use. However, when compared to other kinds of measures, interview techniques tend to yield rich and important idiosyncratic information that may not emerge when employing more rigidly developed psychometric and actuarial methods. This is particularly true when gathering information to plan for intervention programs.

In his work with adolescents, Hass (1979) perceived that they required a reference point for understanding not only their own sexuality but also what other people were thinking and feeling about sex. In response to this need Hass developed an extensive questionnaire with both male and female forms. Over 600 teenagers between the ages of 15 and 18 participated in the study, which was evenly composed of males and females; 125 of these subjects were minority, 90% from California and 10% representing the rest of the country. Results of the study are summarized in *Teenage Sexuality: A Survey of Teenage Sexual Behavior* (Hass, 1979). This report provides a frame of reference for assessing adolescent sexuality by covering its myths and realities in a presentation similiar to the 1948 Kinsey report. Topics covered include a range of topics rarely discussed in the professional literature, including sex or romance, dating, petting, oral sex, intercourse, masturbation, fantasies, homosexuality, and performance anxiety.

Results of the Hass study are presented by sex and age (15-16; 17-18). Although the specific findings included in the Hass study are quite numerous, a few of the major results should be highlighted. With regard to sexual intercourse, 53% of girls irrespective of age indicated that they would become involved if "I was in love with him," while 29% of males indicated that love would be the motivation. Twenty-three percent of 15- to 16-year-old males and 13% of 17- to 18-year-old males indicated that the first or second date would be the desirable time. Seventy-five percent of the younger males indicated that they masturbated; 80% of the males and 59% of the females in the older group responded affirmatively. More males than females had sexual performance anxiety. There were no indications of double standards, and over 70% of all respondents indicated that they approved of same-sex relationships if "that's what they both wanted to do" (Hass, 1979, p. 143).

What is so striking about the Hass findings is the contrast between the sexual sophistication often attributed to adolescents and their actual lack of knowledge or possession of distorted information. Much of the information shared among adolescents is grossly inaccurate. Examiners newly introduced to the assessment of adolescent sexuality are advised to refer to the Hass study to compare how teenagers generally view the sexual issues covered before drawing diagnostic conclusions based on an adult perspective. Although there are no explicit norms, cutoff scores, or diagnostic categories associated with Hass's questionnaire, the data provide a useful frame of reference for the examiner to investigate normative adolescent issues and concerns as well as serving as a source of reading and discussion material useful in bibliotherapy with the adolescent.

A self-report instrument designed to assess teens' attitudes about adolescent sexuality is the previously mentioned Inventory of Attitudes Toward Sex (Eysenck, 1970), which presents 98 items in a "Yes," "No," or "Questionable" response format. Nine hundred 16- to 20-year-old unmarried students were administered the instrument and their responses were factor analyzed, yielding 15 factors: Sexual Satisfaction, Sexual Nervousness, Premarital Sex, Prudishness, Homosexuality, Promiscuity, Guilt, Dual Standard, Sexual Excitement, Sexual Curiosity, Repression, Sexual Experimentation, Censorship, Sexual Hostility, and Inhibition. These 15 factors were then clustered into three higher order factors (Bergen, 1979): 1) Sexual Inhibition, a factor designed to reflect hesitancy, reticence, or a general discomfort towards sexual matters; 2) Sexual Orientation, a factor designed to reflect a positive orientation toward sexual matters; and 3) Sexual Allowance, a factor designed to reflect openness, comfort, or an experimental attitude toward sexual matters.

One of the advantages of the Inventory of Attitudes Toward Sex is that it is less threatening to the teenager than a face-to-face interview and most certainly permits privacy. Such an inventory may prove useful in providing insight into the adolescent's problem-solving processes and in helping to highlight some of the problematic areas that the adolescent either is not aware of or is too troubled or embarrassed to discuss openly. For example, in reviewing the results of an experimental questionnaire distributed to 150 female college freshmen (Katz & Kaufman, 1985), many of these young women reported retrospectively that in secondary school they had many sexual concerns. Some concerns were generated by flirtatious attitudes on the part of their male teachers, which they felt unable to discuss with anyone. At least 12% reported having sexual relationships with or knowing about friends sexually involved with their high school teachers.

Good assessment practice, then, requires that the clinician not only note the age and sex of the referred individual, but he or she also must be cognizant of the client's socioeconomic status, ethnicity, and sociocultural context before drawing any generalizations about atypicality or normality of the observed, expressed, or reported behavior. The expectations of the adolescent's peer group and family may influence the teenager's responses, with the result of obscuring their personal feelings. In these situations self-report questionnaires may represent an excellent technique for studying general trends and speculating about normative behavior, as long as their results are never used as the sole indicator of pathological patterns of adjustment.

The Rorschach, the Thematic Apperception Test (TAT), and figure drawings represent indirect assessment techniques that also may provide insight into the emotional attitude of the adolescent toward sexual development, despite the questionable validity and reliability of such instruments. Through these indirect assessment techniques defense mechanisms, personal conflicts, and difficulties in self-identity and sexuality may be highlighted. An extensive discussion of such instruments is not the intent of this chapter, which focuses on instrumentation used specifically to assess factors related to adolescent sexuality; however, there are several books that provide excellent overviews, such as Goldstein and Hersen (1984) and Groth-Marnart (1984).

SPECIAL ISSUES AND TOPICS IN ASSESSING ADOLESCENT SEXUALITY

Self-Concept

Self-concept or self-esteem is an integrating variable for all human behavior (Wylie, 1961). As such, its consideration may prove useful as a global issue in assessing adolescent sexuality; as a construct, however, self-concept is particularly problematic. A brief review of self-concept as it relates to adolescent sexuality is presented here, though a more extensive discussion of its assessment may be found in chapter 3 of this volume.

In a classic review of the research literature on self-concept, Wylie (1961) pointed out the difficulties associated with an empirical study, most of which still applies today. Reflecting on the diversity of the research, he wrote:

> When one reads the empirical literature pertaining to the self-concept theories, one finds that a bewildering array of hypotheses, measuring instruments and research designs has been used. As a consequence, one cannot prepare a simple synthesis of the established results. . . . The theories are in many ways ambiguous, incomplete, and overlapping and no one theory has received a large amount of systematic empirical exploration. (1961, p. 3)

One of the major problems in self-concept assessment lies in the very nature of the phenomenological construct itself. The researcher appears to be confronted with an inherent contradiction: self-concept theorists require that a specific class of variables be measured, namely conscious self-perceptions; however, in keeping within an internal frame of reference, these self-perceptions are private, personal, and unique to each individual. Consequently, such self-perceptions elude direct observation and due to their uniqueness are not easily measured using standardized instruments. The fact that there is no one definition of the self poses yet another difficulty in assessing this construct empirically.

Researchers define self-concept differentially and devise measuring instruments accordingly. Of the many scales developed to assess self-esteem and self-concept, the most commonly cited for use with adolescents are the Coopersmith Self-Esteem Inventories (1967) and the Piers-Harris Children's Self-Concept Scale (1984). These scales and comparable others contain questions focusing on the adolescent's physical self-concept or sense of attractiveness. In fact, on one of the six subscales of the Piers-Harris there are items that cluster around the variable of physical self and can give some indication of how the adolescent perceives his or her own attractiveness in relation to others of similar age. It is interesting to note that the physical development scale correlates significantly with school achievement; that is, the higher the school achievement, the higher the physical self-concept (Conger & Petersen, 1984), indicating the impact of accepting the physical self for both males and females. The Piers-Harris has recently been revised and its norms expanded. A positive feature of the scale is that it is written at fifth-grade reading level and thus may be administered to adolescents who appear to be having academic difficulties.

Perhaps the most extensive self-concept scale specifically designed to assess self-perceptions in adolescent populations is the Offer Self-Image Questionnaire (OSIQ; Offer, Ostrov, & Howard, 1981b). The OSIQ was developed as a means of gathering information about adolescents' "phenomenal selves." It is untimed and appropriate for group administration. Subjects are asked to indicate how well each item describes them based on a 6-point Likert-type dimension, where 1 indicates the item "describes me very well" and 6 means that the item "does not describe me at all." Based on theory, clinical practice, and research, items were written to cover 11 areas important to the psychological life of the adolescent: impulse control, emotional tone, body and self image, social relationships, morals, sexual attitudes, family relationships, mastery of the external world, vocational and educational goals, psychopathology, and superior adjustment.

One of the two subscales of the OSIQ focusing on adolescent sexuality is the Body and Self Image subscale, which reflects the extent to which the adolescent has adjusted to or feels awkward about body boundaries or body changes that take place in early adolescence. A low standard score on this subscale indicates continuing confusion or awkwardness about body boundaries, while a high score shows a well-structured self-concept with well-defined body boundaries. Sexual Attitudes, the second subscale of interest here, is concerned with feelings, attitudes, and behaviors toward the opposite sex. A low standard score on this subscale would reflect a relatively conservative attitude towards sexuality and a high standard score would reflect relative openness. The OSIQ has been studied using large samples of "typical" adolescents and has generated new speculations about self-perceptions and behavior during this developmental period. Research employing these subscales of the OSIQ has yielded findings depicting generally healthy self-perceptions of sexual behavior among teenagers and thus permitting a broader definition of "typical" adolescent sexuality, which is not supportive of the notion that adolescence is a time of "trauma" in regard to normal sexual development.

The 11 OSIQ subscales have been shown to cluster on five higher order domains, one of which has special significance for the assessment of adolescent sexuality. Offer et al.'s (1981b) research findings based on this Sexual Self domain have indicated that, in general, normal adolescents are not overly anxious about their sexuality, but boys are more open than girls. For example, boys report that they think about sex more often and attend "sexy" shows more often than do girls. In contrast to earlier studies (Zelnik & Kanter, 1977), recent research (Offer et al., 1981b) has identified no significant differences across cultural and ethnic backgrounds in sexual attitudes based on the Sexual Self domain. In interpreting these research findings it should be noted, however, that the current research results are based on the OSIQ, which evaluates self-reported attitudes and perceptions, while previous studies examined observable behavior. These differences in research design could account for the differences in findings. For example, while individual adolescents may report that early sexual intercourse or frequent masturbation is acceptable to them, they may not actually engage in such behavior.

The Offer Self-Image Questionnaire is a good example of its genre. Psychometrically, it is quite adequate, showing a stability coefficient for the total score of .73 and good predictive and construct validity. Longitudinal studies have demonstrated that the OSIQ may be useful in discriminating subgroups of adolescents ranging in personality characteristics and adolescents differing in psychological adjustment, based on their self-images (Dudley, Craig, & Mason, 1981). A questionnaire of this type allows for relative comparisons among adolescents. The multicultural, multiage sample employed in its standardization permits the clinician to compare an individual's scores to the appropriate reference group. The OSIQ must be computer-scored by the publisher and results in a computer-generated profile with appropriate means and standard deviations for each of the subscales and domains. For this reason, it may be difficult under emergency circumstances for the clinician to include the OSIQ in an individual battery unless local norms are generated within a clinic, school, or community.

Sex-Role Identification and Gender Identification

Sex-role identification and gender identity, particularly as they solidify in adolescence, are integral components within the assessment of adolescent self-concept. The literature is replete with critiques of sex-role and gender stereotyping, and thus it is not surprising that scales assessing these concepts also have had their difficulties. With the burgeoning interest in the concept of androgyny and the deemphasis on sex-role expectations, the Bem Sex-Role Inventory (BSRI) has been widely applied (Gayton, Flava, Ozman, & Tavormina, 1977). Bem (1981) has argued that because masculinity and femininity have been conceptualized traditionally as unipolar constructs, they have been measured as two distinctly independent dimensions. When both dimensions are exhibited within the same individual, his or her sex role may be called "androgynous."

The BSRI consists of 20 masculine, feminine, and neutral adjectives, which adolescent subjects rate on a 7-point Likert-type scale regarding how well each adjective describes their self-perceptions of their sex-role. The BSRI is scored by deriving a masculinity and femininity score and then comparing them with the median masculinity and femininity scores for the age group of interest. Subjects who score above both masculine and feminine medians may be characterized as androgynous; those who score above the masculine median and below the female median are classified as masculine; those who score above the feminine median and below the masculine median are classified as feminine; and those who score below the median on both the masculine and feminine dimensions are considered undifferentiated. Currently, there are no national norms for the BSRI, but only median scores derived for the group to which the individual is being compared. The absence of a national reference group (and thus an overall objective national standard) limits the interpretation of BSRI scores.

Another scale focusing on androgyny is the PRF ANDRO scale (Berzins, Welling, & Wetter, 1978), adapted from Jackson's Personality Research Form (PRF) and employing 63 of its original items. The PRF ANDRO scale is scored by deriving masculinity and femininity scores for individuals in much the same way as the BSRI and comparing these scores with the median masculinity and femininity scores for a particular group (Gayton et al., 1977).

The Personal Attributes Questionnaire (PAQ) is a self-report inventory of socially desirable gender-linked traits designed to assess sex-role identification

(Spence & Helmreich, 1978; 1980). All traits measured on the PAQ are categorized as either instrumental or expressive and considered stereotypically more characteristic of males or females respectively. The PAQ views masculinity-femininity as dualistic rather than bipolar dimensions and provides an opportunity for androgynous sex-role identification. This instrument consists of three scales: Masculinity, containing eight items judged significantly more characteristic of men than of women; Femininity, comprised of eight items judged more characteristic of females; and Masculinity-Femininity, also with eight items, consisting of qualities judged equally desirable for both males and females.

Respondents are asked to rate each PAQ item on a 5-point Likert scale in terms of how much they agree with the item. A median cutoff score is employed in the same way as in the previously mentioned scales to determine masculinity, femininity, and androgyny in sex-role functioning. High levels of test-retest reliability have been reported. Furthermore, considerable evidence has been accrued to suggest that the PAQ has construct and predictive validity in measuring instrumental (Masculine) and expressive (Feminine) behaviors. However, the attempt to relate these types of behaviors to other qualities that might be considered masculine or feminine has not proven as successful (Spence & Helmreich, 1980).

The scales just described for assessing sex-role identity and others like them share similar reliability, validity, and norming problems. In addition, the question may be raised whether it is efficacious to measure gender identity in adolescents, who are in the midst of integrating new sex-role expectations, their own sexuality, and a changing body image. Conceivably these kinds of gender identification scales may be useful in identifying the more deviant adjustment patterns in an informal manner, but it must be stressed that normative data generally are lacking for such scales. Findings from the BSRI, PRF ANDRO, and PAQ should be interpreted with caution; they may be quite useful in research studies, but not necessarily in clinical assessment batteries unless applied in a supplemental, informal manner.

Body Image

Evaluations of body image may be particularly important in an assessment of adolescent sexuality because for adolescents the body can reflect self-image and over-all mental health. Distortions in body image can represent an adolescent's difficulties in accepting his or her emerging sexuality. As substantiation for this position, Offer et al. (1981b) have defined body image operationally as part of the adolescent's sexual self as measured by the OSIQ, while others (e.g., Levenkron, 1982) report that body image may be distorted in anorexic adolescents as a defense against emerging sexuality. Two effective techniques for evaluating body image are the Image Marking Method (Askevold, 1975) and the Body Cathexis Scale (Secord & Jourard, 1953).

Askevold's image-marking method is simple and direct. The examinee stands within reaching distance of a piece of wrapping paper and is asked to imagine standing in front of a mirror looking at him- or herself. Standing behind the individual, the evaluator firmly touches those points on the examinee's body that he or she is to outline on the paper. Next, the individual is asked to turn around and move back against the paper while the evaluator records the actual body points. The differences between the actual and perceived body size are compared, and distortions are reflected along a continuum. Both obese and anorexic youngsters may be expected to experience body distortions, and the more disturbed the individual, the greater the body size distortions (Askevold, 1975).

The Body Cathexis Scale (Secord & Jourard, 1953) may be used in conjunction with the image marking method. This scale was developed for assessing the strength of feelings toward one's body. The original Body Cathexis Scale evaluated 46 body parts and functions, although shortened and modified versions have been employed. Using a 5-point Likert continuum, individuals are asked to rate their degree of satisfaction or dissatisfaction with specified body parts. A total Body Cathexis Scale score is derived by summing the subject's ratings for each of the items and dividing by the number of items.

Adjustment to Menstruation

Along with the general developmental tasks faced by all adolescents, females must adjust to the onset of menstruation, which in itself is a major developmental milestone. Menarche is associated with major changes in the female self-concept, eventually culminating in the consolidation of feminine identification and gender identity. For some adolescents the onset of menstruation may symbolize the separation and individuation process, identification with mother as a woman, and integration of gender identity. It is interesting to note that one symbol of control for anorexic adolescents is amenorrhea. (The reader is referred to chapter 7 in this volume for a comprehensive discussion of anorexia nervosa.)

Popular characterizations of menstruation have ranged from the most joyful and fruitful attribute of womankind to describing it as "the curse." Assessing an adolescent's attitude toward and personal meaning attributed to menstruation can be critical in assessing her overall adjustment. Although currently there are no standardized instruments to address these concerns, certain methods have been developed in the context of research studies. Of these, a questionnaire developed by Greenman (1985) seems the most comprehensive and representative. Items were developed from a review of the literature on adolescent females' responses to menarche. The questionnaire covers areas such as relationship with mother, identification with mother's attitudes toward menstruation, affective responses to the onset of menarche, attainment of developmental landmarks, heterosexual interest, and satisfaction with gender. The questionnaire is quite extensive and subscales might be abstracted and employed, depending on the kinds of information sought. Norms are not available at present, but results may aid in generating clinical hypotheses when used in conjunction with other measures.

Adolescent Pregnancy

Adolescent pregnancy and the number of teenagers at risk for pregnancy has increased significantly in the past 10 years and has reached epidemic proportions in certain areas of the country (McAnarney & Schreider, 1984). Using 1978 census data as a base, the incidence of pregnancy among adolescents now exceeds one million a year; 49% result in birth, 38% are terminated by abortion, and 13% miscarry (Alan Guttmacher Institute, 1981). The consequences of pregnancy are most severe for the youngest adolescents and may be viewed as a "syndrome of failure," primarily in terms of failure to fulfill the developmental tasks of adolescence (Waters, 1969). Alternatively, carrying a baby to term may be seen as signifying an alternative means of attaining recognition and status (Fischman, 1977).

Psychological, interpersonal, and social factors contribute to an adolescent's vulnerability to becoming pregnant early. Self-perception is a major factor. The sense of who or what one is, can be, and wants to become represents a standard against which the idea of becoming pregnant is weighed. A high need for achievement and plans for future educational goals have been correlated with effective contraceptive use; lack of educational ambition has been associated with early intercourse and risk for pregnancy (Furstenberg, 1976). In this regard, adolescents coming from more highly educated families are more likely to be educationally ambitious.

The more control a young adolescent feels over her environment, the less vulnerable she is to an unplanned pregnancy. An interesting finding in this regard is that birth control users tend to have higher levels of self-esteem and feelings of control than pregnant adolescents. Furthermore, adolescents who become pregnant tend to come from families with absent fathers or families that have experienced a loss of someone close to them (Von der Ahe, 1969). Teenagers may be more vulnerable to unplanned pregnancy when they are severely depressed and seeking attention, affection, and nurturance. Under these circumstances pregnancy may be used to counteract extreme stress reactions.

Although demographic factors, socioeconomic status, and ethnicity have been well documented as contributers to vulnerability, intrapsychic factors have not. Ego and superego development, the organization of defense mechanisms, ego identity, nature of attachments, separation/individuation, and gender identity are among the areas frequently cited as contributing to vulnerability, although empirical findings are still equivocal. A number of techniques may be used to assess and identify youngsters who may be particularly vulnerable to "too early mothering" (i.e., pregnancy).

Self-concept scales and gender-identity measures described earlier in this chapter have been employed frequently to assess these areas of concern. Another common technique used to assess ego development is the Washington University Sentence Completion Test (Loevinger, 1970), on which the individual responds to 36 items that are scored according to one of nine developmental levels: impulsive, self-protective, transition, conformist, post-conformist, conscientious, individualistic, autonomous, and integrated. The scoring schema is based on Loevinger's (1970) conception of the development of ego functions.

The Washington University Sentence Completion Test is difficult to score and requires considerable practice in order to establish interjudge reliability. The technique, however, is remarkably substantial in its predictive and construct validity and reliability. Although the test has proven itself to be a good predictor of those adolescents at risk, it should not be used casually or by an untrained assessor. Youngsters who carry their pregnancies to full term and those who do not use birth control typically will fall within the lower levels of ego development (the conformist to post-conformist levels). Birth control users will score much higher, between conscientious and individualistic. These diagnostic criteria apply to sexually active females only and show the relationship between vulnerability to unplanned pregnancy and female ego development.

Females who experience difficulty in separating from their mothers or feel rejected also are at greater risk for pregnancy as a means of compensating for perceived losses in interpersonal relationships. These females may view the birth process as a way of attempting a reunion with their mothers. It is challenging for the professional to operationalize and measure object relations and personal attachments; most frequently object relation scales are applied to Rorschach responses (Jrist, 1977). Although such measures are applicable with psychiatric populations, they do not seem to be effective with essentially normal adolescents. Such questionable measurement approaches seem to compound validity and reliability problems when they are used to assess relatively untested constructs. From a theoretical perspective the notion of assessing object relations as a risk factor appears quite worthy at first, but given the psychometric obstacles that goal has yet to be achieved.

One of the most interesting approaches for examining the influence and consequences of parental acceptance/rejection is the Parental Acceptance/Rejection Questionnaire (PARQ; Rohner, 1975, 1980). The PARQ is a self-report inventory designed to assess an individual's perception of parental acceptance and rejection. The three versions of the PARQ include the adult version, which measures the adult's perceptions about how he or she was treated by mother; the mother version, which assesses the way mothers currently treat their children; and the child version, which evaluates the way children feel about how their mothers treat them. On each version of the PARQ the individual is asked to respond to items on a Likert continuum, ranging from "almost always true" to "almost never true." Items cluster into four scales: Perceived Parental Warmth/Affection, Perceived Parental Hostility/Aggression, Perceived Parental Neglect/Indifference, and Perceived Parental Rejection. Reliability coefficients for the PARQ are good, while validity coefficients are modest, although with increased use of the scale the statistics are becoming more impressive. Adolescents who show an imbalance between low warmth and affection scores and high scores on the other PARQ scales should be considered at risk for interpersonal adjustment problems. One of the advantages of the PARQ is that its items are phrased in terms of maternal *behavior* instead of maternal *attitudes*.

Evidence of a low level of ego development, immature object relations, and feelings of rejection on the PARQ profile does not always indicate that a particular teenager is sexually active or that she does not use birth control or that she will become pregnant and carry the baby to term; however, such a profile does signify increased risk for any of these outcomes. Instruments such as the PARQ that are capable of isolating vulnerability factors should be considered when planning primary prevention and/or early intervention programs for adolescents at risk for early pregnancy. In addition to the psychometric approaches discussed, clinical interview and "clinical judgment" should not be overlooked as valuable adjuncts to complete the diagnostic process.

Homosexuality

The most commonly applied definitions describe homosexuality as a phenomenon arising in early childhood characterized by emotional attachments and erotic fantasies directed toward individuals of the same gender. Typically, homosexual responsiveness culminates in overt sexual expression, but this does not preclude heterosexual experiences (Marmor, 1980; Saghir & Robins, 1980). Because of the associated stigma, it is impossible to ascertain accurately what proportion of the population is homosexual. Incidence figures suggest that at least 25% of American men have had a significant homosexual experience between age 16 and 55, 10% have been predominantly homosexual for at least 3 years, and 4% remain homosexual throughout their lives (Ross-Reynolds & Hardy, 1985). Current data suggest that approximately 185 of every 500 male high-school-age adolescents have experienced at least one homosexual act resulting in orgasm.

Although theories of homosexuality abound in the literature, no strong empirical evidence unequivocally supports one theory or another. Causality has been attributed typically to disturbed parent/child relationships (Hooker, 1969), biological factors (Hendryx, 1980), and genetic origins (Money, 1980). Despite these theories, personality assessment research has not provided a standard personality profile useful in distinguishing male homosexuals from heterosexuals; they may be no less masculine in appearance, nor may they appear to engage in any more feminine activity while growing up than their heterosexual counterparts (Saghir & Robins, 1980).

"Coming out" among adolescent homosexuals is marked by individuals identifying themselves as gay, becoming attracted to and sexually interested in partners of the same sex (McDonald, 1982). On the average, boys are first aware of same-gender attraction at age 13 and may have their first homosexual experience between ages 13-15. However, most do not label themselves as homosexual until ages 19-21. Sexual awakening for the homosexual adolescent in a heterosexual culture can prove traumatic, and he or she must cope with fear of discovery, isolation, guilt, and a sense of stigma.

Several general considerations arise when homosexuality is an assessment issue. The first, problem definition, involves determining whether the homosexuality itself actually comprises the presenting problem for a particular adolescent. The second issue involves defining the personal meaning of homosexuality for the adolescent. Is the homosexuality fantasized, the result of a single isolated same-sex experience, or is it an integral part of the individual's identity? The *Diagnostic and Statistical Manual of Mental Disorders* (DSM-III; American Psychiatric Association, 1980) distinguishes ego-syntonic from ego-dystonic homosexuality. *Ego-dystonic homosexuality* is a term reserved for those homosexuals for whom heterosexual arousal is persistently absent or weak and who state that the unwanted homosexual arousal is a persistent source of distress. On the other hand, *ego-syntonic homosexuality* is not considered a psychopathology according to DSM-III and refers to individuals who wish to remain homosexual. Having ascertained the meaning homosexuality has for the adolescent, the next step is to determine its integration into the individual's self-concept. The state of the art is such that specific assessment instruments have not been developed to assess whether or not an individual is "truly" homosexual. Furthermore, it would be absurd to think that such an instrument would be meaningful. As in any other area of development, some individuals will adjust successfully and others will not (Hart, 1984).

How the professional reacts to the adolescent who may have questions and concerns about sexual preference is of critical importance, because homosexuality is perceived as a taboo topic in many sectors of society. Using an experimental questionnaire, Scherma (1984) ascertained that a large percentage of urban school psychologists held what seemed to be myths about homosexuality. Although those in the helping professions may express generally liberal attitudes, many in the Scherma study reported that they would feel uncomfortable treating a 17-year-old homosexual, primarily because of a lack of knowledge in treatment procedures, but also because of questions regarding their own attitudes about homosexuality. What becomes clear is that before clinicians can begin to deal with issues of homosexuality with clients, they need to clarify their own subjective feelings about the topic. What is most important to assess is not whether a certain adolescent is homosexual or heterosexual, but rather how well and to what extent that individual has adjusted to his or her sex-role choice, regardless of the clinician's personal views about homosexuality. Assessment techniques that focus on self-esteem, defensive strategies, needs, and conflicts are most effective in evaluating the individual's adjustment.

Sexual Abuse

Statistics indicate that females are more likely to be victims of sexual abuse while males are more likely to be the offenders. Most abuse is not reported, but recent surveys have revealed that one out of four girls under the age of 14 has been sexually molested in some way (Walker, 1981). It is not usually the "devious stranger" who victimizes adolescents; instead, sexual abusers are often relatives or family friends. Although males are the most common abusers, females may be involved as well. Male victims, however, often are abused in a homosexual context. Initial research suggests that the more the male parent is involved in the parenting process, the less likely that sexual abuse will occur. The children most vulnerable to sexual abuse are females who reside in homes (a) with no stable male figures, (b) where there are frequent "visitors," and (c) where they as well as the mother are viewed as sexual objects.

There are no standardized instruments to assess whether an adolescent has been sexually abused. Some attempts have been made to develop TAT-like pictures to help victims discuss their painful experiences, although clinical interview and behavior observation probably still represent the best approach. Warning signals that might emerge through observation and interview (and sometimes through indicators on a psychological battery) include demonstrating undue dependency on and clinging to trusted guardians. Victims also may become school phobic, socially withdrawn, and isolated, may cut themselves off from an existing peer group network, and may experience sleep disturbances.

Depending on the level of trauma experienced as a result of the abuse, adolescents may be at risk to develop depressive and suicidal tendencies. When such symptoms appear with a sudden onset and cannot be traced to a readily known cause, sexual abuse might be considered as one hypothesis. When more chronic abuse is prevalent, there may be marked learning problems in school, and sometimes the adolescent will engage in delinquent behavior, seemingly without any fear of the consequences. These symptoms suggest the possibility of sexual abuse only when there has been no prior evidence of such behavior patterns.

The ability to survive the unhealthy consequences of such stress is dependent on a number of issues, all of which must be evaluated. The adolescent's intrapsychic resources are critical, as is available social support. There is nothing more devastating than having suffered from sexual abuse and then being blamed for provoking the assault. Therefore, it is critical that the psychological examiner not only ascertain whether an adolescent is suffering from sexual abuse, but also how he or she has integrated the experience psychologically and what social supports are available in order to help the individual deal with the experience in the most adaptive way. Further, in most states psychologists are legally required to report suspected cases of sexual abuse. Psychologists should be aware of their legal and ethical obligations in cases of sexual abuse, acting both in accordance with the requirements of state law as well as in the best interest of the child.

CASE STUDIES

In order to illustrate the potential difficulties in adjusting to sexuality and sexual development, two cases are presented with suggested evaluation strategies.

George

16-year-old George was having difficulty with his school work and was thinking about dropping out of school. His homeroom teacher referred him to the school psychologist, as he appeared to be quite bright but extremely troubled. Soon after the initial interview with the psychologist, George began staying away from school. When his parents were questioned by the school authorities, they could not understand what was going on. Subsequently it was discovered that George had started carrying a gun illegally; in fact, he was arrested for illegal possession of a firearm and for threatening a 60-year-old man with it.

As part of the routine court hearing, George was given a complete psychological battery. What began to unfold was that much of George's behavior was an attempt to camouflage an attraction to other boys. He was terrified of his homosexual feelings, but could not stop himself from thinking about certain boys. His greatest fear was that he would lose control and try to touch another boy. This information began to emerge in a clinical interview as well as through projective tests. All of his responses were brief and unelaborated.

Although his assessed intelligence was high, these feelings and his confused reaction to them had spurred George's school learning difficulties. As he stayed away from school more and more, he began to be suspicious of men, thinking that he might be attacked by them. It was at this time that George purchased an illegal gun and lost all objectivity and judgment about others. However, he also was seeking a way of asking for help and control.

Through a clinical interview and by asking retrospective questions, it became clear that George was at risk as he entered adolescence. He described himself as a shy child, with few friends and a rich fantasy life, which Rorschach material subsequently substantiated. The Piers-Harris Self-Concept Scale showed that George had a poor sense of himself in all areas. When he reached sexual maturity, his battle against his homosexual feelings collapsed, and he spent most of his time at home with his parents and his stamp collection. At home his difficulties went unnoticed, and his parents were unaware that he was displaying atypical adolescent behavior patterns. The first real sign of George's pain and panic was displayed in school.

George's problem illustrates the problem whereby sex-role identity and homosexual panic may become confounded with the onset of puberty. In future sessions, the examiner discovered that the sexual difficulty and confusion that George experienced were having major impacts on other domains of functioning, including his school work and interpersonal relationships. George reported he felt isolated from his peer group and felt as if he could not talk to anyone. As a result of the psychological assessment, George's parents and teachers were made more aware of his isolation so that appropriate interventions could be developed. A program in sex education was constructed to deal with George's difficulties, and his parents became more sensitive to his needs.

Lisa

Lisa, a 17-year-old female, was recommended to the school psychologist by her teacher, who indicated that although she participated in class and appeared motivated, she seemed happy one day and quite upset the next. The teacher indicated that Lisa's mood swings were more extreme than the typical teenager's. She also stayed away from school two or three days at a time. Lisa did not share her feelings, but was overheard saying to a classmate that she didn't care if she were dead.

Lisa presented herself to the psychologist as a very depressed person. She answered questions with a single word, if at all, and appeared to be on the verge of tears. When her parents were interviewed, they expressed concern but thought she might outgrow it, as "all adolescents feel depressed." Through clinical interview, projectives, and body image and self-concept scales, the following information was revealed.

Lisa said she had been happy up until the age of 14, and then "she just couldn't be bothered getting out of bed in the morning." Shortly before her 14th birthday she began to menstruate, and she hated her body for producing "dirty blood." She began to feel that she was overweight, not as pretty as her friends, and that nobody would ever like her. At 15 she had intercourse with her boyfriend, which did not improve her negative self-concept. After sex proved to be no "cure," and in fact made her feel "dirtier," she became extremely depressed and began talking about suicide. Lisa did not have a peer group or friend to talk with and felt that her parents did not take her feelings seriously. Although she did not experience sexual desire, she agreed to intercourse thinking it would make her boyfriend love her more and prove to her that she was "normal." By comparing Lisa's responses to those of other teenagers, it was clear that she saw herself as "abnormal."

Lisa's problems had culminated with the onset of puberty. Based on the results of psychological assessment, it was clear that Lisa used her sexuality in an attempt to alleviate her distress over menstruation and to gain affection and normality. However, for her the solution, sexual intercourse, also became part of the problem. Through interviewing mother and daughter together, it became apparent that her relationship with her mother was extremely complex. As long as Lisa saw herself as a child, her mother saw her as "clean and good." Once she began to menstruate and have "the curse" as her mother referred to it, she became "dirty" and "bad," as well as unlovable. Through identifying with her mother, Lisa developed a fear of femininity and ensuing womanhood. The examiner was able to use this assessment information to develop an appropriate treatment plan to strengthen Lisa's self-esteem, clarify her relationship with her mother, and increase her understanding of menarche, thereby enabling a successful adjustment to this biological change.

SUMMARY

There are many who feel that the sexual revolution has altered the entire fabric of society and created the "death of innocence" (Janus, 1981). The underlying premise is that there are no parameters for acceptable behavior remaining and that those relaxed standards can have tragic consequences for the adolescent. There is no question that sexuality and knowledge about sexual issues are having an impact on children at increasingly earlier ages. Instead of playing childhood games, many children are playing sexual games, long before they are ready for them. Clinicians cannot avoid these issues and their consequences.

Adolescents in general, by virtue of theoretical, empirical, and clinical data, can be viewed as an "at risk" population. However, not all adolescents are vulnerable and susceptible. Vulnerability is dependent on the interaction of a number of factors. A multifactorial approach is critical to the assessment of adolescent sexuality, a vital component of the teenager's adjustment. Good assessment should evaluate the individual based on the integration of three primary dimensions: 1) the personal, which includes developmental history, intrapsychic and personality factors, and physical factors; 2) the interpersonal, which includes peer group involvement, familial relationships, and perception of the family structure; and 3) social-contextual, which includes social supports, networks, and demographics. The earlier an adolescent is identified as having problems adjusting physically and sexually, the more likely one can intervene and enable that individual to move on to a healthy, sexually well-adjusted adulthood.

REFERENCES

Alan Guttmacher Institute. (1981). *Teen pregnancy: The problem that won't go away.* New York: Author.

American Psychiatric Association. (1980). *Diagnostic and statistical manual of mental disorders* (3rd ed.). Washington, DC: Author.

Anthony, J. (1969). The reactions of adults to adolescents and their behavior. In G. Kaplan & S. Lebovic (Eds.), *Adolescence: Psychosocial perspectives* (pp. 218-235). New York: Basic.

Askevold, F. (1975). Measuring body image: Preliminary report on a new method. *Psychotherapy, Psychosomatics, 26,* 71-77.

Bem, S. L. (1981). Gender schema theory: A cognitive account of sex-typing. *Psychological Review, 88,* 354-364.

Bergen, V. A. (1979). Relationship of early father absence on sexual attitudes and self-concept of adult women. *Dissertation Abstracts International, 41,* 5528B-5529B.

Berzins, J. I., Welling, M. A., & Wetter, R. E. (1978). A new measure of psychological androgyny based on the Personality Research Form. *Journal of Consulting and Clinical Psychology, 46,* 126-138.

Blos, P. (1962). *On adolescence.* New York: Free Press.

Coleman, J. (1980). *The nature of adolescence.* New York: Methuen.

Conger, J. J., & Petersen, A. C. (1984). *Adolescence & youth* (3rd ed.) New York: Harper & Row.

Dudley, H. K., Jr., Craig, E. M., & Mason, J. M. (1981). The measurement of adolescent personality dimensions—The MMPI and the Offer Self-Image Questionnaire for Adolescents. *Adolescence, 16,* 453-469.

Eysenck, H. J. (1970). Personality and attitudes to sex: A factoral study. *Personality, 4,* 355-377.

Finkel, M. L., & Finkel, D. J. (1975). Sexual and contraceptive knowledge, attitudes and behavior of male adolescents. *Family Planning Perspectives, 7,* 256-260.

Fischman, S. H. (1977). Delivery or abortion in inner-city adolescents. *American Journal of Orthopsychiatry, 47,* 127-133.

Furstenberg, F. F. (1976). *Unplanned parenthood: The social consequences of teenage child bearing.* New York: Free Press.

Gartner, A. F. (1985). Countertransference issues in the psychotherapy of adolescents. *Child and Adolescent Psychotherapy, 2*(3), 187-196.

Gayton, W. F., Flava, G. F., Ozman, K. L., & Tavormina, J. (1977). A comparison of the Bem Sex-Role Inventory with the PRF ANDRO Scale. *Journal of Personality Assessment, 41,* 6.

Goldstein, G., & Hersen, A. R. (1984). *Handbook of psychological assessment.* New York: Pergamon.

Greenman, A. M. (1985). *Menarche—Its developmental consequences for the female self.* Unpublished doctoral dissertation, Ferkauf Graduate School, New York.

Groth-Marnat, G. (1984). *Handbook of psychological assessment.* New York: Van Nostrand Reinhold.

Hart, J. (1984). *So you're attracted to the same sex.* Middlesex, England: Penguin.

Hass, A. (1979). *Teenage sexuality: A survey of teenage sexual behavior.* New York: Macmillan.

Hendryx, W. W. (1980). In defense of the homosexual teacher. *Viewpoints in Teaching and Learning, 56,* 74-84.

Hooker, E. (1969). Parental relationships and male homosexuality in patient and non-patient samples. *Journal of Consulting and Clinical Psychology, 33,* 140-142.

Janus, S. (1981). *The death of innocence.* New York: Wm. Morrow.

Jrist, J. (1977). The Rorschach test and the assessment of object relations. *Journal of Personality Assessment, 41*(1), 3-9.

Kanter, J. F., & Zelnik, M. (1972). Sexual experience of young unmarried women in the United States. *Family Planning Perspectives, 4,* 9-18.

Katz, K., & Kaufman, J. (1985). *Sexual experiences: A retrospective survey of college women.* Unpublished manuscript.

Kaufman, J. (1983, March). *The standard and not so standard deviations of adolescence.* Paper presented at the annual convention of the National Association of School Psychologists, Philadelphia.

Kaufman, J. (in press). *Assessment and intervention with adolescents.* Hillsdale, NJ: Lawrence Erlbaum.

Kiestenbaum, C. J. (1979). Current sexual attitudes, societal pressure and the middle class adolescent girl. In S. C. Feinstein & P. L. Giovacchini (Eds.), *Adolescent psychiatry* (Vol. 7, pp. 146-156). Chicago: University of Chicago Press.

Kinsey, A. C., Pomeroy, W. B., & Martin, C. E. (1948). *Sexual behavior in males.* Philadelphia: Saunders.

Levenkron, S. (1982). *Treating and overcoming anorexia nervosa.* New York: Warner.

Loevinger, J. (1970). *Measuring ego development* (Vols. 1 & 2). San Francisco: Jossey-Bass.

Marmor, J. (1980). Overview: The multiple roots of homosexual behavior. In J. Marmor (Ed.), *Homosexual behavior* (pp. 3-22). New York: Basic.

McAnarney, E. R., & Schreider, C. (1984). *Identifying social and psychological antecedents of adolescent pregnancy.* New York: W. T. Grant Foundation.

McDonald, G. J. (1982). Individual differences in the coming out process for gay men: Implications for theoretical models. *Journal of Homosexuality, 8,* 47-60.

Miller, P., & Simon, W. (1974). Adolescent behavior: Context and shape. *Social Problems, 22,* 58-76.

Money, J. (1980). Genetic and chromosomal aspects of homosexual etiology. In J. Marmor (Ed.), *Homosexual behavior* (pp. 59-72). New York: Basic.

Offer, D., Ostrov, E., & Howard, K. (1981a). *The adolescent: A psychological self-portrait.* New York: Basic.

Offer, D., Ostrov, E., & Howard, K. (1981b). *The Offer Self-Image Questionnaire for Adolescents: A manual.* Chicago: Michael Reese Hospital.

Rohner, R. (1976). *They love me, they love me not: A world-wide study of parental acceptance-rejection.* New Haven, CT: HRAF.

Rohner, R. (1980). *Handbook of the study of parental acceptance and rejection.* Storrs, CT: Center for Study of Parental Acceptance and Rejection.

Ross-Reynolds, G., & Hardy, B. S. (1985). Crisis counseling for disparate adolescent sexual dilemmas: Pregnancy and homosexuality. *School Psychology Review, 14*(3), 300-312.

Saghir, M. T., & Robins, E. (1980). Clinical aspects of female homosexuality. In J. Marmor (Ed.), *Homosexual behavior* (pp. 280-295). New York: Basic.

Scherma, R. (1984). *Homosexuality and the homosexual adolescent: Current attitudes and beliefs of school psychologists and school psychologists in training.* Unpublished Psy.D. project, Ferkauf Graduate School, New York.

Secord, P. F., & Jourard, S. M. (1953). The appraisal of body cathexis: Body cathexis and self. *Journal of Consulting Psychology, 17,* 343-347.

Sondheimer, A. (1982). Mid-adolescent sexual concerns. In S. C. Feinstein, J. G. Looney, A. Z. Schwartzberg, & A. D. Sorosky (Eds.), *Adolescent psychiatry* (Vol. 10, pp. 208-227). Chicago: University of Chicago Press.

Spence, J. T., & Helmreich, R. L. (1978). *Masculinity and femininity.* Austin: University of Texas Press.

Spence, J. T., & Helmreich, R. L. (1980). Masculine instrumentality and feminine expressiveness: Their relationships with sex-role attitudes and behaviors. *Psychology of Women Quarterly, 15,* 147-163.

Von der Ahe, C. V. (1969). The unwed teenage mother. *American Journal of Obstetrics-Gynecology, 104,* 279-287.

Walker, L. E. (1981). Battered women: Sex roles and clinical issues. *Professional Psychology, 12*(1), 81-91.

Waters, J. L. (1969). Pregnancy in young adolescents, a syndrome of failure. *Southern Medical Journal, 62,* 655-658.

Wylie, R. C. (1961). *The self-concept: A critical survey of the research literature.* Lincoln, NE: University of Nebraska Press.

Zelnick, M., & Kanter, J. F. (1977). Sexual and contraceptive experience of young unmarried women in the United States, 1976 and 1971. *Family Planning Perspectives, 9,* 55-71.

7

Assessment of Eating Disorders in Adolescence

JOAN P. CESARI, PH.D.

The appearance of eating disorders in adolescents is in no way a recent phenomenon. One of the earliest clinical descriptions of anorexia nervosa was presented in 1689 by Dr. Richard Morton, in which a 17-year-old girl suffering from "nervous consumption" was described by Dr. Morton as ". . . (like a Skeleton only clad with skin) yet there was no fever, but on the contrary, a coldness of the whole Body . . ." (Lucas, 1981, p. 255). Similarly, reports of binge eating and purging stem from as far back in history as the Roman Empire.

The increased attention directed to eating disorders in the last decade has been prompted by alarming estimates of their prevalance in the United States. Obesity is estimated to affect 15-30% of adolescents and increases with age (Brownell & Stunkard, 1978; Canning & Mayer, 1966). Further, Stunkard and Burt (1967) have found that childhood obesity, if not controlled by the end of adolescence, increases the odds of adult obesity by 28 to 1. Although large-scale epidemiological studies are not available, anorexia nervosa is estimated to involve 1-5% of girls ages 10 to 20, and the incidence of bulimia (binge-purge syndrome) has been estimated at 5-30% of adolescent and young adult females. Because all eating disorders occur in females more often than in males, the feminine gender will be used to identify individuals discussed in this chapter. It is difficult to determine whether the actual incidence of eating disorders such as anorexia nervosa or bulimia is increasing or if, instead, the increased attention of helping professionals and the media fosters a more informed, less threatening environment that is conducive to reports of eating disorders.

Whatever the reason, public awareness and concern in this area have risen. Today, almost everyone who works with adolescents will encounter the issue of eating disorders at some point; consequently, a strong argument can be made for the necessity of synthesized knowledge in assessing and working with these disorders in a variety of settings.

The goal of this chapter is to provide useful background knowledge about eating disorders and practical assessment procedures for screening, diagnosis, and treatment intervention planning. Theories of etiology will be briefly discussed, but the reader interested in therapeutic intervention strategies beyond assessment will find excellent reviews in Neuman and Halvorson (1983), Mitchell (1985), Coates and Thoreson (1978), and Hawkins, Fremouw, and Clement (1984).

147

DEFINITIONS AND CONCEPTUAL ISSUES

The most recent *Diagnostic and Statistical Manual of Mental Disorders* (DSM-III; American Psychiatric Association, 1980) defines anorexia nervosa and bulimia as separate entities. Although these are not the only definitions employed to diagnose and describe eating disorders, they are used widely in research and applied settings.

The DSM-III lists the following diagnostic criteria for anorexia nervosa:

A. Intense fear of becoming obese, which does not diminish as weight loss progresses.
B. Disturbance of body image, e.g., claiming to "feel fat" even when emaciated.
C. Weight loss of at least 25% of original body weight or, if under 18 years of age, weight loss from original body weight plus projected weight gain expected from growth charts may be combined to make the 25%.
D. Refusal to maintain body weight over a minimal normal weight for age and height.
E. No known physical illness that would account for the weight loss. (p. 69)

This definition is considered an improvement over earlier diagnostic criteria such as Feighner's (Feighner et al., 1972), which accounted for anorexia nervosa only if the onset occurred prior to age 25, but it has been criticized for its exclusion of amenorrhea (Mitchell, 1985). Amenorrhea, the cessation of the menstrual cycle, is a frequent symptom of anorexia nervosa and that which is often the first sign of anorexia for physicians or parents. The exclusion of amenorrhea in the DSM-III criteria appears to ignore the importance of this symptom for diagnostic purposes.

The DSM-III diagnostic criteria for bulimia are:

A. Recurrent episodes of binge eating (rapid consumption of a large amount of food in a discrete period of time, usually less than two hours).
B. At least three of the following:
    1. consumption of high-caloric, easily ingested food during a binge
    2. inconspicuous eating during a binge
    3. termination of such eating episodes by abdominal pain, sleep, social interruption, or self-induced vomiting
    4. repeated attempts to lose weight by severely restrictive diets, self-induced vomiting, or use of cathartics or diuretics
    5. frequent weight fluctuations greater than ten pounds due to alternated binges and fasts
C. Awareness that eating pattern is abnormal and fear of not being able to stop eating voluntarily.
D. Depressed mood and self-deprecating thoughts following eating binges.
E. The bulimic episodes are not due to Anorexia Nervosa or any known physical disorder. (pp. 70-71)

It is important to note that bulimia, as defined by DSM-III criteria, does not automatically include purging (e.g., vomiting, laxative abuse). This is important because the term *bulimia* and the phrase *binge-purge syndrome* have become almost synonymous, and individuals who "merely" binge are at risk of being considered less serious if not viewed as meeting the diagnostic criteria of bulimia.

A note on use of the term *binge* is indicated. Bingeing has become something of a catch phrase in our society, and it is not uncommon to hear all sorts of people confess to a "binge" when they have eaten more than they wish they had. The term has replaced popular phrases such as "pigging out" or "stuffing your face." The DSM-III criteria do not operationalize the phrase "rapid consumption of a large amount of food." Polivy, Herman, Olmsted, and Jazwinski (1984) discriminate between binge eating and overeating by defining a binge as a "truly prodigious consumption of food" that goes beyond hunger and satiation and has a compulsive quality (p. 105). Attempts at describing binges by caloric intake (Mitchell, Pyle, & Eckert, 1981) indicate a range of 1,200-11,500 calories per binge, with a few individuals consuming as many as 50,000 calories per day. Dykens (1982) lists typical binges reported by bulimic individuals. In 30 minutes to an hour, one woman consumed 18 doughnuts, a double hamburger, a portion of french fries, a chocolate shake, three scoops of ice cream, and one package of snack cakes. Another individual ate six or seven chocolate bars and a large pizza in 15-20 minutes (Dykens, 1982). Despite these efforts at clarifying what constitutes a binge, the operational definitions of terms such as *large amount of food* and *rapid consumption* are still left open to individual interpretation.

The identification and definitions of eating disorders become even more confused when one is faced with the following controversy. Some believe that anorexia nervosa and bulimia are discrete phenomena under the global heading of eating disorders. This position is reflected in the segregation of the DSM-III diagnostic criteria. Others, such as Hamilton, Gelwick, and Meade (1984), caution against fostering an arbitrary dichotomy between anorexia nervosa and bulimia until more is known of the interrelationship between the two disorders. Further, researchers warn that there may be specific subtypes and/or heterogeneity among those with anorexia nervosa (Eckert, 1985) and bulimia (Hamilton et al., 1984).

Unlike anorexia nervosa and bulimia, obesity is not considered a mental disorder; hence, it is not included in the DSM-III diagnostic criteria. Rather, obesity is defined more appropriately as a medical or metabolic issue, not a psychological disorder (Brewerton, Heffernan, & Rosenthal, 1986). Obesity is an "excessive amount of subcutaneous, nonessential fat" (Abramson, 1977, p. 7), which is usually determined when an individual's body weight exceeds height/weight standards by 10-20%. There are four categories of obesity using these standards: obese (10% or more over ideal recommended weight), mildly obese (10-29% overweight), moderately obese (30-49% overweight), and severely obese (50% or more overweight). Other methods for identifying obesity range from simple self-identified dissatisfaction with body weight (Kelly & Patten, 1985) to the measurement of percent of body fat with sophisticated laboratory instruments. While the self-identified dissatisfaction with body weight raises some interesting issues to be discussed later, the height/weight standard definition of obesity is the most commonly used identifier.

There has been some controversy regarding the height/weight standards used to determine ideal recommended weight. The most commonly used of these have been developed from insurance company data (Metropolitan Life Insurance Company, 1959), which provides a 10-pound range of ideal weight according to height, gender, and body frame size. However, in 1983, the Metropolitan Life Insurance Company issued new charts, which they believed provided more realistic weight ranges based on health-related data. These new charts increased the recommended weight ranges 2-12 pounds over the 1959 standards. Although some have hailed the newer standards as a more accurate reflection of reasonable ideal body weights, others have criticized the newer data as too tolerant of our overweight society and urge a return to the 1959 data (American Heart Association, 1983). This controversy is particularly relevant for the adolescent population, whose self-selected ideal weights may be grossly underestimated (Kelly & Patten, 1985) and who may be confused by conflicting standards.

Whether all three eating disorders are discrete phenomena or manifestations of the same behaviors that can be placed on a continuum of severity is impossible to answer with our current knowledge. Certainly, the similarities in abuse of food, abuse of body, compulsions, and irrational beliefs are difficult to ignore, but the differences are readily apparent as well, including family history information, personality characteristics, and the course of the disorders. This chapter will consider anorexia nervosa, bulimia, and obesity separately, with the knowledge that future insight may alter this perspective.

The current state of knowledge itself in this area poses another issue. The practitioner must look hard to find practical, useful information that is not geared toward research strategies. Although the uses of assessment instrumentation in eating disorders cannot be covered exhaustively here, the most widely recognized and utilized procedures will be applied to the most commonly found situations in which assessment can benefit the client and the professional.

ANOREXIA NERVOSA

Etiology

There are diverse theories about the causes of anorexia nervosa. Some experts stress the psychodynamic factors, requiring both an understanding of the forces that motivate an individual and attention to the reciprocal relationship between an individual and her environment (Josephson, 1985). In this vein, Strober (1981) describes recent opinion that anorexia nervosa is a combination of some pre-existing psychological disability and a psychological compensation aimed at suppressing maturational (pubertal) changes. The psychodynamic explanation that anorexia nervosa represents the individual's unconscious attempts to deny womanhood has been a popular and enduring theory in this area.

Other psychodynamic theories have focused on the families of girls with anorexia nervosa. Bemis's (1979) review of current approaches in the field maintains that most inquiries into this area noted a relatively high incidence of psychoneurotic disturbances in the family, a peculiar or indifferent relationship between mothers and daughters, and fathers who were passive and ineffectual. Josephson (1985) describes anorexic families as ones that suppress individuals' self-interest, thereby stunting psychological development in young adults. This stunting, according to Josephson, could foster childlike, immature reactions such as anorexia nervosa.

Others have described a link between anorexia nervosa and depression (Cantwell, Sturzenberger, Burroughs, Salkin, & Green, 1977). It is difficult to tell if the relationship is casual, but at least one article has decried this view as merely more understandable and more manageable for physicians, who might otherwise be uncomfortable with a diagnosis of anorexia nervosa (Altschuler & Weiner, 1985).

Theories on anorexia nervosa have also focused on causes external to the individual. Damlouji and Ferguson (1985) suggest that anorexia nervosa can be secondary to real or perceived physical distortion, and may sometimes be caused by actual physical distortion. This contention was based on their case study of several women who developed anorexia nervosa after being involved in accidents that caused physical injury (distortion). The distinction then between real and perceived physical or cosmetic deficits may be of little importance to the development of anorexia nervosa. Another external cause that has been postulated is misinformation about proper dietary practices. Smead (1983) pointed out that many young women may have incorrect or incomplete information about normal eating and dieting practices. She also states:

> Perhaps the starting point for anorexia is not within the individual but the diet. Perhaps over-controlled and inappropriated [*sic*] food intake may produce pathology in both strong and weak individuals. (p. 24)

Much attention has been given to the effect of societal and cultural emphases on thinness and female attractiveness and their relationship to anorexia nervosa. Body image is the way in which people view and judge their physical selves. Having a positive body image often depends on how closely one believes her body resembles the current societal norm. Garner, Garfinkel, Schwartz, and Thompson (1980) studied the steady metamorphosis in *Playboy* magazine centerfolds and Miss America contestants. During the period of 1959-1978, they found the weight of the *Playboy* models decreased significantly and that Miss America contestants had an average weight decrease of .28 pounds per year, with an average .37 pounds per year decline for the contest winners. Chernin (1981) and Boskind-White (1983) are excellent resources describing the relationship between America's over-valuation of thinness and the occurrence of eating disorders among our young, peer-conscious adolescents.

Incidence

The incidence of anorexia nervosa has been estimated at anywhere from 1 to 5% of the adolescent population, with one study indicating that as many as 10% of the female adolescent population could be considered mildly anorexic (Nylander, 1971). While estimates vary, the number of cases reported each year is increasing (Mitchell, 1985). The Anorexia Nervosa and Related Eating Disorders Organization (ANRED; Andersen, 1981) predicts that about one in every 100 females ages 12-18 is anorexic; Button and Whitehouse (1981) reported a 6.3% incidence rate in their college population. Some researchers are attempting to identify subgroups at risk of developing anorexia nervosa, such as dance and theater majors (Joseph, Wood, & Goldberg, 1982).

Assessment Procedures

Psychological assessment in any area can be categorized into at least two types: informal and formal. Informal assessment techniques in the area of eating disorders include interviewing, response to interviewing, and observational techniques. Formal assessment techniques include 1) standardized instruments designed specifically for eating-disordered individuals; 2) standardized instruments for a broader population that address eating issues rather than clinical disorders; and 3) standardized instruments designed for use in other areas, but applicable to eating disorders as well. Discussion follows of informal and formal assessment techniques as they apply to screening, differential diagnosis, and treatment intervention planning.

Screening. Professionals who come into contact with adolescents are apt to wonder how one determines who suffers from anorexia nervosa and who is at risk for developing this disorder. The appropriate informal assessment techniques are likely to be indirect, as few girls with anorexia nervosa will respond to direct interviewing techniques. Romeo (1984) lists several areas in which informal, observational techniques would be helpful. He points out that, unlike normal teenagers who complain about having to diet or lose weight, the anorexic develops an unusual eagerness to talk about food and diet, also developing an interest in solitary physical exercise that becomes ritualistic and compulsive. The once-compliant individual becomes negativistic and, when it is commented on, she will deny her thinness.

Heron and Leheup (1984) suggest that observational cues also stem from a perfectionistic attitude and that more cases of anorexia nervosa can be found in families that are close-knit, have few external stressors, and profess a high degree of exclusivity. Leon (1984) warns that athletes who restrict their food intake may be indistinguishable from individuals who use athletics and food restriction compulsively to maintain body image; this suggests that sensitivity to athletes who may be at risk of developing an eating disorder is warranted. All of these characteristics can be used as informal screening cues for anorexia nervosa.

Formal assessment techniques for screening anorexia nervosa will most likely be applied in the school setting, where groups can be evaluated with relative ease. The most logical screening method in such a situation is an instrument designed to distinguish between anorexia nervosa and normal eating habits and body image. Obviously, such instruments also can be used in settings other than school, such as mental health centers. Two such instruments can be used in mass or individual screenings: the Eating Disorder Inventory (EDI) and the Eating Attitudes Test (EAT; Garner & Garfinkel, 1979).

A 64-item self-report inventory, the EDI was developed to tap the psychological dimensions of eating disorders, not just the behavioral dimensions. It provides normed scores on eight subscales: Drive for Thinness, Bulimia, Body Dissatisfaction, Ineffectiveness, Perfectionism, Interpersonal Distrust, Interoceptive Awareness, and Maturity Fears. Normative data are reported for anorexia nervosa patients, female college students, female high school students, and male college students. Garner and Olmsted (1984) suggest that the EDI may be used to identify individuals who are weight preoccupied (hence, maybe eating disordered) by noting elevations on the Drive for Thinness, Bulimia, and Body Dissatisfaction subscales. Elevations on all eight scales may indicate anorexia nervosa.

The EAT is a 40-item self-report measure designed to differentiate females with anorexia nervosa from those of normal weight and those who are overweight. This assessment serves as a good screening device to detect attitudes and symptoms of anorexia. Garner and Garfinkel (1979) specify that a score of 30 or more on the EAT constitutes anorexia nervosa. Unfortunately, both the EDI and the EAT are subject to faking, and without clear instructions regarding the intent of the mass screening instrument, students with anorexia nervosa would probably respond with response distortion, uncooperation, and some hostility.

Broad measures of adjustment may be employed as indirect screening measures of eating disorders. Such personality tests or adjustment measures are, to some extent, more imprecise than either the EDI or the EAT, but they are less intrusive and less subject to faking. Strober (1981) used the High School Personality Questionnaire to discriminate anorexia nervosa and affective disorders and found that students with anorexia nervosa scored in a pattern toward greater regulatory control over emotions on scales C (affected by feelings), G (conscientiousness), O (apprehensive), and Q3 (self-controlling). These students also indicated higher social conformity and anxiety. Using the Devereux Adolescent Behavior Rating Scale, Colligan, Ferdinande, and Rasmussen (1984) found that individuals with anorexia nervosa displayed less heterosexual interest, more timidity, more physical inferiority, and more ability to delay gratification. Furthermore, results from a study using a symbol-digit paired-associates learning test (Witt, Ryan, & Hsu, 1985) indicate that individuals with anorexia nervosa can be distinguished by a deficit in learning ability, but cannot be distinguished from others via measures of attention, immediate or delayed visual memory, or psychomotor ability. This result would indicate that a learning disability can be viewed as a signal to screen for a possible eating disorder, but learning disabilities cannot be concluded to cause anorexia.

Further research may identify other unobtrusive, reliable screening measures that are not susceptible to faking. Until such time, however, the best available formal screening mechanisms are those, such as the EAT and the EDI, that are specifically designed to assess eating disorders. In addition, careful observation of changes in an individual's appearance and demeanor provides good clues regarding the development of anorexia nervosa. Physical changes include weight loss and preoccupation with appearance. In later stages of anorexia, weight loss is accompanied by some hair loss on the head, growth of fine body hair on torso and extremities, chronic fatigue and, paradoxically, vigorous exercising. Emotional changes include withdrawal from others, sullenness or hostility, and formerly cooperative individuals perhaps becoming unreliable or irresponsible. Many individuals with anorexia become preoccupied with food, cooking, dieting, fashion magazines, and so on; these are typical adolescent female interests, which become exaggerated.

Differential diagnosis. Once an individual is suspected of having anorexia nervosa, assessment techniques can be employed to understand further the nature of the situation. First, however, it is imperative that a medical evaluation be completed to rule out the possibility of organic explanations for extreme weight loss, such as ulcers, obstructions of the digestive tract, intestinal parasites, and so on.

Informal assessment procedures in this phase usually center around interviewing techniques. Because of the inherent denial and concomitant hostility found with anorexia nervosa, interviewing the affected individual is only successful if a sufficiently trusting relationship is established. For this purpose, it is sometimes preferable to engage a trusted, respected adult of the patient's acquaintance to gather information using the DSM-III criteria. When the adolescent's cooperation cannot be obtained, it is often useful to interview others about her behavior, including peers, parents, siblings, teachers who might have the opportunity to notice physical changes (e.g., home economics or physical education instructor), and cafeteria aides.

Formal techniques for differential diagnosis commonly include using the EAT, the EDI, and the Minnesota Multiphasic Personality Inventory (MMPI). The EAT and the EDI can be used as described previously, and a one-to-one discussion of the reasons for the assessment may reduce the uncooperation, faking, or manipulation sometimes associated with taking these instruments. Further, the EDI has been used to differentiate between individuals with anorexia nervosa and those who are weight preoccupied but not clinically eating disordered. Garner, Olmsted, Polivy, and Garfinkel (1984) found that the anorexic group was best differentiated from the weight-preoccupied group by higher scores on the Ineffectiveness, Interpersonal Distrust, and Lack of Interoceptive Awareness subscales. Individuals with anorexia nervosa can be differentiated from those with bulimia by their scores on the Bulimia subscale of the EDI; individuals with anorexia generally will score within the normal range on this subscale.

Greene (1980) indicates that the MMPI, although intended primarily for adult populations, is also an appropriate instrument for use with adolescents. There appears to be agreement that individuals with anorexia nervosa elevate MMPI scales 2 (Depression) and 4 (Psychopathic Deviate) (Skoog, Andersen, & Laufer, 1984), although other studies also show an elevation of scale 8 (Schizophrenia), reflecting disordered thinking (Small et al., 1981; Verberne, 1984). The indications, then, are that the typical MMPI profile for someone with anorexia nervosa is an overall 2-4-8 profile, which is associated with individuals suffering from chronic difficulties such as hostility and resentment, often stemming from familial discord. Individuals with this profile are frequently seen as alcohol or substance abusers. They may also display excellent cognitive insight into their difficulties and express a desire to change, but the chronicity of their problems may be difficult to overcome (Greene, 1980).

The information on MMPI profiles associated with anorexia nervosa is presented as a corollary to other assessment techniques; at the present time, the MMPI alone should not be used to diagnose this disorder. In particular, the 2-4-8 profile associated with anorexia is not uncommon in normal adolescents who are experiencing age-related transitions toward autonomy from the family. The resulting tensions that accompany growth and change (often viewed as "normal adolescent rebellion") may be what is reflected on an MMPI profile. Thus, using the MMPI alone to diagnose anorexia may produce many false positives and should be used to corroborate other assessment instruments only.

Treatment planning. The range of treatment options for anorexia nervosa is enormous. Neuman and Halvorson (1983) provide an excellent discussion of professional efforts and adjunctive aids. Research in this area is just beginning to focus on identifying the most effective treatment approaches; however, when dealing with anorexia nervosa in an adolescent population, the more salient issue becomes how to elicit cooperation from the patient in order to initiate whatever treatment strategy is indicated. Romeo (1984) and Smead (1984) both discuss the reinforcing properties of anorexia nervosa; that is, being thin and dieting are socially acceptable behaviors. When the dieting becomes out of control, the denial and hostility present may seem insurmountable.

One particularly helpful informal assessment technique can be used to challenge this barrier in instigating treatment. Eckert and Labeck (1985) suggest the use of instruments such as the EAT, where high scores can be shown to the individual and used to help her acknowledge that she has a problem. They also recommend a body distortion measure for the same purpose. The Draw-A-Person projective test has been used with eating-disordered individuals, who more often left off parts of the figure they were drawing (e.g., the hands) than did control subjects (Kalliopouska, 1982). Using a projective drawing technique in conjunction with a measure like the EAT may increase the individual's understanding of her problem by giving her and the counselor a tangible, immediate, yet indirect (hence, potentially less threatening) forum for discussion.

Formal assessment procedures for treatment planning are not widely used. Many treatment strategies, however, include gathering of formal assessment data such as objective personality measures, projective personality measures, a measure of intelligence, a social history, and data on any available eating disorder measures. In addition, many treatment facilities include their own assessment measures. Much of this information will be used to chart progress through treatment. For example, Skoog et al. (1984) report that successful inpatient treatment of anorexia nervosa results in a significant decrease in MMPI scale scores on 2 (Depression) and 3 (Hysteria), and a decrease of social introversion. This decrease might be expected as a sign of increased psychological functioning following treatment. Future research aimed at defining and describing effective treatment interventions will undoubtedly spawn assessment techniques designed to identify the different types of anorexic clients who can benefit from different interventions.

BULIMIA

Etiology

The causes of bulimia (literally translated *ox hunger*) are as yet unknown. The disorder is a relatively recent addition to the psychological literature, with most information becoming available in the last five to seven years.

Psychoanalytic theories of bulimia stress overidentification with the feminine role, as opposed to the anorexic's denial of the feminine role. Others view bulimia as acting-out the fear of losing control. Swift and Letven (1984) postulate that severely bulimic women demonstrate a basic ego dysfunction and that the consequent inability to regulate internal tension results in bingeing and purging. Less is known about the familial contributions to bulimia than to anorexia nervosa (Josephson, 1985), but some have found a relationship between maternal or familial obesity and a higher incidence of bulimia (Grace, Jacobson, & Fullager, 1985). This leads to speculation about familial preoccupation with food and weight issues as a predisposition to bulimia.

The social and cultural contexts for thinness and attractiveness have also been cited as possible causes of bulimia. Smead (1984) describes how, once begun, bulimic behaviors become cyclical: restrictive dieting can trigger binge eating, and the need to vomit or purge can interfere with normal social relationships, thus the individual withdraws. Others have made a strong and controversial case for the theory that bulimic behaviors are a manifestation of biochemical imbalances of depression, asserting that these behaviors can be managed with antidepressant medication (Pope & Hudson, 1984). However, the evidence presented by Pope and Hudson is preliminary, their method of research is open to criticism, and their results are not at all convincing from a counseling standpoint.

Whatever the social, physical, or psychological causes, individuals who display bulimic behaviors also exhibit low self-esteem and fear or rejection. It has been said that food is not the primary issue for these individuals (Sugarman & Kurash, 1981); rather, the catalysts for developing and maintaining bulimic behaviors may include the individuals' misguided beliefs about themselves and their inability to control their environment. Saying that food is not the issue merely implies that dieting and weight loss are not the core factors in bulimia. Although bulimic behavior may begin as a weight-control strategy, maintenance of such self-destructive behavior is not solely determined by the desire to master food and weight loss.

Incidence

The onset of bulimia is usually somewhat later than the onset of anorexia nervosa, the former occurring in the later teenage years or early 20s and the latter usually around puberty. The incidence figures for bulimia vary somewhat, and Mitchell and Pyle (1985) caution that writers and researchers may use different definitions or terminology to refer to bulimia. Further, reliance on self-report data-gathering techniques and the focus on the college populations may combine to distort the incidence figures of bulimia in the general population. Halmi, Falk, and Schwartz (1981) found that 13-20% of a normal college population (men and women) displayed DSM-III criteria for bulimia. The national self-help organization, Anorexia Nervosa and Associated Disorders (ANAD), estimates that 20-30% of college women engage in bulimic behaviors (Neuman & Halvorson, 1983), and others have concurred (English & Papalia, 1984).

Several attempts have been made to describe the rate of bulimic behaviors in high school populations. In a study by Carter and Duncan (1984), 9% of the 421 females studied were self-induced vomiters, 89% of whom said that they would use another means of weight control if it were as effective as vomiting. Johnson, Lewis, Love, Lewis, and Stuckey (1984) reported a 4.9% incidence of bulimia in a racially and economically mixed high school population. Moss, Jennings, McFarland, and Carter (1984) used two criteria to define bulimia—those who binge only and those who binge and vomit—and reported an incidence range of 6-17% in tenth-grade girls when combining the criteria. VanThorre and Vogel (1985) tested 1,093 high school girls using the EDI and found incidence rates between 12.5-20.1%, depending on the ages of the respondents. Further, LeClair and Berkowitz (1983) point out that the inherent secrecy and few overt symptoms of bulimia could contribute to a deflated estimate of the incidence of the behavior.

Bulimia has often been considered a rich white girl's disorder, but research has shown almost no socioeconomic or racial differences (Carter & Duncan, 1984; Johnson et al., 1984; VanThorre & Vogel, 1985), and 5-10% of individuals with bulimia are males (ANAD, as cited in Neuman & Halvorson, 1983).

Assessment Procedures

It is important to note that our understanding of bulimia is so relatively new that unified practices are not yet established. Some researchers are at work at the creation of newer, improved assessment devices (e.g., Smith & Thelen, 1984); others feel that there may be utility in using combinations of better-validated instruments when attempting to assess patterns of behavior in bulimia (Hamilton et al., 1984). It is sure to be some time before professional expertise will match the growing and varied need for reasonable assessment practices in this area.

Screening. Given the estimates of incidence rates of bulimia in adolescents, it behooves professionals who work with this group to be able to screen for the presence of bulimic behavior. Informal screening through observation or interviewing is even more difficult for bulimia than it is for anorexia nervosa. Most of the physical indicators of the disorder are not readily apparent; indeed, individuals engaging in bulimic behavior are usually either of normal weight or 10-15 pounds overweight. Dental enamel erosion, brittle and discolored fingernails, and loss of hair luster may not be evidenced until the disorder is in advanced stages, and facial blemishes (due to binges on junk food) are common enough among adolescents that they do not necessarily attract attention. Bingeing and/or purging are intensely secretive, shameful behaviors for the bulimic individual, so it is difficult for others to perceive the behavioral cues that could initiate discussion.

Formal screening procedures include Hawkins and Clement's (1980) Binge Scale and the EDI. As discussed previously, using direct measures of eating disorders in a group setting may foster faking and/or distrust of the assessment. Although such measures can provide the most reliable information for screening purposes, compliance with the assessment intent may be low when anonymity cannot be guaranteed.

Some indirect formal assessment techniques that can provide warning cues in screening for bulimia include the use of measures such as the 1) Sixteen Personality Factor Questionnaire (16PF), on which low self-esteem scores are associated with bulimia (Boskind-Lodahl & White, 1978); 2) the California Psychological Inventory (CPI), on which individuals with bulimia indicate more self-doubt and are more impatient, changeable, deceitful, inattentive, and forgetful than their peers (Maceyko & Nagelberg, 1985); and 3) the Beck Depression Inventory (BDI), an especially good indirect screening device. Like the 16PF and the CPI, the Beck Depression Inventory does not diagnose or predict bulimia, but high BDI scores have been associated with the disorder (Katzman & Wolchik, 1984). One should always consider that high scorers on the Beck inventory merit at least the attention of an individual screening interview to account for the depression score.

Differential diagnosis and treatment planning. The task of discriminating bulimia from other disorders is difficult, due to the variability of criteria for determining bulimia itself (e.g., the operational definition of a binge, the similarities and differences between bulimia and anorexia nervosa, the fact that purging is not a necessary criterion to diagnose bulimia, etc.). Hamilton et al. (1984) state that "until there is agreement on a diagnosis of that term, there can be no unified research on bulimia" (p. 20). Assessment in bulimia, too, awaits such diagnostic agreement.

As with anorexia nervosa, the value of indirect assessment measures lies in the degree of "fit" between an individual's assessment profiles and those generated through research with bulimic individuals. Norman and Herzog (1983) found that bulimia is associated with an elevated 2-4 MMPI profile, much like what was reported earlier for anorexia. This profile is characteristic of someone with "poor impulse control, chronic depression, exaggerated guilt, and low tolerance for frustration" (p. 49). The relationship between bulimia and depression has been demonstrated consistently with various populations and measures. Using a battery of nine psychological measures (SCL-90, Piers-Harris Self-Concept Scale, Nowicki-Strickland Locus of Control scale, Maudsley Obsessive-Compulsive Inventory, Holmes and Rahe Social Readjustment Rating Scale, Social Network Index, Anorectic Attitude Questionnaire, Goldberg Situational Discomfort Scale, and the WAIS Vocabulary subtest), Weiss and Ebert (1983) observed a pattern of depression, obsessional traits, and feelings of inadequacy in bulimic subjects as compared to normal controls. When comparing bulimics with binge eaters, the former group evidenced higher scores of depression, binge eating, and demand for approval, as measured by a different battery of instruments that included the Revised Restraint Scale, Beck Depression Inventory, Levenson and Gottman Dating and Assertion Questionnaire, Hawkins and Clement Binge Eating Scale, Rosenberg Self-Esteem Index, Jones Survey of Beliefs and Feelings, Kurtz Body Attitude Scale, and the short form of the Personality Assessment Questionnaire (PAQ) (Katzman & Wolchik, 1984). Depression, then, is a common theme in bulimia, and though certainly an indirect assessment criterion, the incidence of depression is probably the most helpful warning signal available at this time.

Direct assessment measures of bulimia are becoming more plentiful and more popular as professionals learn more about the disorder. The most widely discussed and utilized measures are the previously mentioned Binge Scale and the Eating Disorder Inventory. Other measures are reviewed in Hamilton et al. (1984), but appear less frequently in the clinical literature on bulimia. These include the Compulsive Eating Scale (Ondercin, 1979), which is a 32-item self-report instrument that gathers information about emotional states associated with eating, physical characteristics, and bingeing behaviors. Smith and Thelen (1984) have devised the Bulimia Test (BULIT) for clinical and non-clinical use in differentiating between 1) individuals with bulimia and those who do not have an eating disorder, 2) individuals with bulimia and those with other eating disorders, and 3) possible subgroups of bulimia (e.g., those who binge only versus those who binge and purge, etc.). The BULIT represents an attempt to assess bulimia primarily, rather than as a subgroup or category of anorexia nervosa.

The Binge Scale is a questionnaire used for measuring behaviors and attitudes associated with bulimia that attempts to distinguish the severity of the symptoms and place them along a continuum. The items ask for specific information about bingeing, purging, and the individual's emotional state before and after a binge. This self-report measure is most useful after a probable diagnosis of bulimia has been made.

Other efforts in this area have begun focusing on possible subtypes of bulimia. Grace et al. (1985) found no significant differences between purging and non-purging bulimics on measures of self-esteem, anxiety, and locus of control. Although research into subgroup differences is relatively new and Grace et al. (1985) found no significant personality differences, at least one attempt has been described using clinical assessment to differentiate subgroups. Cesari (1986) has proposed the term "fad bulimia" to describe a group of individuals who display bulimic symptoms with far less intensity than clinical bulimics. These individuals could also be called "social bulimics," as their behavior is analogous to social drinking versus alcoholism. On some college campuses, "bulimia" has become a status symbol of sorts, and college women are heard comparing binge and purge behaviors or wishing that they could learn how to "become bulimic." It is possible that these individuals could have a predisposition to developing clinical bulimia (Cesari, 1986; English & Papalia, 1984; Hamilton et al., 1984).

Clinical assessment has proven crucial in the differentiation of fad-bulimic clients from their clinical counterparts, and this differentiation is essential in treatment planning. Fad-bulimic individuals do not display the characteristic MMPI profile; rather, they do not elevate any clinical scales and they typically show a very low scale 5 (Masculinity-Feminity). Such profiles are usually associated with a strong identification with the traditional feminine role (Greene, 1980). It is possible that fad-bulimic individuals strongly identify with the traditional female role in an effort to gain attention and acceptance in a society that values physical appearance. The absence of depressive features on the MMPI is confirmed in interviews with fad-bulimic individuals, and this is a critical distinction when planning therapy. As noted earlier, depression itself is not a sufficient diagnostic indicator of bulimia, but is frequently a strong correlate. Further, the fad-bulimic individuals do not elevate the Bulimia subscale of the EDI, but show elevations on the Drive for Thinness and Body Dissatisfaction subscales. Such EDI profiles would be expected of young women who place a strong emphasis on physical attractiveness and conformity to societal standards of beauty, and the lack of endorsement of items on the Bulimia subscale is a strong indicator that these individuals are engaging in some behavior other than clinical bulimia. Intervention planning that takes this into account should prove more successful than interventions that assume an individual has a mild form of bulimia (Cesari, 1986). These phenomena have been observed in several college populations, typically in the 18- to 20-year-old age range, and similar patterns may be present in younger age groups as well.

OBESITY

Etiology

Theories of obesity range from psychodynamic causes to society's influence on the individual. Abramson (1977) divides these theories into biological and psychosocial categories. The biological theories of obesity provide the most logical starting point, given that obesity is defined as a medical/physical issue. However, it should be noted here that Kaplan and Kaplan (1957) found no relationship between metabolic factors and obesity in their review of the literature; in fact, fewer than 5% of the total number of obesity cases reviewed were found to have glandular imbalances.

The set-point theory of obesity (Nisbett, 1972) postulates a fixed number of fat cells in the body, predetermined by heredity and early nutritional considerations. Weight loss can only occur by a reduction in the size of these cells, which cannot be destroyed. Reduction in cell size, according to the set-point theory, probably can only be accomplished by semistarvation diets; thus, individuals may be well advised to learn to adapt to a higher set-point than their present ideal.

One particular biological theory of obesity has the most supporting evidence. Johnson, Burke, and Mayer (1956) found that 9% of children of nonobese parents were obese, 40% of children with one obese parent were obese, and 80% of children with two obese parents were categorized as obese. A more recent study (Plutchik, 1976) found that the number of overweight relatives in one's immediate family (e.g., parents, siblings, grandparents) was significantly related to obesity. It is difficult to know whether such findings indicate genetic factors or environmental ones, such as modeling. Mayer (1968) reported a greater variability in body weight among fraternal twins raised together than in identical twins, which lends support for the theory that heredity may play an important role in the development of obesity.

Psychological theories of obesity span a variety of potential causes (Gormally, 1984). The psychoanalytic theories stress a deficit in the psychic structure, along with underlying personality problems. These dynamic issues create anxiety and psychic conflict, which the person attempts to manage or dispel by the consumption of food rather than by confronting the anxieties in a "mature," direct fashion (Rubin, 1970). Further, the psychoanalytic perspective postulates that an individual who receives too little or too much gratification at the oral stage of psychosexual development may fixate or regress to that stage in later years and continue to seek oral gratification via eating. The difficulty with such theories is that insight into the dynamic motivations of one's behavior is usually not enough to engender a change in that behavior (Gormally, 1984).

The behavioral model explains obesity as a result of learning poor eating habits (Gormally, 1984), such as responding to external cues to eat rather than to internal hunger cues (Schacter, 1971). For example, Ferster, Nurnberger, and Levitt (1962) found that obese people condition themselves to eat snacks, resulting in bad habits that are paired with environmental cues such as socializing or watching television. Schacter and Gross (1968) manipulated the external cue of time and found that obese subjects consumed twice as much food when they believed it was dinner time than when they were told it was prior to mealtime. From such studies, Schacter (1971) concluded that "Obviously, the actual state of the stomach has nothing to do with the eating behavior of the obese" (p. 130).

Gormally (1984) labels his psychological theory of obesity as *skill deficit*. Like the psychodynamic theories, this one postulates that obese people eat in order to cope with unpleasant emotions and that they set impossibly high standards for themselves and for controlling their eating. The skill deficit lies in the inability to handle emotion. Hamberger (1951) classified four types of "emotional eaters": 1) those who eat in response to nonspecific emotional discomfort, 2) those who eat in response to chronic emotional distress, 3) those who have an underlying emotional illness, such as depression, and 4) those who are addictive or compulsive eaters. Such categories are common in recent literature on obesity, especially with girls and women who are affected. Hooker and Convisser (1983) pointed out that "many women, regardless of their size, often turn to eating as a means of coping with uncomfortable feelings that are related to difficult aspects of their lives" (p. 236). In Gormally's (1984) view, these women have yet to learn the "skill" needed to cope with uncomfortable feelings in a way that is not related to food.

The Hooker and Convisser categories include (a) the compulsive eater who uses food as a coping mechanism, (b) the binge eater who plans and organizes the consumption of large amounts of food, (c) the low-grade eater who snacks throughout most of the day, and (d) someone with obessive food thoughts that interfere with normal functioning (e.g., anorexic or bulimic). The salient part of this theory of categories is the split between mind and body so often seen with the obese female. This mind-body split serves to alienate women from their bodies, so much so that they may not know objectively how they look; thus, these individuals project a feeling of disgust toward themselves and their bodies that is difficult to overcome. Eating becomes both a nurturing activity to stifle unpleasant emotions and a way to perpetuate one's feelings of failure (Hooker & Convisser, 1983).

A variant of the emotional eating theories is the restraint theory of obesity, according to which eating behavior is determined by both physiological characteristics and voluntary restraint. Restrained eaters are characterized as vigilant and concerned about eating, and they tend to eat in cycles of restraint versus overeating. Restrained eaters, then, may be typical dieters who break their diet when they have made the slightest deviation. Restrained eaters often overeat for emotional reasons; unrestrained eaters are described as relaxed and spontaneous. Overweight individuals are more often restrained eaters, due to their cyclical eating habits and eating in response to distressing emotions (Ruderman, 1985).

Finally, the causes of obesity can also be viewed from a sociocultural perspective. In a study of 2,276 American adolescents, Kelly and Patten (1985) found that 71% of their sample (male and female) were dissatisfied with their body weight. Further, female subjects feared being or becoming overweight in the absence of any indication of obesity. Female subjects reported weighing themselves more than once a day and viewed themselves as less attractive than their peers. In 1967, Dwyer, Feldman, and Mayer reported that 37% of their sample of high school girls were currently dieting; almost 20 years later, Kelly and Patten (1985) found that 48.1% of female high school students were dieting. Such interest in weight loss does not appear to be based in a need to lose weight, but rather appears to be related to the sociocultural standards of beauty and attractiveness.

These findings relate to obesity in two ways. First, one definition of obesity is self-reported dissatisfaction with body weight (Abramson, 1977); literally, every adolescent who so reports would be considered obese. While the medical criteria of obesity may not be fulfilled in all such cases, those who work with adolescents may find themselves confronted with a curious group of nonobese teenagers who perceive themselves as "obese." Self-report may artificially inflate the reported incidence rates of obesity, but more importantly, it may identify a distinct group of individuals requiring interventions that are *not* directed at "curing" a nonexistent condition. The "cause" of this type of "obesity" must be considered in the intervention plan.

Sociocultural emphases can be viewed as causing obesity in a second way. The current American ideal of female attractiveness was reviewed in the earlier section on anorexia nervosa. Such standards of acceptability are difficult for most girls to attain or maintain because 1) the standards are unrealistic for most body types and 2) there is a competing message in society about food consumption, portrayed as fun, healthy, and acceptably worthwhile (note the plethora of fast-food advertising in the media). Overeating, then, may become a means of expressing one's feelings of failure to measure up to society's standards or a way to manage one's feelings of hopelessness in achieving the proffered ideal. When the overeating results in obesity, a vicious cycle of self-hatred is perpetuated, not only because one's own standards have not been met, but because one's own standards were set by an unrealistic sociocultural model. Anorexia nervosa, bulimia, and obesity may all be variants on the same theme of attempting to fulfill unreasonable sociocultural norms.

Incidence

The onset of obesity is not associated with any particular age. Obesity is more likely to begin in childhood if either one or both parents are obese (Johnson et al., 1956). Childhood-onset obesity that is not controlled prior to the end of adolescence is more likely to persist into adulthood (Stunkard & Burt, 1967).

Estimates of the incidence of obesity in this country are varied. Chernin (1981) reports data from the Metropolitan Life Insurance Company stating that 12% of men and women ages 20-29 could be considered overweight. Further data on obesity were reported for women only: 25% in the 30-39 age group, 40% in ages 40-49, 46% obesity in those from 50-59. The increase of obesity with age is clearly demonstrated by these data. Others have estimated that obesity affects 58% of the overall population (Wyden, 1965).

Obesity in adolescents has been estimated at 15-30%, with a higher frequency in females than in males (Brownell & Stunkard, 1978). Dwyer et al. (1967) surveyed 446 high school females and found that 15.2% were obese. Canning and Mayer (1966) found a 23.3% incidence rate among high school females. Kelly and Patten (1985) found that 38.6% of their teenage female subjects wanted to weigh less, regardless of their current weight. Kagan and Squires (1984a) reported that 19% of their college-age sample believed that they were obese. Thus, incidence rates (objective and self-reported) are varied in adolescent populations as well as in adult populations.

Assessment Procedures

Because obesity is defined as a physiological issue and not (primarily) as a psychological one, the uses of psychological assessment in this area will vary from those presented in the earlier sections on anorexia nervosa and bulimia. In particular, screening and differential diagnosis of obesity are considered primarily medical/ physical issues, and thus such types of assessments should be conducted before any psychological assessments. Brownell (1982) stresses the need for a multifaceted assessment plan when working with the obese, encompassing the definition and measurement of obesity and its biological and genetic determinants; an evaluation of the individual's level of physical activity and fitness; an evaluation of eating habits; the assessment of independent (e.g., psychological) variables; and treatment planning/ evaluation assessments.

The latter three categories lend themselves to the type of work most readers of this chapter will find useful. A note of caution must be provided, however. The physical aspects of obesity should not be ignored, and if one does not have the expertise to deal with those aspects, collaboration with medical and/or nutritional experts is dictated. While its harmful physical effects may be somewhat overrated (Chernin, 1981), obesity is still primarily a physical issue and must be treated as such.

Eating habits. The evaluation of eating habits is an important component in the assessment of obesity, which is caused and maintained, in part, by maladaptive eating patterns (e.g., overeating or an imbalance of nutrients). Schorr, Sanjur, and Erickson (1972) recommended the use of 24-hour food recalls, 3- to 7-day food records, and diet history questionnaires to assess eating patterns.

Food records are subject to the same imprecision as any self-report measure, and the examiner must check the consistency of the self-report to ensure the reliability of the self-assessment. Furthermore, food records are often used to provide baseline information about a person's eating habits; thus, subjects should be encouraged to maintain their regular diet eating habits, avoiding a change to more "socially appropriate" consumption because the record will be shared with someone else. Of course, self-monitoring may always be subject to reactivity, and subjects may actually reduce the amount they eat when self-monitoring begins. The helping professional must be alert to this possibility to minimize the loss of important information.

In a 24-hour food recall, respondents are asked to remember everything they have consumed for the past 24 hours; these can be somewhat inaccurate, as items such as the precise number of beverages consumed may not be recalled accurately. The 3- to 7-day food record requires the individual to maintain an ongoing tally of all substances consumed (including beverages and chewing gum) and often requires additional information such as where the food was eaten, who the person was with, or the mood state before and after eating. This additional information reveals patterns of adaptive and maladaptive eating, such as learning that the subject only overeats when alone or feeling angry.

Diet history questionnaires assess both a subject's typical eating practices and the frequency and types of weight loss programs she has attempted. Dwyer et al. (1967) note that it is as important to consider adolescent dieting as it is to know the prevalence of obesity because the dieting information gives an indication of successful and unsuccessful weight control efforts, whereas the obesity figures only reflect unsuccessful attempts at weight loss. Diet history questionnaires may include questions about the type of diet engaged in, age and weight at the initiation of the diet, successful and unsuccessful aspects of each diet, and so on. This information can be used to assist in understanding both the relative success and the individual context (e.g., support system, goals) of each dieting attempt.

Other self-report measures include informal questionnaires about weight, eating practices, and body image (Miller, Coffman, & Linke, 1980), self-reported frequency of binges (Gormally, 1984), and reports of daily activities and mood states in addition to food consumption (Leon & Chamberlain, 1973). While an interview procedure can provide useful information about eating practices, it is generally considered more accurate for the person to monitor food intake outside of the helper's office as well.

The Eating Practices Inventory (EPI; Helms, Domke, & Simons, 1981) was developed to assess the eating habits of women of varying weight levels, rather than to focus solely on the symptom (i.e., overweight). Its developers considered the cognitive, affective, and interpersonal influences on eating practices as well as the notion that eating practices can be stable or situational. For example, a person might overeat if she is anxious, but if anxiety is not a common state for that person, the eating due to anxiety may be considered a situational eating practice rather than a stable or common practice. The EPI consists of four separate scales for a total of 102 items. The Common Habits scale has 17 items, which assess typical, stable eating practices. The 40-item Uncommon Habits scale was designed to assess internal and external circumstances associated with a person's atypical eating habits. For these two scales, respondents use a 5-point Likert-type scale ranging from "rarely" to "usually." The Common Cognitions (17 items) and Uncommon Cognitions (28 items) scales measure stable and atypical thoughts that increase or decrease one's eating practices. These scales also use a 5-point response system, ranging from "rarely effective" to "usually effective." Helms et al. (1981) report that research using the EPI with college-age normal weight versus overweight women differentiated the two groups, particularly with respect to eating habits. Further, the results suggested no differences between the two groups in the use of eating related cognitions to increase or decrease eating habits. Thus, the EPI may be most useful in determining maladaptive, stable and atypical eating habits for overweight females.

The Binge Eating Scale (BES; Gormally, Black, Daston, & Rardin, 1982) was developed to assess the severity of binge eating among obese individuals. The BES contains 16 items that identify binge behaviors and the feelings that trigger and/or follow a binge. Like the EPI, the BES focuses on both eating practices and cognitions. Gormally et al. (1982) report developing the Cognitive Factors Scale to assess both individual dieting standards and the person's beliefs about her dieting stamina. Used together, the BES and the Cognitive Factors Scale can replace lengthy interview procedures now used to identify moderate and serious binge eaters and to plan appropriate treatment courses for each (Gormally, 1984). In planning treatment diets, Gormally et al. (1982) found that moderate bingers (as measured by the BES) tended to react to lapses in diet resolve by eating more food, but were more tolerant of their lapses. The serious binge eaters reported (a) eating more food, (b) feelings of self-hatred, and (c) extreme dieting methods after a lapse in control. Thus, the BES can be used to assess eating habits and cognitions in a productive context.

Social/psychological aspects. Brownell (1982) points out that little is known either about the social and psychological concomitants of obesity or about the effects of weight loss on the individual. Measures of self-esteem, psychological adjustment, and body image should be included in the assessment of obesity, to assist in understanding both the individual and the disorder.

The research on assessment of self-esteem in obese adolescents has yielded unexpected results. Wadden, Foster, Brownell, and Finley (1984) administered the Piers-Harris Self-Concept Scale to 716 children in Grades 3-8. Obese subjects (20% or more over ideal weight) did not differ in self-concept scores from nonobese subjects. This result corroborated earlier research by Mendelson and White (1982) with the Piers-Harris, using subjects in a similar age range (7-12); self-esteem was not related to overweight. Jacobs and Wagner (1984) used the Tennessee Self Concept Scale with 99 subjects identified as currently obese, previously obese, and never obese, and found no difference in self-concept scores among the three groups. Wolf and Crother (1983) also did not find differences in self-concept between normal weight and overweight college women using the Tennessee Self Concept Scale.

These results are somewhat surprising because low self-concept often has been thought to be a major part of obesity, either as a precursor to obesity ("I don't like myself so I will eat for comfort") or as a correlate ("I don't like myself because I am overweight"). The lack of substantiating research evidence may be due to several factors. First, it is possible that standard measures of self-concept such as the Tennessee and Piers-Harris may not accurately measure the affective experience associated with obesity. Kagan and Squires (1984b) surveyed over 2,000 high school students with a nonstandardized multiple-choice questionnaire and found that adolescents with "disordered eating patterns" routinely felt that they had met neither their own expectations for themselves nor others' expectations for them; they felt inadequate. Whether this affective variable could be labeled as low self-concept is not clear, but the negative attitude about self clearly is present in these subjects. Perhaps the traditional self-concept measures are too global.

The second possible explanation is that low self-concept is related to obesity in adulthood but not in childhood or adolescence. The development of a low self-image may begin in the teenage years and come to fruition in adulthood, after the individual has struggled for years with weight issues or is currently faced with physical complaints or social disapproval.

The third hypothesis is that low self-concept in obesity is a clinical myth, or only affects those who seek professional help for their weight problems. For interesting reading about obese individuals who struggle to like themselves in a world that expects low self-concept in the overweight, see Millman (1980) and Schoenfielder and Wieser (1983). The assessment of the self-concept variable is still to be recommended, if only to verify or disconfirm a stereotypic assumption that may not be valid for all adolescents.

The assessment of general personality adjustment in adolescent obesity also appears to have been predicated on the assumption that obesity is related to some form of emotional maladjustment. Few correlates between obesity and personality characteristics have been supported. Wolf and Crother (1983) found that neither the Beck Depression Inventory, the Rotter Locus of Control Scale, nor the Body Cathexis Scale were significant predictors of overweight in normal weight and obese college women. Williamson, Kelly, Davis, Ruggiero, and Blouin (1985) also did not find any differences in levels of depression between obese and the normal-weight individuals using the Beck Depression Inventory. Brewerton et al. (1986) reviewed research relating obesity with affective disorders (e.g., depression), concluding that "a paucity of scientifically based information exists on the relationship between eating and mood in obese individuals" (p. 78).

Studies attempting to establish MMPI profiles of obesity have not provided conclusive results. Williamson et al. (1985) found that although obese subjects score higher than normal-weight subjects on scales 7 (Psychasthenia) and 8 (Schizophrenia), only 33% of these obese subjects evidenced clinical psychopathology on the MMPI. Halmi, Long, Stunkard, and Mason (1980) assessed 80 severely obese individuals scheduled for gastric bypass surgery, a weight-loss treatment intervention. Using DSM-III diagnostic criteria, these researchers found no evidence of increased prevalence of major psychiatric disorders among the severely obese. Similarly, a study of the MacAndrew Addiction Scale, a subscale of the MMPI designed to assess addictive disorders, found no difference between obese and normal weight individuals (Leon, Kolotkin, & Korgeski, 1979).

The assessment of psychological adjustment, then, should not be based on an assumption of emotional instability or personality deficit. As with the self-esteem variable, assessment of psychological adjustment will be helpful if it is directed toward understanding the individual and not toward diagnosing psychopathology. The assessment of body image appears to be one of the most salient psychological factors related to obesity. The two most widely used instruments for this purpose are the Body Cathexis Scale and the Body Esteem Scale.

The Body Cathexis Scale originally was developed by Secord and Jourard (1953) as a measure of self-esteem. According to these developers, feelings about oneself are related to feelings about one's body: self-feelings are projected (cathected) onto one's physical self, and the measurement of feelings about the body then also yield information about self-esteem. The Body Cathexis Scale consists of 40 items, listings of various body parts or functions (e.g., hair, face, weight, stamina, keenness of senses). Respondents indicate their feelings about those parts of themselves using a 5-point scale that ranges from strong positive feelings to strong negative feelings. Early research indicated that low body cathexis scores were related to insecurity (Secord & Jourard, 1953). Although the Body Cathexis Scale has not been useful in discriminating between obese and normal weight people (Wolf & Crother, 1983), it can be used to help the overweight individual identify specific aspects of her physical self that she does and does not like. Overweight young women have a tendency to depersonalize themselves from their bodies (Chernin, 1981), and the specificity of the items on the Body Cathexis Scale will encourage the subject to look at herself aside from her weight alone; therefore, this scale can be a useful clinical tool to initiate an interview.

The Body Esteem Scale is a relatively new measure of attitudes toward certain body characteristics (Franzoi & Shields, 1984). In a late adolescent population, females' body esteem depended on attitudes toward their sexual attractiveness, weight concern, and perceived physical condition. Body Esteem scores have been found to relate to obesity in young adolescent populations (Mendelson & White, 1982). The Body Esteem Scale can be used to measure attitudes toward physical self and to identify which aspects (sexuality, weight, and/or condition) are salient for each individual.

Treatment planning. Despite the plethora of treatment programs that have been developed to combat obesity, current treatment approaches do not appear to have produced promising results. Coates and Thoreson (1978) reviewed the prominent intervention plans in use with adolescents, and their review is somewhat discouraging. Calorie restriction programs have been found to be ineffective and an inefficient use of client and professional time. This may be due in part to the fact that the typical caloric intake of obese adolescents has been found to be comparable *or lower* than that of nonobese adolescents of the same height and age; the obese adolescents simply appear to have lower activity levels (Dwyer et al., 1967). In this vein, Coates and Thoreson (1978) ascribed some value to exercise programs, but noted the difficulty in generating motivation for them. Anorectic drugs (amphetamines), fasting, and bypass surgery are all regarded as risky and without lasting effects. Even behavior therapy, with its emphasis on extinguishing bad habits and rewarding appropriate eating behaviors, has been shown to have limited long-term effects.

In view of the discouraging record of weight loss programs, assessment measures can be particularly useful in helping professionals tailor interventions that maximize the potential for success. Wilson (1976) suggests that professionals need to identify *all* the pertinent variables that serve to maintain the individual's obesity, such as environmental support or stress, cognitive beliefs, and emotional states.

One such pertinent variable might be one's health-related locus of control. The Health Locus of Control scale is an 11-item questionnaire that surveys health-related situations and beliefs (Wallston, Wallston, Kaplan, & Maides, 1976). People with an internal health-related locus of control were found to lose significantly more weight than those with an external health locus of control (Chavez & Michaels, 1980). Similarly, the Weight Locus of Control Scale (Saltzer, 1982) was developed to predict behavior associated with weight reduction. On this 4-item measure of locus of control regarding personal weight, individuals with an internal locus of control regarding weight were more likely to complete a weight loss program than those with an external locus of control regarding weight.

Polivy et al. (1984) emphasized that determining the cause of overeating and addressing treatment programs to that issue will be more effective than simply treating the symptom (i.e., focusing on weight). Until the causes of obesity are better understood, the most beneficial assessment procedures will assist the examiner in understanding the client's individual "causes" of being overweight so that treatment programs are not based on stereotypic assumptions (e.g., universal low self-concept in obesity) or inappropriate goals (e.g., reduction of caloric intake vs. increased exercise). Thus, Brownell's multifaceted assessment plan is essential in the understanding and treatment planning of adolescent obesity.

CASE EXAMPLE

A case example documenting the uses of assessment with a bulimic individual is presented here. After reviewing all three common eating disorders in adolescents, the area of bulimia appears to benefit the most from assessment-based understanding.

Pat is an 18-year-old white college freshman at a midwestern university. She was referred to the Counseling Service by one of her instructors, who reported that Pat excuses herself from class at least once a week because she "feels sick." The class meets in the early afternoon, and the instructor was concerned that Pat may be feeling overly anxious about her performance in this class, thus "feeling sick" immediately after lunch. The instructor also reported that Pat usually returns to class within 15 minutes, looking pale and shaky, and is not receptive to expressions of concern regarding her health from either the instructor or her classmates. The instructor strongly recommended to Pat that she seek counseling, before her apparent anxiety negatively affected her academic performance.

Pat concurred with her instructor's concern over academic progress in this class. She appeared quite worried about whether she would pass the course and agreed to "try anything, even counseling" if the instructor so wished. Pat's expectations of counseling were twofold: to fulfill her instructor's request and to explore anxiety-reduction strategies and academic success strategies.

History

Pat is the second of three children in an upper-middle-class, well-educated family. Her family lives in a major city, about 400 miles from where she attends school. Pat's father is a bank vice president, and her mother has a small, private interior decorating firm. Both parents hold college degrees. Although Pat's parents currently live together, she reports that twice in the past five years they have separated for six-month intervals and their marriage still is not secure. During both separation periods, the children resided with their mother.

Pat has a 21-year-old brother and a younger sister, age 15. Her brother is a college senior at a different university. Pat reports that she and her brother have few interests in common and that they rarely see one another except on school vacations. The younger sister is just beginning high school. According to Pat, although her sister is bright and talented, she does only average work in school and has been something of a discipline problem for the parents. Pat attributes her sister's behavior to difficulty in dealing with their parents' marital discord. Pat reports being the "peacemaker" among the family members, and she finds it easy to see all sides of an issue and to act as a mediator. She also believes that her family would not approve of her seeking counseling because of their belief that "one should work things out on one's own."

Current Context

Despite the imagined disapproval of her family, Pat was candid and cooperative with the counselor. She describes herself as "smart but lazy," does not appear to have much self-confidence, and does not have a positive self-image. Pat came to college because "that's what all my friends did when they graduated." She was a good student in high school and has maintained a B+ average so far in college courses. She has not chosen a major area of study and appears to be vacillating between business courses (which is her father's wish) and elementary education, chosen because she likes "the spontaneity of little kids and the chance to have a major impact in their lives." She did not report experiencing any distress over her lack of college major at this time.

Besides her fear of academic failure, which is not substantiated by her performance thus far, Pat also expressed concern about her interpersonal relationships. She has had difficulty in overcoming her shyness in meeting new people since coming to campus and has relied primarily on the company of two or three high school friends who also came to the campus this year. These friends, however, are also pursuing other relationships, and Pat often feels abandoned by them. She lives in a women's residence hall on campus where, she reports, "most of the girls are just interested in diets, dates, and gossip." She does not have a roommate, she eats alone, and she tends to spend her leisure time alone, either reading or watching television. She does not actively seek companionship at the residence hall or on campus.

Pat has had several dates since the beginning of school, but is not "going steady" with anyone at this time. Her mother in particular has stressed that Pat should date more, while also saying that, in order to attract desirable men, Pat should lose another

10 pounds. Pat appears to believe that this would help her dating potential because her mother is overweight and, in Pat's opinion, unattractive.

Pat is 5'9" tall and reports weighing 139 pounds; she would like to weigh 125 pounds. She is an attractive blond with a well-proportioned figure; she has a round face, however, accentuated by her use of exaggerated cosmetics that emphasize that roundness. She appears to relate much of her negative body image to "fat chipmunk cheeks." Pat has attempted dieting and weight loss at least three times per year since the age of 14. In her opinion, her dieting attempts were not successful.

A recent physical examination indicates that Pat is in good health and there are no physical reasons for her "feeling sick." Pat reports having a "nervous stomach" and often vomits after meals. She says that it is difficult for her to enjoy the dining hall food and she often purchases fast food in town, but the expense of such habits is high. In fact, Pat admitted to having overdrawn her checking account three times this semester in order to purchase fast food and snacks. On occasion, she has contemplated shoplifting from the grocery store, but fears the consequences. These thoughts and the overdrawn checking account appear to cause Pat considerable alarm. She wondered aloud if she were "crazy," then refused to talk more about either these topics or about feeling nauseated in class.

Counselor Conceptualization

There are several pieces of information that lead the counselor to suspect the presence of an eating disorder in this case. The absence of an organic explanation for Pat's "feeling sick" supports the belief that her distress is psychological in nature. Simple anxiety over academic and/or social performance could account for her symptoms, as the instructor who referred her to Counseling Services believed; however, the presence of other factors warrant the need to consider an eating disorder as a possible explanation as well.

1. *Family history.* It is not unusual for an eating disorder to develop in response to emotional trauma or discord. Pat's parents' marital difficulties may have triggered a need in Pat to exercise control over something in her environment that is totally hers (i.e., her body). Also, the history of maternal obesity and focus on weight/attractiveness issues as a self-validator in families is a correlate of the development of eating disorders. Pat's sister's overt discipline problems may have contributed to Pat's "silent" struggle with an eating disorder.

2. *Family pressures.* Pat's family appears to be success and achievement oriented, which puts pressure on Pat to succeed, to be "perfect." She may be struggling with the future issue of defying her father in the choice of a major. External pressures such as these may result in unusual coping strategies, such as an eating disorder.

3. *Internal evaluation of self.* Pat has a low self-concept in the face of positive objective data such as good grades and talents. Low self-concept, near-impossible standards for self, and inability to evaluate achievements accurately are correlated with eating disorders.

4. *Interpersonal skills.* Pat's isolation from others in general and her current withdrawal from established relationships in particular are often seen in young women with eating disorders. Also, her inability to judge her body image accurately in relation to potential dating situations is significant.

5. *Physical signs.* Pat is at an appropriate weight but continues to diet; thus she experiences weight fluctuations. The continued attempts at dieting alone might have led her at some point to attempt drastic, eating-disordered measures. She has inconsistent eating habits. She wants to lose weight and dislikes institutional food, but appears to consume some quantity of "junk food." Vomiting after eating without evidence of physical disorder should always be considered a sign of a potential eating disorder.

6. *Other signs.* An eating disorder such as bulimia is expensive to maintain; Pat's overdrawn checking account and spending most of her allowance on food without apparent weight gain could be signs that she is bingeing and purging. At times, individuals with bulimia will also shoplift or steal food or money from others when they feel the need to binge. Further, after admitting to these thoughts and behaviors, Pat's distress in the session increased and she refused to talk further. Bulimia is a secretive, shameful syndrome for almost all who have the symptoms, and Pat's refusal to reveal further information is indicative of that secrecy and shame.

Use of Assessment

The counselor has formulated a reasonable hypothesis that the cause of Pat's absences from class are due to behaviors associated with an eating disorder. Assesment measures can be used in three ways: 1) to gain confirmation for this diagnosis, 2) to elicit cooperation from the client and provide a framework for talking about painful issues, and 3) to identify issues that need to be considered in treatment strategy planning.

The counselor presents the need for objective assessment data in order to help understand Pat's concerns, drawing the analogy that just as a physician might perform certain physical tests when presented with certain symptoms, the counselor would like to use psychological measures to confirm or rule out psychological factors in this case. Pat needed reassurance that this did not mean she was "crazy"; in fact, these measures could confirm that she is a normal adolescent experiencing rather common symptoms for her age group.

The counselor chose to administer the MMPI, 16PF, and EDI for the purposes of diagnosis, eliciting cooperation, and intervention planning. Each measure was described to Pat, and the inclusion of the EDI was explained as necessary in light of the evidence that she either has or soon could develop a clinical eating disorder.

Pat's MMPI profile was consistent with and typical of the diagnosis of bulimia (though not in itself conclusive of such a diagnosis). The validity scale configuration reflected a moderate amount of distress coupled with the client's willingness to admit to painful things. The clinical scales showed a 2-4 elevation, coupled with a low score on scale 5 (Masculinity-Femininity).

The profile of Pat's 16PF scores reflected someone who is warm, intelligent, affected by feelings, shy, tenderminded, apprehensive, imaginative, and somewhat tense. These characteristics are consistent with the bulimic individual, who has been found to be bright, with tendencies to withdraw from others (shy) and to rely on self for support/protection about the "secret" (imaginative), and who is in distress (tense, apprehensive). The 16PF profile is used to highlight characteristics that Pat likes in herself (e.g., being imaginative), while also pointing out the costs of other characteristics (e.g., tension). A case is then made that those undesired characteristics could be causing Pat a great deal of distress and that an objective, empathic counseling experience could help her to learn to cope with her distress or to eliminate the stressors.

Interpretation of Pat's responses on the EDI indicates scores above the 95th percentile on Drive for Thinness, Bulimia, and Body Dissatisfaction. This profile is consistent with a diagnosis of bulimia. Pat was uncomfortable with the discussion of the EDI profile, so the counselor took the opportunity to point out a pattern in her responses. In particular, Pat indicated on the inventory that she always or usually thinks about dieting, eats when she is upset, is terrified of gaining weight, eats in secret, and has thought about vomiting in order to lose weight. Pat also indicated that she rarely or never feels satisfied with her body, secure about herself, or like a worthwhile person. The counselor pointed out that, whether or not Pat has an eating disorder, those responses indicate that she experiences some very distressing thoughts and feelings. Counseling was presented as a way to help alleviate the pain that Pat reported via the assessment instruments. Pat endorsed the distress that was indicated in her assessment results and agreed to continue in counseling.

Treatment goals and intervention strategies were specified on the basis of assessment results. Pat's profiles confirmed that she has low self-esteem, is anxious, and handles her stress in maladaptive ways; thus, therapy goals were aimed at reassessing and raising Pat's self-esteem, instructing her in relaxation techniques, and teaching her other ways to deal with stress. As assessment measures indicated that Pat's case was not atypical of an adolescent with an eating disorder, the shared benefits of a group therapy process aimed at self-concept and stress issues for bulimics emerged as the treatment of choice.

RECOMMENDATIONS

Adolescent eating disorders do not appear to be subsiding. In fact, as professionals in our various fields, we may be among the first to identify a case of anorexia nervosa or bulimia simply by our varied roles in the lives of adolescents around us (Colligan et al., 1984; Peters, Swassing, Butterfield, & McKay, 1985; Romeo, 1984). This chapter has focused on the most widely known uses of psychological assessment in eating disorders. The future of assessment in this area should be threefold: defining the disorders, furthering epidemiological surveys, and establishing better treatment intervention planning.

First, although the definitions of anorexia seem straightforward, the relationship between anorexia nervosa and bulimia needs to be better understood. Psychological assessment can play a major role in this endeavor by direct and indirect measures. In particular, the indirect measures (i.e., those that were not developed specifically for use with eating disorders) can figure prominently by providing criteria against which individuals with each disorder can be compared. Further, the intuitive belief that obesity may be related to anorexia and bulimia can be studied in this way.

Second, it is important to develop an understanding of the base rates and characteristics of individuals who suffer from eating disorders. Again, indirect assessment measures could be helpful, especially if there were a reliable yet inobtrusive way in which to assess the symptoms and occurrence of eating disorders. As discussed earlier, affected individuals may be reluctant to admit to an eating disorder unless absolute anonymity is guaranteed by the assessment measure. Although it is not necessarily advisable to construct and administer assessment measures with a deceptive purpose in mind, it is important to be able to access information about eating disorders in a reliable and uniform manner, and thus indirect assessment measures could play a prominent role.

Third, and most importantly, a major role of any assessment is the planning of appropriate intervention strategies. Of necessity, many intervention strategies have been developed prior to completely understanding eating disorders and the individuals involved. It is now apparent to some that eating disorders are even more complex than originally thought. The appearance of subtypes of bulimia, the occurrence of anorexia nervosa with bulimic-like symptoms, the observations of pseudobulimic behaviors such as fad bulimia, and the failure of traditional treatments of obesity all point to the need for more differentiated intervention strategies. The future of assessment in the area of eating disorders will undoubtedly lie in making those discriminations among variations of eating disorders in order to implement more suitable and effective interventions.

One particularly interesting area for future research and clinical inquiry will be in how eating disorders develop across the life span. Longitudinal direct and indirect assessment strategies that address themselves to this issue are greatly needed and will boost the understanding and treatment of these disorders afflicting so many adolescents.

Much effort appears to be concentrated on research aspects at the moment. Practitioners should look to this research for clues on how to proceed until the eating disorders field is more clear. One warning to practitioners and researchers alike, however: Do not translate your current assessment needs or clinical impatience into yet another "homegrown" psychological measure of eating disorders. Many treatment facilities produce their own such measures, and researchers have decried the lack of comprehensive assessment measures of the disorders. The result is more likely a mass of information about eating disorders that cannot be generalized or synthesized, and that could serve only to further confuse an already confusing area of inquiry. Instead, like Hamilton et al. (1984), this author would suggest concentrating on gathering information with the assessment knowledge we have and creating new instruments only when our accumulated knowledge is confronted with an information gap that would best be addressed by a new approach.

REFERENCES

Abramson, E. E. (1977). An overview of etiology and traditional treatments. In treatments. In E. E. Abramson (Ed.), *Behavioral approaches to weight control* (pp. 3-13). New York: Springer.

Altschuler, K. Z., & Weiner, M. F. (1985). Anorexia nervosa and depression: A dissenting view. *American Journal of Psychiatry, 142,* 328-332.

American Heart Association. (1983, March 14). American Heart Association. *Time Magazine.*

American Psychiatric Association. (1980). *Diagnostic and statistical manual of mental disorders* (3rd ed.). Washington, DC: Author.

Andersen, A. (1981). Psychiatric aspects of bulimia. *Directions in Psychiatry, 14,* 1-7.

Bemis, K. M. (1979). Current approaches to the etiology and treatment of anorexia nervosa. In S. Chess & A. Thomas (Eds.), *Annual progress in child psychiatry and child development* (pp. 486-523). New York: Brunner/Mazel.

Boskind-Lodahl, M., & White, W. C. (1978). The definition and treatment of bulimarexia in college women—A pilot study. *Journal of American College Health Association, 27,* 84-86, 97.

Boskind-White, M., & White, W. C. (1983). *Bulimarexia: The binge-purge cycle.* New York: W. W. Norton.

Brewerton, T. D., Heffernan, M. M., & Rosenthal, N. E. (1986). Psychiatric aspects of the relationship between eating and mood. *Nutrition Reviews,* 78-88.

Brownell, K. D. (1982). Obesity: Understanding and treating a serious, prevalent, and refractory disorder. *Journal of Consulting & Clinical Psychology, 50,* 820-840.

Brownell, K. D., & Stunkard, A. J. (1978). Behavioral treatment of obesity in children. *American Journal of Diseases of Children, 132,* 403-412.

Button, E. J., & Whitehouse, A. (1981). Subclinical anorexia nervosa. *Psychological Medicine, 11,* 509-616.

Canning, H., & Mayer, J. (1966). Obesity: Its possible effect on college acceptance. *New England Journal of Medicine, 275,* 1172.

Cantwell, D. P., Sturzenberger, S., Borroughs, J., Salkin, B., & Green, J. K. (1977). Anorexia nervosa—An affective disorder? *Archives of General Psychiatry, 34,* 1087-1093.

Carter, J. A., & Duncan, P. A. (1984). Binge-eating and vomiting: A survey of a high school population. *Psychology in the Schools, 21,* 198-203.

Cesari, J. P. (1986). Fad bulimia: A serious and separate counseling issue. *Journal of College Student Personnel, 27,* 255-259.

Chavez, E. L., & Michaels, C. (1980). Evaluation of the Health Locus of Control for obesity treatment. *Psychological Reports, 47*(3, Pt. 1), 709-710.

Chernin, K. (1981). *The obsession: Reflections on the tyranny of slenderness.* New York: Harper & Row.

Coates, T. J., & Thoreson, C. E. (1978). Treating obesity in children and adolescents: A review. *American Journal of Public Health, 68,* 143-151.

Colligan, R. C., Ferdinande, R. J., & Rasmussen, N. H. (1984). Anorexia nervosa: Academic-behavioral management and mainstream dismissal planning for hospitalized adolescents. *Residential Groups Care & Treatment, 2*(3), 45-55.

Damlouji, N. F., & Ferguson, J. M. (1985). Three cases of posttraumatic anorexia nervosa. *American Journal of Psychiatry, 142,* 362-363.

Dwyer, J. T., Feldman, J. J., & Mayer, J. (1967). Adolescent dieters: Who are they? *American Journal of Clinical Nutrition, 20,* 1045-1056.

Dykens, E. (1982). *Bulimia: Psychological profiles of bulimics, repeat dieters, and controls.* Unpublished master's thesis, University of Kansas, Lawrence.

Eckert, E. D. (1985). Characteristics of anorexia nervosa. In J. E. Mitchell (Ed.), *Anorexia nervosa and bulimia: Diagnosis and treatment* (pp. 3-28). Minneapolis, MN: University of Minnesota Press.

Eckert, E., & Labeck, L. (1985). Integrated treatment program for anorexia nervosa. In J. E. Mitchell (Ed.), *Anorexia nervosa and bulimia: Diagnosis and treatment* (pp. 152-170), Minneapolis, MN: University of Minnesota Press.

English, J. Z., & Papalia, A. S. (1984). *An educator's guide for dealing with eating disorders among students* (Report No. P 608). Moravia, NY: Chronical Guidance Professional Subscription Publications.

Feighner, J. P., Robins, E., Guze, S. B., Woodruff, R. A., Jr., Winokur, G., & Munoz, R. (1972). Diagnostic criteria for use in psychiatric research. *Archives of General Psychiatry, 26,* 57-63.

Ferster, C. B., Nurnberger, J. I., & Levitt, E. (1962). The control of eating. *Journal of Mathetics, 1,* 87-109.

Franzoi, S. L., & Shields, S. A. (1984). The Body Esteem Scale: Multidimensional structure and sex differences in a college population. *Journal of Personality Assessment, 48,* 173-178.

Garner, D. M., & Garfinkel, P. E. (1979). The Eating Attitudes Test: An index of the symptoms of anorexia nervosa. *Psychological Medicine, 9,* 273-279.

Garner, D. M., Garfinkel, P. E., Schwartz, D., & Thompson, M. (1980). Cultural expectations of thinness in women. *Psychological Reports, 47,* 483-491.

Garner, D. M., & Olmsted, M. P. (1984). *Manual for Eating Disorders Inventory (EDI).* Odessa, FL: Psychological Assessment Resources.

Garner, D. M., Olmsted, M. P., Polivy, J., & Garfinkel, P. E. (1984). Comparison between weight preoccupation in women and anorexia nervosa. *Psychosomatic Medicine, 46,* 255-266.

Gormally, J. (1984). The obese binge eater: Diagnosis, etiology, and clinical issues. In R. C. Hawkins, W. J. Fremouw, & P. F. Clement (Eds.), *The binge-purge syndrome: Diagnosis, treatment, and research* (pp. 47-73). New York: Springer.

Gormally, J., Black, S., Daston, S., & Rardin, D. (1982). The assessment of binge eating severity among obese persons. *Addictive Behaviors, 7,* 47-55.

Grace, P. S., Jacobson, R. S., & Fullager, C. J. (1985). A pilot comparison of purging and non-purging bulimics. *Journal of Clinical Psychology, 41,* 173-180.

Greene, R. L. (1980). *The MMPI: An interpretive manual.* Orlando, FL: Grune & Stratton.

Halmi, K. A., Falk, J. R., & Schwartz, E. (1981). Binge eating and vomiting: A survey of a college population. *Psychological Medicine, 11,* 697-706.

Halmi, K. A., Long, M., Stunkard, A. J., & Mason, E. (1980). Psychiatric diagnosis of morbidly obese gastric bypass patients. *Journal of American Psychiatry, 137,* 470-472.

Hamberger, W. (1951). Emotional aspects of obesity. *Medical Clinics of North America, 35,* 483.

Hamilton, M. K., Gelwick, B. P., & Meade, C. J. (1984). The definition and prevalance of bulimia. In R. C. Hawkins, W. J. Fremouw, & P. F. Clement (Eds.), *The binge-purge syndrome: Diagnosis, treatment, and research* (pp. 3-26). New York: Springer.

Hawkins, R. C., & Clement, P. F. (1980). Development and construct validation of a self-report measure of binge eating tendencies. *Addictive Behaviors, 5,* 219-226.

Hawkins, R. C., Fremouw, W. J., & Clement, P. F. (1984). The binge-purge syndrome: Diagnosis, treatment, and research. New York: Springer.

Helms, J. E., Domke, J. A., & Simons, J. A. (1981). Development of an inventory to measure the eating practices of college women. *JSAS Catalog of Selected Documents in Psychology, 11*(2), 28.

Heron, J. M., & Leheup, R. F. (1984). Happy families? *British Journal of Psychiatry, 145,* 136-138.

Hooker, D., & Convisser, E. (1983). Women's eating problems: An analysis of a coping mechanism. *Personnel and Guidance Journal, 62,* 236-239.

Jacobs, S. B., & Wagner, M. K. (1984). Obese and nonobese individuals: Behavioral and personality characteristics. *Addictive Behaviors, 9,* 223-226.

Johnson, C., Lewis, C., Love, S., Lewis, L., & Stuckey, M. (1984). Incidence and correlates of bulimic behavior in a female high school population. *Journal of Youth and Adolescence, 13,* 15-26.

Johnson, M. L., Burke, B. S., & Mayer, J. (1956). Relative importance of inactivity and over-eating in the energy balance of obese high school girls. *American Journal of Clinical Nutrition, 4,* 37-44.

Joseph, A., Wood, I. K., & Goldberg, S. C. (1982). Determining populations at risk of developing anorexia nervosa based on selection of college major. *Psychiatry Research, 7,* 53-58.

Josephson, A. M. (1985). Psychodynamics of anorexia nervosa and bulimia. In J. E. Mitchell (Ed.), *Anorexia nervosa and bulimia: Diagnosis and treatment* (pp. 78-101). Minneapolis, MN: University of Minnesota Press.

Kagan, D. M., & Squires, R. L. (1984a). Compulsive eating, dieting, stress, and hostility among college students. *Journal of College Student Personnel, 25,* 213-220.

Kagan, D. M., & Squires, R. L. (1984b). Eating disorders among adolescents: Patterns and prevalence. *Adolescence, 19,* 15-29.

Kalliopouska, M. (1982). Body-image disturbances in patients with anorexia nervosa. *Psychological Reports, 51*(3, Pt. 1), 715-722.

Kaplan, H. I., & Kaplan, H. S. (1957). The psychosomatic concept of obesity. *Journal of Nervous and Mental Disorders, 125,* 181-201.

Katzman, M. A., & Wolchik, S. A. (1984). Bulimia and binge eating in college women: A comparison of personality and behavior characteristics. *Journal of Consulting and Clinical Psychology, 52,* 423-428.

Kelly, J. T., & Patten, S. E. (1985). Adolescent behaviors and attitudes toward weight and eating. In J. E. Mitchell (Ed.), *Anorexia nervosa and bulimia: Diagnosis and treatment* (pp. 191-204). Minneapolis: University of Minnesota Press.

LeClair, N. J., & Berkowitz, B. (1983). Counseling concerns for the individual with bulimia. *Personnel and Guidance Journal, 61,* 352-355.

Leon, G. R. (1984). Anorexia nervosa and sports activities. *Behavior Therapist, 7,* 9-10.

Leon, G. R., & Chamberlain, K. (1973). Comparison of daily eating habits and emotional states of overweight persons successful or unsuccessful in maintaining weight loss. *Journal of Consulting & Clinical Psychology, 41,* 108-115.

Leon, G. R., Kolotkin, R., & Korgeski, G. (1979). MacAndrews Addiction Scale and other MMPI characteristics associated with obesity, anorexia, and smoking behavior. *Addictive Behaviors, 4,* 401-407.

Lucas, A. R. (1981). Toward the understanding of anorexia nervosa as a disease entity. *Mayo Clinic Proceedings, 56,* 254-264.

Maceyko, S. J., & Nagelberg, D. B. (1985). The assessment of bulimia in high school students. *Journal of School Health, 55,* 135-137.

Mayer, J. (1968). *Obesity: Causes, cost, and control.* Englewood Cliffs, NJ: Prentice-Hall.

Mendelson, B. K., & White, D. R. (1982). Relation between body-esteem and self-esteem of obese and normal children. *Perceptual & Motor Skills, 53*(3, Pt. 1), 899-905.

Metropolitan Life Insurance Company. (1959). New weight standards for men and women. *Statistical Bulletin, 40,* 1-4.

Miller, T. M., Coffman, J. G., & Linke, R. A. (1980). Survey on body image, weight and diet of college students. *Journal of the American Dietetic Association, 77,* 561-566.

Millman, M. (1980). *Such a pretty face: Being fat in America.* New York: Berkley Books.

Mitchell, J. E. (Ed.). (1985). *Anorexia nervosa and bulimia: Diagnosis and treatment.* Minneapolis, MN: University of Minnesota Press.

Mitchell, J. E., & Pyle, R. L. (1985). Characteristics of bulimia. In J. E. Mitchell (Ed.), *Anorexia nervosa and bulimia: Diagnosis and treatment* (pp. 29-47). Minneapolis, MN: University of Minnesota Press.

Mitchell, J. E., Pyle, R. L., & Eckert, E. D. (1981). Frequency and duration of binge-eating episodes in patients with bulimia. *American Journal of Psychiatry, 138,* 835-836.

Moss, R. A., Jennings, G., McFarland, J. H., & Carter, P. (1984). Binge eating, vomiting, and weight fear in a female high school population. *Journal of Family Practice, 18,* 313-320.

Neuman, P. A., & Halvorson, P. A. (1983). *Anorexia nervosa and bulimia: A handbook for counselors and therapists.* New York: Van Nostrand Reinhold.

Nisbett, R. E. (1972). Hunger, obesity, and ventromedial hypothalamus. *Psychological Review, 79,* 433-453.

Norman, I. K., & Herzog, D. B. (1983). Bulimia, anorexia nervosa, and anorexia nervosa with bulimia: A comparative analysis of MMPI profiles. *International Journal of Eating Disorders, 2*(2), 43-52.

Nylander, I. (1971). The feeling of being fat and dieting in a school population: Epidemiologic, interview investigation. *Acta Sociomed Scand, 3,* 17-26.

Ondercin, P. (1979). Compulsive eating in college women. *Journal of College Student Personnel, 20,* 153-157.

Peters, C., Swassing, C. S., Butterfield, P., & McKay, G. (1984). Assessment and treatment of anorexic nervosa and bulimia in school-age children. *School Psychology Review, 13,* 183-191.

Plutchik, R. (1976). Emotions and attitudes related to being overweight. *Journal of Clinical Psychology, 32,* 21-24.

Polivy, J., Herman, C. P., Olmsted, M., & Jazwinski, C. (1984). Restraint and binge eating. In R. C. Hawkins, W. J. Fremouw, & P. F. Clement (Eds.), *The binge-purge syndrome: Diagnosis, treatment, and research* (pp. 104-122). New York: Springer Publishing.

Pope, H. G., & Hudson, J. I. (1984). *New hope for binge eaters.* New York: Harper & Row.

Romeo, F. F. (1984). Early identification of anorexia nervosa in the classroom. *High School Journal, 67,* 81-85.

Rubin, D. (1970). *Forever thin.* New York: Grammercy.

Ruderman, A. J. (1985). Restraint, obesity, and bulimia. *Behavior Research & Therapy, 26,* 151-156.

Saltzer, E. B. (1982). The Weight Locus of Control (WLOC) Scale: A specific measure for obesity research. *Journal of Personality Assessment, 46,* 620-628.

Schacter, S. (1971). Some extraordinary facts about obese humans and rats. *American Psychologist, 26,* 129-144.

Schacter, S., & Gross, L. (1968). Eating and manipulation of time. *Journal of Personality & Social Psychology, 10,* 98-106.

Schoenfielder, L., & Wieser, B. (1983). *Shadow on a tightrope: Writings by women on fat oppression.* Iowa City, IA: Aunt Lute Book Co.

Schorr, B. C., Sanjur, D., & Erickson, E. C. (1972). Teenage food habits: A multidimensional analysis. *Journal of the American Dietetic Association, 61,* 415.

Secord, P., & Jourard, S. (1953). The appraisal of body-cathexis: Body-cathexis and the self. *Journal of Consulting Psychology, 17,* 343-347.

Skoog, D. K., Andersen, A. E., & Laufer, W. S. (1984). Personality and treatment effectiveness in anorexia nervosa. *Journal of Clinical Psychology, 40,* 955-961.

Small, A. C., Madero, J., Gross, H., Teagno, L., Leib, J., & Ebert, M. (1981). A comparative analysis of primary anorexics and schizophrenics on the MMPI. *Journal of Clinical Psychology, 37,* 733-736.

Smead, V. S. (1983). Anorexia nervosa, bulimarexia, and bulimia: Labeled pathology and the Western female. *Women & Therapy, 2,* 19-35.

Smead, V. S. (1984). Eating behaviors which may lead to perpetuate anorexia nervosa, bulimarexia, and bulimia. *Women & Therapy, 3,* 37-49.

Smith, M. C., & Thelen, M. H. (1984). Development and validation of a test for bulimia. *Journal of Consulting and Clinical Psychology, 52,* 863-872.

Strober, M. (1981). A comparative analysis of personality organization in juvenile anorexia nervosa. *Journal of Youth and Adolescence, 10,* 285-295.

Stunkard, A. J., & Burt, V. (1967). Obesity and the body image: II. Age at onset of disturbances in the body. *American Journal of Psychiatry, 123,* 1443-1447.

Sugarman, A., & Kurash, C. (1981). The body as a transitional object in bulimia. *International Journal of Eating Disorders, 1,* 57-67.

Swift, W. J., & Letven, R. (1984). Bulimia and the basic fault: A psychoanalytic interpretation of the bingeing-vomiting syndrome. *Journal of the American Academy of Child Psychiatry, 23,* 489-497.

VanThorre, M. D., & Vogel, F. X. (1985). The presence of bulimia in high school females. *Adolescence, 20*(77), 45-51.

Verberne, T. J. (1984). Do anorexics and schizophrenics look alike on the MMPI? A critique. *Journal of Clinical Psychology, 40,* 1433-1434.

Wadden, T. A., Foster, G. D., Brownell, K. D., & Finley, E. (1984). Self-concept in obese and normal weight children. *Journal of Consulting & Clinical Psychology, 52,* 1104-1105.

Wallston, B. S., Wallston, K. A., Kaplan, G. D., & Maides, S. A. (1976). Development and validation of the Health Locus of Control (HLC) Scale. *Journal of Consulting & Clinical Psychology, 44,* 580-585.

Weiss, S. W., & Ebert, M. H. (1983). Psychological and behavioral characteristics of normal weight bulimics and normal weight controls. *Psychosomatic Medicine, 45,* 293-303.

Williamson, D. A., Kelly, M. L., Davis, C. J., Ruggiero, L., & Blouin, D. C. (1985). Psychopathology of eating disorders: A controlled comparison of bulimic, obese, and normal subjects. *Journal of Consulting & Clinical Psychology, 53,* 161-166.

Wilson, G. T. (1976). Obesity, binged eating and behavior therapy: Some clinical observations. *Behavior Therapy, 7,* 700-701.

Witt, E. D., Ryan, C., & Hsu, L. G. (1985). Learning deficits in adolescents with anorexia nervosa. *Journal of Nervous and Mental Disease, 173,* 182-184.

Wolf, E. M., & Crother, J. H. (1983). Personality and eating habit variables as predictors of severity of binge eating and weight. *Addictive Behaviors, 8,* 335-344.

Wyden, P. (1965). *The overweight society.* New York: William Morrow.

8

Assessment of Adolescent Substance Abuse

THORANA NELSON, M.A., DAVID ROSENTHAL, PH.D., ROBERT G.
HARRINGTON, PH.D., DANNY MITCHELSON, M.A., MS.ED.

Adolescent substance abuse is frequently misunderstood by the public and often misrepresented by the popular press. Despite reports to the contrary, the overall number of adolescents abusing substances in the past 5 years has not increased (Bennett & Vourakis, 1983). In fact, in a study of over 16,000 high school seniors conducted by the National Institute on Drug Abuse (NIDA), Johnston, O'Malley, and Bachman (1986) reported that overall drug use, except for cocaine, has declined from previous years. Marijuana use also has declined. Five percent of the seniors surveyed in 1985 used marijuana at least 20 times in the previous month compared to 11% in 1978. Teenage disapproval of regular marijuana use increased, with 85% of the seniors disapproving in 1985 compared with 65% in 1977. In the same study, Johnston et al. (1986) reported that 61% of the high school seniors surveyed had used an illicit drug at least once and 92% had tried alcohol; 67% had used alcohol in the previous month, 5% daily. Further, it was reported in 1982 that of those high school seniors who used alcohol, 9% tried it for the first time in sixth grade. Despite reports that substance abuse has either stabilized (Bennett & Vourakis, 1983) or declined (L. D. Johnston, personal communication, January, 1985; Johnston et al., 1986), the adolescent drug problem is still enormous.

Table 1 shows the incidence rates by recency of use for 16 types of drugs as reported in the previously mentioned national sample of high school seniors (Johnston et al., 1986). Alcohol users represent the largest category of substance users. The number of high schoolers who have ever used marijuana also represent a substantial number (54.2%). Over 17% of the teenagers reporting in this study said that they had used cocaine at least once. The reported incidence of heroin use is low (1.2%), but given the repercussions of its use this percentage is still of great concern.

Controversy also exists among researchers about the health costs of substance abuse. For example, some studying marijuana use have reported significant irreversible changes in brain structure and function, genetic or prenatal damage to unborn children, and suppression of pituitary sex hormones involved in reproduction (National Academy of Sciences, 1982). On the other hand, each of these charges have been challenged in many instances by the results of other research studies (Pollin, 1980). Certainly the financial and social costs are immense. Ten thousand youths between the ages of 16 and 24 are killed yearly in alcohol-related car crashes (NIDA, 1983). An additional 300,000 youths are seriously injured in such accidents.

This chapter reflects the cooperative efforts of the authors.

TABLE 1*

PREVALENCE (PERCENT EVER USED) AND RECENCY OF USE OF SIXTEEN TYPES OF DRUGS (1985)
(Approx. N = 16,000)

	Ever used	Past month	Past year, not past month	Not past year	Never used
Marijuana/Hashish	54.2	25.7	14.9	13.6	45.8
Inhalants[a]	15.4	2.2	3.5	9.7	84.6
Inhalants Adjusted[b]	*17.9*	*2.9*	*4.3*	*10.7*	*82.1*
Amyl & Butyl Nitrites[c]	7.9	1.6	2.4	3.9	92.1
Hallucinogens	10.3	2.5	3.8	4.0	89.7
Hallucinogens Adjusted[d]	*12.2*	*4.2*	*3.5*	*4.5*	*87.8*
LSD	7.5	1.6	2.8	3.1	92.5
PCP[c]	4.9	1.6	1.3	2.0	95.1
Cocaine	17.3	6.7	6.4	4.2	82.7
Heroin	1.2	0.3	0.3	0.6	98.8
Other opiates[e]	10.2	2.3	3.6	4.3	89.8
Stimulants Adjusted[e,f]	*26.2*	*6.8*	*9.0*	*10.4*	*73.8*
Sedatives[e]	11.8	2.4	3.4	6.0	88.2
Barbiturates[e]	9.2	2.0	2.6	4.6	90.8
Methaqualone[e]	6.7	1.0	1.8	3.9	93.3
Tranquilizers[e]	11.9	2.1	4.0	5.8	88.1
Alcohol	92.2	65.9	19.7	6.6	7.8
Cigarettes	68.8	30.1	(38.7)[g]		31.2

*From Johnston, L. D., O'Malley, P. M., & Bachman, J. G. (1986). *Drug use among high school students, college students and other young adults.* Rockville, MD: National Institute on Drug Abuse.

[a]Data based on four questionnaire forms. N is four-fifths of N indicated.
[b]Adjusted for underreporting of amyl and butyl nitrites. See text [Johnston, O'Malley, & Bachman, 1986] for details.
[c]Data based on a single questionnaire form. N is one-fifth of N indicated.
[d]Adjusted for underreporting of PCP. See text [Johnston, O'Malley, & Bachman, 1986] for details.
[e]Only drug use which was not under a doctor's orders is included here.
[f]Adjusted for the inappropriate reporting of non-prescription stimulants.
[g]The combined total for the two columns is shown because the question asked did not discriminate between the two answer categories.

Over 12,000 13- to 14-year-olds and nearly 19,000 15-year-olds were arrested in 1980 for drug abuse violations (Flanagan & McLeod, 1983). Approximately 30,000 16-year-olds were arrested for drug-related violations in 1980, excluding drunk driving. More that 31,500 adolescents were admitted to federally funded substance-abuse programs in 1980, at substantial cost to taxpayers and with emotional costs to adolescents and their families.

CONSIDERATIONS IN ADOLESCENT SUBSTANCE ABUSE ASSESSMENT

The assessment of adolescent problems in general and substance abuse behaviors in particular calls for knowledge in the fields of adolescent behavior, substance abuse, and family dynamics. The authors of this chapter wish to emphasize a family systems perspective for adolescent substance abuse assessment and refer the reader to Stanton and Todd (1982), Kaufman (1985), and Ault-Riché and Rosenthal (1986) for additional readings in this area. This focus on family issues when assessing adolescent chemical dependency is particularly necessary when one considers that 1) most of the research on chemically dependent adults has been inappropriately applied to adolescents, 2) assessment procedures designed for adults are not appropriate for use with adolescents, particularly when they ignore family issues, and 3) previous research has suggested the usefulness of working with the entire family rather than an individual on substance abuse issues (Gurman & Kniskern, 1979). Furthermore, adolescent substance abuse is considered a major issue in family assessment and therapy because of the physical and social consequences associated with it and because hospitalization of the adolescent may be involved.

This chapter is offered as a guide for practitioners, especially as they confer with other professionals, and not as a comprehensive treatise on the topic. Adolescent substance abuse is a complex problem, calling for the team efforts of a variety of professionals for successful assessment and treatment. School counselors, psychologists, therapists, and medical personnel must work together to determine the extent and severity of a variety of issues, including physical, behavioral, emotional, social, and familial. Practitioners who are not already experienced in working with adolescents or substance abusers may find their initial encounters with the substance-abusing adolescent and/or family to be rather difficult. Some may feel uncomfortable using slang or drug jargon and may not appear credible. Professionals must rely on their own personal styles and on other professionals in such situations.

Practitioners should be cautious about using any single measure to evaluate the severity or etiology of substance use. For example, Marlatt (1983) clearly states that urinalyses or the use of a "dipstick" method for evaluating substance use only indicates whether an individual is "wet" or "dry" at a fixed point in time. That is, a urinalysis may detect the presence of a substance in a person's body, but it cannot suggest etiology or treatment or even whether the usage is a problem. Similarly, personality tests may provide information that suggests an addictive personality, but they cannot predict future behavior. Moberg (1983) concurs with Marlatt, suggesting that any unidimensional assessment process may result in a misclassification of an adolescent as an abuser. Professionals must strive to distinguish occasional chemical use or misuse from a pattern of abuse or dependency.

Because of the significant relationship between assessment and treatment, it is necessary to develop procedures that facilitate both processes. Treatment providers and assessment professionals may find information lacking regarding the particular developmental, physical, and treatment needs of adolescents as compared to those of adults and children. Consequently, it is important 1) to define clearly the various behaviors that lead to diagnoses of adolescent substance use, abuse, and/or dependency, 2) to specify the uses and misuses attendant with various assessment measures, and 3) to ensure that treatment matches the various diagnoses of substance use. Long-term hospitalization of adolescent substance abusers is controversial, and professionals should be cautious of diagnostic labels that could mandate such treatment. Diagnostic activities should be conducted within the definitional contexts of the problem, distinguishing whether it is a legal, physical, developmental, school, or familial issue, as each context suggests a different criterion for diagnosis and treatment.

The clinician should also keep ethical and legal points in mind when utilizing the information in this chapter. Ethical codes and state regulations related to substance abuse and juvenile versus adult definitions of such should be a part of substance abuse assessment education. For example, clinicians may need to inform substance abusers that if they suspect illegal activity or that which may bring harm to others, it may become necessary to report this to the proper authorities (Steininger, Newell, & Garcia, 1984).

Understanding the Nature of the Problem

Experimentation versus Chronic Substance Abuse

Before assessing an adolescent for possible substance abuse, the professional must become familiar with definitional features of use and abuse of as well as dependency on mood-altering chemical substances. These definitional features affect the assessment of adolescent problems and the treatment decisions made regarding these individuals and their families. For example, the impact of substance abuse may influence behaviors differentially among younger children, adolescents, and adults. In such situations, labels that could apply to adult behavior, for instance, may be inappropriate for teenagers.

It is important to consider differences between "experimentation" and "problematic" substance abuse, as these are the key issues that separate adolescent from adult substance abusers. Without this viewpoint, practitioners experienced with adult abusers may conclude that one-time misuse or overuse of a chemical is part of an adolescent's established behavior pattern, when this may not be so. Self-destructive patterns of substance abuse should always be treated with extreme caution and concern; however, adolescent experimentation may be treated more conservatively in the context of other adolescent developmental problems (Weil, 1972). Indeed, overreaction (e.g., inpatient treatment) for a single case of adolescent experimentation may do as much to establish a pattern of substance misuse or abuse as does peer pressure.

Definitions of Substance Abuse

According to the *Diagnostic and Statistical Manual of Mental Disorders* (DSM-III; American Psychiatric Association, 1980), a distinction must be made between pathological substance *abuse* and nonpathological substance *use*. The DSM-III manual cautions against overly strict uses of the criteria and recommends the consideration of contextual features such as cultural and social norms. There are three criteria that distinguish pathological substance abuse from nonpathological use: 1) a pattern of pathological use; 2) impairment in social or occupational functioning related to the pattern of pathological use; and 3) duration. Several components comprise each of these criteria.

Criterion 1, a pattern of pathological substance abuse, is considered met when (a) the substance or substances are used repeatedly; (b) the efforts to cut down or stop the use are unsuccessful; (c) there is frequent use despite knowledge that it is harmful; (d) there is a need for the substance in order to function adequately; and/or (e) there have been episodes of intoxication complications, such as blackouts or overdoses. In addition, the examiner should ascertain what type of drug is being abused ("hard" versus "soft"), as hard drug abuse may be more symptomatic of a chronic pattern of abuse.

Criterion 2, an impairment in social or occupational functioning, is considered met when (a) social relations have deteriorated and inappropriate displays of aggressiveness have been reported; (b) substance abuse has been determined to be a contributing factor in legal actions, such as cases involving car accidents, petty theft, and so on; (c) a sudden deterioration in work or school functioning related to the substance abuse is identified; (d) a pattern of personality and affective disorders is observed due to the substance abuse and not to some preexisting mental disorder(s).

Criterion 3, duration, is met when a pattern of substance abuse lasts at least one month. The pattern may be intermittent rather than continuous.

DSM-III associates eight classes of substances with pathological substance abuse: alcohol, barbiturates or similarly acting sedatives or hypnotics, opioids, amphetamines or similarly acting sympathomimetics, cannabis, cocaine, phencyclidine (PCP) or similarly acting arylcyclohexylamines, and hallucinogens.

Further definitional distinctions must be made between pathological substance abuse and dependency. As defined by DSM-III, a diagnosis of the latter requires physiological dependence, in which the client experiences either (a) a tolerance to the substance that requires greater amounts for minimum effects or (b) adverse physiological reactions when withdrawing from the substance. In addition, evidence of social or occupational impairment is required. Tobacco use does not typically impair social or occupational functioning and thus is not associated with definitions of substance abuse by DSM-III standards.

Except for chronic substance abuse and dependency, as defined using DSM-III criteria, most adolescent use is experimental or recreational and may involve substances that are legal for adults. In other words, the behavior may not fit the criteria for substance abuse because it may occur less frequently and/or typically in peer-related situations, may not have a negative association with other behavior, and may involve substances such as alcohol, diet pills, or tobacco. The use of illegal drugs such as marijuana and cocaine should be considered more serious than experimentation with alcohol or diet pills (amphetamines), even when used experimentally, as the former require more effort to obtain, are less acceptable in most social situations, and involve legal consequences.

This is not to suggest that marijuana and cocaine are potentially more harmful physiologically than alcohol or amphetamines, but that their use possibly suggests more serious behavioral and treatment issues.

It should be noted that the absence of a DSM-III criterion diagnosis does not mean necessarily that no problem exists for the adolescent or his or her family. School, police, or family identification alone indicates a need for some kind of assessment and treatment, regardless of negative physiological test results and criterion measures. "No-problem" problems (Eastwood, Sweeney, & Piercy, in press) need treatment, but possibly of a different sort or with a different focus. Fors and Rojek (1983) have attempted to distinguish "no-problem" problems from other chronic forms of substance abuse by identifying three groups of drug-use behaviors: traditional, rebel or "fringe," and hard core. As could be expected, Fors and Rojek consider the recreational use of beer, cigarettes, or stimulants ("traditional" behaviors) less problematic than more frequent use of depressants, cocaine, LSD, or narcotics ("fringe" behaviors). Most problematic are the hard drugs such as narcotics. Dependency on such substances and its associated behaviors, such as auto theft, breaking and entering, and assault, indicate hard-core abuse and are of extreme seriousness.

Adult DSM-III criteria, based on adult normative samples, adult developmental theory and behaviors, and legal and social definitions related to appropriate adult behavior, should be used cautiously when assessing the teenager. The unique nature of adolescent physiology, psychology, and behavior, and factors related to adult responses to adolescent behavior (e.g., coming home drunk), should contribute to the differentiation of assessment definitions and criteria as well as treatment modalities.

Factors Contributing to Adolescent Substance Abuse

The etiology of adolescent substance abuse is multidimensional. Factors such as age, economics, social or ethnic group, peer pressure, developmental issues, and family dynamics all contribute, wholly or in part, to the development of a substance-abuse symptom. One reason adolescents may begin a pattern of abuse is because of the widespread availability of certain substances considered attractive by adolescent populations. According to a national study conducted by the National Institute on Drug Abuse (Johnston et al., 1986), almost 90% of U.S. high school seniors reported that they could obtain marijuana "very easily" or "fairly easily." Furthermore, over 50% reported the same view regarding amphetamines, barbiturates, and tranquilizers. Given adolescents' natural curiosity and interests in experimentation, it is not surprising that they are willing to take the risks involved in using substances that are so readily available.

Peer pressure is a second factor in adolescent substance experimentation and use. Gallup reported in 1977 that this was the most frequently cited reason for drug use among adolescents aged 13 to 18. The most recent NIDA report (Johnston et al., 1986) confirmed these findings: 20% believed that most or all of their friends smoked marijuana in the previous year and 66% indicated that most or all of their friends drank alcoholic beverages in the previous year. Almost 6% thought that most or all of their friends had used cocaine within the previous year. While peers may not always pressure adolescents into experimenting with or using alcohol or drugs, there certainly is a lot of temptation involved in many peer activities. Drugs are often fun, relieve feelings of stress, produce pleasurable feelings or euphoria or relaxation, and are often part of attractive pseudo-adult activity and peer interaction.

A third factor contributing to adolescent substance use involves adolescent rebellion against perceived parental values related to the use of mood-altering substances (Kandel, 1980). Although 95% of the high school seniors surveyed in the 1986 NIDA study (Johnston et al.) reported that their parents disapproved of occasional marijuana smoking, 26% of the same group reported that they had smoked marijuana or hashish in the past month anyway. Similarly, 80% of this same sample indicated that their parents disapproved of adolescents' consuming five or more drinks once or twice each weekend, yet 37% reported that on at least one occasion during the prior 2-week interval, they had consumed at least that amount of alcohol.

A fourth reason for adolescent substance use/abuse cited by 26% of the adolescents in one study (Gilbert, 1979) was to escape from alienation and the pressures of life. Normal adolescent behavior includes extreme responses to normal stresses such as school pressures, peer relations, changing family interactions, individuation, and societal problems (e.g., nuclear armament). Feelings of being overwhelmed, availability of mood-altering substances, and peer encouragement combine with the "high" associated with ingestion to reinforce substance use as a coping response to life.

Family conflict represents a fifth contributing factor. Significant dysfunction in family life may maintain an adolescent substance abuse problem. Among the problem areas that may be experienced by children of alcoholics are the following: 1) unresolved emotional bonds with the family; 2) fear and denial of feelings; 3) poor communication skills; 4) role confusion; 5) problems of identification; 6) lack of trust and avoidance of intimacy; and 7) assumption of excessive responsibility as children. Research has found that, due in part to these dysfunctional family circumstances and the alcoholic role models, children of alcoholics are at a higher risk of becoming alcoholics themselves (Black & Steven, 1986).

FAMILY DYNAMICS AS A CONTEXT FOR ASSESSMENT

Psychological examiners should view the family of the substance abuser as a primary influence on the dynamics of assessing substance abuse as well as on treatment, recovery, and continued abstinence (Stanton & Todd, 1982). The focus of assessment is not on the etiology of the problem but on the interpersonal family dynamics that maintain the symptomatology (Rosenthal, Nelson, & Drake, 1986). Clinicians should be careful not to attribute any one cause to the problem or to blame individual family members, because this may serve to exacerbate, rather than alleviate, the problem. For example, an adolescent may begin using drugs experimentally because he or she enjoys the state of altered consciousness and then may fall into overuse and misuse as a habit unrelated to family or individual problems (Weil, 1972).

With these caveats in mind, the following research is offered to demonstrate how family dynamics might influence or maintain an adolescent substance abuse problem. Research has shown that young adolescents who consume alcoholic beverages may begin to do so at home with the knowledge of their parents (Conger & Petersen, 1984), most often during holidays and special celebrations. In fact, 13% of all high school students are encouraged by their parents to drink alcohol in their homes (NIDA, 1983). As they grow older, the proportions of adolescents drinking within the home remains stable, however these same adolescents may increase the amount of time spent in drinking outside of the home. Adolescents who are heavy drinkers are significantly more likely to have parents who drink heavily than non-drinkers from junior high school to college entrance. In addition, adolescents who are problem or heavy drinkers are apt to report more difficulties with their parents, are less likely to value academic achievement, and, in fact, do obtain lower grades (Kandel, Kessler, & Margulies, 1978).

Further, studies have shown that when both parents smoke cigarettes, the percent of male and female adolescents who become smokers is about double that of homes in which neither parent smokes (National Institute of Health, 1977). The probabilities that an adolescent will begin to smoke are quadruple when an older sibling and both parents smoke (National Institute of Health, 1977).

Not only do parents have a strong influence on their adolescents' drinking and smoking behaviors, but research has shown that they may also influence the use of marijuana, amphetamines, and barbiturates by their attitudes, values, and behaviors. Parents who convey beliefs that marijuana is harmful or morally wrong are less likely to have children who use marijuana (Brook, Lukoff, & Whiteman, 1980). Parental use of tranquilizers, amphetamines, barbiturates, alcohol, or tobacco is positively correlated with adolescent use of these or other (illegal) drugs (Kandel, 1980).

Certain family dynamics make adolescent family members more prone to engage in substance abuse, including emotional distance, parental uninvolvement, low parental expectations for adolescents, parental passivity, and deviant behavior (Kandel, 1980). The influence of dysfunctional families on maintaining adolescent drug abuse may be strong in some cases. The families of drug-abusing adolescents engage in more scapegoating, are more authoritarian, and converse less openly and equally than do normal families (Gantman, 1978). All of these communication factors and the familial factors mentioned earlier may contribute to the prevalence of substance abuse among adolescents. Of course, there will be those cases in which the family dynamics do not serve to maintain the adolescent substance abuse problem, but these cases are in the minority.

Individual Development

The close affinity between family relationships and substance abuse that has been identified for adolescents seems to endure through adulthood. For example, one third of adult abusers surveyed by Stanton and Todd (1982) were still living with their family-of-origin. Another substantial number continued to list their mother's street address as their primary residence, indicating emotional, if not physical, ties with their families. These facts support previous research that has shown substance abusers' long-term dependency on physical ties with their families rather than seeking their own individuality. Stanton has called this situation *pseudoindividuation;* that is, the individual sustains the illusion of independence from his or her family while remaining dependent on them.

For adolescents, this means that the critical individuation process is especially troublesome. In some families, it is more difficult to separate and maintain intimacy at the same time, as family loyalty is tremendously important (Boszormenyi-Nagy & Spark, 1984). Within these families, the conflict between remaining loyal and close on the one hand and individuating on the other is resolved (by both adults and adolescents) by using substances. In this way, an adolescent may appear separated, staying away from home and appearing to value peer and drug activities over family activities, but he or she remains dependent upon the family economically and emotionally, unable to care for him- or herself and needing the family to assist in the resolution of difficulties.

Substance abuse as a means of resolving the loyalty-individuation conflict produces problems of its own for the adolescent. Achievement of independence from the family is the primary task of adolescence (Ackerman, 1980; Weidman, 1983); however, when drug usage interferes with normal adolescent development, not only may transitions to independent living be delayed, but also the time needed for the acquisition of important developmental skills may be lost (Birmingham & Sheehy, 1984). Thus, even after treatment and recovery habitual substance abusers may not have the social skills necessary to develop job skills or heterosexual relationships and often appear immature.

The significance of these observations is that assessment should begin by identifying the highest level of development that the adolescent substance abuser has achieved, what age-appropriate skills he or she should have achieved if development had not been interrupted, and the developmental tasks still to be accomplished. Developmental skills include 1) identification with role models, 2) identification with and responsibility for family processes, 3) interpersonal skills, 4) systemic skills, and 5) judgmental skills (Glenn & Warner, 1977). The implications of the developmental perspective for treatment is that remediation of developmental delays may be helpful (Spoth & Rosenthal, 1980).

Family Life Cycle

In addition to adolescent developmental issues, family life-cycle stages should also be considered in assessing substance abuse situations. (For a full explication of family life cycles, see Carter & McGoldrick, 1980, particularly chapters 4 and 7). Typically, families progress through a series of life stages that involve a variety of family transitions and adaptations. If one of these stages has been particularly problematic, the transition to the succeeding stage may be more difficult (Haley, 1980). Solutions used during one stage may not be effective in the next stage, and new solutions must be developed. Adolescent acting out may signal such stage-transition difficulties. Additionally, some adolescents may use drugs as a way of both escaping from and distracting their parents from unresolved family problems.

Parenting Behavior

Parenting behavior is part of the context of adolescent substance abuse. It is important to note, however, that this does not mean that adolescent substance abuse is "caused" by "bad" parental behavior (Dell, 1980). Parenting techniques that were appropriate for a younger, dependent child may no longer be effective with an adolescent. It is often difficult for parents and children to work through the changes needed for young people to learn negotiation of rules and consequences. Parents may over-respond to normal adolescent "stretching" with extreme punishments. Parents may disagree with each other about appropriate parenting, undermine each other, and unintentionally exacerbate the problems. Subsequently, an otherwise minor problem, such as staying out too late, may be seen as something more severe (Watzlawick, Weakland, & Fisch, 1974). Parenting that is inattentive to adolescent developmental changes may also be accompanied by problematic behavior. Adolescents need guide-lines, limits, and clear consequences for their behavior in order to develop a sense of self within a secure environment.

Family Conflict

Marital or other family problems also may be part of the context of adolescent substance abuse. As stated previously, during adolescence the individual must resolve the dilemma of dependence on versus independence from the family. Marital conflict can be precipitated or exacerbated by this phenomenon and drug usage may escalate in response to the marital conflict, particularly if the adolescent behavior has served to distract the parents in other ways earlier in the family's development. Par-ents in these families who have had difficulty resolving their disagreements may find the typical stresses that accompany adolescent movement toward independence diffi-cult to cope with and may fight "through the child" by blaming the other parent for the child's current behavior. The adolescent's substance abuse may serve to distract the parents so that they avoid or postpone their marital crisis and focus on the problematic behavior of the child. Another parental reaction can be to display a "united front" (Minuchin, 1974), in which the spouses appear to be in agreement with each other about their "awful" child. If the child were to become drug-free and asymptomatic without the resolution of the parents' marital conflict, it is possible that the family unit might dissolve. In either case, the adolescent may "cooperate" by developing symp-toms.

Disturbing adolescent behavior also may mask or distract family members from attending to other kinds of family problems as well. Madanes (1981) and Minuchin (1974) have suggested that sometimes a problem adolescent's behavior can be viewed as sacrificial and protective of another family member or the family as a whole. Addi-tionally, the behavior may serve as a means for dealing with other family problems, such as difficulties with extended family members, work-related issues, and involve-ment with other systems (e.g., schools, protective services, police). In the more for-tunate cases, this scapegoating serves to bring the family to treatment. If family issues are not addressed, however, it is possible that substance abuse treatment will be unsuccessful (Gurman & Kniskern, 1979). Whether the clinician begins to concep-tualize a case with the family's poor problem-solving attempts or with the adolescent's substance abuse, both are part of the same cycle.

PRELIMINARY ASSESSMENT CONSIDERATIONS

Jacobson (1983) differentiates between substance abuse detection, assessment, and diagnosis. Detection provides a *yes* or *no* answer to the question of the presence of drug abuse. This approach may be rather limiting, as it provides no information about the parameters of the substance abuse problem. Assessment provides a continuum profile of the pattern, severity, and duration of substance use behavior. Diagnosis should provide implications for the treatment of a disorder or problematic behavior pattern. It is recommended that assessment, diagnosis, and treatment be considered simultaneously when assessing adolescent substance abuse.

Stein and Davis (1982) advocate the use of progressive criteria rather than bivariate decision-making, which would classify an adolescent as either a user or a nonuser of drugs. They postulate a progression of drug use that moves from (a) experimentation through (b) escape from depressive or anxious thoughts/situations to (c) relief from a threat of breakdown. A category of substance dependence specifically for adolescents is not included, although Stein and Davis do include a category of pleasure from alteration of mood, which may apply to adolescent substance use. These researchers further suggest that a comprehensive assessment of drug use should consider patterns within the family, the adolescent's ability to make discriminations (e.g., appropriate decision-making), and factors in the adolescent's environment that may be reinforcing the substance abuse.

Symptoms and Signs

The symptomatology associated with substance abuse is comprised of physical, physiological, and behavioral patterns. Physical symptoms include bloodshot, dull-looking, or watery eyes, runny nose, coughing, needle marks, weight loss, some forms of acute acne, and tremors. Physiological signs include positive tests for certain substances in the urine or blood, positive alcohol levels in breathalyzer tests, and abnormal respiration, heart rate, and blood pressure. Behavioral signs include drowsiness; manic/hyper behavior; hallucinations; delusions; irresponsible behavior at home, with peers, or at school; excessive argumentative behavior; mood swings; lack of motivation; solitary behavior; frequent absence from home; nonparticipation in family activities; new, unusual friends; forgetfulness; lying; changes in speaking patterns, such as slowed or slurred speech; and legal problems. Other signs that may accompany substance abuse include drugs missing from medicine cabinets, alcohol missing from liquor cabinets, falling grades, truancy, car accidents, missing clothing or possessions, strange phone calls, and use or possession of drug paraphernalia.

The professional psychologist should be aware that many of the aforementioned symptoms may be associated with normal variability in behavior or with non-drug-related health problems. Consequently, the signs do not in themselves constitute proof of substance abuse. Adolescents who exhibit sudden changes in their daily routines or personality patterns should be examined for problems such as sexual abuse as well as for evidence of substance abuse. Conclusions must be based on multiple sources of information so that false positives as well as undue family conflict may be avoided.

Physiological Evaluation

The first step in the assessment of adolescent substance use/abuse is referral for urinalysis or blood testing to determine the presence and extent of any toxic substances. Laboratory results should be obtained as part of a physician/clinician team approach to assessment and treatment. Professionals involved in the assessment and treatment of adolescent substance abusers should be somewhat familiar with physiological assessment data in general, but should rely on medical personnel for interpretation and assistance; this strengthens the therapeutic system and is compulsory when detoxification or hospitalization is necessary. When interpreting physiological tests, one must keep in mind that urine and blood testing indicate only the presence or absence of a substance in a person's system (a high concentration implies nothing about frequency of use), that the effects of drugs or alcohol on a young person's body are different than on an adult's, and that the adolescent may respond to these effects in different ways.

In addition, criterion levels and measurement accuracy greatly affect the kind of information the clinician may receive and interpret. For example, a different criterion is needed for assessing addiction than for assessing the occasional use of a particular substance. While initial screening of blood or urine may result in a 65-95% accuracy rate for specific drugs, Cohen (1984) suggests that these tests be followed by gas chromatography in order to reduce further the possibility of false positives or negatives. Others (Bernhardt, Mumford, Taylor, Smith, & Murray, 1984) suggest that laboratory tests ordered and interpreted by physicians should be combined with structured interviews by clinicians because the laboratory results may be accurate only 30% of the time. A number of variables affect the results of physiological tests and must be considered, including body weight, fluid intake, urine acidity, diet, level of physical activity, quantity of drug ingested, and time elapsed since the substance was consumed (Cohen, 1984).

For treatment to be successful, the professional must obtain clear information and agreement that a problem exists from everyone involved, including parents and teachers. When an adolescent suspected of drug use denies or minimizes the use of illegal substances, it may be beneficial for the family to be instructed to gather behavioral data on usage as a supplement to physiological measures. This method of assessment involves the abuser and his or her family, as well as significant others such as school personnel, as part of the assessment/treatment team and provides information about family dynamics associated with the problem. It also serves to enlist the cooperation and involvement of the family in treatment, which thus becomes part of an ongoing assessment and treatment process.

In conclusion, physiological tests, although often necessary and ordered by a physician, should be interpreted cautiously as part of the whole clinical picture to avoid false positive identifications. The possible misuse of these tests and their results in developing treatment plans should be considered. Telling parents that their children have used unspecified amounts of drugs for unspecified periods of time will not help either the parent or the child; the continued involvement of clinicians is necessary in the interpretation of such test results and in the careful planning of interventions.

SPECIALIZED INSTRUMENTATION TO ASSESS SUBSTANCE ABUSE

Most of the available instrumentation for assessing substance abuse deals with the use/abuse of alcohol. As this is the major form of substance abuse among teenagers, these instruments should prove helpful. Although measures for assessing other forms of substance abuse are almost nonexistent, many of the instruments for assessing alcohol abuse have been adapted for other substances. However, the examiner must be cautious: many of the available instruments have not been normed appropriately with adolescent populations, and their normative results may not be valid when used to assess adolescents. Consequently, many should be used informally with adolescent subjects.

In the initial phases of substance abuse assessment it may be useful to determine the extent and frequency of drug use after the presence of drugs or alcohol in the adolescent's system has been verified. The Drug Use Index (DUI; Douglass & Khavari, 1978) was developed as a quantitative index of multiple drug use that covers 19 various drugs, including alcohol, marijuana, cocaine, amphetamines, and tranquilizers. The drugs listed in the DUI are grouped according to their psychopharmacological characteristics, providing the clinician with a view of the overall pattern of drug use. Respondents are asked if they have ever tried each drug and how frequently they use them. In scoring, the DUI assigns less weight to the more commonly used drugs, creating a classification for experimental use of drugs such as alcohol and marijuana. This is an important consideration in the assessment of substance use in adolescents, who may experiment with drugs on an occasional and infrequent basis. The DUI Assessment Profile describes the extent of drug use in four major categories (Psychedelics, Euphorics-Analgesics, Depressants-Tranquilizers, and Stimulants), with separate indicators for antidepressants (more commonly used by prescription), over-the-counter drugs, tobacco, and alcohol. The Assessment Profile also provides an opportunity for reports of other drugs. This type of profile used in conjunction with other assessment procedures may aid in the identification of particular patterns of drug use and possible concomitant psychological problems (e.g., depression as a side effect of barbiturates).

It is important to determine the severity of drug use as well as whether an adolescent is a polydrug user. The Addiction Severity Index (ASI; Erdlen, McLellan, & LaPorte, 1978) was developed for this purpose. According to Erdlen et al., it is assumed that the addictive behavioral pattern associated with alcoholism parallels that associated with other types of drug abuse; therefore, the ASI may be used to assess a wide variety of addictions in addition to alcoholism. The instrument provides for sociological as well as psychological assessment information. The ASI assesses the severity of behavioral characteristics associated with specific chemical use, related medical issues, personality patterns, possible legal issues, family/sociological issues, and employment/support issues. The ASI can be used in conjunction with related information from referral sources, family members, school personnel, and so on for diagnostic purposes and treatment planning. Furthermore, if DSM-III criteria (American Psychiatric Association, 1980) are being used in the assessment process, the ASI may be helpful to clinicians in determining a diagnosis, as it assesses patterns of abuse, social functioning, and duration of use.

Specific characteristics and patterns of drug use may be investigated using the Michigan Alcoholism Screening Test (MAST; Selzer, 1971), a widely used alcohol detection instrument. The MAST is a 25-item questionnaire that deals with a person's drinking history in a yes/no format. The MAST includes such concepts as whether the respondent feels he or she is a normal drinker, whether he or she drinks before noon, and whether he or she can stop drinking without a struggle after one or two drinks. The MAST has the advantages of brief administration time (about 10 minutes), objective scoring, a multivariate profile, and suitability for individual or group administration. Its usefulness in polydrug assessment has not been established and its validity with adolescent populations needs to be tested. The MAST can be administered simultaneously to other family members to increase reliability and to assess family dynamics around the problem.

In summary, probably the best use of the MAST is to place respondents along a continuum of severity of general alcoholic deterioration or involvement. Clinicians may find it useful as well to review specific MAST item responses with the referred adolescent as a point of departure for a diagnostic inteview. A shortened version of the MAST, called the BMAST (Pokorny, Miller, & Kaplan, 1972), is also available, containing 10 of the items found on the original. High correlations have been reported between scores on the MAST and BMAST, making the shortened version a possible substitute for the MAST when quick screening is necessary.

The Minnesota Multiphasic Personality Instrument (MMPI) has been revised to provide separate scales and/or subscales for many specific assessment purposes. Using the MMPI with 600 male subjects (300 alcoholics and 300 psychiatric inpatients), MacAndrew (1965) developed the MacAndrew Scale (MAC) for screening alcoholics. This scale is composed of 49 MMPI items that can be either derived from an administration of the whole test or administered separately as a self-contained instrument. The MAC's reliability, validity, and clinical as well as research usefulness have been documented (Jacobson, 1983). Of particular importance here is the scale's usefulness as an assessment device for measuring multiple drug use, not merely as a screening tool for alcoholism, because it does not seem to discriminate between alcoholism and other drug abuse patterns (Jacobson, 1983).

The items on the MAC are not obviously related to chemical use, making it reliable for use with a "savvy" population. It also is very accurate for classification purposes, yielding few false positives or false negatives (Jacobson, 1983). Because it was normed on adult males, the scale's usefulness with females and with adolescents has been questioned (Friedrick & Loftsgard, 1978; Jacobson, 1983). The MAC seems to be a more reliable assessment device for older, less educated, unemployed males than for females and younger adolescents. Jacobson (1983), however, recommends its use in conjunction with other assessment methods, including laboratory analyses and interviews. In general, clinicians should be cautious when interpreting MMPI profiles for adolescents, as they may appear to be spuriously abnormal; however, Klinge (1983) has found that there is a significant relationship between the MAC and the extent of substance use in adolescents.

Rathus, Fox, and Ortins (1980) have developed an abbreviated MAC using the first 20 items of the original scale for specific use with adolescents. They have found that it predicts thievery and the use of alcohol, cigarettes, and marijuana in this age group. The scale seems to indicate "thrill-seeking" behaviors such as the use of amphetamines, depressants, LSD, and cocaine as well as vandalism and stealing cars. For this reason, it may predict general delinquency rather than alcoholism or drug use per se.

The Adolescent Alcohol Involvement Scale (AAIS; Mayer & Filstead, 1979) is a 40-item self-administered questionnaire designed to differentiate adolescent alcohol abusers from nonproblem drinkers. The AAIS relates drinking to the areas of psychological functioning, social relations, and family living, including items relating to quantity and frequency of drinking, situations when drinking occurs, the consequence of drinking, and the particular beverage consumed.

Moberg (1983) has questioned whether Mayer and Filstead (1979) have been successful in creating a multidimensional measure that assists in defining alcoholism in an empirical manner. Moberg has argued that the AAIS does not examine the different patterns and meanings of alcohol use across the various stages of adolescent development and is concerned that the instrument does not demonstrate stability over time. It could thus falsely identify an adolescent as an abuser without sufficient long-term data. Additionally, Moberg expresses concern that the process of labeling a young person based on such an assessment could be detrimental to the adolescent and his or her family. Moberg concludes that the AAIS may be useful for research, but it should be used cautiously as a supplemental clinical assessment device. The AAIS is included here because it is one of the few instruments that specifically examine adolescent alcohol use.

FAMILY ASSESSMENT

Assessment of family dynamics related to adolescent substance abuse should begin with a family history, including the family's structure and life-cycle stage, a social history of the parents, family-of-origin data, the developmental levels of siblings, and a drug/alcohol history of extended family members. The parents' attitudes toward drugs and alcohol in general should be determined, as well as the approach they take toward discipline, including the level of agreement regarding rules and consequences for infractions. Family problem-solving methods may be observed by asking the parents to decide the next step in the treatment process and then observing the family's interaction. The significance of the adolescent's substance abuse for the parents should be clarified, as well as their goals for the adolescent and the family. When an adolescent's problem-solving capabilities seem impaired, these skills actually may be masked by the presence of the chemicals in the system. At such times, it may be useful to delay assessment of individual or family coping patterns until after a detoxification period.

Stress in the family also requires assessment. Minuchin (1974) describes three kinds of stresses that can contribute to the development of a family's dysfunctional system: normal transitional stresses in the family life cycle; internal stress, such as unresolved family conflict; and external stress, such as unemployment of a family member. It is important to assess the presence of one or more of these stressors, alone and in combinations, as this may suggest different treatments. In some cases, the family has been able to solve the normal problems of life, but becomes dysfunctional under the extraordinary stress associated with financial difficulties, serious illness, or the death of a parent. The adolescent's drug use or abuse may at such times be a way of assisting the family, by bringing attention to them through authorities or professionals.

In addition to assessing current and recent stressors, the current life-cycle position of the family should be ascertained, including an inquiry into the ways the family passed through earlier stages and transitions. The presence of unresolved conflict or unsuccessful task development could suggest issues for exploration in treatment. For example, if parents were not able to agree on disciplining methods when their children were young, it is unlikely that they could incorporate necessary parenting changes for disciplining adolescents. The parents may find it difficult in the current situation to discuss their adolescent's behavior without further distancing each other and exacerbating the substance use/abuse.

The nature and severity of the family's concerns should be assessed so that a plan of treatment appropriate to their situation can be developed. For example, it may not be helpful to the family to confront real or imagined issues if change can be brought about by having the parents reach some agreement about their child's current difficulties and the resolution of the problem. One must remember that the abuse itself may have contributed to the level of family stress and dysfunction. Modifying the family's dysfunctional behaviors may not eradicate the substance use; drug use may involve individual behaviors that are unrelated to family dysfunction. Similarly, eradicating the substance abuse may not, by itself, allow the family to begin functioning successfully. It is necessary in most cases to treat both the substance-abusing adolescent and his or her entire family. Assessment procedures must take into account the kinds of treatment available for different diagnoses, and the clinician must be careful to assess a variety of dynamics related to the adolescent's behavior. (For a comprehensive introduction to family assessment, see Nichols, 1984; Stanton & Todd, 1982; and chapter 2 in this volume.)

Family Assessment Instruments

The Family Adaptability and Cohesion Evaluation Scales (FACES-III; Olson, Portner, & Lavee, 1985) were designed to assess the structural-functional dimensions of family cohesion and adaptability. The cohesion scale measures the balance of closeness and autonomy of individuals in the family, an important issue during adolescence as this is when a child moves out of the family while needing to remain a part of it. The adaptability scale measures the flexibility of a family in problem-solving during various kinds of stress periods, including life-cycle transitions. Excessive cohesion may indicate both an inability to let a child develop relationships outside the family and an overinvolvement with family members' problems. Inadequate cohesion in the family may indicate a lack of awareness about the adolescent's activities, including substance use. A family with inadequate adaptability may find it difficult to alter parenting techniques for adolescents; one with excessive flexibility may not know how to place limits on the adolescent's activities.

FACES-III is the product of several refinements and revisions. It has been normed on a national sample and seems to discriminate functional from nonfunctional families (Olson et al., 1985). The instrument includes questionnaires for both parents and adolescents to complete and includes items regarding the family as the individual views it presently (the real) and as he or she would like it to be (the ideal). Discrepancy scores between the real and the ideal family provide information about levels of satisfaction in the family. In addition, comparisons may be made between parental and adolescent reports by referring to the separate norms tables provided for adults and adolescents (Olson et al., 1985).

Used in conjunction with other assessment tools, the FACES-III may facilitate the assessment of total family functioning and assist in the development of appropriate treatment plans. For example, when no severely dysfunctional family patterns are identified on the FACES-III profile, but the examiner is aware of excessive peer influence in the experimental use of amphetamines, inpatient treatment may not necessarily be the most appropriate therapeutic intervention. Instead, treatment might include assisting the parents to establish appropriate limits and consequences for their adolescent. If the profile indicates a family with overly close relationships (enmeshment) and inability to adapt easily during times of stress, the examiner might assist the family members in separating from each other and in developing new problem-solving skills appropriate for families with adolescents.

Another tool for assessing the family communication patterns of adolescent substance abusers is the Family Assessment Device (FAD; Epstein, Baldwin, & Bishop, 1983). The FAD is a 53-item questionnaire completed by individual family members and composed of seven scales: Problem Solving, Communication, Roles, Affective Responses, Affective Involvement, Behavior Control, and General Functioning. The FAD also provides a multidimensional profile of the family and can suggest content areas for attention in treatment. Differences between family members in particular areas may indicate specific areas of interest to the clinician as well as provide an overall picture of the family's functional level.

Like most self-report inventories, the FACES-III and the FAD may be criticized because they are based on subjective impressions rather than objective criteria. On the other hand, the subjective nature of these instruments may be their strength in assessing cases of adolescent substance abuse. The mere presence/absence of either substance use activity or knowledge about its extent or severity does not suggest treatment issues from a family systems point of view. Instruments such as FACES-III and FAD provide subjective, multidimensional views of reality, which serve both to elicit family member's responses to related family issues and to facilitate change in their family systems. Each family member has his or her own perception or "reality" of the family, which combines with other "realities" to produce the family "reality." None is more real than any of the others. When FACES-III and FAD are used as part of a multidimensional, multilevel assessment that includes a family interview, behavior observations, objective physiological data from laboratory tests, substance inventories such as the DUI and the ASI, and subjective inventories such as the MAST and MAC, such a family-based assessment represents an excellent starting point for suggesting treatment in cases of adolescent substance abuse.

The development of an assessment and treatment contract should include a discussion of the options the family has and a description of potential outcomes. The initial goal and contract should be based on the family's original reason for referral once the presence and definition of the problem has been discussed. Having accomplished the initial treatment goal, the focus of treatment may switch to other concerns if necessary and agreed upon by the family. If the family is adamant about denying the adolescent substance abuse problem, assisting the adolescent in extricating him- or herself from family problems may be the best, albeit last resort, solution (Madanes,

1981). Treatment of substance abuse problems in a context of family therapy is presented in greater depth in Haley (1980), Minuchin, Rosman, and Baker (1978), and Stanton and Todd (1982).

CASE STUDY: A FAMILY-BASED ASSESSMENT OF ADOLESCENT SUBSTANCE ABUSE

No case presentation can typify all the options involved in the assessment or treatment of adolescent substance abuse. The following case offers an illustration of one possible situation and sequence of assessment.

Rick was a 17-year-old high school junior referred by his teacher to the school counselor because of recently falling grades, inattentiveness in class, and absenteeism. When the counselor first met with Rick, she observed some behaviors atypical for him, including bloodshot eyes, irritability, and a poor personal appearance. The initial interview revealed that he liked school and his teachers and could offer no explanation for his changes in behavior and falling grades other than being tired lately. After reviewing Rick's educational file, the counselor phoned his home to schedule a meeting with Rick and his parents.

Rick, his 12-year-old sister, and their parents arrived at the scheduled appointment together. The counselor noted a faint odor of beer on Rick's breath and asked him what he had been drinking. Rick denied any drinking, and his parents expressed alarm with both his drinking and lying. After discussing Rick's recent school behavior, his parents expressed concern that he might have a drinking problem. They recalled other unusual behavior, including lethargy, unkempt appearance, and frequent late-night trips "out." Rick also had begun to snap at them when questioned about his activities. He always had been a rather quiet "loner" with few friends. He had never dated. Rick's parents had not been alarmed, attributing his behavior to school pressures and normal adjustments to adolescence. Rick's father recalled that he had gone through similar periods in his teenage years, though he had not started drinking until his senior year in high school. Rick at first denied any problems, asserting that he was fine and just wanted to be left alone. When asked to describe the last fight he was involved in at home, he admitted leaving the house angry and feeling misunderstood and harassed.

Family members agreed to observe Rick's and the family's behavior during the next week to gather baseline data about issues that had been raised, including Rick's drinking-related behavior and family arguments concerning the children's privileges and responsibilities. Rick further agreed to a urine test "to get my parents off my case." The parents expressed relief with this plan, wishing to clarify the kind and extent of Rick's possible drug and/or alcohol use. They agreed, however, that if the laboratory tests were negative, they were concerned enough with Rick's changed behavior and other family problems to seek further family treatment.

During the next session with the school counselor, the parents reported that although Rick's behavior seemed to improve somewhat, they were concerned with his attitude and withdrawal from the family. There had continued to be some arguing about his responsibilities in the home and activities outside the home. The family physician had reported to the parents the presence of alcohol in Rick's urine and had suggested that they bring him in for a complete physical examination. Rick admitted that the tension at home was high and that he would like to have some help dealing with his parents' arguing with him and over him. He and his parents decided to follow the counselor's recommendation for further testing of the family and referral for family therapy.

Rick and his family met with a psychologist and a family therapist for an assessment session, where Rick was administered the Adolescent Alcohol Involvement Scale (AAIS). He and his family also completed the FACES-III and FAD. The AAIS results revealed some interesting patterns in the family, including regular father-son drinking at home since Rick was 12 years old. The scale also revealed that Rick enjoyed drinking with friends, but believed that his mother would be upset if she knew this. The FACES-III revealed low adaptability, indicating that Rick's family might have difficulty changing rules as children became older or during other times of stress, and high cohesion, indicating that it might be difficult for members to engage in outside activities without appearing disloyal to the family. This measure also showed a difference between Rick and his parents regarding the optimal distance desired in the family. Rick's "ideal" cohesion score indicated that he would prefer more distance in the family than his parents. Differences between the "real" and "ideal" scores of adaptability and cohesion indicated that, for the most part, the family was satisfied with the way things were, though Rick's mother's scores showed that she would like greater family closeness than did other family members.

The FAD results indicated that the family tended to avoid problems and talking with each other when angry, that rules and consequences were often unclear to Rick and his sister, but that, in general, the family was functioning fairly well. When questioned about family patterns, the family agreed that Rick's father was often uninvolved in arguments between Rick and his sister or Rick and his mother, but that when he was involved, he exhibited extreme responses such as shoving and shouting. They reported that Rick's paternal grandfather was alcoholic and his maternal grandfather was a "closet" drinker whose wife had tended to avoid him and tried to keep peace in the family by taking care of everything herself. Rick's mother expressed concern that she would be very lonely when Rick left home; the rest of the family concurred that she would miss Rick the most. Rick and his sister thought that their parents would fight more after Rick left unless the sister did something to prevent it. The family members agreed that Rick's going "out" occurred most frequently after family arguments about rules, and that arguments about rules followed times that he had been "out."

The family agreed to more sessions with the counselor, who began by assisting the parents in agreeing on one or two rules and consequences for Rick and for his sister for the coming week. The psychologist also suggested that Rick attend a substance abuse education/support group at school to help him learn new ways of interacting with peers.

REFERENCES

Ackerman, N. H. (1980) The family with adolescents. In E. A. Carter & M. McGoldrick (Eds.), *The family life cycle: A framework for family therapy* (pp. 147-170). New York: Gardner Press.

American Psychiatric Association. (1980). *Diagnostic and statistical manual of mental disorders* (3rd ed.). Washington, DC: Author.

Ault-Riché, M., & Rosenthal, D. M. (in press). Family therapy with adolescent-focused problems. In G. K. Leigh & C. W. Peterson, *Adolescents in families.* Cincinnati, OH: South-Western.

Bennett, G., & Vourakis, C. (1983). *Substance abuse: Pharmacologic, developmental and clinical perspectives.* New York: John Wiley.

Bernhardt, M. W., Mumford, S., Taylor, C., Smith, B., & Murray, R. M. (1982). Comparison of questionnaire and laboratory tests in the detection of excessive drinking and alcoholism. *Lancet, 1*(8267), 325-328.

Birmingham, W. G., & Sheehy, M. S. (1984). A model of psychological dependence in adolescent substance abusers. *Journal of Adolescence, 1,* 17-27.

Black, C., & Steven, B. F. (1986). The interpersonal and emotional consequences of being an adult child of an alcoholic. *International Journal of the Addictions, 21,* 213-231.

Boszormenyi-Nagy, I., & Spark, G. (1984). *Invisible loyalties.* New York: Brunner/Mazel.

Brook, J. S., Lukoff, J. F., & Whiteman, M. (1980). Initiation into adolescent marijuana use. *Journal of Genetic Psychology, 137,* 133-142.

Carter, E. A., & McGoldrick, M. (1980). The family life cycle and family therapy: An overview. In E. A. Carter & M. McGoldrick (Eds.), *The family life cycle: A framework for family therapy* (pp. 3-20). New York: Gardner Press.

Cohen, S. (1984). Drugs in the work place. *Journal of Clinical Psychiatry, 45,* 4-8.

Conger, J. J., & Petersen, A. C. (1984). *Adolescence and youth.* New York: Harper & Row.

Dell, P. F. (1980). The Hopi family therapist and the Aristotelian parents. *Journal of Marital and Family Therapy, 6,* 123-130.

Douglass, F. M., & Khavari, K. A. (1978). The Drug Use Index: A measure of the extent of polydrug usage. *International Journal of the Addictions, 13,* 981-993.

Eastwood, M., Sweeney, D., & Piercy, F. (in press). A "no-problem" problem: A family therapy approach for certain first-time adolescent abusers. *Family Relations.*

Epstein, N. B., Baldwin, L. M., & Bishop, D. S. 1983. The McMaster Family Assessment Device. *Journal of Marital and Family Therapy, 9,* 171-180.

Erdlen, R., McLellan, A. T., & LaPorte, D. J. (1978). *Instruction manual for the administration of the Addiction Severity Index.* Philadelphia: Veterans Administration Press.

Flanagan, T. J., & McLeod, M. (Eds.). (1983). *The sourcebook of criminal justice statistics 1982.* Washington, DC: U.S. Government Printing Office.

Fors, S. W., & Rojek, D. B. (1983). The social and demographic correlates of adolescent drug use patterns. *Journal of Drug Education, 13,* 205-222.

Friedrick, W. N., & Loftsgard, S. D. (1978). A comparison of the MacAndrew Alcoholism Scale and the Michigan Alcohol Screening Test in a sample of problem drinkers. *Journal of Studies on Alcoholism, 39,* 1940-1944.

Gallup, G. (1977, May 29). The Gallup youth survey. *Denver Post,* p. 16.

Gantman, C. A. (1978). Family interaction patterns among families with normal, disturbed, and drug-abusing adolescents. *Journal of Youth and Adolescence, 7,* 429-440.

Gilbert, D. G. (1979). Paradoxical tranquilizing and emotion-reducing effects of incentive. *Psychological Bulletin, 86,* 643-661.

Glenn, H. S., & Warner, J. W. (1977). *The developmental approach to preventing program dependencies.* Bloomington, IN: Social Systems.

Gurman, A. S., & Kniskern, D. P. (1979). Research on marital and family therapy: Progress, perspective and prospect. In S. L. Garfield & A. E. Bergin (Eds.), *Handbook of psychotherapy and behavior change: An empirical analysis* (pp. 817-902). New York: John Wiley.

Haley, J. (1980). *Leaving home: The therapy of disturbed young people.* New York: McGraw-Hill.

Jacobson, G. R. (1983). Detection, assessment, and diagnosis of alcoholism: Current techniques. *Recent Developments in Alcoholism, 1,* 377-413.

Johnston, L. D., O'Malley, P. M., & Bachman, J. G. (1986). *Drug use among high school students, college students and other young adults: National trends through 1985.* Rockville, MD: National Institute on Drug Abuse.

Kandel, D. B. (1980). Drug and drinking behavior among youth. *Annual Review of Sociology, 6,* 235-288.

Kandel, D. B., Kessler, R. C., & Margulies, R. Z. (1978). Antecedents of adolescent initiation into stages of drug abuse: A developmental analysis. In D. B. Kandel (Ed.), *Longitudinal research on drug use: Empirical findings and methodological issues* (pp. 73-79). Washington, DC: Hemisphere.

Kaufman, E. (1985). *Substance abuse and family therapy.* New York: Grune & Stratton.

Klinge, V. (1983). A comparison of parental and adolescent MMPIs as related to substance use. *International Journal of the Addictions, 18,* 1179-1185.

MacAndrew, C. (1965). The differentiation of male alcoholic outpatients from nonalcoholic psychiatric outpatients by means of the MMPI. *Quarterly Journal of Studies on Alcoholism, 26,* 238-246.

Madanes, C. (1981). *Strategic family therapy.* San Francisco: Jossey-Bass.

Marlatt, G. A. (1983, October). Controlled drinking controversy: A commentary. *American Psychologist,* pp. 1097-1110.

Mayer, F., & Filstead, W. G. (1979). The Adolescent Alcohol Involvement Scale: An instrument for measuring adolescents' use and misuse of alcohol. *Journal of Studies on Alcohol, 40,* 291-300.

Minuchin, S. (1974). *Families and family therapy.* Cambridge, MA: Harvard University Press.

Minuchin, S., Rosman, B. L., & Baker, L. (1978). *Psychosomatic families.* Cambridge, MA: Harvard University Press.

Moberg, D. P. (1983). Identifying adolescents with alcohol problems, a field test of the Adolescent Alcohol Involvement Scale. *Journal of Studies on Alcohol, 44,* 701-721.

National Academy of Sciences. (1982). *Marijuana and health.* Washington, DC: National Academy Press.

National Institute of Health. (1977). *Teenage smoking: National patterns of cigarette smoking.* Washington, DC: U.S. Department of Health Education and Welfare, Public Health Services.

National Institute on Drug Abuse. (1983). *National Institute on Alcohol Abuse and Alcoholism fact sheet.* Rockville, MD: National Institute on Drug Abuse.

Nichols, M. P. (1984). *Family therapy: Concepts and methods.* New York: Gardner Press.

Olson, D. H., Portner, S., & Lavee, Y. (1985). *FACES III.* St. Paul, MN: University of Minnesota, Department of Family Social Sciences.

Pokorny, A. O., Miller, B. A., & Kaplan, H. B. (1972). The Brief MAST: A shorthand version of the Michigan Alcohol Screening Test. *American Journal of Psychiatry, 129,* 342-345.

Pollin, W. (1980). *Health consequences of marijuana use: Statement before the Subcommittee on Criminal Justice, Committee of the Judiciary, U.S. Senate.* Rockville, MD: National Institute on Drug Abuse.

Rathus, S. A., Fox, J. A., & Ortins, J. B. (1980). The MacAndrew Scale as a measure of substance abuse and delinquency among adolescents. *Journal of Clinical Psychology, 36,* 579-583.

Rosenthal, D., Nelson, T., & Drake, N. (1986). Adolescent substance use and abuse: A family context. In G. K. Leigh & C. W. Peterson (Eds.), *Adolescents in families.* Cincinnati, OH: South-Western.

Selzer, M. L. (1971). The Michigan Alcohol Screening Test: The quest for a new diagnostic instrument. *American Journal of Psychiatry, 127,* 1653-1659.

Spoth, R., & Rosenthal, D. (1980). Wanted: A developmentally oriented alcohol prevention program. *Personnel and Guidance Journal, 59,* 212-216.

Stanton, M. D., & Todd, T. C. (1982). *The family therapy of drug abuse and addiction.* New York: Guilford.

Stein, M. D., & Davis, J. K. (1982). *Therapy for adolescents.* San Francisco: Jossey-Bass.

Steininger, M., Newell, J. D., & Garcia, L. T. (1984). *Ethical issues in psychology.* Homewood, IL: Dorsey.

Watzlawick, P., Weakland, J., & Fisch, R. (1974). *Change: Principles of problem formation and problem orientation.* New York: Norton.

Weidman, A. (1983). The compulsive adolescent substance abuser: Psychological differentiation and family process. *Journal of Drug Education, 13,* 161-172.

Weil, A. (1972). *The natural mind.* Boston: Houghton Mifflin.

9

Assessment of Divorce Adjustment and Custody Arrangements

JOHN GUIDUBALDI, D.ED., JOSEPH D. PERRY, PH.D.

Mental health professionals today increasingly are called on to assess youth's divorce adjustment (Kurdek, 1985, in press) and to perform evaluations that the courts will use to determine which parent will gain custody following a divorce (Derdeyn, 1976; Lowery, 1981; Woody, 1977). The relevance of this area of assessment is illustrated by the repeated finding that children of divorce are overrepresented in referrals to mental health agencies (Felner, Stolberg, & Cowen, 1975; Kalter, 1977; McDermott, 1970; Morrison, 1974) as well as in referrals to school psychologists (Guidubaldi, Perry, & Cleminshaw, 1984). Moreover, the sheer prevalence of divorce indicates an unprecedented need for assessment of this phenomenon as a psychosocial stressor for adolescents. Census data indicate, for example, that the divorce rate doubled from 1970 to 1981 and that single-parent child rearing increased from 11.9% in 1970 to 22.5% in 1983 (U.S. Bureau of the Census, 1982a, 1982b; National Center for Health Statistics, 1984). The census data are likely to underestimate the actual incidence of divorce as remarried persons are not counted in the divorce frequencies, even though about 83% of men and 75% of women who are divorced remarry and about 40% of these experience a second divorce (Glick, 1980; Moss & Moss, 1975). Moreover, epidemiological data do not include the 23% to 30% of divorce petitions that are withdrawn in instances of periodic separation and discord (Kitson & Langlie, 1984). It is estimated that about 40% to 50% of children born in the past decade will experience marital disruption and a single-parent family by late adolescence (Bane, 1976; Bumpass & Rindfuss, 1979; Furstenberg, Nord, Peterson, & Zill, 1983; Glick, 1979).

IMPACT OF DIVORCE ON ADOLESCENTS

Despite this profound social change, a dearth of empirically sound research persists concerning the impact of divorce on adolescents. A recent comprehensive research project with a nationwide sample (the National Association of School Psychologists and Kent State University [NASP-KSU] study) has demonstrated more conclusively than previous studies that during middle childhood and early adolescence (6-13 years), youth are adversely affected by divorce (Guidubaldi, 1983, in press; Guidubaldi & Cleminshaw, 1985a, 1985b; Guidubaldi, Cleminshaw, & Perry,

1985a, 1985b; Guidubaldi, Cleminshaw, Perry, & McLoughlin, 1983; Guidubaldi, Cleminshaw, Perry, & Nastasi, 1984; Guidubaldi, Cleminshaw, Perry, Nastasi, & Lightel, in press; Guidubaldi & Perry, 1984, 1985; Guidubaldi, Perry, & Cleminshaw, 1984). This study improved on past research by including 699 randomly selected children from schools in 38 states and by gathering extensive multifactored and multisource data in a longitudinal research design. The sample included 341 children from divorced families and 358 from intact families who served as age-related comparison groups in first, third, and fifth grades. Assessments included standardized tests (Wechsler Intelligence Scale for Children-Revised and Wide Range Achievement Test), teacher rating scales, parent and child interviews, psychologist ratings, and school records information.

Analyses of the multifactored, longitudinal data are ongoing; however, findings identify specific measurement criteria on which children and young adolescents from divorced homes perform more poorly than those from intact homes: (a) social-behavioral measures of dependency, anxiety, aggressive acting out, withdrawal, inattention, peer popularity, and locus of control; (b) mental health indices (e.g., hostility to adults, nightmares, anxiety) obtained from parental interviews as well as the total number of maladaptive behaviors from Achenbach and Edelbrock's Child Behavior Checklist; (c) Wechsler IQ scores; (d) Wide Range Achievement Test scores in reading, spelling, and math; (e) school-related measures, such as grades in reading and math, as well as repeating a school grade; (f) adaptive behaviors of daily living, social skills, and communication; and (g) physical health ratings of the child as well as of parents and siblings.

Defining the sequelae of divorce is a complex process, and assessment must therefore include not only multidimensional aspects of child and parent adjustment, but also an interactive, ecological approach. Major findings in this regard from the NASP-KSU study follow:

1. The negative, differential effects of divorce on children and young adolescents are long-term (the average length of time since divorce was 6.41 years [S.D. = 2.35] at Time-2 of this study). This does not support the recency or stressor hypotheses implicit in DSM-III, which implies that the negative impact of divorce is a temporary, short-term adjustment problem.

2. Children's reactions to divorce are especially influenced by sex and age, with young adolescent boys being more adversely affected on multiple criteria than 6- and 7-year-old boys and young adolescent girls much better adjusted than those at the 6- and 7-year age level.

3. Single-parent divorced-family households have significantly less income than intact families, and this difference accounts for significant academic achievement variance between children of divorced and intact families.

4. Parents' educational and occupational levels also moderate some of children's divorce adjustment, and this is especially apparent with regard to the educational level of the same-sex parent.

5. A positive relationship with both the custodial and noncustodial parents predicts positive adjustment for both girls and boys, both concurrently and across time; however, the noncustodial parent-child relationship is noticeably more important for boys.

6. Frequent and reliable visitation with the noncustodial parent (typically, the father) is associated with better adjustment for both girls and boys.

7. A diminished degree of conflict between custodial and noncustodial parents predicts children's adjustment, especially for boys across time to early adolescence.

8. An authoritarian (i.e., punitive) child-rearing style in comparison to authoritative (i.e., more democratic) and permissive styles predicts more adverse child adjustment, especially for boys.

9. Home routines of less television viewing, regular bedtimes, maternal employment, and helpfulness of maternal grandfather predict positive adjustment for both boys and girls.

10. The family support factors that promote positive post-divorce adjustment are availability of helpful relatives (including in-laws), availability of friends, paid child-care assistance such as nursery schools and babysitters, and participation in occupational and educational endeavors by the custodial parent.

11. Smaller school population, safe and orderly atmosphere, fewer miles bused to school, and traditional rather than open classroom structure are the school-environment variables associated with better divorce adjustment.

Research concerning the impact of divorce on older adolescents (i.e., 14-20 years of age) is less definitive. This period typically is described as a time of parent-child conflict due to independence-seeking (Coleman, 1961; Musgrove, 1964), and divorce is likely to exacerbate this conflict. Kelly and Wallerstein's 10-year longitudinal study probably has contributed the most to our understanding of divorce's long-term aftereffects on adolescents (Wallerstein & Kelly, 1980a, 1980b; Wallerstein, 1984, 1985). Using a semi-structured interview format, this study found that at the time of divorce, adolescents react by early disengagement from their parents due to anxieties about future marriage and parental sexuality and to worry about how to meet future needs. A five-year follow-up indicated that over a third of the original sample continued to present moderate to severe depression, with no differences found by age and sex. The 10-year follow-up included 31 adolescents aged 12 to 18 from an original group of 34 children who were between 2½ and 6 years of age at the time of divorce. A primary finding was that those who were younger at the time of divorce experienced fewer divorce-specific adjustment problems than older siblings. Even 10 years later, 30% of the adolescents were found to report sadness and loneliness directly attributed to the divorce. Moreover, 25% continued to disapprove of the divorce very strongly, and about 50% maintained hopes of parental reconciliation. Relative to custody, 90% remained with their mother and 53% were residing in homes where the custodial parent had remarried. A salient sex difference was that as girls reached adolescence, there was an increased need to establish relationships with the absent fathers. The findings were interpreted to indicate generally that divorce "is not a single, circumscribed event but a multistage process of radically changing family relationships that begin in the failing marriage and extend over several, sometimes many, years that may be marked by continued instability in family structure, as well as lasting change in social and economic circumstance" (Wallerstein, 1984, p. 445).

The preponderance of related studies with more restricted scopes and widely different methodologies confirm that older adolescents of divorced families have higher deviance rates than those from intact families. This includes negative adjustment in such areas as antisocial behavior and juvenile delinquency (Kalter, 1977; McDermott, 1970); self-esteem (Fry & Trifiletti, 1983; Kurdek & Blisk, 1983; Parish & Wigle, 1985; Slater, Stewart, & Linn, 1983); health-risk behavior, such as substance abuse (Saucier & Ambert, 1983); school achievement and behavior (Brown, 1980; Kurdek & Sinclair, 1985; Lazarus, 1980; Zakariya, 1982); and negative perceptions of the noncustodial father (Ambert & Saucier, 1983). Sex differences for adolescents have been indicated recently, with girls reporting higher internalizing problems (e.g., anxiety, depression, sensitivity) and lower self-concepts, while boys were found to have more negative attitudes toward school (Kurdek & Sinclair, 1985; Slater, Stewart, & Linn, 1983). Parental discord in divorced, intact, and remarried families as compared to low-conflict intact families has been found to predict psychopathology in adolescents (Dornbusch et al., 1985; Farber, Felner, & Primavera, 1985; Kurdek & Sinclair, 1985; Schwartz & Getter, 1980; Slater & Haber, 1984).

Methodological limitations clearly relevant to research concerning the divorce adjustment of older adolescents have been pointed out by recent evaluations of the literature (e.g., Clingempeel & Repucci, 1982; Emery, 1982; Kurdek, 1981, 1985, in press; White & Mika, 1983). Major criticisms include: (a) small and biased samples are primarily restricted to white middle-class families wherein the mother has child custody; (b) critical ecological variables, such as socioeconomic status and community support systems, typically are not controlled; (c) control groups of intact families often are lacking totally or are inadequate in terms of identifying parental discord and remarriage; (d) samples often include more than one child from a single-parent family, with questionable independence of assessments; (e) intraindividual age effects usually are not assessed due to a lack of longitudinal studies; (f) age at the time of divorce and length of time residing in single-parent family often are not reported; and (g) the retrospective nature of most studies may result in a biased report of past divorce-related experiences. Considering assessment, the reader is cautioned that most studies lack psychometrically sound criterion measures in terms of reliability and validity. Moreover, false positives may be reported in studies without multifactored criterion measures (e.g., Bernard & Nesbitt, 1981; Colletta, 1979; Reinhard, 1977; Rosen, 1977).

IMPACT OF CUSTODY ARRANGEMENTS ON ADOLESCENTS

While there are severe limitations in the knowledge about adolescent adjustment to divorce in general, even less is known concerning the impact of custody arrangements. For example, there is considerable uncertainty regarding the current incidence of custody types. Many writers report an increase in father and joint custody, while census data indicate that the relative frequency of maternal custody arrangements has not changed since 1970, remaining at approximately 90% of all custody decisions (U.S. Bureau of the Census, 1979, 1982a, 1982b). However, more fathers are seeking custody (Bodenheimer, 1977), which has been attributed to societal changes such as the feminist movement, the Equal Rights Amendment lobby, and maternal employment, with the resultant change in sex-of-parent bias by the courts (Derdeyn, 1976). Joint custody has recently become an alternative, and over half of the states have established legislation favoring this arrangement (Clingempeel &

Repucci, 1982; Derdeyn & Scott, 1984). This reflects an application of the "best interest" of the child rather than a "tender years" (i.e., young children "belong" with their mothers) conceptualization. However, the adversarial and competitive approach to the 10% of contested custody decisions often continues to be based on finding one parent inadequate or unfit (Foster & Freed, 1980), which heightens parental discord and typically results in ongoing litigation (Saposnek, 1983).

Joint custody has been defined as both parents sharing responsibility for decisions about their child's welfare rather than just sharing physical custody (Ahrons, 1980; Cox & Cease, 1978). The consensus of the few recent studies on this topic is that no difference was found in psychological adjustment (e.g., depression, aggression, self-esteem, psychosomatic symptoms) between children and adolescents of maternal and joint custody (Luepnitz, 1979; Wolchik, Braver, & Sandler, 1985). However, both boys and girls were found to report more positive experiences from joint custody rather than maternal custody homes (Wolchik et al., 1985). This data base supports the earlier reviews of research supporting joint over maternal custody (Clingempeel & Repucci, 1982; Roman & Haddad, 1978; Stack, 1976; Steinman, 1981). A cautionary note regarding these findings is that selection bias may influence the results, in that parents who select joint custody may have less discord and greater involvement in parenting than those selecting sole custody (Wolchik et al., 1985). Hence, degree of parental discord rather than custody arrangements may account for the favorable finding of joint custody groups. There also is a consensus in related research that reduced parental discord as well as increased contact with the non-custodial parent and extended family are associated with more positive adjustment (e.g., Furstenberg & Spanier, 1984; Guidubaldi, Cleminshaw, Perry, & Nastasi, 1984; Guidubaldi, Perry, & Cleminshaw, 1984; Hetherington, 1979; Wallerstein & Kelly, 1980a, 1980b).

Derdeyn and Scott (1984) point out that due to the limitations of current studies, research results do not necessarily support the rapid growth of joint custody. Many of the limitations reported for divorce adjustment research also are cited as typical of the few studies concerning the aftereffects of joint versus maternal custody on adolescents. A principal limitation is the lack of current evidence on the relationship between joint custody and parental discord, as the latter variable repeatedly has been found an optimal predictor of children's divorce maladjustment (e.g., Dornbusch et al., 1985; Farber, Felner, & Primavera, 1985; Guidubaldi, Cleminshaw, Perry, & Nastasi, 1984; Guidubaldi, Perry, & Cleminshaw, 1984; Kurdek & Sinclair, 1985; Slater & Haber, 1984). Clearly, such a limited data base leaves many unanswered questions about the impact of custody arrangements on adolescents.

ASSESSMENT OF ADOLESCENTS' DIVORCE ADJUSTMENT

At present, there is no single conceptual or data-based approach to the assessment of adolescents' divorce adjustment. Based on the diverse measures used in research, Kurdek (1985, in press) has dichotomized the strategies typically employed. These are (a) the use of standardized measures of adolescents' general or objective psychological adjustment and (b) the use of more restricted instrumentation evaluating adolescents' divorce-specific adjustment. There are advantages and disadvantages to each approach, but at present both are recommended. Standardized measures include information on reliability and validity in addition to providing normative data for comparing the degree to which a divorced sample differs from peers of the same age and sex. However, these assessments do not measure adequately the relevant factors found to be associated with divorce. Conversely, divorce-specific assessments provide more relevant information about adjustment to divorce itself, but typically are not standardized and lack evidence of reliability and validity (U.S. Department of Health and Human Services, 1980). Moreover, because divorce adjustment is a complex, multidimensional process, it requires the evaluation not only of the adolescent's characteristics, but also of parents and of ecological variables pertaining to the social support systems in the family, community, and school. Hence, multimethod and multifactored evaluation of the adolescents' adjustment and information about the total ecology is necessary.

Divorce-Specific Instrumentation

Table 1 lists parental and adolescent direct-report instruments that are used in research to evaluate the divorce-specific adjustment of adolescents. As shown in the table, five types of measures have been identified: open-ended clinical interviews, structured interviews, child self-report scales, projective techniques, and parent rating scales. These measures are not commercially available to practitioners, but one may be able to obtain them from the authors listed; however, they must be interpreted cautiously due to the lack of standardization, reliability, and validity data. Nevertheless, the assessments listed in Table 1 represent recent progress and the present state of the art in evaluating adolescents' reactions to divorce itself.

Open-ended clinical interviews. These measures are best used to gain a preliminary, qualitative review of adjustment to divorce. Wallerstein (1984), for example, included this kind of criterion in the 10-year longitudinal studies of the divorced sample cited earlier. The initial questions in an open-ended clinical interview deal with experiences and responses to divorce, including the adolescent's thoughts and emotional reactions, defenses used to cope, and reactions to specific situations (e.g., change in residence or visitation schedule). Next, the child is asked to assess his or her relationship with both the custodial and noncustodial parent. Finally, one should review the social support available to the adolescent (e.g., siblings, peers, extended family, school environment, extracurricular activities). This kind of measure has been criticized for use in research due to its subjective nature (Emery, 1982), but it may be helpful for initial data gathering in clinical assessment.

Structured interviews. Recent research frequently has used this form of assessment. Unlike its open-ended counterpart, the structured interview provides specific questions, and positive interrater reliability has been reported for most of the structured interview scales listed in Table 1. The Divorce Adjustment Child Interview (DACI) comprises material from several sources, including the Harvard University Stress and Family Survey (Belle, 1982), an Optimism vs. Pessimism scale developed by Stipek, Lamb, and Zigler (1981), and 130 items constructed by the authors (Guidubaldi, Perry, & Cleminshaw, 1981). These items include questions to assess peer relations, locus of control, parent-child interaction, support systems, life changes, worries, leisure-time activities, divorce arrangements, and emotional reac-

TABLE 1

ASSESSMENTS OF ADOLESCENTS' DIVORCE-SPECIFIC ADJUSTMENT IN RESEARCH

Type of Assessment	Instrument	References*
Open-ended clinical interviews	Nonstandardized general questions for adolescents and parents	Gardner, 1976; Tessman, 1978; Wallerstein & Kelly, 1980a, 1980b; Wallerstein, 1984
Structured interviews	Nonstandardized specific questions for adolescents and parents	Fry & Leahy, 1983; Kalter & Plunkett, 1984; Kurdek & Siesky, 1980
	Divorce Adjustment Child Interview	Guidubaldi, Perry, & Cleminshaw, 1981
Self-report scales for adolescents	Children's Separation Inventory	Kurdek & Berg, 1983; Berg & Kurdek, 1983a
	Divorce Experiences Schedule for Children	Wolchik, Braver, & Sandler, 1985
	Structured questionnaires of divorce adjustment	Ambert & Saucier, 1983; Emery & O'Leary, 1982; Fry & Trifiletti, 1983; Hingst, 1981; Plunkett & Kalter, 1984; Reinhard, 1977
Projective assessments	Family Story Test	Kelly & Berg, 1978
	Projective Story Task	Warshak & Santrock, 1983
Parent rating scales	Divorced Parent Questionnaire	Hodges & Bloom, 1984; Hodges, Tierney, & Buschbaum, 1984
	Fisher Divorce Adjustment Scale	Fisher, 1978; Stolberg & Bush, 1985
	Parent Separation Inventory	Berg & Kurdek, 1983b
	Parent Response Inventory	Stolberg & Cullen, 1983
	Single Parenting Questionnaire	Stolberg & Ullman, 1985

*These refer both to the developers of the scales and to divorce research using the instruments.

tions to divorce. At present, data concerning the psychometric properties of this instrument have not been examined; hence, it is recommended currently only for gathering qualitative data from interviews with young adolescents of divorce.

The 13-item interview developed by Kurdek and Siesky (1980) focuses on comprehension of divorce as a concept, reasons for and acceptance of divorce, blame for divorce, reconciliation of parents, feelings about divorce, description of both parents, influence of divorce in peer relationships, activities while with parents, and child's current beliefs about his or her own future marital status. The interview devised by Fry and Leahey (1983) asks for adolescents' ratings of positive and negative events associated with the custodial parent interactions. Kalter and Plunkett's (1984) study included a 10-question interview concerning general adjustment in the areas of behavior, feelings, peer relations, and the future. Although these structured interviews provide relevant data, they were used with populations that greatly restrict their generalizability. In contrast, the Divorce Adjustment Child Interview was used with a large, randomly selected nationwide sample.

Self-report scales. This kind of assessment has been developed only recently and is directed at providing objective measurement of adolescents' divorce perceptions. The typical format requires a written response to structured questions, which lends itself to study of reliability and validity. Measures of this sort could provide objective assessment of adolescents' adjustment specifically related to divorce.

The scale presently thought to provide the most relevant and practical direct assessment is the Children's Separation Inventory (CSI) developed by Berg and Kurdek (1983a). The 48 CSI items require a yes or no answer and can be used with children aged 8 years and older. The scale also could be administered orally to younger children and to adolescents with low reading levels. The manual provides a structured scoring system for the six scales, labeled Peer Ridicule and Avoidance, Paternal Blame, Maternal Blame, Self-Blame, Fear of Abandonment, and Hope of Reunification. The CSI represents a revision of Berg's (1979) Children's Attitudes toward Parental Separation Inventory (CAPSI). Although the CSI manual reports no reliability or validity data, the CAPSI was found to have high retest reliability (e.g., total scale intercorrelation = .83). Evidence of construct validity also was indicated by Kurdek and Berg (1983). Because of the lack of well-documented psychometric properties, cautious interpretation of the CSI is necessary. However, this inventory does provide qualitative data concerning salient divorce-specific criteria and would be useful as a self-report measure for adolescents.

Other self-report scales used as research measures include the Divorce Experiences Schedule for Children (Sandler, Wolchik, & Braver, 1984; Wolchik, Braver, & Sandler, 1985). Its 62 items measure divorce-related events found to affect children and adolescents (e.g., custody arrangements) through subjects' ratings of the occurrence, impact, and quality of each item. A more general focus is contained in Hingst's (1981) 49-item scale for ratings of feelings, in ratings of parents on a seven-point polar adjective scale (Ambert & Saucier, 1983), and through identification of divorce-related stressors (Fry & Trifiletti, 1983). A comprehensive scale developed by Reinhard (1977) includes 99 items on which adolescents rate the degree of agreement in several areas: news of divorce, acceptance of parents, loss of parent, changes in family relationships, post-divorce conflict, emotional responses, peer reactions, need for counseling, and maturity. Plunkett and Kalter (1984) include 25 items rating the extent of agreement in the domains of Sad/Insecure, Active Coping, and Abandonment. These self-report measures typically report positive reliability findings, but currently lack adequate validity and standardization data.

Projective assessments. Projective measures of children's divorce perceptions are recommended as supplemental tools in the assessment process due to their traditional lack of psychometric data. Kurdek (in press) recommends that in practice they may be helpful as "warm up" for the more objective measures and in eliciting responses from children who are reluctant to discuss the topic of divorce. The Projective Story Task devised by Warshak and Santrock (1983) uses pictures of divorce-related situations to elicit children's stories. The scoring criteria include attribution of blame, reconciliation beliefs and wishes, attitudes toward custody arrangements, and attitudes toward parental remarriage. The Family Story Test (Kelly & Berg, 1978) also uses drawings of divorce-related situations, but, in contrast to other projective devices, includes structured questions for adolescents' responses as well. The questions from this test were revised for inclusion in the CSI, described previously.

Parent-rating scales. Objective parent-rating scales have been used in research to provide assessment of adolescents' reactions to divorce as well as descriptive data about the divorce itself and parents' adjustment to divorce. The most comprehensive such instrument is the Parent Separation Inventory (PSI), developed by Berg and Kurdek (1983b). This inventory includes 131 items concerning the parents' experience of marriage and separation in addition to 189 items concerning adolescents' adjustment. Part I of the PSI covers a comprehensive review of demographic data, family environment, home routines, visitation, custody arrangements, parent relationships, and parent support systems. Part II includes a comprehensive review of the adolescent's reaction to the predivorce home environment, post-divorce parent management, custody, visitation, and support systems. Most items include a Likert-type scale for frequency-of-occurrence ratings. At present, there is no manual or report of psychometric data for this scale. Table 2 lists examples of information typically included in parent interviews.

The Single Parenting Questionnaire (SPQ) is unique among the divorce-specific assessments because reliability and validity are reported (Stolberg & Ullman, 1985). The SPQ does not provide a parent rating of adolescents' divorce adjustment, but rather purports to measure the parent-child relationship, which has been found to be a principal mediator of youths' post-divorce adjustment. The 88 items are behaviorally referenced for frequency of occurrence and are divided into six dimensions of parent-child relations: problem-solving skills, parental warmth, discipline procedures, parental rules, enthusiasm for parenting, and parent support systems. The SPQ includes both a computer- and hand-scoring format for converting raw scores to norm-based T-scores for each factor in addition to a total score. Reliability and validity studies were conducted on a group of 239 divorced, custodial parents. Alpha coefficients ranged from .59 to .85 for each factor score. Test-retest and interrater reliability were inadequate, ranging from .54 to .71 and .00 to .59, with means of .59 and .32, respectively. Evidence of concurrent validity was demonstrated by significant correlations of the SPQ with the Fisher Divorce Adjustment Scale and the Child Behavior Checklist.

TABLE 2

EXAMPLES OF INFORMATION IN PARENT INTERVIEWS AND QUESTIONNAIRES

Divorce/Custody Information

Date of divorce.
Child's/children's age(s) at time of divorce.
Parent who initiated divorce.
Reason for divorce.
Nature of legal proceedings for divorce and custody.
Current custody arrangements.
Changes in custody arrangements.
Current visitation schedule of non-custodial parent.
Parents' satisfaction with custody and visitation.
Length of time parents were married.
Degree of predivorce parental discord.
Degree of post-divorce parental discord.
Nature of divorce property/payment settlement.
Remarriage or remarriage plans of parents.

Socioeconomic Status

Income of both custodial and non-custodial parent.
Educational level of parents.
Occupation of parents.
Time at work and work hours.
Job satisfaction of both parents.
Availability and type of transportation of both parents.

Family Environment

Number, ages, and gender of children.
Time residing at current residence.
Number of moves by both parents.
Type of residence/neighborhood.
Frequency and type of alternative child care.
History of nontraditional marriages in extended family.
Parents' time spent with children per day.
Parents' child-rearing styles (e.g., authoritarian, authoritative, permissive)
Home routines and schedules (e.g., bed-time, TV, etc.).
Presence or visitation of step-siblings if there is a remarriage.
Quality of child interactions with each parent.

Support Systems

Availability and helpfulness of extended family (custodial and noncustodial parent).
Availability and helpfulness of friends and neighbors.
Parent participation in organizations and activities.
Use of pre- or post-divorce counseling.

The other parent rating scales used in recent divorce research are similar to the PSI and SPQ, but are judged to be less comprehensive and relevant to adolescents' divorce adjustment. These include the Divorced Parent Questionnaire (Hodges & Bloom, 1984; Hodges, Tierney, & Buschhaum, 1984), the Parent Response Inventory (Stolberg & Cullen, 1983), and the Fisher Divorce Adjustment Scale (Fisher, 1978).

Standardized Measures

Table 3 offers a compendium of standardized measures used in research to evaluate adolescents' divorce adjustment. This grouping reflects multimethod assessment, and the instruments are categorized by type of evaluation, including self-report scales, parent rating scales, teacher rating scales, scholastic achievement tests, and

TABLE 3

STANDARDIZED OBJECTIVE MEASURES OF ADOLESCENTS' DIVORCE ADJUSTMENT
IN RESEARCH

Type of Assessment	Instrument	Divorce Research using These Measures
Child self-report scales	Adolescent-Coping Orientation for Problem Experience	Kurdek & Sinclair, 1985
	Children's Depression Inventory	Wolchik, Braver, & Sandler, 1985
	Coopersmith Self-Esteem Inventories, Piers-Harris Self-Concept Scale, and Tennessee Self Concept Scale	Kelly & Berg, 1978; Kurdek & Blisk, 1983; Lowenstein & Koopman, 1978; Slater, Stewart, & Linn, 1983; Stolberg & Bush, 1985
	Locus of Control	Kurdek & Siesky, 1980
	Perceived Competence Scale	Copeland, 1985; Wyman, Cowen, Hightower, & Pedro-Carroll, 1985
	Revised Children's Manifest Anxiety Scale	Wolchik, Braver, & Sandler, 1985
	SCL-90-R	Kurdek & Sinclair, 1985
Parent-rating scales	Child Behavior Checklist	Copeland, 1985; Guidubaldi & Perry, 1985; Kurdek & Sinclair, 1985; Stolberg & Cullen, 1983; Stolberg & Bush, 1985; Wolchik, Braver, & Sandler, 1985
	Louisville Behavior Checklist	Jacobson, 1978
	Personal Adjustment and Role Skills Scale	Pett, 1982
	Personality Inventory for Children	Kurdek, Blisk, & Siesky, 1981
Teacher-rating scales	Child Behavior Checklist-Teacher Form	Guidubaldi & Perry, 1985
	Hahnemann Elementary School Behavior Rating Scale;	Guidubaldi et al., 1983; *Continued*

TABLE 3 (CONT.)

Type of Assessment	Instrument	Divorce Research using These Measures
	Hahnemann High School Behavior Rating Scale	Guidubaldi, Perry, & Cleminshaw, 1984; Guidubaldi & Perry, 1985
	Health Resources Inventory	Kurdek & Berg, 1983
	Sells and Roff Peer Status Scale	Guidubaldi et al., 1983; Guidubaldi, Perry, & Cleminshaw, 1984
	Vineland Adaptive Behavior Scales-Classroom Edition	Guidubaldi et al., 1983; Guidubaldi, Perry, & Cleminshaw, 1984
Scholastic achievement	Wide Range Achievement Test-Revised and school grades	Brown, 1980; Guidubaldi et al., 1983; Guidubaldi, Perry, & Cleminshaw, 1984; Lazarus, 1980; Zakariya, 1982
Intelligence	Wechsler Intelligence Scale for Children-Revised	Guidubaldi et al., 1983; Guidubaldi, Perry, & Cleminshaw, 1984

intelligence tests. A multifactored approach, including measures of social-emotional, behavioral, self-esteem, health, and cognitive functioning, also is reflected by this listing. Research indicates that these assessments have generally been effective in identifying deficits in the adjustment of adolescents from divorced families. Researchers, however, have been especially interested in the assessment of general emotional adjustment to divorce, and only a few studies have included cognitive measures; thus, current research is not adequate for postulating a standard battery. Multimethod evaluation using reports from both of the parents, adolescents themselves, and teachers provides cross-validation and is particularly necessary because parents involved in the divorce process frequently disagree in their descriptions of family relationships (Elwood & Jacobson, 1982; Spanier & Thompson, 1984).

Child self-report scales. The most frequently used of the self-report scales are self-concept instruments, which include the Coopersmith Self-Esteem Inventories, the Piers-Harris Children's Self-Concept Scale, and the Tennessee Self Concept Scale. These provide a report of global self-concept as well as subscales of self-ratings with regard to family, peers, and school. It is suggested that practitioners use the subscales related to family functioning when evaluating adolescents' perceptions of divorce, although standardized subscale scores are not often reported. The Piers-Harris scale is especially recommended for this reason, because it does provide relevant subscale scores. The more recently developed Perceived Competence Scale (Harter, 1979, 1982), which is recommended for younger adolescents and children, provides an indication of perceived cognitive, social, and physical abilities in addition to general self-esteem.

The Adolescent-Coping Orientation for Problem Experiences scale recently has been found to provide a salient criterion measure of adolescents' divorce adjustment (Kurdek & Sinclair, 1985). The scale's 54 items yield a self-report score of coping in the following 12 areas: Ventilation ("letting off steam"); Low Activity (e.g., reading); Self-Reliance and Positive Appraisal (e.g., trying to figure out problems); Emotional Connections (e.g., crying); Family Problem Solving (e.g., talking to family members); Passive Problem Solving (e.g., alcohol); Spiritual Support (e.g., praying); Close Friendship Support; Professional Support; High Activity Level; Humor; and Relaxation (e.g., listening to music). This assessment has been found to have positive reliability with a mean Cronbach's alpha of .64 for the composite score. The data provided by this scale would be especially relevant for practitioners who provide counseling for divorced-family adolescents.

Self-report scales concerning locus of control (e.g., Nowicki & Strickland, 1973) have been used to gain an assessment of self-efficacy and motivation as they relate to divorce adjustment. Self-report measures that may be helpful for assessing psychological maladjustment include the Children's Depression Inventory, the Revised Children's Manifest Anxiety Scale, and the SCL-90-R. These could be applied selectively for a direct measure of specific areas of psychopathology. Although not used in divorce research, the Minnesota Multiphasic Personality Inventory is frequently used in clinical practice for assessing psychopathology in older adolescents.

Parent-rating scales. The parent-rating scale most frequently used in divorce research is the 118-item Child Behavior Checklist (CBCL) developed by Achenbach and Edelbrock. The wide use of the CBCL reflects its utility for providing a comprehensive profile of social-emotional functioning. This instrument includes broad-based scales of internalizing and externalizing pathology as well as a total problem score and subscales of specific maladaptive areas (e.g., depression). In addition, a standardized measure of positive functioning also is included (i.e., activity, social competence, and school performance ratings). Additional positive features are economy in terms of completion time by parents, computerized scoring, and well-established psychometric properties for a parent-rating scale. The CBCL is highly recommended as an optimal measure for gaining an objective parental assessment of adolescents' emotional reactions to divorce.

Several other parent-rating scales listed in Table 3 are of less utility. Although the Personality Inventory for Children is a standardized and comprehensive measure, only an abridged form has been used in divorce research (Kurdek, Blisk, & Siesky, 1981), which limits its interpretation for divorced samples. Form E-2 of the Louisville Behavior Checklist has been used in only one study of adolescents' divorce adjustment (Jacobson, 1978). This 163-item scale provides parent ratings of both positive and prosocial behavior. Another parent scale of personal-social functioning less frequently used and with a more restricted scope is the Personal Adjustment and Role Skills Scale (Pett, 1982).

Teacher-rating scales. Assessment data from teachers concerning the adolescent's school-related behavior and academic performance as well as his or her general personal-social functioning is highly desirable in a comprehensive evaluation of reactions to divorce. The primary advantage to including such measures is objectivity, in view of the evidence cited previously concerning possible bias in ratings by divorcing parents. Moreover, teacher-rating scales recently have been well standardized and found to have positive reliability and validity (Perry, Guidubaldi, & Kehle, 1979; Stevenson, Parker, Wilkinson, Hegion, & Fish, 1976).

A standardized profile for the Child Behavior Checklist-Teacher Form (CBCL-TF) developed by Achenbach and Edelbrock in 1983 has been used to assess young adolescents' divorce adjustment (Guidubaldi & Perry, 1985). This scale provides scores similar to the ones derived from parent ratings on the CBCL. Cross-validation in the reporting of maladjustment for adolescents was found when both the teacher and parent forms were used. Hence, the CBCL-TF combined with the parent version of the CBCL are highly recommended because of the objectivity of ratings and the opportunity for cross-validation in the ratings of adolescent reactions to divorce. It should be noted that an adolescent self-report form of the CBCL is available from Achenbach and Edelbrock, but currently is not standardized.

Other teacher-rating scales with utility for assessing positive and negative school-related behavior of either young or older divorced-family adolescents are the Hahnemann Elementary School Behavior Rating Scale and the Hahnemann High School Behavior Rating Scale. These instruments are an expansion of the frequently used Devereux Elementary School Behavior Rating Scale, with the number of items increased from 47 to 60. The 16 subscales include four positive behavioral domains (e.g., independent learning), 10 negative domains (e.g., inattention and failure anxiety), and two ratings of academic achievement. These scales are considered the best available instruments of their kind and have been found effective in assessing not only school adjustment but also general behavioral functioning (Guidubaldi & Perry, 1985).

Additional teacher ratings that are helpful in documenting the divorce adjustment of adolescents are the Health Resources Inventory (Gesten, 1976), the Sells and Roff Peer Status Scale (Sells & Roff, 1966), and the Classroom Edition of the Vineland Adaptive Behavior Scales. The Health Resources Inventory includes 46 items that measure children's personal and social competence. The peer status ratings cover seven levels describing the degree to which the child is accepted or rejected by peers. Psychometric data reported by the authors for both scales are adequate. The Vineland scale is a measure of four adaptive behavior factors, labeled Daily Living Skills, Social Skills, Communication, and Motor Development; however, as it was designed for use with an upper-age range of sixth grade, its applicability is limited to very early adolescence.

Scholastic achievement. Measures of basic achievement such as the Wide Range Achievement Test-Revised and school grades should be routinely included in the battery of assessments of adolescents' divorce adjustment. This enables the evaluator to gain an indication of the degree to which an adolescent's academic achievement skills and performance at school are affected by divorce.

Intellectual assessment. A comprehensive individual intelligence instrument such as the Wechsler Intelligence Scale for Children-Revised provides a reliable and valid indication of scholastic ability. Kurdek's (1985, in press) rationale for including this measure covers the need for a cognitive-developmental explanation, whereby divorce adjustment is mediated not only by age but also by intelligence. In addition, it is desirable to know the adolescent's intellectual level for selecting counseling approaches.

At present, this core battery of standardized instruments (WISC-R, WRAT-R, CBCL, CBCL-TF, Adolescent-Coping Orientation for Problem Experiences scale, and Hahnemann High School Behavior Rating Scale), when combined with the previously recommended divorce-specific assessments, provides comprehensive indices of not only adolescents' reactions to divorce but also major mediators of these reactions. Such a battery would require three to four evaluation sessions with an adolescent and his or her parents in addition to scoring, interpretation, and report writing. However, considering the importance of this area of adjustment and its evaluation complexity, such a comprehensive approach is warranted.

ASSESSMENT OF CUSTODY ARRANGEMENTS

Evaluation for the purpose of determining which parent will gain custody of an adolescent following divorce is especially challenging, and mental health practitioners may be handicapped in this function due to the frequently adversarial nature of custody litigation. Ideally, evaluation for custody determination should be based on a body of knowledge that is concerned with the impact of custody arrangements on adolescents' adjustment relevant to the best interests of the child. As noted in the earlier research review, such a knowledge base does not exist at present. Although there are limited data to guide the assessment process in mediation of custody disputes, the following discussion attempts to apply what is presently available and relevant to this topic.

Although there is no single conceptual or methodological mode of evaluation concerning custody arrangements, past practice has tended to focus on clinical parent interview and a very limited set of standardized personality inventories administered to parents. The most frequently used of these has been the Minnesota Multiphasic Personality Inventory (MMPI), an objective measure of parental pathology. Such a focus was consistent with the former judicial orientation that stressed identification of the "unfit" parent; however, in current custody determinations, a more balanced and realistic approach to identifying the more suitable parent limits the utility of such methods. Furthermore, although the MMPI has been used in a wide variety of clinical research, it has not been validated for specific use in divorce evaluations and custody decision making. The recommendations included herein are based on the assumption that determinations of "more suitable" custody arrangements require a comprehensive understanding both of relationships between adolescents and their parents, siblings, peers, and teachers as well as of the suitability of the match between the adolescent's needs and the ability of each parent to structure a home environment that responds to those needs.

In support of this assessment approach, a recent study by Stolberg and Bush (1985) found that

> Personal adjustment [of the parent] was certainly no guarantee of good parenting, predicting only a modest predisposition toward this skill. Significantly, no

direct relationship was found between mothers' and children's adjustment after parenting skills were considered. Mothers coming to grips with their divorces and personally achieving healthy readjustment was reflected in improved parenting practices. Parenting skills was found to be the single most significant influence on children's postdivorce adjustment. (p. 53)

Thus, a limited, unvalidated search for parental pathology cannot serve as a recommended best practice in custody determination. In contrast, the recommendations that follow are oriented toward less inference from assessments to actual behavior in natural settings and toward more consideration of general ecological determinants of adjustment.

It is suggested that custody and related issues such as visitation should be routinely addressed in the divorce-specific assessments reviewed earlier. The Single Parenting Questionnaire (SPQ) is most relevant where salient characteristics of the parent are evaluated. Although intended primarily for use with the custodial parent, the SPQ also could be applied to the noncustodial parent at the time of divorce, when custody determination typically takes place. The SPQ generally provides a measure of the criteria for custody evaluation frequently recommended in the clinical literature (e.g., Gardner, 1982; Ramos, 1979; Woody, 1977), including quality of the individual parent's relationship with the child, parental ability to function effectively in the parenting role, and parent's ability to provide continuity of care for the child. The Parent Separation Inventory (PSI) provides a parental report of type of custody agreement, future custody plans, parental desires for custody visitation, and parental rating of the child's reaction to these topics. The Children's Separation Inventory (CSI) also provides relevant child self-report of attitudes toward parents.

Another relevant instrument, not reviewed previously in this chapter but utilized in the aforementioned NASP-KSU nationwide study, provides data on three critical dimensions of the parenting process. Entitled the Cleminshaw-Guidubaldi Parent Satisfaction Scale (CGPSS; Guidubaldi & Cleminshaw, 1985b, in press), this parent self-report device yields data on three aspects of parent satisfaction: 1) satisfaction with spouse support, 2) satisfaction with the parent-child relationship, and 3) satisfaction with one's parenting skills. These dimensions have been generated through factor analyses on two large samples of parents, including the 699 parent respondents in the nationwide study. Such characteristics of satisfaction represent global summarizations of parents' perceived effectiveness in the parenting process. Statistical support for this instrument is substantial: Cronbach's alpha exceeded .82 for each of the scales and concurrent validity coefficients were substantial in comparisons with other criteria in both normative studies (e.g., parent-child relationship scores correlated .62 with Lee's [1978] Life Satisfaction Scale).

Current Criteria in Custody Evaluation

In current practice, Lowery (1985) points out that custody decisions are not based on psychological assessments alone, but also on legal or practical criteria. Reportedly, these criteria include (a) child preferences; (b) parents' preferences, health, financial sufficiency, moral character, and biological relationship to the child;

(c) educational aspects of the home environment; and (d) provision of a two-parent home. Lowery (1985) also provides the following rank-ordering of criteria currently used by mental health practitioners for custody evaluation:

1. Quality of the parent-child relationship
2. Parent's sense of responsibility to the child
3. Parent's mental stability
4. Parenting skills
5. Amount of contact with the child by custodial parent
6. Parent's affection for the child
7. Parents' wishes
     when the parents agree
     when the parents disagree
8. Maintaining sibling relationships
9. Parent's moral character
10. Stable community involvement
11. Child's wishes
12. Access to schools
13. Professional recommendations
14. Relationship with ex-spouse
15. Amount of contact with the child by noncustodial parent
16. Parent's physical health
17. Parent's financial sufficiency
18. Child's access to peers
19. Length of temporary custody
20. Child's contact with other relatives
21. Biological parents vs. stepparents
22. Keeping a young child with the mother
23. Biological parent vs. adoptive parent
24. Keeping the child with the same-sex parent
25. Availability of a two-parent home (p. 37)

Practitioners could improve their assessment procedures by reviewing these criteria when conducting custody evaluations. In the absence of a formal instrument, the review could be conducted as a structured interview with parents and adolescents. However, interpretation should not be based solely on this hierarchical arrangement as listed, but rather should be guided by research-based findings indicating the degree to which the criteria do, in fact, mediate adolescents' subsequent adjustment. The high rankings of quality of parent-child relationships, parent's sense of responsibility, and parenting skills have been supported by replicated research findings. However, the relatively low ranking of financial sufficiency is not supported, because a recent study has demonstrated that family income of the custodial home *is* a major influence on youth's divorce adjustment (Guidubaldi, Cleminshaw, Perry, & Nastasi, 1984; Guidubaldi, Perry, & Cleminshaw, 1984; Guidubaldi & Perry, 1985). Hence, the practitioner should be familiar with continued refinements in the body of knowledge concerning the complex, interactive ecological mediators of divorce adjustment illustrated earlier.

Ethical and Procedural Issues

In addition to structured assessments and a review of specific custody criteria, there are many ethical and clinical issues that confront evaluators. Gardner's 1982 text provides a system for addressing many of these concerns. Especially helpful is the inclusion of a sample policy statement that a mental health professional could provide to parents, lawyers, and judges prior to accepting the task of custody evaluation. This document stipulates the following: (a) the evaluator's function as an impartial expert rather than an advocate for one parent; (b) a parent waiver of traditional confidentiality rules concerning release of information gained in the evaluation process; (c) parents' willingness to sign releases for access to information from all relevant sources; (d) fee schedules for both evaluation and testifying in court; (e) a payment plan for an advanced retainer; (f) time schedules; and (g) parental consent for release of the report to each other and to the court. The provisos also specify a post-evaluation conference with the parents before releasing the report to both attorneys and the court, which would offer a final opportunity for mediation prior to the custody litigation. The policy statement promotes objectivity, mediating functions, and resolution of such critical ethical issues as the noncustodial parent withholding fees in an attempt to influence the evaluator. Moreover, Gardner provides guidelines for interacting with attorneys, conducting clinical interviews, and testifying in court, in addition to a sample parent questionnaire for assessing custody-related criteria. One of the most helpful documents in his book is a sample custody-evaluation report format.

CASE FORMULATION

The Integrative Model of Socialization

One of the most serious problems in childhood and adolescent assessment is the absence of accepted theoretical models that can be used to integrate evaluation results, predict future adjustment, and identify precise areas of intervention to facilitate healthy development. The inclusion of an ecological-developmental context is particularly needed in divorce cases because the assessment is (a) initiated as a result of major ecological changes and (b) intended to provide assistance in decision making about ecological interventions for children and adolescents. Parental divorce and its aftermath obviously represent major disruptions in the ecology of an adolescent's life, and infusing objectivity into custody determination can pose quite a challenge for psychologists, who are increasingly called upon to assist parents and judicial personnel in custody decisions. Ecological considerations such as these have led the senior author of this chapter to construct the Integrative Model of the Socialization Process (IMS) as a guide to diagnosis and intervention for individuals of any age.

Model description. The model in Figure 1 is a simplified rendition of a very complex process; however, it provides a framework for integrating assessment findings and is based on individual and ecological characteristics. Generally, the model outlines the following process. The subject's social environment consists of potential *reference groups* and individual socializing agents such as parents, peers, siblings, and teachers (see Sherif & Sherif, 1964). Socializing agents, individually or in groups, promote certain *standards* and values. The values and standards of one agent

FIGURE 1. AN INTEGRATIVE MODEL OF THE SOCIALIZATION PROCESS

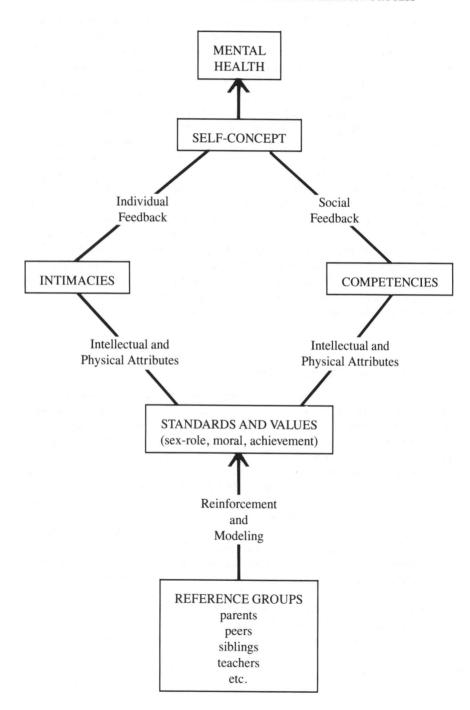

or group may be in conflict with those of another or they may be congruent. Parents and peers may promote conflicting standards, while parents and teachers may reinforce each other. The value hierarchy of a given socializing agent or group may be stable across time, as with a religious leader's set of moral prescriptions, or it may vary considerably, as in the case of a peer group's set of requirements for successful sex-role performance. Some agents, such as parents, may exert their influence over a long time interval, while others may operate for comparatively brief periods of time, as in the case of a science teacher or a Cub Scout pack. In addition, the influence of any particular individual or group may wax or wane depending on such factors as increasing or descreasing contact and changes in the stimulus value of the reinforcements they have to offer.

Reference groups and individuals influence standards and values through *reinforcement* of accepted behavior and *modeling*. Although the observable impact of this influence may be the acquisition of specific *competencies* (e.g., catching a baseball), the more significant effects of informal learning center about the development of standards and values (e.g., adapting standards for male and female sex-role identification). Sex-role standards, moral values, academic achievement orientation, and so on are all influenced by standards and values inculcated by the socialization process. Of course, the individual's physical and intellectual capabilities will have considerable bearing on the realization of any given competence, as well as on his or her expectations of success but the desire to acquire the competency is often independent of any personal qualification or limitation, depending almost entirely on the standards and values adopted from socializing agents.

In addition to the development of socially valued competencies, successful socialization requires the ability to establish viable *intimacy* relationships, intended to validate personal worth. One's standards and values serve a dual role in the establishment of intimacy relationships. These learned guidelines mediate the selection of intimate partners by serving as evaluative dimensions on which to rate the suitability of a prospective partner and, in addition, serve to enhance or detract from the attractiveness of the individual himself. For example, a male's conceptualization of sex-role standards may include the notion that males should be dominant and females submissive. The likelihood of his selecting a dominant female as an intimate partner consequently would be low, and such females correspondingly would have a decreased attraction to him.

Physical and *intellectual attributes* also play a large part in determining success in establishing intimacy relationships. In addition, competencies play a major role in interpersonal attraction. For example, an intelligent man or woman is likely to capitalize on his or her intellectual skills by securing a socially valued job, thereby enhancing interpersonal attractiveness. A physically powerful man may utilize his physical advantage by becoming a professional athlete. Both intimacy relationships and areas of competency derive largely from informal learning of values and standards.

The model further describes intimacy relationships and competencies as the two primary determinants of a positive self-concept. Intimacy partners provide a special kind of feedback, in that they care for each other and are truly concerned about each other's well-being. The competencies that one has developed provide a basis for feedback from a much broader segment of the social environment and are, in fact, those aspects of the individual that are held up for public display. Thus, the complementarity of *individual feedback* from established intimate partners and *social feedback* non-intimate evaluators of socially valued competencies provides the foundation for *self-concept*. In the absence of a more descriptive term, *mental health* has been considered by many writers as the ultimate objective of this socialization process.

Application of the model. Applying this model to the assessment of post-divorce adjustment and custody determination requires the following procedural considerations. First, determination of the most salient reference agents is critically important in measuring post-divorce adjustment. For example, allegiance or alienation in relations with the custodial or noncustodial parent is a significant issue, as is removal or continuation of influence from grandparents and other extended-family reference agents. Moreover, degree of peer influence can often be increased to disproportionate levels because of a lack of adult role models, which is frequently observed in post-divorce households. Conversely, in remarried households new reference agents are introduced, and the child's behaviors may be affected by an even wider extended family of multiple grandparents, aunts, uncles, and so on. Clearly, issues of proximity, degree of contact, relative reinforcement power, and consistency of socializing messages are relevant dynamics of the post-divorce reference system assessment. Examples of instruments that can contribute to such assessment include the Cleminshaw-Guidubaldi Parent Satisfaction Scale, which offers information about the quality of the custodial parent-child relationship and the degree of parenting support from the noncustodial parent; the Hahnemann High School Behavior Rating Scale, which yields information about teacher and peer relationships; the Divorce Adjustment Child Interview, which assesses relationships with parents, peers, siblings, and other relatives; and both parent and teacher forms of the Child Behavior Checklist (Part I), which give information about relationships with peers, siblings, parents, and teachers.

Although no formalized instrument is herein recommended to assess the child's modeling strategies or susceptibility to various reinforcers, issues such as these need to be determined through interviews with the child and his or her caretakers. These factors are particularly salient in post-divorce households in which lower SES levels and absence of same-sex models may present reinforcement and observational-learning problems.

With regard to assessment of standards and values, a variety of cognitive mediators should be assessed. For example, determination of sex-role standards can be approximated by an examination of activity items from the CBCL and of problem-solving approaches from the A-COPE. Achievement standards can be assessed through teacher-rating factors on the HHSBR, parent and teacher CBCL ratings, and through more direct measurement of achievement levels from the WRAT-R. Assessment of some moral standards can be accomplished through the delinquency scale of the CBCL. Assessments of both current cognitive mediators and changes in standards and values throughout the post-divorce period may be critical indices of the adolescent's coping strategies.

Intellectual attributes can be assessed through the WISC-R, and some of the physical characteristics through CBCL ratings on somatization and physical activity.

As described in the model, attainment of intimacy relations and socially valued competencies can be facilitated or obstructed by these characteristics. Socially valued competencies and meaningful intimacy relationships represent the two best indices of successful adjustment to family disruption. Such accomplishments not only offer evidence of successful past problem solving, but they also preview the adolescent's future coping skills and likelihood of success. Recommended procedures include academic achievement indices, such as the WRAT-R, peer acceptance and adult relations measures such as the Sells and Roff Scale, the HHSBRS, the DACI, the CBCL, the PSI, and A-COPE.

Obviously, the adolescent's self-image may be particularly vulnerable in the post-divorce family context. Recommended self-concept assessments include the A-COPE, the HHSBRS, the CSI, the Locus of Control and Worry scales from the DACI, as well as more specific self-concept assessments such as the Coopersmith, Piers-Harris, and Tennessee scales.

CONCLUSIONS

This chapter has focused on applying recent research findings and theoretical concepts to evaluation of adolescents' adjustment to divorce and custody arrangements. The intent has been to provide a model for current assessment practice, including a variety of suggested instruments, in addition to a theoretical model for synthesizing and interpreting the data. The practices and instruments recommended were derived from a review of the rapidly expanding literature on this topic. Although progress is evident from the recent development of assessments that specifically delineate adolescents' reactions to divorce, the knowledge base concerning custody evaluation remains at a rudimentary level.

Two general approaches are recommended for assessment of adolescents' divorce adjustment: 1) the recently developed but psychometrically unsubstantiated measures of divorce-specific reactions and 2) established standardized measures of objective functioning in several domains. The combined core battery currently recommended as providing the most relevant criteria follows:

1. Adolescent-Coping Orientation for Problem Experiences (A-COPE)
2. Child Behavior Checklist (CBCL)
3. Child Behavior Checklist-Teacher Form (CBCL-TF)
4. Children's Separation Inventory (CSI)
5. Cleminshaw-Guidubaldi Parent Satisfaction Scale (CGPSS)
6. Divorce Adjustment Child Interview (DACI)
7. Hahnemann High School Behavior Rating Scale (HHSBRS)
8. Parent Separation Inventory (PSI)
9. Single Parenting Questionnaire (SPQ)
10. Wechsler Intelligence Scale for Children-Revised (WISC-R)
11. Wide Range Achievement Test-Revised (WRAT-R)

The primary rationale for selecting these assessments is their enhanced generalizability and interpretation, as they have been found in research to be related to adolescents' divorce adjustment. This comprehensive approach is multifactored in nature, combining personal-social adjustment, school-related behavioral performance, cognitive abilities, academic achievement, family background, parent-child interaction, and divorce-specific criteria. The battery is also multimethod, in that direct standardized assessments plus child self-report, parent self-report, child interviews, parent-rating scales, and teacher-rating scales are included.

This approach to assessment enables the evaluator to gain relevant criteria for counseling interventions with adolescent clients and, additionally, generates a foundation for consultation with parents, teachers, and other professionals. An adolescent's perceptions and feelings about divorce could be assessed by the DACI and CSI. These instruments provide a review of multiple issues concerning divorce that includes salient topics for counseling adolescents following evaluation. The A-COPE provides data about the client's specific style of coping with divorce, thus yielding essential information for applying a cognitive, social problem-solving approach to counseling. Such information would be helpful when the evaluator directly provides counseling or when consulting with other professionals and parents. The parent- and teacher-rating scales yield additional data concerning how the adolescent performs at home and school, enabling the evaluator to interpret results in terms of relevant problems and maladaptive symptoms. This type of specific information facilitates the establishment of goals for behavorial counseling and management approaches when consulting with parents and teachers.

Although there is presently no single parent interview scale available that could be recommended, the parent-rating scales and questionnaires listed previously (i.e., CGPSS, PSI, and SPQ) could be administered to parents as a structured interview, with additional topics as presented in Table 2. Specific topics for custody evaluation interviews were suggested earlier, and selected procedures for minimizing ethical and procedural issues in custody evaluation were also presented.

Although this core battery appears lengthy, most of the instruments are self-report rating scales and questionnaires that require a minimum of the evaluator's time. The multiple scales for parents to complete are especially comprehensive and lengthy, but provide essential information about the interactive, ecological aspects of divorce and custody. It is suggested that these be presented sequentially over the recommended three evaluation sessions. For example, the PSI and CBCL could be completed by the parent(s) during the initial evaluation session while the practitioner administers direct assessments to the adolescent. The CGPSS and SPQ could be completed by parents in subsequent evaluation sessions. Other standardized instruments listed in Table 3 could also be used as needed.

Psychometric issues and data-based assessments have been emphasized in this review, along with a theoretical model for case formulation. It is tempting to stray within this discussion into some of the more controversial areas embedded within this highly charged topic; however, such forays extend beyond the scope of this chapter. Some recommendations have been made in prior publications of the NASP-KSU study concerning public policy, litigation, and home-environment alternatives. For example, findings alluded to in this chapter about the more adverse post-divorce reactions of boys have led to the suggestion that the highly disproportionate maternal custody decisions may require careful reexamination.

The art of assessing divorce adjustment and custody arrangements is at an early stage of development. Continued refinement of divorce-specific assessment instruments requires a commitment to well-designed studies of divorce adjustment that can generate an improved data base for identification of salient personal and ecological predictors of adjustment. These assessment items then need to be incorporated within a socialization model that stresses individual-environment interactions, cognitive mediation, and attainment of life goals. The recommended assessment practices in this chapter are presented as modest but promising beginnings.

REFERENCES

Ahrons, C. R. (1980). Joint custody arrangements in the post-divorce family. *Journal of Divorce, 3,* 189-205.

Ambert, A. M., & Saucier, J. F. (1983). Adolescents' perception of their parents and parents' marital status. *Journal of Social Psychology, 120,* 101-110.

American Psychological Association. (1985). *Standards for educational and psychological testing.* Washington, DC: Author.

Bandura, A. (1982). Self-efficacy mechanism in human agency. *American Psychologist, 37,* 122-147.

Bane, M. J. (1976). Marital disruption in the lives of children. *Journal of Social Issues, 32,* 103-117.

Barker, R. G. (1968). *Ecological psychology.* Stanford, CA: Stanford University Press.

Belle, D. (1982). *Lives in stress: Women and depression.* Beverly Hills: Sage Publications.

Berg, B. (1979). *Children's Attitudes toward Parental Separation Inventory.* Dayton, OH: University of Dayton Press.

Berg, B., & Kurdek, L. A. (1983a). *Children's Separation Inventory.* Unpublished manuscript, Wright State University, Department of Psychology, Dayton.

Berg, B., & Kurdek, L. A. (1983b). *Parent Separation Inventory.* Unpublished manuscript, Wright State University, Department of Psychology, Dayton.

Bernard, J. M., & Nesbitt, S. (1981). Divorce: An unreliable predictor of children's emotional predispositions. *Journal of Divorce, 4,* 31-42.

Blechman, E. A. (1982). Are children with one parent of psychological risk? A methodological review. *Journal of Marriage and Family, 44,* 179-195.

Bodenheimer, B. M. (1977). Progress under the Uniform Child Custody Jurisdiction Act and remaining problems: Punitive decrees, joint custody, and excessive modifications. *California Law Review, 65,* 978-1014.

Brown, B. F. (1980). A study of the school needs of children from one-parent families. *Phi Delta Kappan, 62,* 537-540.

Bumpass, L., & Rindfuss, R. R. (1979). Children's experiences of marital disruption. *American Journal of Sociology, 85,* 49-65.

Clingempeel, W. G., & Reppucci, N. D. (1982). Joint custody after divorce: Major issues and goals for research. *Psychological Bulletin, 91,* 102-127.

Coleman, J. S. (1961). *The adolescent society.* New York: Free Press.

Colletta, N. (1979). The impact of divorce: Father absence or poverty? *Journal of Divorce, 3,* 27-35.

Copeland, A. P. (1985). Individual differences in children's reactions to divorce. *Journal of Clinical Child Psychology, 14,* 11-19.

Cox, M. J., & Cease, L. (1978). Joint custody: What does it mean? *Family Advocate, Summer,* 10-13.

Derdeyn, A. P. (1976). Child custody contests in historical perspective. *The American Journal of Psychiatry, 133,* 1369-1376.

Derdeyn, A. P., & Scott, E. (1984). Joint custody. *American Journal of Orthopsychiatry, 54,* 199-209.

Dornbusch, S. M., Carlsmith, J. M., Bushwall, S. J., Ritter, P. L., Leiderman, H., Hastorf, A. H., & Gross, R. T. (1985). Single parents, extended households, and the control of adolescents. *Child Development, 56,* 326-341.

Elwood, R. W., & Jacobson, N. S. (1982). Spouse's agreement in reporting their behavioral interactions. *Journal of Consulting and Clinical Psychology, 50,* 783-784.

Emery, R. E. (1982). Interparental conflict and the children of discord and divorce. *Psychological Bulletin, 92,* 310-330.

Emery, R. E., & O'Leary, K. D. (1982). Children's perceptions of marital discord and behavior problems of boys and girls. *Journal of Abnormal Child Psychology, 10,* 11-24.

Farber, S. S., Felner, R. D., & Primavera, J. (1985). Parental separation/divorce and adolescents. *American Journal of Community Psychology, 13,* 171-185.

Felner, R. D., Stolberg, A. L., & Cowen, E. L. (1975). Crisis events and school mental health referral patterns of young children. *Journal of Consulting and Clinical Psychology, 43,* 305-310.

Fisher, B. (1978). *When your relationship ends.* Boulder: Family Relations Learning Center.

Foster, H. H., & Freed, D. J. (1980). Joint custody: Legislative reform. *Trial, 16,* 22-27.

Fry, P. S., & Leahey, M. (1983). Children's perceptions of major positive and negative events and factors in single-parent families. *Journal of Applied Developmental Psychology, 4,* 371-388.

Fry, P., & Trifiletti, R. (1983). An exploration of the adolescent's perspective: Perceptions of major stress dimensions in the single parent family. *Journal of Psychiatric Treatment and Evaluation, 5,* 101-111.

Furstenberg, F. F., Nord, C. W., Peterson, J. L., & Zill, N. (1983). The life course of children of divorce: Marital disruption and parental contact. *American Sociological Review, 48,* 656-668.

Furstenberg, F. F., & Spanier, G. B. (1984). *Recycling the family.* Beverly Hills: Sage Publications.

Gardner, R. A. (1976). *Pyschotherapy with children of divorce.* New York: Jason Aronson.

Gardner, R. A. (1982). *Family evaluation in child custody litigation.* Creekskill, NJ: Creative Therapeutics.

Gesten, E. L. (1976). A Health Resources Inventory: The development of the personal and social competence of primary-grade children. *Journal of Consulting and Clinical Psychology, 44,* 775-786.

Glick, P. (1979). Children of divorced parents in demographic perspective. *Journal of Social Issues, 35,* 170-182.

Glick, P. C. (1980). Remarriage: Some recent changes and variations. *Journal of Family Issues, 1,* 455-478.

Guidubaldi, J. (1969). *An integrative model of the socialization process.* Unpublished manuscript, Harvard University, Harvard Preschool Project, Boston.

Guidubaldi, J. (1983, July). Divorce research clarified issues: A report on NASP's nationwide study. *Communique,* pp. 1-3.

Guidubaldi, J. (in press). Differences in children's divorce adjustment across grade level and gender: A report from the NASP-Kent State University Nationwide Project. In S. Wolchik & P. Karoly (Eds.), *Children of divorce: Perspectives on adjustment.* Lexington, MA: Lexington Books.

Guidubaldi, J., & Cleminshaw, H. K. (1985a). Divorce, family health and child adjustment. *Family Relations, 34,* 35-41.

Guidubaldi, J., & Cleminshaw, H. K. (1985b). The development of the Cleminshaw-Guidubaldi Parent Satisfaction Scale. *Journal of Clinical Child Psychology, 14,* 293-298.

Guidubaldi, J., & Cleminshaw, H. K. (in press). The Cleminshaw-Guidubaldi Parent Satisfaction Scale. In M. E. Fine (Ed.), *Advances in parent education.* New York: Plenum.

Guidubaldi, J., Cleminshaw, H. K., & Perry, J. D. (1985a). The effects of parental divorce on children's and their parents' health. *Special Services in the Schools, 1*, 73-81.

Guidubaldi, J., Cleminshaw, H. K., & Perry, J. D. (1985b). The relationship of parental divorce to health status of parents and children. In J. E. Zins, D. I. Wagner, & C. A. Maher (Eds.), *Health promotion in the schools: Innovative approaches to facilitating physical and emotional well-being* (pp. 73-88). New York: Haworth Press.

Guidubaldi, J., Cleminshaw, H. K., Perry, J. D., & McLoughlin, C. S. (1983). The impact of parental divorce on children: Report of the nationwide NASP study. *School Psychology Review, 12*, 300-323.

Guidubaldi, J., Cleminshaw, H. K., Perry, J. D., & Nastasi, B. K. (1984). Impact of family support systems on children's academic and social functioning after divorce. In G. Rowe, J. DeFrain, H. Lingrin, R. MacDonald, N. Stinnet, S. Van Zandt, & R. Williams (Eds.), *Family strengths 5: Continuity and diversity* (pp. 191-207). Newton, MA: Education Development Center.

Guidubaldi, J., Cleminshaw, H. K., Perry, J. D., Nastasi, B. K., & Lightel, J. (in press). The role of selected family environment factors in children's post-divorce adjustment. *Family Relations.*

Guidubaldi, J., & Perry, J. D. (1984). Divorce, socioeconomic status, and children's cognitive-social competence at school entry. *American Journal of Orthopsychiatry, 54*, 459-468.

Guidubaldi, J., & Perry, J. D. (1985). Divorce and mental health sequelae for children: A two-year follow-up of a nationwide sample. *Journal of the American Academy of Child Psychiatry, 24*, 531-537.

Guidubaldi, J., Perry, J. D., & Cleminshaw, H. K. (1981). *The Divorce Adjustment Child Interview.* Unpublished manuscript, Kent State University, Department of School Psychology, Kent, OH.

Guidubaldi, J., Perry, J. D., & Cleminshaw, H. K. (1984). The legacy of parental divorce: A nationwide study of family status and selected mediating variables on children's academic and social competencies. In B. B. Lahey & A. E. Kazdin (Eds.), *Advances in clinical child psychology* (Vol. 7; pp. 109-151). New York: Plenum Press.

Harter, S. (1979). Perceived Competence Scale for Children: Manual, Form O. Denver: University of Denver.

Harter, S. (1982). The Perceived Competence Scale for Children. *Child Development, 53*, 87-97.

Hingst, A. G. (1981). Children and divorce: A child's view. *Journal of Clinical Child Psychology, 6*, 161-164.

Hodges, W. F., & Bloom, B. L. (1984). Parents' report of children's adjustment to marital separation. *Journal of Divorce, 8*, 33-50.

Hodges, W. F., Tierney, C. W., & Buschbaum, H. K. (1984). The cumulative effect of stress on preschool children of divorced and intact families. *Journal of Marriage and the Family, 46*, 611-617.

Hunt, J. M. (1961). *Intelligence and experience.* New York: Ronald Press.

Huntington, D. S. (1985). Theory and method: The use of psychological tests in research on divorce. *Journal of American Academy of Child Psychiatry, 24*, 583-589.

Jacobson, D. S. (1978). The impact of marital separation/divorce on children. *Journal of Divorce, 1*, 341-360.

Jones, N. B. (Ed.). (1972). *Ethological studies of child behavior.* New York: Cambridge University Press.

Kalter, N. (1977). Children of divorce in an outpatient psychiatric population. *American Journal of Orthopsychiatry, 47*, 40-51.

Kalter, N., & Plunkett, J. W. (1984). Children's perception of causes and consequences of divorce. *Journal of the American Academy of Child Psychiatry, 23*, 326-334.

Kelly, R. R., & Berg, B. (1978). Measuring children's reactions to divorce. *Journal of Clinical Psychology, 34,* 215-221.

Kitson, G. C., & Langlie, J. D. (1984). Couples who file for divorce but change their minds. *American Journal of Orthopsychiatry, 54,* 469-489.

Kurdek, L. A. (1981). An integrative perspective on children's divorce adjustment. *American Psychologist, 36,* 856-866.

Kurdek, L. A. (1985). Children's reasoning about parental divorce. In R. D. Ashmore & D. M. Brodinsky (Eds.), *Perspectives on the family* (pp. 1-48). Hillsdale, NJ: Lawrence Erlbaum Associates.

Kurdek, L. A. (in press). Cognitive mediators of children's adjustment to divorce. In S. Wolchik & P. Karoly (Eds.), *Children of divorce: Perspectives on adjustment.* New York: Gardner Press.

Kurdek, L. A., & Berg, B. (1983). Correlates of children's adjustment to their parents' divorces. In L. A. Kurdek (Ed.), *Children and divorce* (pp. 47-60). San Francisco: Jossey-Bass.

Kurdek, L. A., & Blisk, D. (1983). Dimensions and correlates of mothers' divorce experiences. *Journal of Divorce, 6,* 1-24.

Kurdek, L. A., Blisk, D., & Siesky, A. E. (1981). Correlates of children's long-term adjustment to their parents' divorce. *Developmental Psychology, 17,* 565-579.

Kurdek, L. A., & Siesky, A. E. (1980). Sex-role self-concepts of single divorced parents and their children. *Journal of Divorce, 3,* 249-261.

Kurdek, L. A., & Sinclair, R. (1985). *The relation between adolescent adjustment and family structure, grade, and gender.* Unpublished manuscript, Wright State University, Department of Psychology, Dayton.

Lazarus, M. (1980). One-parent families and their children. *Principal, 60,* 31-37.

Lee, G. R. (1978). Marriage and morale in later life. *Journal of Marriage and the Family, 40,* 131-139.

Lowenstein, J. S., & Koopman, E. J. (1978). A comparison of the self-esteem of boys living with single parent fathers. *Journal of Divorce, 2,* 195-208.

Lowery, C. R. (1981). Child custody decisions in divorce proceedings: A survey of judges. *Professional Psychology, 12,* 492-498.

Lowery, C. R. (1985). Child custody evaluations: Criteria and clinical implications. *Journal of Clinical Child Psychology, 14,* 35-41.

Luepnitz, D. A. (1979). Which aspects of divorce affect children? *Family Coordinator, 28,* 79-85.

McCandless, B. R. (1967). *Children: Behavior and development* (2nd ed.). New York: Holt, Rinehart & Winston.

McDermott, J. J. (1970). Divorce and its psychiatric sequelae in children. *Archives of General Psychiatry, 23,* 421-427.

Morrison, J. R. (1974). Parental divorce as a factor in childhood psychiatric illness. *Comparative Psychiatry, 15,* 95-102.

Moss, S. Z., & Moss, M. S. (1975). Surrogate mother-child relationships. *American Journal of Orthopsychiatry, 45,* 382-390.

Musgrove, F. (1964). *Youth and the social order.* Bloomington: Indiana University Press.

National Center for Health Statistics. (1984). Births, marriages, divorces, and deaths for 1983. *Monthly vital statistics* (Report No. 23, PHS-84-1120). Washington, DC: U.S. Government Printing Office.

Nowicki, S., & Strickland, B. R. (1973). A locus of control scale for children. *Journal of Consulting and Clinical Psychology, 40,* 148-155.

Parish, J. S., & Wigle, S. E. (1985). A longitudinal study of the impact of parental divorce on adolescents' evaluation of self and parents. *Adolescence, 20,* 239-244.

Perry, J. D., Guidubaldi, J., & Kehle, T. J. (1979). Kindergarten competencies as predictors of third-grade classroom behavior and achievement. *Journal of Educational Psychology, 71,* 443-450.

Pett, M. G. (1982). Correlates of children's social adjustment following divorce. *Journal of Divorce, 5,* 25-39.

Plunkett, J. W., & Kalter, N. (1984). Children's beliefs about reactions to parental divorce. *Journal of the American Academy of Child Psychiatry, 23,*616-621.

Ramos, S. (1979). *The complete book of child custody.* New York: Putnam.

Reinhard, D. W. (1977). The reaction of adolescent boys and girls to the divorce of their parents. *Journal of Clinical Child Psychology, 6,* 21-23.

Roman, M., & Haddad, W. (1978). *The disposable parent.* New York: Holt, Rinehart & Winston.

Rosen, R. (1977). Children of divorce: What they feel about access and other aspects of the divorce experience. *Journal of Clinical Child Psychology, 6,* 24-27.

Sandler, I. N., Wolchik, S. A., & Braver, S. L. (1984). *The Divorce Experiences Schedule for Children.* Unpublished manuscript, Arizona State University, Department of Psychology, Tempe.

Saposnek, D. T. (1983). *Mediating child custody disputes.* San Francisco: Jossey-Bass.

Saucier, J. F., & Ambert, A. M. (1983). Parental marital status and adolescents' health-risk behavior. *Adolescence, 18,* 403-411.

Schwartz, J. C., & Getter, H. (1980). Parental conflict and dominance in late adolescent maladjustment. *Journal of Abnormal Psychology, 89,* 573-580.

Sells, S. B., & Roff, M. (1966). *Peer acceptance–rejection and personality development.* Washington, DC: U.S. Department of Health, Education and Welfare.

Sherif, M., & Sherif, C. W. (1964). *Reference groups.* New York: Harper & Row.

Slater, E. J., & Haber, J. D. (1984). Adolescent adjustment following divorce as a function of family conflict. *Journal of Consulting and Clinical Psychology, 52,* 920-921.

Slater, E. J., Stewart, K. J., & Linn, M. W. (1983). The effects of family disruption on adolescent males and females. *Adolescence, 18,* 931-942.

Spanier, G. B., & Thompson, L. (1984). *Parting: The aftermath of separation and divorce.* Beverly Hills: Sage Publications.

Stack, C. B. (1976). Who owns the child? Divorce and child custody decisions in middle-class families. *Social Problems, 23,* 505-515.

Steinman, S. (1981). The experience of children in a joint-custody arrangement. *American Journal of Orthopsychiatry, 51,* 403-414.

Stevenson, H. W., Parker, T., Wilkinson, A., Hegion, A., & Fish, E. (1976). Predictive validity of teachers' ratings of young children. *Journal of Educational Psychology, 68,* 507-517.

Stipek, D., Lamb, M., & Zigler, E. (1981). OPTI: A measure of children's optimism. *Educational and Psychological Measurement, 41,* 131-150.

Stolberg, A. L., & Bush, A. L. (1985). A path analysis of factors predicting children's divorce adjustment. *Journal of Clinical Child Psychology, 14,* 49-54.

Stolberg, A. L., & Cullen, P. M. (1983). Preventive interventions for families of divorce: Divorce Adjustment Project. In L. A. Kurdek (Ed.), *Children and divorce* (pp. 71-82). San Francisco: Jossey-Bass.

Stolberg, A. L., & Ullman, A. J. (1985). Assessing dimensions of single parenting: The Single Parenting Questionnaire. *Journal of Divorce, 8,* 31-45.

Sullivan, H. S. (1953). *The interpersonal theory of psychiatry.* New York: W. W. Norton & Company.

Tessman, L. H. (1978). Children of parting parents. New York: Jason Aronson.

U.S. Bureau of the Census. (1979). *Divorce, child custody, and child support* (Current Population Reports, Series P-23, No. 84). Washington, DC: U.S. Government Printing Office.

U.S. Bureau of the Census. (1982b). *Marital status and living arrangements: March 1981* (Current Population Report, Series P-20, No. 372). Washington, DC: U.S. Government Printing Office.

U.S. Bureau of the Census. (1982b). *Marital status and living arrangements: March 1981* (Current Population Report, Series P-20, No. 372). Washington, DC: U.S. Government Printing Office.

U.S. Department of Health and Human Services. (1980). *Helping youth and families of separation, divorce, and remarriage.* Washington, DC: U.S. Government Printing Office.

Wallerstein, J. S. (1984). Children of divorce: Preliminary report of a ten-year follow-up of young children. *American Journal of Orthopsychiatry, 54,* 444-453.

Wallerstein, J. S., & Kelly, J. B. (1980a, January). California's children of divorce. *Psychology Today,* pp. 66-67.

Wallerstein, J. S., & Kelly, J. B. (1980b). *Surviving the break-up: How children and parents cope with divorce.* New York: Basic Books.

Warshak, R. A., & Santrock, J. W. (1983). The impact of divorce on father-custody and mother-custody homes: The child's perspective. In L. A. Kurdek (Ed.), *Children and divorce* (pp. 29-46). San Francisco: Jossey-Bass.

White, S. W., & Mika, K. (1983). Family divorce and separation: Theory and research. *Marriage and Family Review, 6,* 175-192.

Wolchik, S. A., Braver, S. L., & Sandler, I. N. (1985). Maternal versus joint custody: Children's post-separation experiences and adjustment. *Journal of Clinical Child Psychology, 14,* 5-10.

Woody, R. H. (1977). Behavioral science criteria in child custody determinants. *Journal of Marriage and Family Counseling, 3,* 11-18.

Wyman, P. A., Cowen, E. L., Hightower, A. D., & Pedro-Carroll, J. L. (1985). Perceived competence, self-esteem, and anxiety in latency-aged children of divorce. *Journal of Clinical Child Psychology, 14,* 20-26.

Zakariya, S. B. (1982). Another look at the children of divorce: Summary report of the study of school needs of one-parent children. *Principal, 62,* 34-37.

10

The Assessment of Adolescent Psychopathology

HELEN REINER, PH.D.

During adolescence, a teenager undergoes more drastic changes than occur during any other time in life. Within this context, concern about acne, weight problems, menstruation, late or early development, sexual arousal, school pressures, boredom, "hassles" with adults, peer pressures, and money problems serve to produce confused feelings, particularly in relationships with parents. Adolescents will fight for independence, yet fear too much freedom; they may resent overprotection, but need and want parental attention. This process of development and reorganization entails forging a new image of self and becoming independent of home—emotionally, socially, and economically—through the acquisition of education or training.

Our culture places the adolescent under a great deal of stress in terms of sexual inhibition, limitations of freedom, and pressure for success. The stress of adolescence is evident in that more adolescents than adults report only a low level of happiness (Conger & Petersen, 1984). Demographic data indicate that suicide ranks as a leading cause of death among the 15- to 19-year-old age group. In addition, three quarters of persons with schizophrenia develop the disorder between 16 and 25 years of age (Torrey, 1983). When psychological problems occur during adolescence, they must be viewed within the context of ongoing development. This is in sharp contrast to the psychological disorders of adulthood, which typically are considered within a framework of stable adaptation that has either broken down or been disrupted. While most adolescents successfully make the transition into adulthood, a significant number present psychological problems, which will require intervention.

Adolescent referrals to psychiatric and psychological clinics peak between ages 14 to 16 (Anthony, 1970). The overall purpose of this chapter is to describe the use of appropriate psychological instrumentation and techniques, both formal and informal, that aid in the assessment of adolescent psychopathology, specifically affective disorders, anxiety disorders, and schizophrenic disorders. The discussion will attempt to relate such diagnostic assessments to criteria specified in the *Diagnostic and Statistical Manual of Mental Disorders* (DSM-III; American Psychiatric Association, 1980). The DSM-III is acknowledged as the most extensive and detailed attempt in psychiatric history to develop not only a comprehensive diagnostic system, but more significantly, a universal agreement on the criteria for identifying certain child and adult psychopathological disorders. Not only is reliable classification of conse-

229

quence to insurance companies for reimbursement purposes, but relatively homogenous categories such as these are important for research purposes, determination of etiology and epidemiology, treatment specification, and the identification of social, biological, and other factors that may exacerbate or mitigate the effects of a disorder (Harrington, 1984).

AFFECTIVE DISORDERS IN ADOLESCENCE

Symptomatology and Classification: Major Depression versus Manic-Depressive Syndrome

The subject of affective disorders in adolescence has been especially controversial because of the presumed difficulties in understanding the problem of adolescent turmoil (Carlson & Strober, 1983). That is, some authorities contend that adolescent depression is an identifiable diagnostic entity similar to that seen in adults (Carlson & Strober, 1978); others suggest the need for identifying nontraditional, adolescent-specific "equivalents" of depressive disorders (Glaser, 1967). For many young people, the phenomenology of their depressive disorder is similar to that of adults. The conflicts presented by this particular developmental period coexist with, but do not seem to alter substantially, the primary features of depression and mania.

All of the DSM-III Affective Disorders share the common denominator of a primary and preponderant disturbance in mood, a prolonged and pervasive emotional state that affects the total person: feelings, outlook, attitude, self-regard, activity level, homeostatic balance, and trends in thinking. Major affective disorders, according to DSM-III, include Bipolar Disorder, also known as *manic-depressive disorder,* and Major Depression, sometimes referred to as *unipolar depression.* It is important to note that both of these syndromes are clinical clusters of symptoms that might be produced by a number of causes.

There is no question that depression occurs in adolescence; in fact, it has been suggested that depressive illness in adolescence is considerably more prevalent and identifiable than current opinion and available epidemiological data suggest (Carlson & Strober, 1983). Two major issues have been highlighted in recent literature on adolescent depression. First, while research has begun to suggest that the descriptive features of unipolar depression in adolescents do resemble those found in adults (Carlson & Strober, 1983), these data also indicate considerable heterogeneity of symptom patterns among youngsters who share a label of depressive disorder. Secondly, there is a growing sentiment that manic-depressive disorder, or bipolar depression, is more common in adolescence than once believed; thus it will also be addressed here.

The features of the unipolar depressive syndrome (Webb et al., 1981) can be grouped into four areas: mood, vitality, agitation, and consolation-seeking behaviors. The affected adolescent will often display sadness, demoralization, loss of enthusiasm, boredom, and feelings of listlessness. He or she may demonstrate anxiety and worry, with accompanying difficulty in sleeping. Behavior may appear reckless and even self-destructive, with the individual often seeking escape in excessive intake of or reliance on food, drugs, or alcohol.

Dysphoric mood or a loss of interest or pleasure in all or most usual activities and pastimes constitutes the first DSM-III diagnostic criterion for a major depressive episode. Characterized by symptoms such as sadness, feeling blue, hopelessness, feeling low, and so on, the mood disturbance must be prominent and relatively persistent. It is not necessarily the most dominant symptom, however, and does not include momentary shifts from one dysphoric mood to another (e.g., anxiety to depression to anger), such as one sees in states of acute psychotic turmoil. In addition, for a period of at least two weeks, at least four of the following symptoms should have been present nearly every day: 1) poor appetite or significant weight loss (when not dieting), or increased appetite or significant weight gain; 2) insomnia or hypersomnia; 3) psychomotor agitation or retardation (but not merely subjective feelings of restlessness or being slowed down); 4) loss of interest or pleasure in usual activities or decrease in sexual drive, not limited to a period when delusional or hallucinating; 5) loss of energy or fatigue; 6) feelings of worthlessness, self-reproach, or excessive or inappropriate guilt (either may be delusional); 7) complaints or evidence of diminished capacity to think or concentrate, such as slowed thinking, or indecisiveness not associated with marked loosening of associations or incoherence; and 8) recurrent thoughts of death, suicidal ideation, wishing to be dead, or attempted suicide. Furthermore, neither bizarre behavior nor a preoccupation with a mood-incongruent delusion or hallucination can dominate the clinical picture when an affective syndrome (i.e., specified in the previously described mood disturbance and symptom pattern criteria) is not present (i.e., before it developed or after it has remitted). Finally, the depressive syndrome must not be superimposed on either a schizophrenic or paranoid disorder and must not be due to any organic mental disorder or uncomplicated bereavement.

What distinguishes a major depression from the bipolar disorders is the absence of a manic episode, the features of which include elation, expansiveness, and increased appetite, stamina, and well-being. However, behavior is often restless, loud, physically aggressive, and high spirited; much of this misbehavior will be pleasure-seeking and is often indiscreet and excessive. The diagnostic criteria for a manic episode require one or more distinct periods with a predominantly elevated, expansive, or irritable mood, which must be a prominent and relatively persistent part of the illness, though it may alternate or intermingle with depressive mood. Secondly, for at least one week (or any duration of necessary hospitalization), for most of the time, at least three of the following symptoms should persist (four if the mood is only irritable) and should be present to a significant degree: 1) increase in activity (either socially, at work, or sexually) or physical restlessness; 2) more talkative than usual or pressure felt to keep talking; 3) flight of ideas or the subjective experience that thoughts are racing; 4) inflated self-esteem (grandiosity, which may be delusional); 5) decreased need for sleep; 6) distractibility (i.e., attention too easily drawn to unimportant or irrelevant external stimuli); and 7) excessive involvement in activities that have a high potential, which is not recognized, for painful consequences (e.g., buying sprees, sexual indiscretions, foolish business investments, reckless driving, etc.). As with the depressive syndrome, neither preoccupation with a mood-incongruent delusion or hallucination nor bizarre behavior can dominate the clinical picture when the manic-depressive syndrome is not present. The final criteria stipulate that the manic episodes are not superimposed on either schizophrenic or paranoid disorders and that they are not due to any organic mental disorder, such as substance intoxication.

Though the existence and phenomenology of manic-depressive illness in early childhood remain unclear, the appearance of this disorder in adolescence is accepted. Precise epidemiological figures on its incidence are unavailable, however, because episodes of mania and depression are often overlooked or misinterpreted. First episodes, for example, may be mild and thus not come to psychiatric attention. It is only when an episode occurs in later years requiring treatment that past history often reveals mood swings beginning around puberty.

Carlson's (1983) review of the literature on early-onset bipolar manic-depressive illness concludes that while no particular premorbid personality seems to predispose the disorder, family histories positive for affective disorder are often noted. In a study of manic-depressive illness in children, Anthony and Scott (1960) found family histories positive for depression, manic depression, alcoholism, suicide, or cyclothymia in 75% of all cases. In addition, onset of the full-fledged disorder is often acute and dramatic, even when there is an earlier history of problems. Psychosis and psychomotor retardation are frequently part of the episodes of illness. These observations are particularly useful in predicting whether an adolescent first presenting with depressive symptomatology may be at possible risk for a bipolar course. It should be noted that, given the extended period of risk for bipolar manic-depressive illness, a diagnosis of unipolar depression in an adolescent suffering a first episode of depression cannot be made with absolute certainty. In practice, adolescents often are diagnosed as having unipolar depression if they have no other preceding or concurrent psychiatric diagnosis, if there is no family history of manic-depressive illness, and if they meet DSM-III operational criteria for a major depressive disorder.

Depression and Suicidal Behavior

Although the suicide rate among young people has fluctuated in the past, it has captured the attention of mental health professionals and the public in the last two decades because of its alarming increase. Suicide and homocidal incidents are now the second and third leading causes of death in the 15- to 24-year age group (Holinger, 1978). Suicide in children under the age of 15 is still considered a low-frequency phenomenon.

Recent research has suggested that depression has a contributory but not constant relationship to a suicide attempt, being neither a requisite nor a sufficient cause (Carlson, 1983). Although a psychiatric diagnosis is not enough to explain a suicide attempt, we do know that individuals meeting criteria for a major affective disorder do carry a higher risk of suicide. Therefore, it is important to assess depressive disorders systematically, gathering data from the subject, family, and/or friends and using all the DSM-III inclusionary and exclusionary criteria.

If an adolescent has made a suicide attempt, assessment should focus on the imminent risk to his or her life as well as on the evaluation and clarification of the whole family system. Specific factors such as a family history of psychiatric illness (especially depression and alcoholism) and histories of suicidal behaviors help in confirming a diagnosis and in getting a sense of the family's coping skills (Carlson, 1983). This information should assist the psychologist in understanding and possibly remediating certain familial factors, with the goal of improving the ultimate prognosis. Finally, it is also recommended that the adolescent's interpersonal, social, and school functioning be evaluated.

PROCEDURES FOR THE ASSESSMENT OF AFFECTIVE DISORDERS

It is generally agreed that psychiatric disorders in children and adolescents are probably of multifactorial etiology. In order for the diagnostic process to be multifac-tored and multisourced, clinicians must use a variety of tools. Cantwell (1983) classi-fies the tools available for the assessment of depression into four general types: 1) interviews with the parent about the child; 2) interviews with and observations of the child him- or herself; 3) rating scales, including the self-rating variety as well as those completed by parents, teachers, peers, and clinicians; and 4) laboratory stud-ies, here used in the broadest sense to include not only biological measures (e.g., physical or neurological examinations) but psychological testing as well. In general, the definition of any clinical syndrome in childhood begins in the parental interview, the interview with the child, and behavior rating scales.

Interviews

Most clinical researchers interested in adolescent depression strongly empha-size the diagnostic importance of the interview with the child to measure reliably all symptoms in the depressive syndrome. In one of the few studies of reliability and validity of the diagnostic procedures in child psychiatry, Rutter, Tizard, and Whit-more (1970) found that the interview with the parents was the single best instrument for detecting children with psychiatric disorders. Interviews for use with the child or parents to detail symptomatology include the Schedule for Affective Disorders and Schizophrenia for School-Age Children (Kiddie-SADS), the Diagnostic Interview for Children and Adolescents (DICA), the Diagnostic Interview Schedule for Chil-dren-Parent Form (DISC-P), and the Interview Schedule for Children (ISC), parent form. Some of these procedures are geared toward assessing general psycho-pathology, while others are more specific for depression, such as the Kiddie-SADS. Probably the most comprehensive interview is the DISC-P (a NIMH-generated [1980] interview analogous to the adult Diagnostic Interview Schedule), which is keyed to the DSM-III diagnostic categories. While some instruments assess only the present depressive episode, the most widely used instruments, described hereafter, are developmental in scope, obtaining data on the child's history and not only the present depressive episode.

At the present time, there are three diagnostic instruments most often recom-mended to measure the depressive syndrome in clients under the age of 18:

1. The Diagnostic Interview for Children and Adolescents (DICA; Herjanic & Campbell, 1977) was designed to diagnose children aged 6-17 years according to the DSM-III. Separate forms are provided for the child and parent.

2. The Interview Schedule for Children (ISC) developed in 1981 by Kovacs for use with children 8-13 years of age also records the interview with the child. Data is obtained only from the child, but the interview may be administered to parents by altering the format of the questions.

3. The Schedule for Affective Disorders and Schizophrenia for School-Age Children (Kiddie-SADS), developed by Chambers, Puig-Antich, and Tabrizi in 1978. This schedule records information from the interview with both the child and the parent and is one of the most widely used psychiatric interviews with children ages 6 to 16.

In addition, Hodges, McKnew, Cytryn, Stern, and Kline (1982) have developed the Child Assessment Schedule (CAS), a standardized diagnostic interview for children that consists of two parts. The first is a series of 75 questions asked of the child, covering multiple topics such as school, friends, hobbies, concerns, and so on. The second part is observational, in which the interviewer can record observations and judgments made after completing the interview with the child. The Child Assessment Schedule is designed for clinical assessment as well as collection of research data. The CAS provides a systematic and comprehensive method for obtaining information and is intended primarily as a clinical tool to be analyzed qualitatively by a clinican.

Rating Scales

Rating scales have been devised to be completed by the client (self-report) and by significant others in the client's environment, such as parents, teachers, and peers. In addition, clinician-completed rating scales are also available. While some of these scales are designed to assess general psychopathology, others address the depressive symptomatology more specifically.

Self-report inventories. Of the self-report inventories, the Children's Depression Scale (CDS) and the Children's Depression Inventory (CDI) are most often recommended for clinical use. The CDS, developed by Lange and Tisher (1978), measures depression in children aged 9-16 years. The full inventory contains 66 items, 48 depressive ("Often I feel lonely") and 18 positive ("I enjoy myself most of the time"). The two sets of items are retained as independent scales and scored separately, yielding a Depressive score and a Positive score.

Within the two main scales of the CDS, certain items that refer to similar features of childhood depression have been grouped together as subscales. The Depressive scale contains five such subscales and the Positive scale contains one. These subscales are identified as Affective Response, Social Problems, Self-Esteem, Preoccupation With Own Sickness and Death, Guilt, and Pleasure. Items in each are mutually exclusive; that is, each item belongs to only one subscale. The CDS subscales offer the clinican a clearer understanding of the nature of the child's depression by providing scores across different areas of depression. (In addition, the CDS Adult Form can be used with parents, siblings, or teachers, permitting a comparison of the child's responses with those of parents or others, thus relating the child's depression to the context of his or her life.) The CDS developers report high internal consistency and reliability, asserting that scores on the CDS do differentiate depressed children from both normals and other diagnostic groups.

The Children's Depression Inventory (CDI) is a 27-item severity measure of overt symptoms of depression, such as sadness, anhedonia, suicidal ideation, and sleep disturbance, in children aged 10 through 17. The CDI was created by Kovacs and Beck (1977) by modifying certain items on the Beck Depression Inventory. Each of the 27 items consists of three sentences ranging from normalcy to mild symptomatology to severe and clinically significant symptoms. Each item is read aloud to the child and he or she marks an answer based on feelings experienced over the previous 2 weeks. Each item is then scored on a 0- to 2-point scale, resulting in a range of scores from 0 to 54 that indicate the severity of the depressive episode. The average score in nonpsychiatric populations is 9, while a cutoff score of 19 identifies children whose scores deviate significantly from the "normal" population. The original CDI has been modified several times by Kovacs, with regard to both scoring format and item content. Kovacs (1978) reports interrater consistency estimates from .71 to .87, with fair to excellent test-retest reliability depending on sample characteristics and retest interval. The CDI is presently the most widely used self-rating scale for assessing the severity of depression.

It should be noted that some authors question whether self-report inventories are as useful with children as they are with adults. These inventories are subject to certain general sources of bias and distortion with both age groups, but with children, language and cognitive skills at different age levels probably influence the child's interpretation of the items and may contribute to variance among scores more than with adults (Cantwell, 1983; Harrington & Follett, 1984).

Parent-rating scales. Achenbach and Edelbrock's Child Behavior Checklist (CBCL) is often used as a means of assessing childhood depression via parental report. The four-page checklist contains questions regarding the child's social history, interests, and school performance. The last two pages present 118 items describing a variety of problem behaviors, which parents rate from 0 (not true) to 2 (very true) according to their child's behavior over the past 6 months. Scores are yielded for Social Competence scales and Behavior Problem scales, as well as for Internalizing, Externalizing, and Total Problem.

The Children's Depression Scale (CDS) as well as the Children's Depression Inventory (CDI) both have versions that can be completed by the child's parents. Sensitive parents are usually the best informants for observable behavior, including past verbal statements by the child, and for providing the interviewer with a chronological framework for the unfolding of the present episode.

Cantwell (1983) notes a word of caution here. The diagnosis of depressive disorder in childhood is heavily dependent on subjective phenomena and not on observable behavior; therefore, its presence cannot be identified by rating scales developed for use by parents and teachers alone.

Peer-rating scales. In addition to the observations of parents and teachers, peer ratings have been used to measure a variety of aspects of childhood behavior. Lefkowitz and Tesiny's Peer Nomination Inventory of Depression (PNID) requires an individual child to be evaluated by many peers in his or her classroom setting. The 20 items on the PNID cover four areas related to depression: affective, cognitive, motivational, and vegetative. The scale items are represented by three factors: loneliness, inadequacy, and dejection. While reliability studies have been impressive, validity studies are somewhat lacking. The PNID appears to be predictive of school performance, self-concept, teacher rating of work skills and social behavior, peer rating of happiness and popularity, and loss of control. From the standpoint of psychometric work, the PNID is one of the better scales developed. However, its utility should be restricted to school rather than clinical settings, because accurate ratings require stable peer groups familiar with the child being evaluated.

Projective Techniques

Cytryn and McKnew (1972) have used projective techniques to measure fantasy in children with depression. Projective tests such as the Rorschach, the Thematic Apperception Test (TAT), figure drawings, and others can be scored for depressive themes. However, these techniques have not been applied extensively or systematically to the study of child and adolescent depression. Whether they would add anything beyond what might be gathered from other forms of evaluation is questionable. Gittleman's (1980) review of the use of projective techniques in differential diagnosis in child psychiatry gives less than enthusiastic support for their reliability and validity in these applications.

In assessing affective disorders in adolescence, several special considerations must be made in contrast to assessing similar disorders in adults. First, although depressed youngsters may have symptomatology similar to adults, its form of expression relates to the developmental level of the child and thus may differ from adults. Secondly, some depressed adolescents present problems suggestive of behavior disorder or some other psychiatric disorder, and only on careful examination does depressive symptomatology become apparent. Third, and most importantly, information from a variety of sources must be obtained before making a diagnosis. Evidence suggests that parents and children correspond fairly well in reporting symptoms of depression, but children, parents, and teachers often differ on the presence and severity of specific symptomatology (Kazdin, French, & Unis, in press). Although it is important to gather data from a variety of sources, the adolescent must be the primary source of information when making a final diagnosis.

Current best practices for assessing adolescent depression, as described in this chapter, include diagnostic interviews, self-report inventories, parent- and peer-rating scales, and projective techniques. The choice of specific instrumentation will vary, of course, depending on the skills of the clinician, the age of the informant, and the availability of parents, teachers, and significant others.

ANXIETY DISORDERS IN ADOLESCENCE

Symptomatology and Classification

According to the DSM-III, an anxiety reaction is characterized by apprehension, fearfulness, and tenseness, either acute or chronic. An acute anxiety reaction comes quickly and may last from a few minutes to several hours. Among the symptomatology of acute anxiety are sudden fearfulness, restlessness, fatigue, dizziness, headache, nausea, vomiting, limited attention span, sleep disturbances, and muscle tension symptoms. Chronic reactions entail persistent tenseness that may last for weeks, months, or, with fluctuations, for years. Most of the symptomatology associated with acute anxiety also applies to the chronic form (which in fact may result from unresolved acute anxiety). Anxiety reactions tend to occur more frequently in children over the age of 10 and become more common in early adolescence. During middle and late adolescence these reactions increase in clinical frequency, and in early adulthood constitute the most common emotional symptom seen in medical practice.

In early adolescence, episodes of depression and marked anxiety may be associated with an increasing need to separate from parents and family, increased pressure for peer approval, and increased academic demands. In mid-adolescence, anxiety and regressive behavior may be associated with increased demands to establish heterosexual relationships and with concern about sexual adequacy. The late adolescent may experience considerable stress moving from home to a college environment and in turn needing to choose a career, belong to a group, and establish relationships with the opposite sex.

Usually the diagnostician will attempt to classify symptoms of adolescent psychopathology within the DSM-III category entitled Disorders Usually First Evident in Infancy, Childhood or Adolescence. In this classification, the Anxiety Disorders of Childhood or Adolescence include three subclasses: Separation Anxiety, Avoidant Disorder, and Overanxious Disorder. The main characteristics of these groups is excessive anxiety manifested by fear of separation, social avoidance, or persistent and excessive worry. If this classification is unsuccessful then the clinician should turn to the appropriate adult classification schemes for anxiety disorders, affective disorders, schizophrenic disorders, and so on. DSM-III does not set rigid or arbitrary age boundaries for infancy, childhood, or adolescence. Although the disorders under discussion here usually occur in childhood or adolescence, they also can develop in early or later adulthood.

Anxiety Disorders

Many of the conditions formerly labeled "neurosis" in DSM-II are now classified under the heading of Anxiety Disorders in DSM-III. The basic features of anxiety, the core of this group of disorders, are described in DSM-III as follows: 1) motor tension demonstrated by jumpiness, trembling, or inability to relax; 2) autonomic hyperactivity evidenced by dizziness, racing heart, or perspiring; 3) apprehensive expectation demonstrated by anxious rumination; and 4) vigilance and scanning evidenced by hyperattentiveness. In DSM-II, anxiety was the *signal* of neurosis. By contrast, only disorders in which anxiety is experienced *directly* are included in the DSM-III Anxiety Disorders. Of all the subclasses of anxiety disorders (Phobic, Obsessive-Compulsive, Panic, Generalized Anxiety, Post-Traumatic Stress, and Atypical Anxiety), those that are most significant in relation to adolescence are Phobic, Panic, and Generalized Anxiety.

Phobic disorders comprise the most specific subclass of the anxiety disorders. The essential features of all the phobic disorders are persistent avoidance behavior secondary to irrational fears; recognition of the fear as unreasonable and unwarranted; and avoidance behavior and fear causing subjective distress or interfering with the individual's social or role functioning.

Although the term "school phobia" does not appear in the traditional nomenclature of psychological disorders and is usually regarded as a problem more of childhood than adolescence, adolescent school phobia merits attention in any consideration of adolescent psychopathology. In a great many adolescents brought for professional help in connection with anxiety, headache, abdominal pain, nausea, vomiting, and so on, refusal to go to school has been the event that crystallized parental concern. School phobia or refusal may occur in the absence of any other psychological disturbances or in combination with various neurotic or psychotic disorders. In fact, in order to categorize school phobia into its acute and chronic forms, the examiner must consider the psychological disturbances associated with it. Research has shown that the initial indications of the school-phobic adolescent include progressive school aversion and accompanying withdrawal from social and peer-group activities. In chronic cases, the associated psychological problems may be deeply imbedded, and the prognosis is not as positive as in acute cases (Chapman, 1974). The prevalence of school phobia for boys versus girls is about equal (Achenbach & Edelbrock, 1981).

Panic Disorder and Generalized Anxiety Disorder comprise the condition identified as "anxiety neurosis" in DSM-III. The essential features of a panic disorder are recurrent panic attacks marked by a sudden onset of intense apprehension, fear, or terror, often accompanied by feelings of impending doom. One of the diagnostic criteria for Panic Disorder entails three panic attacks in three weeks in non-life-threatening circumstances. Secondly, the attacks are manifested by discrete periods of apprehension and at least four of the following symptoms appear during each attack: dyspnea; palpitations; chest pain; choking sensation; dizziness; feelings of unreality; paresthesias (tingling in hands/feet); hot and cold flashes; sweating; faintness; trembling or shaking; and fear of dying, going crazy, or doing something uncontrolled. Finally, Panic Disorder is not due to a physical disorder or another mental disorder. Of note, while persistent anxiety of at least one month is the basic element of the Generalized Anxiety Disorder, to receive this diagnosis an individual must be 18 or older.

PROCEDURES FOR THE ASSESSMENT OF ANXIETY DISORDERS

Assessment material pertinent to adolescent anxiety disorders suggests a multimethod approach to provide the most comprehensive view of the disorder. An accurate classification according to DSM-III criteria and the development of the most effective treatment program for the adolescent require a careful comparison of data from several different assessment instruments, informants, and stimulus situations. The types of data available to a clinician may include behavior observation, interview material from the child, parents, and sometimes a teacher or other significant person, test material relevant to intellectual and academic functioning, various projective and self-report instruments, questionnaires, and checklists.

Rating Scales

A number of rating scales exist to measure childhood and adolescent anxiety. The most popular clinical scale is the Devereux Adolescent Behavior Rating Scale (DAB), which was designed to evaluate and describe a wide range of readily observable behavior problems in adolescents between the ages of 13 and 18. The Devereux scale was not intended to provide a measure of personality traits, but rather to profile 15 problem behavior dimensions characteristic of youngsters aged 13-18. The DAB yields 12 factor scores (Unethical Behavior, Defiant-Resistive, Domineering-Sadistic, Heterosexual Interest, Hyperactive Expansive, Poor Emotional Control, Need

Approval and Dependency, Emotional Distance, Physical Inferiority-Timidity, Schizoid Withdrawal, Bizarre Speech and Cognition, Bizarre Action), three cluster scores (Inability to Delay Paranoid Thought, Anxious, Self-Blame), and 11 item scores (Persecution, Plotting, Bodily Concern, External Influences, Compulsive Acts, Avoids Competition, Withdrawn, Socialization, Peer Dominance, Physical Coordination, Distraction).

In selecting items for inclusion, the authors attempted to cover the broad spectrum of problem behaviors that may be found among typical adolescents. In addition, the scale is designed to be usable by nonprofessionals. Rating time is estimated at 15 minutes, and test results are displayed in a conveniently constructed profile of scores.

Parent-rating scales. The Behavior Problem Checklist (BPC; Quay, 1977) and the Personality Inventory for Children (PIC) are valuable instruments when one suspects that the anxiety disorder is affecting functioning in a variety of areas (e.g., school, interpersonal functioning, social skills, etc.). These global instruments provide a broad description of personality functioning. The BPC consists of 55 items describing problem behavior traits occurring in childhood and adolescence. Each of the problem behaviors is rated on a 3-point scale (no problem, mild problem, severe problem) by the parent or other respondents. The checklist measures four primary constructs: Conduct Problems, Personality Problems, Inadequacy-Immaturity, and Socialized Delinquency. The BPC is convenient and efficient, permitting a descriptive analysis of the child's problem(s) as viewed by the adult caretaker (parent and/or teachers). In addition, interrater and test-retest reliabilities have been shown to be high, and a number of validation studies have been performed (Touliatos & Lindholm, 1975; Victor & Halverson, 1976).

The PIC is a paper-and-pencil, true/false inventory filled out by a parent, providing comprehensive profiles based on the model of the MMPI. Three validity scales, an Adjustment Scale, and 12 clinical scales are displayed on the profile form. The PIC is easy to administer and is appropriate for subjects aged 3-16. The manual provides a considerable amount of information about test development and profile analysis, including empirical validity data. The major advantage of the PIC is that it can serve as a preliminary screening device, drawing the clinician's attention to areas that might otherwise be overlooked. In addition, it may be used to confirm impressions derived from the intake interview. In cases where ambiguity exists about a diagnosis, the PIC may also prove helpful.

Self-rating scales. In contrast to the previously described global instruments, a narrow-band, self-report measure such as the Revised Children's Manifest Anxiety Scale (RCMAS) is designed specifically to evaluate childhood anxiety. In 1978, Reynolds and Richmond revised the original Children's Manifest Anxiety Scale (CMAS). The resulting RCMAS utilizes 37 items (28 Anxiety and 9 Lie items), consisting of statements to which the child responds by circling "yes" or "no." The score for the Anxiety items and Lie items is calculated by summing the number of items circled "yes." The RCMAS is appropriate for children aged 6-19 and may be administered individually or in a group. Concurrent validity measures have been obtained by correlating the RCMAS with the State-Trait Anxiety Inventory for Children (STAIC). A significant correlation ($r = .85, p = .001$) was found between the RCMAS and the Trait Scale of the STAIC, but not between the RCMAS and the

STAIC State Scale, leading Reynolds (1980) to conclude that the RCMAS may constitute a measure of trait anxiety, but not state anxiety. Levels of internal consistency and test-retest reliability are considered within acceptable ranges. In addition, a factor analysis of the RCMAS yielded three factors: Physiological Anxiety, Worry and Oversensitivity, and Concentration Anxiety.

Interviews

The informal interview may represent one of the most efficient approaches for the assessment of adolescent anxiety disorders. Because adolescents may be able to think more abstractly than younger children, they may be able to provide more ideas about the underlying causes of the anxiety disorder they confront. Despite their analytic abilities, however, the motivation for sharing and expressing viewpoints about existing problems depends on the adolescent's perception of the interviewer. For an interview to be successful, the interviewer must be identified as empathic, open-minded, and receptive to the adolescent's opinions. The clinician must convey the attitude that the adolescent's opinion is valuable and will affect some outcome important to him or her.

In a two-parent household, interviewing both parents will help establish their reliability as informants. The interview should establish some factual information (e.g., developmental history), which will contribute to the diagnostic formulation resulting from the assessment process. In addition, it would be helpful to learn how the family operates as a group (Satir, 1967). Because family therapy is a major therapeutic consideration in dealing with adolescents, gaining an understanding of the family's dynamics helps determine the appropriateness of this therapeutic modality.

SCHIZOPHRENIC DISORDERS IN ADOLESCENCE

Symptomatology and Classification

Psychotic reactions in adolescence appear almost exclusively as schizophrenic disturbances. DSM-III uses the term *psychotic* to mean a condition that includes a loss of contact with reality. Historically, schizophrenia has been defined inconsistently in this country. Diagnostic criteria used in research contributing to the development of the DSM-III over the past decade have assisted in defining this psychopathology in a manner that provides for more general agreement and understanding. Because schizophrenia is the most frequently occurring adolescent psychotic disorder, it is important that the clinician understand the features by which it is differentially diagnosed.

According to DSM-III, Schizophrenic Disorders comprise serious illnesses, producing widespread personality dysfunction and affecting a range of behaviors. Features associated with schizophrenia include familial transmission, onset in early adulthood, a precipitate drop from an established level of functioning, a characteristic set of symptoms that involve abberrations in an array of mental functions, and a high probability of recurrences and further disability.

An adolescent with schizophrenia will have had, at some point in time, "normal" personality functioning. The onset of the schizophrenic disorder may be sudden or gradual. No single symptom establishes the diagnosis of adolescent schizophrenia; disturbances in several areas can be symptomatic. DSM-III diagnostic criteria for schizophrenia include various types and combinations of delusions and hallucinations, incoherence, markedly illogical thoughts, and marked poverty of content in speech (if associated with blunted, flat, or inappropriate affect, catatonic or grossly deranged behavior, etc.). There is a deterioration in adaptive functioning, and presenting symptoms must have been continuous for more than 6 months. The age of onset should have been before age 45, and affective disorders, organicity, or mental retardation should not be present.

In addition, DSM-III delineates five types of schizophrenia: Disorganized, Catatonic, Paranoid, Undifferentiated, and Residual. Each type must first meet the criteria for the class of Schizophrenia. Next, the differential diagnosis is based on the differentiation of the presenting cluster of symptoms into some distinctive pattern. The Disorganized type is evidenced when verbalizations are incoherent, delusions are evidenced and blunted, and inappropriate affect is displayed. Features of the Catatonic type include stupor or mutism, negativism, rigidity, and posturing. The Undifferentiated type includes grossly disorganized behavior, hallucinations, incoherence, or prominent delusions; this category is used when criteria for other types are not met, or when an individual meets the criteria for more than one of the other types. Residual type is the diagnosis used when the client presents no prominent symptoms, but such have been present at least one time in the past. The Residual type often applies to chronic outpatients who are still exhibiting some symptoms of the disorder. Features of the Paranoid type are persecutory and grandiose delusions, delusional jealousy, and persecutory and grandiose hallucinations.

It is important for the clinician to distinguish schizophrenic and paranoid disorders. Like schizophrenic disorders, paranoid disorders also present psychotic states. What differentiates the two is that paranoid disorders do not have all the symptoms to meet the criteria for schizophrenic. Paranoid disorders simply feature an organized delusional system in an individual who is coping otherwise. These cases feature no prominent hallucinations, only persecutory delusions or delusional jealousy. In addition, one does not see the marked drop in functioning found in schizophrenia. It should also be noted that the onset of paranoid disorders does tend to occur somewhat later in life than schizophrenia.

Procedures for the Assessment of Schizophrenic Disorders

For adolescents, the diagnosis of schizophrenic psychosis is established through formal assessment in addition to the history and interview. Significant observational material can be described from the interpersonal contact attained during the assessment sessions; the adolescent's manner of relating is of primary importance. Formal assessment techniques often involve both cognitive and affective components. Most clinicians will include an individually administered intelligence test, such as a Wechsler (WISC-R or WAIS-R) or the Stanford-Binet, projective techniques, such as the Rorschach, and a personality inventory, such as the Minnesota Multiphasic Personality Inventory (MMPI).

No single source of data should be considered sufficient to diagnose adolescent schizophrenia. Rather, consistency across several data sources—observational, historical, and test material—provides the most reliable estimate of functioning. Additional diagnostic data from the following sources can be of significant value in the differential diagnosis of the adolescent who presents a mixed clinical picture.

Clinical History

The clinical history as collected from the adolescent and his or her parents, school records, family doctor, and so on can contribute significantly to the identification of schizophrenia. In addition, peer-group relationships should be evaluated to determine the presence of "peculiar ideas or behavior" associated with schizophrenia (Weiner, 1970).

Family History

A family history of schizophrenia is always important in alerting the clinician to the possibility of schizophrenia. In addition, indications of prior disturbance or deviation in the child's developmental history are helpful in assessing schizophrenia.

Interview Behavior

When an adolescent is interviewed for the first time, the examiner should discuss the adolescent's perception and understanding of the situation in comparison with the interviewer's frank statement of his or her understanding. All interviews should have a goal, and so the interviewer must determine what he or she wants to learn or convey. Success or failure of an attempt to help an adolescent may well depend on the initial interview and the relationship established. Although the interview may well be structured and formal, much can be learned about the adolescent by observing speech patterns, appearance, style of relating, and the quality of his or her affect and judgment.

In adolescents, anxiety may be manifested by fidgeting, walking around, sitting at the edge of the seat, and the like. Responses may be curt or flippant. Appearance and demeanor may reflect depression, as evidenced by slouched posture, flat affect, slow speech, or listlessness. In the seriously disturbed youngster, one may note during the course of the interview inappropriate affect, confused speech and thought processes, and possibly delusions and/or hallucinations.

Psychological Test Findings

The MMPI is the most widely used self-administered questionnaire. It establishes a diagnostic category and behavioral potential by comparing the test profiles of known diagnostic groups. Marks, Seeman, and Haller (1974) gathered MMPI data for adolescent code types from over 1,800 normal adolescents as well as 834 adolescents who were involved in psychotherapy of one form or another. The availability of adolescent code types makes the MMPI a valuable tool in the assessment of adolescents.

Human figure drawings yield information about self-concept and internalized body image. For the adolescent, attitudes towards sexual maturation and acceptance of a sexual role are revealed. The Kinetic Family Drawing yields information regarding attitudes towards family and the adolescent's place within that system.

Often the clinician can clarify more readily the extent to which peculiar content in an adolescent's fantasy is accompanied by peculiarities in formal thought processes through structured and projective techniques. Psychodiagnostic tests additionally allow some qualitative assessment of aspects of ego functioning that are significant for the differential diagnosis of schizophrenia. The use of projective tests in the evaluation is generally worth the time when employed by a well-trained and experienced practitioner. Though research overall has not supported the claims for reliability and validity of projective tests, they still can provide information that will enable the examiner to clarify diagnostic dilemmas, as well as contributing to the developing picture of the adolescent in distress.

In summary, when assessing schizophrenic disorders in adolescence, there is some danger in assigning a clinical diagnosis to the adolescent because developmental adjustments are occurring in so many domains. Certain diagnoses such as schizophrenia carry powerful implications for future functioning and, in effect, represent predictions that the adolescent's problems may be chronic and prognosis poor. For this reason, it is important to exercise caution. This cautionary statement does not alter the fact, however, that certain adolescents will be confronting serious psychiatric disability. Some investigators feel that early onset of schizophrenic symptoms, coupled with a history of childhood problems and poor peer relationships, suggests a poor prognosis for the schizophrenic youngster (Offord & Cross, 1969). The outlook for treatment is best when the family accepts the problem, and there is adequate planning for future treatment, school work, and living arrangements (Weiner & Elkind, 1972).

TEST RESULT COMMUNICATION

When the diagnostic information is complete, it is necessary to arrange one or more conferences with the parent and adolescent to discuss findings and recommendations. The communication of test results is a vital step in setting the stage for successful treatment. Without a clear diagnostic conception, however, the therapist cannot hope for effective communication. By integrating clinical observations, clinical interviews, current psychological test data, information from schools, medical reports, and results from previous testing, the examiner can make a meaningful diagnosis and formulate an appropriate treatment plan.

It is the role of the therapist to outline a treatment plan with objectives, strategies, and estimated length of time for psychotherapeutic intervention. Possible goals of treatment may be 1) intrapsychic modification, 2) alterations in intrafamilial functioning, 3) alteration of peer-group interaction, 4) modification of school or community adjustment, or 5) removal of the adolescent from his or her family, with placement in a therapeutic environment (i.e., hospital or residential treatment). Often these goals are not mutually exclusive, and recommendations may include combined modalities of treatment.

A CASE STUDY: ACUTE ANXIETY

Jenny was a 16-year-old high school sophomore who, on her way home from school one day, was involved in a minor car accident in which no one was hurt. Following that accident, she experienced nightmares, complained of shortness of breath, became agoraphobic, and refused to go anywhere. Jenny's parents became very concerned about her behaviors and referred her for evaluation to the child development clinic at the university medical center. They believed that her "strange" behaviors could have something to do with her car accident.

The psychologist began by interviewing Jenny regarding the onset, frequency, and duration of her fears and nightmares. It soon became clear that these were long-term problems and not necessarily directly associated with the car accident. When Jenny's parents were interviewed, they revealed that they had been discussing divorce. In addition the parents expressed concern that Jenny had been apprehended in sex play with a boyfriend a few weeks earlier. They also confessed that they recently had confronted Jenny about spending lengthly periods of time in the bathroom and had handled their accusations of masturbation rather poorly, which Jenny had in turn tearfully denied. Before leaving, the psychologist asked each of the parents to complete the Devereux Adolescent Behavior Rating Scale independently in order to learn more about factors that could be related to Jenny's problem.

When Jenny returned to the psychologist for her next visit, they discussed her parents' concerns about her sexual behavior and masturbation. He also asked her to complete the Revised Children's Manifest Anxiety Scale.

Upon comparing the results of the child and parent interviews with the standardized test data, it appeared that Jenny's anxiety had been chronic. She evidenced a high level of trait anxiety on the RCMAS, much of which was due to the consternation in her family and her parents attitudes about her sexuality. However, it was her minor car accident that precipitated the acute anxiety attack involving nightmares and agoraphobia. The psychologist was able to use the results of the Devereux Adolescent Behavior Rating Scale in designing a family-based intervention to deal with Jenny's symptomatology of acute anxiety as well as deal with her generally high level of anxiety resulting from the family dysfunction.

SUMMARY

The task of assessing adolescent psychopathology is made difficult by the fact that adolescents typically evidence signs of stress due to normally occurring developmental changes. While disturbances may originate in earlier periods of development, in many cases they become manifested or exacerbated during adolescence (Rutter, 1980). This emergence is associated with the rapid physical, physiological, sexual, and cognitive changes that take place in adolescence and that must be resolved in order for the adolescent to cope and to achieve a positive self-concept.

The state of knowledge in adolescent psychopathology, specifically in the area of adolescent depression, is seriously underdeveloped. What are the factors contributing to the development of depression, anxiety, and/or psychosis? In what ways are the cognitive, emotional, and behavioral characteristics of disturbed adolescents significantly different from their peers? What are the most effective methods for treatment and prevention efforts? Even prevalence estimates are quite inconsistent. In addition, as the assessment of adolescents has received much less research attention than that of children or adults, the availability of appropriate psychometric instrumentation is limited. The psychological examiner must examine new instruments consistently as aids to diagnosis. Only through the use of a multifactored diagnostic process can the clinician obtain useful assessment information and formulate an appropriate treatment plan.

REFERENCES

Achenbach, T. M., & Edelbrock, C. S. (1981). Behavioral problems and competencies reported by parents of normal and disturbed children aged four through sixteen. *Monographs of the Society for Research in Child Development, 46*, 1-82.

American Psychiatric Association. (1980). *Diagnostic and statistical manual of mental disorders* (3rd ed.). Washington, DC: Author.

Anthony, E. J. (1970). The behavior disorders of children. In P. H. Mussen (Ed.), *Carmichael's manual of child psychology* (Vol. 2, pp. 667-764). New York: John Wiley.

Anthony, J., & Scott, P. (1960). Manic-depressive psychosis in childhood. *Journal of Child Psychology and Psychiatry, 1*, 53-72.

Cantwell, D. P. (1983). Assessment of childhood depression. In D. Cantwell & G. Carlson (Eds.), *Affective disorders in childhood and adolescence: An update*. New York: Spectrum.

Carlson, G. (1983). Bipolar affective disorders in childhood and adolescence. In D. Cantwell & G. Carlson (Eds.), *Affective disorders in childhood and adolescence: An update*. New York: Spectrum.

Carlson, G. A., & Strober, M. (1978). Manic-depressive illness in early adolescence: A study of clinical and diagnostic characteristics in six cases. *Journal of the American Academy of Child Psychiatry, 17*(1), 138-153.

Carlson, G., & Strober, M. (1983). Affective disorders in adolescence. In D. Cantwell & G. Carlson (Eds.), *Affective disorders in childhood and adolescence: An update*. New York: Spectrum.

Chambers, W., Puig-Antich, J., & Tabrizi, M. (1978). *The ongoing development of the Kiddie-SADS (Schedule for Affective Disorders and Schizophrenia) for school-age children*. Paper presented at the American Academy of Child Psychiatry, San Diego, CA.

Chapman, A. H. (1974). *Management of emotional problems of children and adolescents*. Philadelphia: Lippincott.

Cytryn, L., & McKnew, D. H., Jr. (1972). Proposed classification of childhood depression. *American Journal of Psychiatry, 129*(2), 149-155.

Conger, J. J., & Petersen, A. C. (1984). *Adolescence and youth* (3rd ed.). New York: Harper & Row.

Gittleman, R. (1980). Role of psychological tests for differential diagnosis in child psychiatry. *Journal of the American Academy of Child Psychiatry, 19*(3), 413-438.

Glaser, K. (1967). Masked depression in children and adolescents. *American Journal of Psychotherapy, 21*, 565-574.

Harrington, R. G. (1984). Assessing childhood anxiety and depressive disorders. In S. J. Weaver (Ed.), *Testing children: A reference guide for effective clinical and psychoeducational assessments* (pp. 161-184). Kansas City, MO: Test Corporation.

Harrington, R. G., & Follett, G. M. (1984). The readability of child personality assessment instruments. *Journal of Psychoeducational Assessment, 2*(1), 37-48.

Herjanic, B., & Campbell, W. (1977). Differentiating psychiatrically disturbed children on the basis of a structured interview. *Journal of the Association of Child Psychology, 5*, 127-134.

Hodges, K., McKnew, D., Cytryn, L., Stern, L., & Kline, J. (1982). The Child Assessment

Schedule (CAS) Diagnostic Interview: A report on reliability and validity. *Journal of the American Academy of Child Psychiatry, 21*(5), 468-473.

Holinger, P. C. (1978). Adolescent suicide: An epidemiologic study of recent trends. *American Journal of Psychiatry, 135,* 754-756.

Kazdin, A., French, N., & Unis, A. (in press). Child, mother, and father evaluations of depression in psychiatric inpatient children. *Journal of Abnormal Child Psychology.*

Kovacs, M. (1978). *Interview Schedule for Children (ISC).* Unpublished manuscript.

Kovacs, M. (1981). Rating scales to assess depression in school-aged children. *Acta Paedopsychiatrica, 46,* 305-315.

Kovacs, M., & Beck, A. T. (1977). An empirical-clinical approach toward a definition of childhood depression. In J. G. Schulterbrandt & A. Raskin (Eds.), *Depression in childhood: Diagnosis, treatment and conceptual models.* New York: Raven.

Lange, M., & Tisher, M. (1978). *Children's Depression Scale.* Melbourne, Australia: Australian Council for Educational Research.

Marks, P., Seeman, W., & Haller, D. (1974). *The actuarial use of the MMPI with adolescents and adults.* Baltimore: Williams & Wilkins.

National Institute of Mental Health. (1980). *Diagnostic Interview Schedule for Children-Parent Form* (DHHS Publication No. ADM 80-1037). Washington, DC: U.S. Government Printing Office.

Offord, D. R., & Cross, L. (1969). Behavioral antecedents of adult schizophrenia. *Archives of General Psychiatry, 21,* 267-283.

Quay, H. C. (1977). Measuring dimensions of deviant behavior: The Behavior Problem Checklist. *Journal of Abnormal Child Psychology, 5,* 277-287.

Reynolds, C. R. (1980). Concurrent validity of What I Think and Feel: The Revised Children's Manifest Anxiety Scale. *Journal of Consulting and Clinical Psychology, 48,* 774-775.

Rutter, M. (1980). *Changing youth in a changing society: Patterns of adolescent development and disorder.* Cambridge, MA: Harvard University Press.

Rutter, M., Tizard, J., & Whitmore, K. (1970). *Education, health and behavior.* London: Longman.

Satir, V. (1967). *Conjoint family therapy.* Palo Alto: Science & Behavior Books.

Torrey, E. F. (1983). *Surviving schizophrenia: A family manual.* New York: Harper & Row.

Touliatos, J., & Lindholm, B. W. (1975). Relationships of children's grade in school, sex, and social class to teacher's ratings on the Behavior Problem Checklist. *Journal of Abnormal Child Psychology, 3,* 115-126.

Victor, J. B., & Halverson, C. F., Jr. (1976). Behavior problems in elementary school children: A follow-up study. *Journal of Abnormal Child Psychology, 4,* 17-29.

Webb, L. J., DiClemente, C. C., Johnstone, E. E., Sanders, J. L., & Perley, R. A. (Eds.). (1981). *DSM-III training guide for use with the American Psychiatric Association's diagnostic and statistical manual of mental disorders (3rd ed.).* New York: Brunner/Mazel.

Weiner, I. (1970). *Psychological disturbance in adolescence.* New York: John Wiley.

Weiner, I. B., & Elkind, D. (1972). *Child development: A core approach.* New York: John Wiley.

11

Assessment of Suicidal Risk among Adolescents

BRIAN W. McNEILL, PH.D., ROBERT G. HARRINGTON, PH.D.

The developmental stage of adolescence is associated with a number of critical tasks and conflicts. According to developmental theorists, these tasks involve establishing a personal identity (Chickering, 1969; Erikson, 1968), fostering intimate interpersonal relationships (Perry, 1970; Loevinger, 1976) and choosing a future career (Havighurst, 1972). When these developmental hurdles are not resolved successfully, however, adolescence often is characterized as a time of emotional conflicts, social pressures, and stresses in the home and school (Conger & Petersen, 1984). The increasing frequency with which authors characterize adolescence as a period of storm and stress seems to be related to the increasing number of adolescent suicides (Davis, 1980). Indeed, suicide has been identified as the second highest cause of death in 15- to 24-year-olds for the period of 1960 to 1982.

While statistics for 1980-82 indicate that more than three times as many male adolescents commit suicide than females, there has been a steady increase in the number of suicides for both groups (Vital Statistics of the United States, 1982). The higher incidence of male suicides probably reflects their preference for more lethal methods. Recent statistics also indicate that, compared to the incidence among black adolescents, a higher percentage of white adolescents commit suicide (Vital Statistics of the United States, 1982).

As Anderson (1981) points out, the benefit of such demographic information is that it helps to identify groups of individuals at higher risk for suicide; however, it also increases the likelihood that a practitioner using this information may make a false positive identification (i.e., identifying an individual as suicidal who, in fact, is nonsuicidal). Thus, in the absence of supporting clinical data, statistics alone may be of little assistance in diagnosing the individual case.

The primary purpose of this chapter is to introduce the reader to the major issues involved in the assessment of adolescent suicide risk. A multidimensional approach will be presented, taking into consideration the multitude of variables that may increase the likelihood of an adolescent taking his or her own life. Included among the assessment strategies that will be discussed are biographical and psychological data, the clinical interview, and formal psychological assessments, as well as recently developed instrumentation specifically designed to assess suicidal risk.

METHODOLOGICAL AND ETHICAL CONSIDERATIONS IN SUICIDE ASSESSMENT

Because the implications of decisions associated with assessing adolescent suicide risk are so profound, it is important for the practitioner to understand clearly the methodological and ethical considerations involved with these types of referrals. Certain methodological problems associated with adolescent suicide assessment create ethical dilemmas for the psychological examiner. The first concern relates to how the practitioner should assess and deal with suicidal risk, which involves underidentification and overidentification.

Beck, Kovacs, and Weissman (1979) define suicidal risk as a predictive statement regarding the probability of a fatal suicide attempt, based on suicidal ideation, lethality of method, and access to lethal methods, as well as on any number of variables hypothesized to predict suicidal occurrence. As Neuringer (1974a) suggests, successful suicide prevention depends on the clinician's ability to recognize and utilize these factors in predicting self-destructive behavior.

Greene (1980) emphasizes that the initial hurdle encountered when using any assessment device to predict suicide risk is the problem of the very low base rate (extremely low frequency) at which suicide occurs in the population. In other words, any index of suicide will yield a large number of false positives. For example, even if a test were 75% accurate in predicting suicide, which would be unusually high for most tests, a more accurate prediction would be made if all adolescent referrals were considered nonsuicidal because the frequency of suicide would surely be less than 25% in any group. Such a position would result in underidentification of a small number of adolescents who would be at risk for suicide. Obviously, there will be case referrals in which certain adolescents will commit suicide if not identified; consequently, the clinician may have little choice but to identify a certain number of false positives, if among the presumed negatives even one true positive otherwise would be overlooked.

Conversely, overidentification has its methodological as well as ethical ramifications. For example, clinicians and counselors in training typically are advised regarding suicide risk to be cautious and, when in doubt, to make a Type I error (i.e., identify adolescents as at risk when they may not be suicidal). In many cases, making an error of this type may be the prudent course of action. In other cases, however, mislabeling clients as suicidal risks can provoke interventions that inadvertently violate client confidentiality and result in the infringement of civil rights through involuntary hospitalization. In addition to these ethical problems, Cull and Gill (1982) stress that when inappropriate interventions are developed, not only are limited and expensive clinical resources wasted, but an opportunity is lost to intervene in a more clinically relevant manner with these cases.

The low base rate of adolescent suicide also makes it difficult for researchers to conduct predictive studies of individuals identified as potential high risks for suicide, as these types of investigations are complex, costly, and require extremely long follow-up intervals (Beck et al., 1979). Thus, researchers have tended to rely on self-reports from unsuccessful suicide attemptors as well as on suicide notes, biographical information, and case notes on those who have completed suicides. As both of these methods yield postdictive conclusions, they may have limited utility in the development of strategies to predict adolescent suicide. Lester, Beck, and Mitchell (1979) illustrate this problem in their recent study, which found that the psychological characteristics of suicide attemptors may, in fact, differ from those who complete suicide. In this study, only those who attempted suicide and were "highly intent" on killing themselves were similar on measures of hopelessness and depression to those who completed suicide. Another factor that arises here and confounds the validity of research on adolescent suicide is the ethical responsibility to provide treatment in these cases. The result is that researchers never have the opportunity to study the totality of predictive factors associated with adolescent suicide (Anderson, 1981).

Beyond the problems associated with under- and overidentification of suicide risk, the examiner must also be aware of the questionable reliability of informal assessments based on primarily self-reported information (e.g., case history or interview data). For example, Strosahl, Linehan, and Chiles (1984) have demonstrated that social desirability may distort self-reports of past or present suicidal ideations or behaviors as well as future intentions. In addition, self-reports of suicidal risk on various standardized psychological tests may also be subject to distortion or social desirability factors. The methodological problems involved in using self-report data to differentiate nonsuicidal clients from suicide attemptors present ethical implications similar to those detailed previously; that is, misidentification may result in the unnecessary violation of client confidentiality as well as hospitalization on a voluntary or involuntary basis. In such cases, Hipple and Cimbolic (1979) offer specific guidelines: if a client makes a statement such as "I will kill myself before 9 a.m. with a drug overdose no matter what you or anybody else does," the examiner is left with no other choice but to break confidentiality, report the case, and take steps to hospitalize.

In the majority of situations, however, such clearcut indications of suicidal intentions may be rare, and thus the practitioner may have to rely on clinical judgment to determine whether to break confidentiality and refer. For these reasons, examiners cannot rely on base rates or self-reports alone, but rather must blend both empirical data and clinical skills to assess the probability of suicide. In this effort, it is important to understand both the variables posited to improve predictive skills along with specific assessments useful in gathering diagnostic information related to these variables. The following discussion will delineate and evaluate such procedures.

BIOGRAPHICAL AND PSYCHOLOGICAL FACTORS IN THE DIAGNOSIS
OF SUICIDAL RISK

The current *Diagnostic and Statistical Manual of Mental Disorders* (DSM-III; American Psychiatric Association, 1980) does not include a unique category for the formal diagnosis of suicidal risk. Instead, suicidal ideations, gestures, or behaviors often are identified in clients over 18 in the context of Borderline Personality Disorders, Histrionic Personality Disorders, Major Depressive Episodes, and Dysthymic Disorders. Despite the appearance of suicidal ideations or gestures in these various DSM-III classifications, most empirical research has focused on specific client behaviors (current or previous) that may be predictive of self-destructive behavior rather than emphasizing global diagnostic categories. For example, Cosand, Bourque, and Kraus (1982) recently investigated adolescent suicides in Sacramento, California, from the period 1950 to 1979. These investigators reported that one third to one half of adolescent suicides had shown evidence of "emotional instability" and "despondency."

Other investigators have cited depression as the most common diagnosis associated with suicide in adolescent populations (Peck, 1977). However, as has been found in studies of adult suicides (e.g., Beck, Kovacs, & Weissman, 1979), hopelessness has been a factor more often associated with suicidal ideation and behavior than depression per se (Hawton, 1986). Recent studies (Kazdin, French, Unis, Esveldt-Dawson, & Sherick, 1983; Topol & Resnikoff, 1982) are supportive of this notion. For example, Hawton, Cole, O'Grady, and Osborn (1982) found that the most frequent reasons cited by adolescents for self-poisoning included the following: "Get relief from a terrible state of mind . . ."; "Escape for awhile from an impossible situation . . ."; and "Make people understand how desperate you were feeling." Likewise, Peck (1977) states that a common characteristic across adolescent suicides is "a nagging lack of optimism and hope for the future and an overwhelming sense of unhappiness" (p. 169).

Previous "emotional problems" (Cosand et al., 1982) as well as previous psychological treatment also have been identified consistently as contributing factors in adolescent suicide attempts (Peck, 1977; Hawton, 1986). Hawton et. al. (1982) examined adolescent suicide attemptors' feelings that preceded the attempts, and over half reported having felt angry with someone, lonely, or unwanted. Older adolescents reported more worry about the future. Cohen-Sandler, Berman, and King (1982) found that in the 12 months prior to hospitalization, suicide attemptors had experienced twice as much stress as compared to depressed nonsuicidal individuals and nondepressed psychiatric controls, all of whom were admitted to a psychiatric inpatient unit. These individuals also had reported greater amounts of "early" stressors (e.g., disruptive family events).

These early stressors moved investigators to focus on the role of family influences and interactions in adolescent suicide. For example, family disruption by death, separation, or divorce has been associated with suicidal behavior (Cosand et al., 1982; Cohen-Sandler et al., 1982). Hawton (1986) has noted that a psychiatric disorder in the family, such as alcoholism or drug abuse, may represent a frequent precursor to these family disruptions. Furthermore, previous suicidal behavior by an immediate family member or relative has been found to be more prevalent among suicide attemptors than individuals who have not attempted suicide. Hawton (1986) hypothesizes that suicidal acts by other family members may serve as a model for coping with stress, with the result that these adolescents may be more likely to resort to suicide attempts to cope with bouts of severe stress.

Frequently, drug and/or alcohol abuse have been identified in cases of adolescent suicide (Peck, 1977). Hawton et al. (1982) have noted school or work difficulties as significant factors in suicide attempts; however, such difficulties do not appear to be immediate causes, but more often are a reflection of general interpersonal difficulties and low self-esteem that have impaired the ability to cope with life stresses (Hawton, 1986). Problems with boyfriends or girlfriends represent another interpersonal variable contributing to the increased likelihood of an adolescent suicide attempt.

Anderson (1981) views many of the foregoing suicidal indicators within a developmental framework in which suicide is the final stage in the sequence; thus, Anderson believes that assessment of suicidal risk ought to include a detailed developmental history as a first step. In conceptualizing this developmental history it may be helpful to refer to the three stages Anderson has identified in the development of suicidal behavior in adolescents.

The first stage involves a long-standing history of problems from childhood to adolescence, primarily consisting of social and familial instability (e.g., significant and/or repeated object losses; unstable, hostile family environments, with little opportunity to establish and maintain meaningful relationships). The second stage begins with the onset of adolescence and involves an escalation of problems and acute behavioral changes (e.g., a breakdown in social contacts and peer relations; neurotic, depressive symptoms and hopelessness). The third and final stage immediately precedes the suicide attempt and often involves a total breakdown of interpersonal situations, which dramatically increase immediate suicidal risk (e.g., failing on the job or in academic coursework). Using this developmental conceptualization, the practitioner may be better able to gather and organize biographical and psychological data that will identify the current stage of an adolescent client who appears to be at higher risk for suicide.

SELECTING AND IMPLEMENTING APPROPRIATE ASSESSMENT TECHNIQUES

Clinical Interview

When an adolescent client is first referred, the practitioner may not have immediate access to the types of biographical and/or psychological data previously discussed. This is certainly the case under emergency or crisis circumstances. As a result of the extreme emotional turmoil in such circumstances the client would probably report unreliable biographical or psychological data anyway. In fact, for the examiner to focus on eliciting this kind of clinical interview data from such a client may be considered unethical. Thus, good clinical judgment in crisis or emergency situations dictates that the examiner attend to present conditions and stressors and the assessment of immediate suicidal ideation and risk.

While there are no specific guidelines for the examiner interviewing for suicide risk in adolescents, a number of authors have provided guidelines for the crisis assessment of suicide risk in general populations. Such guidelines appear to be applicable for adolescent clients as well. For example, Hipple and Cimbolic (1979) have suggested that early in the interview the clinician should be sensitive to veiled cues of suicidal ideation, such as "Sometimes I just want it to be over" or "I'm tired of the whole thing; I just want to sleep."

Most previous work on the use of the clinical interview has focused on assessing the presence of any suicidal intent or a plan, which Hatton, Valente, and Rink (1977) define as "those suicidal ideations or conceptualizations of suicide and the ways and the means of suicide that can lead a person to the final act of taking his or her life" (p. 52). Several authors (Hatton, Valente, & Rink, 1977; Hipple & Cimbolic, 1979) stress that four criteria need to be considered in the assessment of a suicidal plan. The first of these involves assessment of the *method*. For example, has the client specified a method of choice, such as pills or shooting? Such an assessment may be done by simply asking the client how he or she envisions carrying out the suicide. The second criterion requires establishing the *availability* of the method. For example, does the client own a gun? The third component, *specificity* of the suicidal plan, involves investigating the degree to which the client provides details (e.g., the time or the day of the planned suicide). The more specific the plan and the more proximate the intended suicide is to the present, the greater the suicidal risk (Hipple & Cimbolic, 1979). The fourth criterion requires the psychologist to assess the *lethality* of the method. Of the common methods used to commit suicide, the most lethal is shooting and the least lethal is slashing one's wrists (Hatton et al., 1977). Obviously, the higher the lethality of the proposed method, the greater the suicidal risk.

Freeman, Wilson, Thigpen, and McGee (1974) further elaborate the notion of lethality by conceptualizing it in terms of intention to die. Within this framework, intentionality is evaluated by 1) the method of self-destruction employed and 2) the expected proximity of other people (the probability of intervention by others in the victim's environment). These two components determine reversibility of method, which refers to the ease with which a suicidal action can be stopped or reversed once the potential victim has set it into motion. Freeman et al. (1974) provide a 5-point rating scale on which 1 indicates a method with complete reversibility (e.g., aspirin ingestion) and 5 represents a method with a remote or no chance for reversibility (e.g., gunshot). This model also includes a probability rating, which is a function of the proximity or expected proximity of other people in the victim's immediate environment who could intervene. As with the reversibility rating, this scale ranges from 1 to 5, with 1 signifying certain intervention (e.g., acts committed in the presence of another person) and 5 denoting that the chances of intervention are remote (e.g., acts committed in isolated places without access to telephone). Practitioners may find this paradigm helpful in the clinical assessment of suicidal intention.

In addition to the variables already discussed, investigators cite a number of other "high risk" factors that may aid the practitioner in the clinical interview process. These factors include previous suicide attempts, especially when attempts are numerous and highly lethal. Regardless of the client's current crisis, sex, or age, when one sees evidence of multiple, highly lethal attempts the client should be placed in the highest category of risk (Hatton et al., 1977). In a parallel manner, the frequency and duration of suicidal thoughts and feelings should be assessed because if long-term suicidal intent can be documented, the client should be considered at greater risk (Hipple & Cimbolic, 1979; Hawton, 1986).

Hatton et al. (1977) recommend that a client's current cognitive or thinking processes also should be considered in the course of the clinical interview. Suicide risk increases when the client exhibits a confused state of mind or demonstrates distorted or disorganized thought processes with little orientation to reality. Levenson (1974) cites rigid, inflexible, or dichotomous thinking patterns as examples of cognitive features that may confuse a client's logic and increase suicide risk. This cognitive style results in narrowed thinking, which reduces the individual's range of conceptualization and openness to perceiving alternatives to suicide. As stress increases, the more restricted the suicidal clients' cognitive structure becomes, resulting in a higher probability that he or she will attempt suicide.

Personality Assessment

The Minnesota Multiphasic Personality Inventory (MMPI) is one of the most useful measures to assess personality variables related to suicide risk. Numerous attempts have been made to use the MMPI to predict the occurrence of suicide through the application of special scales, profile analysis, and clinical judgment (Greene, 1980). Most studies investigating suicide risk are based on adult samples; consequently, standard practice has been to use adolescent norms to generate an MMPI profile and then refer to an adult interpretive system for analysis of the profile. For example, significant elevations (i.e., T-scores above 70) on Scales 2 (Depression) and/or 7 (Psychasthenia) have been associated with increased likelihood of suicide attempts (Graham, 1977). Increased suicide risk has also been associated with a "spike 2 profile" (i.e., Scale 2 [Depression] is the only scale above 70), especially when the client denies depressive thoughts and feelings (Dahlstrom, Welsh, & Dahlstrom, 1972). Clopton, Pallis, and Birtchnell (1979) found that among clients with 7-8/8-7 high-point codes (i.e., significant elevations on Psychasthenia and Schizophrenia), the relative elevation of Scales 1 (Hypochrondriasis) and 2 (Depression) was significantly associated with previous suicide attempts. Scale 1 was greater than Scale 2 in 60% of the nonsuicidal clients, while Scale 2 was greater than Scale 1 in 64% of suicidal clients.

One of the few studies to examine MMPI scores in suicidal adolescents below age 18 was performed by Marks and Haller (1977). In this study, adolescent suicide attemptors were found to score significantly higher than non-attemptors on Scales 1 (Hypochondriasis) and 5 (Masculinity-Femininity). For females, higher scores were obtained for attemptors on Scales 2 (Depression) and 3 (Hysteria) when compared to non-attemptors. These research results require replication in other adolescent populations.

Despite all of these findings, recent empirical reviews of the use of the MMPI in predicting suicidal risk via special scales, profile analysis, and so on have concluded that the MMPI has not been able to differentiate *consistently* between suicidal and nonsuicidal individuals (Clopton, 1979; Greene, 1980). Such disappointing results have led some reviewers (e.g., Anderson, 1981) to conclude that the MMPI may be of limited value in the identification of suicidal risk. These investigators appear to assume that suicidal gestures/attempts and completed suicides result from a single cause, without fully appreciating the multitude of factors that may lead a client to attempt or commit suicide (Greene, 1980).

Rather than question whether the MMPI is sufficient to predict suicide, researchers should ask whether the MMPI increases the accuracy of prediction (Clopton, 1979). For example, when the MMPI is utilized by a skilled practitioner, it may yield information relevant to a client's current levels of depression, anxiety, cognitive functioning, and so on. The MMPI may be especially useful in uncovering factors associated with adolescent suicide risk, including familial discord, conflicts with authorities, social alienation, impulse control, and lack of good interpersonal relationships. In addition, the MMPI includes various scales/indices useful in assessing the validity of self-reports (e.g., faking bad, faking good), and thus it addresses the problem of social desirability prevalent in the unstructured interview and other formal measures. In sum, the MMPI should be used as part of a multidimensional assessment to derive information relevant to the many factors associated with adolescent suicidal attempts. (For more information on assessment of adolescent depression and anxiety see chapter 10 in this book.)

Projective Techniques

The Rorschach Inkblot Test is another traditional measure of personality functioning often used in suicide assessment, though its utility in standard psychological assessments has been widely debated (Kaplan & Saccuzzo, 1982). Exner and Wylie (1977) examined a number of indices derived from Exner's Rorschach scoring system for their utility in the prediction of suicide in adults. Results indicated that a constellation of eight scoring indices (e.g., CF + C > FL; X + < 70%) identified 75% of suicides and 45% of attempted suicides, with relatively low percentages of false positives. On the other hand, there have been no recent investigations testing the usefulness of the Rorschach for predicting suicidal risk in adolescent populations. Neuringer (1974b) has recommended that the examiner using the Rorschach Inkblot Test to assess suicide risk rely primarily on response content rather than on specific indices derived from various scoring systems. When the Rorschach is used in this way, clients may respond to specific stimulus cards revealing suicidal intentions and feelings. Like the MMPI, when the Rorschach is interpreted by a skilled clinician, it may yield helpful information relevant to the assessment and treatment of suicidal clients.

Another projective measure often employed in the assessment of adolescent ideation is the Thematic Apperception Test (TAT). In a review of the relevant literature, McEvoy (1974) concluded that the TAT has not demonstrated usefulness in the study of assessment of suicidal risk. This conclusion appears to be based both on the variety of methodological problems associated with suicide risk assessment as well as on a lack of systematic investigations of the TAT for this purpose. Similar to the Rorschach, best use of the TAT may be as a stimulus for eliciting suicidal ideation or as a general personality assessment measure in which implications are drawn about an individual's needs, motivations, conflicts, and dynamics. Cards 3BM, 6BM, and 13MF may be the most useful in assessing suicidal ideation via the TAT. Card 3BM, traditionally referred to as the "suicidal" card, can be expected to address feelings of loneliness, loss, guilt, and aggression, 6BM taps the degree of adolescent independence, and 13MF assesses death and aggressive ideations.

Suicide-Specific Instrumentation

While the MMPI, the Rorschach, and the TAT may provide clues to suicidal ideation, they are probably best employed in gathering information about personality dynamics that will be useful in planning ongoing therapeutic interventions. Given the limitations of global personality measures in assessing suicide risk, specialized instruments have been developed to assess suicide potential. Among these specialized psychological scales are the Suicide Probability Scale (SPS), the Scale for Suicide Ideation (SSI), and the Modified Scale for Suicidal Ideation (MSSI). Although none of these scales have been validated exclusively on adolescent populations, they represent the state of the art in suicide-specific assessment scales.

The Suicide Probability Scale. Cull and Gill's 1982 Suicide Probability Scale (SPS) is a 36-item self-report measure that assesses suicide risk in examinees aged 14 years and older. According to the authors, the SPS is intended for a variety of settings where a quick routine assessment of suicide risk is important (the scale can be administered, scored, and interpreted in less than 20 minutes). Designed to yield a global index of suicide risk, SPS-derived information should generate hypotheses and open areas for clinical exploration as well. Suicide Ideation, one of the four rationally derived SPS subscales, reflects the extent to which an individual reports thoughts or behaviors associated with suicide. The Hopelessness subscale assesses one's overall dissatisfaction with life and negative expectations regarding the future. Negative Self-Evaluation yields information regarding an individual's subjective appraisal that things are not going well. The Hostility subscale measures the tendency to break or throw things when angry or upset and appears to tap feelings of isolation and impulsivity. Raw scores are tallied to derive T-scores ($X = 50; SD = 10$) for each of the subscales as well as for the overall total score. Cull and Gill (1982) report that reliability of the SPS total scores is close to .90 for internal consistency, split-half, and test-retest measures. Negative Self-Evaluation had the lowest subscale reliability; Suicide Ideation had the highest. In terms of validity, the various subscales of the SPS have not been corroborated fully by factor analysis. Discriminant validity has been demonstrated by the ability of the SPS to discriminate attemptors from nonattemptors in a postdictive manner, but as Golding (1985) notes, in practical use the SPS needs to discriminate high-risk from low-risk individuals in a predictive manner. Whether the SPS is predictive of high risk for suicide is unknown. Construct validity has been established by significantly correlating SPS scores with MMPI scales supposedly related to suicide prediction (e.g., Scale 2—Depression). Significant correlations of SPS scores with an experimental MMPI scale designed to assess suicide risk (i.e., the Suicide Threat Scale; Farberow & Devries, 1967) have been less helpful because, as previously noted, the development of specific MMPI suicide scales has not been fruitful. The authors acknowledge that one of the major limitations of the SPS is its lack of predictive validity.

In interpreting the SPS, Cull and Gill recommend analysis and interpretation of the SPS total scores, probability scores, subscale elevations, and responses to individual items. In general, a total score of 70 or above is viewed as a significant elevation and provides strong evidence for taking suicide precautions (Cull & Gill, 1982). The probability score indicates the likelihood that an individual's responses on the SPS are similar to a criterion group of lethal suicide attemptors. Additionally, the SPS answer sheets include convenient categories for identifying pertinent demographic information along with the clients' self-report of major stresses occurring in the past 2 years. The clinician should also note the nature, time frame, and severity of the reported stressors. Previous suicide attempts are recorded, and the examiner may wish to complete the checklist of indicators for the DSM-III diagnosis of a Major Depressive Episode included on the SPS protocol.

Cull and Gill (1982) provide sound recommendations for the overall clinical use of the SPS and offer relevant case examples in the manual, emphasizing corroboration of SPS results through the use of a clinical interview. Despite its limitations, especially in the areas of construct and predictive validity, the SPS represents one of the few structured methods of suicide-risk assessment that is especially useful in crisis/emergency situations where a quick assessment may be necessary. The SPS also may be helpful in examining the client who has been reluctant to reveal suicidal ideation, yet appears to be at risk (Bardwell, 1985). Future research on the SPS should study its predictive validity in order to substantiate its use in identifying individuals at risk for suicide.

The Scale for Suicide Ideation. A 19-item scale designed to quantify and assess suicidal intention, the Scale for Suicide Ideation (SSI; Beck, Kovacs, & Weissman, 1979) was designed to assess 1) the extent of suicidal thoughts and the client's attitude toward them; 2) how intent the individual is on completing the suicide act, including details or plans for committing suicide and deterrents to an active attempt; and 3) feelings of control and/or "courage" regarding a proposed attempt. Typically, a clinician completes the SSI within the context of a clinical interview; that is, he or she structures the interview in such a way that the client provides information relevant to the SSI. Each item consists of three alternative statements graded in intensity from 0 to 2. For example, on item 4 the clinician would assess the client's desire to make an active suicide attempt as "0" (none), "1" (weak), or "2" (moderate to strong desire). Higher scores on the SSI indicate higher levels of suicidal ideation leading to higher suicidal risk.

Beck et al. (1979) report internal consistency and interrater reliability coefficients of .89 and .83, respectively. In terms of construct validity, SSI items correlate positively (r = .41; Beck et al., 1979) with the self-harm items of the Beck Depression Inventory (BDI). The SSI also has been used successfully to discriminate between groups of clients hospitalized for suicidal ideation and outpatients who sought psychiatric treatment for depression (Beck et al., 1979). The authors of the SSI also tested the hypothesis that hopelessness is more closely related than depression to the extent of suicidal ideation. Hopelessness, as measured by the Hopelessness Scale (Beck, Weissman, Lester, & Trexler, 1974), and depression, as measured by the BDI, have been correlated positively with the extent of current suicidal ideation tapped by the SSI. When the BDI score was partialled out, the correlation between hopelessness and suicidal ideation remained significant, while the correlation between the BDI and ideation scores was not significant. Thus, the SSI appears to be tapping an important component of suicidal ideation (i.e., feelings of hopelessness) that seems distinct from global depression. The SSI also appears to be sensitive to changes in the level of suicidal ideation paralleling changes in feelings of depression and hopelessness over time (Beck et al., 1979).

Although the authors describe the SSI as a primarily clinical research instrument, given the dearth of reliable, valid instruments specifically designed to assess suicidal ideation and risk, the SSI may be useful in structuring and quantifying information gathered in an interview situation relevant to suicidal ideation and risk. While Beck et al. (1979) do not provide cutoff scores or profile analyses indicative of suicidal risk, the clinician may find it useful to refer to the authors' findings regarding factor analysis of the instrument. Factor analysis of the SSI has identified three item clusters, which may be interpreted informally by the examiner: Active Suicidal Desire,

Preparation, and Passive Suicidal Desire. While the SSI authors acknowledge the current lack of predictive validity, they are to be commended in undertaking a 10-year longitudinal predictive study.

Modified Scale for Suicidal Ideation. Recently, a group of investigators have developed a Modified Scale for Suicidal Ideation (MSSI; Miller, Norman, Bishop, & Dow, 1986), which differs from the SSI in a number of practical ways. First, the MSSI includes four items at the beginning of the scale designed to screen for suicidal ideation. Patients who are assessed at this point as demonstrating significant suicidal ideation are then administered the remainder of the MSSI. Interrater reliability for the screening items ranges from .86 to 1.0. Interrater agreement regarding the screening decision (i.e., to continue or stop the interview) was reported at 100%. Subjects who met the screening criteria (i.e., ideators) also received significantly higher ratings from expert clinicians regarding likelihood of suicide. The four screening items, when added to the 14 remaining items on the MSSI, yield a total score that also has been shown to be highly reliable ($r = .94$). Concurrent validity of the MSSI total score has been established through high correlations with expert clinicians' ratings of the likelihood of suicide. Evidence of construct validity has been demonstrated by correlating MSSI scores with the BDI and the Hopelessness Scale. Furthermore, MSSI scores have been used successfully to discriminate between suicide attemptors and non-attemptors prior to hospitalization.

The authors of the MSSI have added standardized prompt questions for each item, enabling paraprofessionals to administer the MSSI. Thus, the scale appears to have great potential in the assessment of suicidal risk. The addition of the screening items increases the time effectiveness of the scale, which may be of great help for clinicians facing crisis or emergency situations. Furthermore, the MSSI provides a score that is in concordance with expert clinicians' judgments regarding suicidal ideation (Miller et al., 1986).

CASE EXAMPLES

What follows are two case studies demonstrating the application of the assessment procedures presented in this chapter. The first study demonstrates assessment techniques used in a crisis situation; the second illustrates the assessment of suicidal ideations in the early stages of ongoing counseling.

Sharon

A counselor on emergency duty at a university counseling center received a call from Dr. Jones, a faculty member at the university. Dr. Jones reported her concerns regarding what she described as "suicidal talk" by a student who had confided in her. The student was distraught and was sitting in Dr. Jones's office at the time of the call. As this was her first encounter with a potentially suicidal student, she was very alarmed. The counselor recommended that Dr. Jones encourage the student to come to the counseling center immediately and to walk over with her. Furthermore, the counselor suggested that if the student resisted, Dr. Jones should call back immediately.

A few minutes later, Dr. Jones arrived at the counseling center with Sharon, a 19-

year-old female in her first semester at the university. At this point the counselor began a semistructured clinical interview. Sharon was visibly distraught, sobbing heavily as she described her recent breakup with a boyfriend back home. Sharon also reported that her parents reside in another state, that she is currently struggling academically at the University, and that she has made few friends. It seemed to the counselor that Sharon had not made the full transition from home to the university environment. She appeared tired and reported not having slept or eaten in the past two days. She described current feelings of nervousness and anxiety and repeatedly mentioned the need to "stop" these feelings. She consistently blamed herself for the failure of her relationship with her boyfriend and alluded to a past history of failure in interpersonal relations, especially heterosexual relationships.

After gathering data relevant to Sharon's current circumstances and crisis, the counselor inquired about current suicidal ideation, method, lethality, and past suicidal attempts. Although Sharon confided that 2 years ago she "half-heartedly" attempted suicide by cutting her wrists, she became quiet and vague in her responses to direct questions about current suicidal ideations and refused to disclose much information. At this point the clinician continued the information-gathering process, but in a facilitative, nonthreatening manner.

Once Sharon regained some composure, the counselor administered the Suicide Probability Scale, a measure of suicidal intent. The results showed T-scores of 75, 76, 79, and 55 for the Hopelessness, Suicide Ideation, Negative Self-Evaluation, and Hostility subscales. These subscale scores yielded a total weighted score of 75; thus, three of the four were clearly and significantly above the mean. The total weighted score of 99 and a Probability score of 90 indicated that, given Sharon's present psychological state, she was a severe suicide risk.

When interpreting the SPS subscales, the counselor was most concerned with Sharon's current sense of hopelessness and high level of suicidal ideation. Her high level of negative self-evaluation appeared to reflect her pervasive, perhaps long-term feelings of low self-esteem. Sharon did not appear to be expressing her suicidal ideation through hostile rage; rather, her responses to individual SPS items reflected strong feelings of loneliness, worthlessness, pervasive unhappiness, and a lack of feelings of closeness. These item responses substantiated other findings on the SPS, showing that Sharon was a serious suicide risk.

Additionally, the number and severity of psychosocial stressors impacting Sharon were considered severe for a university student (i.e., academic problems, breakup of a significant relationship). Furthermore, she evidenced a number of symptoms of an impending Major Depressive Episode as described by DSM-III (e.g., sleep disorders, appetite disturbances, feelings of worthlessness, recurrent thoughts of suicide).

When the counselor discussed the implications of the SPS results, Sharon acknowledged the severity of her current ideation and hopelessness, but denied any present active plan to harm herself. She also acknowledged that, given her current psychological as well as physical state, voluntary hospitalization would be an appropriate alternative. Sharon was referred for hospitalization to the Student Health Service, where she received medication in response to a DSM-III diagnosis of Major Depressive Episode. After her dismissal from the hospital, Sharon returned to the university counseling center for treatment, and the counselor continued to monitor her suicidal ideations closely.

Joel

Joel was a 15-year-old male referred for outpatient counseling by his mother. In an initial interview with Joel's mother, she reported that he had always been somewhat of a shy "loner." Within the past year, however, she had noticed Joel spending an increasing amount of time alone, lacking close interpersonal relationships and exhibiting a general sense of apathy. She also reported that he was currently failing a number of classes in which he previously had been a high average student. Joel's mother also confided that 2 years ago she and her husband had divorced.

After gathering developmental/biographical information from his mother, Joel was seen for an initial intake/information-gathering interview. During the initial interview, Joel resisted providing information and answering questions. He was openly resentful of his mother's referral for counseling. He acknowledged that he did not have a close relationship with either of his parents, but would prefer to live with his father. Joel denied that any problems existed and said that school is "just hard." Toward the end of the interview he disclosed the wish to belong to a "group" at school and to have a girlfriend; however, he still seemed reluctant to communicate more in-depth information.

Up to this point, the clinician had collected a developmental, biographical history suggestive of significant problems and suicidal risk. However, because Joel was reluctant to self-disclose during the interview, the clinician found it helpful to administer certain formal assessment instruments, including the MMPI. The results of the MMPI indicated that Joel had completed the test reliably. His MMPI profile yielded a 2(Depression)—8(Schizophrenia) high-point code. This configuration is indicative of severe depression with associated anxiety and agitation and frequently results in fears of loss of control (Greene, 1980). Other features associated with this type of profile include depression and agitation sufficient to produce confusion, forgetfulness, and difficulties in concentration and attention. Obsessive ruminations and isolation from interpersonal relationships and activities may occur. Suicidal ruminations also may be present and should be evaluated carefully. Elevations of other scales on the MMPI were suggestive of family conflicts, social alienation, and interpersonal sensitivity.

The initial reports provided by Joel's mother were corroborated further by the MMPI. The clinician's next step was to perform a careful evaluation of Joel's suicidal ideation and intention using the structured interview format of the Modified Scale for Suicidal Ideation (MSSI). Results of the MSSI indicated that overall Joel expressed a moderate degree of suicidal ideation. For example, he expressed that in the last 48 hours he had thought about suicide for long periods of time, had a strong wish to die, could think of no deterrents to an active attempt, and could think of no reasons to continue living. On the other hand, however, Joel had not worked out a specific plan of action and did not have immediate access to a highly lethal method. He was unsure of his ability and courage to carry out a suicide and had neither prepared for a suicide attempt nor thought about leaving a suicide note.

After the administration of the MSSI, Joel seemed more willing to discuss his problems and expressed that he had indeed been depressed in the last year. He felt that he did not fit in socially with various peer groups at school and felt rejected by others. His parents' divorce had put a strain on his relationship with both his mother and father, because he strongly felt that neither of them understood or cared about him.

The clinician did not take steps to hospitalize Joel because he was not seen as an immediate threat to himself. However, because he was a 15-year-old minor, Joel's mother was informed of the degree of his suicidal ideation. The examiner recommended that Joel continue to be seen on an individual outpatient basis in order to monitor him closely and evaluate his potential for suicide. Family therapy for Joel and his parents was recommended as a future option, once suicidal risk had been reduced. (For more information on family assessment, see chapter 2 in this volume.)

SUMMARY

It should be clear that there does not appear to be any "suicidal personality type." Furthermore, adolescent suicidal referrals originate from a variety of sources, including family members or friends, mental health agencies, or crisis counseling centers. Depending on the referral source, the clinician may or may not have access to the various background data needed to make a determination of suicidal risk. For example, while working on an ongoing outpatient basis with a severely depressed client, a clinician may have access to biographical information, weekly changes in attitudes and behavior, and psychological test information. In contrast, the clinician who encounters a client demonstrating suicidal ideation on an "emergency shift" may need to make a quick determination of suicidal risk without the benefit of in-depth information, thus relying on data easily gathered in a brief clinical interview. Consequently, the choice of instrumentation reviewed here will depend on the circumstances of the referral.

Obviously, one's judgment will play a major role in adolescent suicide assessment. However, the reliability of clinical judgment may be improved substantially when applied in the context of a multifactored assessment. In this process, formal measures of general personality adjustment and specific measures of suicide potential are combined to add further insight into the idiosyncratic factors that may lead an adolescent to consider taking his or her own life. Because the determination of whether an adolescent is at risk for suicide probably constitutes one of the most significant decisions a clinician may ever face, knowledge of the various assessment approaches presented in this chapter should assist in making these decisions with a higher degree of reliability and accuracy.

REFERENCES

American Psychiatric Association. (1980). *Diagnostic and statistical manual of mental disorders* (3rd ed.). Washington, DC: Author.

Anderson, D. R. (1981). Diagnosis and prediction of suicidal risk among adolescents. In C. F. Wells & I. R. Stuart (Eds.), *Self-destructive behavior in children and adolescents* (pp. 45-60). New York: Van Nostrand.

Bardwell, R. (1985). Suicide Probability Scale. In D. J. Keyser & R. C. Sweetland (Eds.), *Test critiques* (Vol. IV, pp. 649-655). Kansas City, MO: Test Corporation.

Beck, A. T., Kovacs, M., & Weissman, A. (1979). Assessment of suicidal intention: The Scale for Suicide Ideation. *Journal of Consulting and Clinical Psychology, 47*, 343-352.

Beck, A. T., Weissman, A., Lester, D., & Trexler, L. (1974). The measurement of pessimism: The Hopelessness Scale. *Journal of Counsulting and Clinical Psychology, 42*, 861-865.

Chickering, A. W. (1969). *Education and identity.* San Francisco: Jossey-Bass.

Clopton, J. R. (1979). The MMPI and suicide. In C. J. Newmark (Ed.), *MMPI: Clinical and research trends.* New York: Praeger.

Clopton, J. R., Pallis, D. J., & Birtchnell, J. (1979). MMPI profile patterns of suicide attemptors. *Journal of Consulting and Clinical Psychology, 47*, 135-139.

Cohen-Sandler, R., Berman, A. L., & King, R. A. (1982). Life stress and symptomatology: Determinants of suicidal behavior in children. *Journal of the American Academy of Child Psychiatry, 21*, 178-186.

Conger, J. J., & Petersen, A. C. (1984). *Adolescence and youth* (3rd ed.). New York: Harper & Row.

Cosand, B. J., Bourque, L. B., & Kraus, J. F. (1982). Suicide among adolescents in Sacramento County, California 1950-1979. *Adolescence, 17*, 917-930.

Cull, J. G., & Gill, W. S. (1982). *Suicide Probability Scale (SPS) manual.* Los Angeles: Western Psychological Services.

Dahlstrom, W. G., Welsh, G. S., & Dahlstrom, L. E. (1972). *An MMPI handbook: Vol. 1. Clinical interpretation* (rev. ed.). Minneapolis: University of Minnesota Press.

Davis, P. A. (1980). *Suicidal adolescents.* Springfield, IL: Charles C. Thomas.

Erikson, E. H. (1968). *Identity: Youth and crisis.* New York: Norton.

Exner, J. E., & Wylie, J. (1977). Some Rorschach data concerning suicide. *Journal of Personality Assessment, 4*, 339-349.

Farberow, N. L., & Devries, A. G. (1967). An item differentiation analysis of MMPIs of suicidal neuropsychiatric hospital patients. *Psychological Reports, 20*, 607-617.

Freeman, D. J., Wilson, K., Thigpen, J., & McGee, R. K. (1974). Assessing intention to die in self-injury behavior. In C. Neuringer (Ed.), *Psychological assessment of suicidal risk* (pp. 18-42). Springfield, IL: Charles C. Thomas.

Golding, S. L. (1985). Suicide Probability Scale. In J. V. Mitchell, Jr. (Ed.), *The ninth mental measurements yearbook* (pp. 1500-1501). Lincoln, NE: Buros Institute.

Graham, J. R. (1977). *The MMPI: A practical guide.* New York: Oxford University Press.

Greene, R. H. (1980). *The MMPI: An interpretive manual.* New York: Grune & Stratton.

Hatton, C. L., Valente, S. M., & Rink, A. (1977). Assessment of suicidal risk. In C. L. Hatton, S. M. Valente, & A. Rink (Eds.), *Suicide assessment and intervention* (pp. 40-61). New York: Appleton-Century-Crofts.

Havighurst, R. J. (1972). *Developmental tasks and education.* New York: McKay.

Hawton, K. (1986). *Suicide and attempted suicide among children and adolescents.* Beverly Hills: Sage.

Hawton, K., Cole, D., O'Grady, J., & Osborn, M. (1982). Motivational aspects of deliberate self-poisoning in adolescents. *British Journal of Psychiatry, 141*, 286-291.

Hipple, J., & Cimbolic, P. (1979). *The counselor and suicidal crisis: Diagnosis and intervention.* Springfield, IL: Charles C. Thomas.

Kaplan, R. M., & Sacuzzo, D. P. (1982). *Psychological testing: Principles, applications and issues.* Monterey, CA: Brooks/Cole.

Kazdin, A. E., French, N. H., Unis, A. S., Esveldt-Dawson, K., & Sherick, R. B. (1983). Hopelessness, depression and suicidal intent among psychiatrically disturbed inpatient children. *Journal of Consulting and Clinical Psychology, 51*, 504-510.

Lester, D., Beck, A. T., & Mitchell, B. (1979). Extrapolation from attempted suicides to completed suicides: A test. *Journal of Abnormal Psychology, 88*, 78-80.

Levenson, M. (1974). Cognitive correlates of suicidal risk. In C. Neuringer (Ed.), *Psychological assessment of suicidal risk* (pp. 150-160). Springfield, IL: Charles C. Thomas.

Loevinger, J. (1976). *Ego development: Conception and theories.* San Francisco: Jossey-Bass.

Marks, P. A., & Haller, D. L. (1977). Now I lay me down for keeps: A study of adolescent suicide attempts. *Journal of Clinical Psychology, 33,* 390-400.

McEvoy, T. L. (1974). Suicidal risk via the Thematic Apperception Test. In C. Neuringer (Ed.), *Psychological assessment of suicidal risk.* Springfield, IL: Charles C. Thomas.

Miller, I. W., Norman, W. H., Bishop, S. B., & Dow, M. G. (1986). The Modified Scale for Suicidal Ideation: Reliability and validity. *Journal of Consulting and Clinical Psychology, 54,* 724-725.

Neuringer, C. (1974a). Problems of assessing suicidal risk. In C. Neuringer (Ed.), *Psychological assessment of suicidal risk* (pp. 3-17). Springfield, IL: Charles C. Thomas.

Neuringer, C. (1974b). Rorschach Inkblot Test assessment of suicidal risk. In C. Neuringer (Ed.), *Psychological assessment of suicidal risk* (pp. 74-94). Springfield, IL: Charles C. Thomas.

Peck, M. (1977). Adolescent suicide. In C. L. Holton, S. M. Valente, & A. Rink (Eds.), *Suicide assessment and intervention* (pp. 165-174). New York: Appleton-Century-Crofts.

Perry, W. G. (1970). *Forms of intellectul and ethical development in the college years.* New York: Holt, Rinehart & Winston.

Strosahl, K. D., Linehan, M. M., & Chiles, J. A. (1984). Will the real social desirability please stand up? Hopelessness, depression, social desirability and the prediction of suicidal behavior. *Journal of Consulting and Clinical Psychology, 52,* 449-457.

Topol, P., & Resnikoff, N. (1982). Perceived peer and family relationships, hopelessness, and locus of control as factors in adolescent suicide attempts. *Suicide and Life Threatening Behavior, 12,* 141-150.

Vital statistics of the United States. (1982). Washington, DC: U.S. Department of Health and Human Services, Public Health Services.

12

Assessing Adolescent Conduct Disorders and Oppositional Behaviors

RANDAL P. QUEVILLON, PH.D., STEVEN LANDAU, PH.D.,
W. B. APPLE, M.A., PATRICIA PETRETIC-JACKSON, PH.D.

The importance of any behavior disorder arises from its personal and social significance. Boyle and Jones (1985) suggest three criteria by which to judge this importance: *frequency* (prevalence in the population and number of referrals), *seriousness* (the burden of suffering to the individual and family), and *relevance* (societal costs in terms of disorder effects and remediation expenses). By these benchmarks, conduct disorders and oppositional behaviors attain a preeminent position among adolescent problems. These difficulties are common and have a striking impact on affected individuals, families, and society. Moreover, their effects often continue over time. In short, the pattern of violence, rule violation, provocation, lying, stealing, and/or noncompliance found in conduct and oppositional disorders is of crucial importance for those professionals who must assess and understand adolescents in turmoil.

To document the impact of conduct disorders and oppositional behaviors, one needs only to turn to the local news. Reports of homicides, robberies, arson, assaults, and an alarming variety of other offenses illustrate the more extreme manifestations of these problems and the consequences, in adulthood, of uninterrupted adolescent conduct problems. In addition, statistics on juvenile arrests for property crimes and violence indicate that the 13-17 age range is greatly overrepresented, accounting for 43% of the crimes while making up only 10% of the U.S. population (Strasberg, 1978; see also chapter 13 in this volume).

Conduct disorders and oppositional behaviors warrant attention in part because they occur frequently in the population. La Greca and Quay (1984) reviewed prevalence studies for conduct disorders and concluded that a 6% estimate for the disorder was indicated in the child population, and although estimates for adolescent prevalence per se are not well established, there is good reason to assume that they exceed the 6% figure (La Greca & Quay, 1984). Furthermore, adolescents with conduct and oppositional disorders constitute the largest number of referrals to clinics. Most estimates indicate that one-half to one-third of all referrals from parents and teachers are

---

The authors wish to thank Phil Bornstein for his critical review of and earlier draft of this paper and Tom Jackson for his technical assistance.

the result of conduct and oppositional disorders (Patterson, Reid, Jones, & Conger, 1975; Roach, 1958; Wiltz & Patterson, 1974; Wolff, 1961). Indeed, unresponsiveness to parental and/or community controls appears implicated in the majority of treatment efforts reported in the behavioral literature (Atkeson & Forehand, 1981). Finally, these cases are much more likely than other adolescent outpatient disorders to demand attention from several professionals (i.e., clinical psychologists, social workers, school psychologists, probation officers, the courts), thereby magnifying the societal costs.

Perhaps the most disheartening aspect of conduct disorders and oppositional behaviors is their temporal stability. Studies of antisocial, aggressive, and delinquent behavior show that these problems tend to persist into adulthood (Epstein, Kauffman, & Cullinan, 1985; Farrington, 1978; Loeber, 1982; Morris, 1956; Robins, 1966). Although some acting out and noncompliance is probably typical for this age group, high rates of antisocial behavior, especially covert acts such as lying and stealing, are associated with greater problem stability and greater risks of legal entanglements (Loeber, 1982; Moore, Chamberlain, & Menkes, 1979). In one recent study (Loeber & Schmaling, 1985), adolescent boys who stole but were not aggressive and boys who were "versatile" in their antisocial behaviors (i.e., including aggressive) were significantly more likely to be involved in delinquency than boys who were exclusively aggressive or those who were neither. Aggression per se, although moderately stable (e.g., Lefkowitz, Eron, Walder, & Huesmann, 1977; Moskowitz, Ledingham, & Schwartzman, 1985), appears less often implicated in adjudication for delinquent status. Finally, early onset has been identified as a contributing factor to ongoing and even escalating rates of conduct disturbance and oppositional behavior (Loeber, 1982). Thus, adolescents who show a substantial history of disturbed behaviors and/ or those who are frequent offenders and versatile in their specific antisocial acts are at risk for developing a chronic course of deviant behavior and societal conflict. As conduct disorders and oppositional behaviors constitute such a compelling area of professional concern for those affected adolescents, the challenge of conducting adequate assessments merits careful attention.

DESCRIPTIONS AND DEFINITIONS

As Quay (1979) has pointed out, most of the symptoms of conduct disorder are directly observable. The wide range of these activities includes the extreme forms of homicide and violent aggression, murder of one's parents, parent battering, and fire setting. More common albeit less extreme forms include aggressive/coercive interactions, stealing, and classroom/study hall disruptions and rule violations.

In a major review of 37 multivariate studies of childhood psychopathology conducted through 1978, Quay (1979) identified the most frequently found characteristics describing conduct-disordered individuals. In order of frequency, these are fighting/ assaultiveness, temper tantrums, disobedience/defiance, destructiveness of property, impertinence/impudence, uncooperativeness/lack of consideration, disruptiveness via interruptions and disturbing others, negativism and refusing direction, restlessness, and boisterousness/noisiness. Also included in Quay's 26-item list were irritability, use of profane or abusive language, stealing, and denial of mistakes/blaming of others.

Given the range of problem behaviors seen, it is useful to abstract some themes around which these acts appear to cluster. An obvious one is aggression, which is defined by Hartup (1974) as the "intentional physical and verbal responses that are directed toward an object or another person and that have the capacity to damage or injure" (p. 339; see also Bandura, 1973). A somewhat overlapping but likewise important issue is antisocial behavior, which Loeber (1982) defines as "acts that maximize a person's immediate gain through inflicting pain or loss on others" (p. 1432). A final area to consider is that of oppositional behavior. This subclass of noncompliant behavior is distinguished by the fact that the adolescent *has the required competence* to comply with the rule or directive, but fails to do so (Doke & Flippo, 1983). This would exclude noncompliance due to inability to comply or skill deficits.

As indicated, conduct disorders and oppositional behavior cover a wide range of acts reflecting aggressive and antisocial behavior. As will be discussed, it is by no means clear that conduct problems and oppositional disorders represent distinct clinical entities; therefore, this chapter will consider these two diagnoses together as representing a range of problems found in adolescents in varying degrees and with specific "symptom" emphases. No efforts will be made to provide parallel or equal coverage for differential classifications, as it is the present authors' position that the assessment of adolescents who present these problems can be handled best by concurrently examining conduct disorders and oppositional behaviors as a singular unit. Juvenile delinquency, covered in detail in chapter 13 of this volume, will be considered here as a legal term, apart from the psychological orientation of this chapter.

CLASSIFICATION

Until recently, the study of psychopathology has been an adult-centered activity (Achenbach, 1974). As most efforts to describe and categorize child and adolescent deviant behavior and emotional disturbance have a history of less than two decades, it is not surprising that the area is fraught with controversy and confusion. Despite these ambiguities, advances have been made in the classification of adolescent conduct disturbance and oppositional behavior. The functions of classification are two-fold. First, for descriptive purposes, classification should aid in record keeping, add to epidemiological studies, and contribute to existing information and theory about the particular disorders. Secondly, for prescriptive purposes, classification should direct treatment efforts, allow predictions of both future behavior and unassessed areas of current performance, and should suggest possibilities for prevention. As will be seen, more than one classification system shows promise for these purposes. Although a thorough examination of all existing taxonomies is beyond the scope of this chapter, brief discussion is warranted.

Clinically Derived Systems

This group of classification systems is comprised of diagnostic schemes that evolved out of the day-to-day observations of clinicians working with affected individuals. It is presumed that syndromes will emerge from these observations of common symptoms and client characteristics, involving: 1) consensually validated clusters of symptoms, which form and describe the diagnostic entities; 2) specific patterns of symptom course, which standardize expectations of onset, typical duration, and severity fluctuations; and 3) specific etiological factor(s) (typically organic) that, if present, will cause the syndrome to be manifested and if absent mean that observed symptoms must be related to alternative conditions or diagnoses (see Feighner et al., 1972).

Currently, the most widely used of the clinically derived systems is the third edition of the *Diagnostic and Statistical Manual of Mental Disorders* (DSM-III; American Psychiatric Association, 1980). DSM-III differs from earlier editions in providing many more categories appropriate for children and adolescents and by including categories relevant for diagnosing adolescent conduct and oppositional disorders. Two major categories on Axis I of DSM-III are Conduct Disorder and Oppositional Disorder. Conduct disorders are divided into four categories along two dichotomous dimensions (Aggressive/Nonaggressive and Socialized/Undersocialized): 1) undersocialized, aggressive, 2) undersocialized, nonaggressive, 3) socialized, aggressive, and 4) socialized, nonaggressive.

Oppositional disorder, by DSM-III standards, involves a similar pattern of disobedience, negativism, and provocative opposition to authority. It is distinguished from conduct disorder, however, in that no violation of others' basic rights or societal norms is observed. Instead, adolescents in this category tend to exhibit minor rule violations, temper tantrums, argumentativeness, provocative behavior, or stubbornness.

Other DSM-III categories that might have relevance for the assessor of conductdisturbed adolescents include adjustment reactions, V-codes (categories set aside for individuals who show no evidence of a clear-cut mental disorder, but who have exhibited behavior extreme enough to prompt attention from mental health personnel), and the adult Antisocial Personality Disorder, which extends down to age 18.

Although the DSM-III is the established system for American psychiatrists and most mental health workers, several criticisms of this system are warranted. A major issue concerns the reliability of diagnoses (see Strober, Green, & Carlson, 1981; Werry, Methven, Fitzpatrick, & Dixon, 1983; Mattison, Cantwell, Russell, & Will, 1979). Werry et al. (1983) make the interesting point that using the Oppositional Disorder category appeared to introduce "noise" into the system and combining this diagnosis with conduct disorders improved reliability of the broad classification.

Other criticisms of the DSM-III relate to its limited utility, as in the dubious validity of the conduct disorder diagnosis for hospitalized adolescents suggested by Lewis, Lewis, Unger, and Goldman (1984) and in the fact that its child and adolescent categories often may obscure more appropriate adult diagnoses (Weller, Weller, & Herjanic, 1983). However, the risk of classifying adolescents using adult diagnostic categories (Garber, 1984) makes the practice of assigning adult diagnoses to children and adolescents questionable.

Empirically Derived Systems

The empirically derived systems have been based on studies using multivariate statistical methods. These methods rest on the determination of correlations among various problems or symptoms, which are then summarized by predetermined quantitative methods. As major alternatives to clinically derived systems, these empirically derived taxonomies reflect a dimensional rather than a categorical approach to describing psychopathology. These dimensional systems tend to represent behavior disorders as existing on continua; that is, an individual's behaviors are examined for relatively high or low rates across several factors rather than for an "either/or" fit within a particular diagnosis.

Empirical systems have the major advantage of placing the individual in the context of his/her peers, and some systems (e.g., that of Achenbach) compare according to age and sex strata. In addition, these systems draw on empirical support from multivariate statistical methods to form their taxonomies rather than on clinical observation and theory. To date, a rather impressive body of research has been gathered supporting various empirical classification systems (see Quay, 1979). The central weakness of this approach, however, is that the results of empirical classification studies are influenced by many idiosyncratic factors, such as sample selection, measurement procedures, and data analysis techniques.

An excellent example of an empirically derived system is found in Quay's research on the Behavior Problem Checklist (La Greca & Quay, 1984; Quay, 1979; Quay & Peterson, 1979; Peterson, 1961). Quay has clustered childhood and adolescent behavioral problems and traits into five broad-band patterns of disorder that make up the categories of his system (Conduct Disorder, Socialized Aggressive, Attention Deficit Disorder, Anxiety-Withdrawal, and Psychotic Disorder). Each of these broad-band patterns is described by a set of characteristics arising from the checklist items that formed the factors. For example, in Conduct Disorder, the characteristics include fighting, disobedience, temper tantrums, uncooperativeness, attention seeking, bullying, irritability, hyperactivity, and blaming others.

A second empirically derived system has been developed by Achenbach and Edelbrock (Achenbach, 1978; Achenbach & Edelbrock, 1983; Edelbrock & Achenbach, 1980) using their Child Behavior Checklist (CBCL). Their system is similar to Quay's in that both broad-band and narrow-band factors have been identified. Narrow-band factors represent the more specific personality characteristics that compose the broad-band factor. Achenbach's two broad-band factors are Externalizing (undercontrolled) behavior and Internalizing (overcontrolled) behavior. This system differs from Quay's in that narrow-band factors (e.g., Hyperactive, Aggressive, etc.) were taken from separate factor analyses for each sex and three age groups; thus, six sets of categories (sex by age) are reported.

CONDUCT DISORDERS IN THE CONTEXT OF ADOLESCENCE

While conduct-disordered behavior includes a broad variety of specific symptoms such as fighting, stealing, lying, loss of temper, and noncompliance exhibited in an extreme and persistent manner, it is important to recognize that many of these same behaviors are manifested over the course of normal development. Thus, they must be viewed in comparison to their age appropriateness during normal adolescent development. Epidemiological, longitudinal, and cross-sectional studies have provided a pattern of symptom development for samples of children and adolescents in the general population. Although the studies differ with respect to populations, methodologies, definition of behaviors, and the source of behavioral information, thus making comparisons difficult, a consistent developmental picture does emerge. This suggests that there are predictable trends in the development of specific antisocial behaviors.

Research findings support the view that behavior problems in a normal sample decrease with age. Parental ratings collected in the Berkeley Guidance Study (MacFarlane, Allen, & Honzik, 1954) indicated that children averaged five to six problems at each age level between 21 months and 11 years. However, the frequency dropped to between two and four problems at ages 12 and 13 and between one and two problems at age 14. Sex differences were found, with the incidence of temper tantrums and lying significantly greater in males across the age range.

A cross-sectional study by Achenbach and Edelbrock (1981), for example, has provided useful information regarding the distribution of antisocial behaviors. These researchers found, based on parental reports, that the percentage of children who engage in fighting decreases as a function of age. High rates of fighting behavior may be observed during the preschool years, then stabilizes at a level of 20% in the 10- to 13-year-old age group, and then decreases to approximately 1% by the age of 16. Teacher ratings of fighting (Loeber, Patterson, & Dishion, 1982) indicate similar frequencies. While 8% of children at age 13 are reported to engage in fighting, this number decreases to 1% by age 16. Similar trends have been found in the Isle of Wright (Rutter, Tizard, & Whitmore, 1970/1981) and in the Manhattan (Gersten, Langner, Eisenberg, Simcha-Fagan, & McCarthy, 1976) longitudinal studies. In contrast to this trend, Zimring (1979) found that arrests for serious violent offenses peaked at age 18. Taken together these findings suggest that despite overall declines in the rate of fighting, a subgroup of highly aggressive youths emerges by about age 13. Adolescents in this group are responsible for the vast majority of violent acts perpetrated in late adolescence. Another consideration is that while much of the research examining high levels of adolescent aggression included samples of arrested youths, such samples may reflect not only conduct-disordered subjects, but schizophrenic, hyperactive, and organically impaired adolescents as well (Lewis, Shanok, Pincus, & Glaser, 1979).

Gersten et al. (1976) found that the rates of bullying and teasing behavior among adolescent groups decreased from age 7 through 16. Achenbach and Edelbrock (1981), however, found a stable rate (i.e., approximately 40%) of such behaviors for boys from age 10 through 16. This percentage was only slightly lower than rates in a clinical sample. The percentage of girls who engaged in such behaviors was found to decrease between ages 10 to 16.

While disobedience in the home generally decreases from 50% at ages 6-7 to 30% at age 10, a new increase is indicated at ages 12 and 13 (Loeber, 1982), followed by a decline. This behavior pattern has been interpreted as indicating temporary antisocial or noncompliant behavior rather than a diagnosis of conduct disorder.

Other overt behaviors show less clear patterns of temporal decline. Rates of argumentative behavior, for example, remain stable during this period. While teasing remains stable for boys, it declines for girls after age 12. In contrast, the base rates for threatening behavior tend to be low, markedly decreasing percentages are not found.

Although cruelty drops substantially for girls, the percentage of boys showing such behavior between 10 and 16 remains stable (Achenbach & Edelbrock, 1981).

The changes in such overt behaviors can be contrasted with rates for covert anti-social behaviors during adolescence. Achenbach and Edelbrock (1981) report that the frequency of children who engage in lying remains stable, with approximately 20% of those aged 10 to 16 showing such behaviors. Stealing in the home seems to increase between the ages of 8 or 9 to age 16, a finding substantiated by adolescent self-reports (Farrington, 1973). Disobedience in school peaks for boys at ages 12 and 13, and decreases until age 16 for both sexes (Achenbach & Edelbrock, 1981; Loeber, 1982). Running away from home, association with bad companions, truancy, alcohol use, and vandalism show slight increases (Farrington, 1973; Robins & Wish, 1977; Shapland, 1978), although in most cases no more than 10% of normal children at age 16 engage in such behaviors based on parental report (Achenbach & Edelbrock, 1981).

Parental reports most likely provide an underestimate of the true prevalence of covert antisocial behaviors, as parents may not be aware of the actual frequency of lying and stealing in their adolescent children (Loeber, 1982). Additionally, there appears to be a considerable amount of hidden delinquency in the adolescent population (Achenbach, 1982), particularly when adolescent self-report data are considered (Cernkovich & Giordano, 1979). However, important differences exist between the minor delinquent behaviors frequently exhibited by 13- or 14-year-old males and the persistent antisocial behavior typical of conduct-disordered adolescents (Wadsworth, 1979; West & Farrington, 1977). These differences include severity, persistence, and ultimate costs to society.

How can one distinguish between the symptoms of diagnosable conduct distur-bance and normal development? The results of the aforementioned studies indicate that at some point the average adolescent may exhibit a few symptoms of various types of disorders, but infrequently will show many symptoms of one disorder (Garber, 1984). Also, although such behaviors as fighting, destructiveness, lying, and disobedience may be relatively frequent occurrences at different points in time, the simple occurrence of these behaviors is not enough in itself to warrant a diagnosis of conduct disturbance. Instead, conduct disorders are identified only when the behav-ior deviates significantly from age and sex norms in terms of age of onset, course, frequency, and intensity.

A recognition of the developmental perspective in the assessment process is cru-cial given that similar behaviors are evaluated differently as a function of the age of the child. Because most overt aggressive acts occur in decreasing numbers as the adolescent matures, the presence of such behaviors is interpreted as more deviant and indicative of a poorer prognosis than if exhibited by a preadolescent (Schechtman, 1970). Conversely, many more adolescents exhibit covert acts during this period, although the frequency, intensity, duration, and variety differ between normal and conduct-disordered samples, and such differences serve to distinguish the two groups.

Sex Differences

Not surprisingly, research consistently has found disturbances of conduct more common in males than females. This significant sex difference is found for both normal and clinical samples and in all age groups for the range of conduct-disordered behaviors, beginning at age 5 and continuing through adolescence (Graham & Rutter, 1973; Lavik, 1977; Rutter et al., 1970/1981; Werry & Quay, 1971). This sex difference is particularly evident with overt aggressive behaviors. For covert behaviors, such as truancy, lying, and stealing, the degree of difference between males and females is not as dramatic. Similar findings are present in studies sampling delinquent adolescents. While the sex ratio difference for delinquency has been reduced by one-half over the past 20 years, it is unclear whether this trend applies to nondelinquent, conduct-disordered adolescents (i.e., those meeting diagnostic criteria for conduct disorders but who have not been adjudicated) (Rutter & Garmezy, 1983).

Several explanations have been offered to account for the observed effects of gender (Rutter & Garmezy, 1983). These include biological/genetic differences between the sexes, differential exposure rates of male and female adolescents to marital discord (i.e., the parents of male adolescents tend to argue more openly), differential reactions of adolescent males and females to parental discord, and different response styles on the part of parents to the problem behaviors shown by male or female adolescent children (i.e., differences in referral patterns).

Risk Factors

Research findings suggest that although the presence of antisocial behaviors during childhood is highly predictive of adolescent conduct disturbance, other risk factors exist that apparently also predispose the adolescent to such a diagnosis. Although risk factors do not show as strong an association with a diagnosis of adolescent conduct disorders as problem behaviors, these variables are significant: they suggest concomitant problems that may mediate and maintain conduct disorders, and thus should be addressed in both assessment and treatment.

School-related factors. Several investigations of conduct-disordered adolescents have shown a strong, bidirectional relationship between this disorder and academic performance deficiencies, lower scores on intelligence and academic achievement tests, and specific skill deficits, especially in the areaas of reading and mathematics. Academic deficiencies typically are identified early in the academic history, and though no single explanation for the IQ-conduct disorders association can be offered, Rutter and Garmezy (1983) suggest two likely possibilities. First, cognitive deficits and conduct disorders may share a common etiology, probably a temperamental characteristic or family problem. Second, as educational failure leads to self-esteem problems and emotional disturbance, these may in turn lead to the development of a conduct disorder. Unfortunately, the bulk of evidence favoring either one of these hypotheses results primarily from the lack of support for other discounted hypotheses.

The characteristics of the school itself comprise another school-related risk factor. Rutter and his colleagues (1979) found that teacher classroom-management style, rewards, academic emphasis, and the expectations for and responsibilities placed on students were predictive of academic performance, school climate, and delinquency rates.

A final school-related factor concerns peer relationships. Although they do not contribute significantly to the initiation of early aggressive behaviors in a social context (e.g., agonistic behaviors), peers play an important role in the maintenance of aggression. Peers serve as models, reinforcing agents, and targets of aggression. Additionally, the management of interpersonal conflict in the peer group has important consequences for social acceptance, and consequently exerts a significant influence on long-term social adjustment (Rutter & Garmezy, 1983). Much adolescent delinquent activity occurs in the presence of friends, and status in delinquent gangs often is associated with skillful performance of antisocial acts (Miller, 1958).

Although a peer subculture may reinforce certain antisocial behaviors, most conduct-disordered adolescents have poor peer relationships. They are rejected by the larger peer group and are judged to have poor social skills (Behar & Stewart, 1982; Lesser, 1959; Roff, 1972). Bellack and Hersen (1977, 1978) have hypothesized that if behaviorally disordered youth could better express their wishes, respond positively to criticism, and engage in positive social interaction, then aggression would decrease. The success of interpersonal skills training programs with aggressive adolescents (Elder, Edelstein, & Narick, 1979; Fridler, Orenstein, Chiles, Fritz, & Breitt, 1979; Lee, Halberg, & Hassard, 1979) appears to provide indirect support for such a social-skills deficit hypothesis.

Cognitive aspects. In the last several years, increasing attention has focused on the cognitive characteristics of conduct-disordered children. Specifically, it is hypothesized that cognitive-skill deficits are present in such a population, and such deficits mediate social behaviors. Unfortunately, the primary evidence supporting this hypothesis is indirect and comes from the positive response of conduct-disordered adolescents to cognitively oriented treatment.

Little and Kendall (1979) have provided a review suggesting that conduct-disordered children have specific skill deficits in the areas of problem solving, role-taking, and self-control. Research has focused on the relationship between delays in the development of social perspective-taking skills and the development of socially deviant behavior (Chandler, 1972, 1973). These studies support the view that pro-social behavior is related to perspective-taking skills and that social egocentrism (i.e., the inability to take another's perspective) is involved in the development and maintenance of antisocial behavior (Chandler, 1973).

Family variables. Studies of both delinquent and nondelinquent manifestations of conduct disturbance indicate similar family correlates. Those correlates that have been investigated and implicated include parent-child interactions (e.g., characterized by harsh discipline practices, positive attention for deviant behavior, inconsistent management skills, child abuse, and poor supervision); parental characteristics and psychopathology (e.g., maternal distress and depression, parental substance abuse, and criminal behavior); and the marital relationship (e.g., domestic violence and discord). In general, family variables are thought to play a more important role for adolescents showing moderate levels of antisocial behavior as opposed to high levels of these behaviors (Robins, 1978).

Families with conduct-disordered adolescents are disorganized, often described as chaotic, and provide poor supervision. Parents engage in less monitoring of children's activities and less frequently make arrangements for temporary care in their physical absence. In such families there is a deficiency of family rules and standards and children more frequently are allowed to roam the streets and engage in considerable independent and unsupervised activity (Garmezy, 1974; Hetherington, Cox, & Cox, 1978). Communication patterns in families with delinquent adolescents differ from those with nondelinquent adolescents. The former are described as having defensive rather than supportive communication patterns, which include power-assertive, evaluative messages meant to make others feel inferior or indifferent to the feelings of others. Behaviors toward others are threatening and produce defensive behaviors in response. Defensive communications also reduce the effectiveness of interpersonal problem solving.

An additional dimension of family functioning associated with conduct disorders involve personality characteristics and psychopathology present in other family members, particularly parents. These parental characteristics include social difficulties, such as alcoholism, criminal behavior, particularly antisocial behavior on the part of the father, and personality abnormalities such as indications of inconsistent explosive anger. Siblings also show a high incidence of conduct-disordered behaviors, especially when the referred adolescent is identified as both delinquent and conduct disturbed. These families tend to be isolated and are often described as insular, particularly when mothers also show signs of mental distress.

In summary, the concurrent family variables most often present with conduct disorders include marital discord, deviant parental models, a harsh, inconsistent parent-child relationship, and poor supervision and discipline. It appears that parent, family, and educational variables, in addition to the presence of conduct-disturbed behaviors in childhood and adolescence, are the most robust predictors of conduct-disordered behaviors in adolescence (Loeber & Dishion, 1983; Rutter & Giller, 1983; West, 1982).

AN ORIENTATION TO THE ASSESSMENT PROCESS FOR CONDUCT-DISORDERED ADOLESCENTS

As noted by Mash and Terdal (1981), assessments are conducted for a number of different purposes, each of which will guide and influence the process in several ways. Depending on the assessment's purpose, the diagnostician, clinician, or researcher will attend to different adolescent behaviors, capabilities, and behavioral settings. Even the working assumptions, hypotheses, and conceptualizations about the adolescent will be influenced by, and influence, the purposes of the psychological assessment. Furthermore, the specific referral questions, whether explicit or implied, well formed or vague, will have an important impact on the nature of the assessment and the methods employed during the ongoing assessment process. As in all other areas of clinical and research involvement with adolescents, assessments improve in efficiency and quality if their referral questions are stated clearly and their aims and purposes are well planned before the process begins. The examiner must consider the appropriateness and limitations of his or her preferred approaches and methods vis-à-vis the assessment purposes and referral questions under investigation. As noted by Costello (1985), "it is as important for clinical practice as for research that an assessment is of acknowledged validity, and that the conclusions drawn are not merely the individual clinician's idiosyncratic responses to the findings" (p. 15).

General Approaches and Purposes of Assessment

There are three distinct approaches to assessment, corresponding loosely to major theoretical orientations: projective, objective, and behavioral. Mash and Terdal (1981) have outlined the common purposes of assessment that are not specific to any one theoretical, methodological, or therapeutic orientation. These include diagnosis, design, and evaluation. Diagnostic assessments are concerned with differential diagnosis, determining the nature and extent of a problem, and administrative decision making. For example, following the assessment/intake interview at a mental health center, clinicians are often expected to have adequate information to make a DSM-III diagnosis for classification, record keeping, and possible payment purposes. Gathering information that will be relevant for selecting and formulating models of behavioral change is characteristic of the design phase of assessment. Evaluation assessments are performed for the purpose of evaluating the effectiveness of treatment, whether the changes have endured, and whether the treatments have been acceptable to the participants, both economically and subjectively. Other possible purposes for assessment include making cross-referral or placement decisions and answering legal questions, such as an adolescent's ability to understand charges being brought against him or her.

Whatever the reason for referral, for conduct-disordered adolescents the assessment of history and problem development is vital. Obviously, as adolescents are in a transitional and therefore special period of development, normative comparisons to same-age peers provide important information about appropriate psychosocial functioning. As few adolescents will present conduct problems for the first time during this period, a thorough history of the development of their disturbed conduct is essential. Releases must be signed in order to obtain results of past evaluations. In this way, it is possible to answer such questions as: What is the history of the problem behaviors? What has been tried before? Did it work? Why or why not? What interventions have not been tried?

Referral Questions

Often clinicians receive assessment requests with vaguely formed or nonspecific referral questions. One may be asked very general questions about the adolescent, such as "What makes this guy tick?", only to discover later that the assessment results are intended to form the basis of a specific decision-making process, such as a school placement, custody decision, or treatment selection. Referrals may come from the court system, a lawyer, the school system, a parent, or a mental health agency, and each expects to receive different diagnostic and prognostic information about the client.

Furthermore, the referral *source* of the conduct-disordered adolescent will greatly influence the nature and clarity of the referral question, as well as the assessment strategies selected. Court system workers may pose questions such as: "Is this boy a danger to society?" "Do you think we can trust his account or story?" "Is he telling the truth?" "Do you think he will honor the conditions of probation?" "In what situations might he become violent or dangerous?" "Did he know the difference between right and wrong when he committed the offense?" A school system may ask: "Can this student make it in a regular classroom?" "What might help maintain this boy in our school system rather than referring him for out-of-school placement?" "What are the factors that might explain his achievement problems?" A counselor or other therapist may ask: "Tell me about the underlying dynamics or personality issues relevant to treatment." "Can this kid make use of treatment?" "How can I help this guy?" "Do you think he is a sociopath?" "Does he have a conscience or feel any guilt?" "What is he capable of emotionally and in relationships?" "Can we push her in treatment, or will she fall apart?" "Do you think he needs inpatient therapy?" Finally, a parent might ask: "What's wrong with him?" "Why does she act the way she does?" "Do you think my boy is on drugs?" "Is he crazy?" "Where have I gone wrong?" "Doesn't she understand how she makes so much trouble for herself?" "His dad was just the same. Could it be genetic?"

Clearly, many of these referral questions have little utility in guiding the assessment process because there are no reliable and valid ways to answer them. As noted by others (e.g., Palmer, 1983; Sattler, 1982), it is essential to discuss the reasons for the assessment and the specific referral questions with the referral source rather than relying on referral forms or brief discussion. During this consultation, the skilled clinician can familiarize the referring agent with the inherent values and limitations of conduct disorder assessment. The referral source should be informed of the nature of the results that he or she can realistically expect for this assessment. As such, the referral discussion can be used as a negotiation process, whereby the clinician and referral agent work toward increasingly realistic referral questions.

As a specific example, assume that a court probation officer wants to know if a 15-year-old male is lying about his denial of involvement in a vandalism incident. Clearly, the referral agent should be informed that there is no way that this information can be gathered from psychological or behavioral assessment, unless the boy decides to confess in the process. On the other hand, it is possible, by comparing historical information gathered in the referral process to interview data gathered from the adolescent, to note incidences or tendencies to misrepresent, forget, deny, distort, or minimize past events. By using various interview techniques or behavioral observations, the assessor might be able to determine if the boy is "rebellious or negativistic" to the extent that he might lie. Similarly, the use of a personality inventory may reveal a tendency to "fake good" or to present himself in an unrealistically favorable light, conforming to social conventions. Behavior checklists and rating scales, completed by various significant adults who know the adolescent, might provide some converging evidence about how others perceive the boy's past behavioral tendencies.

Domains

The domains pertinent for assessment of conduct disorders can range from "narrow band, high fidelity" to "broad band, low fidelity." Narrow-band, high-fidelity approaches assess very specific personality characteristics, such as temper tantrums, whereas broad-band, low-fidelity approaches tap comprehensive or "whole person" characteristics such as overall adjustment (Kleinmuntz, 1982). These two approaches are often used to complement each other.

To begin, the clinician must become aware of the cardinal indicators of conduct-disordered behaviors and assess for the presence or absence of these. According to factor analytic studies (e.g., Achenbach & Edelbrock, 1979), there are at least nine frequently found characteristics of aggressive conduct in males aged 12 to 16 years: threatens people, temper tantrums, cruel to others, disobedient at home, swears, argues, attacks people, stubborn, and teases. For 12- to 16-year-old girls, the following behaviors are characteristic: temper tantrums, loudness, stubbornness, screaming, teasing, threatening people, arguing, excessively demanding attention, cruel to others, and disobedient at home. The presence or absence of these behaviors can be assessed by administering behavior rating scales to significant adults who know the adolescent well, and/or by using standardized observation forms, interview data, or self-report information. As noted by Kazdin (1985), some of these behaviors may, as a function of developmental maturation and the course of the disorder, decline while others emerge over time. This makes a broader assessment necessary in order to evaluate the nature and stability of change.

Clinicians should also be aware of the previously described principal correlates of the "typical" adolescent referred for conduct disorders or oppositional behaviors. Such knowledge allows for "educated guesses" and more efficient predictions about domains of behavior and functioning to be considered during the assessment. Usually these adolescents have multiple problems, not just one maladaptive behavior. Therefore, conduct-disordered adolescents are clearly at risk for problems in many other areas as well (Kazdin, 1985), and these should not be overlooked in the assessment process. For example, the clinician should always consider exploring collateral problems in the following areas: substance abuse; peer relationship difficulties; sexual difficulties or inappropriate sexual behaviors (acting-out, exploitive); academic difficulties; vocational problems; medical complications or contributing factors requiring referral for medical screening (such as seizures or neurological difficulties); neuropsychological problems; legal difficulties; family system difficulties; parental alcoholism or drug abuse; other forms of parental psychopathology; and the presence of emotional, physical, or sexual abuse of the adolescent. Finally, the assessor should attend to other forms of adolescent psychopathology, such as attention deficit disorder, psychotic behaviors, or impulsiveness. Even seemingly incompatible problems, such as dysphoria, depression (Puig-Antich, 1982), or suicidal behavior/ideation (Husain & Vandiver, 1984), may coexist with adolescent conduct disorders.

In assessing the presence or absence of the cardinal indicators and associated difficulties of adolescent conduct disorders, it is important to remember that the behavioral data reflecting disordered conduct are specific to the setting and the informant (source), in that there are specific "response topographies" (Mischel, 1972). In other words, negative findings about the presence of threats to others, temper tantrums, or acts of cruelty and disobedience in school should not lead the examiner to rule out automatically their occurrence in the home. Ollendick and Hersen (1984) note that moderate behavioral consistency (for any behavior) can be expected across situations that (a) share similar stimulus and response characteristics and (b) are temporally related. Nonetheless, the possible cross-situational specificity of problem behaviors requires an assessment process that includes multiple informants (numerous teachers at school, both parents), across multiple settings (school, home, playground, clinic), using multiple methods of assessment (inventories, interviews, rating scales, observations).

The Assessment Process

The assessment process for adolescents displaying conduct problems should not be a rigid, mechanical process, but rather a creative endeavor that occurs in several stages within a complex interpersonal and/or interagency context (Sundberg, 1977). Following a decision to accept the referral, the clinician makes a choice of appropriate strategies and methods. As these are employed, the assessor actively processes and interprets the information gained, and this feedback may lead to a reevaluation of methods. This decision, such as opting to include an assessment of the family environment, may need to be communicated to the referral source. Finally, the assessor organizes the elicited information and chooses a method for presenting the results to all concerned parties. Ideally, the assessor should also receive feedback or reactions to the assessment report.

It is important to acknowledge that during the assessment a "triangular relationship" may develop between the assessor, the referral source, and the adolescent client. These relationships can be even more complex, as they often include several agencies and the adolescent's parents. Frequently the factors that require understanding and clarification reside not only in the nature of the adolescent's problems, but equally in the nature of the relationships between the adolescent, his or her parents, and the various social agencies or legal services that have become involved in their lives (Kaplan, 1969).

A basic difficulty between the assessor and the referral source can be the negotiation or clarification of the role each will take in dealing with the adolescent's problems. Along with the referral questions and the purposes for the evaluation, the assessor should become aware of the referral agent's attitudes toward and relationship with the adolescent. Most importantly, the assessor must take steps to distinguish his or her relationship with the referral source from the pending relationship with the client (Palmer, 1983). Relevant questions to address prior to assessment are "Should the adolescent or someone else be considered the client?", "What are the client's due process rights?", and "Whose interests are being served by conducting this assessment?"

For reasons that include professional ethics, client trust, and examiner and family cooperation, one must explain carefully the reasons the referral source has requested the assessment. This obviously must be done in a manner that the adolescent can understand. For example, "I've been asked by your caseworker to find out more about your angry outbursts. He said that you've been in several fights recently and may get kicked out of school. I'd like to talk to you about this and hopefully help you by offering some recommendations. What do you think about this? Do you think we can work together to make things better for you?" Success of the assessment depends heavily on the cooperation of the adolescent client, and that cooperation depends, in part, on being fully informed.

Ethical Issues

As implied previously, there are significant complex ethical issues involved in the assessment of adolescents with conduct disorders. As noted by Rekers (1984) and as stated in the *Ethical Standards for Psychologists* (American Psychological Association, 1981), the professional must protect the client's welfare by 1) providing full and appropriate information about the assessment or intervention planned, 2) providing for confidentiality, and 3) assuring the client's freedom of choice with regard to participation in the procedures.

When assessing adolescents, the implications of these standards are often ambiguous and complex. Legal and ethical issues, such as the client's right to confidentiality, the right to consent or dissent to assessment or treatment, and the right to know the results of the evaluation are complicated by several factors: (a) whether the adolescent can make voluntary, informed, and competent decisions; (b) whether his or her parents have total access to test results; and (c) the occasional inconsistency between ethical standards and the legal codes within the state concerned. Clearly, these are issues the clinician should explore before assessment begins. While a general review of these issues is beyond the scope of this chapter, the reader is referred to Glenn (1980), Grisso and Vierling (1978), Melton (1981), Plotkin (1981), and Ross (1980).

Selecting and Using Appropriate Assessment Instruments

Aside from the considerations previously highlighted, there are other important factors in selecting appropriate tests for the assessment of an adolescent's functioning. Although a test's general psychometric properties are important, it is more crucial that the test be reliable and valid for the specific purposes and populations to be examined by the clinician. A related issue with adolescent clients concerns selecting assessment techniques that were developed for use with children or adults. Even if a given procedure has demonstrated validity when utilized with 6- to 10-year-old children, for example, the results derived from use with adolescents would be of unknown validity. By failing to make such considerations, the clinician potentially introduces a large degree of error into his or her conclusions.

Interviews. The interview is such a widely used assessment procedure across settings, professional orientations, problems, and populations that it has been termed the universal method of data collection (O'Leary & Johnson, 1979). One reason for this popularity is the fact that interviews (at least the unstructured variety) require no formal test materials and can be conducted in the clinician's office. However, they also have some advantages beyond convenience. Interviews are broad-band data collection methods in that they (a) permit a survey of a wide variety of topics and (b) allow for behavioral observations (e.g., verbal style, social skills) that supplement the content of client responses. Further, interviews are flexible enough to allow in-depth coverage of selected topics that might be missed or summarily covered by another assessment device. In addition, some individuals may be more willing to divulge information orally than to provide a permanent written record (Linehan, 1977). In short, the interview can be an excellent data source for understanding presenting problems, certain exacerbating conditions, parent-child interactions, and the context of family circumstances. Interviews can be useful in suggesting treatment regimens and in providing clues about motivation for change.

Interviews can be set up to include the client and/or members of the family. With conduct-disordered adolescents, it is useful also to include an interview with the parents, preferably both, without the client present (Doke & Flippo, 1983). This allows for a freer discussion of symptoms and complaints, while a subsequent conjoint interview allows for observation of parent-child interaction. An interview with the adolescent alone is also recommended to gain his or her perspectives on the problems and process.

Interview procedures, of course, are subject to problems with cooperation, inaccuracy, or falsification of reports. For example, information provided by parents may be biased toward precocity (Hetherington & Martin, 1979) or simply be inaccurate (Schnelle, 1974). It has been suggested that having parents report specific elements (e.g., verbal threats) rather than trait labels or global judgments (e.g., negativism or defiance) will result in increased accuracy (O'Leary & Johnson, 1979).

Whether the adolescent, the parents, or the entire family is being interviewed, the interviewer should be concerned initially with facilitating rapport. A light, relatively neutral tone should characterize early interchanges, and discussions of confidentiality and its limits should be included. It is often useful to begin by having interview subjects express their perceptions of why the referral was made. It may be informative to investigate the causal attributions of the perceived problems. Parents, for example, might describe home conditions or societal influences, or they may stress genetic/organic factors. This technique provides information about how plausible the individuals involved will find initial treatment suggestions. Along the same line, it is also important to ascertain what has been tried previously to remediate the problem. Parents also can report useful data on the feelings family members hold for each other, family stressors and resources, and the degree of family insularity (Wahler, 1980).

With the adolescent, the interviewer should also inquire about patterns of interest and recreation, peer relations, and social awareness (see Simmons, 1974). It is unclear how the degree of formality of interview style and setting affects a child's self-disclosure (see Mader & Quevillon, 1984). Current recommendations are to establish rapport carefully and to balance professional decorum with a relaxed interview style. Although research on the validity of interview data has produced contradictory findings (Gross, 1984), interviews have the wide range and flexibility to be extremely useful assessment procedures, particularly if used in conjunction with other devices.

In addition to the basic, unstructured interview, a number of structured and semistructured procedures exist. Of these, certain diagnosis-oriented interviews are relevant to conduct disorders. The Schedule for Affective Disorders and Schizophrenia for School-Age Children (Kiddie-SADS or K-SADS; Chambers, Puig-Antich, & Tabrizi, 1978) is a semistructured interview requiring separate discussions with both the adolescent and his or her parents regarding the presence of symptoms. The K-SADS takes 45-90 minutes to complete and leads to a tentative diagnosis. Some symptoms are rated for severity on a 1-4 or 1-7 scale, while others are noted simply as "present" or "absent." Modeled after the adult SADS (Endicott & Spitzer, 1978), the K-SADS includes a Conduct Disordered category.

Herjanic and Welner's Diagnostic Interview for Children and Adolescents (DICA; see Herjanic, 1980) is a structured interview designed to be used with individuals aged 9 to 17. A parent form also exists. The DICA takes 1 to 1½ hours to complete and assesses psychiatric symptomatology through the adolescent's history. It begins with questions about demographics and progresses to school functioning, home relations, and interpersonal conduct. The DICA also yields information related to diagnostic categorization, including conduct disorders.

A third appropriate instrument was developed with particular reference to the DSM-III classification system. This structured interview, the Diagnostic Interview Schedule for Children (DIS-C; Radloff, 1982) was designed to aid in diagnosis when used by trained paraprofessionals or clinicians. Now in its second revision, the DIS-C is being developed by the National Institute of Mental Health as part of its Children's Epidemiology Program for mental disorders.

More work is needed on all of these interviews before their potential for wide clinical usage is realized. For more information on structured interviews, the reader is encouraged to consult a recent review (National Institute of Mental Health, 1980).

Self-report measures. Omnibus personality measures and problem-oriented self-report scales for adolescents are not central to the assessment of psychological disturbance as are their adult counterparts. Although most adolescents can complete these devices without assistance, the fact that these clients have not been self-referred in most cases and may not recognize a personal problem can affect their ability or willingness to describe their problems accurately. When attention is paid to the client's motivation, response set, and reading level, the self-report modality can provide considerable assessment information.

The following discussion will focus on four relevant self-report measures for the assessment of adolescent conduct disorders. The reader is referred to Finch and Rogers (1984) for more exhaustive converage of general child and adolescent self-report methods, to Bornstein, Schuldberg, and Bornstein (in press), and to Doke and Flippo (1983) for additional inventories appropriate for data-gathering on aggression, oppositional behavior, or conduct disorders.

The Minnesota Multiphasic Personality Inventory (MMPI) was developed as an aid to adult psychiatric diagnosis. In this context, it continues to be the most widely used and thoroughly studied personality test for both clinical assessment and psychopathology research. More importantly for this chapter, the MMPI has attained both wide usage with older adolescents (Archer, 1984) as well as strengths that warrant examination. Use of the MMPI with adolescents referred for conduct problems follows the same practices recommended for adults (Graham, 1977; Lachar, 1974). Separate norms exist for 14-, 15-, 16-, and 17-year-old males and females, while subjects 18 and older are compared to adult norm groups.

Some controversy exists about the validity of scales and normative comparisons when the MMPI is used with adolescents. With adult profiles, significant elevations obtained on the Cannot Say (?), Lie (L), Frequency (F), and Correction (K) scale invalidate the clinical profile, confining interpretation to a discussion of unusual response sets or test administration problems. Although unusual validity indices obtained from adolescents continue to be of concern, it is not clear that adult cutoffs should prompt the examiner to "throw out" the clinical profile. For example, Meehl (1956) has suggested that a raw score of 16 or greater on scale F should cause the results to be considered invalid. In the experience of these chapter authors, however, this criterion causes the invalidation of an inordinate number of adolescent profiles (see also Archer, White, & Orvin, 1979). In the major interpretative guide for adolescents, Marks, Seeman, and Haller (1974) make no specific provisions for invalidation on the basis of ?, L, and K scales, proposing only that F raw scores of 26 or greater are cause for validity concerns. The present recommendation is that the assessor working with adolescents be aware of validity indices, but be flexible with regard to specified adult cutoffs.

The issue of whether to use age-appropriate or adult norms is also important and somewhat controversial (Archer, 1984). Some writers (e.g., Hathaway & Monachesi, 1963) have stated that adult norms are preferred primarily because 1) most code type correlates and discriptors have been generated on adult samples, 2) special age norms serve to reduce the contrast between adults and adolescents, and 3) high base-rate psychopathological traits in adolescents might be obscured. However, despite these arguments, the present authors agree with Archer (1984), who endorses the use of age-appropriate norms to increase the accuracy of interpretations and reduce the risk of over-diagnosing pathology. In some cases, however, it will be of additional interest to compare an adolescent's MMPI responses to adult criteria. The specific referral or research questions under investigation and the nature of the criterion to be predicted will determine the choice of an adolescent or adult norm group.

The major MMPI resource when working with conduct-disordered adolescents is the Marks et al. (1974) text, which includes narratives and descriptive data on 29 adolescent code types. Not surprisingly, most code types relevant to conduct disorders involve Scale 4 (Psychopathic Deviate, PD), which originally was derived on adolescents and young adults who were court-referred for delinquent or antisocial acts (Hathaway & McKinley, 1940). Examples of items similar to those keyed on Scale 4 include "My parents are on my back more often than they should be" (keyed true), "No one understands me" (keyed true), and " I enjoyed school" (keyed false).

Many experts (see, for example, Graham, 1977) suggest that MMPI interpretation should involve a two-point code approach; that is, an examination of the two highest clinical scales in the profile. If Scale 9 (Mania; Ma) is elevated significantly along with Scale 4 (4-9/9-4 profiles), a range of antisocial and/or aggressive acts is suggested, though often in an adolescent who has some social skills and attachments (peers rather than family). The 4-5/5-4 code type is similar, but if drug abuse is present, it may more often be multiple-drug experimentation. Many of the adolescents in the Marks et al. (1974) sample obtaining 4-0/0-4 high point codes were less sociable, but still experiencing authority problems.

A particular strength of the MMPI lies in its ability to suggest additional topics warranting exploration. For example, an adolescent with a Scale 3 (Hysteria; Hy) along with and elevated Scale 4 (i.e., 3-4/4-3) should be carefully assessed for suicide risk. This is also true of 4-8/8-4 and 2-8/8-2 profiles, according to the Marks et al., (1974) narratives. The latter profile also illustrates the utility of the MMPI in suggesting diagnostic alternatives. Although an adolescent showing the 2-8/8-2 code type might be referred for conduct problems such as truancy or drug use, they are in fact more likely to be involved with difficulties outside the conduct disorder realm. Thought disorder, severe depression, social eccentricities, and alienation are characteristic of 2-8/8-2 adolescents. Thus, the MMPI may uncover an alternative explanation to conduct-problems referral.

Unlike the MMPI, the multiple-scale California Psychological Inventory (CPI) is designed to measure normal personality styles and traits rather than psychopathology. The 480-item CPI was constructed in a fashion similar to the MMPI, shares a number of items with the latter, and as such also shares most of the test construction weaknesses attributed to the MMPI. However, the CPI normative sample (high school and college students) makes it easier to relate to adolescent clients. The CPI scales with relevance to conduct-disordered adolescents include Socialization (So), which was developed using delinquent and nondelinquent contrast groups, Self-control (Sc), and Responsibility (Re). In addition, Megargee (1972) has written a handbook for the CPI in which he reports significant differential responding by delinquent groups on several scales. Besides the scales already mentioned, one also should note the Well-being (Wb), Tolerance (To), and Achievement via Conformity (Ac) scales, which tend to reflect lower scores for conduct-disordered groups. Like the MMPI, the CPI is subject to deviant response sets and problems in test-taking cooperation. It can, however, provide a wide range of descriptive statements regarding client traits and response tendencies (see, for example, Megargee, 1972).

A number of other self-report instruments are available for the assessment of adolescent conduct disorder (see Bornstein et al., in press; Doke & Flippo, 1983; Wells, 1981), and two will be briefly described here. The 155-item Jesness Inventory has particular relevance for delinquent behavior. Examples of its scales are Manifest Aggression and Social Maladjustment. Although much of the validation work with the Jesness Inventory has involved the California I-Level classification system (Jesness & Wedge, 1984), its focus on conduct-disordered youth may make it a scale of more general interest. Secondly, the Child Behavior Checklist (CBCL) includes a Youth Self-Report Form, designed to be filled out by youngsters aged 11 to 18 years. This form includes 102 behavioral problem items from the CBCL that have been reworded into a first-person format and 16 (unscored) neutral self-referent statements. Items are scored 0 (not true), 1 (somewhat or sometimes true), or 2 (very or often true). The reliability data reported in the manual (Achenbach & Edelbrock, 1983) are sparse and there are no provisions yet for scoring profiles. However, use of the Youth Self-Report Form allows for a direct comparison of self-reports with parent and teacher ratings of symptomatic behaviors.

Rating scales. In the assessment of conduct disorders, several useful devices exist that involve the ratings of significant others regarding the adolescent client. Many of these instruments offer high levels of objectivity, reliability, and validity, making them important additions to any assessment battery. By drawing information from significant others, rating scales can circumvent many problems with cooperation and/or falsification of responses, which can foil assessment efforts when the adolescent is the informant. Many rating scales are brief and convenient to administer, making them amenable to repeated administrations to assess short-term changes in conduct problems and aggressiveness. Unfortunately, empirical support for the sensitivity of these measures to behavior changes over brief time periods is lacking at present, making their usefulness as measures of treatment effects tenuous.

One criticism of this popular methodology is inaccuracy, in that informants report impressions based on unsystematic observations and recall. As such, ratings reflect the problems usually attributed to retrospective data collection. Further, these scales vary widely in their item objectivity (Walls, Werner, Bacon, & Zane, 1977). However, with clearly specified objective referents, informants can do a better job of accurately describing the adolescent's behavior. The most reliable rating scales emphasize observable and discrete problem behaviors in their items rather than trait-like terms. A related criticism of this method reflects the relative lack of correspondence between ratings and direct behavioral observations. Home observations by trained observers often differ from parent ratings of child deviance (Lobitz & Johnson, 1975), possibly suggesting that rating scales are subject to influence by additional factors, such as marital dissatisfaction (see Oltmanns, Broderick, & O'Leary, 1977).

In defense of rating scales, however, it should be noted that they perform well in sorting deviant and normal youth when defined by referral status. While behavioral observations of samples of normal and deviant children have tended to show considerable overlap among the two groups (Delfini, Bernal, & Rosen, 1976), rating scales have proven highly accurate in discriminating normal from clinic-referred conduct-disturbed youth (Lobitz & Johnson, 1975). Thus, although rating scale scores might indeed be influenced by external factors leading to negative attitudes on the part of raters, these "extraneous" factors may play an important role in the process of referral and therefore should be considered an integral part of the assessment.

Although the range of possible informants includes hospital staff (e.g., Curtiss et al., 1983) and sociometric ratings by peers (e.g., Prinz, Swan, Liebert, Weintraub, & Neale, 1978), this discussion will cover only those scales involving teacher and parent reports, as these are the most extensively developed instruments. Because many include both a teacher and a parent form, or else use the same scale for either respondent, both types of rating scales will be considered together. More information is available elsewhere regarding scales for psychopathology research (National Institute of Mental Health, 1980), epidemiology (Boyle & Jones, 1985), and measures of adaptive functioning (National Institute of Mental Health, 1984).

On Achenbach and Edelbrock's Child Behavior Checklist (CBCL), appropriate for children aged 4-16, parents or surrogates respond to a total of 130 items. Initial questions concern activities, social functioning, and school performance/academic problems; the remaining 118 items involve problem behaviors occurring in the past 6 months, such as teasing and threatening others. Responses are then plotted on the Child Behavior Profile, which provides an overview of the adolescent's behavior, shows how problems cluster, and makes comparisons to age/sex group norms. Norms, separated by sex, are available for 4- to 5-, 6- to 11-, and 12- to 16-year-olds. The CBCL is also available in a Teacher's Report Form (TRF), designed to be completed by the youth's teacher using a 2-month reference period. Most TRF items are identical to those on the parent form, although some have been reworded and others replaced to reflect behaviors more accessible to teachers. For example, the item relating to allergies was dropped and one about making odd noises in class added.

Edelbrock and Achenbach (1984) are in the process of constructing profiles based on these teacher ratings. The Externalizing scales for boys aged 6 to 11 years, the only group for which teacher norms are currently available, are Aggressive, Nervous-Overactive, and Inattentive.

The 55-item Behavior Problem Checklist (BPC), a scale for assessing behavioral/emotional disturbance, was designed for 5- to 17-year-olds and is typically used with parents, teachers, or other professionals serving as informants. Examples of items similar to those on the BPC are "stays out past curfew," "is noisy," and "gets in fights." Completion time of approximately 10 minutes and brief scoring time make the BPC applicable as a screening instrument as well as part of the assessment battery. The BPC has four subscales: Conduct Problem, Personality Problem, Inadequacy-Immaturity, and Socialized Delinquency. A fifth scale, Psychotic Behavior, consists of four items that are less important in quantifying a construct than they are in serving as "flag" or "critical" items; if any are present (e.g., incoherent speech), a comprehensive evaluation of the adolescent is indicated. Recently, the BPC has undergone another revision (Aman & Werry, 1984; Quay, 1983; Quay & Peterson, 1983), which has increased the number of items to 150, increased the number of factors to six, and expanded the rating format. However, until the psychometric characteristics of the BPC-R have been fully established, its clinical utility remains to be seen.

C. Keith Conners has developed rating scales using parent and teacher reports to screen for behavior disorders, particularly hyperactivity, in children and adolescents. The Conners Parent Symptom Questionnaire (PSQ) is a revision of an earlier instrument that included 93 behavior problem items (eating problems, sleep difficulties, etc.) and a final global rating of problem severity. The revised 48-item version includes items similar to "Talks back to grown-ups" rated on a 4-point scale. Factor analysis has yielded six factors, including Conduct Anxiety, and Impulsivity/Hyperactivity (Goyette, Conners, & Ulrich, 1978). The PSQ is brief and has attained rather wide usage, especially in research settings. It is a useful screening device in general, and provides a means to judge the adolescent's level of hyperactivity if the clinician is interested in ruling out these problems. The original 39-item Conners Teacher Rating Scale (TRS) contains clusters for classroom behavior, group participation, and attitudes toward authority. The revision shortened the TRS to 28-items (Goyette et al., 1978). The factors obtained on the revised scale yield three indices: Conduct Problems, Hyperactivity, and Inattentive/Passive. Psychometric studies using both Conners scales have produced positive results (Barkley, 1981). These scales are convenient and especially appropriate for externalizing types of problems.

Two other rating scales that merit attention are the Louisville Behavior Checklist (LBC) and the Personality Inventory for Children (PIC). The 164 behaviors rated on the LBC comprise eight subscales, including Antisocial, Infantile Aggression, and Social Withdrawal. Despite the fact that the LBC has, to date, obtained a less impressive psychometric background than some of the previously discussed scales, its clinical derivation and potential utility make it a useful instrument. A teacher-completed version measuring school behaviors is also available (Miller, 1972), but its age ceiling of 12 years restricts its utility in the present context.

The PIC queries behavior, attitudes, and family relationships and yields three validity scales, one screening scale of general maladjustment, and 12 clinical scales, including Delinquency, Social Skills, Achievement, and Family Relations. Supplemental scales are also available, with Aggression, Asocial Behavior, Adolescent Maladjustment, Externalization, and Delinquency Prediction being of particular relevance to the diagnosis of conduct disorders. The PIC would be of most benefit here if validation studies were conducted with conduct-disordered adolescents. Additionally, this inventory may be too long, especially when readministered to monitor treatment gains. Furthermore, the PIC may be difficult for parent informants with low reading levels. However, the excellent range of coverage and its thorough initial standardization make the PIC well worth considering as part of an assessment battery.

Projective techniques. The use of projective tests to assess childhood behavior disorders is a controversial topic. While numerous criticisms of their use have been voiced (e.g., Gittleman, 1980), these procedures continue to be very popular among personality researchers, clinicians, and school psychologists (e.g., Goh & Fuller, 1983). However, if these instruments are to be useful, the evaluator must be skilled in their interpretation. Projective techniques are often better for generating hypotheses about aspects of an adolescent's functioning than for making specific behavioral predictions, such as the likelihood of future aggressive outbursts (see Gittleman, 1980). Because of the increased level of inference involved in projective testing, the assessor must gather convergent evidence from various instruments before placing confidence in a case interpretation.

The Rorschach Inkblot Test can provide substantial information about conduct-disordered adolescents. Because of the developmental differences in the validity of Rorschach signs, Exner and Weiner (1982) point out that one must take age carefully into account when interpreting obtained results. New norms for the Comprehensive System have been compiled (Exner, 1985) to aid in this process. Using Exner's scoring system (for clients aged 12 or above), Rorschach signs of interest include white space (S) responses, suggesting need for autonomy/oppositional tendencies; color-dominated responses (C or CF), suggesting impulsivity; and high egocentricity index scores, suggesting self-absorption. Also important are indicators of response style such as the "Four Square" indices (see Exner, 1978). Use of specific indices is a more defensible approach than impressionistic interpretations not based on normative comparisions.

The Thematic Apperception Test (TAT) has been used extensively with aggressive and conduct-disturbed adolescents. Although research findings regarding overt aggression predictions based on TAT themes have ranged from mixed to nonsupportive (Gittleman, 1980; Matranga, 1976), the test may be useful in gauging need states, attitudes toward authority, interpersonal orientation, and family issues (Holt, 1978). Interpretation of TAT stories must be tempered by knowledge that some cards pull certain contents, like aggression or family conflict (see Holt, 1978); that is, a story's aggressive theme may have been elicited to a degree by the stimulus card. In addition, cultural influences, examiner biases, and special client characteristics (e.g., IQ) influence TAT results (Dana, 1966, 1985).

Although most projective techniques have not been sufficiently validated with conduct-disordered youth to warrant their inclusion, one possible exception is the 40-item Rotter Incomplete Sentences Blank (ISB). Objective scoring, an adjustment index, and extensive high school norms make the ISB attractive to an examiner, although cooperation on the part of the adolescent subject is obviously necessary. Like all projectives, the ISB lacks evidence to support its diagnostic accuracy.

Behavioral observations. Systematic behavioral observation offers the most direct method of assessing the behavior of conduct-disordered adolescents. Using this procedure, which is based on observing problem behaviors over time and recording some aspect(s) of the response (e.g., frequency, duration, etc.), very little inference is required to bridge the gap between the measurement results and the actual behavior/problems of the referred youth. This feature is a major advantage, and behavioral observations have been a dominant method of assessing the effects of behavior modification programs. Direct observations, thorough, can be technically demanding and difficult to implement, particularly with target behaviors of extremely low frequency or those that are difficult to observe (e.g., fire setting, stealing).

Behavioral observations can be conducted in the home, school, community, or clinic. Either trained observers or parents and teachers can record responses. In either case, though, clear operational definitions specifying the behaviors to be observed are an important element for accurate recording. Specifying the behaviors of interest in desirable terms can contribute to valid, reliable measurement (see Johnson & Bolstad, 1973, for a review of issues in observation accuracy). Tailoring an observation scheme to individual needs can also contribute to a useful data collection. For example, if frequency over time is being used, the length of the appropriate time interval depends on the characteristics of the behavior. Low frequency events, such as running away from home or physical aggression, require a broader time scale to be representative of the adolescent's status. While frequency counts are most useful for moderately low-base-rate behaviors, alternative observation schemes are suited to other circumstances.

For behaviors that are continuous or of very high frequency, time sampling or spot-check strategies can be employed. At regular intervals or predesignated points cued by a timer, observers can code whether a behavior is present or absent. Usually the output is in terms of percentage of observations in which the target behavior was present (Barlow, Hayes, & Nelson, 1984). Formal behavior coding systems, which will be discussed, often employ time sampling.

At times it is possible to enhance observational assessment by determining optimal times to observe the behavior of interest, such as compliance with requests and instructions (see Browning & Stover, 1971). Cuing observation to the opportunities to comply and recording the percent of requests obeyed can provide an accurate index of this target behavior. In other instances, target responses might be primed to occur. If the assessor is aware of setting conditions that might elicit the response of interest (e.g., verbal aggression), steps may be taken to ensure their presence. One example involves bringing in mother-adolescent dyads to discuss topics that characteristically produce conflict (see Bright & Robin, 1981).

Finally, some target behaviors might be assessed best via temporal indices rather than frequency or presence/absence. For example, duration may be important, as in timing the length of arguments or verbal tirades. Latency might also be employed, such as recording the amount of time it takes to comply with instructions.

At its best, behavioral observation provides assessment data with unparalleled directness and treatment relevance. However, such schemes tax the assessor's ingenuity in making them practical. The formal coding systems outlined hereafter illustrate the extension of this modality to the point where exemplary assessment occurs, but the systems are so complex that trained observers and substantial resources are a prerequisite. For this reason, despite their obvious strengths, these procedures are seldom used in clinical settings except for research purposes.

Although several available behavioral coding systems are relevant to conduct-disordered youth (see Wells, 1981, for a review), only two will be covered here. The first, developed by Patterson and others at the Oregon Research Institute, was designed to assess parent-child interactions in the homes of families with aggressive youth. As detailed by Reid (1978), this coding system includes 29 target behavior types, geared primarily for home observations although other settings (i.e., school and clinic) have been employed. Interval time-sampling (30-second periods) is used, and observers record symbols representing the behaviors of the target adolescent and other family members interacting with him or her. Behaviors such as aggression, yelling, and compliance are coded present or absent for the adolescent, while parent codes involve ignoring, put-downs, or showing approval. Although the Oregon coding system is highly complex and requires trained observers, an impressive case for its validity has been established (Patterson, 1982) that makes the system worth considering.

Substantial work on a second behavioral coding system has been carried out by Forehand and his colleagues at the University of Georgia. This system is somewhat specialized and therefore limited in generalizability. The Georgia group has focused on compliance/noncompliance and has developed few codes for other conduct disturbances (see Forehand et al., 1979). In addition, they have employed a clinic setting most often for the dyadic interactions, though the home is also a possible observation site. The strength of the Georgia system is in the match between parent behaviors and child compliance or lack thereof. Further, these researchers distinguish between parental commands where compliance is appropriate and those that are ineffective or unrealistic. If oppositional behavior is of central importance in the assessment, consideration of this coding system is recommended (see Forehand & McMahon, 1981, for training materials).

CASE STUDY

An integrative approach using multiple data sources is clearly superior to any of the previously described approaches used alone. The following case report illustrates such an integrative assessment.

Nina S., a 16-year-old girl from a midwestern city, was seen for a comprehensive psychological evaluation and therapy at the request of her father. Presenting problems at the time of evaluation included a three-year history of progressively escalating noncompliant and conduct-disordered behaviors. During this period Nina was in the custody of her biological mother, following the divorce of her parents. In the month prior to the evaluation, Nina had engaged in a variety of especially problematic antisocial behaviors. Her mother characterized her behavior during this time as increasingly oppositional, unmanageable, violent, and argumentative. Nina also was frequently truant from school, was staying out all night, and was suspected of thefts of money from the home. Her mother reported a series of escalating arguments in which

Nina was physically violent toward her, pushing and shoving her across the room. These arguments appeared to be in part precipitated by discussions about her mother's decision not to take Nina along when she moved to another state for employment. The week before Nina's father contacted the clinic, Nina had stolen merchandise valued at over $4,000 from the store in which she and her mother were employed. She then pawned the merchandise, using part of the money to reimburse her mother for an outstanding debt of $200. The theft was discovered in a routine police check. Following the discovery of the theft by the authorities, Nina disappeared from her mother's home before police could interview her. Two days after the authorities had contacted her mother, Nina telephoned both parents, admitted her guilt, and agreed to return home.

History

Nina's developmental history appeared relatively unremarkable with the exception of two hospitalizations, the first for an electrolyte imbalance at age 1 and the second for an appendectomy and resultant infection at age 6. Developmental milestones were achieved within normal limits. No disturbances of sleep, eating, or elimination were noted. Nina's father, the primary informant, did, however, report a history of high activity level during infancy and early childhood. He also indicated that Nina had experienced difficulty in relating to other children from early childhood on and continued to have difficulty maintaining friendships that lasted for more than a few months. Academically her performance in elementary school had been average (Cs and Bs), although she had received remediation for an identified reading disability in the second and third grades. Nina's academic performance changed substantially when she entered high school, however, with grades dropping sharply (Cs, Ds, and Fs and a class rank of 173/222). Truancy also became a greater problem (30 days of absence in the tenth grade), and there was an increase of behavior problems in the classroom. School difficulties prompted a transfer to a private school during the first semester of ninth grade, but Nina's mother was asked to remove her daughter from the school after one year of enrollment due to recurring problems. Nina then completed the remainder of tenth grade at a third school, before her move to the community in which her father lives.

When Nina was 7 her parents began to experience difficulties in their marriage. A turbulent period followed, characterized by alcohol abuse, open infidelity, and frequent arguments. Over a five-year period the parents separated and reconciled several times. Nina's father, a successful businessman, also underwent individual treatment for alcohol abuse and eventually recovered, although the marriage ended in divorce. Nina's parents divorced when she was 12 and arranged for joint custody of their two children. Her older brother, aged 14, lived with her father in their hometown and Nina moved to another city with her mother. Soon after the divorce Nina's father became involved with another woman, whom he married three years later. Nina visited her father and stepmother frequently and appeared to get along well with her stepmother. The nature of her relationship with her mother appeared to be more that of a friend-roommate than a mother-daughter relationship. Although her mother was active socially, she did not remarry. While living with her mother Nina was not given a curfew or any other rules. She was expected to hold a part-time job, contribute to her tuition at the private school she attended, and pay for some of her clothes and basic necessities (haircuts, toothpaste, shampoo, etc.).

Nina's father indicated that although he did not criticize Nina's mother in front of her, he felt that she had not done an adequate job in supervising their daughter. Although he had wanted to retain custody of her at the time of the divorce, he had been told by his attorney that he would be unlikely to get custody of both children and so did not pursue it. He had, however, informally indicated to his wife that he would like to have Nina live with him. He stated in an individual interview that he believed his former wife was immature and self-centered. He also indicated that she had told him in the year prior to her impending move that she did not want the responsibility of caring for Nina any longer. He reported that since moving in with him and his second wife Nina was well-behaved, but he was being very strict, providing a highly structured environment, and had established a set of rules for Nina to follow. He did feel some anxiety that he might not be able to control Nina and might have to send her to a residential treatment center, because all the professionals he had consulted recently indicated a poor prognosis. He reported that they believed Nina probably could not be maintained in the community, based both on her history of disregard for rules at home and school on the increase in the number and frequency of antisocial behaviors in the past months.

Current Status

At the time of the psychological evaluation, Nina seemed to be a pleasant, verbal, yet somewhat guarded young girl. She was slightly apprehensive and expressed concern about what the clinician might think of her. During the initial interview, in which Nina, her father, and stepmother were all present, the family members spoke openly about their concerns and the goals they hoped to accomplish as a family. Nina's father and stepmother indicated that they believed Nina had a problem with low self-esteem that contributed to her behavior problems, but stated they were optimistic that they all could make the effort to work family problems out. They appeared quite motivated. When interviewed individually, both the father and stepmother expressed considerably more concern about the seriousness of Nina's problems, especially her chronic lying, and indicated a lack of confidence in their ability to control her. They reported that they wanted Nina to have a "fresh start" and hoped the move could accomplish this. They also stated that they felt it was important to show Nina that they were aware of her accomplishments and strengths as well as her problems and could support such positive behaviors. They consequently were hesitant to express directly to Nina their doubts that she could change her problem behavior.

Nina was quite verbal during her individual interview, more so than in the presence of her father. She indicated that she felt her father was quite strict and that she was afraid of him, knowing that he would "check up" on her and distrust her due to her history of lying. Nina was clearly uncomfortable in being the identified patient and stated that her brother also had problems, although their father did not treat him in the same way. She also indicated that her father himself had had problems in the past and that she was uncertain whether he had changed, even though it appeared he had. At the time of her interview Nina was physically healthy and showed good personal hygiene and considerable attention to her appearance. Although she was open and honest in her responses to questions, she was defensive at times and tended to minimize the extent of her presenting problems while projecting blame for actions onto others or situational factors.

Nina was administered the WISC-R and obtained a Verbal IQ score of 128, a Performance IQ score of 120, and a Full Scale IQ score of 127, indicating overall functioning in the Superior range of intellectual functioning. Subtest scaled score performance ranged from Average to Superior scores. To assess academic achievement, the Wide Range Achievement Test (WRAT) was administered. Her WRAT scores indicated reading and spelling skills within normal limits, given her grade placement (Reading = 58th percentile and Spelling = 42nd percentile). However, her arithmetic score (30th percentile; grade equivalent = 8.1) indicated a marked deficiency. Comparing Nina's WISC-R and WRAT scores, it is evident that she did not show academic achievement at a level commensurate with her true ability. It was felt that to some extent Nina's lack of confidence in her abilities may have hampered her test performance. During test taking, she appeared quite anxious and concerned about her performance, making deprecatory self-evaluations. In receiving feedback about her performance, she appeared to have considerable difficulty accepting how well she had done on the WISC-R, suggesting that she "was not at all smart." She also indicated that she probably was not smart enough to attend college, in contrast to her older brother, who had been an honor student all through high school.

Nina's responses on the MMPI indicated a valid profile, with honest and accurate responses to test items. Test results appeared to corroborate other test data and were consistent with a diagnosis of conduct disorder, socialized nonaggressive. Her MMPI profile corresponded to the low 4-9 profile illustrated in Marks et al. (1974). Adolescents showing a similar test profile have presenting problems of defiant, disobedient, truant, and impulsive behaviors. The predominant presenting problem was excessive lying, which Nina's father felt to be her most serious and pervasive problem. Such adolescents are in conflict with parents over misbehavior and are difficult to control. As was the case with Nina, mothers of such adolescents are often neglectful and have problems with alcohol. Gregarious and having good interpersonal skills, adolescents like Nina are active socially in their peer group. On the basis of the MMPI, typical adjectives that could be used to describe her include *assertive, daring, impulsive, good-natured, bright,* and *pleasure-seeking.* Nina showed a tendency to act out when distressed, often without sufficient deliberation or regard for the consequences of her actions. The typical response to problem behavior is rationalization (e.g., Nina indicated that taking the store merchandise was probably not that bad because her employer had once told her she could take an article of merchandise she might especially want). Highly insecure, Nina had a strong need for approval, was narcissistic, and was overly sensitive to others' opinions of her. Demanding, with a strong need for affection, she valued wealth and material possessions and tended to judge others in those terms. She also showed an egocentrism and inability to take into account the opinions of others (especially adults with whom she came into conflict). Consistent with her MMPI profile, Nina described school as boring and had a history of truant behavior when living in the unstructured environment of her mother's home. Although she presented as healthy and symptom-free due to her use of defenses, she had a strong tendency to be argumentative and to challenge adult rules.

Nina was also administered the Beck Depression Inventory and received a raw score of 9, within the average range for her age and indicating little or mild depression. The mild elevation appeared to reflect Nina's unhappiness with herself over getting caught for the theft. Item analysis showed Nina to be feeling self-critical, disgusted with herself, and mildly guilty.

Nina's responses on the Rotter Incomplete Sentences Blank were consistent with other test data. She showed concern about evaluation by others, was self-critical, showed strong attachment to her father, and had concerns about family issues such as whether or not family members loved her.

Nina also completed the California Psychological Inventory (CPI), so that some level of positive social functioning could be obtained. Comparing her performance to that of typical high school females, eight scale scores were below the expected mean for this age (i.e., 40). Four of these below-average scores were on Class II scales, which would suggest some impairment in interpersonal adjustment, primarily as indicated in below-average socialization skills (i.e., maturity, responsibility, self-control). However, a low score on the Well-being scale indicated basic defensiveness. Above-average scores were obtained on five of the Class I scales, indicating adequately developed social skills (i.e., poised, outgoing, aggressive, and self-centered). The profile revealed an assertive, socially extroverted, self-centered, impulsive, undependable individual who is overly concerned with personal gain. Because of her superior social skills, functioning would appear adequate in the sense that she is capable of achieving her own objectives and ends. However, the deficiencies present in the areas of responsibility and interpersonal maturity would indicate probable future social difficulties. These results were highly consistent with other test data, especially those of the MMPI.

Nina's father and stepmother independently completed the Achenbach Child Behavior Checklist and the Behavior Problem Checklist. On the BPC both parents' scores were highly consistent, with scores on the Conduct Problem (CP) factor being most elevated. The scores of 5 to 7 were comparable to expected scores for a female delinquent adolescent sample. Scores on both the Personality Problem (PP) and the Socialized Delinquency (SD) factors ranged from 2 to 3. Scores on the Child Behavior Checklist were also consistent and, not surprisingly, indicated an Externalizing profile. Nina's scores (61-father; 68-stepmother) approximated the normal cutoff score of 63. The only scales for which Nina obtained a T-score greater than 70 were Scale VI, the Delinquency scale (T = 73), and Scale VIII, the Cruel scale (T = 71). This profile, with the Delinquency scale as the high point, is consistent with a DSM-III diagnosis of conduct disorder, socialized nonaggressive subtype.

This case study illustrates the use of personality inventories, interviews, projective methods (sentence completion), behavioral checklists, and intellectual and achievement measures in the assessment of an adolescent female with both oppositional and conduct-disordered behaviors. Although most test results were highly consistent, perhaps the most useful and descriptive data were obtained from the MMPI, which is likely to be the case with adolescent clients. From an etiological perspective, many of the early signs of academic problems were noted, as were family problems, although early signs of aggression in Nina's preadolescent years were absent, due in part to the primacy of covert as opposed to overt antisòcial behaviors.

A six-month follow-up indicated that Nina was functioning adequately in her new home environment, due in large part to the application of strict controls and structure by her father and stepmother. Nina was making slow but steady progress in examining values and developing social perspective taking skills in individual therapy. (See chapter 4 for an examination of the assessment of values and moral development.)

SUMMARY

There is little doubt that all psychologists eventually will encounter adolescents who present conduct disorders, as they are clearly overrepresented in the clinical setting. Even though prevalence estimates suggest a rate of approximately 6% in the general population (La Greca & Quay, 1984), these adolescents may reflect, in some settings, up to one-half of all referred children. Their presenting problems are even more compelling when one realizes that these clients are at great risk for adult anti-social and law-violating behaviors.

In a descriptive context, conduct disturbance involves physical and verbal assaults, coercive control tactics (such as tantrums), disobedience and oppositional behaviors, property destruction, and sexual acting out. These disturbed adolescents create stress for others and engage in these problem behaviors to such a frequent degree as to be considered unmanageable by parents, teachers, and, in some cases, the legal system.

In terms of assessment strategies, the challenge for the clinician is not to determine if the adolescent client is, in fact, one with diagnosable conduct disturbance; the problem behaviors are so compelling that a symptom history derived from interviews alone could establish diagnosis. The challenge instead is to perform a multifaceted assessment, in order to establish strengths and weaknesses, behavioral excesses and deficits, as targets for treatment. The assessment model promoted by this chapter reflects an evaluation plan that recognizes that the source of assessment data, the methods or tests by which they are derived, and the settings from which they originate influence the outcome of the psychological evaluation. As a result, the psychologist must define problem behaviors in terms of multiple informants, multiple methods or procedures, and from a multisituational perspective.

Finally, after all assessment results are in, the assessor is faced with the sometimes overwhelming task of integrating complex and often contradictory results (Kazdin, French, Unis, & Esveldt-Dawson, 1983; Nelson, Hayes, Felton, & Jarrett, 1985; Orvaschel, Puig-Antich, Chambers, Tabrizi, & Johnson, 1982). There is at present no way to evaluate which is the "best" or most representative source of information (adolescent self-report, parent or teacher ratings, observations). Lack of agreement in ratings about adolescent behaviors appears to be a function of the sources of information, different perspectives or values, and types of behaviors rated (Kazdin, 1985). Nonetheless, the clinician is left with the task of combining and integrating information, which presents another point in the assessment process where subjective inference may introduce error and bias (Sawyer, 1966). Although most psychologists in field-based situations do not have access to statistical procedures for collecting and combining information, Sundberg (1977) suggests that the assessor attempt to develop local base rates, expectancy tables, and norms for behaviors and outcomes in order to generate a normative perspective for those presenting problems.

When confronted with an adolescent who presents the problems of violence, property crimes, or extreme disobedience, it is easy to be overwhelmed by the prominence of these symptoms and lose sight of the need for a holistic approach to problem identification. One must remember that the conduct-disturbed adolescent is also at risk for a disordered academic history, peer problems, substance abuse, and victimization by incompetent and disturbed parenting strategies (occasionally characterized by physical and sexual assaults). Only after all facets of adaptive functioning are assessed and integrated can the complex task of intervention be planned.

REFERENCES

Achenbach, T. M. (1974). *Developmental psychopathology*. New York: Ronald.
Achenbach, T. M. (1978). Psychopathology of childhood: Research problems and issues. *Journal of Consulting and Clinical Psychology, 46*, 759-776.
Achenbach, T. M. (1982). *Developmental psychopathology* (2nd ed.). New York: John Wiley & Sons.
Achenbach, T. M., & Edelbrock, C. S. (1979). The Child Behavior Profile: II. Boys aged 12-16 and girls aged 6-11 and 12-16. *Journal of Consulting and Clinical Psychology, 47*, 223-233.
Achenbach, T. M., & Edelbrock, C. S. (1981). Behavioral problems and competencies reported by parents of normal and disturbed children aged 4-16. *Monograph of Social Research in Child Development, 46*(1, Serial No. 188).
Achenbach, T. M., & Edelbrock, C. S. (1983). *Manual for the Child Behavior Checklist and Revised Child Behavior Profile*. Burlington, VT: Queen City Printers.
Aman, M. G., & Werry, J. S. (1984). The revised Behavior Problem Checklist in clinic attenders and nonattenders: Age and sex effects. *Journal of Clinical Child Psychology, 13*, 237-242.
American Psychiatric Association. (1980). *Diagnostic and statistical manual of mental disorders* (3rd ed.). Washington, DC: Author.
American Psychological Association. (1981). Ethical principles of psychologists. *American Psychologist, 36*, 633-638.
Archer, R. P. (1984). Use of the MMPI with adolescents: A review of salient issues. *Clinical Psychology Review, 4*, 241-251.
Archer, R. P., White, J. L., & Orvin, G. H. (1979). MMPI characteristics and correlates among adolescent psychiatric inpatients. *Journal of Clinical Psychology, 35*, 498-504.
Atkeson, B. M., & Forehand, R. (1981). Conduct disorders. In E. J. Mash & L. G. Terdal (Eds.), *Behavioral assessment of childhood disorders* (pp. 185-210). New York: Guilford.
Bandura, A. (1973). *Aggression: A social learning analysis*. Englewood Cliffs, NJ: Prentice-Hall.
Barkley, R. A. (1981). *Hyperactive children: A handbook for diagnosis and treatment*. New York: Guilford.
Barlow, D. H., Hayes, S. C., & Nelson, R. O. (1984). *The scientist practitioner: Research and accountability in clinical and educational settings*. New York: Pergamon.
Behar, D., & Stewart, M. A. (1982). Aggressive conduct disorder of children. *Acta Psychiatrica Scandinavia, 65*, 210-220.

Bellack, A. S., & Hersen, M. (1977). *Behavioral modification: An introductory textbook.* Baltimore: Williams & Wilkins.

Bellack, A. S., & Hersen, M. (1978). Chronic psychiatric patients: Social skills training. In M. Hersen & A. S. Bellack (Eds.), *Behavior therapy in the psychiatric setting.* Baltimore: Williams & Wilkens.

Bornstein, P. H., Schuldberg, D. A., & Bornstein, M. T. (in press). Conduct disorders. In V. B. Van Hasselt & M. Hersen (Eds.), *The handbook of adolescent psychology.* New York: Pergamon.

Boyle, M. H., & Jones, S. C. (1985). Selecting measures of emotional and behavioral disorders of childhood for use in general populations. *Journal of Child Psychology and Psychiatry, 26,* 137-159.

Bright, P. D., & Robin, A. L. (1981). Ameliorating parent-adolescent conflict with problem-solving communication training. *Journal of Behavior Therapy and Experimental Psychiatry, 12,* 275-280.

Browning, R. M., & Stover, D. O. (1971). *Behavior modification in child treatment: An experimental and clinical approach.* Chicago: Aldine.

Cernkovich, S. A., & Giordano, P. C. (1979). A comparative analysis of male and female delinquency. *Sociological Quarterly, 20,* 131-145.

Chambers, W. J., Puig-Antich, J., & Tabrizi, M. A. (1978). *The ongoing development of the Kiddie-SADS (Schedule for Affective Disorders and Schizophrenia for School-Age Children).* Paper presented at the American Academy of Child Psychiatry, San Diego.

Chandler, M. J. (1972). Egocentricism in normal and pathological child development. In F. Monks, W. Hartup, & J. DeWitt (Eds.), *Determinants of behavioral development* (pp. 569-576). New York: Academic Press.

Chandler, M. (1973). Egocentricism and anti-social behavior: The assessment and training of social perspective-taking skills. *Developmental Psychology, 9,* 326-332.

Costello, A. J. (1985). Assessment of children and adolescents: An overview. *Psychiatric Annals, 15,* 15-24.

Curtiss, G., Rosenthal, R. H., Marohn, R. L., Ostrov, E., Offer, D., & Trujillo, J. (1983). Measuring delinquent behavior in inpatient treatment settings: Revision and validation of the Adolescent Antisocial Behavior Checklist. *Journal of the American Academy of Child Psychiatry, 22,* 459-466.

Dana, R. H. (1966). Eisegesis and assessment. *Journal of Projective Techniques and Personality Assessment, 30,* 215-222.

Dana, R. H. (1985). Thematic Apperception Test (TAT). In C. S. Newmark (Ed.), *Major psychological assessment instruments* (pp. 89-134). Boston: Allyn & Bacon.

Delfini, L. F., Bernal, M. E., & Rosen, P. M. (1976). Comparison of defiant and normal boys in home settings. In E. J. Mash, L. A. Hamerlynck, & L. C. Handy (Eds.), *Behavior modification and families* (pp. 228-248). New York: Brunner/Mazel.

Doke, L. A., & Flippo, J. R. (1983). Aggressive and oppositional behavior. In T. H. Ollendick & M. Hersen (Eds.), *Handbook of child psychopathology* (pp. 323-356). New York: Plenum.

Edelbrock, C. S., & Achenbach, T. M. (1980). A typology of Child Behavior Profile patterns: Distribution and correlates for disturbed children aged 6-16. *Journal of Abnormal Child Psychology, 8,* 441-470.

Edelbrock, C. S., & Achenbach, T. M. (1984). The teacher version of the Child Behavior Profile. I: Boys aged 6-11. *Journal of Consulting and Clinical Psychology, 52,* 207-217.

Elder, J. P., Edelstein, B. A., & Narick, M. M. (1979). Adolescent psychiatric patients: Modifying aggressive behavior with social skills training. *Behavior Modification, 3,* 161-178.

Endicott, J., & Spitzer, R. L. (1978). A diagnostic interview: The Schedule of Affective Disorders and Schizophrenia. *Archives of General Psychiatry, 35,* 837-844.

Epstein, M. H., Kauffman, J. M., & Cullinan, D. (1985). Patterns of maladjustment among the behaviorally disordered. II: Boys aged 6-11, boys aged 12-18, girls aged 6-11, and girls aged 12-18. *Behavioral Disorders, 10,* 125-135.

Exner, J. E. (1978). *The Rorschach: A comprehensive system: Vol. 2. Current research and advanced interpretation.* New York: John Wiley & Sons.

Exner, J. E. (1985). *A Rorschach workbook for the comprehensive system* (2nd ed.). (Available from Rorschach Workshops, Bayville, NY 11709)

Exner, J. E., & Weiner, I. B. (1982). *The Rorschach: A comprehensive system: Vol. 3. Assessment of children and adolescents.* New York: John Wiley & Sons.

Farrington, D. (1973). Self-reports of deviant behavior: Predictive and stable? *Journal of Criminal Law and Criminology, 64,* 99-110.

Farrington, D. P. (1978). The family backgrounds of aggressive youths. In L. A. Hersen & M. Berger with D. Shaffer (Eds.), *Aggression and antisocial behaviours in childhood & adolescence* (pp. 73-93). Oxford: Pergamon.

Feighner, J. P., Robins, E., Guze, S. B., Woodruff, R. A., Winokur, G., & Munoz, R. (1972). Diagnostic criteria for use in psychiatric research. *Archives of General Psychiatry, 26,* 57-63.

Finch, A. J., Jr., & Rogers, T. R. (1984). Self-report instruments. In T. H. Ollendick & M. Hersen (Eds.), *Child behavioral assessment: Principles and procedures* (pp. 106-123). New York: Pergamon.

Forehand, R., & McMahon, R. J. (1981). *Helping the noncompliant child: A clinician's guide to parent training.* New York: Guilford.

Forehand, R., Peed, S., Roberts, M., McMahon, R., Griest, D. L., & Humphreys, L. (1979). *Coding manual for scoring mother-child interaction* (3rd ed.). Unpublished manuscript, University of Georgia, Department of Psychology, Athens.

Fridler, P. E., Orenstein, H., Chiles, J., Fritz, G., & Breitt, S. (1979). Effects of assertiveness training on hospitalized adolescents and young adults. *Adolescence, 14,* 523-528.

Garber, J. (1984). Classification of childhood psychopathology: A developmental perspective. *Child Development, 55,* 30-48.

Garmezy, N. (1974). Children at risk: The search for the antecedents of schizophrenia. *Schizophrenia Bulletin, 8,* 14-90.

Gersten, J., Langner, T., Eisenberg, J., Simcha-Fagan, O., & McCarthy, E. (1976). Stability in changes in types of behavioral disturbances of children & adolescents. *Journal of Abnormal Child Psychology, 4,* 111-127.

Gittleman, R. (1980). The role of psychological tests for differential diagnoses in child psychiatry. *Journal of the American Academy of Child Psychiatry, 19,* 413-438.

Glenn, C. M. (1980). Ethical issues in the practice of child psychotherapy. *Professional Psychology, 11,* 613-619.

Goh, D. S., & Fuller, G. B. (1983). Current practices in the assessment of personality and behavior by school psychologists. *School Psychology Review, 12,* 240-243.

Goyette, C. H., Conners, C. K., & Ulrich, R. F. (1978). Normative data on revised Conners parent and teacher rating scales. *Journal of Abnormal Child Psychology, 6,* 221-236.

Graham, J. R. (1977). *The MMPI: A practical guide.* New York: Oxford University Press.

Graham, P. J., & Rutter, M. (1973). Psychiatric disorder in the young adolescent: A follow-up study. *Proceedings of the Royal Society of Medicine, 66,* 1226-1229.

Grisso, T., & Vierling, L. (1978). Minor's consent to treatment: A developmental perspective. *Professional Psychology, 9,* 412-427.

Gross, A. M. (1984). Behavioral interviewing. In T. H. Ollendick & M. Hersen (Eds.), *Child behavioral assessment: Principles and procedures* (pp. 61-79). New York: Pergamon.

Hartup, W. (1974). Aggression in childhood: Developmental perspectives. *American Psychologist, 5,* 336-341.

Hathaway, S. R., & McKinley, J. C. (1940). A multiphasic personality schedule (Minnesota): I. Construction of the schedule. *Journal of Psychology, 10*, 249-254.

Hathaway, S. R., & Monachesi, E. D. (1963). *Adolescent personality and behavior.* Minneapolis: University of Minnesota Press.

Herjanic, B. (1980). *Washington University Diagnostic Interview for Children and Adolescents (DICA).* St. Louis: Washington University School of Medicine.

Hetherington, E. M., & Martin, B. (1979). Family interaction and psychopathology in children. In H. Quay & J. Werry (Eds.), *Psychopathological disorders of childhood* (pp. 30-82). New York: John Wiley & Sons.

Hetherington, E. M., Cox, M., & Cox, R. (1978). The aftermath of divorce. In J. H. Stevens & M. Mathews (Eds.), *Mother-child, father-child relations.* Washington, DC: National Association for the Education of Young Children.

Holt, R. R. (1978). *Methods in clinical psychology: Vol. 1. Projective assessments.* New York: Plenum.

Husain, S. A., & Vandiver, T. (1984). *Suicide in children and adolescents.* New York: SP Medical and Scientific Books.

Jesness, C. F., & Wedge, R. F. (1984). Validity of Jesness Inventory I—Level classification with delinquents. *Journal of Consulting and Clinical Psychology, 52*, 997-1010.

Johnson, S. M., & Bolstad, O. D. (1973). Methodological issues in naturalistic observation: Some problems and solutions for field research. In L. A. Hamerlynck, L. C. Handy, & E. J. Mash (Eds.), *Behavior change: Methodology, concepts, and practice* (pp. 7-67). Champaign, IL: Research Press.

Kaplan, M. (1969). Problems between a referral source and a child guidance clinic. In S. A. Szurek & I. N. Berlin (Eds.), *The antisocial child: Her family and his community* (pp. 116-131). Palo Alto, CA: Science and Behavior Books.

Kazdin, A. E. (1985). *Treatment of antisocial behavior in children and adolescents.* Homewood, IL: Dorsey.

Kazdin, A. E., French, N. H., Unis, A. S., & Esveldt-Dawson, K. (1983). Assessment of childhood depression: Correspondence of child and parent ratings. *Journal of the American Academy of Child Psychology, 22*, 157-164.

Kleinmuntz, B. (1982). *Personality and psychological assessment.* New York: St. Martin's.

Lachar, D. (1974). *The MMPI: Clinical assessment and automated interpretation.* Los Angeles: Western Psychological Services.

La Greca, A. M., & Quay, H. C. (1984). Behavior disorders of children. In N. S. Endler & J. McV. Hunt (Eds.), *Personality and the behavior disorders* (2nd ed.) (pp. 711-746). New York: John Wiley & Sons.

Lavik, N. J. (1977). Urban-rural differences in rates of disorder: A comparative psychiatric population study of Norwegian adolescents. In P. J. Graham (Ed.), *Epidemiological approaches in child psychiatry.* London: Academic Press.

Lee, D. V., Halberg, E. T., & Hassard, H. E. (1979). Effects of assertion training on aggressive behavior of adolescents. *Journal of Counseling Psychology, 26*, 459-461.

Lefkowitz, M. M., Eron, L. D., Walder, L. O., & Huesman, L. R. (1977). *Growing up to be violent: A longitudinal study of the development of aggression.* New York: Pergamon.

Lesser, G. S. (1959). The relationships between various forms of aggression and popularity among lower-class children. *Journal of Educational Psychology, 50*, 20-25.

Lewis, D. O., Lewis, M., Unger, L., & Goldman, C. (1984). Conduct disorder and its synonyms: Diagnosis of dubious validity and usefulness. *American Journal of Psychiatry, 141*, 514-519.

Lewis, D. O., Shanok, S. S., Pincus, J. H., & Glaser, G. H. (1979). Violent juvenile delinquents: Psychiatric, neurological, psychological and abuse factors. *Journal of the American Academy of Child Psychiatry, 18*, 307-319.

Linehan, M. M. (1977). Issues in behavioral interviewing. In J. D. Cone & R. P. Hawkins (Ed.), *Behavioral assessment: New directions in clinical psychology* (pp. 30-51). New York: Brunner/Mazel.

Little,V., & Kendall, P. (1979). Cognitive-behavioral interventions with delinquents: Problem-solving, role-taking, & self-control. In P. Kendall & S. Hollon (Eds.), *Cognitive-behavioral interventions: Theory, research, and procedures* (pp. 81-116). New York: Academic Press.

Lobitz, G. R., & Johnson, S. M. (1975). Normal versus deviant children: A multimethod comparison. *Journal of Abnormal Child Psychology, 3,* 353-374.

Loeber, R. (1982). The stability of antisocial and delinquent child behavior: A review. *Child Development, 53,* 1431-1446.

Loeber, R., & Dishion, T. J. (1983). Early predictors of male delinquence: A review. *Psychological Bulletin, 94,* 68-99.

Loeber, R., Patterson, G., & Dishion, T. (1982). *Boys who fight: Familial and antisocial correlates.* Unpublished manuscript, Oregon Social Learning Center, Eugene.

Loeber, R., & Schmaling, K. B. (1985). The utility of differentiating between mixed and pure forms of antisocial child behavior. *Journal of Abnormal Child Psychology, 13,* 315-336.

MacFarlane, J., Allen, L., & Honzik, M. (1954). *A developmental study of the behavior problems of normal children between twenty-one months and fourteen years.* Berkeley: University of California Press.

Mader, L., & Quevillon, R. P. (1984). *Effects of interviewing appearance on a child behavior interview* (Report No. C 6016475). Vermillion, SD: University of South Dakota, Department of Psychology. (ERIC Document Reproduction Service No. ED 226 282)

Marks, P. A., Seeman, W., & Haller, D. L. (1974). *The actuarial use of the MMPI with adolescents and adults.* Baltimore: Williams & Wilkins.

Mash, E. J., & Terdal, L. G. (1981). *Bahavioral assessment of childhood disorders.* New York: Guilford.

Matranga, J. T. (1976). The relationship between behavioral indices of aggression and hostile content on the TAT. *Journal of Personality Assessment, 40,* 130-134.

Mattison, R., Cantwell, D. P., Russell, A. T., & Will, L. (1979). A comparison of DSM-II and DSM-III in the diagnosis of childhood psychiatry disorders: II. Interrater agreement. *Archives of General Psychiatry, 36,* 1217-1222.

Meehl, P. E. (1956). Wanted—A good cookbook. *American Psychologist, 11,* 263-272.

Megargee, E. I. (1972). *The California Psychological Inventory handbook.* San Francisco: Jossey-Bass.

Melton, G. B. (1981). Children's participation in treatment planning: Psychological and legal issues. *Professional Psychology, 12,* 246-252.

Miller, L. C. (1972). School Behavior Checklist: An inventory of deviant behavior for elementary school children. *Journal of Consulting and Clinical Psychology, 38,* 138-144.

Miller, W. B. (1958). Lower class culture as a generating milieu of gang delinquency. *Journal of Social Issues, 14,* 5-19.

Mischel, W. (1972). Direct versus indirect personality assessment: Evidence and implications. *Journal of Consulting and Clinical Psychology, 38,* 319-324.

Moore, D. R., Chamberlain, P., & Menkes, L. H. (1979). Children at risk for delinquency: A follow-up comparison of aggressive children and children who steal. *Journal of Abnormal Child Psychology, 7,* 345-355.

Morris, H. H. (1956). Aggressive behavior disorders in children: A follow-up study. *American Journal of Psychiatry, 112,* 991-997.

Moskowitz, D. S., Ledingham, J. E., & Schwartzman, A. E. (1985). Stability and change in aggression and withdrawal in middle childhood and early adolescence. *Journal of Abnormal Psychology, 94,* 30-41.

National Institute of Mental Health. (1980). *The assessment of psychopathology and behavioral problems in children: A review of scales suitable for epidemiological and clinical research (1967-1979)* (DHHS Publication No. ADM 80-1037). Washington, DC: U.S. Government Printing Office.

National Institute of Mental Health. (1984). *The assessment of adaptive functioning in children: A review of existing measures suitable for epidemiological and clinical services research* (DHHS Publication No. ADM 84-1343). Washington, DC: U.S. Government Printing Office.

Nelson, R. O., Hayes, S. C., Felton, J. L., & Jarrett, R. B. (1985). A comparison of data produced by different behavioral assessment techniques with implications for models of social skills inadequacy. *Behaviour Research and Therapy, 23,* 1-11.

O'Leary, K. D., & Johnson, S. M. (1979). Psychological assessment. In H. C. Quay & J. S. Werry (Eds.), *Psychopathological disorders of childhood* (2nd ed.) (pp. 210-246). New York: John Wiley & Sons.

Ollendick, T. H., & Hersen, M. (Eds.). (1984). *Child behavioral assessment: Principles and procedures.* New York: Pergamon.

Oltmanns, T. F., Broderick, J. E., & O'Leary, K. D. (1977). Marital adjustment and the efficacy of behavior therapy with children. *Journal of Consulting and Clinical Psychology, 45,* 724-729.

Orvaschel, H., Puig-Antich, J., Chambers, W., Tabrizi, M. A., & Johnson, R. (1982). Retrospective assessment of prepubertal major depression with the Kiddie-SADS-E. *Journal of the American Academy of Child Psychiatry, 21,* 392-397.

Palmer, J. O. (1983). *The psychological assessment of children* (2nd ed.). New York: John Wiley & Sons.

Patterson, G. R. (1982). *A social learning approach: Vol. 3. Coercive family process.* Eugene, OR: Castalia.

Patterson, G. R., Reid, J. B., Jones, R. R., & Conger, R. E. (1975). *A social learning approach to family intervention: Families with aggressive children* (Vol. 1). Eugene, OR: Castalia.

Peterson, D. R. (1961). Behavior problems of middle childhood. *Journal of Consulting Psychology, 25,* 205-207.

Plotkin, R. (1981). When rights collide: Parents, children, and consent to treatment. *Journal of Pediatric Psychology, 6,* 121-130.

Prinz, R. J., Swan, G., Liebert, D., Weintraub, S., & Neale, J. M. (1978). ASSESS: Adjustment Scales for Sociometric Evaluation of Secondary School Students. *Journal of Abnormal Child Psychology, 6,* 493-501.

Puig-Antich, J. (1982). Major depression and conduct disorder in prepuberty. *Journal of the American Academy of Child Psychology, 21,* 118-128.

Quay, H. C. (1979). Classification. In H. C. Quay & J. S. Werry (Eds.), *Psychopathological disorders of childhood* (2nd ed.). (pp. 1-42). New York: John Wiley & Sons.

Quay, H. C. (1983). A dimensional approach to behavior disorder: The revised Behavior Problem Checklist. *School Psychology Review, 12,* 244-249.

Quay, H. C., & Peterson, D. R. (1979). *Manual for the Behavior Problem Checklist.* (Available from Herbert Quay, University of Miami, P. O. Box 248074, Coral Gables, FL 33124)

Quay, H. C., & Peterson, D. R. (1983). *Interim manual for the Revised Behavior Problem Checklist.* (Available from Herbert Quay, University of Miami, P. O. Box 248074, Coral Gables, FL 33124)

Radloff, L. (1982). *Diagnostic Interview Schedule for Children* (2nd working draft). Rockville, MD: National Institute of Mental Health.

Reid, J. B. (Ed.). (1978). *A social learning approach to family intervention: Vol. 2. Observation in home settings.* Eugene, OR: Castalia.

Rekers, G. A. (1984). Ethical issues in child behavioral assessment. In T. H. Ollendick & M. Hersen (Eds.), *Child behavioral assessment: Principles and procedures* (pp. 244-262). New York: Pergamon.

Roach, J. L. (1958). Some social psychological characteristics of child guidance clinic caseloads. *Journal of Consulting Psychology, 22,* 183-186.

Robins, L. N. (1966). *Deviant children grown up.* Baltimore: Williams & Wilkins.

Robins, L. N. (1978). Aetiological implications in studies of childhood histories relating to antisocial personality, In R. P. Hane & D. Schalling (Eds.), *Psychopathic behavior.* New York: John Wiley & Sons.

Robins, L. N., & Wish, E. (1977). Childhood deviance as a developmental process: A study of 223 urban black men from birth to 18. *Social Forces, 56,* 448-473.

Roff, M. (1972). A two-factor approach to juvenile delinquency and the later histories of juvenile delinquents. In M. Roff, L. N. Robins, & M. Pollack (Eds.), *Life history research in psychopathology* (Vol. 2, pp. 77-101.). Minneapolis: University of Minnesota Press.

Ross, A. O. (1980). *Psychological disorders of children: A behavioral approach to theory, research, and therapy* (2nd ed.). New York: McGraw-Hill.

Rutter, M., & Garmezy, N. (1983). Developmental psychopathology. In P. Mussen (Ed.), *Handbook of child psychology: Vol. 4. Socialization, personality and social development* (p. 775-911). New York: John Wiley & Sons.

Rutter, M., & Giller, H. (1983). *Juvenile delinquency: Trends and prespectives.* New York: Penguin.

Rutter, M., Maughan, B., Mortimore, P., Ouston, J. W., & Smith, A. (1979). *Fifteen thousand hours: Secondary schools and their effects on children.* Cambridge: Harvard Uinversity Press.

Rutter, M., Tizard, J., & Whitmore, K. (Eds.) (1981). *Education, health & behaviour.* Huntington, NY: Krieger. (Originally published in 1970)

Sattler, J. M. (1982). *Assessment of children's intelligence and special abilities* (2nd ed.). Boston: Allyn & Bacon.

Sawyer, J. (1966). Measurement and prediction, clinical and statistical. *Psychological Bulletin, 66,* 178-200.

Schechtman, A. (1970). Psychiatric symptoms observed in normal and disturbed children. *Journal of Clinical Psychology, 26,* 38-41.

Schnelle, J. F. (1974). A brief report on invalidity of parent evaluations of behavior change. *Journal of Applied Behavior Analysis, 7,* 341-343.

Shapland, J. M. (1978). Self-reported delinquency in boys aged 11 to 14. *British Journal of Criminology, 18,* 255-266.

Simmons, J. E. (1974). *Psychiatric examination of children* (2nd ed.). Philadelphia: Lea & Febiger.

Strasberg, P. A. (1978). *Violent delinquents: A report to the Ford Foundation from Vera Institute of Justice.* New York: Monarch.

Strober, M., Green, J., & Carlson, G. (1981). Reliability of psychiatric diagnosis in hospitalized adolescents: Interrater agreement using DSM-III. *Archives in General Psychiatry, 38,* 141-145.

Sundberg, N. D. (1977). *Assessment of persons.* Englewood Cliffs, NJ: Prentice-Hall.

Wadsworth, M. (1979). *Roots of delinquency: Infancy, adolescence and crime.* Oxford: Martin Robinson.

Wahler, R. G. (1980). The insular mother: Her problems in parent-child treatment. *Journal of Applied Behavior Analysis, 13,* 207-219.

Walls, R. T., Werner, T. J., Bacon, A., & Zane, T. (1977). Behavior checklists. In J. D. Cone & R. P. Hawkins (Eds.), *Behavioral assessment: New directions in clinical psychology* (pp. 77-146). New York: Brunner/Mazel.

Weller, R. A., Weller, R. B., & Herjanic, B. (1983). Adult psychiatry disorders in psychiatrically ill young adolescents. *American Journal of Psychiatry, 140,* 1585-1588.

Wells, K. C. (1981). Assessment of children in outpatient settings. In M. Hersen & A. S. Bellack (Eds.), *Behavioral assessment: A practical handbook* (2nd ed.) (pp. 484-533). New York: Pergamon.

Werry, J. S., Methven, R. J., Fitzpatrick, J., & Dixon, H. (1983). The reliability of DSM-III in children. *Journal of Abnormal Child Psychology, 11,* 341-354.

Werry, J. S., & Quay, H. C. (1971). The prevalence of behavior symptoms in younger elementary school children. *American Journal of Orthopsychiatry, 41,* 136-143.

West, D. J. (1982). *Delinquency: Its roots, careers, and prospects.* London: Heinemann Educational.

West, D. J., & Farrington, D. P. (1977). *The delinquent way of life.* London: Heinemann Educational.

Wiltz, N. A., & Patterson, G. R. (1974). An evaluation of parent training procedures designed to alter inappropriate aggressive behavior of boys. *Behavior Therapy, 5,* 215-221.

Wolff, S. (1961). Symptomatology and outcome of preschool children with behavior disorders attending a child guidance clinic. *Journal of Child Psychology and Psychiatry, 2,* 269-276.

Zimring, F. E. (1979). American youth violence: Issues & trends. In N. Morris & M. Tonry (Eds.), *Crime & justice: An annual review of research* (Vol. 1, pp. 67-107). Chicago: University of Chicago Press.

13

Juvenile Delinquency and Antisocial Personality Disorders

STEWART W. EHLY, PH.D.

Delinquency and *adolescents* are inseparable terms in the world of juvenile justice. The adolescent or youth between the ages roughly of 12-18 may commit acts in the home, school, or community that bring him or her to the attention of juvenile authorities. Such attention is usually not positive; adolescents are seldom recognized by the justice system for acts of prosocial behavior. When a juvenile does commit an act that brings him or her under the purview of the authorities, there is a need to collect valid, reliable information about the youth for assessment purposes. This chapter will review what is known about delinquency and its assessment and will explore current and best practices related to data gathering.

One difficulty with the entire topic of delinquency is in establishing the boundaries for what can be considered "delinquent" behavior. When viewing an action as deviant, there are several alternatives to simply labeling the behavior dichotomously as acceptable or unacceptable. Erikson (1964), for example, noted that

> Deviance is not a property inherent in certain forms of behavior; it is a property conferred upon these forms by the audiences which directly or indirectly witness them. The critical variable in the study of deviance, then, is the social audience rather than the individual actor, since it is the audience which eventually determines whether or not any episode or behavior or any class of episodes is labeled deviant. (p. 11)

There has been disagreement on what qualifies as delinquent behavior and, indeed, why some children who commit certain acts are processed through the juvenile justice system while others go unpunished. The deviant actions of a middle- or upper-class juvenile can result in a placement with mental health officials, while an identical act committed by an inner-city youth may result in prosecution and sentencing. Offer, Marohn, and Ostrov (1979) contend that law enforcement criteria for the identification of and intervention with juvenile delinquents are no satisfactory substitutes for mental health systems designed to treat youthful offenders. A discussion of the interface between the juvenile justice and mental health professions will be addressed later in this chapter.

There are several reasons why it is difficult to establish the actual incidence rate of specific acts considered delinquent. The major problem lies in defining "delinquent behavior." Offer et al. (1979) agree with Kvaraceus's (1960) earlier contention that delinquency is a legal classification that does not represent a meaningful diagnostic category. Furthermore they specify that juvenile delinquent activities may be defined as any behavior that is

in violation of the laws or values of the prevailing society. It can be very serious (murder, violence against other humans); serious—but less so (violence against property which belongs to others: robbery, theft, destruction, etc.); less serious and tending to be more self-destructive, but still defined as delinquent (truancy, run-aways, sexual activity without physically hurting another human being, and drug abuse). (p. 5)

Other authors discriminate between delinquent acts and status offenses, relegating truancy, running away, and sex-related offenses to the latter category. *Status offenses* can be defined as those actions committed by a juvenile that would not elicit consequences from the justice system if the individual were an adult. Behavior disorders represent another related classification category for socially maladjusted children and youth. *Behavior disorders* may be defined as situationally inappropriate behavior that deviates significantly from behavior appropriate to one's age and interferes with the learning process, interpersonal relations, or personal adjustment. The "behavior disorders" label is an educational one and implies assignment to a special education program. It is not, however, synonymous with the delinquency designation; indeed, many children with behavioral disorders never commit delinquent acts.

Efforts at controlling the actions of juveniles have engendered numerous statutes and regulations that attempt to modify the behavior of adolescents. The law and the influences that shape it must be understood by the mental health practitioner who wishes to be prepared to serve delinquents. Laws have changed over the years, modified by an array of court and legislative decisions that have affected not only the specific language of the law but also its intent. The juvenile court or agency responsible for controlling juveniles is influenced by the law and by a more amorphous set of considerations that coincide with community mores. Carey and McAnany (1984) claim that juvenile law has taken longer than adult law to respond to changes in constitutional due process. Often, juvenile justice is an isolated part of broader law enforcement, allowing for a wide range of individual differences in the application of justice to emerge. In some states, such as Illinois, juvenile court judges can be selected from specialists interested in working with children; other states do not take into consideration such specialized training or interest (Carey & McAnany, 1984).

The courts tend to hear juvenile cases falling within four broad categories (which may not be mutually exclusive, depending on the case at hand): delinquency, children in need of supervision (formerly called status offenses), neglect, and dependency cases (Carey & McAnany, 1984). According to these authors,

Delinquency cases involve use of a violated penal law. This may involve also children in need of supervision who are defined as having violated control norms of parents or school, such as running away, being truant, or using alcohol or drugs. (p. 31)

Over the years much legislation has removed status offenses from the category of delinquency and allowed separate agencies, often mental health centers, to work with these youth. The third category of cases, neglect, involves situations in which parents or guardians abuse children either directly or by the omission of appropriate care. Physical abuse can be considered within this category. The final category, dependency, pertains to children either without a parent or guardian or with a parent unable to provide specified care. The law bearing on each of these four types of cases can address the individual needs of children. Because of differences in the characteristics of cases heard by juvenile courts and the special needs of children and families, the mental health professional serving a referred adolescent must be sensitive to the unique aspects of each case. The definitions provided by the court (i.e., delinquency, in need of supervision, neglect, and dependency) are not ones found in mental health classification systems; thus, the interest of the mental health professional must center on the educational, social and emotional, and cognitive needs of the adolescent.

In American society, arrest statistics are often considered valid indicators of the delinquent actions of children and juveniles (in fact, some authors limit definitions of delinquency to the arrested adolescent). There is some indication that delinquency rates as expressed in arrest statistics have risen over the last century, although some (Newman, 1980) have argued that delinquent behavior has existed much longer than our labels and our techniques for measuring the same. Even arrest statistics do not necessarily provide an accurate picture of the encounters that juveniles have with law enforcement agencies; court statistics, victim reports, and victimization studies are other avenues by which information on the actions of delinquents may be reported. Using all of these resources, Carey and McAnany (1984) have collected some recent statistics. Citing data from the National Center for Juvenile Justice (1981), the FBI Uniform Crime reports (Federal Bureau of Investigation, 1980), self-reports from crime victims (Williams & Gold, 1972), and data from the Law Enforcement Assistance Administration (McDermott & Hindelang, 1981), the two authors provide the following findings:

1) "Delinquency rates as measured by the number of cases disposed of by courts with juvenile jurisdiction increased by 111% from 1957 to 1978. Females composed 19% of the cases in 1959 and 22% in 1978" (pp. 9-10).

A second collection of data (National Center for Juvenile Justice, 1981) reveals that most males committed property offenses (49.9%), status offenses (17.3%), violent crimes (9.2%), and drug- or alcohol-related offenses (7.9%). One-fourth of referrals to juvenile authorities represented in the second data set were females, referred primarily for status offenses (43.1%), property offenses (33.2%), and drug- or alcohol-related offenses (5.8%). Carey and McAnany (1984) cite that in 1978 whites accounted for 74% of all cases disposed of, blacks represented 18%, and other racial groups accounted for 8%.

2) According to the FBI (1980), 1979 arrest statistics indicated that juveniles aged 10-17 constituted only 15% of persons arrested, but 40% of those arrested for the most serious crimes, including homicide, rape, robbery, aggravated assault, burglary, larceny theft, motor vehicle theft, and arson. In the most violent crime areas (murder, rape, aggravated assault, and robbery), juveniles constituted only 18% of arrests. Property crimes are clearly the area in which juveniles are arrested most frequently. Female arrests have escalated in recent years. The FBI has argued that many of these arrests have been in connection with acts committed in the presence of a

male, whereas other studies (e.g., National Center for Juvenile Justice, 1981) report more dramatic increases in exclusively female-perpetrated offenses in areas such as property crimes.

3) Adolescent self-reports of delinquency indicate that the actual number of delinquent actions may be 10 times higher than official figures. Williams and Gold (1972) report that serious violations go unreported in 8 out of 10 cases, with even higher proportions of unreported cases when less serious actions were involved. Although no clearcut explanation is offered for why such a high proportion of delinquent actions go unreported, this may reflect the pattern of crime reports in general rather than indicate different community standards or tolerance for crimes committed by youth.

4) Victimization studies contain figures from relatively serious crimes and come from large samples of the general population. Though critics have claimed shortcomings in these studies, the data do indicate shifts in crime rates over time. According to Carey and McAnany (1984),

> The figures indicate that the number of victim reported crimes is far in excess of the number reported to the police and that the 18-20 year old group is the most delinquent. Rates for the 12-17 year old group gradually declined from 1973 to 1977. (p. 15)

Surveying all the data, Carey and McAnany argue that delinquency is not increasing at a rate suggested by other sources of information and in some areas may be actually decreasing.

PREASSESSMENT CONSIDERATIONS

When a juvenile offender is presented for initial screening, the psychologist should begin by collecting history data. With access to previous assessment data, the psychologist will find his or her task simplified. Commonly reported practices during screening involve collecting a wide variety of demographic information on a child, a format for which is shown in Figure 1. The process of documenting facts is an important component of the initial assessment, because such documentation generally precedes the formation of formal assessment hypotheses and subsequent data interpretation and intervention. Information on the child's academic or behavioral status, relations with peers or family, and interactions with community agencies are important data to collect. In some cases, background screening of the delinquent or offender may be all that is required for an assessment. Psychologists working with juvenile law enforcement agencies may restrict their attention to demographic information, with priority attached to identifying mental health or education agencies most suited for a subsequent referral. In agencies that emphasize more extensive evaluation, diagnostic techniques are applied following screening.

The effects of delinquency on families, schools, and communities are extensive. The interaction of community and educational agencies in response to juvenile delinquency can vary from mild to intense. The psychologist who works with delinquents will discover that local and state law enforcement agencies will respond differentially to juvenile crime based on the perpetrator's age. An awareness of local and state

FIGURE 1. SAMPLE SOCIAL HISTORY WORKSHEET

SOCIAL HISTORY WORKSHEET

Name _____ Address _____

Telephone _____ Attorney _____ Court Date _____

Social Security # _____ Age _____ Birthdate: _____

Birthplace _____ Ht ___ Wt ___ Hair ___ Eyes ___

General appearance and health

Previous record _____

PERSONALITY

Officer's opinion of anxieties, overall adjustment:

Child's image of self:

How others see child:

Child's attitude toward referral, authority, parents, life, etc.:

Nature of influence of peer group:

Hobbies/interests:

SCHOOL

School and grade attending:

Achievement vs. ability:

Grades:

Discipline reports:

IQ tests/dates given:

Extracurricular activities:

EMPLOYMENT

Location, hrs., salary, duties:

Use of money earned:

Previous employment/performance:

Future goals:

HOME & FAMILY

FATHER'S full name:

Address:

Social Security #:

Occupation:

Employer:

Length of service:

Salary, hours:

Birthdate/place:

Education:

Marriages/divorces:

Military service:

Police record:

Drinking, other habits:

General health:

Family background:

Opinion of child's problem/causes:

MOTHER'S full name:

Address:

Social Security #:

Occupation:

Employer:

Length of service:

Salary, hours:

Birthdate/place:

Education:

Marriages/divorces:

Military service:

Police record:

Drinking, other habits:

General health:

Family background:

Opinion of child's problem/causes:

STEP-PARENT'S full name:

Address:

Social Security #:

Occupation:

Employer:

Length of service:

Salary, hours:

Birthdate/place:

Education:

Marriages/divorces:

SIBLINGS & OTHERS IN HOME

Name   Relationship   Age   DOB   Birthplace   School/Employed

HOME ENVIRONMENT

Address and description of home; number of people in the home:

Renting/buying; previous residences:

Relationships between family members:

SUMMARY OF SIGNIFICANT FACTORS

RECOMMENDATION

priorities will help the psychodiagnostician in deciding what type of assessment data need to be collected. A recent report (Institute for Judicial Administration & American Bar Association, 1980) on police handling of juvenile problems notes that the younger the child, the less responsibility is assigned to him or her for the actions. A preschool- or grade-school-aged offender might be considered more a nuisance or mischief-maker by the police and thus be referred for short-term behavioral interventions by school psychologists or mental health agencies. Junior high school students committing minor offenses may still elicit an official response short of arrest; referral to community services or citation for actions without incarceration may be the most extreme actions taken. By high school age, offenses generally will produce arrest or referral to the juvenile court system (Carey & McAnany, 1984).

The psychologist working with status offenders or delinquent youth must be aware of the differential functioning of the law enforcement system in terms of juvenile arrests and processing. Wide variations exist across the United States regarding reactions to specific problem behaviors, and recent years have seen a dramatic change in the interventions provided for status-offender children and youth. Few states currently emphasize coherent, ongoing programs for truants, runaways, or sexually involved youth; on the other hand, awareness of drug-related offenses and major crimes has increased (i.e., greater publicity has been attached to drug offenders, etc.). The psychologist in touch with juvenile law enforcement agencies must be cognizant of community standards, local codes, and state policies for the processing of juvenile offenders.

Classification Schemes and Data Gathering

With an awareness of local and state priorities, the psychologist will be faced with the decision about the most appropriate procedures for data gathering. From state to state, the juvenile justice system is seldom consistent in its policies regarding data collection and preintervention assessment; no uniform standards for assessing juvenile offenders exist in the United States. The psychologist desiring information about the offender for treatment planning generally will prefer a clinically derived classification scheme in lieu of law enforcement classification categories.

In a recently published work on classification schemes, family and ecological influences, and intervention options with delinquent offenders (Henggeler, 1982), the *Diagnostic and Statistical Manual of Mental Disorders* (DSM-III; American Psychiatric Association, 1980) emerges as the most widely used classification scheme among mental health professionals serving delinquents. Actions labeled delinquent by law enforcement agencies fall under the DSM-III diagnostic criteria for Antisocial Personality Disorder:

A. Current age at least 18
B. Onset before age 15 as indicated by a history of three or more of the following before that age:
  (1) truancy (positive if it amounted to at least five days per year for at least two years, not including the last year of school)
  (2) expulsion or suspension from school for misbehavior
  (3) delinquency (arrested or referred to juvenile court because of behavior)

(4) running away from home overnight or at least twice while living in parental or parental surrogate home

(5) persistent lying

(6) repeated sexual intercourse in a casual relationship

(7) repeated drunkenness or substance abuse

(8) thefts

(9) vandalism

(10) school grades markedly below expectations in relation to estimated or known IQ (may have resulted in repeating a year)

(11) chronic violations of rules at home and/or school (other than truancy)

(12) initiation of fights

C. At least four of the following manifestations of the disorder since age 18:

    (1) inability to sustain consistent work behavior, as indicated by any of the following: (a) too frequent job changes (e.g., three or more jobs in five years not accounted for by nature of job or economic or seasonal fluctuation), (b) significant unemployment (e.g., six months or more in five years when expected to work), (c) serious absenteeism from work (e.g., average three days or more lateness or absence per month), (d) walking off several jobs without other job in sight (Note: similar behavior in an academic setting during the last few years of school may substitute for this criterion in individuals who by reason of their age or circumstances have not had an opportunity to demonstrate occupational adjustment)

    (2) lack of ability to function as a responsible parent as evidenced by one or more of the following: (a) child's malnutrition, (b) child's illness resulting from lack of minimal hygiene standards, (c) failure to obtain medical care for a seriously ill child, (d) child's dependence on neighbors or nonresident relatives for food or shelter, (e) failure to arrange for a caretaker for a child under six when parent is away from home, (f) repeated squandering, on personal items, of money required for household necessities

    (3) failure to accept social norms with respect to lawful behavior, as indicated by any of the following: repeated thefts, illegal occupation (pimping, prostitution, fencing, selling drugs), multiple arrests, a felony conviction

    (4) inability to maintain enduring attachment to a sexual partner as indicated by two or more divorces and/or separations (whether legally married or not), desertion of spouse, promiscuity (ten or more sexual partners within one year)

    (5) irritability and aggressiveness as indicated by repeated physical fights or assault (not required by one's job or to defend someone or oneself), including spouse or child beating

    (6) failure to honor financial obligations, as indicated by repeated defaulting on debts, failure to provide child support, failure to support other dependents on a regular basis

    (7) failure to plan ahead, or impulsivity, as indicated by traveling from place to place without a prearranged job or clear goal for the period of travel or clear idea about when the travel would terminate, or lack of a fixed address for a month or more

(8) disregard for the truth as indicated by repeated lying, use of aliases, "con-
     ning" others for personal profit
(9) reckless, as indicated by driving while intoxicated or recurrent speeding
D. A pattern of continuous antisocial behavior in which the rights of others are violated, with no intervening period of at least five years without antisocial behavior
   between age 15 and the present time (except when the individual was bedridden or
   confined in a hospital or penal institution)
E. Antisocial Behavior is not due to either Severe Mental Retardation, Schizophrenia
   or manic episodes.

While not the only classification scheme available to the mental health professional, the DSM-III does offer certain parameters within which to establish a
typology of juvenile delinquency. The DSM-III standards provide a structure by
which to consider the actions of youth who are under age 18 but exhibiting behavior
that indicates a probability of future difficulties.

Current national depictions (Institute of Judicial Administration & American
Bar Association, 1977) of sanctions for juvenile offenses classify sanctions according
to maximum consequences to the adolescent. A rough parallel between adult and
juvenile sanctions by offense category follows:

Class 1—*Adult:* 20+ years; *Juvenile:* 36 months conditional or 24 months in secure or
     nonsecure setting.
Class 2—*Adult:* 5-20 years; *Juvenile:* 24 months conditional or 12 months in secure or
     nonsecure setting.
Class 3—*Adult:* 1-5 years; *Juvenile:* 18 months conditional or 6 months in secure or
     nonsecure setting.
Class 4—*Adult:* 6 months; *Juvenile:* 12 months conditional or 3 months secure
     (+ record) or nonsecure setting.
Class 5—*Adult:* under 6 months; *Juvenile:* 6 months conditional or 2 months secure
     (+ record).

According to Henggeler, Brunk, and Haefele (1982), classifying delinquency in
a manner that satisfies both juvenile justice and mental health classification schemes
is difficult at best. The authors note that "the classification of delinquency is further
compounded by the amount of discretion that is available to police, judges, and correctional authorities in deciding which adolescents are adjudicated" (p. 34). Community standards play an important role in influencing how involved a juvenile
becomes in the machinations of the law enforcement system. The mental health professional providing an opinion on a youth's short-term or long-term status will be
responsible for soliciting information about the offender from family, school, and
community sources before offering a prognosis.

The search for data to support intervention decisions may pursue the question of
etiology or may focus on the delinquent acts themselves and the feasibility of interventions to eliminate specific behaviors. (The delinquent's peers and family are the
frequent foci of such investigations and will be addressed in a later section.) The
mental health professional is responsible for balancing the urgency of the presenting
problem (the delinquent act and its immediate consequences) with the expectations of
the family and the law enforcement agency addressing the delinquent act. The profes-

sional is often asked to coordinate data gathering from several sources and to contribute information that will assist schools and community agencies in helping the family work with the delinquent. The reality of this consultative process is that the family or the child may be uncooperative in providing all the information requested.

Offer, Marohn, and Ostrov (1979) have collected a number of case studies in which assessment data from home, school, and community resources are provided on delinquent offenders. One consistent feature in each case is the richness of the data reported. To reach this level of sophistication, much effort and commitment to developing case histories had to be coordinated by various mental health professionals. The influence of background data on the decisions made in the Offer et al. (1979) cases should reinforce the priority that mental health agents must place on data gathering.

If one is attempting to gather information related to the DSM-III criteria described earlier, clear documentation of the individual's past actions is mandated. The DSM-III criteria are sensitive to the various antisocial acts described by juvenile justice legislation as disruptive or offensive to the community at large. The role of data gathering centers on establishing a case history for each referred juvenile, documentation and validation of past and present behaviors, and a collection of information on the child's involvement with other agencies or mental health professionals.

At first, the boundaries drawn by legal or mental health classification systems around children's actions may appear arbitrary. For example, faced with a child who exhibits behaviors that fall under the three categories of (a) delinquency, (b) in need of supervision, and (c) neglect, the psychologist may decide to focus on an ecological or a family-centered intervention, with less emphasis on the individual child's actions. The psychologist must establish his or her treatment agenda early in any consideration of the delinquent, thereby allowing for an ethical review of the needs and priorities of the other agents or agencies involved.

Theoretical and Ideological Orientations

Agendas for the juvenile justice system, school districts, and other youth service agencies may reflect an orientation toward punishment of the child who behaves in a deviant fashion. Assuming that he or she does not qualify for a special education program focused on a behavioral concern, the school, the juvenile justice system, or youth service agency may choose to restrict the offender's actions following the commission of a crime. Over the years the orientation of juvenile law enforcement toward adolescents has alternated between a punitive approach and intervention/rehabilitation. Most recently, however, research evidence has suggested that the orientation of correctional programs has little effect on the later commission of crimes by adolescents. Lipton, Martinson, and Wilks (1975) have argued that punishment without a supportive rehabilitation program has little impact on delinquents' actions. Other evidence confirming such an argument has not prevented the broader public from arguing for stricter sentencing and punishment of delinquents for their actions (Carey & McAnany, 1984).

As Zwier and Vaughan (1984) have noted, the ideological orientations of both change agents and the broader public have an important influence not only on what we do with the delinquent but even what information we consider important about a pardo with the delinquent but even what information we consider important about a particular case. Zwier and Vaughan have proposed three common orientations to describe what is often done when working with children who engage in delinquent actions, specifically vandalism. Table 1 describes their breakdown of three common ideological orientations: conservative, liberal, and radical.

The conservative orientation clearly would argue for a punishment model of justice, while a liberal or radical one would be more interested in involving a broader array of individuals in a change program. The focus is on the child, and restrictions of his or her actions are common recommendations from a conservative orientation. Working with parents, school and community officials, and peer groups would be possibilities under a liberal model. Finally, the radical approach would seek to identify system-level factors that influence the child's actions and therein attempt a remediation. The important point associated with Zwier and Vaughan's (1984) argument is that the professional psychologist must examine both his or her ideological orientation and the assumptions of the broader system claiming responsibility for work with the delinquent. By clarifying values and assumptions associated with all groups focused on the child, the psychologist will have an important set of data to manipulate in any change program.

Related to Zwier and Vaughan's ideological orientation approach is Shoemaker's (1984) review of explanations for delinquency that transcend ideology. After having examined the extensive literature on delinquency, Shoemaker argues that multiple explanations can be provided for any action of the delinquent and that these explanations have important implications for assessment and intervention plans. Shoemaker lists the following alternatives for explaining delinquent behavior: 1) biological and biosocial explanations (somatotypes, inheritance); 2) psychological theories (intelligence, psychiatric-psychoanalytic, general personality); 3) social disorganization and anomie; 4) lower-class-based theories; 5) interpersonal and situational explanations; 6) control theories; 7) labeling theories; and 8) radical theories. The available literature provides an impressive choice for the professional interested in suggestions on intervention programs. Each theoretical position has been challenged. Shoemaker argues that while each theoretical approach requires much additional investigation to establish its utility, no single orientation has provided a coherent system that satisfies all audiences at work with delinquents.

SELECTION AND IMPLEMENTATION OF ASSESSMENT PROCEDURES

The role of assessment in working with delinquents, status offenders, and other youth experiencing difficulty parallels that of assessment in other settings, such as educational and mental health facilities. A widely accepted definition of assessment is that it involves the collection of information about an individual to assist in decision-making or programming considerations (Salvia & Ysseldyke, 1984). So defined, assessment does not merely involve the collection of norm-referenced test scores; the goal is to collect, interpret, and apply data to the individual case and to involve other concerned individuals (such as the parents or educators) in developing programs for the child.

As noted previously, psychologists working with law enforcement agencies operate within a framework and professional agenda that may vary from those of

TABLE 1

SCHOOL VANDALISM: ASSUMPTIONS OF CAUSE AND SOLUTIONS OFFERED BY THREE IDEOLOGICAL ORIENTATIONS*

Ideological Orientation and Assumption of Cause	Type of Solution SPECIFIC ← → DIFFUSE		
	Physical Environment	School System	Community at Large
CONSERVATIVE — Vandals are deviant. They must be caught and punished.	Protection of school and school grounds, employment of security officers and caretakers**	Encouragement and enforcement of school rules, use of contingency contracts	Involvement of community in antivandalism patrols and (parent) restitution programs, dependence on judicial system
LIBERAL — The school system is malfunctioning. Vandals capitalize on this.	(Superficial) improvement of the design, appearance and layout of the school and school grounds	Modifications in school climate, curriculum, and use of special conflict management programs**	Extension of recreational activities, use of school after hours for health and social services.
RADICAL — The school system is debilitating. Vandalism is a response of normal individuals to abnormal conditions.	Promotion of radical changes in the structure and appearance of the school, approval of policy to decrease the size of large schools and maintain small schools	Provision of student involvement in decision-making processes, adoption of changes in assessment procedures, and exploration of alternative schooling methods	Involvement of the whole community in school affairs, installment of community education programs, improvement of social situation in society at large**

*as described in Zwier and Vaughan (1984)
**the solution considered most favorably by the particular ideological orientation

practitioners in mental health agencies and other settings. Service options, whatever the setting, will be extensive. Carey and McAnany (1984), Offer, Marohn, and Ostrov (1979), Henggeler (1982), and Marohn, Dalle-Molle, McCarter, and Linn (1980) review many of the options available to psychologists in working with delinquent students. The Marohn et al. (1980) presentation centers on psychodynamic assessment and hospital treatment, Carey and McAnany (1984) review juvenile justice alternatives, while Offer et al. (1979) and Henggeler (1982) focus on psychologically based alternatives. The expertise of the individual psychologist and his or her professional orientation will influence the strategies selected to collect data, the framework within which the data are interpreted, and the alternatives chosen for intervention with the juvenile. Although this chapter will not review intervention options reported within the psychological literature, the reader can appreciate the wide array of techniques and programs potentially available to serve children who are experiencing difficulty and who have been labeled as delinquent.

In the literature on delinquency and assessment, the areas of data gathering commonly reported include the following: 1) intelligence and achievement; 2) personality, social skills, and adaptive behavior; 3) vocational and career measures; 4) family, peer, and ecological measures; and 5) measures of delinquency. Consideration of the adolescent's responses to any of the formal or informal measures used will be related to the priorities of the psychologist and agency requesting assessment information.

Intelligence and Achievement Measures

Psychology and juvenile justice literature contain extensive references to the relation of intelligence and educational achievement to delinquency. As might be expected, controversy abounds as to whether the relationships between each factor and delinquency are causative or simply correlative. Rutter and Giller (1984) present one school of thought regarding the controversy, arguing that IQ (i.e., the performance of youths on intelligence tests) is related to delinquency. They summarize an extensive array of research that can be interpreted to imply that, in both the United States and Great Britain, IQ appears to have an association with delinquency that "is as strong as that between either social class or race and crime" (p. 164). In contrast, Rutter and Giller argue that problems in educational achievement may be related to delinquent actions in some children, but the direction of influence has yet to be established with all delinquent youths. Indeed, a review of the literature on delinquency indicates that there may be intervening variables (self-esteem, emotional disturbance, etc.) that could mediate the impact of educational attainment on delinquent actions.

Historically, writings on delinquency reveal an extended emphasis on the belief that low intelligence is linked to criminal actions. Carey and McAnany (1984) present an entertaining summary of more than a century of arguments that low intelligence is a cause of or is associated with delinquent actions. More recent studies (also cited in Carey & McAnany, 1984) of children with behavioral difficulties including delinquency have noted the links between IQ scores and forms of psychopathology. In contrast, Shoemaker (1984) presents a collection of research projects that argue against any direct effects of intelligence on delinquency. Shoemaker is cautious to indicate possible relations between the youth's school performance, family life, and psychological makeup and his or her eventual actions.

Consideration of additional literature on the relation of educational attainment to delinquency reaches a similar conclusion; that is, scores from tests of ability may relate to delinquent actions without yielding a basis on which to intervene with a program of mental health services. Being aware of IQ and educational achievement data may assist the professional in recommending an educational program that is within the skill range and abilities of the adolescent performer. On the other hand, IQ and achievement scores are seldom an integral part of the programming considerations within the juvenile law enforcement system. Such data are often important only as one piece of documentation about personal attributes of an offender.

When intelligence and achievement data are solicited by a school or community agency, reliance on established measures would appear warranted. The Stanford-Binet Intelligence Scale, the Wechsler Intelligence Scale for Children-Revised (WISC-R), the Wechsler Adult Intelligence Scale-Revised (WAIS-R), or the Kaufman Assessment Battery for Children (K-ABC) can provide potentially useful information for academic decision making. In conjunction with tests of achievement, such as the Peabody Individual Achievement Test (PIAT), the Wide Range Achievement Test-Revised (WRAT-R), and similar norm- or criterion-referenced instruments, the psychologist can work with school officials to review placement possibilities and special programming options. The unique characteristics of the child as expressed in test performance may, at best, relate to school programming considerations rather than alternative intervention approaches (such as psychotherapeutic or juvenile justice alternatives).

Measures of Personality, Social Skills, and Adaptive Behavior

Personality measures and related behavioral assessment strategies are widely applied, even while being criticized for offering less than acceptable assessment data on the behavior and personality of children (Mowder, 1980). The psychologist functioning in a school or mental health setting may rely on such measures—projective techniques, objective personality techniques, direct behavioral observation, indirect behavioral observation, and indirect objective personality techniques—for a number of reasons, weighing the advantages and disadvantages of each. While studies often have failed to demonstrate the validity of many of the personality techniques, the instruments remain popular.

Certain techniques may help the psychologist to establish rapport with a juvenile during the assessment. The Bender Visual Motor Gestalt Test and strategies that require the student to draw pictures or respond to verbal and visual stimuli can establish rapport between the professional and client before other formal instruments are administered.

The Rorschach, the Children's Apperception Test (CAT), and the Thematic Apperception Test (TAT) are used by many professionals because of the self-report information they provide. Other, more objective sources of data on client behavior are also widely used. The Minnesota Multiphasic Personality Inventory (MMPI) is popular with psychologists working with older adolescents, including delinquents, and has been validated by a variety of authors for this purpose (Mischel, 1968).

An alternative to the MMPI is the Personality Inventory for Children (PIC), an inventory developed for use with clinical populations of children. A number of research projects have led to the development of scales for specific groups of adolescents. Hampton (1969/1970) constructed a scale from the PIC to predict juvenile delinquency in children. Working with data from the original standardization sample, Hampton found a correlation of .79 between her scale's scores and delinquency status. Several other researchers have developed scales that relate performance to a variety of behavioral difficulties. Wirt, Lachar, Klinedinst, and Seat (1977) reported a related delinquency prediction scale on the PIC, developed using the Darlington and Bishop (1966) procedure. The scale they developed correlated highly with the PIC's Adolescent Maladjustment and Asocial Scales. More recent studies have confirmed the utility of both the original PIC and a short form of the instrument with delinquency populations. DeKrey and Ehly (1985) report on the validity of the short form with educational classifications of students. Although their sample was largely elementary-school aged, the implications of their data are clear: the PIC is a useful tool in both clinical and educational environments to confirm a child's behavioral status.

Other avenues to the collection of information about behavior include the numerous checklists that are available for home, school, and self-assessment of children, such as Achenbach and Edelbrock's Child Behavior Checklist and Revised Child Behavior Profile and the Adolescent Behavior Checklist (Fine & Offer, 1965). Although checklists produce data related to other indicators of the child's emotional and behavioral status, they may also be useful as confirmations or validations of a child's status as assessed by more valid methods.

Additional approaches to gathering information concerning a juvenile's social and adaptive behavior skills include social skills interventions, which are being applied increasingly in school settings to enable educators to enhance the communication and behavioral repertoires of children. Approaches such as Goldstein's (Goldstein, Sprafkin, & Gershaw, 1980) skill-streaming program have provided a much-needed intervention in classroom settings, and applications of such programs in clinical settings is increasing similarly. Interest in enhancing the social competence of children and adolescents has led to the development of a number of techniques for use with handicapped as well as nonhandicapped individuals.

Similar growth has occurred with adaptive behavior assessment—strategies to document the ability of the individual to assume responsibility and control over daily activities. Like much of the early social skills programming, adaptive behavior research has centered on handicapped populations. Both social skill and adaptive behavior assessment offer the psychologist an opportunity to collect information on adolescent functioning that can be applied to placement decision-making. Instruments such as the System of Multicultural Pluralistic Assessment (SOMPA) and the Vineland Adaptive Behavior Scales are examples of effective tools available to the professional.

Vocational and Career Measures

A psychologist's interest in collecting data on vocational aptitudes and career interests may relate to a concern for developing an intervention sensitive to the long-term needs of the adolescent. Mental health professionals may routinely seek data from such sources. Interest inventories, such as the Kuder Preference Record, assess an adolescent's awareness of work and career alternatives. Sophisticated computer-scored programs that assess career interest, aptitude, and ability (e.g., General Aptitude Test Battery [GATB], Strong-Campbell Interest Inventory, and Career Assessment Inventory) have become available and indeed are being applied with some incarcerated populations. The GATB is an especially useful tool for professionals, identifying the aptitudes of the adolescent and comparing them to entry requirements in major occupational areas. The aptitudes identified can provide the psychologist with a basis on which to counsel the adolescent and to direct him or her to necessary training, education, or job placement. Carey and McAnany (1984) review the interest of law enforcement professionals in collecting vocational and career information on adolescents to prepare better for their post-institutional placement.

Family and Ecological Options

Interest in the impact of the family and broader environments on adolescents has led to the collection of data on delinquents and other juvenile populations. Instruments available on family life and interactions with peers have been widely reported. Offer, Marohn, and Ostrov (1979) report on a number of case studies that look at delinquent behavior across specific areas. These authors focus primarily on the individual's functioning within the family and in school, notably investigating communication patterns within families of delinquents. Their data-gathering procedures are of interest to psychologists working with delinquents from broken homes.

A recent text edited by Henggeler (1982) focuses on delinquents from a family-ecological systems perspective, covering research on such topics as parent-adolescent interaction, the impact of father absence on children's development, behavioral disorders and the problems of female adolescents, and the influences of peer relations on adolescent behavior. In addition to its analysis of ecological influences on behavior, the volume provides information on assessment issues and on the intervention options within an ecological orientation. Several salient points made in the text are summarized as follows: 1) The process of adaptation between an individual and the environmental context produces that person's behavior. Adaptation is unique, reflecting both the individual and the setting with which the individual interacts. No one exists independent of a context. 2) Interaction between a person and a setting is bidirectional and changes over time as the person and the context evolve. Change is due to maturation and to the effects each has on the other. 3) Environment surrounding behavior includes the immediate situation and other interconnected settings that may indirectly affect or be affected by the individual. Interpersonal, environmental, and institutional factors create the context of behavior (Kralj & Allen, 1982, pp. 226-227).

A related approach to examining family influences on adolescent behavior is that of McCubbin and Patterson (1981). These authors present an array of instruments that focus on family life and its influence on children's perceptions of their environment. Several instruments assess stress in the family environment. One of the more widely studied instruments focusing on stress is the Adolescent-Family Inventory of Life Environments and Changes (A-FILE). Available with the A-FILE is a measure of coping, the Adolescent-Coping Orientation for Problem Experiences (A-COPE).

These and other instruments from McCubbin and Patterson will be useful in school and mental health settings, providing psychologists with information on family dynamics, specifically the members' responses to stress and strategies for coping. The emphasis on the family as a source of information about the delinquent coincides with many professionals' involvement with family members during intervention planning. Marohn, Dalle-Molle, McCarter, and Linn (1980) summarize arguments from practitioners who believe a therapeutic milieu for the delinquent must involve the family. Families are indeed an obvious source of information not only about the adolescent's functioning but about the support systems available following the assessment. There is sufficient evidence to believe that family life does have profound influence on the behavior of many adolescents (Rutter & Giller, 1984).

Measures of Delinquency

The most controversial area involving the assessment of delinquency involves those instruments claiming to measure delinquent behavior or attempting to predict potential occurrences of such actions. The literature includes a few references to instruments such as the Social Prediction scale of Glueck (1956) and the Delinquency Proneness Checklist and Rating Scales (Kvaraceus, 1961), but does not support their use. As noted previously, portions of instruments such as the PIC have been found to relate to delinquent activities. The idea of having an instrument that could predict future delinquent behavior would be attractive to law enforcement agents. As every psychologist is aware, however, the reliability and validity of such approaches must be established prior to their application in school or community settings. It is safe to say that a reliable and valid mesure of delinquency has yet to be established. The usefulness of any such measure would remain for the individual professional to determine within the context of the service environment. The demands of the case, including available time, cooperativeness of the client and family, and assessment hypotheses developed by the professional, will combine to influence the selection of assessment procedures. When such procedures have unproven reliability and validity, as do Glueck's and Kvaraceus's scales, the psychologist is likely to turn to instruments with a more extensive history of successful application (e.g., the PIC).

ASSESSMENT OUTCOMES AND INTERVENTIONS

Planning for intervention that involves use of extensive assessment data will be influenced by the options available at the service site. Interventions with delinquents are extensive, as numerous writers have described, but Dembinsky (1974) provides an overview of several therapeutic approaches commonly used with this population. He describes client-centered therapies (including reality therapy, vocationally oriented psychotherapy, and Adlerian approaches) and milieu-oriented therapies (including community adjustments, educational adjustments, psychoeducational approaches, and social competency models).

Weis (1983) has identified interventions that show promise for delinquency prevention in general and for use with high risk populations, including community improvement projects, parenting training, crisis intervention projects, and alternative schools. Weis notes that these and related interventions may be based in community or school settings and involve mental health and juvenile justice agencies working with youths and their families. A common feature of successful projects is a long-term commitment to change by *all* parties involved.

McDermott (1983) has cautioned that interventions with delinquents work best when they are coordinated across the environments within which the child operates. She notes that relying only on school-based interventions may not significantly lower the incidence of some delinquent actions committed by youths, and states that law and order approaches such as tighter security, stricter rule enforcement, and fortresslike alterations in the school may reduce acts of crime in schools only to displace them to the community. She and other authors have promoted close working relations among the agencies that encounter delinquent youths and their families.

Of critical importance for all forms of intervention is an evaluation component that allows professionals in each service site to review the impact of services selected. Evaluation of services is reported infrequently in the literature, possibly because it is mainly of interest at the local level. Strategies to improve the evaluation of interventions clearly fall within the domain of the professional psychologist, who is trained to conduct such activities, as do strategies for the dissemination of information about project or intervention outcomes. Spreading the word about successful and unsuccessful plans of action allows colleagues to assess the efficacy of approaches being promoted for delinquent youths and their families.

An issue that transcends all of these considerations is the process by which an organization and its agents decide on management procedures in working with delinquents. The decision as to who is responsible for the management of individual cases or groups of cases may involve a formal process in some organizations but an informal one in others. Given the recommendations of previously discussed researchers, the organization that establishes a structure within which delinquents are assigned to a specific professional, who in turn is responsible for collaborating with other agents, will be functioning in a proven mode. Management on a case-by-case basis may be feasible to the psychologist in private practice, in a mental health agency, or a school setting, but is less practical in a juvenile law enforcement agency.

With or without a case management approach for working with delinquents, the assessor is faced with concerns about the use of data collected during screening, diagnosis, and intervention. Standards of best professional behavior (i.e., ethical behavior) may introduce dilemmas in the day-to-day functioning of psychologists. Psychologists practicing outside law enforcement agencies may have been trained to maintain confidentiality of information in almost all circumstances. In law enforcement agencies, however, standards of confidentiality are generally quite different from the standards of the American Psychological Association (APA, 1981). Standards of professional practice have evolved in law enforcement agencies to control action, whereas standards in mental health agencies strive toward personal development and responsibility.

Even within private practice or school settings, the question of who is the primary audience or client may create difficulties for the psychologist—is it the parents, the delinquent, the school, or the involved community agencies in any particular case? The full range of ethical standards offered by professional organizations creates conditions that, if enacted by the individual psychologist, will produce dilemmas in some situations. APA's guidelines for professional responsibility, competency, and practice mandate behavior that treats clients as responsible individuals who merit the practice of informed choice. In the justice system, informed choice may be reduced to a reading of rights, a process foreign to the spirit of informed choice as defined by the APA standards. During assessment, the ethical psychologist works to deliver services sensitively as well as competently. However, following best practices in assessing the delinquent will not eliminate ethical dilemmas; each psychologist is responsible for interpreting ethical standards in light of the realities of the individual cases and service environments.

CASE EXAMPLES

In the following sections, two cases are provided involving delinquents and their contacts with a psychologist. Each can be interpreted as illustrating some of the key considerations already discussed. Implications of the individual cases will be drawn following the presentation of both.

Case 1: John

A 12-year-old Caucasian, John was referred by his mother to a psychologist in private practice. The child had been caught within the local junior high school by school security agents responding to a silent alarm. Upon entering the building, the security personnel found John in a science lab, where he had sprayed chemicals around the room and overturned desks. They notified the school principal, who in turn called the parents. At the building, John confessed to several other acts of vandalism in the school and surrounding community. Local authorities were contacted and met with John and his parents to discuss what should be done.

When documented, John's actions involved significant property damage. The juvenile authorities, school officials, and John's parents agreed to have him assessed by a clinical psychologist. His parents reached an agreement with school officials to reimburse them for much of the damaged property. The juvenile authorities were interested in following through with John's case so that they could determine a feasible program to prevent him from damaging other property in the community. The parents also agreed to participate in a counseling group offered at a community mental health agency that focused on families of delinquents and status offenders who were concerned about their communication with their children. Finally, the school psychologist was notified of John's actions and agreed to engage in counseling with him and two other students similarly apprehended for vandalism.

The clinical psychologist reviewed all existing information on John's academic progress. John had proceeded at a normal pace through elementary school, but had great difficulty in adjusting to life in a junior high. He did not accept the responsibilities of junior high life and became a frequent visitor to the vice-principal's office. There were several reports of his leaving the school without notifying the office. His parents had participated in conferences with the school counselor and school psychologist. Both parents were reluctant to attend such school meetings, but eventually did agree that John was having difficulties. No changes were reported, however, in the parents' interactions with John at home.

The psychologist noted from school records that John was of average intelligence and average academic ability. The school had administered a group intelligence test and was engaged in a program of assessing achievement using the Iowa Test of Basic Skills. The psychologist administered some informal techniques that allowed John to discuss his feelings about school and family. John's parents completed the Personality Inventory for Children and engaged in individual conferences with the psychologist. The psychologist chose not to administer a battery of other instruments because he perceived his major goal in working with John and the family was to determine what course of action would best address John's difficulty in adjusting to junior high. The psychologist became concerned that the parents were not fully aware of the problems that John was having; they appeared more interested in minimizing any long-term difficulties he *could* have. The clinical psychologist contacted the school psychologist and jointly the two agreed that an ongoing program of work with John and his family members would be an important first step in helping John cope with his new responsibilities.

Law enforcement authorities were open to the arrangements offered by the school and private psychologist, so the intervention plan was implemented. Since then, John's long-term adjustment to school and to his family has been positive, with no additional reports of delinquency within a three-year period.

Case 2: George

George, a 16-year-old black youth, had been in contact with juvenile law enforcement authorities for several years without any assessment being conducted beyond documentation of his living arrangements. Juvenile authorities reported that they were frustrated with George's continued acts of delinquency (joy riding, property damage, and drug use). The authorities were open to collaboration with school and community health agencies to determine what could best be done with George to control his actions. In juvenile court within the past year, a judge had considered a motion to place George in an institutional setting until he turned 18, which would have allowed for vocational training while preventing him from interacting with the community at large. At that time, however, George's mother had succeeded in convincing the judge to leave George in her care.

The psychologist assigned by the courts to investigate George's status was a member of a community mental health agency. This psychologist had worked with several delinquents and had been successful in getting family support and input in working with children. The community agency was actively involved in organizing parents and training them to become more effective communicators.

George's mother and her husband, a stepparent to George, were frustrated with their seeming lack of influence over George's activities. George was closely involved with several friends who had similar difficulties with juvenile authorities. His mother and stepfather were both employed and were unavailable most of the day to supervise his actions. Both parents reported that George was seldom at home in the evening and would not cooperate with parental directives about when to report home. George told the psychologist that he seldom came home, especially on weekends, and chose instead to stay at friends' homes. George indicated he was well aware that he could be incarcerated until he was 18 if he did not change his actions. He knew what other people expected of him, but did not want to alter his behavior to be more independent of his friends. The parents, however, told the psychologist that many of the friends' parents considered George the leader of his peer group.

The psychologist determined that George's school attendance was minimal at best. His intelligence and achievement test scores were generally in the average to low-average range, but his school attendance had produced difficulty with school officials. George's parents had been notified that he attended school the previous year approximately 25% of the time and had been suspended because of a school policy related to minimal attendance. His parents were concerned about George's problems, but again felt unable to control his behavior. The school basically had given up with George and had chosen not to pursue his attendance. Because of the large amounts of time that George spent roaming the streets with his friends, his chances of landing in trouble were high.

The psychologist decided that administration of an intelligence or achievement battery would not be critical to any eventual intervention and administered the TAT and a sentence completion task instead, allowing George to elaborate on his perceptions of his environment and his beliefs about his life. The data were not scored in any fashion, but viewed rather as an opportunity to involve George in a discussion.

The psychologist opted next to focus on George's plans for the future. The community offered a special program for adults in difficulty with the law that focused on assessing vocational and career interest and abilities. The psychologist offered to arrange for George to be assessed on these vocational and career measures. He reluctantly agreed to participate, but did present himself to be assessed. As expected, the measures confirmed that George had little interest in most vocations and even less an idea about what he would be doing within the next five years.

Individual counseling sessions with George and his family members did not produce any new insights regarding how to diminish his risk of future difficulty with law enforcement agencies. George did agree that he had problems and would be willing to participate in a group counseling session with other young offenders. Enrolled in this group, he attended about half the time. George was apprehended four months later during a car theft. At that time the judge decided to place him in a juvenile correctional facility.

Implications

As is true with any form of intervention, the client who has made a decision to change is more likely to succeed than one who resists the psychologist's efforts. The two case examples illustrate a narrow range of behaviors associated with delinquents. Although statistics may tell us that there is a "typical" delinquent, in reality the professional will not be confronted with a generic youth. The individual adolescent, with his or her unique history and current behaviors, will challenge the professional to assess circumstances and problems in a way that leads to an intervention with a likelihood of success. As mentioned previously, one reality of working with delinquents is that the older they are, the less flexible the justice system is in response to their behavior. Past offenders especially are more likely to continue to repeat actions than are first offenders (Carey & McAnany, 1984). Similarly, the older the delinquent, the more frustrated the families and the less enthusiastic they are about the eventual success of any intervention. Matching the needs of the delinquent with the broader needs of the family, school, and community is a complex and difficult task. "John" and "George" illustrate that the chances of an intervention succeeding are fragile, requiring the full support of concerned adults and the delinquent youth.

As Gottesman (1981) argues, the juvenile justice system is a major force in shaping the actions of other agents working with the adolescent. Within the justice system, there is a remarkable degree of latitude in which the adolescent's actions and case history can be interpreted to shape interventions. The psychologist working with the adolescent will be able to provide data based on assessment findings that document past and present status as well as family dynamics. The psychological data collected can play a major role in influencing actions of the juvenile justice system at several points: intake, pretrial, trial and disposition, and post-trial treatment.

The psychologist working in service areas involving delinquent and status offender youths is in need of accurate and reliable information on services and programs available for juvenile offenders. As noted previously, the laws affecting juveniles change frequently, based on both court and legislative actions. Psychological services require constant update through inservice and written formats to provide professionals with service directions.

An additional concern of psychologists involves legal testimony, and how best to prepare for involvement with the juvenile courts. Given that the interpretation of the seriousness of a juvenile crime is influenced by the age of the offender, the preparation for a court case involving a young juvenile thus differs from that involving the older adolescent. Professionals must be aware of the weight that courts place on legal testimony from psychologists. The literature in psychological journals has begun to reflect the courts' growing interest in expert psychological testimony.

Professional psychologists will be asked by courts as well as by attorneys prior to court hearings to provide recommendations for the disposition of cases involving delinquency and status offenses. The professional must weigh what he or she has learned through assessment about the adolescent, about the family, and about available school and community services before recommending any plan to the court.

REFERENCES

American Psychiatric Association. (1980). *Diagnostic and statistical manual of mental disorders* (3rd ed.). Washington, DC: Author.
American Psychological Association. (1981). Ethical principles of psychologists. *American Psychologist, 36,* 633-638.
Carey, J. T., & McAnany, P. D. (1984). *Introduction to juvenile delinquency: Youth and the law.* Englewood Cliffs, NJ: Prentice-Hall.
Darlington, R. B., & Bishop, L. H. (1966). Increasing test validity by combining inter-item correlations. *Journal of Applied Psychology, 50,* 322-330.
DeKrey, S. J., & Ehly, S. (1985). The Personality Inventory for Children: Differential diagnosis in school settings. *Journal of Psychoeducational Assessment, 3,* 45-53.
Dembinsky, R. (1974). *Psychoeducational management of disruptive youth* (Treatment of Delinquency Series). Wilkes-Barre, PA: Wilkes College, Educational Development Center. (ERIC Document Reproduction No. ED 170 684)

Erikson, K. T. (1964). Notes on the sociology of deviance. In H. S. Becker (Ed.), *The other side: Perspectives on deviance* (pp. 9-21). New York: Free Press.

Federal Bureau of Investigation. (1980). *Crime in the United States: Uniform crime results—1979.* Washington, DC: U.S. Government Printing Office.

Fine, P., & Offer, D. (1965). Periodic outbursts of antisocial behavior. *Archives of General Psychiatry, 13,* 240-251.

Glueck, E. (1956). Spotting potential delinquents—Can it be done? *Federal Probation, 20,* 7-13.

Goldstein, A. P., Sprafkin, R. P., & Gershaw, N. J. (1980). *Skill-streaming the adolescent: A structured learning approach to teaching prosocial skills.* Champaign, IL: Research Press.

Gottesman, R. (1981). *The child and the law.* St. Paul: West.

Hampton, A. (1970). Longitudinal study of personality of children who become delinquent using the Personality Inventory for Children (Doctoral dissertation, University of Minnesota, 1969). *Dissertation Abstracts International, 30,* 4792B.

Henggeler, S. W. (Ed.). (1982). *Delinquency and adolescent psychopathology—A family-ecological systems approach.* Boston: John Wright.

Henggeler, S. W., Brunk, M. A., & Haefele, W. F. (1982). Classification and epidemiology. In S. W. Henggeler (Ed.), *Delinquency and adolescent psychopathology—A family-ecological systems approach* (pp. 27-41). Boston: John Wright.

Institute for Judicial Administration and American Bar Association. (1977). *Standards relating to juvenile delinquency and sanctions* (Juvenile Justice Standards Project). Cambridge, MA: Ballinger.

Institute for Judicial Administration and American Bar Association. (1980). *Standards relating to police handling of juvenile problems.* Cambridge, MA: Ballinger.

Kralj, M. M., & Allen, L. (1982). Delinquency prevention programs: Models, methods, and social policy. In S. W. Henggeler (Ed.), *Delinquency and adolescent psychopathology—A family-ecological systems approach* (pp. 223-242). Boston: John Wright.

Kvaraceus, W. C. (1960). *Anxious youth: Dynamics of delinquency.* Columbus: Charles E. Merrill.

Kvaraceus, W. C. (1961). Forecasting delinquency: A three-year experiment. *Exceptional Children, 27,* 429-435.

Lipton, D., Martinson, R., & Wilks, J. (1975). *The effectiveness of correctional treatment: A survey of treatment evaluation studies.* New York: Praeger.

Marohn, R. C., Dalle-Molle, D., McCarter, E., & Linn, D. (1980). *Juvenile delinquents: Psychodynamic assessment and hospital treatment.* New York: Brunner/Mazel.

McCubbin, H. I., & Patterson, J. M. (1981). *Systematic assessment of family stress, resources and coping.* St. Paul: University of Minnesota, Family Stress and Coping Project.

McDermott, J. (1983). Crime in the school and in the community: Offenders, victims, and fearful youths. *Crime and Delinquency, 29,* 270-282.

McDermott, M. J., & Hindelang, M. J. (1981). *Juvenile criminal behavior in the United States: Its trends and patterns* (National Institute for Juvenile Justice and Delinquency Prevention, Law Enforcement Assistance Administration). Washington, DC: U.S. Government Printing Office.

Mischel, W. (1968). *Personality and assessment.* New York: Wiley.

Mowder, B. A. (1980). Pre-intervention assessment of behavior disordered children: Where does the school psychologist stand? *School Psychology Review, 9,* 5-13.

National Center for Juvenile Justice. (1981). *Juvenile court statistics, 1976-1978.* Pittsburgh: Author.

Newman, J. (1980). From past to future: School violence in a broad view. *Contemporary Education, 52*(1), 7-12.

Offer, D., Marohn, R. C., & Ostrov, E. (1979). *The psychological world of the juvenile delinquent.* New York: Basic Books.

Rutter, M., & Giller, H. (1984). *Juvenile delinquency—Trends and perspectives.* New York: Guilford Press.

Salvia, J., & Ysseldyke, J. E. (1984). *Assessment in special and remedial education* (3rd ed.). Boston: Houghton Mifflin.

Shoemaker, D. J. (1984). *Theories of delinquency.* New York: Oxford University Press.

Weis, J. G. (1983, January). Focus on youth. In A. Somers (Chair), *National symposium to decrease violence: Youth involvement and juvenile justice programs.* Symposium sponsored by University of Nevada and National Council of Juvenile and Family Court Judges, Reno. (ERIC Document Reproduction No. ED 230 889)

Wirt, R. D., Lachar, D., Klinedinst, J. K., & Seat, P. D. (1977). *Multidimensional description of child personality: A manual for the Personality Inventory for Children.* Los Angeles: Western Psychological Services.

Williams, J. R., & Gold, M. (1972). From delinquent behavior to official delinquency. *Social Problems, 20,* 209-229.

Zwier, G., & Vaughan, G. M. (1984). Three ideological orientations in school vandalism research. *Review of Educational Research, 54,* 263-292.

14

Considerations in Assessing the Psychological Adjustment of Handicapped Adolescents

ANNE B. SPRAGINS, PH.D.

The variability in services currently available for handicapped youth, both in special education and in community resources, may permit some adolescents, with some types of disabling conditions, to "make it" into the mainstream educational system with only minimal needs for psychological services. Others may languish in inappropriate placements waiting to be identified as in need. All will, no doubt, be accompanied by thick educational, medical, and psychological files. The purpose of this chapter is to 1) raise issues involved in the measurement of psychological adjustment of handicapped adolescents and 2) suggest an assessment model, including a brief discussion of instruments, that can be used in evaluating the psychological adjustment of handicapped adolescents.

DEFINITION AND INCIDENCE

Who is included when referring to the "handicapped"? According to federal legislation in the areas of both education and rehabilitation services, the term *handicapped* includes the following categories: mentally retarded, hard of hearing, deaf, speech impaired, visually handicapped, seriously emotionally disturbed, orthopedically impaired, other health impaired, deaf-blind, multihandicapped, and learning disabled (Federal Register, 1977). Federal laws governing what is and is not expected, required, and available in terms of services for these groups are Public Law 94-142 (Education for All Handicapped Children Act of 1975), Public Law 94-482 (Amendments to the Vocational Education Act of 1976), Public Law 93-112, and Public Law 98-221 (Rehabilitation Act of 1973, Sections 503 and 504, and the Rehabilitation Act Amendments of 1984).

Although federal legislation refers to these individuals as *handicapped,* the rehabilitation literature tends to refer to the same students as *disabled.* Included among the disability groups in the rehabilitation literature are all types of disablement—physical, psychiatric, intellectual, and social. It appears that when a handicapped youngster leaves the world of schooling and the legislation that governs school programming, he or she moves into the adult community and receives services as part of the "disabled" adult group. For the purposes of this chapter, the terms *handicapped* and *disabled* will be used interchangeably.

The number of handicapped students receiving education at the secondary and post-secondary age levels clearly is increasing. Hohenshil (1982) notes that more and more handicapped youth are entering high school rather than dropping out prior to reaching that point. National data from 50 states for post-secondary-age handicapped students (ages 18 through 21) showed a 70% increase in the number of those receiving services between the years 1978-79 and 1982-83 (U.S. Department of Education, 1984). Before the passage of the Education for All Handicapped Children Act amendments of 1983, the actual number of secondary-age handicapped students was hidden within the total count for the age group 6 through 17. In contrast, a survey of eight states showed an increase in the number of handicapped students served for ages 12 through 17 in the years 1979 through 1982 that was greater than the increase for the total population of 3- through 21-year-olds in those states surveyed (U.S. Department of Education, 1984).

Accompanying the increase in the numbers of identified handicapped students at the secondary and post-secondary age levels has been an increase in the numbers of programs and services available for these students. Although mildly handicapped students are not generally included in the national data quoted, many of these adolescents may be experiencing adjustment problems. As these mildly handicapped students meet the stresses of adolescence and face challenges to their potential for success in the work place, increasing numbers of them may turn to special education programs at the secondary level for assistance.

ISSUES IN PSYCHOLOGICAL ADJUSTMENT AND DISABILITY

What is meant by psychological adjustment? Lazarus (1969) defines the concept as "man's efforts, successful and unsuccessful, to deal with life in the face of environmental demands, internal pressures, and human potentials" (p. x). Other definitions take varying perspectives and are more or less useful from an evaluation point of view. In Roessler and Bolton's (1978) discussion of psychological adjustment and the disabled, two issues emerge as particularly important: the theoretical model used to describe "healthy" adjustment (e.g., adjustment viewed as achievement vs. process) and the model used for establishing procedures for measuring the level of adjustment (e.g., adjustment viewed from two frames of reference, the client and an external agent).

In the achievement model, adjustment is seen as a "trouble-free state" in which all problems are solvable if one can find the appropriate solutions. Unfortunately, the achievement model of goal-directed behavior and the belief that all is possible in this best of all possible worlds do not prepare one to deal "with the senseless aspects of life such as disability, disease and natural disaster" (Roessler & Bolton, 1978, p. 4). The process model of adjustment focuses both on how one meets stress and what events influence one's efforts to adapt to stress. Existence is seen as a continued process of adjusting or adapting to situations and problems inherent in the situations. Adjustment is defined in terms of adequacy of response to changing life situations. The process model appears preferable to the achievement model of adjustment because it takes into account the changing needs of the individual within the environmental context.

A model for measuring an individual's level of adjustment, or maladjustment, may be viewed in terms of frame of reference: the perspective of the individual being evaluated and that of an external agent (e.g., a psychologist, a psychiatrist, a rehabilitation counselor, a social worker, a family member, etc). Obviously, the critical question to be addressed when evaluating the psychological adjustment of an adolescent is the extent of the convergence between the two perspectives. When the two frames of reference are taken into account, Roessler and Bolton (1978) conclude that the extent to which evaluations of adjustment level are in agreement depends on a number of factors, such as the type of instrument used, the nature of the psychosocial domain, and the purpose of the assessment. In summary, an optimal approach to the measurement of psychological adjustment of handicapped adolescents should be based on a process model of adjustment and should take into consideration the two frames of reference from which the data for decision-making are obtained.

Adjustment and the Handicapped

Having broadly defined the concept of adjustment, the clinician must consider what is meant by adjustment in relation to handicapped adolescents. Is the question one of the student's adjustment to the normal stress and strains of adolescence, or does it concern the student's level of adjustment to his or her handicap? In considering the handicapped student's adjustment to adolescence first, the following characteristic tasks of adolescence must be taken into account.

The adolescent period has been described as divided into three distinct stages (Hamburg, 1974). In early adolescence, the individual must come to terms with his or her body image by integrating the perceptions of significant others with his or her own. In the junior high school years, the child is viewed by self and others as entering the "teen" culture, requiring a new set of behaviors, values, and reference persons. In high school, interpersonal transactions come to the fore and inclusion in the peer group becomes critical. Most researchers would agree that even though Hall's (1904) "storm and stress" description of the period of adolescence may not be true for all individuals, adolescence can be a period of impoverished coping skills, high stress, and high vulnerability. Consider the handicapped youth facing adolescent adjustment. How many of his or her problems in adjustment are non-handicap-related? To what degree do these problems represent a normal adolescent coping response to a changing body and a changing set of values and behaviors?

A second question in the psychological adjustment of the handicapped adolescent relates to the youth's adjustment to the specific handicap. In the rehabilitation literature, numerous studies have explored whether a disability leads to severe emotional maladjustment and whether there are specific effects on personality functioning created by specific disabilities. Three conclusions independently supported by these studies are summarized in Roessler and Bolton (1978): 1) there appears to be no identifiable personality type associated with a specific handicap (e.g., deaf persons do not have a specific personality syndrome, nor does an amputee); 2) there does not seem to be a simple relationship between the degree of psychological impairment and the severity of the handicap (e.g., a multiple amputee may show better adjustment than a youngster with minor, but visible, burn injuries, or a profoundly hearing-impaired student may evidence better adjustment than a hard-of-hearing youngster with a mild loss); and 3) there appears to be a wide range of individual reactions to disability (e.g., although individuals may have exactly the same handicapping condition, their responses to the condition may be at entirely different ends of the response spectrum).

In writing specifically about physical disability, Wright (1960) has identified what she terms *signs of succumbing to* and *signs of coping with* the handicap. Whether the youngster is recently disabled or has lived a lifetime with the handicap, the challenges encountered during adolescence may be new. A handicap the individual has not succumbed to in childhood may require a different, more demanding response in adolescence. Wright (1960) delineates the following signs that may indicate a handicapped person is succumbing to the disability: 1) the individual may attempt to conceal the handicap and act as if it does not exist (i.e., "as if" behavior); 2) the individual may idolize the normal standard, therefore building in failure for him- or herself; 3) the "as if" behavior may eclipse the individual's behavioral possibilities and thus mask viable behavioral options; and 4) the individual may try to compensate for deficiencies by striving unusually hard in another area, which can lead to a general reduction of the individual's self-esteem. A judgment about any student's level of adjustment to his or her disability must discriminate the student who is succumbing to the handicap from the one who is exhibiting adaptive coping behaviors, given the nature of the handicap.

Signs of coping or positive striving in regard to disability can be observed by the sensitive and well-trained clinician in the following ways: 1) the individual may realize that, even given the limitations of the handicap, his or her scope of values may be enlarged and values realized; 2) there may be a realization that learning new social skills and new coping skills will help contain the disability's effect; 3) the disability may be accepted as limiting and inconvenient but not devaluating; 4) the individual may begin attributing value to personality traits such as kindness, wisdom, and effort rather than physical competence and "normality"; 5) the individual may counteract spread by realizing that not all of life is affected by the disability; and 6) the handicapped individual may be able to recognize his or her own personal assets to meet situational demands rather than comparing him- or herself to some external standard of normality (Wright, 1960).

Attitudes toward Disability

Regardless of the adaptiveness of the coping behavior exhibited by the handicapped student, he or she is at a disadvantage "in striving to adjust in a society that values good health, athletic prowess and personal appearance" (Roessler & Bolton, 1978, p. 10). The attitudes of those surrounding the handicapped student, both peers and the professionals who provide service, clearly affect the student's ability to make a healthy adjustment to his or her life's situation. Consequently, the assessment of attitudes toward a person with a disability has generated a large amount of research.

Using attitude questionnaires, Siller (1976) found that adolescents of both sexes tended to be more rejecting than younger or older persons when measured on attitudes toward a variety of handicapping conditions. What does this kind of information imply for peer acceptance of the handicapped adolescent? How is the handicapped adolescent expected to respond in an environment which he or she correctly perceives as non-accepting? Research does indicate rapidly changing societal attitudes. In the more recent studies, attempts have been made to operationalize social/situational-specific and disability-specific factors in the study of acceptance of the handicapped (Strohner, Grand, & Purcell, 1984). Findings do support the often-held contention that the most important factor associated with more favorable attitudes toward disability is the extent of contact with disabled persons. Questions remain regarding how extensive different types of contact must be to influence attitudes significantly, what type of contact is useful, and whether there is an interaction between type of contact and type of disability.

Antonak (1980) used an ordering-theory data analysis to explore attitudes toward school and community integration. Using college students as raters, he found that handicaps requiring mainly environmental modification (as with those who are physically disabled, chronically ill, hearing or visually impaired, communication disordered) were viewed more favorably on the hierarchy of attitudes toward school integration than handicaps requiring more substantial program modification (i.e., those who are behaviorally disordered, mentally retarded, and severely and profoundly impaired). When special education college students were asked to rank acceptability of common disabilities, they ranked organic impairments as most acceptable, followed by sensorimotor impairments, and finally, as least acceptable, psychoeducational or functional impairments (Abroms & Kodera, 1979). This finding suggests the possibility that a disorder's amenability to treatment may determine acceptability.

Generally, it appears that attitudes toward disability cannot be considered in a simplistic, unidimensional fashion. Attention must be given both to the specific disability and to social context. Although research has called into question whether attitudes actually affect behavior, the case for attitudes influencing behavior toward the disabled is strong (Kellman, 1974; Wright, 1974). Does the clinician working with the handicapped student succumb to negativity toward the disability or toward the person with the disability? Siller (1976) maintains that professionals often tend to label and consequently stereotype rather than respond to the individual qualities and competencies of the disabled person. In fact, he points out that in the case of many disabled individuals, "the gravity and pessimistic prognosis of many conditions inhibit involvement and interest on the part of many professionals" (p. 74). Realizing that the relationship between attitude and behavior is highly complex, the clinician responsible for judgments about the psychological adjustment of a disabled student should engage in some healthy personal reflection. The clinician should try to determine what messages he or she is conveying during interactions with the handicapped student and, therefore, what type of behavior he or she is eliciting.

ASSESSMENT FOR PSYCHOLOGICAL ADJUSTMENT

For mainstreamed mildly handicapped adolescents and for the formally identified handicapped adolescent, the question of psychological adjustment becomes increasingly important as schooling advances. Hohenshil (1982) describes the traditional purpose of the high school as preparation for entry-level employment or preparation for the next level of the educational system. In asking parents what they want for their handicapped children as a result of 12 years of schooling, Hohenshil found that the parents reported wanting their children "to be independent, self supporting, self directing individuals" (p. 2). He maintains that this aspiration is virtually impossible in our society "unless a person is *occupationally* independent" (p. 2). Thus, the psychological health of the adolescent must be seen and evaluated not only in relation to the typical tasks of adolescent relationships and identity questions, but also in relation to expectations for the work place.

Assessment has been defined by Ysseldyke and Shinn (1981) as a process of collecting data to make decisions. The purpose of assessment within the schools is to enable educators to make psychoeducational decisions in the areas of screening, identification or placement, intervention or instructional planning, program evaluation, and individual student progress (Salvia & Ysseldyke, 1978). In which of these components will assessment of the psychological adjustment of handicapped adolescents appear? By adolescence it is reasonable to expect that assessment for the purposes of screening, identification, and placement will receive little emphasis. Most students will have a long history of placement decisions and previous testing, including reports by teachers, psychologists, and medical personnel, for reference. A major emphasis at the secondary level should be assessment for the purpose of intervention planning and improvement in educational programming. Clearly, intervention planning in the context of an educational program should include planning for future occupational independence to the greatest extent possible. Before presenting an assessment model, it may be helpful to review the major educational programs available for handicapped youth.

Educational Programming

At the secondary level there are a variety of interventions and school programs available for handicapped adolescents. Epstein (1982), while describing types of programs available, laments that few have been carefully specified and disseminated to others and that the programs have rarely been evaluated to determine their value for the students. Nevertheless, he categorizes four types of programming: 1) alternate learning approaches (e.g., basic skills remediation, functional curriculum, tutorial models, and work-study models); 2) social participation models (e.g., behavioral interventions; reviewed by Epstein, Cullinan, & Rose, 1980) and social skills and social participation curriculums (Zigmond, 1978); 3) career preparation (e.g., programs described by Brolin & Kokaska, 1979); and 4) community participation (e.g., Teaching-Family Model; Epstein, 1982).

Many of these programs provide a method for assessing what might be termed "the student's psychological adjustment" within the program itself. Assessment of the student's level of psychological adjustment as a component of the program then becomes part of the intervention plan. For example, Neff (1976) refers to the need for the individual to develop a "work personality" as part of a total socialization process. He suggests that maladjustment to work may reflect inability to cope with demands inherent in work as a social situation. He suggests that problems of work need not respond necessarily to the same therapeutic techniques as those developed to solve the problems of intimate personal relations.

Neff's (1976) approach would imply that career preparation programs should concentrate their efforts on assessing the psychological adjustment of students to the functional vocational requirements of the work role. Following this line of thinking, Roessler and Bolton (1985) have developed an experimental rating scale (the Work Personality Profile) that provides a profile portraying a student's work personality strengths and weaknesses on dimensions such as "Ability to socialize with co-workers," "Social communication skills," and "Appropriateness of personal relations with supervisor."

Assessment Model

A model of assessment that attempts to describe a youngster's "work personality" would incorporate both formal and informal assessment procedures. The purpose of the assessment would be ongoing measurement, to evaluate either individual student progress, program quality, or both. For example, a number of social-skills training programs are available. Davidow (1974) describes a program for visually impaired students that includes units of instruction in a number of living skills such as personal appearance, table etiquette, and interpersonal relations.

Goldstein and Pentz (1984) describe a structured learning approach to psychological skill training in which specific skills are broken down into five or six different steps. The steps are the operational definition of the given skill. Component behavior steps include such skills as asking for help, giving instructions, expressing a complaint, preparing for a stressful conversation, and so on. The program uses trainers who either act out the skill themselves or use audiovisual modeling displays with actors displaying the skill. Each skill is then modeled by the trainees through role play with feedback sessions following. Although this type of program reportedly has been successful, a problem still remains in the trainees' failure to transfer therapeutic gains from training to the "real-life" setting.

Blevins (1982), in advocating the use of social skill programs for hearing-impaired youths, suggests a type of program that attempts to overcome the difficulties encountered in the transfer of training. The trainee is accompanied by a trained observer as he or she goes into the workplace to get a job application, arrange a future appointment, and so on. Feedback from the participant observer is incorporated as a part of the overall skill training program.

Lack of social skills has been identified as a major difficulty for both mildly and severely handicapped adolescents (Epstein, 1982) and has been found to be a major reason for loss of employment (Brolin, 1973; Hooper, 1980). Because a lack of social skills comprises a part of handicapped students' adjustment problems, an assessment strategy should 1) assess entry level skills according to the ability of the individual to adjust, 2) monitor the development of those skills at stated periods through the intervention program, 3) establish a desired level of mastery for exit from the program, and 4) follow up by monitoring and evaluating the handicapped students as they progress to higher levels of education or the workplace.

The assessment model being proposed is process oriented and makes use of a variety of assessment procedures. The assessment strategies commonly used in social skills programs are both formal and informal and could be adopted easily for use in a process-oriented approach to the evaluation of psychological adjustment of handicapped adolescents.

Assessment strategies both used in social skills assessment and proposed for inclusion in a process-oriented model include behavioral observations (e.g., naturalistic and structured), behavioral analogues (e.g., role play), external reports (e.g., sociometrics and ratings), and self-reports. Although these techniques are probably quite familiar to most clinicians, their use as a means to evaluate the psychological adjustment of handicapped adolescents may not have been considered. A brief review of the techniques should indicate their potential usefulness in determining psychological health.

In a survey of current practices in the assessment of personality and behavior by school psychologists, Goh and Fuller (1983) found that large numbers of school psychologists reported frequent use of some types of informal procedures for assessing behavior. (The use of rating scales was defined as an informal procedure, but other "informal" approaches were not identified.) Moran (1978) and Guerin and Maier (1983) elaborate on types of informal approaches that can be used in preassessment screenings in the educational setting, but these strategies more often relate to assessing academically related behaviors. Harrington (1984) includes in the category of informal assessment strategies observation of behavioral indicators, testing the limits, and criterion-referenced testing. All of these strategies could be useful in assessing the psychological adjustment of handicapped adolescents in a process model.

Observing in the natural environment requires the clinician to identify target behaviors that are indicative of the youngster's level of adjustment. An example of the kind of adjustment behavior that might be observed in a classroom setting is the following. A hearing-impaired adolescent who is dependent on lip reading for information sits in a desk where viewing the teacher is difficult and does not attend to peer communications, but rather monopolizes the interaction. The examiner's role in this instance would be to monitor and verify whether these same maladaptive behaviors occur in other environments. A trained professional using formal behavioral observation techniques could observe this youngster responding to a standard script about what he would do and how he would respond in everyday situations. As another alternative, a role-play situation might be devised that would focus on this youngster's peer-interactional style of monopolizing versus entering into the give and take of communication.

Gresham and Elliott's (1984) review of research on intervention programs indicates that there are serious questions about whether a youngster's performance in role play predicts the degree to which that youngster will perform similar behaviors in different settings. These researchers suggest that role-play measures can provide meaningful, but limited, diagnostic data.

The sociometric techniques most commonly used as assessment tools are either peer nominations (Moreno, 1934) or peer-rating scales (Roistacher, 1974). Both measures appear to be used more often for younger children, but have potential for application with handicapped and nonhandicapped adolescents. In peer nominations, the examiner asks the youngsters to nominate peers according to nonbehavioral criteria such as preferred work partner, physical attributes, most or least liked, and so on. A student's score is determined by dividing the total number of nominations he or she receives by the number who participate in the nomination. The peer-rating approach involves having students rate members of his or her group or class on a 3- or 5-point Likert-type scale covering some specific criteria. The student's score is determined by averaging the ratings he or she receives from other members of the group.

Gresham (1982) suggests that ratings of acceptance by classmates obtained by using peer ratings may provide more realistic outcome measures than the ratings of popularity that result from peer-nomination techniques. Both methods add a social psychological dimension to the diagnostic process and have potential for building social-skills intervention training programs.

Aside from measures developed specifically for handicapped populations, formal and informal assessment procedures often must be adapted for use with these examinees. Paper-and-pencil inventories frequently require some form of modification, if only in their interpretive use with handicapped students. The adaptation simply may consist of developing local norms for a specific handicapped group placed in a particular setting. For example, a referral question may ask whether a mentally retarded adolescent is ready to move from an in-school work program to an out-of-school work placement; local norms (based on previously successful students) for the Vineland Adaptive Behavior Scales may be used to measure how well the existing curriculum has prepared this adolescent to adjust to an available work program.

Another example would be found in certain items on the AAMD Adaptive Behavior Scales, such as "Talks excessively" or "Talks too close to others' faces." These items may need to be reinterpreted as "Signs or attempts his or her mode of communication excessively" or "Signs right in others' faces" for hearing-impaired youngsters who use sign language rather than oral expression. Similarly, on Vineland Adaptive Behavior Scales items such as "Initiates social small talk when meeting acquaintances," one must consider that hearing-impaired students may be reluctant to do so because of their difficulties in communicating with others who do not sign.

The literature does not abound with formal procedures that can be used to evaluate the psychological adjustment of handicapped adolescents. The instruments that are available contain various problems depending on the particular handicapping condition of the examinee. Table 1 offers assessment strategies and sample instrumentation categorized by frame of reference (perspective of the examinee vs. perspective of an external agent). In both frames of reference, the clinical interview is listed as an assessment approach because, whether focused on the youngster, the parents, or other significant caretakers, this component is critical in establishing a factual picture of the important emotional characteristics of the adolescent within the family setting.

Most individuals will resist revealing their emotional scars to an unfamiliar and thus potentially unaccepting person. Thus, the handicapped adolescent's true situation may be revealed in bits and pieces, well masked, in order to give him or her time to gauge the effect of the story on the interviewer. The handicapped adolescent, or the "stigmatized" individual so well described by Goffman (1963), may feel "unsure of how we normals will identify him and receive him" (p. 13). Even in a clinical interview, Barker's (1948) comment holds true in that "the blind, the ill, the deaf, the crippled can never be sure what the attitude of a new acquaintance will be, whether it will be rejective or accepting, until the contact has been made" (p. 34). Establishing trust and gaining the true facts when interviewing a handicapped adolescent may be a lengthy process.

TABLE 1

ASSESSMENT STRATEGIES CATEGORIZED BY FRAME OF REFERENCE

Perspective of the Individual	*Perspective of an External Agent*
1. Self-Report	1. Rating Scales
Minnesota Multiphasic Personality Inventory (MMPI)	Child Behavior Checklist and Revised Child Behavior Profile
Sixteen Personality Factor Questionnaire (16PF)	The Conners Parent Symptom Questionnaire
Adolescent Emotional Factors Inventory	The Conners Teacher Rating Scale
Rotter Incomplete Sentences Blank	Burks' Behavior Rating Scales
Coopersmith Self-Esteem Inventory—Adult	Personality Inventory for Children
Tennessee Self Concept Scale	Bristol Social Adjustment Guides
2. Interview	AAMD Adaptive Behavior Scale, School Edition
	Vineland Adaptive Behavior Scales
	Meadow-Kendall Social-Emotional Inventories for Deaf and Hearing-Impaired Students
	2. Projectives
	House-Tree-Person Technique
	Kinetic Family Drawing Scales
	Rotter Incomplete Sentences Blank
	3. Observation
	4. Sociometry
	5. Interview

In general, a hypothesis-testing approach (i.e., determining what information is wanted and hypothesizing how best to get it) can lead the clinician into creative informal assessments. Before using rating scales, projective techniques, or even structured interviews, certain informal procedures are generally followed by clinicians familiar with the specific handicapping condition. With the blind, low-vision, or visually limited youngster, for example, informal assessment may involve determining whether materials are best placed on a table or a bookstand, which lighting conditions are most effective, and whether print or braille presentation will be required. Youngsters with motor handicaps may need specific supportive equipment in order to respond effectively. Hearing-impaired subjects who depend on lip reading require time to acclimate to the lip movements of a new person and thus would benefit from casual conversation of a nonstressful nature before beginning formal assessment tasks. How well the student can adapt to the new person and discuss past or present problems with lip reading thus becomes part of the evaluation process.

Projective Techniques

Projective techniques historically have been considered useful either to tap underlying personality structures or to measure discrete personality characteristics (Goh & Fuller, 1983). The usefulness of projective techniques as an assessment tool within the educational system is a matter for continuing debate (Conti, 1983; Knoff, 1983; Peterson & Batsche, 1983). Whether these formal methods have any usefulness for evaluating the psychological adjustment of handicapped adolescents in a process model of evaluation is also a matter for debate. Weaver (1984), in writing of assessing the mentally retarded child, firmly states that the use of projectives "by general practitioners with little training and supervised experience cannot be recommended" (p. 60). Placing projective techniques under the "external agent" frame of reference category in Table 1 illustrates the subjective interpretations involved in the use of these tools.

If the clinician plans to use projective techniques of any type in evaluating the psychological adjustment of handicapped adolescents, caution must be observed for specific disabilities. With the hearing impaired, numerous caveats have been given relating to the mode of communication used and the examiner's knowledge of the "deaf culture" (Levine, 1981). For example, the nature of deaf education is such that most hearing-impaired children are exposed to years of highly structured school routines and environments. Later, as adolescents or young adults, they may be part of a close-knit deaf community, with its own clubs, churches, and sporting events. Given this highly structured society of close-knit groupings, it is not surprising to find that hearing-impaired adolescents or young adults may find it difficult to respond to the inherently loosely structured items of projective tasks. Levine points out that some deaf youths are "immobilized by Rorschach inkblots" and may be "inhibited by sentence completion because they feel their language is not good enough" (1981, p. 283).

A clinician untrained in signing should not administer projective techniques to adolescents whose major mode of communication is through sign language. An informal interview with the youngster can be used alternatively to determine the student's major mode of communication and to decide whether the youngster is a good candidate for projective assessment. For example, the student might be asked to describe how the story line of a movie recently seen might change if they were the hero, or they might be asked to develop a fantasy about what their future holds for them.

For the blind and low-vision youth, Bauman (1976) maintains that sentence and story material can be used, even with the totally blind, by oral presentation. She also makes reference to two auditory projective tests, The Auditory Projective Test and the Sound Test, that have a record of moderate acceptance for use with the blind. Both techniques use sound stimuli in creative ways. The Auditory Projective Test includes auditory stimuli and a series of conversations in nonsense syllable form. The conversations purportedly parallel the interpersonal relationships suggested by some of the Thematic Apperception Test (TAT) cards, such that stories given in response can be interpreted as would the TAT stories. The Sound Test (Palacios, 1964) includes stimuli varying from simple sounds such as footsteps to more complex combinations of music, sounds, and voices. Sample responses rather than statistical norms are provided to assist the clinician in analysis of protocols.

Self-Report Inventories

In order to investigate the handicapped individual's own perspective, self-report inventories are often used. Although objective personality inventories of the self-report variety are quantifiable and can be subjected to empirical tests, they are usually lengthy and time-consuming to administer and score. Additionally, these instruments normally produce labels or descriptors rather than the "dynamic" process information that can be used more easily to generate recommendations for intervention.

Alternatively, Cautela and Upper (1976) argue that self-reports are behaviors in themselves and often are the primary response of interest. They also counter arguments concerning the validity of self-reports by offering evidence indicating that self-reports are no more unreliable or invalid than other types of measurement. While Mischel (1977) maintains that these instruments are constrained by the limits of the individual's own awareness, he also points out that the problem with self-report instruments is not that the subject is unreliable, but that the wrong question is asked of him or her.

The Minnesota Multiphasic Personality Inventory (MMPI), regularly employed to assess adolescent and early adult adjustment, has a history of use with a variety of handicapping conditions. Collins-Moore and Osborn (1984) suggest that the MMPI may be used selectively with the blind but recommend that it and other self-report measures be administered through large-print, braille, or tape-recorded versions, which "guarantees privacy in making the response and improves the predictive validity of the results" (p. 151). Cross (1974) and Potter (1950) discuss braille forms of the MMPI and its use. Roessler and Bolton (1978), while reporting that the MMPI is the most-often used instrument with the disabled, state that conclusions gathered from it are often suspect due to the complex relationship between the occurrence of disability and evidence of emotional maladjustment.

For the hearing impaired, the MMPI presents problems due to its language level, the idiomatic expressions included in some items, its high literacy and concept levels (difficult to transpose into sign), and specific item difficulty. For example, how does a deaf person respond (true/false/cannot-say) to questions such as "My hearing is apparently as good as that of most people" or "While in trains, buses, etc., I often talk to strangers"? As Levine (1981) points out, the deaf respondent risks the label of "maladjusted" if he or she answers truthfully. Levine also questions whether such personality tests mean the same thing conceptually to the deaf, and whether they live in the same psychological world as the hearing. Perhaps the same questions can be asked about individuals with other disabilities regarding the items on an inventory designed to elicit responses "not based on the physical but on the psychological attributes of the 'worlds' inhabited by the test subjects" (Levine, 1981, p. 198). One would have to conclude that, although the main value of the MMPI is in differential diagnosis, the major drawback for use with handicapped adolescents is the reading level required. If the youngster has not achieved a sixth-grade reading level and a good understanding of idiomatic constructions, the MMPI is not likely to be the test of choice.

The Sixteen Personality Factor Questionnaire (16PF) has been refined over a number of years and reviewed thoroughly by Bolton (1978). A summary of empirical investigations of the personality characteristics of a range of physically and psychiatrically disabling conditions using the 16PF is presented in Roessler and Bolton (1978). They conclude that the test provides convincing empirical evidence concerning the relationship between disability and personality. Based on studies with hearing-impaired adolescents, Trybus (1973) and Jensema (1975) conclude that the 16PF Form E (low-literate form, requiring third-grade reading level) is one of the better tests currently used for these subjects. It should be noted, however, that Jensema (1975) found the reliability of the 16PF to be low with a sample of teenaged hearing-impaired college freshmen, especially for Factors M and N. Ordinarily, a low score on Factor M indicates a conventional, proper, or careful person, whereas a high score indicates unconventional, eccentric traits. On Factor N, a high score indicates forthright, simple, or unpretentious personality traits; low scores suggest one who is sophisticated or shrewd. Given Jensema's (1975) finding that the items for Factor M and N yielded near-zero and negative correlations, one should view these factors with caution when using the 16PF with hearing-impaired adolescents. For further information, chapter 14 of the *Handbook for the Sixteen Personality Factor Questionnaire* (Cattell, Eber, & Tatsuoka, 1970) includes 16PF profiles for physically disabled, hearing-impaired, visually impaired, and speech-disordered persons. However, sampling procedures and significance tests were not reported for these populations.

In the more specialized areas of formal paper-and-pencil inventories, Bauman (1976) describes her Adolescent Emotional Factors Inventory, which was developed for blind adults and adapted for teenagers. The items were developed as a result of discussions with blind adolescents about their problems; consequently, the test should have good face validity concerning the adolescent problems involved with blindness.

Because self-esteem and identity are discussed in detail in chapter 3 of this volume, the relationship between disability and measures of self-concept will not be discussed further here. Generally, disabled persons report lower self-esteem than nondisabled, and some disabling conditions have greater impact on self-concept than others (Collins, Burger, & Doherty, 1970; Meighan, 1970). Measurements of self-concept, therefore, might be used productively as part of an ongoing assessment process within an intervention program for handicapped adolescents. Lyman and Roberts (1984) report that the Coopersmith Self-Esteem Inventory has been used successfully to assess adjustment to chronic illness, and Meighan (1970) reports use of the Tennessee Self Concept Scale with blind adolescents as a measure of adjustment.

Rating Scales

A number of behavior rating scales and observation devices have emerged within a behaviorally oriented framework over the last 10 to 15 years. The focus has been on the study of observable behavior rather than traits and personality dynamics.

Edelbrock (1983) raises interesting questions about the complexity involved in considering the seemingly simple questions of what is assessed and who is the informant. He agrees that rating scales provide an efficient and cost-effective way to obtain objective and reliable information about a youngster when the scales are used in a "multimethod" assessment (i.e., one including direct observations, psychological testing, and/or clinical interview).

Rating scales that use multiple informants provide a comprehensive picture of the individual's behavior across settings, thus permitting an integration of data. When moving from the assessment process into the planning and building of intervention programs, this cross-situational data is a necessity. In the case of behavioral rating scales for adolescents, there are few from which to select. Although there are a number of scales for the elementary-age child, only a few of these have been developed to assess youngsters up to the age of 16 and even fewer beyond that age. There are indications that a greater number of behavior rating scales are being extended through Grade 12 or age 18.

An example of a revised and extended instrument is the Child Behavior Checklist and Revised Child Behavior Profile by Achenbach and Edelbrock, which includes a means of assessing behavior from the parent and teacher perspective, a form for having an experienced observer rate the youngster during six 10-minute observation periods, and a Youth Self-Report Inventory for subjects aged 11 through 18.

The Burks' Behavior Rating Scale seeks to identify behavior problems for youngsters up to Grade 9 by having either parent or teacher respond to descriptive statements of observed behavior in such categories as aggressiveness, impulse control, anger control and social conformity. Once problem behavior patterns are identified, the test manual provides suggestions for possible intervention approaches for specific disability groups (e.g., orthopedically handicapped, speech and hearing handicapped, educable mentally retarded).

The Conners Parent Symptom Questionnaire and Teacher Rating Scale provide separate scales to be completed by the parent or the teacher for assessing the problem behavior of youngsters from ages 3 to 17. The parent questionnaire focuses on such areas as peer and family relationships, personal habits, and emotional development. The teacher scale assesses classroom behaviors, with a predominate focus on hyperactivity and conduct problems.

The Personality Inventory for Children (PIC) is a rating scale constructed in the tradition of the MMPI to assess the adjustment of youngsters aged 3 to 16. Designed to be completed by a parent using a true/false response format, the PIC provides a battery of reliable personality scores (i.e., adjustment, family relations, anxiety, depression, social skills) and has the advantages of quick scoring, relatively easy interpretation, and objective data that can be reported to parents in interpretive interviews. Because the validity of parent perception can be a concern, the PIC's MMPI-like validity scale (Lie Scale, F Scale) is a useful device.

Experienced clinicians recognize that parents of handicapped adolescents, even though they may have lived for years with their child's handicap, face new adjustments with each developmental period. Although the process of denial can serve a healthy or coping function for parents of a recently handicapped child, this normal grieving process (Moses, 1979) eventually has to move forward. Using the parent's responses on the PIC, the sensitive clinician can better understand the parent's difficult realities and thus help parent and child build a positive relationship.

A rating scale completed by teachers with a focus on the youngster's adequate or poor adjustment in social behavior is the Bristol Social Adjustment Guides. The scale provides a multidimensional approach for assessing school-aged children from 5 to 15 on several dimensions of maladaptive behavior. The profile is interpreted as showing generally adequate or poor adjustment. Degrees of maladjustment are rated as mild, moderate, or severe in terminology compatible with the third edition of the *Diagnostic and Statistical Manual of Mental Disorders* (DSM-III; American Psychiatric Association, 1980). This system (McDermott, 1983) may be used to separate the poorly adjusted youngster from the severely disturbed one.

Another such scale that taps not only social-emotional adjustment but includes items related to adjustment to hearing impairment is the Meadow-Kendall Social-Emotional Assessment Inventories for Deaf and Hearing-Impaired Students (SEAI). The 59-item school-age form provides norms for hearing-impaired youngsters from ages 7 to 21. The SEAI yields percentile scores in three categories: social adjustment, self-image, and emotional adjustment. Items are typical of those one would expect on a social adjustment scale, with the addition of specialized items for deaf and hearing-impaired such as "Tries to communicate with others (both deaf and hearing) by any means necessary: signs, speech writing, pantomime" and "Is willing to interact with hearing people: does not refuse to interact with peers or adults who have normal hearing" (Meadow, Karchmer, Petersen, & Rudner, 1983).

For multihandicapped youngsters, the instrument of choice for gathering formal information about adjustment has often been a measure of adaptive behavior. Estimates of a multihandicapped student's psychological adjustment can be extracted from a review of responses on both Part I and Part II of the AAMD Adaptive Behavior Scale, either the School Edition or the basic edition generally used for institutionalized populations. Although the basic scale was devised for mentally retarded, emotionally maladjusted, and developmentally disabled individuals, Suess, Dickson, Anderson, and Hildman (1981) have provided norms for deaf-blind individuals. Reliability, from all commonly considered perspectives, is adequate on Part I (which measures self-reliance and social development), but interrater reliability on Part II (which measures antisocial or disturbing behaviors) has been found to be low (Nihira, Foster, Shellhaas, & Leland, 1975).

Part II items on the AAMD deal more with behaviors related to psychological adjustment but results must be used cautiously. Each individual's behaviors should be evaluated with considerable knowledge of the setting with which the individual must cope. Nihira et al. (1975) suggest that, generally, the importance of the specific behavior under consideration should be emphasized rather than its frequency when interpreting Part II. Given these cautions, the AAMD scale can be useful in determining a severely handicapped individual's specific needs, in establishing a priority ranking of behavior patterns, and in outlining individual programming.

The advent of the Vineland Adaptive Behavior Scales, a nationally standardized, technically strong measure of social functioning, will no doubt replace the outdated Vineland Social Maturity Scale. Questions on the newer Vineland Adaptive Behavior Scales are to be administered in a semistructured interview fashion and are answered by an adult informant who is quite familiar with the adaptive behavior of the adolescent being evaluated. The scale domains with the most potential for providing information about the youngster's psychological adjustment are Socialization and Maladaptive Behavior. The Socialization domain includes measures of interpersonal relations, play and leisure time use, and coping skills. The Maladaptive Behavior domain (included only on the Survey and Expanded Forms) has two parts, the second of which has supplementary norms for disabled groups. Unfortunately, the supplementary norms for hearing-impaired and visually handicapped children only cover ages 6 through 12 in residential facilities.

Stress response scales represent recent developments in evaluating the psychological adjustment of handicapped adolescents, who very often operate in social environments in which their needs are not well understood, in which there may be hostility toward them, and in which they may feel punished. Knowledge of a youngster's typical response pattern in stressful situations offers valuable information for constructing intervention programs designed to build coping behaviors. French, Rodgers, and Cobb (1974), using a model of adjustment defined as person-environmental fit, describe various types of scales for measuring reaction to stress, adaptation of which, for specific handicapped populations, may be a useful future direction.

The Stress Response Scale (Chandler, 1983; Chandler, Shermis, & March, 1985) was developed for use with children ages 5 to 15 referred for mild to moderate emotional problems and is not regularly used with severely disturbed youngsters. The scale is based on the assumption that symptoms seen in youngsters referred for emotional adjustment problems may often reflect normal coping responses to extremely stressful situations. Common response patterns to stress (e.g., impulsive, dependent, passive-aggressive, repressed) are defined, quantitative data on the assessment of emotional adjustment reactions are provided. Although there are no specific data on the use of the Stress Response Scale with handicapped groups, the possibility of using standard scores on the subscales to construct a profile reflecting a youngster's preferred response pattern is appealing.

Behavioral Observation

Behavioral observation is an essential component of the assessment process. It may take the form of one of the more formal systems, such as frequency recording, duration recording, momentary time sampling, or interval time sampling (Hall, Hawkins, & Axelrod, 1976; Irwin & Bushnell, 1980), or it may involve observation during testing or the clinical interviews. Defining what is to be observed and why, what one hopes to gain, and what to do with the data once collected is always a challenge. In fact, the challenge may be greater when the task involves the measurement of the psychological health of a handicapped adolescent. Blevins (1982), in discussing vocational assessment for hearing-impaired adolescents, delineates the merits of using observational data in work sampling situations or "miniature situations," structured to replicate real life and allow the youngster to interact with a trained observer. In the case of the hearing-impaired adolescent, such observation is only valuable when the observer can communicate in the same mode as the individual being evaluated. Reading body language may be a useful clinical tool, but imagine the non-signing clinician observing a simulated work situation in which the prospective employee and the employer have an angry exchange in sign language. What possible conclusions could the clinician draw about what transpired during the exchange?

In any case, an evaluation that does not include behavioral observation, either in the natural environment or in simulation, can actually be dangerous when handicapped youngsters are the ones being evaluated. Kent and Foster (1977) point out that with a growing interest in the areas of observer training and behavioral code development, there is likely to be a "productive convergence of research on observational recording with the more traditional testing literature" (p. 323).

FUTURE DIRECTIONS

The concept of psychological adjustment has been broadly defined as an individual's efforts, whether successful or unsuccessful, to handle his or her life in the face of demands from the environment, internal pressures, and human potentials. There are several issues to be considered in the evaluation of the psychological adjustment of handicapped adolescents. First, the examiner must differentiate the normal developmental changes experienced by the majority of adolescents from that which can be clearly defined as maladaptive adjustment. Second, the clinician should define healthy coping behavior for handicapped adolescents in terms of adjustment to their specific disability. The effects of attitudes toward the disability adopted by both peers and clinicians providing services are also factors to be considered in the evaluation process.

Mischel (1977), in discussing the future of personality measurement, describes a person-centered focus in which

one tries to describe the particular individual in relation to the particular psychological conditions of his life. . . . the essence of the approach is a functional analysis that investigates in vivo covariations between changes in the individual and changes in the conditions of his or her life. (p. 248)

In elaborating on his perspective, Mischel suggests consideration of both person variables and environmental variables, as their mutual interaction is evident. A process model of evaluation requires the freedom to use both informal and formal data to evaluate the individual handicapped adolescent, his or her present environment, and the reciprocal affects of the person and the environment on each other.

The continued development of specific behaviorally oriented evaluations of psychological adjustment will be beneficial for developing intervention programs for handicapped adolescents. Such behaviorally oriented evaluations would assess career training, social skills and personal psychological adjustment defined in terms of the specific demand within the program. The use of criterion-referenced procedures would be included in the development of such programs. Secondly, emphasis should continue to be placed on ongoing evaluation of the student regarding his or her adjustment. In conjunction with evaluation of the student, there should also be an evaluation of the environment to determine where changes are required.

Finally, there is a need for a smooth transition between school training (special education) and the world of work (rehabilitation services) if the adolescent is to emerge psychologically well. If there is to be a blend between the "work personality" and the "student personality," there must be cooperation and communication between the workplace and the schools, so that goals for the handicapped adolescent's psychological adjustment are mutually defined.

What the parents of the handicapped adolescent wish for their child is, no doubt, what the youngster wishes for him- or herself: to be an independent, self-supporting, self-directed human being. Whatever the handicapping condition, the youngster's ability to cope, to meet situational demands, and to recognize his or her own personal assets can and must be supported by an environment that is responsive to him or to her as an individual.

REFERENCES

Abroms, K. I., & Kodera, T. L. (1979). Acceptance hierarchy of handicaps: Validations of Kirk's statement, "Special Education often begins where medicine stops." *Journal of Learning Disabilities, 12*(1), 24-29.

American Psychiatric Association. (1980). *Diagnostic and statistical manual of mental disorders* (3rd ed.). Washington, DC: Author.

Antonak, R. F. (1980). A hierarchy of attitudes toward exceptionality. *The Journal of Special Education, 14*(2), 231-241.

Barker, R. (1948). The social psychology of physical disability. *Journal of Social Issues, 4*, 30-35.

Bauman, M. K. (1976). Psychological evaluation of the blind client. In B. Bolton (Ed.), *Handbook of measurement and evaluation in rehabilitation* (pp. 249-268). Baltimore, MD: University Park Press.

Blevins, B. (1982). Vocational assessment procedures for the deaf and hearing impaired. In T. H. Hohenshil, W. T. Anderson, & J. F. Salman (Eds.), *Secondary school psychological services: Focus on vocational assessment procedures for handicapped students.* Blacksburg, VA: Virginia Tech. (ERIC Document Reproduction Service No. ED 229 704)

Bolton, B. (1978). Sixteen Personality Factor Questionnaire. In O. K. Buros (Ed.), *The eighth mental measurements yearbook* (pp. 1078-1080). Highland Park, NJ: Gryphon Press.

Brolin, D. E. (1973). Vocational evaluation: Special education's responsibility. *Education and Training of the Mentally Retarded, 8*, 12-17.

Brolin, D. E., & Kokaska, C. J. (1979). *Career education for handicapped children and youth.* Columbus, OH: Charles E. Merrill.

Cattell, R. B., Eber, H. W., & Tatsuoka, M. M. (1970). *Handbook for the Sixteen Personality Factor Questionnaire (16PF).* Champaign, IL: Institute for Personality and Ability Testing.

Cautela, J. R., & Upper, D. (1976). The behavioral inventory battery: The use of self-report measures as behavioral analysis and therapy. In M. Hersen & A. S. Bellack (Eds.), *Behavioral assessment: A practical handbook* (pp. 77-109). New York: Pergamon.

Chandler, L. A. (1983). The Stress Response Scale. *School Psychology Review, 12*, 260-265.

Chandler, L. A., Shermis, M. D., & March, J. (1985). The use of the Stress Response Scale in diagnostic assessment with children. *Journal of Psychoeducational Assessment, 3*, 15-29.

Collins, H. A., Burger, G. K., & Doherty, D. D. (1970). Self-concept of EMR and non-retarded adolescents. *American Journal of Mental Deficiency, 75*, 285-289.

Collins-Moore, M. S., & Osborn, K. N. (1984). Assessing the visually handicapped child. In S. J. Weaver (Ed.), *Testing children: A reference guide for effective clinical and psychoeducational assessments* (pp. 137-161). Kansas City, MO: Test Corporation.

Conti, A. P. (1983). Implementing interventions from projective findings: Suggestions for school psychologists. *School Psychology Review, 12*(4), 435-440.

Cross, O. H. (1974). Braille adaptation of the Minnesota Multiphasic Personality Inventory for use with the blind. *Journal of Applied Psychology, 31,* 189-198.

Davidow, M. E. (1974). *Social competency.* Louisville, KY: American Printing House for the Blind.

Edelbrock, C. S. (1983). Problems and issues in using rating scales to assess child personality and psychopathology. *School Psychology Review, 12*(3), 293-299.

Epstein, M. H. (1982). Special education programs for the handicapped adolescent. *School Psychology Review, 11*(4), 384-390.

Epstein, M. H., Cullinan, D., & Rose, T. L. (1980). Applied behavior analysis and behaviorally disordered pupils: Selected issues. In L. Mann & D. A. Sabatino (Eds.), *The fourth review of special education.* New York: Grune & Stratton.

Federal Register. (1977, Aug. 23). Public Law 94-142. *Regulations implementing the Education for All Handicapped Children Act of 1975, 42,* 42474-42518.

French, L. R., Rodgers, W., & Cobb, S. (1974). Adjustment as person-environment fit. In G. V. Coelho, D. H. Hamburg, & J. E. Adams (Eds.), *Coping and adaptation* (pp. 316-334). New York: Basic.

Goffman, E. (1963). *Stigma.* Englewood Cliffs, NJ: Prentice-Hall.

Goh, D. S., & Fuller, G. B. (1983). Current practices in the assessment of personality and behavior of school psychologists. *School Psychology Review, 12*(3), 240-243.

Goldstein, A. P., & Pentz, M. A. (1984). Psychological skill training and the aggressive adolescent. *School Psychology Review, 13*(3), 311-323.

Gresham, F. M. (1982). *Social skills: Principles, procedures and practices.* Des Moines: Iowa Department of Public Instruction.

Gresham, F. M., & Elliott, S. N. (1984). Assessment and classification of children's social skills: A review of methods and issues. *School Psychology Review, 13*(3), 292-302.

Guerin, G. R., & Maier, A. S. (1983). *Informal assessment in education.* Palo Alto, CA: Mayfield.

Hall, G. S. (1904). *Adolescence: Its psychology and its relation to physiology, anthropology, sociology, sex, crime, religion and education* (Vol. 1). Englewood Cliffs, NJ: Prentice-Hall.

Hall, R. V., Hawkins, R. P., & Axelrod, S. (1975). Measuring and recording student behavior: A behavior analysis approach. In R. A. Weinberg & F. H. Wood (Eds.), *Observation of pupils and teachers in mainstream and special education settings: Alternative strategies* (pp. 193-217). Reston, VA: The Council for Exceptional Children.

Hamburg, B. (1974). Early adolescence: A specific and stressful stage of the life cycle. In G. V. Coelho, D. H. Hamburg, & J. E. Adams (Eds.), *Coping and adaptation* (pp. 101-126). New York: Basic.

Harrington, R. G. (1984). Assessment of learning disabled children. In S. J. Weaver (Ed.), *Testing children: A reference guide for effective clinical and psychoeducational assessments* (pp. 85-103). Kansas City, MO: Test Corporation.

Hohenshil, T. H. (1982). Secondary school psychological services: Vocational assessment proceedings for handicapped students. In T. H. Hohenshil, W. T. Anderson, & J. F. Salman (Eds.), *Secondary school psychological services: Focus on vocational assessment procedures for handicapped students* (pp. 1-8). Blacksburg, VA: Virginia Tech. (ERIC Document Reproduction Service No. ED 229 704)

Hooper, P. G. (1980). Guidance and counseling: Potential impact on youth unemployment. *Journal of Career Education, 6,* 270-287.

Irwin, D. M., & Bushnell, M. M. (1980). *Observational strategies for child study.* New York: Holt, Rinehart & Winston.

Jensema, C. (1975). A statistical investigation of the 16PF Form E as applied to hearing-impaired college students. *Journal of Rehabilitation of the Deaf, 9*(1), 21-29.

Kellman, H. C. (1974). Attitudes are alive and well and gainfully employed in the sphere of action. *American Psychologist, 29,* 310-324.

Kent, R. N., & Foster, S. L. (1977). Direct behavioral procedures: Methodological issues in naturalistic settings. In A. R. Ciminero, K. S. Calhoun, & H. E. Adams (Eds.), *Handbook of behavioral assessment* (pp. 279-328). New York: John Wiley & Sons.

Knoff, H. M. (1983). Personality assessment in the schools: Issues and procedures for school psychologists. *School Psychology Review, 12*(4), 391-398.

Lazarus, R. (1969). *Patterns of adjustment in human effectiveness.* New York: McGraw-Hill.

Levine, E. S. (1981). *The ecology of early deafness.* New York: Columbia University Press.

Lyman, R. D., & Roberts, M. C. (1984). Assessment of children with psychosomatic disorders. In S. J. Weaver (Ed.), *Testing children: A reference guide for effective clinical and psychoeducational assessments* (pp. 37-50). Kansas City, MO: Test Corporation.

McDermott, P. (1983). A syndromic typology for analyzing school children's disturbed social behavior. *School Psychology Review, 12*(3), 250-259.

Meadow, K. P., Karchmer, M. A., Petersen, L. M., & Rudner, L. (1983). *Revised manual: Meadow-Kendall Social-Emotional Assessment Inventory (SEAI) for Deaf and Hearing-Impaired Students.* Washington, DC: Pre-College Programs, Gallaudet Research Institute, Gallaudet College.

Meighan, T. (1970). *An investigation of the self-concept of blind and partially seeing adolescents and of the relation of their self-concepts to academic achievement in language and paragraph reading.* Unpublished doctoral dissertation, Catholic University, Washington, DC.

Mischel, W. (1977). On the future of personality measurement. *American Psychologist, 32*(4), 246-254.

Moran, M. R. (1978). *Assessment of the exceptional learner in the regular classroom.* Denver: Love.

Moreno, J. L. (1934). *Who shall survive? A new approach to the problem of human interrelations* (Monograph No. 58). Washington, DC: Nervous and Mental Disease Publishing.

Moses, K. (1979). Parenting a hearing-impaired child. *The Volta Review, 81*(2), 73-80.

Neff, W. S. (1976). Assessing vocational potential. In H. Rusalem & D. Maliken (Eds.), *Contemporary vocational rehabilitation* (pp. 103-116). New York: New York University Press.

Nihira, K., Foster, R., Shellhaas, M., & Leland, H. (1975). *AAMD Adaptive Behavior Scale manual.* Monterey, CA: CTB/McGraw-Hill.

Palacios, M. H. (1964). *The Sound Test: An auditory technique.* Marion, IN: Author.

Peterson, D. W., & Batsche, G. M. (1983). School psychology and projective assessment: A growing incompatibility. *School Psychology Review, 12*(4), 440-445.

Potter, S. S. (1950). A method for using the Minnesota Multiphasic Personality Inventory with the blind. In W. Donahue & D. Dabelstein (Eds.), *Psychological diagnosis and counseling of the adult blind.* New York: American Foundation for the Blind.

Roessler, R., & Bolton, B. (1978). *Psychosocial adjustment to disability.* Baltimore, MD: University Park Press.

Roessler, R., & Bolton, B. (1985). The Work Personality Profile: An experimental rating instrument for assessing job maintenance. *Work Adjustment Bulletin, 18*(1), 8-11.

Roistacher, R. C. (1974). A microeconomic model of sociometric choice. *Sociometry, 37,* 219-228.

Salvia, J., & Ysseldyke, J. E. (1981). *Assessment in special education* (2nd ed.). Boston: Houghton Mifflin.

Siller, J. (1976). Attitudes toward disability. In H. Rusalem & D. Malikin (Eds.), *Contemporary vocational rehabilitation* (pp. 67-80). New York: New York University Press.

Strohner, D. C., Grand, S. A., & Purcell, M. J. (1984). Attitudes toward persons with a disability: An examination of demographic factor, social control, and specific disability. *Rehabilitation Psychology, 29*(3), 131-147.

Suess, S., Dickson, A., Anderson, H., & Hildman, L. (1981). The AAMD Adaptive Behavior Scale Norms referenced for deaf-blind individuals: Application and implication. *American Annals of the Deaf, 126*(7), 814-818.

Trybus, R. J. (1973). Personality assessment of entering hearing-impaired college students using the 16PF, Form E. *Journal of Rehabilitation of the Deaf, 6*(3), 34-40.

U.S. Department of Education. (1984). *To assure the free appropriate public education of all handicapped children* (Sixth annual report to Congress on the implementation of Public Law 94-142: The Education for all Handicapped Children Act). Washington, DC: Division of Educational Services Special Education Programs.

Weaver, S. J. (1984). Assessment of mentally retarded children. In S. J. Weaver (Ed.) *Testing children: A reference guide for effective clinical and psychoeducational assessments* (pp. 50-70). Kansas City, MO: Test Corporation.

Wright, B. A. (1960). *Physical disability: A psychological approach.* New York: Harper & Row.

Wright, B. A. (1974). An analysis of attitudes: Dynamics and effects. *The New Outlook for the Blind,* 108-118.

Ysseldyke, J. E., & Shinn, M. R. (1981). Psychoeducational evaluation. In J. M. Kauffman & D. P. Hallahan (Eds.), *Handbook of special education* (pp. 418-440). Englewood Cliffs, NJ: Prentice-Hall.

Zigmond, N. A. (1978). A prototype of comprehensive services for secondary students with learning disabilities: A preliminary report. *Learning Disabilities Quarterly, 1,* 39-49.

15

Learning Problems: Making Decisions about Cognitive/Academic Interventions

MICHAEL M. WARNER, PH.D.

Regardless of one's philosophical or political beliefs, it is hard to deny that contemporary American society poses significant challenges and obstacles to any adolescent who wishes to become a self-sufficient adult. Among the obstacles are the break-up of the family, the constant geographic mobility accompanied by severance of established relationships with friends and relatives, the all-too-easy invitation to drugs and criminal activity, plus the sheer complexity of choices that face many youths today.

Significant also among the challenges and obstacles is the highly competitive nature of the market economy. For most adults success, status, and in some cases even survival will depend on obtaining and maintaining employment at a time when secure, well-paying jobs are scarce and competition is often fierce. Access to occupations is, in turn, very dependent on both school success and obtaining the credentials that signify that success. For adolescents who have experienced failure in school settings, sometimes for many years, the stakes are indeed high. Lack of school success can often mean prolonged dependence on one's parents (Vetter, 1983) and its attendant conflicts and constraints, as well as a future of unemployment or underemployment. Educators and members of other helping professions are not likely, in their professional roles, to solve the political, economic, and social problems that lead to poverty and the underutilization of the potential of so many adolescents and young adults. Such professionals, however, can play important roles in assisting individual adolescents with learning problems in their struggle for survival, growth, and self-fulfillment. The assessment of their capabilities, goals, needs, options, and environmental opportunities plays a crucial role in the overall process of educating and helping such adolescents.

This chapter focuses on the assessment of adolescents with learning problems and particularly on those adolescents identified by schools and other agencies as "learning disabled" (LD). These individuals are perceived to have problems adjusting to the learning demands of secondary schools. Also discussed briefly is the occurrence of learning problems among adolescents and young adults in postsecondary settings.

The approach to assessment that will be emphasized here is called a *decision-making approach*. Salvia and Ysseldyke's (1985) emphasis on the importance of a decision-making focus is reflected in their definition of assessment: "the process of

344

collecting data for the purpose of (1) specifying and verifying problems and (2) making decisions about students" (p. 5). Two points are reflected in this definition. First, a decision-making approach is also typically a problem-solving approach. The way that problems are initially structured and conceptualized will have a critical bearing on the nature of assessment activities that follow. Second, within a decision-making approach, persons involved in assessment are encouraged to collect information that has some bearing on actual intervention decisions to be made. It has been documented that this is not always done in practice (see Williams & Coleman, 1982; Ysseldyke, 1983; Ysseldyke & Algozzine, 1983).

This chapter focuses on decisions that are cognitive/academic in nature (which is not intended to undervalue the appropriateness and importance of assessments that focus on decisions about medical treatments and psychotherapeutic interventions, including interventions with families). There are five major types of cognitive/academic decisions that can be made about students with learning problems: 1) pre-referral decisions; 2) decisions about program eligibility under federal and state regulations; 3) decisions about general intervention goals; 4) decisions about specific needs and progress within a particular curriculum (short-term decisions about what and how to teach); and 5) decisions that depend on more long-term intervention outcomes. Methods used to gather the information on which all of these decisions are based include formal testing plus a wide variety of informal procedures, such as conferences and consulting with adolescents and their parents.

Cognitive/academic decision-making often results in some form of cognitive-academic intervention to be provided in an educational setting. The intervention is designed to assist adolescents with learning problems (including those identified as "learning disabled") in attaining one or more of the following five goals: 1) improving basic academic skills; 2) meeting the immediate demands of educational settings; 3) developing general problem-solving skills that can be applied to immediate as well as later developing problems throughout the life span; 4) developing social competence; and 5) developing other capabilities and knowledge necessary for adult independence, including career maturity and vocational skills as well as functional and daily living skills.

A major assumption that underlies the recommendations made in this chapter is that one must avoid overly mechanistic approaches to assessment (see Heshusius, 1982; Poplin, 1984). Although some decision-making approaches place a great deal of emphasis on the quantification and psychometric qualities of assessment procedures, here assessment is viewed as a highly human and social process, and thus inevitably subject to all the uncertainties and complexities of such processes. For example, factors linked with learning problems in school settings involve multiple dimensions associated with societal, school, classroom, family, and student characteristics. Often, the cause(s) of a particular student's learning problems, including neurological causes, remain unknown (Adelman & Taylor, 1983b; Goodman, 1983).

When the variables and conditions that affect assessment involve high levels of complexity, it follows that decisions made concerning interventions for LD adolescents also will be extremely complex, requiring considerable personal and professional judgment. Complexity is further increased when an attempt is made to involve adolescents with learning problems in the decisions that concern them. Because adolescents may be only partially prepared for involvement in this process, actual decisons must be tentative and renegotiated frequently with those affected by them (Adelman & Taylor, 1983a). This can be very time-consuming, involving consumer education and frequent conferencing and consultation.

None of these problem components in LD decision-making lend themselves to standardized, mechanized solutions. As a result, there are no unequivocal decision-rules linking assessment results and the nature of the intervention to be tried. Often interventions are initiated based on "best guesses." Because these guesses may be wrong, frequent monitoring of intervention consequences by all parties concerned is crucial. Lack of recognition and acceptance of the tentative nature of the entire decision-making process can result in failure and frustration for adolescents and professionals alike.

As the foregoing discussion implies, assessment and intervention are viewed as parts of *one* process. It is often difficult to decide whether a given activity is more concerned with assessment or with instruction. Examples of the interrelationship of these twin concepts include such "assessment" procedures as conferencing with students, trial teaching, and asking a student questions in order to determine how he or she makes sense out of a reading passage. Thus, in addition to the major assumption of a nonmechanistic approach to assessment, there are two corollary assumptions. First, assessment of the instructional environment should be an important part of any general approach to cognitive/academic assessment. Second, those conducting cognitive/academic assessments should be intimately familiar with the contents and processes (i.e., the curricula) of intervention programs.

DEFINITION OF LEARNING PROBLEMS AND
PROBLEMS IN DEFINING LEARNING DISABILITIES

Learning Problems

The term *learning problems* is used throughout this chapter to refer to very inadequate achievement in basic academic skills and knowledge in the areas of reading, writing, and mathematics. Low basic skill achievement *may or may not* be accompanied by the following associated characteristics: 1) dysfunctional motivational patterns; 2) poor thinking and problem-solving skills; 3) limited background knowledge associated with one or more aspects of the school curriculum; 4) spoken language problems, including difficulties with listening comprehension and oral communication; 5) deficiencies in social cognition and social skills; 6) behavior problems, including behavioral patterns associated with the categories of Attention Deficit Disorder as presented in the *Diagnostic and Statistical Manual of Mental Disorders* (DSM-III; American Psychiatric Association, 1980); 7) limited career maturity and community living skills. It is important to keep in mind that the absence of these associated characteristics may be a significant source of strength for the adolescent.

Poor mastery of basic skills, often in combination with one or more of the other characteristics listed, can result in a poor match between the adolescent's current performance levels and aspirations and the demands of the school or work settings as they are currently structured. Negative effects of such a poor match may be compounded when an adolescent's cultural or linguistic background differs from the culture being promoted in the school or work setting. It is this mismatch that results in the adolescent being designated as one with a "learning problem." Whenever professionals in a school or other agency seek to address the needs of persons with learning problems, they must endeavor to reduce the person-by-setting-demand mismatch, either by helping the adolescents develop new capabilities or by modifying setting demands and expectations, or both.

The use of the term *learning problems* throughout this chapter is deliberate and is meant to convey a functional approach to be used with all students experiencing significant cognitive/academic problems. Unlike the term *learning disablities,* to be defined shortly, application of the term *learning problems* is not limited only to those students with real or inferred discrepancies between ability and achievement. In addition, *learning problems* conveys neutrality regarding the cause of a particular student's difficulties.

Adolescents with learning problems, so defined, represent an extremely diverse and heterogeneous group. They also comprise a very large group, requiring significant resources from schools and other agencies to meet their needs appropriately.

Learning Disabilities

Although innumerable definitions of learning disabilities exist in the professional literature (Tucker, Stevens, & Ysseldyke, 1983), the term is used in this chapter to refer to those students with learning problems who are judged to have a "handicapping condition" and meet federal and state criteria of eligibility for receiving learning disability services. Most state definitions of learning disability follow closely the federal definitions as published in the regulations accompanying Public Law 94-142:

Specific learning disability means a disorder in one or more of the basic psychological processes involved in understanding or in using language, spoken or written, which may manifest itself in an imperfect ability to listen, think, speak, read, write, spell, or to do mathematical calculations. The term includes such conditions as perceptual handicaps, brain injury, minimal brain dysfunction, dyslexia, and developmental aphasia. The term does not include children who have learning problems which are primarily the result of visual, hearing or motor handicaps, or mental retardation, or emotional disturbance, or of environmental, cultural, or economic disadvantage. (Federal Register, 1977, p. 65083)

This definition is accompanied in the Federal Register by a number of operational criteria that are to be used to identify learning disabled students, summarized as follows: 1) a severe discrepancy must exist between intellectual ability and achievement in one or more of these areas: oral expression, listening comprehension, written expression, basic reading skill, reading comprehension, mathematics calculation, and mathematics reasoning; 2) achievement is not commensurate with the student's age and ability level in the previously mentioned areas when provided with learning experiences appropriate for his or her age and ability levels; 3) the severe discrepancy should not be primarily the result of other handicapping conditions or of disadvantage, as listed in the conceptual definition; and, perhaps most importantly, 4) the decision that a student is eligible for learning disability services is to be made by a team of professionals, rather than by any individual.

Problems Associated with the Definition of Learning Disabilities

As Harrington (1984) and others have pointed out, the federal definition is vague and subject to considerable interpretation, yet the problems associated with this definition extend well beyond its particular formulation by the federal government. Three significant types are sociopolitical, conceptual, and empirical problems. Examination of these will help provide a context for the recommendations made later in the chapter.

Sociopolitical problems. Around the turn of the century, the nature of public schooling in the United States began to change in some significant ways (Lazerson, 1983). Most critically, compulsory school attendance laws began to be enforced. Large groups of children entering the schools at that time, many of them recent immigrants from southern and eastern Europe, created difficulties for the schools. Franklin (1980) provides some interesting evidence that the types of children identified as learning disabled today are similar to those who were of concern to school professionals in the early part of this century. At that time, some students were referred to as "backward" (McQueary, 1910):

> By "backwardness," we refer more to school attainments than to mental status, that is, our emphasis is upon failure to make regular progress in grades with the average group of children, or unbalanced accomplishment. This may be due to a great many causes, such as late entrance into school; the lock-step in promotion; frequent transfer from school to school, or from teacher to teacher, the presence of physical defects, and sickness causing irregular attendance; poor teaching; and home indulgence; in addition to mental incapacity or delayed maturity; so that there may be general all-round retardation; or backwardness may be manifest only in some particular subject or study. (pp. 122-123)

Although students of average or near average ability with uneven development and specific learning problems have existed in schools throughout this century and before, it was not until the late 1950s and early 1960s that small groups of parents began to put significant pressure on the schools to provide special services for their unique children. This parental pressure was met by the rapid expansion of public elementary school programs for the learning disabled in the late 1960s and early 1970s. As Hallahan and Cruickshank (1973) point out, however, there was very little in the way of empirical research forming a basis for this rapid expansion. Beginning in the mid-1970s, public school programs in junior and senior high schools began to be established; thus, the widespread availability of programs in the secondary schools is a very recent phenomenon.

With the rise in availability of school programs, there has been a constant and significant increase in the proportion of school-age students identified as learning disabled, which in turn has caused controversy and a call for stricter eligibility criteria for LD programs (Foster, 1984; Mercer, Hughes, & Mercer, 1985). In several states, as many as 1 of every 20 students is being identified and served under the learning disability category. Schools often feel pressured to serve students with learning problems in learning disability programs because they perceive that no alternative form of special help exists (Telzrow, 1985).

From a sociological point of view, the concept of learning disabilities can be seen as socially constructed (Carrier, 1983a, 1983b). Simply put, this means that one way to understand a phenomenon like the rapid expansion of the learning disability field is to view it as generated by the mix of very complex historical and social forces, many of which are not currently understood. As a society we create the concept of learning disabilities, institutionalize it, and then come to believe that the construct is a *thing* that exists inside the heads of individual persons. Within this social process, numerous conceptions are offered about how learning disabilities should be understood, and those with particular perspectives often struggle for the ascendency of their own conception. As Coles (1978) noted, for example, certain institutions, such as the public schools, may have a strong stake in promoting conceptions of learning failure that avert blame from the institution itself. There are students, of course, whose learning problems can be understood in part by reference to their physical or neurological limitations, but reference to the coexisting reality of social construction processes does help to explain some of the conceptual confusion and some of the complexity that faces those interested in understanding learning disabilities. No one has expressed the current state of confusion more succinctly than Morsink (1985): "Nobody knows exactly what a learning disability is!" (p. 395).

Conceptual problems. Presently there seems to be rather widespread agreement among professionals in the field of learning disabilities that there is or should be a strong relationship between the notion of learning disability and the notion of severe discrepancy. The idea of discrepancy was borrowed from reading specialists, who have been computing "expectancy" scores at least since the 1920s (Bateman, 1964). Many states have in recent years adopted policies that put "more teeth" into the severe discrepancy clause of the federal learning disabilities definition (Mercer, Hughes, & Mercer, 1985); that is, states may require that students have significantly higher intelligence scores than achievement scores based on the administration of norm-referenced tests.

The widespread agreement about the use of discrepancy criteria is surely one of its advantages. Another advantage may be that through the strict enforcement of discrepancy criteria, many students with low measured intelligence will be excluded from learning disability services, thus potentially slowing the increase in the number identified as learning disabled. Yet the concept of discrepancy, the bedrock of current selection practices, is fraught with conceptual difficulties (Sheppard, 1983; Warner, in press). One set of problems includes those associated with the use of intelligence tests. For example, different tests are based on different concepts of what constitutes intelligence. In addition, there is considerable controversy as to whether existing psychometric tests measure intelligence appropriately (Travers, 1982). Further, there are more specific problems with the use of intelligence test scores that are essentially conceptual in nature. For example, when such scores are used to predict academic "potential," how is one to proceed in the case of two different IQ scores (e.g., Verbal and Performance IQs on the WISC-R) giving strikingly different predictions?

A second conceptual problem relates to the dubious assumption, stated in the

Federal Register (1977), that the existence of an ability/achievement discrepancy, in the absence of other handicapping conditions or disadvantage, points to the existence of neurological or "psychological processing" problems. This assumption neglects the fact that other competing explanations, such as depression, poor motivation, or poor learning history, can coexist and are often in practice very difficult to rule out as the primary cause of the observed ability/achievement discrepancy. The converse of this assumption, that the absence of discrepancy implies the absence of neurological impairment or psychological processing problems, is heard frequently as well. Bateman and Schiefelbusch (1969) pointed out several years ago, however, that whatever within-child factors cause one's achievement to be lower than that of one's peers may also cause IQ scores to be depressed. This would of course include neurological or psychological processing problems as a possible etiology of both deficiencies.

The *practical* problem for many students and school personnel is not so much the gap between achievement and measured ability as it is the gap between current academic performance and the current demands of particular classrooms. The focus on ability/achievement discrepancy may in some instances direct attention away from this more functional issue, particularly for slow-learning students with IQ scores that range between the 5th and the 25th percentiles. Put another way, students with low measured intelligence and inadequate mastery of basic academic skills may be even more poorly matched to the demands of regular classrooms (especially at the secondary school level) than students who are substantially "underachieving."

Empirical problems. Given the sociopolitical and conceptual problems as discussed, it is not surprising that those who have conducted empirical research comparing school-identified learning disabled students with other low-achieving students have had difficulty identifying clear differences between these groups (Warner, Schumaker, Alley, & Deshler, 1980; Ysseldyke, Algozzine, Shinn, & McGue, 1982). In addition, it has not been established that low achievers with higher IQs have significantly different associated characteristics and learning needs than low achievers with low IQs (e.g., Friedrich, Fuller, & Davis, 1984; Taylor, Satz, & Friel, 1979). Both groups may be responding to school failure in similar, albeit dysfunctional, ways. In any case, knowing that an adolescent has been labeled one way or another affords little useful information about that individual.

Another problem of an empirical nature is that for much of the research done with learning disabled students, key variables used to describe the make-up of various research samples often are not reported (Keogh, Major-Kingsley, Omori-Gordon, & Reid, 1982); thus, the results of various studies are often difficult to compare. Further, the sheer amount of empirical research done with learning disabled adolescents is still comparatively small.

OVERVIEW OF THE DECISION-MAKING APPROACH

Traditional assessment practices increasingly are criticized for lack of educational relevance (Ysseldyke & Algozzine, 1983). Although considerable time, money, and human energy may be expended in assessment activities, they may yield insufficient information for decisions about cognitive/academic interventions. The discussion that follows here is designed to combat the tendency to collect irrelevant information.

As mentioned previously, the orientation guiding this chapter is the *decision-making approach*. The process begins with the initial formulation of a problem. In assessing learning problems, the focus of consideration is typically a gap perceived to exist (by a student, parent, or professional) between the current educational performance levels and aspirations of a given adolescent and the demands and constraints of given educational settings. Data collection takes place at the stage of initial problem formulation, as well as during other stages in the assessment process. This information gathering can take a wide variety of forms: testing, interviewing, observing, trial teaching, and so on.

At some point in this process, decisions may be made to modify a student's educational program. These modifications may also take a wide variety of forms. For example, a tutor may be found for the student, there may be changes in the format in which information is presented to the student in a regular classroom (e.g., audiotaping textbook materials), or the student may be placed in a special-education classroom for part of the school day. When a change in the student's program is instituted, more information is gathered in an attempt to determine what effects the new program is having on the student. This information is evaluated, and the results may lead to reformulations of the original problem and/or to further modifications in the student's program.

Ideally, as information is gathered across many students, patterns will emerge, suggesting that certain kinds of interventions either are or are not likely to be advantageous to certain kinds of students. In other words, a necessary (but not solely sufficient) pre-condition for placing problem learners in a particular intervention program should be the documented effectiveness of such programs for specific types of learners. Unfortunately, there are almost no good outcome research data available in the learning disabilities literature to indicate the long-term consequences of participation in given types of programs (especially the differential effects of specific programs for identifiable subgroups of students with learning problems) (Horn, O'Donnell, & Vitulano, 1983).

Within the decision-making framework described here, an important element is the involvement of adolescents with learning problems in the actual decision-making process. Student involvement is important for several reasons, demonstrated by a growing body of research identifying the positive consequences of such involvement (Seabaugh & Schumaker, 1981; Stipek, 1982; Taylor, Adelman, & Kaser-Boyd, 1983; Tollefson, Tracy, Johnsen, & Chatman, 1983). Allowing students to participate in decisions affecting their lives may help them to develop a sense of effectiveness and autonomy. It may also lead to an increase in intrinsic motivation. By involving adolescents in decision-making and by encouraging problem learners to take responsibility for their own learning, power struggles between these adolescents and professionals can be minimized. Finally, as students participate in decision-making, they can come to develop more realistic assessments of their own potentials and capabilities vis-à-vis the demands of various settings.

The decision-making approach calls for five major types of decisions during the course of working with problem learners. Any or all of these decisions may need to be repeated according to changes in student and/or environmental status over time. The process leading to implementation of these decisions is discussed in more detail later in the chapter. Briefly, one important group of decisions is incorporated into what has come to be called "pre-referral" procedures, which involve collecting information and trying out some forms of intervention (usually in the regular classroom) before a student is formally referred for testing under PL 94-142 regulations. A second type of decision-making involves the determination of whether a student should be identified as handicapped and placed in a special education program. This is the issue of eligibility. A third type is concerned with identifying which of the five intervention goals mentioned at the beginning of this chapter should become the focus of a student's program. A fourth type of decision involves determining over the short run what and how a student should be taught, once it has been agreed that a particular program emphasis or curriculum should be included in the student's program. Finally, the fifth decision-making process considers the long-term effects of participation in a given instructional program, both for an individual student and for groups of students.

In addition to these elements of the decision-making framework, attention to the following also forms part of the approach: 1) the particular curricular philosophy or theory that undergirds an intervention program (e.g., see Poplin & Gray, 1982; Warner, 1985; Warner & Bull, 1984); 2) cultural and sociopolitical influences; 3) legal constraints; 4) ethical considerations (Adelman & Taylor, 1984b); and 5) the quality of available psychometric instruments and procedures. All of these factors must be considered in order to make sensible decisions.

ADOLESCENTS WITH LEARNING PROBLEMS AND THEIR ENVIRONMENTS

Key Characteristics of Adolescents with Learning Problems

One caution needs to be stated concerning the characteristics described hereafter: only some, not all, students with learning problems will manifest problems in any one of these areas. For a given student, a particular characteristic may in fact be a source of strength rather than of weakness. In addition, before discussing the several areas in which learning problem students characteristically display deficiencies, it should be stressed that the students under consideration here are adolescents. As such, while specific aspects of their growth and development may be delayed (see Hallahan & Bryan, 1981), generally problem learners face all of the same challenges and changes of other adolescents. Some of the important developmental tasks of adolescence that Havighurst (1972) has discussed are 1) achieving emotional independence from parents and other adults; 2) achieving new and more mature relationships with age-mates of both sexes; 3) desiring, accepting, and achieving socially responsible behavior; 4) preparing for family life; and 5) preparing for an economic career. Problems that are associated with these developmental tasks are often compounded for adolescents with learning problems by the presence of deficiencies in the following areas:

Motivation. The motivation of a student is an important variable in any learning situation. Adelman and Taylor (1983a) have pointed out that the role of motivation often has been ignored in the learning disability literature. In order to be motivated, students must both want to reach a particular goal and believe in their ability to reach the goal, given sufficient effort; that is, they must make appropriate attributions concerning the causes of their success and failure. After sustained histories of school failure, attributional patterns may become very dysfunctional. Perhaps the best indicator that motivation is a serious problem for many adolescents is the high drop-out rate that exists in secondary schools, especially among students with learning problems (Zigmond, Kerr, Brown, & Harris, 1984). Although research focusing on the specific motivational characteristics of adolescents with learning problems is both limited and sometimes contradictory (Deshler, Warner, Schumaker, & Alley, 1983), deficiencies have been documented in the appropriateness of some of these adolescents' attributions concerning the causes of their successes and failures (Pearl, Bryan, & Donahue, 1980).

A practical implication of motivational deficiencies is that assessment and intervention procedures for adolescents with learning problems must be structured realistically to enhance student motivation. This enhancement may be accomplished through practices such as providing students with opportunities for success, helping them to identify their successes as the consequences of their efforts, and providing them with opportunities to be involved in decisions about their schooling. That is, adolescents often need to have at least some control over the content and contexts of their learning (Stipek, 1982). The importance of motivation in assessment lies in the fact that the results of particular tests and other assessments may underestimate or overestimate the actual potential of a given student if his or her motivational status is depressed or elevated at the time of assessment. The assessment of student motivation and attributions should be an ongoing part of any intervention program.

Thinking and problem-solving skills. Various types of problem-solving and thinking skill deficiencies have been documented for groups of problem learners. Adolescents with learning problems often fail to monitor or keep track of their own errors or of their comprehension on particular learning tasks (Deshler, Ferrell, & Kass, 1978; DiVesta, Hayward, & Orlando, 1979; Bos & Filip, 1982; Havertape & Kass, 1978; Warner & Bull, 1984; Wong, 1982). Some adolescents with learning problems are less likely than others to engage in mature planning when faced with a novel task (Warner, Schumaker, Alley, & Deshler, 1982). Associated with problem-solving deficiencies is the difficulty that many problem learners seem to have in generalizing or appropriately applying what they have learned to new situations (Schumaker, Deshler, & Ellis, 1985). One important implication of such deficiencies is that interventions that focus only on the initial acquisition of new skills may be insufficient. Deliberate attempts to assist students in applying new learning will be a necessary and important component of any successful learning program (Schumaker, Deshler, & Ellis, 1985). Another implication is that students with learning problems may profit from programming aimed directly at teaching them to be more effective thinkers and problem-solvers (Deshler, Warner, Schumaker, & Alley, 1983).

The difficulties that students with learning problems appear to have in generalizing what they learn also has implications for the content of assessments. For example, the determination of success of particular interventions, particularly long-term outcomes, must include an evaluation of whether a student can apply newly learned skills across settings and situations. At the present time, assessments for this purpose are not commonly conducted in special education programs.

Background knowledge. Many students with learning problems lack background knowledge or information in particular areas of study. For example, there is some evidence to suggest that adolescents identified as learning disabled have significant deficiencies in their degree of prior learning, particularly in the knowledge of word meanings (Deshler, Warner, Schumaker, & Alley, 1983; Myklebust, 1973; Wiig & Semel, 1975). Students with a history of participation in remedial and special education programs may be doubly disadvantaged. When pulled out of regular classes, they may miss valuable content, and, because of reading deficiencies, they are also likely to gain less content information (Schumaker, Deshler, & Ellis, 1985).

Increasingly, cognitive psychologists have come to appreciate the importance of already knowing a great deal about a subject (and having that knowledge well organized) in order to profit from further study (Brown, Campione, & Day, 1981; Pearson & Spiro, 1982). Stated another way, for a student to incorporate new learning, there must not be too great a gap between the knowledge contained in the new learning and what is already known. When secondary- and postsecondary-school students do have major deficiencies in background knowledge, very difficult intervention problems can arise. Interventions will be appropriate only if they do not overwhelm the student with too much new information. In secondary and postsecondary schools this can be accomplished only through the cooperation of all those who are responsible for delivering content. With respect to assessment, it is important to evaluate the current knowledge level of the student in each content area in which instruction is to be provided.

Basic academic capabilities and oral language proficiency. By definition, the key characteristic of students with learning problems is their deficiency in the acquisition of one or more basic academic skills. Areas where lack of capability manifests itself include word recognition and reading comprehension, mathematics calculation and mathematics reasoning, and written expression. In research reported by Warner, Schumaker, Alley, and Deshler (1980), school-identified learning disabled adolescents were found for the most part to have reached fourth- and fifth-grade achievement levels in basic skills. These students' scores in reading, writing, and math achievement were also typically below the 10th percentile.

For some students, problems in areas like reading are associated with identifiable deficiencies in the speed and efficiency with which language codes are manipulated (Reid & Hresko, 1982a). Sometimes, however, basic skill deficiencies are part of a more general language deficiency involving difficulties in the interpretation and expression of spoken language (Blalock, 1982; Wiig & Semel, 1975).

At the secondary level, application of basic academic skills requires the utilization of a number of important study skills, such as notetaking, gathering information from texts, and test taking. Lack of study skills is another deficiency for many adolescents with learning problems (Schumaker & Deshler, 1984). As will be discussed, basic academic skills, oral language skills, and study skills constitute important demands placed on students in most secondary- and postsecondary-school environments. The assessment of such skills will be important in providing critical cognitive/ academic information for decision-making.

Social skills. The social skills and competencies of adolescents with learning problems are difficult to characterize for several reasons. Although deficiencies in this area have been researched extensively and documented for identified groups of elementary-aged learning disabled students (Bryan & Bryan, 1983), the same cannot be said for adolescents with learning problems (Deshler & Schumaker, 1983). Another problem is that one's view of the nature of social skills deficiencies may differ dramatically depending on one's theoretical point of view. For example, cognitive and behavioral perspectives on the nature of social skills deficiencies differ dramatically (see Greenspan, 1981). A third problem, closely related to the second, is the high degree of overlap between those competencies designated as "social" and others such as problem-solving and thinking skills (Clary, 1984) and oral communication skills (Hallahan & Bryan, 1981).

The available research on the social skills and capabilities of adolescents with learning problems suggests that the generalization that all or even most of them are socially incompetent is unwarranted (Deshler & Schumaker, 1983). Nevertheless, a variety of social skills deficiencies have been noted for *some* of these adolescents. These range from difficulties in the interpretation of nonverbal cues and in social perception (e.g., Wiig & Harris, 1974) to difficulties in social problem-solving (Schumaker, Hazel, Sherman, & Sheldon, 1982). Studies of adults identified as learning disabled also indicate that for some the quality of their interpersonal relationships continues to be a serious problem (Blalock, 1981; Vetter, 1983). Increasingly, intervention programs with assessment components are being developed that address social skill deficits of adolescents with learning problems.

Problems associated with post-school adjustment. A final set of characteristics bearing on assessment and intervention with adolescents having learning problems are those associated with post-school adjustment difficulties. Although the exact types of competencies necessary for successful adult living are not well understood, there is growing agreement that the development of knowledge and skill regarding employment and daily life at home and in the community are crucial goals for many adolescents with learning problems. As a group, problem learners have been found to have difficulties with career maturity and career planning, job satisfaction, making good use of community services and resources, and making good use of leisure time (Bingham, 1978; Blalock, 1981; Vetter, 1983; White et al., 1983).

Important Features of Learning Environments

Learning problems are conceptualized in this chapter as gaps between a student's current performance levels and the requirements or demands of specific learning environments; this implies that solutions to such problems may involve teaching the student new skills, modifying setting demands, or both. Within this perspective, a comprehensive approach to assessment requires that the actual setting demands faced by a given student must be assessed.

A problem encountered in describing the setting demands of secondary schools is that considerable variability in demands can be found across different classrooms and in different schools (Schumaker, Deshler, & Ellis, 1985). The discussion that follows is divided into two parts: consideration of the nature and demands of regular classrooms, and consideration of the nature and demands of special education classrooms.

Demands in regular classrooms. When students make the shift from elementary to secondary school, they encounter a change from a child orientation with an emphasis on the development of basic skills to an emphasis on content. In general, adolescent learners are expected to exhibit a great deal more independence in their learning behaviors than their younger counterparts.

There are certain minimal demands made in most secondary-school classrooms (Zigmond, Kerr, Brown, & Harris, 1984). For example, students are expected to attend classes and to arrive on time, to bring appropriate materials and supplies to class, and to exhibit at least some minimal interest in academic work. Zigmond et al. (1984) report that the high school special education students they studied were only marginally deficient in these minimal demands.

More complex academic demands in secondary-school settings have been reported by Schumaker and Deshler (1984). Secondary-school students are expected to gain information from lectures as well as from reading textbooks, many of which are written at very advanced reading levels. These students are expected to listen a great deal more than they talk and to be able to express themselves in writing, although there is especially great variability across classrooms with respect to the latter (see Applebee, 1980). Finally, students are expected to be able to prepare for and take written tests. As Schumaker and Deshler (1984) note, these demands are also found in many post-secondary educational environments.

Regular classrooms will of course differ from one another in a variety of important dimensions, each of which may be of interest in an assessment of the learning environment. Some examples of these dimensions are the overall amount of required academic work, including homework; the difficulty of the assigned reading material; the degree to which (a) lectures are well organized and (b) advanced organizers and rationales are provided to students for the material to be learned (see Lenz & Alley, 1983); and the degree to which the teacher is willing to accommodate and adapt to the needs of students with learning problems.

Nature and demands of special education settings. As with regular classes, considerable variability exists across special programs for the learning disabled. Understanding and assessing the actual contents and processes of the given remedial or special education program is critical when trying to evaluate whether a given student belongs or fits in that program. A more complete discussion of various interventions used with adolescents having learning problems is presented later in this chapter; at this point will follow a few examples of important dimensions along which special education settings might be assessed.

By far the most common format of service delivery for secondary-school students in LD programs is the resource room. Students with this placement typically spend only one or two hours a day in special education classrooms. The rest of the time is spent in mainstream environments. The special education programs across resource rooms differ considerably in terms of their content. For example, they vary in the extent to which remediation of basic skill deficiencies is emphasized and the extent to which career education goals and processes are incorporated into the curriculum. Another dimension along which special education programs vary is the *intensity* of instruction that is delivered (Meyen & Lehr, 1982). For example, intensity may take the form of increasing the extent to which a tutorial model is used (Bloom, 1984). Degree of student choice and options within a given program also make up an important dimension (Adelman & Taylor, 1983a), as does the way in which students are grouped for instruction (Johnson & Johnson, 1978).

INTERVENTION OPTIONS FOR ADOLESCENTS WITH LEARNING PROBLEMS

The cognitive/academic intervention options available for adolescents with learning problems extend well beyond the typical remedial programs provided for elementary-age students. As students become older, time for programming runs short and concerns begin to emerge beyond the development of basic skills. A variety of decisions must be made about the most appropriate program for a given student, and these decisions should extend past the question of eligibility for special education services. In order to collect information with a direct bearing on decisions to be made, *assessors must be familiar with the intervention options available for adolescents with learning problems.*

It is also important to emphasize that the problems encountered by students with learning problems are often multidimensional, and the students themselves need to be involved in decisions concerning interventions. This usually calls for the designation of someone (often the LD teacher) to help coordinate services for the student, to serve as an advocate for the student as he or she attempts to negotiate the demands of various settings, and to work with the student in the role of counselor, helping him or her to understand the program and assisting in the development of autonomous decision-making skills. The coordinator must also pay attention to integrating the curricular interventions with non-curricular ones, such as medical or psychotherapeutic interventions. Such coordination is considered critical for most adolescents identified as "learning disabled."

The discussion of intervention options that follows is meant only to provide a general indication of the scope and variability of existing or recommended program options. For a more in-depth discussion of these options and the issues involved in choosing between them, the reader is referred to reviews by Deshler, Schumaker, Lenz, and Ellis (1984); Schumaker, Deshler, and Ellis (1985); and Woodward and Peters (1983). One must remember that at the local level all program options are not necessarily available under the designation "learning disability program"; of course, realistic assessment requires that the options either do exist as part of designated programs or can be established.

Improving Basic Academic Skills

Among the most common types of secondary-school programs available for adolescents with learning problems are those that emphasize the remediation of basic skills in reading, writing, and mathematics. Often these programs represent an extension of the curriculum offered in elementary school. The rationale for this type of intervention is clear: in contemporary Western culture, basic academic skills are important to success in secondary school and in adult living. However, there are some problems with this type of programming that should be considered (Deshler, Shumaker, Lenz, & Ellis, 1984). Considerable data suggest that, for many problem learners, significant progress in basic skill mastery during the secondary school years is not likely, at least given the nature of current remedial and special education programs (Horn, O'Donnell, & Vitulano, 1983; Warner, Schumaker, Alley, & Deshler, 1980). The question becomes one of how much emphasis and intensity should be placed on this type of remediation, given the pressing nature of other curricular concerns for this age group.

Focusing on Regular Classroom Demands

There are several types of interventions for adolescents with learning problems that focus on helping them meet the demands encountered in regular secondary-school classrooms. Considerable social pressure is placed on most adolescents to meet such demands. Furthermore, in a mainstreaming context, success in regular classrooms is necessary for obtaining a high school diploma. The approaches to helping students meet this goal are quite diverse, and many of them have significant practical and conceptual problems associated with them. Intervention approaches include:

1. Tutoring by the resource room teacher, which assists students in gaining content, finishing work assigned in the regular class, and/or preparing for tests;

2. Teaching traditional secondary-school content by the special education teacher;

3. Teaching minimal school-survival skills, such as arriving at class on time, bringing required materials to class, etc.;

4. Providing parallel alternative curricula in which content is delivered by a content expert (the regular class teacher) in ways that accommodate the special needs of students with learning problems (see Wiseman, Van Reusen, & Hartwell, 1981);

5. Placing students in courses within the regular curriculum that are less academically demanding;

6. Teaching students various study skills;

7. Helping students compensate for deficiencies in basic academic skills through the provision of tape recorders, oral testing, and so on (see Mosby, 1979); and

8. Providing peer tutoring or tutoring by persons other than the special education teacher.

A number of questions arise when considering whether a given student should be supported in the regular curriculum and how such support should be given. Some of the critical questions are 1) Does the student have sufficient cognitive/academic skills to profit from time spent in regular classes? 2) Is a particular course or courses relevant to the student's most pressing learning needs? 3) Is it a good use of the resource-room teacher's time to tutor students in content from their other classes? Does tutoring create an overdependence by the learner on the tutor? 4) Who is the best person to deliver content across the wide variety of areas covered in a comprehensive junior high or high school—the regular teacher, as content expert, or the special education teacher?

Emphasizing the Development of Problem-Solving Skills

There are a number of approaches that make deliberate and systematic attempts to teach adolescents with learning problems how to think and solve problems, including problems encountered in social interactions. These programs include Instrumental Enrichment (Arbitman-Smith & Haywood, 1980), parts of the Strategies

Intervention Model (Schumaker, Deshler, & Ellis, 1985), and other programs focusing on the development of metacognitive and self-control skills (e.g., Brown & Palincsar, 1982). Within these programs students are given experiences in problem-solving and often are taught such skills as planning, predicting, goal setting, and monitoring. The rationale for these interventions is based largely on the desire to teach skills with a very general application. These skills are believed to be important tools that can be used by adolescents to transfer what they learn in one setting to other tasks and settings, both in and out of school.

Focusing on the Development of Social Competence

A number of programs have been developed that concentrate on helping adolescents with learning problems to improve their social functioning. These include programs reported by Cartledge and Milburn (1983), Clary (1984), Deshler and Schumaker (1983), Schumaker and Hazel (1984), and Zigmond and Brownlee (1980). Social skills programs may be direct, involving the isolation and training of specific skills such as "resisting peer pressure," or they may be indirect, focusing more on involving students in cooperative group activities (see Bryan & Bryan, 1983). The rationale for this type of intervention is based on the idea that the possession of social competence is critical to successful adult functioning, including the ability to gain and maintain employment.

The possession of social competence may also be critical to a student's ability to function successfully in mainstream educational settings. However, in a survey reported by Zigmond, Kerr, Brown, and Harris (1984), high school staff members rated social skills among the lowest of several skills in terms of their importance for success in high school.

Focusing on Career Development and Functional Life Skills

A potential limitation of all the interventions previously discussed is that they may be delivered in such a way that students see little relevance between their school experiences (including special or remedial education experiences) and the world outside of school (including that of work). Since the early 1970s, there has been a growing movement to tie all curricular experiences in some way to career development (Clark, 1980; Marland, 1974; Mori, 1982). Also, the difficulties problem learners face in making the transition from school to the world of work have become the focus of considerable recent attention (Schumaker, Deshler, & Ellis, 1985; Wehman, Kregel, & Barcus, 1985). Those who advocate career education for students with learning problems are interested in promoting adult adjustment on the job, at home, and in the community. Programs focusing on career education are wide ranging and include emphasis on developing career maturity (Biller, 1985), vocational competence (Phelps & McCarty, 1984), and various functional and daily living skills (Wimmer, 1981). Vocationally oriented options appropriate for some students with learning problems include cooperative education programs, work-study programs, vocational rehabilitation programs, and programs offered through vocational-technical schools. In many cases the successful implementation of such programs will depend on the cooperation of professionals from many different disciplines.

IMPLEMENTATION OF THE DECISION-MAKING APPROACH

Information-Gathering Procedures

Many different types of information-gathering procedures can be used in the assessment of adolescents with learning problems. The choice of procedures depends on such factors as the decision to be made, the reliability and validity associated with a particular method, and the procedure's practicality and ease of use.

One important traditional procedure involves the administration of commercially available assessment instruments. Many of these are standardized, norm-referenced tests, often referred to as "formal tests." In general, within the approach to assessment being advocated here, formal tests play a relatively minor role in the overall process. This is true for several reasons. As Schumaker and Deshler (1984) have pointed out, "most test instruments typically used with mildly handicapped adolescents do not assess the broad array of skills needed to successfully cope with the curricular demands of secondary school" (p. 23). For example, there are no commercially available tests that assess how a particular student goes about getting information from a lecture or that take into account the complexity of a given student's motivational status. A second point, related to the first, is that tests are often administered and interpreted out of context. By over-relying on a particular test score, one may, for example, fail to consider important non-student factors related to the nature of setting demands and the quality of instruction provided to the student being assessed (see Ysseldyke & Algozzine, 1983). Finally, many formal tests have technical inadequacies that require very cautious interpretation of results (see Salvia & Ysseldyke, 1985; Taylor, 1984).

In spite of these cautions and limitations, the administration of commercially available tests can make some contribution to the assessment of cognitive/academic learning problems. For example, broad survey tests, such as the Peabody Individual Achievement Test, can be used as screening devices to rule out the existence of some academic skill deficits (Salvia & Ysseldyke, 1985). For purposes of establishing a severe discrepancy between ability and achievement as part of the process of determining eligibility for a learning disability program, the following tests can be used. To measure intelligence, either the Wechsler Intelligence Scale for Children-Revised (for students through age 16) or the Wechsler Adult Intelligence Scale-Revised (for students aged 17 and older) is recommended. Care should be taken not to overinterpret patterns of subtest performance on these two tests (Taylor, 1984). Most often, the Full Scale IQ score from these tests will be used to establish whether or not a severe ability/achievement discrepancy exists. To establish achievement performance levels in the areas of reading, mathematics, and written expression, appropriate "clusters" from Part II of the Woodcock-Johnson Psycho-Educational Battery can be used.

For the most part, decision-makers operating within this chapter's approach will rely on a wide variety of information-gathering procedures extending beyond the use of formal tests. These procedures include: 1) conferences and interviews with students, parents, and professionals; 2) rating scales; 3) checklists; 4) structured and unstructured observation of the student in classroom settings; 5) informal and teacher-made tests; 6) trial lessons and diagnostic questioning of students as they are engaged in learning; and 7) student self-assessments. Use of any of these procedures must of course follow consideration of the limitations inherent in each. For extended discussions of these and other informal assessment procedures, see Adelman and Taylor (1983b), Cawley (1985), Howell and Kaplan (1980), McLoughlin and Lewis (1981), Moran (1978), and Zigmond, Vallecorsa, and Silverman (1983).

Pre-referral Decision-Making

A number of authorities in special education and learning disabilities currently emphasize the importance of assessment and intervention processes that occur *before* a student is formally referred for the lengthy and expensive testing and evaluation needed to determine eligibility for special education placement (Adelman & Taylor, 1983b; Messick, 1984; Salvia & Ysseldyke, 1985; Telzrow, 1985; Tucker, 1982). Such assessment and intervention processes have come to be called "pre-referral" processes. The motivation for pre-referral processes comes from a desire to reduce the number of students misplaced in special education programs. Having conceptualized learning problems as arising from the interaction between a student and particular learning environments, it is incumbent on professionals to seek alternative interventions within the regular classroom setting that may solve the learning problem without going to the extreme of labeling the student "handicapped." Assessing the quality and degree of fit of given programs, in this instance regular classroom programs, is therefore an important practical and ethical concern.

Consistent with the decision-making approach emphasized here, pre-referral processes often are described within a problem-solving framework. Based on an initial "call for help," usually from a classroom teacher, a consultant or building-level instructional support team works with the teacher to determine the nature of the problem at hand. Assessments may take the form of observations of the student, peers, and teacher in the problem classroom(s), interviews with the student both outside of class and while he or she is trying to accomplish classroom tasks, discussions with teachers, and so on. Based on the information gathered, a plan is established for making some modification in the way instruction is delivered and/or in the way the student approaches classroom demands. These modifications could extend to removing the student from one regular classroom and placing him or her in another (see Messick, 1984). Especially when this latter step appears necessary, effective counseling with the original teacher becomes critical to ameliorate possible resentment or perceptions of failure. In any case, the regular classroom teacher always should be fully informed of the philosophy behind the decision-making approach in order to maintain the proper perspective about, and involvement in, its procedures. Once the modifications have been made, the effects of these interventions are evaluated and further changes are instituted if needed. Only when alternatives have been exhausted to meet a student's needs effectively outside of the special education system are the expensive and consequential assessment procedures for determining special education eligibility initiated.

The success of pre-referral processes at the secondary level depends on a number of factors. For example, administrative support for the institutionalization of pre-referral processes is essential. Also, these processes call for the presence of knowledgeable, experienced, interpersonally astute consultants who are familiar with the curricular and basic skill demands of various regular classes and with practical intervention options. Finally, successful pre-referral processes depend on the willingness and ability of regular classroom teachers to share in the responsibility of providing appropriate and flexible classroom experiences for students with learning problems.

Decisions Regarding Learning Disability Program Eligibility

Given the previously discussed sociopolitical, conceptual, and empirical problems in the definition of learning disabilities, it is not hard to imagine that determining program eligibility is a process fraught with difficulties. Because of the different types of definitional problems, there are serious weaknesses in all current approaches to selecting those who will be served in learning disability programs. When formal tests are administered and discrepancy criteria applied, a fourth type of problem arises—limitations inherent in various tests and psychometric procedures. Fortunately, there are a number of excellent documents available that give the practitioner advice on how to "make the best" out of what this author considers a bad situation. These include writings on the most technically adequate approaches to measuring discrepancy (e.g., Berk, 1984; Mellard & Deshler, 1984; Reynolds et al., 1984) and writings that provide meaningful suggestions for utilizing discrepancy criteria as one part of a larger process of determining program eligibility (Fox & Telzrow, 1983; Harrington, 1984; Telzrow, 1985). All of these sources discuss the pitfalls to avoid in determining program eligibility, and most of their recommendations directly apply to the adolescents under consideration in this chapter.

The important elements in this particular determination process can be summarized as follows. Ideally, formal procedures for determining program eligibility are begun only after pre-referral processes have been completed. Virtually all of the assessment techniques and procedures discussed earlier, including both formal and informal procedures, may be applied to determining program eligibility. Furthermore, all procedures and processes must proceed within the constraints of federal and state regulations, particularly those found in PL 94-142 regulations. The formal determination of a severe discrepancy is a crucial step in determining eligibility, as is ruling out specific alternative explanations for the discrepancy (i.e., consideration of the federal exclusionary criteria). Because important eligibility and programming decisions must be made based on a student's current functioning in oral expression and listening comprehension, a speech and language specialist should be involved in the decision-making process.

One way to understand the current legally mandated eligibility process is that the implementation of specific procedures for the identification of learning disabled students is based largely on the needs of large bureaucracies that extend all the way to the federal level (Wise, 1979). Necessarily, the perspective of well-meaning bureaucrats is often far removed from the immediate, local, contextually constrained concerns of school personnel (Fenstermacher & Amarel, 1983), such as the pressures of parents and teachers. Considerable local autonomy and flexibility remain embedded in federal- and state-mandated identification procedures, and the effects, both positive and negative, of the current regulations can be debated. The important point here is that regulated identification procedures are probably best understood as necessary for standardization and control within a bureaucratically organized educational system, rather than as valid procedures for selecting out "real" learning disabled students from others with learning problems. The utility of a specific set of procedures for determining program eligibility can be judged only by conducting systematic evaluation studies that provide data both about the specific types of students that are selected and not selected by the procedures and about the short- and long-term effects of the interventions provided to the students selected into the learning disability program. Such studies will require a major commitment of resources from the school districts or other interested agencies.

In any case, within the decision-making approach, the determination of eligibility for a particular program (e.g., "specific learning disabilities") should not be the sole focus of assessment activities with adolescents with learning problems. If a student is not deemed eligible for a learning disability or other special education program, he or she may still be in desperate need of some form of intervention or change in current educational program. On the other hand, if the student *is* eligible for an LD program, it does not necessarily follow that placement in the available LD program is the most appropriate option! For example, it may be determined, as part of a comprehensive assessment process, that the most critical need for a given adolescent with learning problems is a program that focuses on the development of social skills and capabilities, yet the learning disability program in a given school may be directed solely to the remediation of basic academic skill deficits.

Decisions Regarding the Pursuit of Major Intervention Goals

As is apparent from the preceding discussion, decisions about which of the major types of interventions to emphasize in a given student's program are very complex. In addition, there are no unequivocal decision-rules that can be applied in a straightforward fashion. The following suggestions are provided as guidelines for making these kinds of decisions. This list is not comprehensive and is offered merely to indicate further the types of considerations necessary in weighing program alternatives.

1. Any decisions that are made should involve the adolescent and in many cases his or her parents. Parents and the student should be informed of the options before them and helped to be genuine participants in the decision-making (see Van Reusen, 1984). For example, this might include a period of counseling and consultation, before the student enters a special program at the school, when the goal is for the student to examine the options and decide which one(s) he or she would like to try.

2. One should try to implement "trial" placements in programs of interest. This gives the adolescent a chance to size-up a particular program and to back out from a decision made unrealistically or in haste.

3. In programs that focus mainly on the support of the student in the regular curriculum, attention must be paid to factors such as the student's levels of basic skill development, degree of background knowledge, and ability to comprehend the concepts presented in lectures and texts. For example, if one is going to teach a student study skills such as how to get information out of a textbook, a certain minimal level of reading ability on the part of the student is necessary. In general, students who, on standardized reading tests, receive grade equivalent scores below the fourth grade cannot decode enough words to be able to profit from many study skill techniques. On

the other hand, students whose grade equivalent scores range from fourth through sixth grade may be able to apply study skills when reading material written at readability levels higher than sixth grade.

For students who are essentially non-readers (i.e., reading at the second-grade level and below) but who have good listening comprehension ability in the subject matter being covered, the options might include bypassing the reading demands of the curriculum through the use of tape recorders and similar devices. If the student's general listening comprehension ability is low or if the student lacks sufficient background knowledge in the area being covered in class lectures, placement in some regular classes may be very miseducative and a waste of valuable time (Anderson, Mason, & Shirey, 1984). Selection of another intervention goal may be necessary. Student motivation and interest will be key considerations in any decision to support the student in regular classes.

4. The level of a student's development in basic skills is also important when considering placement of problem learners in vocational education programs, as many such programs require very high levels of skill development. Assessment in the area of career and vocational development for students with learning problems is fast becoming a speciality, and persons doing career and vocational assessment should have specialized training. This will often necessitate an interdisciplinary effort between the secondary-school learning disabilities teacher, for example, and a vocational special needs teacher or rehabilitation personnel. (For further discussion of procedures related to career and vocational assessment, the reader is referred to chapter 16 in this book and to Hohenshil, Levinson, & Heer [1985].)

5. If the decision entails a program that emphasizes remediation of basic academic skills, it may be necessary to provide this instruction in a very intensive fashion if any impact is to be made. Intensity in this case might take the form of one-to-one tutoring in frequent tutoring sessions. In order to make such tutoring feasible in a public school setting, peers, teacher's aides, or other volunteers may have to serve as tutors, under the supervision of a teacher experienced in the area being remediated.

6. One must be prepared to make referrals to other agencies or to other professionals at the request of students or parents, when the case at hand exceeds one's expertise, when current attempts at interventions have failed, or when medical or psychotherapeutic intervention is indicated (see Adelman & Taylor, 1984a).

7. For consideration regarding assessment of social skills, see Schumaker and Hazel (1984) and chapter 5 in this book.

Decisions Regarding Specific Needs within a Given Intervention Program

Once one or more of the five major intervention goals has been selected and a student has been placed in a special program or programs, a number of decisions are necessary related to the instruction delivered within that program. Questions such as the following form the basis of information-gathering: Where should the student begin in a particular curriculum? What kind of progress is the student making in the curriculum? Is there a good match between the content that is being delivered and the student's background knowledge and ability to conceptualize within that content area? Is the student motivated to learn particular content?

The way information is gathered to answer such questions will depend heavily on the educational philosophy that underlies the teacher's practice. If the teacher is operating from a behavioral perspective or is engaging in direct instruction, the curriculum is likely to be highly pre-organized and sequenced. Often specific pre-tests are administered prior to beginning each instructional unit. Frequent and continuous measurement of student progress with criterion-referenced tests is intrinsic to this instructional approach (see Rosenberg & Sindelar, 1982). A strong emphasis is put on the collection of objective and reliable data.

If the teacher is operating from a more holistic perspective (also called personalization, experimentalism, cognitive-field, or Deweyan perspective), then information-gathering is likely to take a different form. Within this perspective the emphasis shifts to the teacher and student themselves becoming the "test instrument." Two important kinds of information, both of which are more subjective and interpersonal, are sought: 1) does the information to which the student is being exposed "make sense" to him or her? and 2) does the student maintain his or her interest in the subject matter? To answer the first of these inquiries, the teacher must often ask the student questions while he or she is engaged in learning. The teacher is often less interested in whether a student answers a particular question correctly than in evaluating the thinking the student used to arrive at the answer (Reid & Hresko, 1982b). The question of whether the student maintains interest is evaluated by observing in which activities he or she engages *when given a choice,* as well as by noting his or her affective behavior, both verbal and nonverbal.

Regardless of which of these two substantially different educational philosophies guides a particular teacher's assessment practices, in neither case is much reliance on formal testing recommended. Typically, commercially available tests are not matched closely enough to the particular curriculum being taught to be of much value in assessing short-term educational progress. As McCauley and Swisher (1984) note, norm-referenced tests, many of which are designed to be used for screening and to be administered quickly, often lack sufficient reliability or test items to measure student gains, even over the course of a year. This point is especially true with secondary students.

Assessment to answer questions about what and how to teach is probably best accomplished within a given curriculum by techniques such as trial teaching, informal evaluation of student work products, and student self-evaluations of performance. The quality of the assessments that are produced depends, in part, on the degree to which the teacher understands both the content and the goals of the particular curriculum being implemented.

Decisions Regarding the Long-Term Effectiveness of Interventions

In order to evaluate whether a program is worthwhile or cost-effective, one must ask "What is the long-term impact of this program on the students who participate in it?" The fact is, though, this question is often difficult to answer. There are many reasons for this, but one of the most important involves the determination of what constitutes a successful outcome. Traditional answers to this question, or answers that may be appropriate for younger students, may not be relevant to adolescents with learning problems. For example, as was documented earlier, an adolescent's learning problems are often chronic in nature and very resistent to change. To what extent should the criterion for success be the "remediation" of such a deficiency (e.g., in written expression) versus helping the student "cope" with or adapt to the deficiency? Also, in the professional literature related to students with learning problems, there is increasing awareness and agreement that the real test of a program's effectiveness is whether problem learners can both maintain the capabilities that they have acquired in a program and appropriately apply their new learning to other settings and situations. Although the teacher or other educational professional may find assessment of long-term outcomes difficult, such assessments should be carried out whenever possible. In some cases this will require a cooperative effort between the teacher who originally helped a student acquire a new skill and other adults who subsequently work with the student in different settings. Based on the positive interpersonal relationship that is often established between a teacher and his or her students, the teacher may find it possible and profitable to maintain correspondence or other forms of contact with students who graduate from or otherwise leave a program. Based on follow-up data, collected either formally or informally and including indicators of "consumer satisfaction" with the program, program change and development can follow.

Applying a Decision-Making Approach in Post-secondary Educational Settings

It is beyond the scope of this chapter to consider in any detail the assessment needs of problem learners in post-secondary educational settings. The few comments that follow are designed to assist the reader who may have a particular interest in pursuing this topic further. Although development of programs for students identified as "learning disabled" in junior colleges, colleges, and universities is a very recent phenomenon, concern about and interest in such programs is quite appropriate because the attainment of post-secondary education is rapidly becoming a prerequisite for occupational advancement.

Articulated approaches to the assessment of problem learners in post-secondary schools are only beginning to be developed. The assessment approaches advocated in this chapter may have considerable applicability to students in post-secondary schools for the following reasons. First, increasing numbers of students with learning problems are seeking post-secondary education. Second, many of the deficiencies that these students exhibit in secondary schools are carried with them and exhibited in post-secondary schools (Blalock & Dixon, 1982). Third, many of the most troublesome setting demands of secondary schools are also present in post-secondary educational settings. Fourth, the types of difficulties that will be encountered in establishing and developing post-secondary special education programs are similar in many ways to those in junior and senior high schools. For example, to what degree will instructors in higher education be inclined or even able to accommodate significantly the individual learning needs of students?

It will be interesting to see how institutions of higher education respond to the growing demand for the provision of appropriate education for the many different types of students who are designated as handicapped or who are problem learners. For those who wish to study further the current status of intervention and assessment processes for students with learning problems in post-secondary educational settings, the following sources are recommended: Brolin and Elliot (1984), Cordini (1982),

Mangrum and Strichart (1983a, 1983b), Ostertag, Baker, Howard, and Best (1982), and Vogel (1982).

CASE STUDIES

Note: The case studies that follow represent assessment processes that are accomplished under ideal circumstances. To the extent that these ideas and suggestions make sense, they represent a challenge and a direction to be worked toward.

Two students, Ralph and Alice, live in a Midwestern city of some 400,000 people. They both attend a comprehensive high school in which a student body of some 1,500 students represents variety of cultures and socioeconomic levels. The high school employs two full-time teachers, Ms. Walsh and Mr. Liedig, to manage the Learning Resources Center, which occupies two rooms in the main building. There are also two teacher's aides who are employed full-time in this resource program, which serves about 60 students in Grades 9 through 12.

When Ms. Walsh and Mr. Liedig originally were hired to work in the Learning Resources Center, they met with the principal and explained to him their goals for their program. They expressed the critical necessity of having enough time in which they were not involved directly in instruction. They explained that they each needed the equivalent of two planning periods each day in order to do assessments, conference and consult with students, coordinate students' total programs, and meet with other school personnel and with key persons in other agencies involved in working with high school students.

Ms. Walsh is a special educator by training and has a master's degree in the area of learning disabilities. Mr. Liedig originally taught courses in distributive education, but recently returned to school and became provisionally certified in special education, with an emphasis in vocational special needs. Ms. Walsh and Mr. Liedig have divided their responsibilities in their program to some extent. Ms. Walsh has received specialized training in applying the Strategies Intervention Model (Schumaker, Deshler, & Ellis, 1985), developed at the University of Kansas. Through a series of in-service workshops provided to her school district, she has become familiar with the teaching procedures and the specific content of that approach. As part of the Strategies Intervention Model, she learned how to help students initially acquire a number of specific learning strategies associated with gaining information from lectures and textbooks and improving their writing. She also learned how to help students apply their knowledge of learning strategies to settings other than the Learning Resources Center.

Ms. Walsh's emphasis is thus on assisting students to meet the academic demands of regular high school classes better, primarily through teaching the students specific and general learning strategies. In doing this, she works closely with the content-area teachers in her building. Mr. Leidig sees his role as overlapping with that of Ms. Walsh, but his special emphasis is on career education and the coordination of student experiences in local businesses and at the nearby vocational-technical school. Both teachers believe that critical to the success of their program are 1) regular conferences with students to plan and discuss each student's program and 2) advocacy for the needs of their students with other persons and agencies.

Ralph

Ralph came to the attention of Ms. Walsh when his learning disability teacher in junior high school called her as he was about to exit the eighth grade. Ralph's parents are both school teachers and he is their only child. Ralph had been in learning disability programs since the fourth grade. He had entered the program because of difficulties in reading and writing; math skills were never a problem for him. Ralph had no history of hearing, vision, or other medical problems. In junior high school, the emphasis of Ralph's program had been on further remediation of his reading and writing problems and on helping him with his other classes through a tutoring process. During the eighth grade Ralph received a comprehensive re-evaluation as a basis for determining what type of program might benefit him in high school. At that time, he was administered the Wechsler Intelligence Scale for Children-Revised (WISC-R), the Reading and Written Expression clusters from the Woodcock-Johnson Psycho-Educational Battery (WJPEB), an informal reading inventory, and an informal writing inventory. Ralph was observed by the learning disability teacher in three of the regular classes he was attending. In addition, copies of the work he turned in for those classes were collected systematically and saved by his regular class teachers.

Ralph received a WISC-R Full Scale IQ score of 108. Based on the computation of a 68% confidence band, his IQ score was judged to range between the 62nd and the 75th percentiles. Ralph's scores on two of the WJPEB achievement clusters, provided in the manual as percentile rank ranges, were 14-21%ile for Reading and 8-11%ile for Written Expression. Standard score equivalents (mean = 100, standard deviation = 15) were also recorded for the Reading and Written Expression clusters. According to an actuarial table that had been developed by the state department of education, Ralph was judged to have severe discrepancies in the areas of reading and writing.

Informal assessment of Ralph's reading skills revealed that his silent reading comprehension was adequate for both stories and social studies content when the passages were written at a readability level of fifth grade or below. Ralph's oral reading of passages with higher readability levels was very slow and halting, yet he was able to pick up the gist of a given passage and paraphrase it appropriately. His decoding difficulty appeared to be the source of his impaired silent reading comprehension at levels beyond fifth grade. When passages taken from ninth- and tenth-grade social studies and English texts were read aloud to him, Ralph's comprehension of the passages and his knowledge of particular word meanings was very good. Samples of his writing, collected from the informal writing inventory and from his classroom teachers, revealed that he could be creative when he wrote and that he was trying to express thoughts and concepts that were appropriately complex for someone his age. On the other hand, Ralph had difficulty with the "mechanics" of writing (i.e., punctuation and capitalization) and he had great difficulty with spelling.

Throughout the seventh and eighth grades, Ralph attended math classes for students with average skill levels and received mostly A and B grades. Ralph's grades in his English and social studies classes were more variable. Ralph frequently failed to complete the work that was assigned to him during the school day and often took it home to finish. His parents reported that they spent a great deal of time helping Ralph with his homework most evenings. In general, Ralph's teachers in junior high school reported that he appeared interested, but frequently became frustrated when he did poorly on a test or failed to finish his in-class assignments. Ralph was part of a small circle of friends, not all of whom were in the learning disability program. He usually spent his late afternoon hours playing sports with friends in the neighborhood.

At the end of the eighth grade, Ms. Walsh arranged to have a series of conferences with Ralph and his parents. Ralph's parents were not present for several of these conferences. Ralph's junior-high learning disability teacher had discussed with him the importance and purpose of the conferences. Initially, in the conferencing process, Ms. Walsh's goal was to gain Ralph's trust. She explained her role at the high school and that she was working closely with his junior-high learning disability teacher. She asked Ralph about his learning problems and found that although hesitant at first, he seemed pleased to have an adult to talk to about his problems. She also found Ralph apprehensive about going into the ninth grade and about the pressures of high school. They discussed his plans and his goals, both for high school and thereafter. Ralph said that he really didn't know what he wanted to do in terms of an occupation, but that he thought he would like to go to college. When Ms. Walsh asked him whether he thought he could achieve grades or test scores good enough to enter and stay in college, Ralph wasn't sure. He knew that he did better in math and was curious about college programs in which math was important. Ms. Walsh explained to Ralph a little bit about the Strategies Intervention program and tried to solicit his commitment to trying it out. She explained that if his goal was to enter college, he needed to learn how to study in such a way that he wouldn't have to depend so much on the learning disability program or on his parents in order to learn. Ralph liked the sound of that.

Alice

Seventeen-year-old Alice was another student who received help through the Learning Resources Center and other programs at the high school. In the tenth grade and living at home with her mother, Alice has two older sisters who live and work away from home. Her father lives in a distant city and visits her only occasionally; her mother works on an assembly line in a local factory. When Alice was sent to the school counselor because of attendance problems, a review of her school records revealed that she had a history of receiving low grades, mostly Ds, but that she had never been in a special education program. She had entered the first grade late and had been retained one year in the second grade. Alice was regarded by her peers and by her teachers as something of a loner. Her mother reported that Alice had become increasingly hostile at home.

In discussions with the school counselor, Alice stated her intention to drop out of school, saying that her classes were "boring" and "too hard" and that she didn't have any friends. As part of a pre-referral process, several of Alice's teachers, along with Mr. Leidig and the school psychologist, met to discuss her situation. Some of the teachers agreed to make modifications in the approach they used with Alice. In some cases, the length of her assignments was reduced, and one teacher agreed to provide Alice with a handout each day showing the main topics that would be covered in lectures and providing some simple definitions of key vocabulary terms. In a conference with Alice conducted by the school psychologist, she was told of her teachers' concern about her progress in school and she agreed to improve her attendance and to work hard in her courses.

After a two-month trial period, during which the effects of these changes were carefully monitored by Alice's teachers, it was decided that the changes were having little effect. With the permission of her mother Alice was given a series of tests to determine if she was eligible for special education. The results revealed that both her intelligence test scores and her achievement test scores, when expressed as confidence bands, ranged between the 12th and the 25th percentiles. Other assessment activities included an interview with Alice, examination of the work she was submitting in her classes, and direct observation by Mr. Liedig in two of her classes. Based on both the formal and informal assessments and discussion by the assessment team, it was decided that Alice did not have a "handicapping condition" as defined under federal and state regulations. On the other hand, all believed that she was in immediate danger of dropping out of school. In a series of conferences with Alice and her mother, the following decisions were made: Alice would enter two programs on a trial basis—a social skills training program conducted by one of the high school counselors and a work-study program coordinated by Mr. Liedig of the Learning Resources Center.

For her work-study program, Alice decided that she would like to work in food services. Arrangements were made for her to spend a half day at her school and the other half working at a local cafeteria, initially as a food server. When Alice was at school, she attended some regular classes in English and social studies. For one period per day she alternated attendance at the Learning Resources Center, where Mr. Liedig was her teacher, and at the social skills training program. The focus of her program with Mr. Liedig was on the application of basic skills to her work situation and to various daily living needs.

In the social skills program, Alice worked with a small group of eight other students in the ninth and tenth grades. Within this program, assessment took the form of having Alice role-play a particular situation, such as accepting criticism from an employer, and then having the counselor check off both the number of discrete appropriate behaviors in which Alice engaged and the quality of her responses. Once Alice and other members of her group had mastered a given skill, the emphasis of instruction and assessment shifted to application. For example, through coordination with Mr. Liedig, Alice was evaluated by her employer in terms of how well she accepted criticism from him when he corrected her. She was encouraged to discuss, in her social skills training group, how she was applying her newly learned skills.

On a frequent basis, Mr. Liedig had conferences with Alice to discuss both her progress in and her attitude toward the program. After two months in the new program, Alice stated that she liked school for the first time in a long time. Her mother reported that her attitude and behavior at home had improved, too. Mr. Liedig worked with Alice on the application of basic math skills, particularly handling and counting money and making change. He spent time helping her learn to use a calculator, check her work, and estimate the reasonableness of the answers she obtained using the calculator. Alice continued to do satisfactory work in her part-time job at the cafeteria.

After working there two years, her employer gave her opportunities to learn to work the cash register, and eventually she handled money transactions on a regular basis. She enjoyed the social exchanges she had with the customers, many of whom were regulars.

FUTURE NEEDS

One important point, also made by Schumaker, Deshler, and Ellis (1985), is that a pressing need exists for the development of *comprehensive* models and programs for adolescents with learning problems. Because many of their needs are multifaceted and interrelated, programs are required to address these needs in an integrated and coordinated fashion. Comprehensive programs must be developed that have components related not only to short-term assessments and interventions, but also to assisting adolescents in making the transition out of secondary schools and evaluating long-term program consequences. In this way, information-gathering, interventions, and program outcomes can be integrated into a more encompassing and effective decision-making system.

The second point to be made relates to the larger cultural and political context in which assessments and interventions will be carried out. It should be understood that professionally competent assessment and the provision of cognitive and academic interventions for adolescents can play at best a very partial role in the solution of problems that lie outside of educational and mental health institutions—problems such as unemployment, which are political and economic in nature and which must be solved in those arenas. Education is but one cog in the wheel.

The concept of specific learning disabilities and the activity it has generated have served at least two positive functions. First, the learning disabilities concept has posed an important challenge to the notion that a student's academic potential and performance can be characterized easily by reference to a unitary, all-determining trait called "intelligence." Instead, the reality of inter- and intraindividual differences in student learning characteristics has been highlighted.

The learning disabilities concept has also served a positive function by raising the general level of awareness among lay persons and professionals alike that traditional approaches to schooling are inappropriate for many learners. However, there is considerable progress yet to be made in expanding the flexibility with which educational institutions provide for individual differences among learners, thereby increasing the proportion of students who receive meaningful educational experiences in schools (Senf, 1981). This is true for all levels of education, including both secondary and post-secondary institutions. Today, some flexibility is achieved through special education programming. It remains to be seen, however, how long the provision of flexible educational options will depend on the identification of real or inferred "disorders."

REFERENCES

Adelman, H., & Taylor, L. (1983a). Enhancing motivation for overcoming learning and behavior problems. *Journal of Learning Disabilities, 16*, 384-392.

Adelman, H., & Taylor, L. (1983b). *Learning disabilities in perspective*. Glenview, IL: Scott, Foresman.

Adelman, H. S., & Taylor, L. (1984a). Ethical concerns and identification of psychoeducational problems. *Journal of Clinical Child Psychology, 13,* 16-23.

Adelman, H. S., & Taylor, L. (1984b). Helping clients find referrals. *Remedial and Special Education, 5*(4), 44-45.

American Psychiatric Association. (1980). *Diagnostic and statistical manual of mental disorders* (3rd ed.). Washington, DC: Author.

Anderson, R., Mason, J., & Shirey, L. (1984). The reading group: An experimental investigation of a labyrinth. *Reading Research Quarterly, XX*(1), 6-38.

Applebee, A. N. (1980). *A study of writing in the secondary school* (Final Report NIE-G-79-0174). Urbana, IL: National Council of Teachers of English. (ERIC Document Reproduction Service No. ED 197 347).

Arbitman-Smith, R., & Haywood, H. C. (1980). Cognitive education for learning disabled adolescents. *Journal of Abnormal Child Psychology, 8,* 51-64.

Bateman, B. D. (1964). Learning disabilities—yesterday, today, and tomorrow. *Exceptional Children, 31,* 167.

Bateman, B. D., & Schiefelbusch, R. L. (1969). Educational identification, assessment, and evaluation procedures. In *Minimal brain dysfunction in children: Phase two, educational, medical and health related services* (N and SDCP Monograph, U.S. Public Health Service Publication No. 2015). Washington, DC: U.S. Government Printing Office.

Berk, R. A. (1984). *Screening and diagnosis of children with learning disabilities.* Springfield, IL: Charles C. Thomas.

Biller, E. F. (1985). Career development of the learning disabled adolescent: A focus on career maturity. *Career Development for Exceptional Individuals, 8,* 17-22.

Bingham, G. (1978). Career attitudes among boys with and without specific learning disabilities. *Exceptional Children, 44,* 341-342.

Blalock, J. W. (1981). Persistent problems and concerns of young adults with learning disabilities. In W. Cruickshank & A. Silvers (Eds.), *Bridges to tomorrow: Vol. 2. The best of ACLD* (pp. 35-55). Syracuse, NY: Syracuse University Press.

Blalock, J. W. (1982). Persistent auditory language deficits in adults with learning disabilities. *Journal of Learning Disabilities, 15,* 604-609.

Blalock, G., & Dixon, N. (1982). Improving prospects for the college-bound learning disabled. *Topics in Learning and Learning Disabilities, 2*(3), 69-78.

Bloom, B. S. (1984). The 2 sigma problem: The search for methods of group instruction as effective as one-to-one tutoring. *Educational Researcher, 13*(6), 4-16.

Bos, C. S., & Filip, D. (1982). Comprehension monitoring skills in learning disabled and average students. *Topics in Learning and Learning Disabilities, 2*(1), 79-85.

Brolin, D. E., & Elliot, T. R. (1984). Meeting the lifelong career development needs of students with handicaps: A community college model. *Career Development For Exceptional Individuals, 7,* 12-21.

Brown, A. L., Campione, J. C., & Day, J. D. (1981). Learning to learn: On training students to learn from texts. *Educational Researcher, 10*(2), 14-21.

Brown, A. L., & Palincsar, A. S. (1982). Inducing strategic learning from texts by means of informed, self-control training. *Topics in Learning and Learning Disabilities, 2*(1), 1-17.

Bryan, J. H., & Bryan, T. H. (1983). The social life of the learning disabled youngster. In J. D. McKinney & L. Feagans (Eds.), *Current topics in learning disabilities* (Vol. 1, pp. 57-85). Norwood, NJ: Ablex.

Carrier, J. G. (1983a). Explaining educability: An investigation of political support for the Children with Learning Disabilities Act of 1969. *British Journal of Sociology in Education, 4*(2), 125-140.

Carrier, J. G. (1983b). Masking the social in educational knowledge: The case of learning disability theory. *American Journal of Sociology, 88*(5), 948-974.

Cartledge, G., & Milburn, J. F. (1983). Social skill assessment and teaching in the schools. In T. R. Kratochwill (Ed.), *Advances in school psychology* (Vol. 3, pp. 175-235). Hillsdale, NJ: Lawrence Erlbaum.

Cawley, J. F. (Ed.). (1985). *Practical mathematics appraisal of the learning disabled.* Rockville, MD: Aspen.

Clark, G. M. (1980). Career preparation for handicapped adolescents: A matter of appropriate education. *Exceptional Education Quarterly, 1*(2), 11-17.

Clary, L. M. (1984, February). *Identifying metacognitive social skills in young adults.* Paper presented at the annual convention of the Association for Children and Adults with Learning Disabilities, New Orleans. (ERIC Document Reproduction Service No. ED 249 705).

Coles, G. S. (1978). The learning disabilities battery: Empirical and social issues. *Harvard Educational Review, 48*, 313-340.

Cordini, B. K. (1982). Postsecondary education: Where do we go from here? *Journal of Learning Disabilities, 15*, 265-266.

Deshler, D. D., Ferrell, W. R., & Kass, C. E. (1978). Error monitoring of schoolwork by learning disabled adolescents. *Journal of Learning Disabilities, 11*(7), 10-23.

Deshler, D. D., & Schumaker, J. B. (1983). Social skills of learning disabled adolescents: Characteristics and intervention. *Topics in Learning and Learning Disabilities, 3*(2), 15-23.

Deshler, D. D., Schumaker, J. B., Lenz, B. K., & Ellis, E. (1984). Academic and cognitive interventions for LD adolescents: Part II. *Journal of Learning Disabilities, 17*, 170-179.

Deshler, D. D., Warner, M. M., Schumaker, J. B., & Alley, G. R. (1983). Learning strategies intervention model: Key components and current status. In J. D. McKinney & L. Feagans (Eds.), *Current topics in learning disabilities* (pp. 245-283). Norwood, NJ: Ablex.

DiVesta, F. J., Hayward, K. G., & Orlando, V. P. (1979). Developmental trends in monitoring text for comprehension. *Child Development, 50*, 97-105.

Federal Register. (1977, December 29). Procedures for evaluating specific learning disabilities. *Federal Register, 42*, 65082-65085.

Fenstermacher, G. D., & Amarel, M. A. (1983). Interest of the student, the state, and humanity in education. In L. S. Shulman & G. Sykes, (Eds.), *Handbook of teaching and policy,* (pp. 392-407). New York: Longman.

Foster, S. G. (1984, April 25). Rise in learning-disabled pupils fuels concern in states, districts. *Education Week,* pp. 1, 18.

Fox, E., & Telzrow, C. (Eds.). (1983). *Ohio guidelines for the identification of children with specific learning disabilities.* Columbus, OH: Ohio Department of Education, Division of Special Education.

Franklin, B. M. (1980). From backwardness to L.D.: Behaviorism, systems theory, and the learning disabilities field historically reconsidered. *The Journal of Education, 162*(4), 5-22.

Friedrich, D., Fuller, G. B., & Davis, D. (1984). Learning disability: Fact or fiction. *Journal of Learning Disabilities, 17*, 205-209.

Gallagher, J. J. (1984). Learning disabilities and the near future. *Journal of Learning Disabilities, 17*, 571-572.

Goodman, J. F. (1983). Organicity as a construct in psychological diagnosis. In T. R. Kratochwill (Ed.), *Advances in school psychology* (Vol. 3, pp. 101-139). Hillsdale, NJ: Lawrence Erlbaum.

Greenspan, S. (1981). Defining childhood social competence: A proposed working model. In B. K. Keogh (Ed.), *Advances in special education* (Vol. 3, pp. 1-39). Greenwich, CT: JAI Press.

Hallahan, D. P., & Bryan, T. H. (1981). Learning disabilities. In J. M. Kauffman & D. P. Hallahan (Eds.), *Handbook of special education* (pp. 141-164). Englewood Cliffs, NJ: Prentice-Hall.

Hallahan, D. P., & Cruickshank, W. M. (1973). *Psychoeducational foundations of learning disabilities.* Englewood Cliffs, NJ: Prentice-Hall.

Harrington, R.G. (1984). Assessment of learning disabled children. In S. J. Weaver (Ed.), *Testing children: A reference guide for effective clinical and psychoeducational assessments.* (pp. 85-103). Kansas City, MO: Test Corporation.

Havertape, J. F., & Kass, C. E. (1978). Examination of problem solving in learning disabled adolescents through verbalized self-instructions. *Learning Disability Quarterly, 1,* 94-100.

Havighurst, R. J. (1972). *Developmental tasks of adolescents* (3rd ed.). New York: McKay.

Heshusius, L. (1982). At the heart of the advocacy dilemma: A mechanistic worldview. *Exceptional Children, 49,* 6-13.

Hohenshil, T., Levinson, E., & Heer, K. (1985). Best practices in vocational assessment for handicapped students. In A. Thomas & J. Grimes (Eds.), *Best practices in school psychology* (pp. 215-228). Kent, OH: The National Association of School Psychologists.

Horn, W. F., O'Donnell, J. P., & Vitulano, L. A. (1983). Long-term follow-up studies of learning disabled persons. *Journal of Learning Disabilities, 16,* 542-555.

Howell, K. W., & Kaplan, J. S. (1980). *Diagnosing basic skills.* Columbus, OH: Charles E. Merrill.

Johnson, D. W., & Johnson, R. T. (1978). Cooperative, competitive, and individualistic learning. *Journal of Research and Development in Education, 12*(1), 3-15.

Keogh, B. K., Major-Kingsley, S., Omori-Gordon, H., & Reid, H. P. (1982). *A system of marker variables for the field of learning disabilities.* Syracuse, NY: Syracuse University Press.

Lazerson, M. (1983). The origins of special education. In J. G. Chambers & W. T. Hartman (Eds.), *Special education policies* (pp. 15-47). Philadelphia: Temple University Press.

Lenz, B. K., & Alley, G. R. (1983). *The effect of advanced organizers on the learning and retention of learning disabled adolescents within the contexts of a cooperative planning model.* Final research report submitted to the U.S. Department of Education, Special Education Services.

Mangrum, C. T., & Strichart, S. S. (1983a). College possibilities for the learning disabled: Part one. *Learning Disabilities: An Interdisciplinary Journal, 2*(5), 57-68.

Mangrum, C. T., & Strichart, S. S. (1983b). College possibilities for the learning disabled: Part two. *Learning Disabilities: An Interdisciplinary Journal, 2*(6), 69-81.

Marland, S. P., Jr. (1974). *Career education: A model for reform.* New York: McGraw-Hill.

McCauley, R. J., & Swisher, L. (1984). Use and misuse of norm-referenced tests in clinical assessment: A hypothetical case. *Journal of Speech and Hearing Disorders, 49,* 338-348.

McLoughlin, J., & Lewis, R. (1981). *Assessing special students.* Columbus OH: Charles E. Merrill.

McQueary, T. H. (1910). The relation of the public school and the special school. In *Proceedings of the Seventh Annual Conference on the Education of Backward, Truant, Delinquent and Dependent Children.* Westboro, MA: The Lyman School for Boys.

Mellard, D. F., & Deshler, D. D. (1984). Modeling the condition of learning disabilities in post-secondary populations. *Educational Psychologist, 19,* 188-197.

Mercer, C. D., Hughes, C., & Mercer, A. R. (1985). Learning disabilities definitions used by state education departments. *Learning Disability Quarterly, 8,* 45-55.

Messick, S. (1984). Assessment in context: Appraising student performance in relation to instructional quality. *Educational Researcher, 13*(3), 3-8.

Meyen, E. L., & Lehr, D. H. (1982). Evolving practices in assessment and intervention for mildly handicapped adolescents: The case for intensive instruction. In J. T. Neisworth (Ed.), *Assessment in special education* (pp. 93-100). Rockville, MD: Aspen.

Moran, M. R. (1978). *Assessment of the exceptional learner in the regular classroom.* Denver: Lowe.

Mori, A. A. (1982). School-based career assessment program: Where are we now and where are we going? *Exceptional Education Quarterly, 3*(3), 40-47.

Morsink, C. V. (1985). Learning disabilities. In W. H. Berdine & A. E. Blackhurst (Eds.), *An introduction to special education* (2nd ed.) (pp. 391-425). Boston: Little, Brown.

Mosby, R. J. (1979). A bypass program of supportive instruction for secondary students with learning disabilities. *Journal of Learning Disabilities, 12,* 187-190.

Myklebust, H. R. (1973). *Development and disorders of written language* (Vol. 2). New York: Grune & Stratton.

Ostertag, B. A., Baker, R. E., Howard, R. F., & Best, L. (1982). Learning disabled programs in California community colleges. *Journal of Learning Disabilities, 15,* 535-538.

Pearson, P. D., & Spiro, R. J. (1982). Toward a theory of reading comprehension instruction. In K. G. Butler & G. P. Wallach (Eds.), *Language disorders and learning disabilities* (pp. 71-88). Rockville, MD: Aspen.

Pearl, R., Bryan, T., & Donahue, M. (1980). Learning disabled children's attributions for success and failure. *Learning Disability Quarterly, 3*(1), 3-9.

Phelps, L. A., & McCarty, T. (1984). Student assessment practices. *Career Development for the Exceptional Individual, 7,* 30-38.

Poplin, M. (Ed.). (1984). Holism [Special issue.] *Learning Disability Quarterly, 7*(4).

Poplin, M. & Gray, R. (1982). A conceptual framework for assessment of curriculum and student progress. In J. T. Neisworth (Ed.), *Assessment in special education* (pp. 53-64). Rockville, MD: Aspen.

Reid, D. K., & Hresko, W. P. (Eds.). (1982a). Controversy: Strategy or capacity deficit [Special issue]. *Topics in Learning and Learning Disabilities, 2*(2).

Reid, D. K., & Hresko, W. P. (1982b). Thinking about thinking about it in that way: Test data and instruction. In J. T. Neisworth (Ed.), *Assessment in special education* (pp. 65-75). Rockville, MD: Aspen.

Reynolds, C. R., Berk, R. A., Gutkin, T. B., Boodoo, G. M., Mann, L., Cox, J., Page, E. B., & Willson, V. L. (1983). *Critical measurement issues in learning disabilities.* Washington, DC: U.S. Department of Education, Special Education Programs Work Group on Measurement Issues in the Assessment of Learning Disabilities.

Rosenberg, M. S., & Sindelar, P. T. (1982). Educational assessment using direct, continuous data. In J. T. Neisworth (Ed.), *Assessment in special education* (pp. 83-92). Rockville, MD: Aspen.

Salvia, J., & Ysseldyke, J. E. (1985). *Assessment in special and remedial education* (3rd ed.). Boston: Houghton Mifflin.

Schumaker, J. B., & Deshler, D. D. (1984). Setting demand variables: A major factor in program planning for the LD adolescent. *Topics in Language Disorders, 4*(2), 22-40.

Schumaker, J. B., Deshler, D. D., & Ellis, E. S. (1985). Intervention issues related to the education of LD adolescents. In J. K. Torgesen & B. L. Wong (Eds.), *Learning disabilities: Some new perspectives.* New York: Academic Press.

Schumaker, J. B., & Hazel, J. S. (1984). Social skills assessment and training for the learning disabled: Who's on first and what's on second? Part I. *Journal of Learning Disabilities, 17,* 422-431.

Schumaker, J. B., Hazel, J. S., Sherman, J. A., & Sheldon, J. (1982). Social skill performances of learning disabled, non-learning disabled, and delinquent adolescents. *Learning Disability Quarterly, 5,* 409-414.

Seabaugh, G. O., & Schumaker, J. B. (1981). *The effects of self-regulation training on the academic productivity of LD and NLD adolescents* (Research Rep. No. 37). Lawrence, KS: The University of Kansas Institute for Research in Learning Disabilities.

Senf, G. M. (1981). Issues surrounding the diagnosis of learning disabilities: Child handicap versus failure of the child-school interaction. In T. R. Kratochwill (Ed.), *Advances in school psychology* (Vol. 1, pp. 83-130). Hillsdale, NJ: Erlbaum.

Sheppard, L. (1983). The role of measurement in educational policy: Lessons from the identification of learning disabilities. *Educational Measurement: Issues and Policies, 2*(3), 4-8.

Stipek, D. J. (1982). *Motivating students to learn: A lifelong perspective.* Washington, DC: National Commission on Excellence in Education. (ERIC Document Reproduction Service No. ED 227 111).

Taylor, H. G., Satz, P., & Friel, J. (1979). Developmental dyslexia in relation to other childhood reading disorders: Significance and clinical utility. *Reading Research Quarterly, XY*(1), 84-101.

Taylor, L., Adelman, H. S., & Kaser-Boyd, N. (1983). Perspectives of children regarding their participation in psychoeducational decisions. *Professional Psychology: Research and Practice, 14,* 882-894.

Taylor, R. L. (1984). *Assessment of exceptional students.* Englewood Cliffs, NJ: Prentice-Hall.

Telzrow, C. F. (1985). Best practices in reducing error in learning disability qualification. In A. Thomas & J. Grimes (Eds.), *Best practices in school psychology* (pp. 431-446). Kent, OH: The National Association of School Psychologists.

Tollefson, N., Tracy, D., Johnsen, E., & Chatman, J. (1983). *Teaching learning disabled students goal implementation skills* (Research Rep. No. 69), Lawrence, KS: The University of Kansas Institute for Research in Learning Disabilities.

Tucker, J. A. (1982). Issues and considerations when screening and assessing handicapped pupils. *Measurement and Evaluation in Guidance, 15,* 116-127.

Tucker, J., Stevens, L. J., & Ysseldyke, J. E. (1983). Learning disabilities: The experts speak out. *Journal of Learning Disabilities, 16,* 6-14.

Travers, J. R. (1982). Testing in educational placement: Issues and evidence. In K. A. Heller, W. H. Holtzman, & S. Messick (Eds.), *Placing children in special education: A strategy for equity* (pp. 230-261). Washington, DC: National Academic Press.

Van Reusen, A. K. (1984). *A study on the effects of training learning disabled adolescents in self-advocacy procedures for use in the IEP conference.* Unpublished doctoral dissertation, University of Kansas, Lawrence.

Vetter, A. (1983). *A comparison of the characteristics of learning disabled and non-learning disabled young adults.* Unpublished doctoral dissertation, University of Kansas, Lawrence.

Vogel, S. (1982). On developing LD college programs. *Journal of Learning Disabilities, 15,* 518-528.

Warner, M. M. (1985, April). *Curriculum theory and special education: Implications for dialogue.* Paper presented at the annual meeting of the American Educational Research Association, Chicago.

Warner, M. M. (in press). A critique of the federal definition of learning disabilities and the concept of discrepancy. In D. Robinson & D. Ray (Eds.), *Opening many doors* (Vol. 3). Stillwater, OK: Oklahoma State University, College of Education.

Warner, M. M., & Bull, K. S. (1984, May). *The next step?: Grounding LD definitions and practices in systems of educational thought.* Paper presented at Learning Disabilities: The Next Step conference, St. Paul, MN.

Warner, M. M., & Bull, K. S. (1984). *Putting metacognitive training for the LD adolescent in* perspective: The issues of control and meaning. Unpublished manuscript, Oklahoma State University, Dept. of Applied Behavioral Studies in Education. Stillwater, OK.

Warner, M. M., Schumaker, J. B., Alley, G. R., & Deshler, D. D. (1980). Learning disabled adolescents in the public schools: Are they different from other low achievers? Exceptional Education Quarterly, 1(2), 27-36.

Warner, M. M., Schumaker, J. B., Alley, G. R., Deshler, D. D., (1982). The performance of learning disabled, low-achieving, and normal-achieving adolescents on a serial recall task: The role of executive control (Research Rep. No. 55). Lawrence, KS: University of Kansas Institute for Research in Learning Disabilities.

Wehman, P., Kregel, J., & Barcus, J. M. (1985). From school to work: A vocational transition model for handicapped students. Exceptional Children, 52, 25-37.

White, W. J., Deshler, D. D., Schumaker, J. B., Warner, M. M., Alley, G. R., & Clark, F. L. (1983). The effects of learning disabilities on postschool adjustment. Journal of Rehabilitation, 49(1), 46-50.

Wiig, E., & Harris, S. (1974). Perceptions and interpretation of nonverbally expressed emotions by adolescents with learning disabilities. Perceptual and Motor Skills, 38, 239-245.

Wiig, E., & Semel, E. (1975). Productive language abilities in learning disabled adolescents. Journal of Learning Disabilities, 8, 578-588.

Williams, F., & Coleman, M. (1982). A follow-up study of psychoeducational recommendations. Journal of Learning Disabilities, 15, 596-598.

Wilson, L. R. (1985). Large scale learning disability identification: The reprieve of a concept. Exceptional Children, 52, 44-51.

Wimmer, D. (1981). Functional learning curricula in the secondary schools. Exceptional Children, 47, 610-616.

Wise, A. E. (1979). Legislated learning. Berkeley, CA: University of California Press.

Wiseman, D. G., Van Reusen, A. K., & Hartwell, L. K. (1981). Teaching social studies in the secondary school. In T. Shaw (Ed.), Teaching handicapped students in the content areas (pp. 57-64). Washington, DC: N.E.A. Publications.

Wong, B. (1982). Strategic behaviors in selecting retrieval cues in gifted, normal achieving, and learning disabled children. Journal of Learning Disabilities, 15, 34-37.

Woodward, D. M. & Peters, D. J. (1983). The learning disabled adolescent. Rockville, MD: Aspen.

Ysseldyke, J. E. (1983). Current practices in making psychoeducational decisions. Journal of Learning Disabilities, 16, 226-233.

Ysseldyke, J. E., & Algozzine, B. (1983). On making psychoeducational decisions. Journal of Psychoeducational Assessment, 1, 187-195.

Ysseldyke, J. E., Algozzine, B., Shinn, M. R., & McGue, M. (1982). Similarities and differences between low achievers and students classified as learning disabled. The Journal of Special Education, 16, 73-85.

Zigmond, N., & Brownlee, J. (1980). Social skills training for adolescents with learning disabilities. Exceptional Education Quarterly, 1(2), 77-83.

Zigmond, N., Kerr, M. M., Brown, G. M., & Harris, A. (1984, April). School survival skills in secondary school age special education students. Paper presented at the annual conference of the American Educational Research Association, New Orleans.

Zigmond, N., Vallecorsa, A., & Silverman, R. (1983). Assessment for instructional planning in special education. Englewood Cliffs, NJ: Prentice-Hall.

16

Vocational Assessment for Adolescents

THOMAS H. HOHENSHIL, PH.D.

Adolescence is clearly one of the most volatile and important periods in overall human development, and the rapid changes in the personal, social, and physical aspects of adolescents' lives are well documented. This is also one of the most critical periods in career development, which entails a lifelong process based on an interwoven and sequential series of educational, occupational, leisure, and family choices. Donald Super, the leading career development theorist, has divided this process into five distinct, but somewhat overlapping stages:

1. The *growth* stage extends from birth to age 14, during which time the primary emphasis is on physical and psychological growth. Important components of self-concept are developed in this period as well as knowledge of the general environment, especially the world of work, which will be used later in tentative career decision-making.
2. The *exploratory* stage generally begins at age 15 and extends to the mid-20s. This is a period of exploration of self, tentative occupational choices, career training, and increasing encounters with the world of work. With these exploratory experiences, most individuals focus on more specific occupational and educational choices.
3. During the *establishment* stage, usually described as occurring between the ages of 24-44, the individual attempts to determine if the career choice(s) made during the exploratory stage have long-term significance. Although there may be considerable job and occupational changes early in this period, the occupational pursuits of most persons become more stable toward the latter part of the establishment stage.
4. During the *maintenance* stage, ages 45-64, most adults follow a rather stable occupational pattern. Generally, a single occupation selected during earlier periods is pursued with the goal of "maintaining" and improving oneself within that occupational area.
5. The fifth stage, ages 65 + , is described as a slowing down period, resulting in retirement and more active pursuit of various leisure goals. (Fredrickson, 1982)

The adolescent years span the latter part of the growth stage and the first five years of the exploratory stage of career development. As such, those in early adolescence are perfecting their concept of themselves (self-awareness) and the occupational world around them (career awareness). Entering later adolescence, youths intensify an exploratory process through which their self-concepts are matched against

378

various occupational alternatives. This is a period of both self-concept and vocational exploration, during which the career development goal is to "try out" several occupational and curricular alternatives in order to determine whether one likes them, is proficient with them, and would like to pursue them through additional education and/or training. Most adolescents make a series of "tentative" occupational choices. As interests, values, and self-concepts are rather fluid during this period, it is certainly realistic to expect that most adolescents will choose several occupational areas to explore. The teenager who chooses an occupation at age 13 and maintains that choice through advanced training and/or education is the exception rather than the rule (Hohenshil, 1982a; Hohenshil, 1982b; Seligman, 1980).

The purpose of this chapter is to describe the basic purposes, components, and processes of adolescent vocational assessment, including those individuals with handicapping conditions.

The Career Decision-Making Process

Assessment, like other educational services, should support the primary emphases of the different levels of the educational system. This is such an important point that these emphases should be reviewed briefly:

Elementary school. The basic emphasis of the primary grades traditionally has focused on the acquisition of reading, writing, mathematics, social, and citizenship skills. These basics, along with various career and self-awareness activities, form the foundation for successful career decision-making throughout life. Assessment at this level normally is confined to diagnostic and achievement procedures relating to the acquisition of the basic academic skills.

Junior high school. Traditionally, a primary emphasis of the junior high or intermediate school has been the exploration of various career and curricular options to assist students in the decision-making process as they enter senior high school. Many schools try to facilitate this exploration process by instituting a series of short-term (2-6 week) courses in which all or designated students may be enrolled. These short courses usually are designed to address various career and curricular clusters. For example, short courses might highlight each of several occupations, such as construction, health, agriculture, entertainment, business, and so on. The major goal in exploratory courses is to provide students with an opportunity to "try out" and learn more about various vocational choices. The primary focus of assessment at this level is *not* skill acquisition. Vocational assessment procedures should support the exploratory process and usually involve both interests and aptitudes testing.

Senior high school. The prime concern of the senior high school traditionally has been preparation for entry-level employment and/or the next level of the educational system, accomplished through vocational education programs, college preparatory programs, or some combination thereof. The decision-making process is particularly important at the early high school level, where curricular choices may lock students into a certain track before they have had an opportunity to explore fully the consequences of various curricular options. Vocational assessment procedures at this level support the preparation phase, focusing on the appropriate placement of adolescents in vocational and college preparation courses (Hohenshil, 1982b; Miller & Schloss, 1982).

A major purpose of vocational assessment data is to provide information and assistance in the career and educational planning process. The basic decision-making model is the same whether students make the decisions themselves or whether they are made by placement committees. As presented in Figure 1, the career decision-making process can be broken down into seven steps or components. Probably the

FIGURE 1. CAREER DECISION-MAKING MODEL*

Step 1—*Determine Decision to be Made*
　　Depends on person's level of educational and psychological development

Step 2—*Collect Appropriate Information*
　　Internal Information
　　　　Interests
　　　　Aptitudes
　　　　Values
　　　　Aspirations
　　　　Achievement
　　　　Personality
　　　　Small/large motor coordination

　　External Information
　　　　Types of occupations available
　　　　Personal requirements for entry
　　　　Educational requirements
　　　　Economic & social consequences
　　　　Relation of curriculum to various career options
　　　　Application process for entrance

Step 3—*Generate Alternative Career Options*

Step 4—*Select Primary Alternative & Specify Secondary Alternatives*

Step 5—*Reality Testing in Sheltered Environment*
　　School courses
　　Co-op programs
　　Simulated work experience
　　Observation

Step 6—*Evaluate Results of Reality Testing*

Step 7—*Continue to Pursue Primary Alternative*
　　or
　　Return to Step 4 to consider secondary career alternatives

*From Hohenshil (1982b)

most important component of this model is Step 1—determining the decision to be made with a particular person. If the student is 10 years old, the decision at hand is not what that student will do with the rest of his or her life; rather, additional career and self-awareness activities would be most appropriate. For the 14- to 20-year-old student, career exploration and preparation goals would be the most appropriate considerations. The specific decision regarding career development depends on such factors as age, level of mental ability, achievement in academic skills, social/emotional maturity, occupational experiences, and type of handicapping condition, if any.

Vocational assessment information has the most significance in Step 2 of the model—collection of the appropriate information. Vocational assessment procedures and instruments focus on the internal information aspects of Step 2 by helping students and placement committees learn more about student interests, aptitudes, values, personality, and so on. All are important aspects of this career decision-making process. In fact, the quality of information developed in Step 2 clearly determines the quality of career options generated in Step 3. Vocational assessment data are also important in the evaluation of the results of reality testing, which is considered in Step 6. Through reality testing, the individual tries out or explores tentative career options and attempts to narrow down the choices for additional training. The more adolescents know about themselves and their various tentative career options, the more appropriate and realistic career decisions will be. The same holds true for future education and training recommendations made by placement committees and agency personnel (Hohenshil, 1984a; Hohenshil, 1984b; Hohenshil, Levinson, & Heer, 1985). Reducing the error factor in career decisions tends to reduce subsequent frustration and occupational/curricular changes.

Many adolescents have literally no occupational goals, while others may have unrealistic ones. For these individuals, the primary purpose of vocational assessment is the *generation* of career options. Research indicates that handicapped adolescents, for example, have very little work experience and generally are less mature in the career development process than their age peers (Hohenshil, in press). A second use of vocational assessment data deals with the *selection* of occupational and training alternatives. Some adolescents have established multiple career goals, have explored a few of them, and need assistance in choosing among them. A third purpose of vocational assessment is *confirmation*. Students, and placement committees as well, may request vocational assessment to help confirm a tentative decision. One can view this generation/selection/confirmation model as a continuum through which everyone passes. Handicapped and nonhandicapped adolescents alike need to generate occupational options, select from the alternatives, and confirm decisions tentatively made. Vocational interest, aptitude, and career maturity data can be helpful in this process (Hohenshil, 1982b).

VOCATIONAL ASSESSMENT TECHNIQUES

There are a variety of vocational assessment techniques that counselors, psychologists, vocational evaluators, and others may use to develop information that facilitates the career development process. These techniques can be classified as follows: 1) vocationally oriented interviews; 2) behavioral observations; 3) work experience; 4) simulated work experience; 5) work sampling systems; 6) performance tests; 7) group psychometrics (paper and pencil); and 8) computerized assessment systems.

Vocational assessment is a multidisciplinary process in almost all of the currently functioning programs. Those involved may include various social agency personnel, vocational and special education teachers, school psychologists, school counselors, rehabilitation counselors, medical personnel, vocational/work evaluation specialists, parents, and students. Who does what in the vocational evaluation process depends on the characteristics of the agency or school, the qualifications of the professional staff, and the availability of services from other agencies or schools in a region. Generally, counselors and psychologists play a major role in the assessment of mental ability, personality/social skills, achievement, motor coordination and perception, and traditional assessment of interests, aptitudes, and adaptive behavior. Vocational evaluators and rehabilitation personnel usually administer and interpret work samples. Obviously, teachers, parents, and other significant persons also participate when needed.

Interviewing and Behavioral Observations

Behavioral observation and interviewing are two of the most useful vocational assessment techniques. A vocationally oriented interview should be part of every adolescent assessment, talking about work experiences, likes and dislikes, leisure activities, school subject preferences, and career and life-style aspirations. This is an excellent means of pinpointing an individual in the career decision-making process as well as assisting in the evaluator's formulation of assessment goals.

Vocational assessment goals naturally are quite different for adolescents who have little idea of what they might do as opposed to those who have significant work experience in an occupational field for which they would like to prepare or in which they seek advancement in the future. The same is true with respect to self-knowledge about aptitudes, interests, values, and so on. The framework for vocationally oriented interviews should include the following:

1. Leisure pursuits
2. Previous work experience
3. Social relationships
4. Course preferences
5. Course dislikes
6. Best course performance
7. Poorest course performance
8. Aspirations for future
9. Parent occupations
10. Parent expectations
11. Knowledge of occupational alternatives
12. Knowledge of training programs
13. Occupational day dreams
14. Influential persons in decision making

The behavioral observations of parents and teachers are also beneficial. For example, it is important to know if the data from the interview with the adolescent parallel the observations of teachers, parents, and other sources of assessment information. If not, this finding has implications for additional career counseling, vocational exploration, and assessment (Hohenshil, Levinson, & Heer, 1985).

Work Experience and Simulated Experiences

Actual work experience is viewed by some as one of the most important vocational assessment techniques. Probably there is no better method than work experience to determine whether a person has interests in a vocational area, has an aptitude for the work and can achieve at it, and would like to pursue an occupational area through specific job training. Unfortunately, research has indicated that most handicapped adolescents have little part- or full-time work experience (Miller & Schloss, 1982). In these situations, simulated work experience can be useful. Using this technique, students are placed in a simulated work environment for a particular occupation or cluster of similar occupations. Some would contend that not only career exploration programs at the junior and senior high levels, but also vocational education itself in many instances, are really simulated work experiences. Through these simulations, adolescents can acquire some firsthand experience in several different occupational and curricular areas. This could be viewed as a self-evaluation component of vocational assessment, where students review the experiences in relation to their own interests, values, aptitudes, and so one. The information derived from work experience and simulated work experience can be accessed through the vocationally oriented interview and behavioral observations.

Work Sampling

Work sampling is a process whereby certain job functions from a single occupation or cluster of related occupations are performed by the individual under the observation of a trained evaluator. There are a variety of commercially and locally developed work sampling programs currently in use in agencies and school settings. These programs generally tap vocational aptitudes, vocational interests, and work attitudes and habits, comprising some of the fastest growing types of vocational assessment in the nation. Initially developed and used primarily by vocational rehabilitation personnel, work sampling techniques are increasingly being integrated into public school and adult education settings. As a word of caution, one of the shortcomings of several work sampling systems is the lack of adequate norms and reliability and validity data. A few of the commonly used work sampling systems include the Singer Vocational Evaluation System, the Valpar Component Work Sample System (VALPAR), the Comprehensive Occupational Assessment and Training System (COATS), and the Vocational Information & Evaluation Work Samples (VIEWS).

Performance Tests

Most vocationally oriented performance tests focus on such areas as finger and manual dexterity, eye-hand coordination, and the use of spatial relations/reasoning, all of which are important in a vocational sense. Some of the more popular performance tests include the performance section of the General Aptitude Test Battery, the performance sections of the Wechsler scales, the Crawford Small Parts Dexterity Test, the Purdue Pegboard, and the Pennsylvania Bi-Manual Worksample.

Paper-and-Pencil Tests

Paper-and-pencil techniques often come to mind first when vocational assessment is discussed. This category includes most of the traditional interest inventories, such as the Strong-Campbell Interest Inventory, the Ohio Vocational Interest Survey, and the various forms of the Kuder interest inventories, as well as multiple aptitude tests like the Differential Aptitude Tests. The distinguishing characteristic of these kinds of vocational assessments is that they represent a conventional paper-and-pencil approach and most can be administered on a group basis.

The reading level often presents one of the major problems in using these tests and inventories with handicapped adolescents, as most are written at around the sixth-grade level; many handicapped, disadvantaged, and non-English-speaking adolescents simply do not read at a high enough level to complete these instruments in a valid manner. It may be necessary, therefore, either to use some of the available reading-free or "low" reading inventories, such as the Wide Range Interest-Opinion Test (WRIOT) and the Judgment of Occupational Behavior-Orientation (JOB-O), or to rely on the vocational interview. For orthopedically disabled adolescents or those with some type of sensory deficit, paper-and-pencil instruments may not yield enough useful information about vocational aptitudes and physical factors (e.g., finger and manual dexterity) of vocational significance. Here, work sampling procedures and performance tests would be more appropriate.

Computerized Assessment

Computerized vocational assessment techniques represent a relatively new development. Many of the common paper-and-pencil vocational interest inventories and aptitude tests have been adapted for use with and interpretation by computers. Some of the newer computer programs also include some elements of work sampling procedures and performance tests. The area of computerized vocational assessment is developing rapidly and has many advantages, one of the most significant of which is almost immediate feedback to the client and evaluator. Rather than having to wait for a week or more for the return of a profile on an interest inventory, the time lapse between completing the instrument and getting a printout interpreting the results may be less than 5 minutes (Anderson, 1985; Hohenshil, 1984a; Kapes & Mastie, 1982). Examples of these vocational assessments include the Self-Directed Search: Computer Version™, the Microcomputer Evaluation and Screening Assessment (MESA), and the System for Assessment and Group Evaluation (SAGE) with its follow-up component Job Opportunity Based Search (JOBS).

SELECTING THE VOCATIONAL ASSESSMENT BATTERY

The experienced clinician chooses particular techniques and instruments for specific students/clients, with the composition of the selection dependent on the latter's presenting needs. Most vocational assessment programs in schools and agencies are structured as a two-level system. Level 1 vocational assessment includes such information as mental ability, academic achievement, adaptive behavior, social skills, and physical data, along with information obtained through vocationally oriented interviews with adolescents and their parents. Information from teachers is also critical and should include data about student work habits and attitudes, interests, aptitudes, and achievement. Information from school and agency records, such as group test data, grades, and available medical information, is also useful. In addition, Level 1 assessments should include a formal evaluation of vocational interests and aptitudes utilizing such traditional methods as paper-and-pencil vocational interest inventories and aptitude tests. Level 1 vocational assessment is recommended for *all* adolescents.

There are some situations in which a realistic vocational decision/recommendation cannot be made as a result of Level 1 data. For example, an adolescent may have reading deficiencies that preclude the use of traditional aptitude and interest inventories, or orthopedic and sensory impairments may increase the difficulty of making a reasonable vocational decision. In this case, a Level 2 vocational assessment, which is reserved for handicapped students and can take place at either junior high, senior high, or adult levels, would be in order. In most cases, this assessment will occur in a central location (system-wide center, multi-county vocational assessment center, or agency setting) due to the nature of the equipment and staffing required. Level 2 includes all of the kinds of information obtained in a Level 1 evaluation, plus the administration of work samples and possibly exploratory vocational course experiences. A comprehensive Level 2 assessment may take as long as a week or more to complete due to the extensive time requirements of work sampling procedures (Hohenshil, Levinson, & Heer, 1985; Levinson & Capps, 1985; Texas Education Agency, 1982).

Having considered the various vocational assessment techniques, the clinician can devise a broadly based vocational assessment battery that can be used with adolescents in school, agency, and private practice settings. The following discussion addresses the components of such an appraisal battery.

Mental Ability and Achievement

Measures of mental ability and achievement in the basic academic skills provide essential data in the career-planning process because they are probably the most accurate predictors of success in any vocational or academic program. Mental ability evaluations include both individual and group methods, with the individual methods usually being reserved for adolescents with various degrees of handicapping conditions. The individual mental ability measures of choice are the Wechsler Adult Intelligence Scale-Revised (WAIS-R) and the Wechsler Intelligence Scale for Children-Revised (WISC-R) because the subscale information can be important from an occupational perspective. The diagram below presents a continuum showing the general relationship between mental ability and occupational levels:

Low Ability		*Average Ability*		*High Ability*
Unskilled Occupations	Semi-Skilled Occupations	Skilled Occupations	Technical Occupations	Professional Occupations

As would be expected, professional and technical occupations require the highest level of general mental ability because they require high levels of verbal and spatial reasoning, memory, and general analytical ability. The requirements of unskilled and semi-skilled occupations are not as great, but these vocations may necessitate a fairly high level of manual skills and finger dexterity. In terms of actual employment, it is rare to find a person of low mental ability in a professional or technical occupation because of strenuous academic preparation and occupational performance standards. Persons who hold unskilled and semi-skilled occupations comprise a much more heterogenous group in terms of mental ability. Because entrance requirements for unskilled jobs are most closely related to physical stamina and manual dexterity, a wide range of general mental ability is possible. It is not at all unusual on an assembly line to have someone with an IQ of 120 working beside someone with low mental ability and both doing a credible job. One could say, though, that the individual with the IQ of 120 is probably underemployed from strictly an ability standpoint. As motivation is such an important aspect of educational and occupational performance, it is not possible to indicate valid cutoffs between the different occupational levels in terms of mental ability; the overlap would be too great. In terms of potential, the higher the ability level, the greater the probability for success (i.e., training as well as occupational performance) in higher level occupational areas.

Motor Coordination

Small and large motor coordination are important factors in these assessments because coordination takes a high priority in many vocational areas. For example, many of the vocational training areas require good eye-hand coordination (word processing, carpentry, electronics, plumbing, cosmetology, etc.) and a relatively high level of physical stamina. In addition to traditional techniques for assessing motor skills and perception, such as the Bender Visual Motor Gestalt Test, work sampling and various types of performance tests can be used.

Social Maturity and Personality

Social maturity and personality factors affect job success in most occupations to some degree. Research indicates that the majority of people lose their jobs not because they lack the necessary occupational skills, but because they cannot get along with their co-workers and supervisors (Miller & Schloss, 1982). For example, in marketing and distribution, social skills are critically important, while they are less so in some trade and industrial occupations such as plumber, electrician, or machinist. Thus, social maturity and personality assessment are necessary components of a comprehensive vocationally oriented battery. For handicapped students, many of these factors are addressed when assessing adaptive behavior.

Adaptive behavior measures are used primarily with handicapped clients, and until recently most of these instruments were developed for mentally retarded children or adults. Important vocationally related adaptive behaviors include personal hygiene, ability to use public transportation, reaction to supervision, independence and flexibility, use of tools, money management, and so on. Few vocationally oriented adaptive behavior measures have been developed for use with adolescents, though this situation slowly is being rectified. Some of the commonly used assessments for this purpose are the Vineland Adaptive Behavior Scales, the Social and Prevocational Information Battery, the Scales of Independent Behavior, and the Program for Assessing Youth Employment Skills.

Interest and Aptitude

Interest and aptitude assessment entails efforts to determine vocational likes and dislikes as well as what abilities can be developed with additional training. Frequently, interests and aptitudes can be assessed through traditional paper-and-pencil psychometric techniques, determined by whether a particular handicapping condition or language or cultural factor interferes with the proper use of the instruments. Poor reading ability, various sensory deficits, orthopedic disabilities, and limited English proficiency may require the use of such nontraditional methods as work sampling, reading-free or low reading difficulty measures, and/or vocational interviewing and behavioral observations.

Career Maturity

Career maturity is similar in some respects to the developmental concept of mental maturity. Instruments such as the Career Maturity Inventory and the Career Development Inventory are designed to assess an individual's levels of self-knowledge, career information, and career decision-making skills in relation to others of the same age group. In general, more career maturity inventories lack norms for students with various types of handicapping conditions, the disadvantaged, and non-English-speaking adolescents; therefore, they must be interpreted with caution if they are to be used with these individuals (Andrulis, 1977; Capps, Levinson, & Hohenshil, 1985; Heinlein, Nelson, & Hohenshil, 1984).

The sequencing of the vocational assessment techniques and processes is important and reflects the basic goals of career decision-making. Figure 2 presents a sequencing model. As the overriding goal of vocational assessment is to help adolescents choose appropriate occupational areas where they will be happy and successful, the place to begin the process is with areas of occupational interests, or in other words, likes and dislikes. As noted previously, this can be done through the vocationally oriented interview, the use of vocational interest inventories, behavior observation, work-sampling procedures, or more likely, a combination of these techniques.

After the client tentatively selects an occupational area, Step 2 proceeds to determine whether the person's ability level seems high enough to be successful in such a training/educational program. Assessment in this area may involve general ability and more specific aptitudes, as well as strictly physical factors. Step 2 may require some combination of general ability measures such as the Wechsler scales, multiple-aptitude test batteries like the General Aptitude Test Battery and the Differential Aptitude Tests, work sampling procedures, and appropriate performance tests.

If it appears that the individual has the ability to pursue the tentative occupational choice, then Step 3 involves determining whether the adolescent has achieved the necessary academic and social skills to enter the specified training/educational program. Traditional basic academic achievement tests can be used, along with a review

FIGURE 2. VOCATIONAL ASSESSMENT SEQUENCE

Step 1—*Determine Areas of Interest*
  Interview
  Inventories
  Observation

Step 2—*Determine Ability Levels*
  General Mental Ability
  Vocational Aptitudes
    GATB or DAT
    Work sampling
    Performance tests
  Physical Factors

Step 3—*Determine Achievement Levels*
  Reading
  Mathematics
  Writing
  Social Skills
  Adaptive Behavior

Step 4—*Relate to Vocational/Educational Options*

of the individual's past grades. Attendance records, work and school attitudes, and ability to follow directions and take criticism are also important aspects to consider in this third step. School and agency records, personality inventories, and adaptive behavior measures can be used alone and in combination to help gather these data.

If the adolescent falls short of the requisites revealed by either Step 2 or Step 3, the appropriate course is to return to Step 1 and consider other tentative occupational choices that may be more suitable to the individual's aptitudes and basic skills. Aside from ability, it may be possible that the individual is not yet ready for serious career training and should be referred for additional career awareness/career exploration activities. If, however, the examinee does seem to have the requisite ability and basic academic/social skills, then Step 4 goes on to review the training/education options that will help the student prepare for the occupational choice identified in Step 1. This education or training may be secured through a vocational education program if the occupation does not require post-secondary education. If it does, then a college preparatory curriculum may be the appropriate choice in high school.

INTEGRATION AND INTERPRETATION OF RESULTS

Another way to view vocational assessment data is from a diagnostic perspective. With the proper information it is quite possible to identify adolescents' vocational development levels, which in turn provides direction for psychologists, counselors, and others in planning a post-assessment program for the adolescents being evaluated. The diagram below presents a visual model of the course of this development:

| Awareness | Exploration | Training | Job Placement |

This kind of diagnosis is also important because many adolescents simply are not developmentally ready for placement in an occupational training program (the third stage in the diagram). Often one finds adolescents only vaguely aware of their own interests, aptitudes, values, and so on, and with little idea of the wide range of occupational/educational alternatives. These students would be classified in the Awareness stage of the model. Placing them directly into an occupational training program would not have a high probability of success, regardless of their degree of aptitude and academic achievement.

Other adolescents may have a fairly good view of their own attributes and the alternatives available and may have narrowed their choices to a few occupational areas, but have not had any direct exploratory experiences in those areas. These adolescents would be classified as ready to enter the Exploration stage of vocational development. Placing them directly into a training program could also have less than satisfactory results.

One of the major problems with vocational training programs is that students are required to make a two-to-three-year commitment when they are only 14-16 years of age. Because adolescents' interests and values exist in a rather fluid state, it is quite possible that an accurate vocational placement at age 14 or 15 may be entirely inappropriate two or three years later because of changes in interests and values. High school and agency vocational training programs should expect that, under the best of conditions, adolescents will be using their training programs for exploratory purposes and thus frequently will request transfer from one occupational training program to another. This does not necessarily reflect on the quality of the vocational program, but rather on the nature of adolescence.

If one determines that a particular adolescent is not developmentally ready for any kind of vocational training program (i.e., is in the Awareness or Exploration stages), there are numerous career development activities that may be prescribed, designed to help persons expand awareness and participate in exploratory experiences. The most common techniques toward this end follow:

Frequently used awareness intervention techniques include reading materials such as the *Occupational Outlook Handbook,* which is published every two years by the U.S. Department of Labor. Other self- and career-awareness techniques include the wide variety of films, filmstrips, and audio recordings available through commercial publishers. Interest and aptitude testing, career trips, values clarification, decision-making training, and the use of career speakers bureaus are also useful methods to increase self- and career awareness. The basic purpose of these intervention techniques is to increase the individual's awareness of self and the occupational world, and how the two relate and interact.

Exploration is a process of more intensively investigating the career alternatives reviewed in the awareness phase. Here, the person selects a few occupations (usually one to five) that seem to be of particular interest. The counselor or psychologist then prescribes exploratory activities, which help the individual actually observe and participate in some of the job functions involved in the selected occupations. The most frequently prescribed career exploration activities include short-term, school-based exploratory courses, self-instructional modules, volunteer work experience, shadowing (spending time actually observing a person in an occupation), summer and part-time employment, and cooperative education/work programs.

The need for vocational assessment services in the future will expand significantly due to some recent federal legislation. The 1985 Vocational Education Act mandates that all handicapped students have a vocational assessment prior to entering vocational training programs. This mandate is requiring school systems and agencies throughout the nation to focus more attention and resources on the vocational needs of adolescents. The contents of this chapter should help prepare professionals to become involved in this important process.

REFERENCES

Anderson, W. T. (in press). Prevocational and vocational assessment of handicapped students. In P. J. Lazarus & S. Strichert (Eds.), *Psychoeducational evaluation of school-aged children with low-incidence handicaps.* New York: Grune & Stratton.
Andrulis, R. S. (1977). *Adult assessment.* Springfield, IL: Charles C. Thomas.
Capps, C. F., Levinson, E. M., & Hohenshil, T. H. (1985). The vocational aspects of psychological assessment: Part III. *The NASP Communique, 13*(5), 5-6.
Fredrickson, R. H. (1982). *Career information.* Englewood Cliffs, NJ: Prentice-Hall.
Heinlein, W. E., Nelson, M. D., & Hohenshil, T. H. (1984). The vocational aspects of psychological assessment: Part II. *The NASP Communique, 13*(4), 7.
Hohenshil, T. H. (1982a). School psychology + vocational counseling = vocational school psychology. *The Personnel and Guidance Journal, 61*(1), 11-14.
Hohenshil, T. H. (1982b). Secondary school psychological services: Vocational assessment procedures for handicapped students. In T. H. Hohenshil, W. T. Anderson, & J. F. Salwan (Eds.), *Secondary school psychological services: Focus on vocational assessment procedures for handicapped students.* Blacksburg, VA: Virginia Polytechnic Institute. (ERIC Document Reproduction No. ED 229 704)
Hohenshil, T. H. (1984a). The vocational aspects of psychological assessment: Part I. *The NASP Communique, 13*(3), 6-7.
Hohenshil, T. H. (1984b). The vocational aspects of school psychology: 1974-84. *The School Psychology Review, 13*(3), 503-509.
Hohenshil, T. H. (in press). Vocational assessment for special populations. In H. Drier (Ed.), *Support and placement services for special populations.* Columbus, OH: The National Center for Research in Vocational Education.
Hohenshil, T. H., Levinson, E. M., & Heer, K. B. (1985). Best practices in vocational assessment for handicapped students. In A. Thomas & J. Grimes (Eds.), *Best practices in school psychology* (pp. 215-228). Washington, DC: National Association of School Psychologists.
Kapes, J. T., & Mastie, M. M. (1982). *A counselor's guide to vocational guidance instruments.* Falls Church, VA: National Vocational Guidance Association.

Levinson, E. M., & Capps, C. F. (1985). Vocational assessment and special education triennial reevaluation at the secondary level. *Psychology in the Schools, 22,* 283-292.

Miller, S. R., & Schloss, P. J. (1982). *Career-vocational education for handicapped youth.* Rockville, MD: Aspen Systems Corporation.

Seligman, L. (1980). *Assessment in developmental career counseling.* Cranston, RI: The Carroll Press.

Texas Education Agency. (1982). *Vocational assessment of students with special needs.* Austin, TX: Author.

Appendix: Test Directory and Index

Assesses children aged 3-16 whose adaptive behavior indicates possible mental retardation, emotional disturbance, or other learning handicaps. Used for screening, instructional planning, diagnostic and placement decisions, and formulating general educational goals.

A 95-item, paper-pencil scale completed by the examiner and measuring social and daily living skills and behaviors. Two profiles are available: Instructional Planning Profile (for classroom instructional planning) summarizes student's scores on 21 domains; Diagnostic Profile (for diagnostic and placement decisions and formulating general educational goals) used to group and convert certain item and domain scores into five factor scores and Companion Score. Administration untimed (30 minutes). Examiner required and evaluated. Not for group use. Hand scored. Microcomputer software available. Starter set $22.75. *Publisher: CTB/ McGraw-Hill*

Measures emotional and personality factors for visually handicapped adolescents. Used to assess their personal and emotional adjustment.

A questionnaire-type personality inventory consisting of 150 statements in large print and including instructions for tape recording questions. Provides scores on nine scales: Sensitivity, Somatic Symptoms, Social Competency, Attitudes of Distrust, Family Adjustment, Boy-Girl Adjustment, School Adjustment, Morale, and Attitudes toward Blindness. Validation score also obtained. Administration untimed (varies). Examiner required and evaluated. Paper-pencil version suitable for group use. Test kit $15.00. *Publisher: Associated Services for the Blind*

Identifies behaviors adolescents find helpful in managing problems or difficult situations that happen to them or members of

Refer to page(s)	*Test Title*

their families. Used in counseling, clinical, and research settings.

A 54-item, self-report instrument covering behaviors for coping with problems. Items are grouped conceptually into seven behavioral patterns: developing and maintaining a sense of self-esteem, investing in family relationships and fitting into the family lifestyle, investing in extra-familial relationships and seeking social support, developing positive perceptions about life situations, relieving tension through diversions, relieving tension through substance use and/or expression of anger, and avoiding confrontation and withdrawing. Administration untimed (varies). Examiner administered and evaluated. Suitable for group use. Each test form $0.10, manual $15.00 ($10.00 for students). *Publisher:* Family Stress, Coping and Health Project

314   ADOLESCENT-FAMILY INVENTORY OF LIFE EVENTS AND CHANGES (A-FILE)   *Hamilton I. McCubbin, Joan M. Patterson, Edward Bauman, and Linda H. Harris*

Assesses the accumulation of life events and changes in a family from an adolescent member's perspective. Used in clinical and research settings to assess the stress adolescents may be experiencing as a result of family events and changes, to identify adolescents at risk for experiencing undesirable outcomes, as a pre- and postmeasure of family stress with intervention programs, and as a predictive tool for a wide range of criteria, including adolescent substance use, family member's health status, and family adaptation/maladaptation.

A 50-item, self-report instrument consisting of six scales: Transitions, Sexuality, Responsibilities and Strains, Substance Use, and Legal Conflict. Three scores can be obtained: scale scores, total past life changes, and a weighted stress score. Administration untimed (varies). Examiner required. Hand scored. Suitable for group use. Each test form $0.10, manual $15.00 ($10.00 for students). *Publisher:* Family Stress, Coping and Health Project

14   BALL APTITUDE BATTERY   *Yong H. Sung and Rene V. Davis*

Measures aptitude for a wide variety of occupational and industrial jobs. Used for employee selection, classification, and placement and for individual career planning.

A standardized battery of 14 multiple-item, paper-pencil tests evaluating aptitude based on an individual's performance on selected work samples. The battery consists of the following tests: Clerical, Idea Fluency, Inductive Reasoning, Word Association, Writing Speed, Paper Folding, Vocabulary, Ideaphoria, Numerical Computation, Numerical Reasoning, Finger Dexterity, Grip Test, Analytical Reasoning, and Shape Assembly. Administration timed (3-3½ hours). Examiner required. Computer scored. All tests except Grip, Analytical Reasoning, and Shape Assembly are suitable for group use. Contact publisher for cost. *Publisher:* Ball Foundation

Refer to page(s)	*Test Title*

9

BASIC ACHIEVEMENT SKILLS INDIVIDUAL SCREENER (BASIS) *The Psychological Corporation*

Measures achievement of children (six years and up) and adults in reading, mathematics, and spelling. Used as a screening device in business and industry and as part of a comprehensive case study in correctional institutions, rehabilitation programs, welfare agencies, mental-health clinics, and the courts. Can be modified for testing physically handicapped, hearing-impaired, and blind persons.

Consists of three tests: Reading (reading passages aloud and supplying missing words), Mathematics (solving computation items and dictated word problems), and Spelling (writing words dictated in sentence contexts). Administration untimed (1 hour). Examiner required and evaluated. Not for group use. Hand scored. Examiner's kit $37.50. *Publisher:* The Psychological Corporation

157, 158, 165, 256, 290

BECK DEPRESSION INVENTORY (BDI) *Aaron T. Beck*

Measures the degree of depression of adolescents and adults. Used for treatment planning and evaluation in mental health settings.

A 21-item inventory assessing an individual's complaints, symptoms, and concerns related to their current degree of depression. Scales include sadness, pessimism, sense of failure, dissatisfaction, guilty feelings, sense of being punished, self-dislike, self-accusations, suicidal ideas, crying, irritability, social withdrawal, indecisiveness, change in body image, work difficulty, insomnia, loss of appetite, weight loss, somatic preoccupation, fatigability, and loss of libido. Questions presented on eighth-grade reading level. Administration untimed (15-20 minutes). Examiner required. Not for group use. Consult publisher for cost. *Publisher:* Center for Cognitive Therapy

135, 136

BEM SEX-ROLE INVENTORY *Sandra L. Bem*

Measures masculinity and femininity. Used for research on psychological androgyny.

A 60-item paper-pencil measure of the integration of masculinity and femininity. Items consist of three sets of 20 personality characteristics: masculine, feminine, and neutral. The subject indicates on a 7-point scale how well each characteristic describes him or her. Materials include a 30-item short form. Self-administered (untimed) and suitable for group use. Hand scored. Test kit $13.00. *Publisher:* Consulting Psychologists Press, Inc.

69, 312, 386

BENDER VISUAL MOTOR GESTALT TEST *Lauretta Bender*

Assesses the visual-motor functions of individuals aged three to adult. Used in the evaluation of developmental problems in children, learning disabilities, retardation, psychosis, and organic brain disorders.

A paper-pencil test consisting of nine different Gestalt cards. The individual is given the cards one at a time and asked to

Refer to page(s)	*Test Title*

reproduce on a blank sheet of paper the configuration or design presented on each card. Responses scored according to development of the concepts of form, shape, and pattern, and orientation in space. Analysis of performance may indicate the presence of psychosis or maturational lags. Administration untimed (10-20 minutes). Slides may be used for group administration. Examiner required and evaluated. Scoring service provided by Koppitz and Grune & Stratton. Cards, manual of instruction $5.00. *Publisher:* American Orthopsychiatric Association

9

THE BRIGANCE® DIAGNOSTIC INVENTORY OF
ESSENTIAL SKILLS *Albert H. Brigance*

Assesses and diagnoses strengths and weaknesses of students (Grades 6-12) with special needs. Used to determine minimal competencies in skills necessary for success as citizen, consumer, employee, and family member.

A paper-pencil or oral-response inventory measuring 186 academic and vocational skills in reading, language arts, and life skills, including applied skills and practical assessments. Results identify mastered and unmastered basic skills and instructional objectives for specified skill level. Administration untimed (varies). Examiner required and evaluated. Some sections suitable for group use. Videotape inservice program available on loan. Inventory, 10 record books $99.95. *Publisher:* Curriculum Associates, Inc.

332, 337

BRISTOL SOCIAL ADJUSTMENT GUIDES (BSAG)
D. H. Stott

Screens school maladjustment, identifies deviant trait characteristics through observable behavior disturbance of children and adolescents aged 5-16, and assesses effects of therapies and special school/class placement. Used to provide clinicians and school psychologists with teachers' reports of school adjustment/maladjustment of students and school counselors and social workers with reasons for learning disabilities, to train teachers to recognize and objectively treat deviant behavior, and in research.

A 116-item assessment consisting of phrases describing children's behavior, especially in school situations. Subscales keyed to five Core Syndromes (Unforthcomingness, Withdrawal, Depression, Inconsequence, Hostility) and four Associated Groupings (Peer-maladaptiveness, Non-syndromic over-reaction, Non-syndromic under-reaction, Neurological symptoms), which (except Neurological symptoms) are grouped into two main scales: Under- and Over-reaction. Observer (teacher/caretaker) underlines phrases best describing recent (approximately one month prior) behavior and attitudes of child being assessed, omitting inappropriate ones. Two forms (Boy and Girl) available. Hand scored. Administration untimed (15 minutes, including scoring). Specimen kit, manual $5.50. *Publisher:* Educational and Industrial Testing Service

Refer to page(s)	*Test Title*

158

BULIMIA TEST (BULIT) *Marcia C. Smith and Mark H. Thelen*

Assesses bulimia symptoms in adolescents and adults. Used as screening device to identify individuals suffering from or at risk for bulimia, in clinical settings to aid in prevention and treatment, and in research.

A 36-item, self-report, forced-choice test consisting of five factors (containing a total of 32 summated and scored items) related to binges, feelings, vomiting, food, and weight, and two factors (containing a total of four unscored items) related to laxative/ diuretic abuse and regularity of menstrual cycles. Summated items scored on a 5-point scale. Administration untimed (varies). Examiner required and evaluated. Suitable for group use. Can be scored on separate computer sheet. Contact publisher for cost. *Publisher:* Mark H. Thelen

332, 336

BURKS' BEHAVIOR RATING SCALES *Harold F. Burks*

Identifies patterns of behavior problems in children Grades 1-9. Used as an aid to differential diagnosis.

A 110-item, paper-pencil inventory with parent or teacher rating the child on the basis of descriptive statements of observed behavior; 19 subscales measure excessive self-blame, anxiety, withdrawal, dependency, suffering, sense of persecution, aggressiveness, resistance, poor ego strength, physical strength, coordination, intellectuality, academics, attention, impulse control, reality contact, sense of identity, anger control, and social conformity. The manual discusses causes and manifestations and possible intervention approaches for each of the subscales and use with special groups, such as educable mentally retarded, educationally and orthopedically handicapped, and speech and hearing handicapped. Administration untimed (15-20 minutes). Examiner required and evaluated. Not for group use. Hand scored. Kit $23.50. *Publisher:* Western Psychological Services

157, 281, 290

CALIFORNIA PSYCHOLOGICAL INVENTORY (CPI) *Harrison G. Gough*

Measures personality characteristics important for social living and interaction. Used as an aid to counselors of nonpsychiatrically disturbed adolescents and adults and in personality research.

A 480-item, paper-pencil test containing 18 scales: Dominance, Capacity for Status, Sociability, Social Presence, Self-Acceptance, Sense of Well-Being, Responsibility, Socialization, Self-Control, Tolerance, Good Impression, Communality, Achievement via Conformance, Achievement via Independence, Intellectual Efficiency, Psychological-Mindedness, Flexibility, and Femininity/Masculinity. Self-administered. Administration untimed (45-60 minutes). Suitable for group use. Available in Italian, Spanish, and German. Hand scored; computer scored using prepaid answer sheets. Counselor's kit $25.00. *Publisher:* Consulting Psychologists Press, Inc.

Refer to page(s)	*Test Title*

14, 314 CAREER ASSESSMENT INVENTORY (CAI) *Charles B. Johansson*

Evaluates career goals of students who want immediate, non-college-graduate business or technical training. Used with adolescents and adults for employment decisions, vocational rehabilitation, and self-employment.

A 305-item, paper-pencil test in a 5-response Likert format covering six general occupational themes (Holland's RIASEC), 22 basic occupational interest scales, and 91 occupational scales. Administration untimed. (20-35 minutes). Self-administered. Computer scored. Suitable for group use. Contact publisher for cost. *Publisher:* National Computer Systems/PAS Division

387 CAREER DEVELOPMENT INVENTORY (CDI) *Donald E. Super, Albert S. Thompson, Richard H. Lindeman, Jean P. Jordaan, and Roger A. Myers*

Assesses attitudes and knowledge of high-school and college students concerning vocational decisions. Used in career guidance and counseling programs.

A 120-item, paper-pencil test of eight vocational, decision-making dimensions: career planning, career exploration, decision making, world-of-work information, knowledge of preferred occupational group, career development attitudes, career development knowledge and skills, and career orientation total. Available in two forms: High School (S) and College and University (CU). Administration untimed (55-65 minutes). Examiner required. Suitable for group use. Computer scored. Specimen set $12.00. *Publisher:* Consulting Psychologists Press, Inc.

14 CAREER DIRECTIONS INVENTORY *Douglas N. Jackson*

Evaluates career interests of high school and college students and adults. Used for educational and vocational planning and counseling.

A 100-item, paper-pencil inventory in which each item consists of a triad of statements, each statement describing a job-related activity. The examinee marks the most and least preferred activities. Computer scoring yields a sex-fair profile of 15 basic interest scales, which are compared to the interests of individuals in a variety of occupations. Administration untimed (30-45 minutes). Examiner required. Suitable for group use. Examination kit $10.00. *Publisher:* Research Psychologists Press, Inc.

387 CAREER MATURITY INVENTORY (CMI) *John O. Crites*

Measures students' maturity by examining their attitudes and competencies regarding career decisions. Used by vocational counselors and educators in planning programs.

A paper-pencil test consisting of an Attitude Scale and Competency Test. The Attitude Scale measures students' maturity in regard to feelings, subjective reactions, and dispositions toward

| *Test Title*

making a career. Screening Form A-2 provides an overall measure and Counseling Form B-1 provides scores for Decisiveness, Involvement, Independence, Orientation, and Compromise. The Competency Test contains five subtests: Self-Appraisal, Occupational Information, Goal Selection, Planning, and Problem Solving. Administration untimed (varies). Examiner required. Suitable for group use. Hand or machine scored. Career Maturity Profile also available. Specimen set $8.95. *Publisher:* CTB/McGraw-Hill

CHILD ASSESSMENT SCHEDULE (CAS) *Kay Hodges, Donald McKnew, Leon Cytryn, Linda Stern, and Jeffrey Kline*

Assesses psychological and behavioral dysfunction problems and symptoms in children. Used in clinical assessments to provide information relevant to diagnosis according to DSM-III and to develop good rapport with child, in child psychopathology research, and in training novice clinicians.

A diagnostic interview consisting of three parts. In the first part, the examiner asks the child approximately 75 questions about school, friends, activities and hobbies, family, fears, worries, self-image, mood, somatic concerns, expression of anger, and thought disorder symtomology. In the second part, the interviewer obtains from the child information about the onset and duration of symptoms. The third section contains approximately 53 items inquiring into areas of insight, grooming, motor coordination, activity level, spontaneous physical behaviors, estimate of cognitive ability, quality of verbal communications and emotional expression, and impressions about quality of interpersonal interactions. Administration untimed (45-60 minutes). Examiner required and evaluated. Manual, interview $7.50. *Publisher:* Kay Hodges, Ph.D.

CHILD BEHAVIOR CHECKLIST AND REVISED CHILD BEHAVIOR PROFILE *Thomas M. Achenbach and Craig Edelbrock*

Assess the behavioral problems and competencies of children aged 4-16. Used in clinical and research applications.

Five multiple-item paper-pencil multiple-choice and free-response inventories evaluating child behavioral problems from four perspectives. The Child Behavior Checklist assesses behavior from the parents' point of view, the Teacher Report Form assesses the child's classroom behavior, the Direct Observation Form employs an experienced observer to rate the child on the basis of a series of at least six 10-minute observation periods, and the Youth Self-Report gathers information directly from the child. Administration untimed (varies).

Self-administered (except for the Direct Observation Form). Examiner evaluated. All self-administered forms suitable for group use. Contact publisher for prices. *Publisher:* University of Vermont, College of Medicine, Department of Psychiatry

Refer to page(s)	Test Title

312

THE CHILDREN'S APPERCEPTION TEST (CAT-A)
Leopold Bellak and Sonya Sorel Bellak

Assesses personality in children aged 3-10. Used in clinical evaluation and diagnosis.

A 10-item, oral-response projective assessment procedure measuring the traits, attitudes, and psychodynamics involved in the personalities of children. Each test item consists of a picture of animals in a human social context through which the child becomes involved in conflicts, identities, roles, family structures, etc. The child is presented with the pictures one at a time and asked to tell a story about each one. Administration untimed (20-30 minutes). Examiner required and evaluated. Not for group use. Available in Spanish, Indian, French, German, Japanese, Flemish, Portugese, and Italian. CAT-H (version using human figures instead of animals) and CAT-S (supplement using jigsaw-puzzle-constructed plates and presenting family situations) also available. Complete kit $15.00. *Publisher:* C.P.S., Inc.

210, 212, 234, 235

CHILDREN'S DEPRESSION INVENTORY (CDI)
Maria Kovacs

Assesses severity of depression currently experienced by children aged 8-13. Used for clinical research in childhood depression.

A 27-item, paper-pencil inventory measuring an array of overt symptoms of childhood depression (e.g., sadness, anhedonia, suicial ideation, and sleep and appetite disturbances) by presenting three related statements for each item. The child is asked to select the statement that best reflects own feelings and ideas during the previous two weeks. The three choices for each item are assigned numerical values from 0-2, graded in order of increasing psychopathology. Total score (0-54) obtained by adding the numerical scores of the individual items. Administration untimed (varies). Examiner required and evaluated. Suitable for use with small groups; individual administration advisable with psychiatric populations or if there is any question as to the child's ability to remain on task. Inventory, supplementary materials $2.50. *Publisher:* Maria Kovacs, Ph.D.

234, 235

CHILDREN'S DEPRESSION SCALE
Moshe Lange and Miriam Tisher

Measures depression in children aged 9-16. Used to identify depressed children in need of further evaluation.

A 66-item scale measuring six aspects of childhood depression: effective response; social problems; self-esteem; preoccupation with own sickness, of death; guilt; and pleasure. Items presented on cards that children sort into fives boxes ranging from "very right" to "very wrong" according to how they feel the item applies to them. A separate set of cards, identical in content but appropriately reworded is provided for use with parents, teachers, or other adults familiar with the child. Examiner required and evaluated. Not for group use. Contact publisher for cost. *Publisher:* The Australian Council for Educational Research Limited

Refer to page(s)	Test Title

383

COMPREHENSIVE OCCUPATIONAL ASSESSMENT &
TRAINING SYSTEM (COATS)

Assesses adolescents' and adults' career preferences, experiences, interests, and aptitude; behavioral attitudes in job-seeking and job-keeping situations; and the skills and knowledge required for functional literacy in society.

Four independent multiple-item instruments assessing skills, attitudes, and preferences pertaining to employment and placement in job training programs. Job Matching II is used to match individuals' preferences and experiences to jobs or training programs at the skilled, semiskilled, technical, and professional levels. Work Samples assesses aptitude and provides career exploration in 27 job simulations relating to the 16 USOE clusters. Employability Attitudes assesses, prescribes, and teaches job-seeking and job-keeping attitudes. Living Skills assesses the skill and knowledge areas required for functional literacy in today's society and prescribes objectives to be achieved. Each of these instruments may be purchased and used independently. Administration untimed (varies, depending on instrument). Examiner/self-administered. Computer scored. Work Samples is examiner evaluated. Job Matching II and Employability Attitudes are suitable for group use; Work Samples and Living Skills must be administered individually. Contact publisher for cost. *Publisher:* PREP, Inc.

5

COMPREHENSIVE TEST OF ADAPTIVE BEHAVIOR
Gary Adams

Assesses handicapped individuals' (birth-21 years) adaptive abilities. Used to determine level of adaptive performance and relation to others of the same age or handicap and to aid establishment of scope and sequence of training.

A 529-item, paper-pencil inventory in six adaptive behavior categories (self-help, home living, independent living, social, sensory/motor, and language concepts/academic), with administration based on basal and ceiling procedures. Examiner checks off mastered skills based on observation of subject's abilities, parent/guardian report, and formal testing. Skills sequenced in order handicapped individuals acquire them, not in normal developmental order. Not suitable for normally developing individuals or groups. Administration untimed (varies). Examiner required and evaluated. Contact publisher for cost. *Publisher:* The Psychological Corporation

71, 283, 332, 336

THE CONNERS PARENT SYMPTOM
QUESTIONNAIRE   *C. K. Conners*

Assesses behavior problems of children aged 3-17 as observed by their parents in the home setting. Identifies children with significant behavior problems in need of further evaluation.

A 48-item, paper-pencil, observational, parent-rated inventory assessing behaviors in areas such as family relationships, peer relationships, personal habits, health, and emotional development.

Refer to page(s)	*Test Title*

Parent indicates degree to which the child exhibits the behaviors by rating each item on a 4-point scale. Yields six factor scores: conduct problems, learning problems, psychosomatic problems, impulsivity-hyperactivity, anxiety, and hyperactivity index. Administration untimed (varies). Self-administered. Examiner evaluated. Not for group use. *Source:* Barkley, R.G. (1981). *Hyperactive children: a handbook for diagnosis and treatment.* New York: Guilford Press

71, 283, 332, 336 THE CONNERS TEACHER RATING SCALE (TRS)
C. K. Conners

Assesses the classroom behavior of children from preschool to Grade 12. Identifies children with significant behavior problems and indicates children who are potentially hyperactive.

A paper-pencil observational, teacher-rated inventory assessing 28 problem behaviors frequently encountered in the classroom setting. The teacher indicates the degree to which the child exhibits the behaviors by rating each item on a 4-point scale. Yields four factor scores: conduct problems, hyperactivity, inattention-passivity, and hyperactivity index. Administration untimed (varies). Self-administered. Not suitable for group use. *Source:* Barkley, R. G. (1981). *Hyperactive children: a handbook for diagnosis and treatment.* New York: Guilford Press

69, 70, 133, 210, COOPERSMITH SELF-ESTEEM INVENTORIES
211, 221, 332, 335 (CSEI) *Stanley Coopersmith*

Measures attitudes of children and adults toward the self in social, academic, and personal contexts. Used for individual diagnosis, classroom screening, pre-post evaluations, and clinical and research studies.

A self-report, paper-pencil questionnaire measuring self-attitudes in four areas (social self-peers, home-parents, school-academic, and general-self) related to academic achievement and personal satisfaction in school and adult life. Two forms available: School (8-15 years) and Adult (16 years and up). Administration untimed (15 minutes). Self-administered. Suitable for group use. Hand scored. Specimen set $6.00. *Publisher:* Consulting Psychologists Press, Inc.

383 CRAWFORD SMALL PARTS DEXTERITY TEST
(CSPDT) *John Crawford*

Measures fine eye-hand coordination of adolescents and adults. Used in selecting applicants, such as precision electronic assemblers and engravers, for jobs and in assessing manual dexterity of handicapped persons in special vocational evaluation and training programs.

A two-part performance measure, with Part 1 measuring dexterity in using tweezers to assemble pin and collar assemblies, and Part 2 measuring dexterity in placing and screwing small screws in threaded holes. Can be administered in the work-limit method (sub-

| *Refer to page(s)* | *Test Title* |

ject completes task, and total time is the score) or using time-limit procedure (score is amount of work done in a specified time). Administration is timed (10-15 minutes). Examiner required and evaluated. Suitable for group use. Complete set $325.00. *Publisher:* The Psychological Corporation

89

DEFINING ISSUES TEST (DIT)   *James R. Rest*

Measures adolescents' (13 years and up) and adults' moral judgment concerning social issues.

A 72-item, paper-pencil test consisting of six short stories presenting social problems or moral dilemmas. Each story followed by 12 statements providing a range of actions that are rated for their moral correctness on a 5-point scale by subjects who then indicate (in order of importance) the four they consider most salient. Internal consistency check identifies subjects who randomly check responses or do not understand directions. Fluent English and eighth-grade reading level required. Supplementary material provided in *Development in Judging Moral Issues.* Administration untimed (40 minutes). Examiner required and evaluated. Suitable for group use. Available free of charge to professional and student researchers with recognized institutions. *Publisher:* Minnesota Moral Research Projects

76, 153, 238, 244

THE DEVEREUX ADOLESCENT BEHAVIOR RATING SCALE   *George Spivack, Peter Haimes, and Jules Spotts*

Assesses behavior symptoms of normal and emotionally disturbed adolescents aged 13-18. Used for diagnostic and screening procedures, group placement decisions, and assessment of progress in response to specific programs or procedures.

A paper-pencil instrument containing 84 items rated by someone living with the subject according to how respondent feels subject's behavior compares with normal children the same age. Yields 12 factor scores (unethical behavior, defiant-resistive, domineering-sadistic, heterosexual interest, hyperactive expansive, poor emotional control, need approval and dependency, emotional distance, physical inferiority-timidity, schizoid withdrawal, bizarre action), three cluster scores (inability to delay, paranoid thought, anxious self-blame), and 11 item scores (persecution, plotting, bodily concern, external influences, compulsive acts, avoids competition, withdrawn, socialization, peer dominance, physical coordination, distraction). Administration untimed (10-15 minutes). Self-administered. Examiner required and evaluated. Not for group use. Contact publisher for cost. *Publisher:* The Devereux Foundation

9

DIAGNOSTIC READING SCALES, REVISED (DRS)
George D. Spache

Identifies a child's reading strengths and weaknesses. Used by educators to determine placement and prescribe weaknesses.

A multiple-item verbal test consisting of a series of graduated scales containing 3 word-recognition lists, 22 reading selections,

Refer to page(s)	*Test Title*

and 12 phonics and word analysis tests. The word-recognition lists determine the level at which the student begins the reading selections. The reading selections assess instructional, independent, and potential level. The phonics and word analysis tests assess several phonetic and word analysis skills. Administration timed. Examiner required and evaluated. Not suitable for group use. Specimen set $14.25. *Publisher:* CTB/McGraw-Hill

9   DIAGNOSTIC SPELLING POTENTIAL TEST (DSPT)
John Arena

Assesses the spelling skills of students ages 7 to adult.

A multiple-item, paper-pencil test consisting of four subtests: Spelling, Word Recognition, Visual Recognition, and Auditory-Visual Recognition. Raw scores can be converted to standard scores, percentile ranks, and grade ratings, which then can be plotted on a profile chart that compares spelling efficiency with decoding, utilization of phonetic generalizations, visual recall, and matching auditory with visual representations skills. Two parallel forms are available. Administration untimed (25-40 minutes). Examiner required and evaluated. Suitable for group use. Complete kit $37.50. *Publisher:* Academic Therapy Publications

384, 387, 388   DIFFERENTIAL APTITUDE TESTS (DAT),
FORMS V AND W   *G.K. Bennett, H.G. Seashore, and A.G. Wesman*

Assess scholastic aptitude. Used for educational and vocational guidance in junior and senior high schools.

A multiple-item, paper-pencil test of eight scholastic abilities: verbal reasoning, numerical ability, abstract reasoning, clerical speed and accuracy, mechanical reasoning, space relations, spelling, and language usage. Ninth score obtained by adding Verbal Reasoning and Numerical Ability scores. Two alternate and equivalent forms (V and W) and the Career Planning Questionnaire (optional) are available. Administration timed (3 hours for complete battery). Examiner required. Suitable for group use. Hand or machine scored; computer service available. Specimen set $10.00. *Publisher:* The Psychological Corporation

155   DRAW-A-PERSON (DAP)   *William H. Urban*

Assesses processes and functions, such as developmental level and personality functioning, of individuals aged five years and older. Used in clinical evaluations as a diagnostic, therapeutic, and screening device.

A projective technique, utilizing freehand pencil and crayon drawings of a person. Examiner required and evaluated. Time varies. Not suitable for group use. Draw-A-Person Catalogue for Interpretative Analysis costs $12.40. For cost of drawing forms and protocol booklets contact publisher. *Publisher:* Western Psychological Services

Refer to page(s)	*Test Title*

190, 194
DRUG USE INDEX (DUI)
Frazier M. Douglass and Khalil A. Khavari

Measures polydrug use. Used by researchers, counselors, physicians, and therapists for diagnosis of possible underlying psychiatric problems and treatment strategies.

A self-report questionnaire listing 19 different drugs and drug categories (alcohol, tobacco, and over-the-counter drugs) and requiring subjects to indicate their current use of each on an 8-point scale. Overall drug-use pattern computed by summing across all drugs. Provides predictive measure for use of 18 drugs or drug classes (omits over-the-counter drugs). Administration untimed (varies). Examiner required and evaluated. Suitable for group use. One questionnaire provided free to each user. *Publisher:* Khalil A. Khavari, Ph.D.

9
DURRELL ANALYSIS OF READING DIFFICULTY
(DARD)   *Donald D. Durrell and Jane H. Catterson*

Assesses students' reading behavior. Used for diagnosis, measurement of prereading skills, and planning remedial programs.

A multiple-item series of tests and situations measuring 10 reading abilities: oral reading, silent reading, listening comprehension, listening vocabulary, word recognition/word analysis, spelling, auditory analysis of words and word elements, pronunciation of word elements, visual memory of words, and prereading phonics abilities. Administration untimed (30-45 minutes). Examiner required and evaluated. Not suitable for group use. Examiner's kit $35.00. *Publisher:* The Psychological Corporation

152, 153, 154, 157,
158, 159, 170, 171
EATING DISORDER INVENTORY (EDI)   *David M. Garner, Marion P. Olmsted, and Janet Polivy*

Assesses psychological and behavioral traits common in anorexia and bulimia. Used to distinguish adolescents and adults with serious psychopathology from "normal" dieters and to aid in treatment of those with eating disorders.

A 64-item, paper-pencil, self-report inventory consisting of eight subscales measuring specific cognitive and behavioral dimensions related to eating disorders: Drive for Thinness, Bulimia, Body Dissatisfaction, Ineffectiveness, Perfectionism, Interpersonal Distrust, Interoceptive Awareness, and Maturity Fears. Administration untimed (20 minutes). Examiner required. Suitable for group use. Hand scored. Kit $25.00. *Publisher:* Psychological Assessment Resources, Inc.

38, 193, 194, 196
FAMILY ADAPTABILITY AND COHESION EVALUATION SCALES (FACES III)   *David H. Olson*

Measures family satisfaction with current family system. Used by clinicians as aid in providing family members with goals and direction for therapy, and for research.

A 20-item, self-report inventory measuring two central dimen-

Refer to page(s)	*Test Title*

sions in the "Circumplex Model of Marital and Family Systems": Family Cohesion and Family Adaptability (change). Should be administered twice: once for how family members see their family and once for how they would like it to be to provide perceived-ideal discrepancy. Replaces 30-item FACES II. Administration untimed (varies). Examiner evaluated. Suitable for group use. On completeion of abstract form, scales may be reproduced for research and clinical work. Packet $30.00. *Publisher:* Family Social Science, University of Minnesota

40, 45, 194, 196   FAMILY ASSESSMENT DEVICE (FAD)
Nathan B. Epstein, Laurence M. Baldwin, and Duane S. Bishop

Measures individuals' (aged 12 and older) perceptions of their families and identifies family problem areas. Used as screening instrument only by therapists and researchers to collect directly from family members clinically relevant information on various dimensions of the family system as a whole.

A 53-item, self-report questionnaire containing seven intercorrelated scales: Problem Solving, Communication, Roles, Affective Responsiveness, Affective Involvement, Behavior Control, and General Functioning. Subjects rate each item on a 4-point scale according to how well item describes their family. Administration untimed (15-20 minutes). Individually administered. Examiner evaluated. Kit $20.00. *Publisher:* Brown/Butler Family Research Program

38, 45   FAMILY ENVIRONMENT SCALE (FES)   *Rudolf H. Moos*

Assesses family environment characteristics of adolescents and adults. Used for family therapy.

A 90-item, paper-pencil test measuring 10 dimensions of family environments (cohesion, expressiveness, conflict, independence, achievement orientation, intellectual-cultural orientation, active-recreational orientation, moral-religious emphasis, organization, and control) that are grouped into three sets: Relationship, Personal Growth, and System Maintenance. Administration untimed (varies). Examiner required and evaluated. Suitable for group use. Hand scored. Specimen set $6.50. *Publisher:* Consulting Psychologists Press, Inc.

314, 383, 387, 388   GENERAL APTITUDE TEST BATTERY (GATB)
U.S. Employment Service

Measures vocational aptitudes of literate adolescents (from Grade 9) and adults who need help in choosing an occupation. Used for counseling.

A 434-item, paper-pencil test consisting of 284 multiple-choice, 150 dichotomous choice (same-different) questions, and two dexterity form boards. Twelve subtests measure nine vocational aptitudes: General Learning Ability, Verbal, Numerical, Spatial, Dexterity, and Manual Dexterity. Occupational Aptitude Patterns (OAP) indicate aptitude requirements for groups of occupations; 66

| *Refer to page(s)* | *Test Title* |

OAPs cover 97% of all nonsupervisory occupations. Scored in items of OAPs, with "H"(High), "M"(Middle), or "L"(Low) assigned for each OAP. Results indicate individual's likelihood of being successful in the various occupations. Administration untimed (1 hour). Examiner required. Suitable for group use. Available in Spanish and French. Hand or computer-scored. Use in the U.S. must be authorized by State Employment Security Agencies, and in Canada by the Canadian Employment and Immigration Commission. Directions for administration and scoring in Manual of USES, available from the Superintendent of Documents, U.S. Government Printing Office, Washington, D.C. 20402. Scoring stencil, 250 answer sheets, 25 identification sheets, computer scoring $26.75. *Publisher:* U.S. Department of Labor

210, 211, 213, 214, 220, 221

HAHNEMANN BEHAVIOR RATING SCALES   *George Spivack and Marshall Swift*

Assess social and emotional behavior of elementary and high-school students. Used in research and clinical settings to measure impact of parental divorce on children's adjustment, and aid in uncovering causes of family trauma, in devising children's school-based services that compensate for declining home support, and in interventions to improve adjustment of children handicapped by life circumstances, such as family problems and changes in family ecology (e.g., divorce, maternal employment, family mobility, and child abuse).

Teacher-rated scales consisting of two versions: Elementary School Scale (HESB) and High School Scale (HHSB). Elementary School Scale consists of 15 behavior factors (originality, independent learning, involvement, productive with peers, intellectual dependency with peers, failure anxiety, unreflectiveness, irrelevant talk, disruptive social involvement, negative feelings, holding back/ withdrawn, critical-competitive, blaming, approach to teacher, and inattention), plus one academic factor (academic achievement). High School Scales consist of 13 scores: reasoning ability, originality, verbal interaction, rapport with teacher, anxious producer, general anxiety, quiet-withdrawn, poor work habits, lack intellectual independence, dogmatic-inflexible, verbal negativism, disturbance-restless, and expressed inability. Administration untimed (varies). Examiner evaluated. Not for group use. Manual $8.00, 50 scales $0.30 each. *Publisher:* George Spivack and Marshall Swift

69, 153

HIGH SCHOOL PERSONALITY QUESTIONNAIRE (HSPQ)   *Raymond B. Cattell and Mary D. Cattell*

Measures personality dimensions of adolescents aged 12-18. Used by institutional personnel, counselors, and school psychologists to counsel students; identify dropouts, drug abusers, and low achievers; and to facilitate cooperation between parents and teachers, officers, and/or clinics.

A 142-item, paper-pencil questionnaire requiring 6th-grade reading level and measuring 14 primary personality dimensions, including stability, tension, warmth, and enthusiasm. Scores also obtained for anxiety, extraversion, creativity, leadership, and other broad trait patterns. Available in four equivalent forms: A,B,C, and D. Administration untimed (45-60 minutes). Examiner required. Suitable for group use. Available in Spanish. Hand scored; computer interpretation services available. Introductory kit $15.25. *Publisher:* Institute for Personality and Ability Testing, Inc.

HOUSE-TREE-PERSON (H-T-P) PROJECTIVE TECHNIQUE   *John N. Buck*

Assesses personality disturbances in individuals aged three years and older. Used in schools, clinics, psychotherapy, and research projects, and with the culturally disadvantaged, educationally deprived, mentally retarded, and aged.

A multiple-item, paper-pencil and oral-response test providing a projective study of personality and consisting of two steps: 1) non-verbal, creative, and mostly unstructured (requiring subject to make free-hand drawing of a house, tree, and person); 2) verbal, apperceptive, and more formally structured (subject describes, defines, and interprets other drawings and their respective environments). Administration untimed (15-20 minutes). Examiner required and evaluated. Not for group use. Hand scored. Set $125.00. *Publisher:* Western Psychological Services

JACKSON VOCATIONAL INTEREST SURVEY (JVIS)   *Douglas N. Jackson*

Evaluates career interests of high-school and college students. Used for educational and vocational planning and counseling and for personnel placement.

A 289-item, paper-pencil inventory consisting of paired statements covering 10 occupational themes: expressive, logical, inquiring, practical, assertive, socialized, helping, conventional, enterprising, and communicative. The subject marks one of two responses. Scoring yields a sex-fair profile of 34 basic career clusters. A seventh-grade reading level is required. Administration untimed (45-60 minutes). Examiner required. Hand or computer scored. Suitable for group use. Examination kit $16.00. *Publisher:* Research Psychologists Press, Inc.

THE JESNESS INVENTORY   *Carl F. Jesness*

Assesses personality disorders predictive of asocial tendencies of subjects aged 8-18. Used to classify disturbed children and adolescents for treatment and distinguish delinquents from nondelinquents.

A 155-item, paper-pencil test of 11 personality characteristics: social maladjustment, value orientation, immaturity, autism, alienation, manifest aggression, withdrawal, social anxiety, repression, denial, and asocial. Administration untimed (20-30 minutes). Self- or examiner administered. Cassette tapes for oral administration

Refer to page(s)	*Test Title*

available. Hand or computer scored. Counselor's kit $19.50. *Publisher:* Consulting Psychologists Press, Inc.

384

JUDGMENT OF OCCUPATIONAL BEHAVIOR-ORIENTATION (JOB-O) *Arthur Cutler, Francis Ferry, Robert Kauk, and Robert Robinett*

Assesses aspirations and interests and identifies appropriate career and occupational choices. Used in vocational guidance and career counseling with adolescents and adults.

Multiple-item paper-pencil or computer-administered instrument assessing nine variables related to educational aspirations, occupational interests, and interpersonal and physical characteristics of occupations. The *Dictionary of Occupational Titles*, the *Occupational Outlook Handbook*, and Schutz's FIRO-B provide the theoretical basis. Displays information on the number of people employed, job outlook, training requirements, and job clusters for 120 job titles. Computer programs available for several kinds of computers. An optional filmstrip is also available. Untimed and suitable for group use. The paper-pencil version may be self-administered. Hand or computer scored. Test booklet, answer folder, and manual $3.45; JOB-O dictionary $1.75; filmstrip $32.95; diskettes $59.95. *Publisher:* CFKR Career Materials, Inc.

312

KAUFMAN ASSESSMENT BATTERY FOR CHILDREN (K-ABC) *Alan S. Kaufman and Nadeen L. Kaufman*

Measures intelligence (i.e., ability of children to process information and solve problems) and achievement of children aged 2½-12½. Used for psychological and clinical assessment of the learning disabled and mentally retarded, minority-group and preschool assessment, and neuropsychological research.

Consists of 16 computer-scored subtests of mental-processing skills and achievement: sequential processing (3); simultaneous processing (7); achievement, including acquired knowledge, reading, and arithmetic (6). Using child's native language or gestures if necessary, examiner presents test plate (containing stimulus item) and gives verbal direction to child who then responds. Yields four major scores: Sequential Processing, Simultaneous Processing, Mental Processing Composite, and Achievement. Administration untimed (35-85 minutes, depending on level). Examiner (must have necessary qualifications) required and evaluated. Not for group use. Available in Spanish and with plastic plates. Kit $143.00. *Publisher:* American Guidance Service

9, 16

KAUFMAN TEST OF EDUCATIONAL ACHIEVEMENT (K-TEA) *Alan S. Kaufman and Nadeen L. Kaufman*

Measures achievement in basic skills of reading, mathematics, and spelling of students (Grades 1-12), including those whose primary language is not English. Used in educational placement, instructional program planning, and for continuous assessment of educational achievement from entry level through high school.

Refer to page(s)	Test Title

Consists of two forms: Brief (providing 30-minute measure of global achievement in Reading, Mathematics, and Spelling) and Comprehensive (offering more thorough assessment and consisting of five subtests measuring Reading/Decoding, Reading/Comprehension, Mathematics/Applications, Mathematics/Comprehension, and Spelling). Administration time for Brief Form—15-30 minutes; Comprehensive Form—30-65 minutes. Examiner required and evaluated. Not for group use. Administered from series of test plates. Complete kit $98.00. *Publisher:* American Guidance Service

13, 384

KUDER GENERAL INTEREST SURVEY, FORM E
Frederic Kuder

Assesses students' preferences for various activities related to general interest areas. Used with students (Grades 6-12) to guide their educational planning toward future employment.

A 168-item, paper-pencil test measuring preferences in 10 areas: outdoor, mechanical, scientific, computational, persuasive, artistic, literary, musical, social science, and clerical. Scoring and profile construction can be done by student. Sixth-grade reading level required. Self-administered. Suitable for group use. Administration untimed (30-40 minutes). Hand or machine scored. Specimen set $6.25. *Publisher:* Science Research Associates, Inc.

13, 384

KUDER FORM DD OCCUPATIONAL INTEREST SURVEY, REVISED *Frederic Kuder*

Measures how an individual's interests compare with those of satisfied workers or students in a number of occupational fields. Used with high-school and college students (Grades 10-up) and adults for career planning, vocational guidance, and academic counseling.

A 100-item, paper-pencil inventory assessing subjects' interests in areas related to occupational fields and educational majors. Each item lists three activities, and subjects indicate which they like best and which they like least. Compares subjects' interests with those of satisfied workers in 126 specific occupational groups and satisfied students in 48 college major groups. All respondents receive scores on all scales. Sixth-grade reading level required. Self-administered. Suitable for group use. Administration timed (30-40 minutes). Computer scoring available. Specimen set $6.50. *Publisher:* Science Research Associates, Inc.

314

KUDER PREFERENCE RECORD, VOCATIONAL, FORM C
Frederic Kuder

Evaluates occupational interests of students and adults. Used in vocational counseling and employee screening and placement. Identifies reading subject areas of special interest.

The 168-item paper-pencil test measures interests in 10 occupational areas: outdoor, mechanical, scientific, computational, per-

Refer to page(s)	Test Title
	suasive, artistic, literary, musical, social science, and clerical. Subject uses pin to indicate a "most like" and "least liked" activity for each group of three activities. High-school reading level required. Self-administered. Administration untimed (varies). Suitable for group use. Hand scored. Specimen set $6.30. *Publisher:* Science Research Associates, Inc.
12	**LANGUAGE INVENTORY FOR TEACHERS (LIT)** *Arlene Cooper and Beverly A. School*
	Assesses the language ability of students who have difficulties reading and writing. Used to determine areas of deficiency requiring remedial intervention and to help teachers write comprehensive Individualized Education Programs.
	A multiple-item, paper-pencil sequence of over 500 language tasks corresponding to 13 long-range goals, 5 for spoken language and 8 for written language. Tasks are ordered by type and difficulty to correspond to the hierarchical development of language concepts. Testing begins at a point at which the examinee is expected to succeed and is discontinued when the examinee has made several errors. Administration untimed (30 minutes). Examiner required. Hand scored. Not suitable for group use. Specimen set $12.00. *Publisher:* Academic Therapy Publications
12	**"LET'S TALK" INVENTORY FOR ADOLESCENTS** *Elisabeth H. Wiig*
	Assesses adolescents' and preadolescents' (nine years-adult) ability to formulate speech acts. Used by speech pathologists, special educators, and psychologists to identify and diagnose students having social communication problems.
	A 40-item, verbal test probing peer-peer and peer-authority interactions and ability to formulate speech acts within four communication functions: ritualizing, informing, controlling, and feeling. Administered with picture manual. Subjects given brief description of context depicted and asked to formulate sentence or sentence series; includes 40 additional back-drop items for those having difficulty formulating expected speech acts. Administration untimed (30-40 minutes). Examiner required and evaluated. Not for group use. Contact publisher for cost. *Publisher:* The Psychological Corporation
210, 212, 283	**LOUISVILLE BEHAVIOR CHECKLIST** *Lovick C. Miller*
	Measures entire range of social and emotional behaviors indicative of psychopathological disorders in children and adolescents (4-17 years). Used as an intake screening device or as a tool in evaluating overall behavior.
	A 164-item, paper-pencil, true-false inventory facilitating parents' recordings of their children's behaviors. Available in three forms: E1 (4-6 years), E2 (7-12 years), and E3 (13-17 years). Forms E1 and E2 contain the following scales: Infantile Aggression, Hyperactivity, Antisocial Behavior, Aggression, Social With-

	Test Title

drawal, Sensitivity, Fear, Inhibition, Immaturity, Normal Irritability, Prosocial Deficit, Rare Deviance, Neurotic Behavior, Psychotic Behavior, Somatic Behavior, Sexual Behavior, and Severity Level. In addition, E1 scales include Intellectual Deficit, Cognitive Disability, and School Disturbance Predictor, and E2 scales include Academic Disability and Learning Disability. E3 contains 13 scales: Egocentric-Exploitive, Destructive-Assaultive, Social Delinquency, Adolescent Turmoil, Apathetic Isolation, Neuroticism, Dependent-Inhibited, Academic Disability, Neurological or Psychotic Abnormality, General Pathology, Longitudinal, Severity Level, and Total Pathology. Administration untimed (20-30 minutes). Examiner required. Suitable for group use. Hand scored; computer scoring available. Kit (specify form) $170.00. *Publisher:* Western Psychological Services

McDERMOTT MULTIDIMENSIONAL ASSESSMENT OF CHILDREN (M•MAC)   *Paul McDermott and Marley W. Watkins*

Integrates data from psychological evaluations, classifies childhood exceptionality, and designs Individualized Educational Plans (IEPs). Used by psychologists and educational professionals for diagnostic and prescriptive purposes, including classroom planning.

A comprehensive system of computer programs integrating data from 22 widely used intelligence and achievement tests, adaptive behavior scales, parent/teacher behavior rating scales, and professional judgments to generate multidimensional classifications (exceptional talent, normal intellectual functioning, borderline intellectual functioning, mental retardation, intellectual retardation, educational retardation, commensurate achievement, specific learning disability, developmental learning disorder, possible academic overcompensation, possible communication disorder, possible visual motor problem, good social-emotional adjustment, conduct disorder, anxiety-withdrawal disorder, attention deficit disorder, and disturbance of emotions and conduct). Consists of two major levels: Classification (providing diagnosis of exceptionality along dimensions of general intellectual functioning, academic achievement, adaptive behavior, and social-emotional adjustment) and Program Design (generating appropriate behavioral objectives for individualized educational planning, based on demonstrated skills in reading, mathematics, general learning style, or adaptive skills). Licensed for use to individuals and agencies. Starter set $200.00 *Publisher:* The Psychological Corporation

MEADOW-KENDALL SOCIAL-EMOTIONAL ASSESSMENT INVENTORY FOR DEAF AND HEARING-IMPAIRED STUDENTS   *Kathryn P. Meadow*

Guides teachers' observations and assessments of students' classroom behaviors reflecting social and emotional adjustment. Used for hearing-impaired students aged 7-21.

                                            Test Title

A 59-item inventory consisting of three subscales: Social Adjustment, Self-image, and Emotional Adjustment. Rated by teachers (having at least eight weeks prior contact with students) on a 5-point scale according to observed behavior of student as compared to students same age regardless of their hearing abilities. Administration untimed (varies). Examiner evaluated. Not for group use. Manual, 10 inventories $14.00 *Source:* Available from Gallaudet College Bookstore.

MICROCOMPUTER EVALUATION SCREENING ASSESSMENT (MESA)

Provides baseline data for the development of an individual's education, training, or employment plan or for more extensive vocational evaluation. May be used with adolescents or adults contemplating entering the labor market for the first time or changing fields of work.

Multiple-item computer-administered test measuring 21 factors of the Worker Qualifications Profile as defined in the D.O.T. of the U.S. Department of Labor. The MESA consists of six subtests: Hardware Exercises, Computer Exercises, Perceptual Screening, Talking/Persuasive Screening, Physical Capacities and Mobility, and Vocational/Interest Awareness. The test may be used with Apple and IBM computers. A short form that contains only the Hardware Exercises and the Computer Exercises subtests is available. Administration timed (1½ or 4½ hours, depending on form). Examiner/self-administered. Hand scored, examiner evaluated, and computer scored. Suitable for group use if multiple computer stations are purchased. Apple computer and 1 station $7, 325.00; IBM computer and 1 station $8,925.00. *Publisher:* Valpar International Corporation

THE MINNESOTA MULTIPHASIC PERSONALITY INVENTORY (MMPI)   *Starke R. Hathaway and Charnley McKinley*

Assesses individual personality. Used for clinical diagnosis and research on psychopathology.

An inventory in four different administration formats. Group Form consists of 566 true-false items written at a 6th-grade reading level; Form R covers 14 basic scales with the first 399 test items; Card Form consists of 550 statements that examinee sorts in three groups (true, false, cannot say); Audiocassette Version contains entire Group Form on audio tape (responses are recorded on Group Form answer sheets). Scales included on the hand-scored version cover L (Lie), F (Infrequency), K (Defensiveness), Hs (Hypochondriasis), D (Depression), Hy (Hysteria), Pd (Psychopathic Deviate), Mf (Masculinity-Femininity), Pa (Paranoia), Pt (Psychasthenia), Sc (Schizophrenia), Ma (Hypomania), Si (Social Introversion), A (Anxiety), R (Depression), Es (Ego Strength), and MAC (MacAndrew Addiction). Additional scales available with computer scoring. Administration untimed (45-90 minutes). Examiner

Refer to page(s)	*Test Title*

required and evaluated. Available in 45 languages. For cost information and various services/reports, write to distributor. *Publisher:* University of Minnesota Press—Distributed by National Computer Systems/PAS Division.

5

NORMATIVE ADAPTIVE BEHAVIOR CHECKLIST (NABC) *Gary Adams*

Assesses individual's (birth-21 years) level of behavioral development. Used in identifying students in need of special education programs.

A 160-item, paper-pencil questionnaire completed by person familiar with subject (parent, teacher, caregiver). Determines performance of adaptive behavior in six subject areas: self-help, home living, independent living, social, sensory/motor, and concept/language/academic. Examiner checks off skills mastered by subject. Administration untimed (20 minutes). Examiner required and evaluated. Not for group use. Contact publisher for prices. *Publisher:* The Psychological Corporation

134, 135, 136

THE OFFER SELF-IMAGE QUESTIONNAIRE FOR ADOLESCENTS *Daniel Offer, Eric Ostrov, and Kenneth I. Howard*

Assesses self-image and adjustment of adolescents aged 13-19. Used to indicate self-concept strengths and weaknesses, design and evaluate management plans, and aid in clinical counseling.

A 130-item, paper-pencil test covering five aspects of self-esteem (psychological self, social self, family self, sexual self, and coping self) and containing 11 scales (Impulse Control, Emotional Tone, Body and Self-Image, Social Relationships, Morals, Sexual Attitudes, Family Attitudes, Mastery of the External World, Vocational and Educational Goals, Psychopathology, and Superior Adjustment). Rated on a 6-point scale, with 65 items in positive form and 65 in negative. Administration untimed (40 minutes). Examiner required and evaluated. Suitable for group use. Computer scoring available. Manual $15.00; each questionnaire (specify male or female) $1.00; answer sheet $.15. *Publisher:* Institute for Psychosomatic and Psychiatric Research and Training

384

OHIO VOCATIONAL INTEREST SURVEY: SECOND EDITION (OVIS II) *The Psychological Corporation*

Assesses educational, occupational, and vocational interests of adolescents (Grades 7-college) and adults. Used for assisting students with educational and vocational plans.

A 253-item, paper-pencil test of job-related activities to which subjects respond on a 5-point scale. Occupations grouped (using the data-people-things classification scheme) into 23 interest scales, each of which consist of 11 job activities. Administration untimed (45 minutes). Examiner required. Hand or computer scored; microcomputer version available. Examination kit $6.00. *Publisher:* The Psychological Corporation

Refer to page(s)	Test Title

139

PARENTAL ACCEPTANCE/REJECTION QUESTIONNAIRE (PARQ) *Ronald P. Rohner*

Assesses warmth of parenting (acception/rejection) of children aged seven and up (younger if able to read and understand questions) and adults. Used as an in-depth or screening device with clinical populations, in research studies with school populations, as a tool for parental education programs, and as an aid in the evaluation of family problems (e.g., unwed mothers, drug abuse) and detection of potential child abuse.

A 60-item questionnaire designed to cut across social classes and available in 12-15 languages. Measures parental warmth in four scales: Warmth/Affection, Hostility/Aggression, Indifference/Neglect, and Undifferentiated Rejection. Available in three versions: Mother (includes father; reflects on what they do to child), Adult (reflects back on childhood), and Child (reflects on present actions in family). Can be combined with the Formal Interview and Behavior Observation. Administration untimed (10-15 minutes). Self-administered or examiner required. Suitable for group use. Hand-scored with self-coding pre-established. All materials needed for administration, scoring, and interpretation for questionnaire, interview, and observations included in handbook. Handbook (1984) $15.00; 1980 edition, $10.00 *Publisher:* Center for the Study of Parental Acceptance and Rejection, University of Connecticut

312, 360

PEABODY INDIVIDUAL ACHIEVEMENT TEST (PIAT) *Lloyd M. Dunn and Frederick C. Markwardt, Jr.*

Provides overview of scholastic attainment in individuals aged five and up. Used to screen for areas of scholastic weakness requiring more detailed diagnostic testing.

A 402-item test consisting of two volumes containing five subtests: Volume I (Mathematics and Reading Recognition) and Volume II (Reading Comprehension, Spelling, and General Information, including science, social studies, fine arts, sports). Administration untimed (30-50 minutes). Examiner required and evaluated. Not for group use. Available with plastic plates. Kit $72.50. *Publisher:* American Guidance Service

12

PEABODY PICTURE VOCABULARY TEST-REVISED (PPVT-R) *Lloyd M. Dunn and Leota M. Dunn*

Measures hearing vocabulary for standard American English, estimates verbal ability and scholastic aptitude in individuals aged 2½ and up. Used with non-English-speaking students to screen for mental retardation or giftedness, as part of a comprehensive battery, and to screen applicants for jobs requiring good receptive vocabulary.

A 175-item, "point to," response test measuring receptive vocabulary in English. Test items, arranged in order of increasing difficulty, are plates of four pictures requiring subject to point to the picture that corresponds to a stimulus word. Only those plates within subject's ability range are administered. Two parallel forms

Refer to page(s)	*Test Title*

(L and M) available. Administration untimed (10-20 minutes). Examiner required and evaluated. Not for group use. Available with plastic plates. Kit (specify form) $34.00. *Publisher:* American Guidance Service

235

PEER NOMINATION INVENTORY OF DEPRESSION (PNID) *Monroe M. Lefkowitz and Edward P. Tesiny*

Assesses symptoms of depression in normal, prepubertal children. Used by researchers to collect epidemiological data regarding depression symptoms in general child population.

A group-rated inventory consisting of 23 items measuring depression, happiness, and popularity. Requires child to be rated on each item by peers. Each rated child receives two scores: an item score and total score (sum of item scores). Group administered only. Examiner required and evaluated. Administration untimed (varies). One-time fee of $25.00 per administration or institution. *Publisher:* Monroe M. Lefkowitz

383

PENNSYLVANIA BI-MANUAL WORKSAMPLE *John R. Roberts*

Measures manual dexterity and eye-hand coordination of individuals aged 16 and up. Used for employee placement requiring assembly or similar motor skills.

A multiple-operation, manual-dexterity test in which subject is presented with an 8″x24″ board containing 100 holes (arranged in 10 rows) and a set of nuts and bolts to test finger dexterity of both hands, whole movement of both arms, eye-hand coordination, and bi-manual coordination. Includes 20 practice and 80 timed motions. Disassembly reverses process, adding 100 timed motions. Administration timed (12 minutes). Special supplement allows administration to blind persons. Examiner required and evaluated. Suitable for group use of up to four subjects if each has board. Set $109.00. *Publisher:* American Guidance Service

210, 212, 239, 283, 284, 313, 315, 318, 332, 336, 337

PERSONALITY INVENTORY FOR CHILDREN (PIC), REVISED FORMAT *Robert D. Wirt, David Lachar, James E. Klinedinst, Philip D. Seat, and William E. Broen, Jr.*

Evaluates personality attributes of children aged 3-16. Used by professionals working with children for counseling and identification of learning and social disabilities.

A 600-item, paper-pencil, true-false inventory filled out by parents and consisting of 16 scales: 12 clinical (Achievement, Intellectual Screening, Development, Somatic Concern, Depression, Family Relations, Delinquency, Withdrawal, Anxiety, Psychosis, Hyperactivity, Social Skills) and four validity and screening (Lie, Frequency, Defensiveness, Adjustment). Divided into four parts: Part I provides scores for Lie Scale and four broad-band scales (Undisciplined/Poor Self-Control, Social Incompetence, Internalization/Somatic Symptoms, Cognitive Development); Parts I-II provide Part I scores, plus Development Scale score and shortened

Refer to page(s)	Test Title

versions of remaining 14 scales; Parts I-III provide Part I scores, plus 16 scores for full-scale versions; Parts I-IV provide Parts I-III scores, plus 17 experimental scales. Administration untimed (varies). Examiner required. Not for group use. Hand scored; computer scoring available. Kit (specify age group) $125.00. *Publisher:* Western Psychological Services

69, 70, 133, 142, 158, 164, 165, 210, 211, 221

PIERS-HARRIS CHILDREN'S SELF-CONCEPT SCALE (PHSCS)   *Ellen V. Piers and Dale B. Harris*

Measures self-concept for children (Grades 4-12). Used to identify problem areas in children's self-confidence (including extreme problem areas concerning minority and special education) and for research.

An 80-item, paper-pencil test requiring a third-grade reading level and assessing six aspects of a child's self-esteem: behavior, intellectual and school status, physical appearance and attributes, anxiety, popularity, and happiness and satisfaction. Provides scores for each area and Total Score. Self- or examiner-administered. Administration untimed (15-20 minutes). Suitable for group use. Hand or computer scored. Test kit $43.00. *Publisher:* Western Psychological Services

387

PROGRAM FOR ASSESSING YOUTH EMPLOYMENT SKILLS (PAYES)   *Educational Testing Service*

Measures areas of employment deficiency of youths (especially dropouts and disadvantaged) and assesses their preferences and suitability for employment. Used by accredited educational institutions, specifically approved noneducational agencies, and qualified individuals engaged in testing activities.

Consists of three informally and orally administered booklets: Booklet 1 measures attitudes in job-holding skills, attitudes toward authoritarian figures, and self-confidence in social and business situations; Booklet 2 measures job knowledge and examines job-seeking skills and capacity for comprehension and compliance of directions/assignments on the job; Booklet 3 assesses suitability of jobs according to subject's interest. Administration untimed (varies). Examiner required and evaluated. Subjects mark answers in test booklets. Suitable for group use. Scored locally only. User's guide and two manuals available. Test package $53.30. *Publisher:* Cambridge

383

PURDUE PEGBOARD TEST   *Developed by Purdue Research Foundation under the direction of Joseph Tiffin*

Measures adolescents' and adults' hand-finger-arm dexterity required for certain types of manual work such as assembly and electronic production. Used in educational and industrial settings for the selection of business and industrial personnel and high-school shop trainees.

A multiple-operation test measuring gross-motor ability and finger-tip dexterity ability. Five separate scores: right hand, left

Refer to page(s)	*Test Title*

hand, both hands, right plus left plus both hands, and assembly. Materials consist of a test board with two vertical rows of holes and four storage wells holding 50 pegs, 40 washers, and 20 collars. To test the right hand, subject inserts as many pegs as possible in the holes, starting at the top of the right-hand row. Left-hand test uses left row, moving from top to bottom. Both hands are then used together to fill both rows from top to bottom. Administration timed (5-10 minutes). Examiner required. Suitable for group use. Hand-scored. Complete set $179.00. *Publisher:* Science Research Associates, Inc.

210, 212, 239, 240, 244

REVISED CHILDREN'S MANIFEST ANXIETY SCALE   *Cecil R. Reynolds and Bert O. Richmond*

Measures childhood anxiety of children and adolescents aged 6-19. Used in clinical and educational settings.

A 37-item, true-false scale producing Total Anxiety Score. Includes Lie Scale and three factor-based subscales: Physiological Anxiety, Worry/Oversensitivity, and Social Concerns/Concentration. Administration untimed (10-15 minutes). Examiner evaluated. Suitable for group use. Hand scored. Kit $33.00 *Publisher:* Western Psychological Services

44, 69, 132, 139, 142, 236, 241, 254, 284, 312, 333

RORSCHACH PSYCHODIAGNOSTIC TEST *Hermann Rorschach*

Evaluates personality through projective technique in individuals aged three and older. Used in clinical evaluation.

A ten-card, oral-response, projective personality test. Subjects asked to interpret what they see in 10 inkblots, based on the assumption that the individuals' perceptions and associations are selected and organized in terms of their motivations, impulses, and other underlying aspects of personality. Extensive scoring systems developed. Although many variations are in use, this entry refers only to the Psychodiagnostic Plates first published in 1921. Administration untimed (varies). Trained examiner required and evaluated. Contact publisher for cost. *Publisher:* Hans Huber—Distributed by Grune & Stratton (U.S.A.)

284, 285, 290, 332

ROTTER INCOMPLETE SENTENCES BLANK *Julian B. Rotter*

Assesses personality of adolescents and adults. Used as a method of studying personality and as a gross screening device for group or individual clinical examination.

A 40-item, paper-pencil test, with items (sentence stems) completed by subjects. Responses classified into three categories: conflict or unhealthy, neutral, and positive or healthy. Self-administered. Administration untimed (20-40 minutes). Examiner evaluated. Suitable for group use. Three forms available: High School, College, and Adult. Manual, 25 blanks (specify form) $16.00. *Publisher:* The Psychological Corporation

Refer to page(s)	*Test Title*

5, 387

SCALES OF INDEPENDENT BEHAVIOR (SIB) *Robert H. Bruininks, Richard W. Woodcock, Richard F. Weatherman, and Bradley K. Hill*

Measures adaptive and problem behavior and social adjustment from infancy through adult. Used in school, community, and industrial settings for determining eligibility for special services, program planning, and individual and program evaluation.

A multiple-item interview with test domains in motor skills, social interaction and communication skills, personal independence skills, community independence skills, and problem behaviors. Four indexes measure general, externalized, internalized, and asocial maladaptive behaviors. Structurally and statistically related to Woodcock-Johnson Psycho-Educational Battery. Administration untimed (45-50 minutes). Examiner required and evaluated. Not for group use. Test kit $99.00. *Publisher:* DLM Teaching Resources

158, 210, 212

SCL-90-R *Leonard R. Derogatis*

Evaluates psychological symptomatic distress of medical and psychiatric patients. Used in mental-health settings for psychological screening and in treatment planning and evaluation of adolescents and adults.

A 90-item, paper-pencil, self-report inventory consisting of nine symptom dimensions (somatization, obsessive-compulsive, interpersonal sensitivity, despression, anxiety, paranoid ideation, and psychoticism) and three global indices (global severity index, positive symptom index, and positive symptom total). Score/profile forms available by sex for four populations: non-patient adult, non-patient adolescent, outpatient psychiatric, and inpatient psychiatric. Administration untimed (12-15 minutes). Examiner required and evaluated. Suitable for group use. Machine scored; microcomputer scoring program available. Manual $16.00; 100 test forms $30.00. *Publisher:* Clinical Psychometric Research

384

SELF-DIRECTED SEARCH: COMPUTER VERSION *John L. Holland; interpretive report by Robert Reardon, Ph.D.*

Assesses the abilities and interests of adolescents and adults. Used for career planning and guidance.

Multiple-item, computer-administered (paper-pencil version also available) test yielding six interest scores (Realistic, Investigative, Artistic, Social, Enterprising, and Conventional) and a three-letter occupational code used for exploring over 1,100 occupational possibilities. The interpretive report includes a list of the user's vocational aspirations, descriptions of Holland's code types, and suggested steps for educational or vocational planning. The program also allows the user to take My Vocational Situation. Administration untimed (30-45 minutes). Self-administered. Computer scored. Suitable for group use. 50 Apple or IBM PC uses $125.00. *Publisher:* Psychological Assessment Resources, Inc.

Refer to page(s)	Test Title

69

SELF-OBSERVATIONAL SCALES   *William G. Katzenmeyer and A. Jackson Stenner*

Assesses social maturity, self-acceptance, self-security, and affiliations (school, teacher, peer) of children from kindergarten through high school and handicapped subjects. Used by school systems, hospitals, and in research.

Four forms are available according to grade: Primary (K-3), Intermediate (4-6), Junior High (7-9), and Senior High (10-12). Items are questions concerning areas of social maturity, social confidence, self-acceptance, self-security, school affiliation, teacher affiliation (except on Primary), and peer affiliation (except on Primary), all of which are answered "yes" or "no" (with yes/no alternatives portrayed pictorially by smiling/frowning faces on Primary Form) and given value in each scale. Administration untimed (25-30 minutes). Primary Form requires examiner for administration; other forms self-administered. Suitable for group use. Only machine scoring by publisher available. Answers marked directly on test booklet and factor-analysis scored by matrix. Complete set $42.00. *Publisher:* NTS Research Corporation

9

SEQUENTIAL ASSESSMENT OF MATHEMATICS INVENTORY (SAMI)   *Fredricka K. Reisman*

Assesses strengths and weaknesses of students' (Grades K-8) mathematics skills. Used by professionals working with children to set classroom or individual goals.

A multiple-item test employing paper-pencil, oral interview, and concrete representation in eight areas: mathematics language, ordinality, number/notation, measurement, geometry, computation, word problems, and mathematical applications. Administration untimed (30-60 minutes). Components available for classroom (intended for group use) and individuals (not for group use). Examiner required. Hand scored. Contact publisher for cost. *Publisher:* The Psychological Corporation

69, 157, 170, 332, 335

SIXTEEN PERSONALITY FACTOR QUESTIONNAIRE   *Raymond B. Cattell and IPAT Staff*

Assesses normal adult personality of adolescents and adults aged 16 and older. Used in diagnostic and therapeutic settings to facilitate diagnosis and treatment; business and industry for personnel selection, placement, promotion, and prediction of job-related criteria; education for college advisement and identifying students with problems; in marriage counseling; and research.

A paper-pencil test measuring levels of 16 primary personality traits: emotional maturity, assertiveness, shrewdness, tension, self-sufficiency, intelligence, seriousness, conscientiousness, shyness, tough-mindedness, suspiciousness, imaginativeness, self-assurance, conservatism, self-control, and reserve. Five forms available: A and B (seventh-grade reading level; 187 items each), C and D (sixth-grade reading level; 105 items each), and Form E (third-grade reading level; 128 items) in a forced-choice format with large type

Refer to page(s)	*Test Title*

and shorter, more concrete items. Form A videotape in American sign language, Form E cassette tape, computer reports, and Spanish and German editions available. Examiner required. Suitable for group use or self-administered. Administration untimed (25-60 minutes). Introductory kit $11.40. *Publisher:* Institute for Personality and Ability Testing, Inc.

387   SOCIAL AND PREVOCATIONAL INFORMATION BATTERY   *A. Halpern, P. Raffeld, L.K. Irvin, R. Link, and Jacqueline D. Becklund*

Assesses knowledge of skills and competencies considered important for the ultimate community adjustment of educable mentally retarded (EMR) students. Used for evaluation in programs for EMR junior and senior high school students, including career education.

A true-false, orally administered battery consisting of five areas containing nine tests: employability (Job Search Skills, Job Related Behavior), economic self-sufficiency (Banking, Budgeting, Purchasing), family living (Home Management, Physical Health Care), personal habits (Hygiene and Grooming), and communication (Functional Signs). Directly related to five secondary-school, work-study, or experience-program goals. Also measures short-term objectives of work-experience and community programs for mildly retarded adolescents. Administration untimed (15-25 minutes). Examiner required and evaluated. Not for group use. Hand or machine scored. Specimen set $8.95. *Publisher:* CTB/McGraw-Hill

105   SOCIAL BEHAVIOR ASSESSMENT (SBA)   *T.M. Stephens*

Assesses school-related social skills of children (Grades K-8). Used in research and educational settings to delineate nature of children's difficulty or specific behavior deficits, provide precise classification and descriptive information of their social behaviors, and select those in need of social skills training.

A 136-item, teacher-rated, observation tool containing 30 subcategories arranged under four broad behavior categories: environmental, interpersonal, task-related, and self-related. Using observation or recall, teachers rate each student on each item on a 4-point scale according to how that item pertains to the student's exhibited behavior. Total scores obtained for each of the 30 subcategories by replacing 0-rated items with average of scorable items for that category; sum of subcategories yields total SBA score. Administration untimed (varies). Examiner evaluated. Suitable for group use. Hand scored. For further information contact publisher. *Publisher:* Cedars Press

11, 241, 312   STANFORD-BINET INTELLIGENCE SCALE: FORM L-M *Lewis M. Terman and Maud A. Merrill*

Measures mental abilities of individuals aged two and older and identifies children and adults who would benefit from spe-

Refer to page(s)	*Test Title*

cialized learning environments. Used to substantiate questionable scores from group tests and when the subject has physical, language, or personality disorders that rule out group testing.

A 142-item, verbal and nonverbal IQ test assessing the following factors: language, memory, conceptual thinking, reasoning, numerical reasoning, visual motor, and social reasoning. In most cases, only 18-24 test items need be administered to a given subject. After basal age is established testing continues until ceiling age is reached. Responses are then scored according to established procedures to yield mental age and IQ. Administered only by professionally trained, certified examiners. Administration untimed (45-90 minutes). Examiner evaluated. Not for group use. Examiner's kit $189.00. *Publisher:* The Riverside Publishing Company

338   STRESS RESPONSE SCALE   *Louis A. Chandler*

Assesses emotional adjustment reactions of children (Grades 1-8) with nonorganic, mild to moderate emotional problems (not appropriate with mentally retarded, psychoneurologically learning disabled, or severely emotionally handicapped). Used in clinical settings as a screening device to identify high-risk children and in diagnostic assessment.

A 40-item test containing five subscale: Impulsive (Acting Out), Passive-Aggressive, Impulsive (Overactive), Repressed, and Dependent. Items rated on 6-point scale by adult making the referral. Administration untimed (varies). Examiner required and evaluated. Not for group use. Hand scored. Sample kit $15.00. *Publisher:* Louis A. Chandler, Ph.D.

13, 314, 384   STRONG-CAMPBELL INTEREST INVENTORY (SCII)   *E. K. Strong, Jr. and David P. Campbell*

Measures occupational interests in a wide range of career areas usually requiring advanced technical or college training. Used to make long-range curricular and occupational choices, employee selection and placement, and vocational rehabilitation placement.

A 325-item, paper-pencil, multiple-choice test asking subject to respond either to items covering a broad range of familiar occupational tasks and day-to-day activities. General topics include occupations, school subjects, activities, amusements, types of people, preference between two activities, and "your characteristics." Administration untimed (30-40 minutes). Responses analyzed by computer to yield a profile that presents scores on a number of scales and offers interpretive advice. Respondent scored on Six General Occupational Themes (based on Holland's RIASEC themes), 23 Basic Interest Scales (measuring strength and consistency of specific interest areas), and 162 Occupational Scales (reflecting degree of similarity between respondent and people employed in particular occupations). Scoring services provide 11 additional non-occupational and administrative indexes. Computer scoring required and available from a number of sources. Self-administered. Suitable for group use. Available in Spanish. Contact

Refer to page(s)	*Test Title*

publisher for cost. *Publisher:* Stanford University Press—Distributed exclusively by Consulting Psychologists Press, Inc.

86   STUDY OF VALUES   *G. Allport, P. Vernon, and G. Lindzey*

Measures relative prominence of adolescents' (Grade 10 and up) and adults' basic interests or personality motives. Used for student educational and vocational planning, guidance, personnel selection, and research.

A 45-item, paper-pencil test measuring six factors: theoretical, economic, aesthetic, social, political, and religious. Self-administered, requiring supervision, guidance, and interpretation by individuals experienced in psychological testing and personality theory. Administration untimed (20 minutes). Suitable for group use. Hand scored. Manual, 35 test booklets $16.86. *Publisher:* The Riverside Publishing Company

254, 255, 256, 258   SUICIDE PROBABILITY SCALE (SPS)   *John G. Cull and Wayne S. Gill*

Predicts the probability of suicidal behavior. Used by clinicians to assess the risk of suicidal behavior in adolescents (aged 14 and up) and adults.

A paper-pencil test consisting of 36 items to which subjects respond on a 4-point scale according to how statements describe their behavior or feelings. Test format makes no mention of suicide. Validated on normals and clinical groups with documented, serious suicide attempts. Weighted scoring procedure designed to discriminate maximally between suicidal and nonsuicidal groups. Probability that a subject belongs to a suicidal group reflected in the Suicide Probability Score providing four clinical subscales: Hopelessness, Suicide Ideation, Negative Self-Evaluation, and Hostility. Cutoff scores indicate level of probable suicide behavior. Administration untimed (5-10 minutes). Examiner required. Suitable for group use. Hand-scored. Complete kit $31.50. *Publisher:* Western Psychological Services

313   SYSTEM OF MULTICULTURAL PLURALISTIC ASSESSMENT (SOMPA)   *Jane R. Mercer and June F. Lewis*

Assesses cognitive abilities, sensorimotor abilities, and adaptive behavior of children aged 5 to 11. Used for assessment of children from varied cultural backgrounds.

Consists of two major components: The Parent Interview (takes place in the home, and includes administration of the Adaptive Behavior Inventory for Children, Sociocultural Scales, Health History Inventories) and the Student Assessment with data collected in the school environment and including the Physical Dexterity Tasks, Weight by Height, Visual Acuity, Auditory Acuity, Bender Visual Motor Gestalt Test (sold separately), and the WISC-R or WPPSI (sold separately). Interpretation by psychologist or a qualified team only. Administration untimed; (Parent Interview 60 minutes; individual interview 20 minutes plus additional time for

Refer to page(s)	*Test Title*

the Wechsler and Bender-Gestalt). Examiner required. Not for group use. Parent Interview available in Spanish. Basic kit $95.00 *Publisher:* The Psychological Corporation

69, 70, 164, 165, 210, 211, 221, 332, 335

TENNESSEE SELF CONCEPT SCALE (TSCS) *William H. Fitts*

Measures self-concept of psychologically healthy and disturbed adolescents and adults (12 years or older with sixth-grade reading level) in terms of identity, feelings, and behavior. Used in clinical and educational settings.

A 100-item, paper-pencil, self-rating test available in two forms and consisting of self-descriptive statements rated on 5-point scale. Counseling Form (C) is appropriate if results are used directly with subject, requires no scoring key, and includes measures of response defensiveness, total score, and self-concept scales (Identity, Self Satisfaction, Behavior, Physical Self, Moral-Ethical Self, Personal Self, Family Self, and Social Self); Clinical and Research Form (C & R) requires scoring key and yields additional measures, including six empirical scales (Defensive Positive, General Maladjustment, Psychosis, Personality Disorder, Neurosis, and Personality Integration). Administration untimed (10-20 minutes). Self-administered. Suitable for group use. Hand or computer scored. Kit $49.50. *Publisher:* Western Psychological Services

12

TEST OF ADOLESCENT LANGUAGE (TOAL) *Donald D. Hammill, Virginia L. Brown, Stephen C. Larsen, and J. Lee Wiederholt*

Assesses language abilities of students (Grades 6-12). Used to identify problems of spoken and written language, specify areas in need of intervention/goal planning, and make comparisons between language and cognitive abilities or academic achievement and among different kinds of language measured.

A paper-pencil, oral-response test measuring a broad spectrum of language abilities, including vocabulary (semantics) and grammar (syntax) in listening, speaking, reading, and writing. Provides 10 subtest scores (listening, speaking, reading, writing, spoken language, written language, vocabulary, grammar, receptive language, and expressive language), the sum of which provides one overall index of language abilities. Administration untimed (100 minutes). Examiner required. Not for group use. Hand scored. Complete kit $72.00. *Publisher:* PRO-ED

9

TEST OF MATHEMATICAL ABILITIES (TOMA) *Virginia L. Brown and Elizabeth McEntire*

Assesses mathematical attitudes and aptitudes of students (Grades 3-12). Used for instructional strategies for individuals, for comparative assessment of mathematical programs, and to differentiate diagnostically between student groups with problems in mathematics and those without.

Consists of two major skill areas (story problems and computa-

Refer to page(s)	*Test Title*

tion) and five subtests providing information related to expressed attitudes toward mathematics; level of understanding vocabulary when used in a mathematical sense; degree of understanding functional use of mathematical facts and concepts as applied in general culture; whether mathematical attitudes, vocabulary, and/or understanding of cultural applications differ markedly from those of age peers; and how these relate to the general level of basic skills shown in both areas. Administration untimed (varies). Examiner required and evaluated. Suitable for group use. Complete kit $43.00. *Publisher:* PRO-ED

11   TEST OF NONVERBAL INTELLIGENCE (TONI)
Linda Brown, Rita J. Sherbenu, and Susan J. Dollar

Measures intelligence and reasoning in subjects suspected of having reading, writing, speaking, or listening difficulties, especially in the mentally retarded, stroke patients, bilingual and non-English-speaking persons, speech or language-handicapped individuals, and the learning disabled.

A 50-item response test assessing intellectual capacity. The examiner pantomimes the instructions, and the subject responds by pointing to the answer. Test items use abstract symbols to present a variety of reasoning tasks arranged in increasing order of difficulty and complexity. Two equivalent forms are available. Administration untimed (20-30 minutes). Examiner required. Hand scored. May be administered to small groups of up to five subjects. Complete kit $69.00. *Publisher:* PRO-ED.

14   TEST OF PRACTICAL KNOWLEDGE (TPK)
J. Lee Wiederholt and Stephen C. Larsen

Assesses students' (Grades 8-12) knowledge concerning important daily-living skills. Used to determine students' particular strengths and weaknesses in this area and to document their progress in special programs.

A paper-pencil test consisting of three subtests: Personal Knowledge, Social Knowledge, and Occupational Knowledge. Administration untimed (35-40 minutes). Examiner required. Suitable for group use. Hand scored. Complete kit $46.00. *Publisher:* PRO-ED

43, 44, 88, 132,   THEMATIC APPERCEPTION TEST (TAT)
236, 254, 284, 312,   *Henry Alexander Murray*
319, 334
Assesses personality in individuals aged 14-40 through projective technique focusing on dominant drives, emotions, sentiments, complexes, attitudes, and conflicts. Used as a preface to a series of psychotherapeutic interviews or a short psychoanalysis, in any comprehensive study of personality, and in the interpretation of behavior disorders, psychosomatic illnesses, neuroses, and psychoses.

A 20-item, projective-type test in which a subject is shown pictures one at a time and asked to make up a story about each picture. Examiner records subject's stories for later analysis. Measurements

Refer to page(s)	*Test Title*

include subject's temperament, level of emotional maturity, observational ability, intellectuality, imagination, psychological insight, creativity, sense of reality and factors of family and psychic dynamics. Generally subject is asked to make up stories based on 10 cards in each of two sessions. Trained examiner required for administration and evaluation. Testing time is one hour per series. Not for groups. Specimen set $11.50; manual $1.50. *Publisher:* Harvard University Press

383

VALPAR COMPONENT WORK SAMPLE SYSTEM (VCWS)

Measures vocational aptitudes, interests, and physical capacities relating to training or work. Used by counselors, evaluators, psychologists, and other professionals working with adolescents and adults, particularly with handicapped individuals, entering training programs for the labor market.

19 manual tests measuring skills relating to the world of work: Small Tools (Mechanical), Size Discrimination, Numerical Sorting, Upper Extremity Range of Motion, Clerical Comprehension and Aptitude, Independent Problem Solving, Multi-Level Sorting, Simulated Assembly, Whole Body Range of Motion, Tri-Level Measurement, Eye-Hand-Foot Coordination, Soldering & Inspection (Electronic), Money Handling, Integrated Peer Performance, Electrical Circuitry and Print Reading, Drafting, Pre-Vocational Readiness Battery, Conceptual Understanding Through Blind Evaluation (CUBE), and Dynamic Physical Capacities. Scores are used to generate the Worker Qualifications Profile as defined by the *Dictionary of Occupational Titles*. Scores also can be compared to special norm groups. Administration timed (varies). Examiner required and evaluated. Some tests suitable for group use. Complete set of VCWS 1-16 $17,020.00; VCWS 17 $3,680.00; VCWS 18 $2,600.00; VCWS 19 $1,395.00. *Publisher:* Valpar International Corporation

6

THE WAKSMAN SOCIAL SKILLS RATING SCALE (WSSRS) *Steven Waksman*

Assesses social skills deficits. Used by teachers and clinicians for selecting students for social skills training or special counseling programs and for evaluating the effectiveness of those programs.

A 21-item rating scale identifying specific social skill deficits in children and adolescents by surveying aggressive and passive domains. The examiner rates the behavior of the targeted student(s) on a 4-point scale. Administration untimed (5-10 minutes). Examiner required and evaluated. Not suitable for group use. Complete kit $29.95. *Publisher:* ASIEP Education Company

106

WALKER PROBLEM BEHAVIOR IDENTIFICATION CHECKLIST *Hill M. Walker*

Identifies prekindergartners through sixth-graders with behavior problems. Used to evaluate children for counseling and possible referral.

A 50-item, paper-pencil, true-false inventory consisting of behavior statements that are applied to the child being rated. The checklist can be completed by anyone familiar with the child, although it is used primarily by teachers. The test provides a Total Score, a cut-off score for classifying children as disturbed, and scores for the following five scales: Acting-Out, Withdrawal, Distractibility, Disturbed Peer Relations, and Immaturity. Administration untimed (5 minutes). Examiner required. Hand scored. Suitable for group use. Complete kit $35.00. *Publisher:* Western Psychological Services

     VALUE SURVEY   *Milton Rokeach*

Measures personal values of adolescents (11 years and up) and adults. Used to provide objective feedback about subjects in comparison with reference group, for value therapy and values clarification, and to change socially undesirable values.

A 36-item test requiring minimum literacy. Values printed on gummed labels that respondent arranges in rank order. Assessed values divided into terminal (comfortable life, world peace) and behavioral (loving, ambition). Self-administered. Administration untimed (15 minutes). Examiner evaluated. Suitable for group use. Available in approximately 12 languages. Computer scoring available. Contact publisher for cost. *Publisher:* Halgren Tests

     VINELAND ADAPTIVE BEHAVIOR SCALES
Sara S. Sparrow, David A. Balla, and Domenic V. Cicchetti

Measure personal and social sufficiency of individuals from birth to adulthood. Used in clinical, educational, and research settings, including evaluation of mentally retarded and physically handicapped individuals.

Three forms assess adaptive behavior: Interview Edition, Survey Form (297 items) provides general assessment obtained in semi-structured interview of parent/caregiver; Interview Edition, Expanded Form (577 items) is more comprehensive to prepare individual educational, habilitative, or treatment programs; Classroom Edition (244 items) focuses on classroom assessment, including basic academic functioning, obtained by questionnaire completed by teachers. Adaptive Behavior Composite derived from four domains: Communication, Daily Living Skills, Socialization, and Motor Skills. Administration untimed (20-90 minutes, depending on form). Examiner required and evaluated. Not for group use. Hand scored. Audiocassette (presenting sample interviews) and microcomputer scoring and profiling programs available for Survey and Expanded Forms. Starter set $68.50. *Publisher:* American Guidance Service

     VOCATIONAL INFORMATION AND EVALUATION WORK SAMPLES (VIEWS)   *Vocational Research Institute-J.E.V.S.*

Assesses vocational interests and abilities of mentally retarded adults. Used for vocational guidance.

Multiple-item performance tests of abilities consisting of 16

Test Title

work samples. Tasks include sorting, cutting, collating, assembling, weighing, tying, measuring, using hand tools, tending a drill press, and electric machine feeding. Assessment process includes client orientation, demonstration by examiner, training, and timed assessment. Observation of client helps distinguish between learning and performance and gives information concerning learning, quality of work, and productivity. Requires no reading ability. Administration untimed (4-5 days). Examiner required and evaluated. Not for group use. Contact publisher for cost. *Publisher:* Vocational Research Institute

WECHSLER ADULT INTELLIGENCE SCALE-REVISED (WAIS-R)   *David Wechsler*

Assesses capacity for intelligent behavior of adolescents and adults (16-74 years). Used by trained clinical examiners.

Consists of two major scales: Verbal, containing six subtests (Informative, Similarities, Arithmetic, Vocabulary, Comprehension, and Digit Span), and Performance, containing six subtests (Digit Symbol, Picture Completion, Block Design, Picture Arrangement, and Object Assembly). Deviation IQs provided for Verbal, Performance, and Full Scales. Requires verbal responses and demonstration of performance ability. Administration untimed (75 minutes). Examiner required and evaluated. Not for group use. Available in Spanish. Complete set $120.00. *Publisher:* The Psychological Corporation

WECHSLER INTELLIGENCE SCALE FOR CHILDREN-REVISED (WISC-R)   *David Wechsler*

Assesses mental ability in children (ages 6-16). Used by psychologists and other trained clinical examiners to measure a child's capacity to understand and cope with the world.

Consists of two major scales: Verbal, containing six subtests (Information, Similarities, Arithmetic, Vocabulary, Comprehension, and Digit Span), and Performance, containing six subtests (Picture Completion, Picture Arrangement, Block Design, Object Assembly, Coding, and Mazes). Deviation IQs provided for Verbal, Performance, and Full Scales. Requires verbal responses and demonstration of performance ability. Administration untimed (1 hour). Examiner required and evaluated. Not for group use. Available in Spanish. Complete set $135.00. *Publisher:* The Psychological Corporation

WIDE RANGE ACHIEVEMENT TEST-REVISED (WRAT-R)   *Joseph F. Jastak and Sarah Jastak*

Measures basic educational skills of word recognition, spelling, and arithmetic, and identifies individuals with learning difficulties. Used for educational placement, measuring school achievement, vocational assessment, job placement and training, and (when used in conjuction with other tests) determining personality structure.

A paper-pencil test containing three subtests of 50-100 items: Reading, Spelling, and Arithmetic. Two levels presented on separate forms: Level I (5-12 years) and Level II (12-75 years). Optional word lists on plastic cards for both levels of Reading and Spelling, recorded pronunciation of lists on cassette tape for Spelling, and large-print edition are available. Administration timed (15-30 minutes, depending on level). Examiner required and evaluated. Spelling and Arithmetic suitable for group use. Hand scored. Specimen set $29.00. *Publisher:* Jastak Assessment Systems.

384

WIDE RANGE INTEREST-OPINION TEST (WRIOT)
Joseph F. Jastak and Sarah Jastak

Assesses self-projected ability and aspiration levels and social conformity. Used with individuals aged five and up (including educationally and culturally disadvantaged, learning disabled, mentally retarded, and visually and hearing-impaired) in vocational/ career planning and counseling, employee selection and placement, and to help coordinate instruction/therapy plans with interest/ attitude patterns.

A paper-pencil test containing 150 sets of three pictures each and measuring individuals' occupational motivation according to their likes and dislikes. Results presented on report form graphically showing individual's strength of interest in 18 interest and eight attitude clusters. Administration untimed (40 minutes). Examiner required. Suitable for group use except when individuals are unable to complete answer sheet. Hand or computer scored. Picture film strip and supplementary Job Title List available. Specimen set $39.00. *Publisher:* Jastak Assessment Systems.

360, 368

WOODCOCK-JOHNSON PSYCHO-EDUCATIONAL
BATTERY (WJPEB)   *Richard W. Woodcock and Mary Bonner Johnson*

Evaluates cognitive ability, scholastic achievement, and interest level of individuals aged 3-80. Used to diagnose learning disabilities and for instructional planning, vocational rehabilitation counseling, and research.

A four-part battery administered in its entirety or as single tests or clusters to meet specific appraisal needs. Part One (12 subtests) measures a range of cognitive ability, including visual matching, auditory blending, concept formulation, and reasoning with analogies. Part Two (10 subtests) measures achievement in reading; mathematics; written language; and knowledge in science, social studies, and humanities. Part Three (5 subtests) measures level of participation preference in scholastic and nonscholastic activities. Part Four measures adaptive behavior with the Scales of Independent Behavior. Administration untimed (2 hours for first three parts). Examiner required and evaluated. Not for group use. Available in Spanish. Microcomputer scoring available. Complete set $155.00. *Publisher:* DLM Teaching Resources

Test Publisher/Distributor Directory

ACADEMIC THERAPY PUBLICATIONS, 20 Commercial Boulevard, Novato, California 94947; (415)883-3314

AMERICAN GUIDANCE SERVICE, Publishers' Building, Circle Pines, Minnesota 55014; (800)328-2560

THE AMERICAN ORTHOPSYCHIATRIC ASSOCIATION, INC., 19 West 44th Street, Suite 1616, New York, New York 10036; (212)354-5770

ASIEP EDUCATION COMPANY, 3216 N.E. 27th Street, Portland, Oregon 97212; (503)281-4115

ASSOCIATED SERVICES FOR THE BLIND, 919 Walnut Street, Philadelphia, Pennsylvania 19107; (215)627-0600

THE AUSTRALIAN COUNCIL FOR EDUCATIONAL RESEARCH LIMITED (ACER), Radford House, Frederick Street, Hawthorn, Victoria 3122, Australia; (03)819-1400

BALL FOUNDATION, Suite 206, Building C, 800 Roosevelt Road, Glen Ellyn, Illinois 60137; (312)469-6270

BROWN/BUTLER FAMILY RESEARCH PROGRAM, 345 Blackstone Boulevard, Providence, Rhode Island 02906; (401)456-3700

CAMBRIDGE, The Adult Education Company, 888 7th Avenue, New York, New York 10106; west of the Mississippi or Louisiana, Alabama, Mississippi, and the Florida panhandle (800)221-4764, east of the Mississippi (except New York) (800)221-4600, in New York (212)957-2563

CEDARS PRESS, P. O. Box 29351, Columbus, Ohio 43229; (614)846-2849

CENTER FOR COGNITIVE THERAPY, 133 South 36th Street, Room 602, Philadelphia, Pennsylvania 19104; (215)898-4100

CENTER FOR THE STUDY OF PARENTAL ACCEPTANCE AND REJECTION, The University of Connecticut, Storrs, Connecticut 06268; (203)486-4513

CFKR CAREER MATERIALS, INC., P.O. Box 437, Meadow Vista, California 95722; (800)553-3313, in California (916)878-0118

CHANDLER, LOUIS A., Ph.D., 5D Forbes Quadrangle, Pittsburgh, Pennsylvania 15260; (412)624-1244

CLINICAL PSYCHOMETRIC RESEARCH, 1228 Wine Spring Lane, Towson, Maryland 21204; (301)321-6165

CONSULTING PSYCHOLOGISTS PRESS, INC., 577 College Avenue, P. O. Box 60070, Palo Alto, California 94306; (415)857-1444

C.P.S., INC., P. O. Box 83, Larchmont, New York 10538; no business phone

CTB/McGRAW-HILL, Publishers Test Service, Del Monte Research Park, 2500 Garden Road, Monterey, California 93940; (800)538-9547, in California (800)682-9222 or (408)649-8400

CURRICULUM ASSOCIATES, INC., 5 Esquire Road, North Billerica, Massachusetts 08162-2589; (800)225-0248, in Massachusetts (617)667-8000

THE DEVEREUX FOUNDATION, 19 South Waterloo Road, P. O. Box 400, Devon, Pennsylvania 19333; (215)964-3000

DLM TEACHING RESOURCES, P. O. Box 4000, One DLM Park, Allen, Texas 75002; (800)527-4747, in Texas (800)442-4711

EDUCATIONAL AND INDUSTRIAL TESTING SERVICE (EdITS), P. O. Box 7234, San Diego, California 92107; (619)222-1666

ELBERN PUBLICATIONS, P. O. Box 09497, Columbus, Ohio 43209; (614)235-2643

FAMILY STRESS, COPING AND HEALTH PROJECT, School of Family Resources and Consumer Sciences, University of Wisconsin, 1300 Linden Drive, Madison, Wisconsin 53706; (608)262-5712

GALLAUDET COLLEGE BOOKSTORE, Kendall Green, P. O. Box 103-B, Washington, D.C. 20002; no business phone

GRUNE & STRATTON, INC., Orlando, Florida 32887-0018; (305)345-4100

THE GUILFORD PRESS, A Division of Guilford Publications, Inc., 200 Park Avenue S., New York, New York 10003; (800)221-3966 or (212)674-1900

HALGREN TESTS, 873 Persimmon Avenue, Sunnyvale, California 94807; (408)738-1342

HANS HUBER, Langgassstrasse 76, 3000 Bern 9, Switzerland; no business phone

HARVARD UNIVERSITY PRESS, 79 Garden Street, Cambridge, Massachusetts 02138; (617)495-2600

HODGES, KAY, Ph.D., Duke University Medical Center, P. O. Box 2906, Durham, North Carolina 27710; (919)684-3044

INSTITUTE FOR PERSONALITY AND ABILITY TESTING, INC. (IPAT), P. O. Box 188, 1602 Coronado Drive, Champaign, Illinois 61820; (217)352-4739

INSTITUTE FOR PSYCHOSOMATIC & PSYCHIATRIC RESEARCH & TRAINING, c/o Daniel Offer, Michael Reese Hospital and Medical Center, Lake Shore Drive at 31st Street, Chicago, Illinois 60616; (312)791-3826

JASTAK ASSESSMENT SYSTEMS, 1526 Gilpin, Wilmington, Delaware 19806; (302)652-4990

KHAVARI, KHALIL A., Ph.D., Midwest Institute on Drug Use, Vogel Hall, University of Wisconsin-Milwaukee, Milwaukee, Wisconsin 53201; (414)963-4747

KOVACS, MARIA, Ph.D., University of Pittsburgh, School of Medicine, Western Psychiatric Institute and Clinic, 3811 O'Hara Street, Pittsburgh, Pennsylvania 15213-2593; no business phone

LEFKOWITZ, MONROE M., Ph.D., 106 Cliffwood Street, Lenox, Massachusetts 01240; (413)637-2113

MINNESOTA MORAL RESEARCH PROJECTS (MMRP), 206 Burton Hall, 178 Pillsbury Drive S.E., University of Minnesota, Minneapolis, Minnesota 55455; (612)373-5539 or (612)373-5213

NATIONAL COMPUTER SYSTEMS/PAS DIVISION, P. O. Box 1416, Minneapolis, Minnesota 55440; (800)328-6759, in Minnesota (612)933-2800

NTS RESEARCH CORPORATION, 1821 Chapel Hill Road, Durham, North Carolina 27707; (919)493-3451

PREP, INC., 1007 Whitehead Road Extension, Trenton, New Jersey 08638; (800)257-5234, in New Jersey, Alaska, Hawaii, and Canada (609)882-2668

PRO-ED, 5341 Industrial Oaks Boulevard, Austin, Texas 78735; (512)892-3142

PSYCHOLOGICAL ASSESSMENT RESOURCES, INC., P. O. Box 98, Odessa, Florida 33556; (800)331-TEST or (813)977-3395

THE PSYCHOLOGICAL CORPORATION, A Subsidiary of Harcourt Brace Jovanovich, Inc., 555 Academic Court, San Antonio, Texas 78204; (512)299-1061

PSYCHOLOGICAL DOCUMENTS, American Psychological Association, 1200 17th Street N.W., Washington, D.C. 20036; (202)955-7600

RESEARCH PSYCHOLOGISTS PRESS, INC., 1110 Military Street, P. O. Box 984, Port Huron, Michigan 48060-0984; (800)265-1285, in Michigan (313)982-4556

THE RIVERSIDE PUBLISHING COMPANY, 8420 Bryn Mawr Avenue, Chicago, Illinois 60631; (800)323-9540, in Alaska, Hawaii, or Illinois call collect (312)693-0040

SCIENCE RESEARCH ASSOCIATES, INC. (SRA), 155 North Wacker Drive, Chicago, Illinois 60606; (800)621-0664, in Illinois (312)984-2000

SPECIAL CHILD PUBLICATIONS (SCP), P. O. Box 33548, Seattle, Washington 98133; (206)771-5711

SPIVACK, GEORGE, and SWIFT, MARSHALL, Department of Mental Health Sciences, Hahnemann University, 1505 Race Street, Philadelphia, Pennsylvania 19102; no business phone

STANFORD UNIVERSITY PRESS. See CONSULTING PSYCHOLOGISTS PRESS, INC.

THELEN, MARK H., Ph.D., Department of Psychology, 210 McAlester Hall, University of Missouri, Columbia, Missouri 65211; no business phone

UNIVERSITY OF MINNESOTA PRESS, 2037 University Avenue S.E., Minneapolis, Minnesota 55414; (612)373-3266

UNIVERSITY OF VERMONT, College of Medicine, Department of Psychiatry, Section of Child, Adolescent, and Family Psychiatry, 1 South Prospect Street, Burlington, Vermont 05401; (802)656-4563

U.S. DEPARTMENT OF LABOR, Division of Testing, Employment and Training Administration, Washington, D.C. 20213; (202)376-6270

VALPAR INTERNATIONAL CORPORATION, P. O. Box 5767, Tucson, Arizona 85703; (800)528-7070

VOCATIONAL RESEARCH INSTITUTE, 2100 Arch Street, Philadelphia, Pennsylvania 19103; (215)893-5911

WESTERN PSYCHOLOGICAL SERVICES, A Division of Manson Western Corporation, 12031 Wilshire Boulevard, Los Angeles, California 90025; (213)478-2061

General Index

About the Contributors

W. B. APPLE, M.A. received his graduate training in clinical psychology at the University of South Dakota. From 1974 to 1981 he was a treatment coordinator and outreach therapist at the Southern Oregon Child Study and Treatment Center, working primarily with conduct-disordered children and adolescents and their families. Currently he is a clinical child psychology intern at the Virginia Treatment Center for Children. Mr. Apple's other clinical interests include the assessment and prevention of suicidal behavior among children and adolescents. His research activities have been in the areas of child and adolescent depression and adolescent substance abuse.

TIMOTHY A. CAVELL, M.S. is an Alumni Federation Fellow in the Department of Psychology at Louisiana State University, where he is earning a doctoral degree in clinical child psychology. His recent publications have examined teachers' judgments of psychologists' use of single-case research designs and paradoxical interventions when working with adolescent students. His other published works have focused on assessment of academic problems in multidisciplinary settings, child and adolescent eating disorders, and use of structured interviews with child and adolescent populations. Mr. Cavell's current research projects include the nature of the relation between adolescent cognitive distortion and emotional disturbance, and the validation of recently constructed measures of adolescent social competency.

JOAN P. CESARI, PH.D. is an assistant professor in the Counseling Psychology Department at the University of Kansas and a staff psychologist at the University Counseling Center. Dr. Cesari received her Ph.D. in psychology from Texas Tech University and completed a psychology internship at the University Counseling Center at Southern Illinois University-Carbondale. Her areas of specialization include psychotherapy and assessment of young women with bulimia, as well as other concerns presented by women in therapy. Her research interests include the professional socialization process of women entering careers, and she has published several articles in the area of career indecision. In addition to her academic and therapy duties, Dr. Cesari serves on the Steering Committee of the Douglas County (Kansas) Anorexia Nervosa and Associated Disorders chapter and has conducted informational workshops on eating disorders with a wide variety of audiences.

STEWART W. EHLY, PH.D. is Associate Professor of Special Education and coordinator of the school psychology program at the University of Iowa. Dr. Ehly received his Ph.D. in school psychology at the University of Texas at Austin in 1975. From 1975 to 1977, he worked in the Education in Living Program, providing psychological services to emotionally disturbed children between the ages of 6 and 16. Dr. Ehly has provided both direct and consultative services in a range of educational and juvenile justice settings and has served for two years at the Career Planning Academy, a program for status offender and delinquent youth. His special interests include children's personality development, peer cooperation and learning, staff development, and organizational change processes. He is the author of a number of publications, including two books, one on peer tutoring and a second on working with parents of exceptional children.

KATHRYN C. GERKEN, PH.D. is an associate professor in the School of Human Development at the University of Texas at Dallas, where she is also the director of the Office of

Teacher Education. Dr. Gerken received her Ph.D. at Southern Illinois University. She began her academic career at the University of Iowa, where she served as the coordinator of the school psychology program and as the co-director of the J. B. Stroud Educational Services Center. Dr. Gerken has worked as a psychologist in a state mental hospital, a medical setting, and public and private schools. Her publications and teaching have focused on the assessment of academic, intellectual, and affective variables.

FRANK M. GRESHAM, PH.D. is Professor of Psychology and director of the school psychology training program at Louisiana State University. Dr. Gresham received his Ph.D. in school psychology from the University of South Carolina in 1979. His major research interests include social skills assessment and training with children, mainstreaming and social skills assessment of handicapped children, assessment of childhood and adolescent depression, non-biased assessment of mildly handicapped children, and behavioral assessment. Dr. Gresham is the author of numerous articles and reviews and has served on the editorial boards of several journals.

JOHN GUIDUBALDI, D.ED. is the director of the Early Childhood School Psychology Program and Professor of Early Childhood Education and Counseling and Personnel Services at Kent State University. Dr. Guidubaldi received his doctoral degree in human development from Harvard University, where he was employed as an assistant on the Harvard Preschool Project for four years. He has served as the president of the National Association of School Psychologists (1981-82) and as the Ohio delegate to NASP for two consecutive terms. Dr. Guidubaldi has published numerous articles and is co-author of the Battelle Development Inventory, a multifactored assessment device for children. He was the originator and editor of both *School Psychology Digest* (later renamed *School Psychology Review*) and the *Newsletter of Parenting.*

ROBERT G. HARRINGTON, PH.D. is Associate Professor of Educational Psychology and Research at the University of Kansas. He received his Ph.D. in school psychology at the University of Iowa and has practiced as a school psychologist in Iowa. Dr. Harrington is the current president of the Trainers of School Psychologists as well as the president of the Association for Psychological and Educational Research in Kansas. He teaches graduate courses in intelligence testing, child and adolescent behavior problems and personality assessment, and preschool assessment in the school psychology program at the University of Kansas. His areas of special interest include the effects of family and home environments on development and the use of test information to diagnose child and adolescent adjustments. His publications include book chapters and over 40 journal articles, focusing primarily on the psychometric characteristics of various psychoeducational tests and their use in developing therapeutic intervention programs.

THOMAS H. HOHENSHIL, PH.D. is Associate Dean of the College of Education and Professor of School Psychology and Counseling at Virginia Polytechnic Institute and State University. He received his doctoral degree from Kent State University. His graduate training emphasized counseling, school psychology, and vocational education. Dr. Hohenshil is an experienced school psychologist in both public school and mental health settings. He has published extensively in school psychology, counseling, and vocational education. In addition, he has served on the editorial boards of *School Psychology Review, Journal of Psychoeducational Assessment, Personnel and Guidance Journal,* and *Vocational Guidance Quarterly.* Dr. Hohenshil serves as a column editor for the *Journal of Counseling and Development* and recently completed a two-year term as Southeast Regional Director and Executive Board Member of the National Association of School Psychologists.

E. PETER JOHNSEN, ED.D. is Professor of Educational Psychology and Research at the University of Kansas. He received his doctoral degree at the University of Rochester. His recent publications have focused on the correlates of play in the development of young children.

Dr. Johnsen's interests include a life-span approach to intellectual and social development, especially as they influence the responsibilities of social agencies and their programs.

JUDITH KAUFMAN, PH.D. is Professor of Psychology and the director of the school psychology training program at Ferkauf Graduate School of Psychology. She received her Ph.D. in school psychology from Yeshiva University. Dr. Kaufman previously taught at the University of Bridgeport and was a visiting professor at the University of Wisconsin-Madison, the Institute of Education at the University of London, and the Hatfield Polytechnic Institute in England. Her areas of specialization include adolescent development and preventive intervention with children and adolescents. Dr. Kaufman has conducted workshops and presented scholarly papers in the area of adolescent behavior in a variety of settings. She is currently Northeast Regional Director of the National Association of School Psychologists and has served in leadership roles in many other organizations.

HOWARD M. KNOFF, PH.D. is Assistant Professor of School Psychology in the Department of Psychological and Social Foundations at the University of South Florida, where he specializes in consultation and intervention processes. He received his Ph.D. from Syracuse University in 1980 and has worked in the field of school psychology for the past eight years. Dr. Knoff maintains a private practice for children and adolescents and is active in the American Psychological Association and the National Association of School Psychologists, in which he chairs and co-chairs several committees. He is the author of *Assessment of Child and Adolescent Personality,* co-author of *The Kinetic Drawing System for Family and School,* and a guest editor of *School Psychology Review.* Dr. Knoff's current research interests include personality assessment, consultation processes, training issues in school psychology, and the development of effective child study teams.

STEVEN LANDAU, PH.D. is an associate professor in the Department of Psychology at Illinois State University and is on the faculty of the school psychology training program. Dr. Landau received his doctoral training at the University of Iowa, where he gained research experience in the Department of Child Psychiatry. He has published and presented papers on externalizing behavior disorders and peer perceptions of deviance and has reviewed for the *Journal of Consulting and Clinical Psychology, School Psychology Review,* and *Child Development.* He is currently on the editorial board of the *Journal of Clinical Child Psychology.*

BRIAN W. McNEILL, PH.D. is Assistant Professor of Counseling Psychology and a counselor in the University Counseling Center at the University of Kansas. He received his doctorate in counseling psychology from Texas Tech University and completed an internship at the University Counseling Service at the University of Iowa. Dr. McNeill currently teaches courses in psychological assessment at the master's and doctoral levels at the University of Kansas. His research and writing interests include attitude change in counseling/psychotherapy and developmental models of clinical supervision and training of professional psychologists.

DANNY MITCHELSON, M.A., M.S.ED. is a doctoral candidate in school psychology at the University of Kansas and has worked for several years as a youth counselor at a residential treatment center for emotionally disturbed adolescents. His teaching responsibilities at the University of Kansas involve undergraduate education courses in child development and classroom management. Mr. Mitchelson's research experience and interests have focused on the role of paraprofessionals in special education, diagnosis and treatment of learning problems in young adult community college students, and the education and training of parents with physically, emotionally, or intellectually handicapped children.

THORANA NELSON, M.A. is a Ph.D. candidate in the Division of Counselor Education at the University of Iowa. She received her master's degree in counseling and human development from the University of Iowa, specializing in marital and family therapy. She assisted in the development of the Marriage and Family Therapy Clinic at the University of

Iowa and has served as a practicum supervisor in the Clinic. Ms. Nelson maintains a private practice in marriage and family therapy and divorce mediation and is a Clinical member of the American Association for Marital and Family Therapy.

JOSEPH D. PERRY, PH.D. is the supervisor of school psychology in the Trumbull County Schools in Warren, Ohio. Dr. Perry was previously Assistant Professor of Rehabilitation Counseling at Kent State University and the Northeastern Ohio University College of Medicine. He also has worked as a pediatric psychologist, school psychologist, counselor, and special education teacher. His research has been directed primarily at the psychosocial sequelae of divorce as an original team member of the ongoing nationwide study of divorce adjustment. Dr. Perry's other publications and presentations at national meetings have focused on multifactored assessment and child health psychology. He has served as co-chair of the Research Committee for the National Association of School Psychologists.

PATRICIA A. PETRETIC-JACKSON, PH.D. is currently an associate professor in the Department of Psychology at the University of South Dakota. A member of the graduate faculty of the clinical psychology doctoral training program, she is also the coordinator of Child and Family Services at the University Psychological Services Center. Dr. Petretic-Jackson received her Ph.D. in developmental psychology from Bowling Green State University in Ohio. She completed a postdoctoral fellowship in clinical psychology at the University of South Dakota and a residency in child clinical psychology at the Children's Memorial Hospital/ Northwestern University. She is active in private practice, specializing in the treatment of adolescents and their families, and serves as a consultant to the juvenile court system. Her research interests include family violence, divorce, and appetitive disorders in adolescents.

RANDAL P. QUEVILLON, PH.D. is Associate Professor of Psychology at the University of South Dakota and is on the faculty of the clinical psychology doctoral training program. Dr. Quevillon received his Ph.D. from the University of Montana and completed his internship at the University of Oklahoma Health Sciences Center. He has published several papers in the areas of self-control, classroom behavior management, depression, and rural mental health. He was co-coordinator of the Community Psychology Special Interest Group of the Association for Advancement of Behavior Therapy and is editor of *Behavioral Community Psychology*.

HELEN REINER, PH.D. is a clinical child psychologist in private practice in Wichita, Kansas. Dr. Reiner received her Ph.D. from Teachers College, Columbia University. She previously served as the director of children's outpatient services and as a supervising psychologist at the Jersey City Medical Center in New Jersey and has extensive experience in community mental health and school settings. Dr. Reiner was Assistant Professor of School Psychology at Wichita State University, where she developed and taught courses in assessment techniques for children and adolescents. She also served as consultant psychologist and clinical supervisor at the Juvenile Court Clinic in Wichita. Dr. Reiner's research and clinical interests include assessment and therapeutic intervention with children and adolescents, as well as clinical supervision and training of pre- and postdoctoral students in psychology.

DAVID ROSENTHAL, PH.D. is an associate professor in the Department of Family Practice/College of Medicine and in the Division of Counselor Education at the University of Iowa. He is the co-director of the Marriage and Family Therapy Clinic in the Division of Counselor Education and co-director of the Family Stress Clinic in the Department of Family Practice. Dr. Rosenthal received his doctorate from the Department of Counselor Education, State University of New York in Buffalo and received two years of training in marriage and family therapy from the Menninger Foundation (Des Moines Program). He is a Supervisory member in the American Association of Marital and Family Therapy. His current research interests include examination of family therapy outcomes and other clinical and family-related issues.

ANNE B. SPRAGINS, PH.D. is Professor of Psychology and director of the school psychology program at Gallaudet College in Washington, D.C. Dr. Spragins received her Ph.D. from the University of South Carolina and completed her school psychology internship in the Montgomery County, Maryland, public school system. She directs a school psychology graduate program that emphasizes a training specialization in the provision of psychological services for deaf and hard-of-hearing children and youth. Her experience with hearing-impaired and multihandicapped children includes psychoeducational assessment, individual counseling, parent education, and parent counseling. Her interests also include cognitive development. Dr. Spragins's publications have focused on the psychoeducational evaluation of deaf and hard-of-hearing youngsters and the organization and development of psychological services for hearing-impaired clients.

MICHAEL M. WARNER, PH.D. is an associate professor in the Department of Applied Behavioral Studies in Education at Oklahoma State University, where he teaches courses in special education, including one on assessment of exceptional children. After receiving his Ph.D. in special education from the University of Kansas, Dr. Warner joined the faculty at Wichita State University, where he developed a graduate program in learning disabilities at the secondary level. He later served on the core staff of the Institute for Research in Learning Disabilities at the University of Kansas. Dr. Warner's scholarly interests have focused recently on the role of curriculum theory in special education and on the education of teachers preparing to work with mildly handicapped students.